Heroes to Remember

Heroes to Remember

Brandon R. Sanders

Writers Club Press
San Jose New York Lincoln Shanghai

Heroes to Remember

All Rights Reserved © 2000 by Brandon R. Sanders

No part of this book may be reproduced or transmitted in any form or by any means, graphic, electronic, or mechanical, including photocopying, recording, taping, or by any information storage retrieval system, without the permission in writing from the publisher.

Writers Club Press
an imprint of iUniverse.com, Inc.

For information address:
iUniverse.com, Inc.
5220 S 16th, Ste. 200
Lincoln, NE 68512
www.iuniverse.com

ISBN: 0-595-14206-0

Printed in the United States of America

*This book is dedicated to Donna and Fred Barker,
James and Betty Sanders,
Dara, Bryan, Robert, Major Buntyn, and
Clay, Beth, and Logan Sanders and
Melody "Jackie" Warner*

Contents

Acknowledgements ix

Introduction xi

World War II European Timeline 1

World War II Pacific Timeline 22

World War II Casualties 37

John Burkhalter, 2nd Lieutenant, Chaplain 39

D-Day Recollections, of Jim Wilkins the Queen's Own Rifles of Canada, B Company 48

Guadalcanal Journal Guadalcanal Island 56

From Pearl Harbor to Guadalcanal 86

Dennis M. Parker 99

Bataan Death March 189

William Collins—USS Indianapolis 212

PFC Mason Herrin 134th Infantry 35 Division Company A General Patton's 3rd Army 245

World War II Medal of Honor Recipients 247

Acknowledgements

I have many people to thank and a limited space to thank them. Many gave invaluable leads, emails, stories, and personal artifacts to help me tell this story. They believe as I believe that remembering the men of that terrible conflict is imperative to our future success as a country. The following are some of those individuals who helped in ways I cannot express in words.

I wish I could have told every story that was relayed to me. The real difficult task was selecting who to leave in, and who had to be left out. I wish I could have finished two interviews before the men passed away, but I hope in these stories all will find a common bond of brotherhood.

Thanks to Emma Vinson, for sharing her family's personal letters. Dennis Brand of the VFW led me to several stories, as well as Steve Manning of the Fort Worth Star Telegram who found a few of the stories in this book.

I would also like to thank the following for help, great and small. Rick and Kristi Staples, Peggy Luh, Andrew Hall, Jeff and Diane Hardin, Trey Moran, Adrian Allison, Suzanne Vlassis, Sharyn Jordan, Scott Fischer, Larry, Patti, James, Jason, and Jacob Duncan.

I would also like to thank the author Terry Davis, Julie Gardner, Ima Allison, the Donald Sanders family, and the Underwood family.

Also, Peggy Craft, Deborah Lacroix, Valerie Johnson, Patrick and Christine Barker, Jennifer Carter, Donnie and Pam Siegler, John Starnes, and my grandmothers who saw it all, Lela Calloway and Mabel Durfey.

If I forgot anyone I promise to dedicate a whole page to you next time.

INTRODUCTION

In December of 1997 I was watching the news on television, when a disturbing report came on. The news anchor said that an average of one thousand veterans of World War II was passing away every day. Something clicked inside of me. There it was, in cold, hard numbers, an inevitable fact that I had been avoiding for a long time. These were the people I looked at as grandparents my whole life. They had always been there, and in my inability to accept reality, always would be. They were the ones who didn't understand my "X" generation. They were the ones who were fun to poke fun with about the "old days". Now, they were passing away, and I realized I didn't even take the time to know them at all.

I started reading everything I could about the war, and it began to creep on me that these people I silently took with a grain of salt, had lived more in four years than I would in my entire life. While I was trying to get five more minutes of sleep before freshman English Literature class, at the same age, these men were fighting for their lives in places like Omaha beach, Iwo Jima, and Nancy, France. I felt very ashamed. They gave up the most productive years of their lives, and in many cases, their lives themselves, because they were asked to defend our country and the people that would follow. With few exceptions, they are largely forgotten. For the most part because they do not see that they did anything special. They did it because they had to, and that was that. I heard that to a man.

The movie "Saving Private Ryan", seemed to help the nation refocus to that time, but it was short lived. We could walk away from the movie theatres, shake our heads, shudder to ourselves, and go about our business. They could not. They had to live every day of that movie for the duration of the war or the duration of their lives, whichever came first.

I know for a fact that the people of my generation take our freedom for granted. John Helprin, in a speech last year, put it this way,

"Nearly four hundred years of America's hard-earned accounts—the principles we established, the battles we fought, the morals we upheld for century after century, our very humility before God—now

flow promiscuously through our hands, like blood onto sand, squandered and laid waste by a generation that imagines history to have been but a prelude for what it would accomplish…Though most people cannot believe at this moment that the United States of America will ever again fight for its survival, history guarantees that it will. And, when it does, most people will not know what to do. They will believe of war, as they did of peace, that it is everlasting."

While this may appear pessimistic, it only goes to solidify how special the men who fought that war were. It goes to the heart of this book. There will come a time when all the voices from that time are silent. When at last they will rest with the brothers and all who went before them. People may ask, "Was it ever real, did it really happen?"

It did happen. It was real, and to avoid it happening again, we must remember those that came before us, and honor their sacrifices. We owe it to them, we owe it to ourselves, and we owe it to the future to remember.

"Old men forget: yet all shall be forgot, But he'll remember with advantages What feats he did…."
Shakespeare, Henry V

"Silly people and there were many…might discount the force of the United States. Some said they were soft, others that they would never be united. They would fool around at a distance. They would never come to grips. They would never stand blood letting. They would just be a vague blur on the horizon to friend and foe. Now we should see the weakness of this numerous but remote, wealthy, and talkative people. But I had studied the American Civil War…American blood flowed in my veins."—

Winston Spencer Churchill on the Americans, after Pearl Harbor and US entry in World War II. Taken from "The Second World War, Vol. III"

WORLD WAR II EUROPEAN TIMELINE

1918

Nov 11—World War One ends with German defeat.

1919

April 28—League of Nations founded.

June 28—Signing of the Treaty of Versailles.

1921

July 29—Adolf Hitler becomes leader of National Socialist 'Nazi' Party.

1923

Nov 8/9—The Beer Hall Putsch.

1925

July 18—Hitler's book "Mein Kampf" published.

1926

Sept 8—Germany admitted to League of Nations.

1929

Oct 29—Stock Market on Wall Street crashes.

1930

Sept 14—Germans elect Nazis making them the 2nd largest political party in Germany.

1932

Nov 8—Roosevelt elected President of the United States.

1933

Jan 30—Adolf Hitler becomes Chancellor of Germany.

Feb 27—The Reichstag burns.

March 12—First concentration camp opened at Oranienburg outside Berlin.

March 23—Enabling Act gives Hitler dictatorial power.

April 1—Nazi boycott of Jewish owned shops.

May 10—Nazis burn books in Germany.

In June—Nazis open Dachau concentration camp.

July 14—Nazi party declared only party in Germany.

Oct 14—Germany quits the League of Nations.

1934

June 30—The "Night of the Long Knives."

July 25—Nazis murder Austrian Chancellor Dollfuss.

Aug 2—German President Hindenburg dies.

Aug 19—Adolf Hitler becomes Führer of Germany.

1935

March 16—Hitler violates the Treaty of Versailles by introducing military conscription.

Sept 15—German Jews stripped of rights by Nuremberg Race Laws.

1936

Feb 10—The German Gestapo is placed above the law.

March 7—German troops occupy the Rhineland.

May 9—Mussolini's Italian forces take Ethiopia.

July 18—Civil war erupts in Spain.

Aug 1—Olympic games begin in Berlin.

Oct 1—Franco declared head of Spanish State.

1937

June 11—Soviet leader Stalin begins a purge of Red Army generals.

Nov 5—Hitler reveals war plans during Hossbach Conference.

1938

March 12/13—Germany announces 'Anschluss' (union) with Austria.

Aug 12—German military mobilizes.

Sept 30—British Prime Minister Chamberlain appeases Hitler at Munich.

Oct 15—German troops occupy the Sudetenland; Czech government resigns.

Nov 9/10—Kristallnacht—The Night of Broken Glass.

1939

Jan 30, 1939—Hitler threatens Jews during Reichstag speech.

March 15/16—Nazis take Czechoslovakia.

March 28, 1939—Spanish Civil war ends.

May 22, 1939—Nazis sign 'Pact of Steel' with Italy.

Aug 23, 1939—Nazis and Soviets sign Pact.

Aug 25, 1939—Britain and Poland sign a Mutual Assistance Treaty.

Aug 31, 1939—British fleet mobilizes; Civilian evacuations begin from London.

Sept 1, 1939—Nazis invade Poland.

Sept 3, 1939—Britain, France, Australia and New Zealand declare war on Germany.

Sept 4, 1939—British Royal Air Force attacks the German Navy.

Sept 5, 1939—United States proclaims neutrality; German troops cross the Vistula River in Poland.

Sept 10, 1939—Canada declares war on Germany; Battle of the Atlantic begins. Sept 17, 1939—Soviets invade Poland.

Sept 27, 1939—Warsaw surrenders to Nazis; Reinhard Heydrich becomes the leader of new Reich Main Security Office (RSHA).

Sept 29, 1939—Nazis and Soviets divide up Poland.

In Oct—Nazis begin euthanasia on sick and disabled in Germany.

Nov 8, 1939—Assassination attempt on Hitler fails.

Nov 30, 1939—Soviets attack Finland.

Dec 14, 1939—Soviet Union expelled from the League of Nations.

1940

Jan 8, 1940—Rationing begins in Britain.

March 12, 1940—Finland signs a peace treaty with Soviets.

March 16, 1940—Germans bomb Scapa Flow naval base near Scotland.

April 9, 1940—Nazis invade Denmark and Norway.

May 10, 1940—Nazis invade France, Belgium, Luxembourg and the Netherlands; Winston Churchill becomes British Prime Minister.

May 15, 1940—Holland surrenders to the Nazis.

May 26, 1940—Evacuation of Allied troops from Dunkirk begins.

May 28, 1940—Belgium surrenders to the Nazis.

June 3, 1940—Germans bomb Paris; Dunkirk evacuation ends.

June 10, 1940—Norway surrenders to the Nazis; Italy declares war on Britain and France.

June 14, 1940—Germans enter Paris.

June 16, 1940—Marshal Pétain becomes French Prime Minister.

June 18, 1940—Hitler and Mussolini meet in Munich; Soviets begin occupation of the Baltic States.

June 22, 1940—France signs an armistice with the Nazis.

June 23, 1940—Hitler tours Paris.

June 28, 1940—Britain recognizes Gen. Charles de Gaulle as the Free French leader.

July 1, 1940—German U-boats attack merchant ships in the Atlantic.

July 5, 1940—French Vichy government breaks off relations with Britain.

July 10, 1940—Battle of Britain begins.

July 23, 1940—Soviets take Lithuania, Latvia and Estonia.

Aug 3-19—Italians occupy British Somaliland in East Africa.

Aug 13, 1940—German bombing offensive against airfields and factories in England.

Aug 15, 1940—Air battles and daylight raids over Britain.

Aug 17, 1940—Hitler declares a blockade of the British Isles.

Aug 23/24—First German air raids on Central London.

Aug 25/26—First British air raid on Berlin.

Sept 3, 1940—Hitler plans Operation Sealion (the invasion of Britain).

Sept 7, 1940—German Blitz against England begins.

Sept 13, 1940—Italians invade Egypt.

Sept 15, 1940—Massive German air raids on London, Southampton, Bristol, Cardiff, Liverpool and Manchester.

Sept 16, 1940—United States military conscription bill passed.

Sept 27, 1940—Tripartite (Axis) Pact signed by Germany, Italy and Japan.

Oct 7, 1940—German troops enter Romania.

Oct 12, 1940—Germans postpone Operation Sealion until Spring of 1941.

Oct 28, 1940—Italy invades Greece.

Nov 5, 1940—Roosevelt re-elected as U.S. president.

Nov 10/11—A torpedo bomber raid cripples the Italian fleet at Taranto, Italy.

Nov 14/15—Germans bomb Coventry, England.

Nov 20, 1940—Hungary joins the Axis Powers.

Nov 22, 1940—Greeks defeat the Italian 9th Army.

Nov 23, 1940—Romania joins the Axis Powers.

Dec 9/10—British begin a western desert offensive in North Africa against the Italians.

Dec 29/30—Massive German air raid on London.

1941

Jan 22, 1941—Tobruk in North Africa falls to the British and Australians.

Feb 11, 1941—British forces advance into Italian Somaliland in East Africa.

Feb 12, 1941—German General Erwin Rommel arrives in Tripoli, North Africa.

Feb 14, 1941—First units of German 'Afrika Korps' arrive in North Africa.

March 7, 1941—British forces arrive in Greece.

March 11, 1941—President Roosevelt signs the Lend-Lease Act.

March 27, 1941—A coup in Yugoslavia overthrows the pro-Axis government.

April 3, 1941—Pro-Axis regime set up in Iraq.

April 6, 1941—Nazis invade Greece and Yugoslavia.

April 14, 1941—Rommel attacks Tobruk.

April 17, 1941—Yugoslavia surrenders to the Nazis.

April 27, 1941—Greece surrenders to the Nazis.

May 1, 1941—German attack on Tobruk is repulsed.

May 10, 1941—Deputy Führer Rudolph Hess flies to Scotland.

May 10/11—Heavy German bombing of London; British bomb Hamburg.

May 15, 1941—Operation Brevity begins (the British counter-attack in Egypt).

May 24, 1941—Sinking of the British ship Hood by the Bismarck.

May 27, 1941—Sinking of the Bismarck by the British Navy.

June 4, 1941—Pro-Allied government installed in Iraq.

June 8, 1941—Allies invade Syria and Lebanon.

June 14, 1941—United States freezes German and Italian assets in America.

June 22, 1941—Germany attacks Soviet Union as Operation Barbarossa begins.

In June—Nazi SS Einsatzgruppen begin mass murder.

June 28, 1941—Germans capture Minsk.

July 3, 1941—Stalin calls for a scorched earth policy.

July 10, 1941—Germans cross the River Dnieper in the Ukraine.

July 12, 1941—Mutual Assistance agreement between British and Soviets.

July 14, 1941—British occupy Syria.

July 26, 1941—Roosevelt freezes Japanese assets in United States and suspends relations.

July 31, 1941—Göring instructs Heydrich to prepare for the Final Solution.

Aug 1, 1941—United States announces an oil embargo against aggressor states.

Aug 14, 1941—Roosevelt and Churchill announce the Atlantic Charter.

Aug 20, 1941—Nazi siege of Leningrad begins.

Sept 1, 1941—Nazis order Jews to wear yellow stars.

Sept 3, 1941—First experimental use of gas chambers at Auschwitz.

Sept 19, 1941—Nazis take Kiev.

Sept 29, 1941—Nazis murder 33,771 Jews at Kiev.

Oct 2, 1941—Operation Typhoon begins (German advance on Moscow).

Oct 16, 1941—Germans take Odessa.

Oct 24, 1941—Germans take Kharkov.

Oct 30, 1941—Germans reach Sevastopol.

Nov 13, 1941—British aircraft carrier Ark Royal is sunk off Gibraltar by a U-boat.

Nov 20, 1941—Germans take Rostov.

Nov 27, 1941—Soviet troops retake Rostov.

Dec 5, 1941—German attack on Moscow is abandoned.

Dec 6, 1941—Soviet Army launches a major counter-offensive around Moscow.

Dec 7, 1941—Japanese bomb Pearl Harbor; Hitler issues the Night and Fog decree.

Dec 8, 1941—United States and Britain declare war on Japan.

Dec 11, 1941—Germany declares war on the United States.

Dec 16, 1941—Rommel begins a retreat to El Agheila in North Africa.

Dec 19, 1941—Hitler takes complete command of the German Army.

1942

Jan 1, 1942—Declaration of the United Nations signed by 26 Allied nations.

Jan 13, 1942—Germans begin a U-boat offensive along east coast of USA.

Jan 20, 1942—SS Leader Heydrich holds the Wannsee Conference to coordinate the "Final Solution of the Jewish Question."

Jan 21, 1942—Rommel's counter-offensive from El Agheila begins.

Jan 26, 1942—First American forces arrive in Great Britain.

In April—Japanese-Americans sent to relocation centers.

April 23, 1942—German air raids begin against cathedral cities in Britain.

May 8, 1942—German summer offensive begins in the Crimea.

May 26, 1942—Rommel begins an offensive against the Gazala Line.

May 27, 1942—SS Leader Heydrich attacked in Prague.

May 30, 1942—First thousand bomber British air raid (against Cologne).

In June—Mass murder of Jews by gassing begins at Auschwitz.

June 4, 1942—Heydrich dies of wounds.

June 5, 1942—Germans besiege Sevastopol.

June 10, 1942—Nazis liquidate Lidice in reprisal for Heydrich's assassination.

June 21, 1942—Rommel captures Tobruk.

June 25, 1942—Eisenhower arrives in London.

June 30, 1942—Rommel reaches El Alamein near Cairo, Egypt.

July 1-30—First Battle of El Alamein.

July 3, 1942—Germans take Sevastopol.

July 5, 1942—Soviet resistance in the Crimea ends.

July 9, 1942—Germans begin a drive toward Stalingrad in the USSR.

July 22, 1942—First deportations from the Warsaw Ghetto to concentration camps; Treblinka extermination camp opened.

Aug 7, 1942—British General Bernard Montgomery takes command of Eighth Army in North Africa.

Aug 12, 1942—Stalin and Churchill meet in Moscow.

Aug 17, 1942—First all-American air attack in Europe.

Aug 23, 1942—Massive German air raid on Stalingrad.

Sept 2, 1942—Rommel driven back by Montgomery in the Battle of Alam Halfa.

Sept 13, 1942—Battle of Stalingrad begins.

Oct 5, 1942—A German eyewitness observes SS mass murder.

Oct 18, 1942—Hitler orders the execution of all captured British commandos.

Nov 1, 1942—Operation Supercharge (Allies break Axis lines at El Alamein).

Nov 8, 1942—Operation Torch begins (U.S. invasion of North Africa).

Nov 11, 1942—Germans and Italians invade unoccupied Vichy France.

Nov 19, 1942—Soviet counter-offensive at Stalingrad begins.

Dec 2, 1942—Professor Enrico Fermi sets up an atomic reactor in Chicago.

Dec 13, 1942—Rommel withdraws from El Agheila.

Dec 16, 1942—Soviets defeat Italian troops on the River Don in the USSR.

Dec 17, 1942—British Foreign Secretary Eden tells the British House of Commons of mass executions of Jews by Nazis; U.S. declares those crimes will be avenged.

Dec 31, 1942—Battle of the Barents Sea between German and British ships.

1943

Jan 2/3—Germans begin a withdrawal from the Caucasus.

Jan 10, 1943—Soviets begin an offensive against the Germans in Stalingrad.

Jan 14-24—Casablanca conference between Churchill and Roosevelt. During the conference, Roosevelt announces the war can end only with an unconditional German surrender.

Jan 23, 1943—Montgomery's Eighth Army takes Tripoli.

Jan 27, 1943—First bombing raid by Americans on Germany (at Wilhelmshaven).

Feb 2, 1943—Germans surrender at Stalingrad in the first big defeat of Hitler's armies.

Feb 8, 1943—Soviet troops take Kursk.

Feb 14-25—Battle of Kasserine Pass between the U.S. 1st Armored Division and German Panzers in North Africa.

Feb 16, 1943—Soviets re-take Kharkov.

Feb 18, 1943—Nazis arrest White Rose resistance leaders in Munich.

March 2, 1943—Germans begin a withdrawal from Tunisia, Africa.

March 15, 1943—Germans re-capture Kharkov.

March 16-20—Battle of Atlantic climaxes with 27 merchant ships sunk by German U-boats.

March 20-28—Montgomery's Eighth Army breaks through the Mareth Line in Tunisia.

April 6/7—Axis forces in Tunisia begin a withdrawal toward Enfidaville as American and British forces link.

April 19, 1943—Waffen SS attacks Jewish resistance in the Warsaw ghetto.

May 7, 1943—Allies take Tunisia.

May 13, 1943—German and Italian troops surrender in North Africa.

May 16, 1943—Jewish resistance in the Warsaw ghetto ends.

May 16/17—British air raid on the Ruhr.

May 22, 1943—Dönitz suspends U-boat operations in the North Atlantic.

June 10, 1943—'Pointblank' directive to improve Allied bombing strategy issued.

June 11, 1943—Himmler orders the liquidation of all Jewish ghettos in Poland.

July 5, 1943—Germans begin their last offensive against Kursk.

July 9/10—Allies land in Sicily.

July 19, 1943—Allies bomb Rome.

July 22, 1943—Americans capture Palermo, Sicily.

July 24, 1943—British bombing raid on Hamburg.

July 25/26—Mussolini arrested and the Italian Fascist government falls; Marshal Pietro Badoglio takes over and negotiates with Allies.

July 27/28—Allied air raid causes a firestorm in Hamburg.

Aug 12-17—Germans evacuate Sicily.

Aug 17, 1943—American daylight air raids on Regensburg and Schweinfurt in Germany; Allies reach Messina, Sicily.

Aug 23, 1943—Soviet troops recapture Kharkov.

Sept 8, 1943—Italian surrender is announced.

Sept 9, 1943—Allied landings at Salerno and Taranto.

Sept 11, 1943—Germans occupy Rome.

Sept 12, 1943—Germans rescue Mussolini.

Sept 23, 1943—Mussolini re-establishes a Fascist government.

Oct 1, 1943—Allies enter Naples, Italy.

Oct 4, 1943—SS Reichsführer Himmler gives speech at Posen.

Oct 13, 1943—Italy declares war on Germany; Second American air raid on Schweinfurt.

Nov 6, 1943—Russians recapture Kiev in the Ukraine.

Nov 18, 1943—Large British air raid on Berlin.

Nov 28, 1943—Roosevelt, Churchill, Stalin meet at Teheran.

Dec 24-26—Soviets launch offensives on the Ukrainian front.

1944

Jan 6, 1944—Soviet troops advance into Poland.

Jan 17, 1944—First attack toward Cassino, Italy.

Jan 22, 1944—Allies land at Anzio.

Jan 27, 1944—Leningrad relieved after a 900-day siege.

Feb 15-18—Allies bomb the monastery at Monte Cassino.

Feb 16, 1944—Germans counter-attack against the Anzio beachhead.

March 4, 1944—Soviet troops begin an offensive on the Belorussian front; First major daylight bombing raid on Berlin by the Allies.

March 15, 1944—Second Allied attempt to capture Monte Cassino begins.

March 18, 1944—British drop 3000 tons of bombs during an air raid on Hamburg, Germany.

April 8, 1944—Soviet troops begin an offensive to liberate Crimea.

May 9, 1944—Soviet troops recapture Sevastopol.

May 11, 1944—Allies attack the Gustav Line south of Rome.

May 12, 1944—Germans surrender in the Crimea.

May 15, 1944—Germans withdraw to the Adolf Hitler Line.

May 25, 1944—Germans retreat from Anzio.

June 5, 1944—Allies enter Rome.

June 6, 1944—D-Day landings.

June 9, 1944—Soviet offensive against the Finnish front begins.

June 10, 1944—Nazis liquidate the town of Oradour-sur-Glane in France.

June 13, 1944—First German V-1 rocket attack on Britain.

June 22, 1944—Operation Bagration begins (the Soviet summer offensive).

June 27, 1944—U.S. troops liberate Cherbourg.

July 3, 1944—'Battle of the Hedgerows' in Normandy; Soviets capture Minsk.

July 9, 1944—British and Canadian troops capture Caen.

July 18, 1944—U.S. troops reach St. Lô.

July 20, 1944—German assassination attempt on Hitler fails.

July 24, 1944—Soviet troops liberate first concentration camp at Majdanek.

July 25-30—Operation Cobra (U.S. troops break out west of St. Lô).

July 28, 1944—Soviet troops take Brest-Litovsk. U.S. troops take Coutances.

Aug 1, 1944—Polish Home Army uprising against Nazis in Warsaw begins; U.S. troops reach Avranches.

Aug 4, 1944—Anne Frank and family arrested by the Gestapo in Amsterdam, Holland.

Aug 7, 1944—Germans begin a major counter-attack toward Avranches.

Aug 15, 1944—Operation Dragoon begins (the Allied invasion of Southern France).

Aug 19, 1944—Resistance uprising in Paris.

Aug 19/20—Soviet offensive in the Balkans begins with an attack on Romania.

Aug 20, 1944—Allies encircle Germans in the Falaise Pocket.

Aug 25, 1944—Liberation of Paris.

Aug 29, 1944—Slovak uprising begins.

Aug 31, 1944—Soviet troops take Bucharest.

Sept 1-4—Verdun, Dieppe, Artois, Rouen, Abbeville, Antwerp and Brussels liberated by Allies.

Sept 4, 1944—Finland and the Soviet Union agree to a cease-fire.

Sept 13, 1944—U.S. troops reach the Siegfried Line.

Sept 17, 1944—Operation Market Garden begins (Allied airborne assault on Holland).

Sept 26, 1944—Soviet troops occupy Estonia.

Oct 2, 1944—Warsaw Uprising ends as the Polish Home Army surrenders to the Germans.

Oct 10-29—Soviet troops capture Riga.

Oct 14, 1944—Allies liberate Athens; Rommel commits suicide.

Oct 21, 1944—Massive German surrender at Aachen.

Oct 30, 1944—Last use of gas chambers at Auschwitz.

Nov 20, 1944—French troops drive through the 'Beffort Gap' to reach the Rhine.

Nov 24, 1944—French capture Strasbourg.

Dec 4, 1944—Civil War in Greece; Athens placed under martial law.

Dec 16-27—Battle of the Bulge in the Ardennes.

Dec 17, 1944—Waffen SS murder 81 U.S. POWs at Malmedy.

Dec 26, 1944—Patton relieves Bastogne.

Dec 27, 1944—Soviet troops besiege Budapest.

1945

Jan 1-17—Germans withdraw from the Ardennes.

Jan 16, 1945—U.S. 1st and 3rd Armies link up after a month long separation during the Battle of the Bulge.

Jan 17, 1945—Soviet troops capture Warsaw.

Jan 26, 1945—Soviet troops liberate Auschwitz.

Feb 4-11—Roosevelt, Churchill, Stalin meet at Yalta.

Feb 13/14—Dresden is destroyed by a firestorm after Allied bombing raids.

March 6, 1945—Last German offensive of the war begins to defend oil fields in Hungary.

March 7, 1945—Allies take Cologne and establish a bridge across the Rhine at Remagen.

March 30, 1945—Soviet troops capture Danzig.

In April—Allies discover stolen Nazi art and wealth hidden in salt mines.

April 1, 1945—U.S. troops encircle Germans in the Ruhr; Allied offensive in North Italy.

April 12, 1945—Allies liberate Buchenwald and Belsen concentration camps; President Roosevelt dies. Truman becomes President.

April 16, 1945—Soviet troops begin their final attack on Berlin; Americans enter Nuremberg.

April 18, 1945—German forces in the Ruhr surrender.

April 21, 1945—Soviets reach Berlin.

April 28, 1945—Mussolini is captured and hanged by Italian partisans; Allies take Venice.

April 29, 1945—U.S. 7th Army liberates Dachau.

April 30, 1945—Adolf Hitler commits suicide.

May 2, 1945—German troops in Italy surrender.

May 7, 1945—Unconditional surrender of all German forces to Allies.

May 8, 1945—V-E (Victory in Europe) Day.

May 9, 1945—Hermann Göring is captured by members of the U.S. 7th Army.

May 23, 1945—SS Reichsführer Himmler commits suicide; German High Command and Provisional Government imprisoned.

June 5, 1945—Allies divide up Germany and Berlin and take over the government.

June 26, 1945—United Nations Charter is signed in San Francisco.

July 1, 1945—U.S., British, and French troops move into Berlin.

July 16, 1945—First U.S. atomic bomb test; Potsdam Conference begins.

July 26, 1945—Atlee succeeds Churchill as British Prime Minister.

Aug 6, 1945—First atomic bomb dropped, on Hiroshima, Japan.

Aug 8, 1945—Soviets declares war on Japan and invade Manchuria.

Aug 9, 1945—Second atomic bomb dropped, on Nagasaki, Japan.

Aug 14, 1945—Japanese agree to unconditional surrender.

Sept 2, 1945—Japanese sign the surrender agreement; V-J (Victory over Japan) Day.

Oct 24, 1945—United Nations is officially born.

Nov 20, 1945—Nuremberg war crimes trials begin.

1946

Oct 16—Hermann Göring commits suicide two hours before his scheduled execution.

WORLD WAR II PACIFIC TIMELINE

1941

Dec 7, 1941—Japanese bomb Pearl Harbor, Hawaii; also attack the Philippines, Wake Island, Guam, Malaya, Thailand, Shanghai and Midway.

Dec 8, 1941—U.S. and Britain declare war on Japan. Japanese land near Singapore and enter Thailand.

Dec 9, 1941—China declares war on Japan.

Dec 10, 1941—Japanese invade the Philippines and also seize Guam.

Dec 11, 1941—Japanese invade Burma.

Dec 15, 1941—First Japanese merchant ship sunk by a U.S. submarine.

Dec 16, 1941—Japanese invade British Borneo.

Dec 18, 1941—Japanese invade Hong Kong.

Dec 22, 1941—Japanese invade Luzon in the Philippines.

Dec 23, 1941—Gen. MacArthur begins withdrawal from Manila to Bataan; Japanese take Wake Island.

Dec 25, 1941—British surrender at Hong Kong.

Dec 26, 1941—Manila declared an open city.

Dec 27, 1941—Japanese bomb Manila.

1942

Jan 2, 1942—Manila and U.S. Naval base at Cavite captured by the Japanese.

Jan 7, 1942—Japanese attack Bataan in the Philippines.

Jan 11, 1942—Japanese invade Dutch East Indies and Dutch Borneo.

Jan 16, 1942—Japanese begin an advance into Burma.

Jan 18, 1942—German-Japanese-Italian military agreement signed in Berlin.

Jan 19, 1942—Japanese take North Borneo.

Jan 23, 1942—Japanese take Rabaul on New Britain in the Solomon Islands and also invade Bougainville, the largest island.

Jan 27, 1942—First Japanese warship sunk by a U.S. submarine.

Jan 30/31—The British withdraw into Singapore. The siege of Singapore then begins.

Feb 1, 1942—First U.S. aircraft carrier offensive of the war as YORKTOWN and ENTERPRISE conduct air raids on Japanese bases in the Gilbert and Marshall Islands.

Feb 2, 1942—Japanese invade Java in the Dutch East Indies.

Feb 8/9—Japanese invade Singapore.

Feb 14, 1942—Japanese invade Sumatra in the Dutch East Indies.

Feb 15, 1942—British surrender at Singapore.

Feb 19, 1942—Largest Japanese air raid since Pearl Harbor occurs against Darwin, Australia; Japanese invade Bali.

Feb 20, 1942—First U.S. fighter ace of the war, Lt. Edward O'Hare from the LEXINGTON in action off Rabaul.

Feb 22, 1942—President Roosevelt orders Gen. MacArthur out of the Philippines.

Feb 23, 1942—First Japanese attack on the U.S. mainland as a submarine shells an oil refinery near Santa Barbara, Calif.

Feb 24, 1942—ENTERPRISE attacks Japanese on Wake Island.
Feb 26, 1942—First U.S. carrier, the LANGLEY, is sunk by Japanese bombers.

Feb 27-March 1—Japanese naval victory in the Battle of the Java Sea as the largest U.S. warship in the Far East, the HOUSTON, is sunk.

March 4, 1942—Two Japanese flying boats bomb Pearl Harbor; ENTERPRISE attacks Marcus Island, just 1000 miles from Japan.

March 7, 1942—British evacuate Rangoon in Burma; Japanese invade Salamaua and Lae on New Guinea.

March 8, 1942—The Dutch on Java surrender to Japanese.

March 11, 1942—Gen. MacArthur leaves Corregidor and is flown to Australia. Gen. Jonathan Wainwright becomes the new U.S. commander.

March 18, 1942—Gen. MacArthur appointed commander of the Southwest Pacific Theater by President Roosevelt.

March 18, 1942—War Relocation Authority established in the U.S. which eventually will round up 120,000 Japanese-Americans and transport them to barb-wired relocation centers. Despite the internment, over 17,000 Japanese-Americans sign up and fight for the U.S. in World War II in Europe, including the 442nd Regimental Combat Team, the most decorated unit in U.S. history.

March 23, 1942—Japanese invade the Andaman Islands in the Bay of Bengal.

March 24, 1942—Admiral Chester Nimitz appointed as Commander in Chief of the U.S. Pacific theater.

April 3, 1942—Japanese attack U.S. and Filipino troops at Bataan.

April 6, 1942—First U.S. troops arrive in Australia.

April 9, 1942—U.S. forces on Bataan surrender unconditionally to the Japanese.

April 10, 1942—Bataan Death March begins as 76,000 Allied POWs including 12,000 Americans are forced to walk 60 miles under a blazing sun without food or water toward a new POW camp, resulting in over 5,000 American deaths.

April 18, 1942—Surprise U.S. "Doolittle" B-25 air raid from the HORNET against Tokyo boosts Allied morale

April 29, 1942—Japanese take central Burma.

May 1, 1942—Japanese occupy Mandalay in Burma.

May 3, 1942—Japanese take Tulagi in the Solomon Islands.

May 5, 1942—Japanese prepare to invade Midway and the Aleutian Islands.

May 6, 1942—Japanese take Corregidor as Gen. Wainwright unconditionally surrenders all U.S. and Filipino forces in the Philippines.

May 7-8, 1942—Japan suffers its first defeat of the war during the Battle of the Coral Sea off New Guinea—the first time in history that two opposing carrier forces fought only using aircraft without the opposing ships ever sighting each other.

May 12, 1942—The last U.S. troops holding out in the Philippines surrender on Mindanao.

May 20, 1942—Japanese complete the capture of Burma and reach India.

June 4-5, 1942—Turning point in the war occurs with a decisive victory for the U.S. against Japan in the Battle of Midway as squadrons of U.S. torpedo planes and dive bombers from ENTERPRISE, HORNET, and YORKTOWN attack and destroy four Japanese carriers, a cruiser, and damage another cruiser and two destroyers. U.S. loses YORKTOWN.

June 7, 1942—Japanese invade the Aleutian Islands.

June 9, 1942—Japanese postpone further plans to take Midway.

July 21, 1942—Japanese land troops near Gona on New Guinea.

Aug 7, 1942—The first U.S. amphibious landing of the Pacific War occurs as 1st Marine Division invades Tulagi and Guadalcanal in the Solomon Islands.

Aug 8, 1942—U.S. Marines take the unfinished airfield on Guadalcanal and name it Henderson Field after Maj. Lofton Henderson, a hero of Midway.

Aug 8/9—A major U.S. naval disaster off Savo Island, north of Guadalcanal, as eight Japanese warships wage a night attack and sink three U.S. heavy cruisers, an Australian cruiser, and one U.S. destroyer, all in less than an hour. Another U.S. cruiser and two destroyers are damaged. Over 1,500 Allied crewmen are lost.

Aug 17, 1942—122 U.S. Marine raiders, transported by submarine, attack Makin Atoll in the Gilbert Islands.

Aug 21, 1942—U.S. Marines repulse first major Japanese ground attack on Guadalcanal.

Aug 24, 1942—U.S. and Japanese carriers meet in the Battle of the Eastern Solomons resulting in a Japanese defeat.

Aug 29, 1942—The Red Cross announces Japan refuses to allow safe passage of ships containing supplies for U.S. POWs.

Aug 30, 1942—U.S. troops invade Adak Island in the Aleutian Islands.

Sept 9/10—A Japanese floatplane flies two missions dropping incendiary bombs on U.S. forests in the state of Oregon—the only bombing of the continental U.S. during the war. Newspapers in the U.S. voluntarily withhold this information.

Sept 12-14—Battle of Bloody Ridge on Guadalcanal.

Sept 15, 1942—A Japanese submarine torpedo attack near the Solomon Islands results in the sinking of the Carrier WASP, Destroyer O'BRIEN and damage to the Battleship NORTH CAROLINA.

Sept 27, 1942—British offensive in Burma.

Oct 11/12—U.S. cruisers and destroyers defeat a Japanese task force in the Battle of Cape Esperance off Guadalcanal.

Oct 13, 1942—The first U.S. Army troops, the 164th Infantry Regiment, land on Guadalcanal.

Oct 14/15—Japanese bombard Henderson Field at night from warships then send troops ashore onto Guadalcanal in the morning as U.S. planes attack.

Oct 15/17—Japanese bombard Henderson Field at night again from warships.

Oct 18, 1942—Vice Admiral William F. Halsey named as the new commander of the South Pacific Area, in charge of the Solomons-New Guinea campaign.

Oct 26, 1942—Battle of Santa Cruz off Guadalcanal between U.S. and Japanese warships results in the loss of the Carrier HORNET.
Nov 14/15—U.S. and Japanese warships clash again off Guadalcanal resulting in the sinking of the U.S. Cruiser JUNEAU and the deaths of the five Sullivan brothers.

Nov 23/24—Japanese air raid on Darwin, Australia.

Nov 30/31—Battle of Tasafaronga off Guadalcanal.

Dec 2, 1942—Enrico Fermi conducts the world's first nuclear chain reaction test at the University of Chicago.

Dec 20-24—Japanese air raids on Calcutta, India.

Dec 31, 1942—Emperor Hirohito of Japan gives permission to his troops to withdraw from Guadalcanal after five months of bloody fighting against U.S. forces.

1943

Jan 2, 1943—Allies take Buna in New Guinea.

Jan 22, 1943—Allies defeat Japanese at Sanananda on New Guinea.

Feb 1, 1943—Japanese begin evacuation of Guadalcanal.

Feb 8, 1943—British-Indian forces begin guerrilla operations against Japanese in Burma.

Feb 9, 1943—Japanese resistance on Guadalcanal ends.

March 2-4—U.S. victory over Japanese in the Battle of Bismarck Sea.

April 18, 1943—U.S. code breakers pinpoint the location of Japanese Admiral Yamamoto flying in a Japanese bomber near Bougainville in the Solomon Islands. Eighteen P-38 fighters then locate and shoot down Yamamoto.

April 21, 1943—President Roosevelt announces the Japanese have executed several airmen from the Doolittle Raid.

April 22, 1943—Japan announces captured Allied pilots will be given "one way tickets to hell."

May 10, 1943—U.S. troops invade Attu in the Aleutian Islands.

May 14, 1943—A Japanese submarine sinks the Australian hospital ship CENTAUR resulting in 299 dead.

May 31, 1943—Japanese end their occupation of the Aleutian Islands as the U.S. completes the capture of Attu.

June 1, 1943—U.S. begins submarine warfare against Japanese shipping.

June 21, 1943—Allies advance to New Georgia, Solomon Islands.

July 8, 1943—B24 Liberators flying from Midway bomb Japanese on Wake Island.

Aug 1/2—A group of 15 U.S. PT-boats attempt to block Japanese convoys south of Kolombangra Island in the Solomon Islands. PT-109, commanded by Lt. John F. Kennedy, is rammed and sunk by the Japanese Cruiser AMAGIRI, killing two and badly injuring others. The crew survives as Kennedy aids one badly injured man by towing him to a nearby atoll.

Aug 6/7, 1943—Battle of Vella Gulf in the Solomon Islands.

Aug 25, 1943—Allies complete the occupation of New Georgia.

Sept 4, 1943—Allies recapture Lae-Salamaua, New Guinea.

Oct 7, 1943—Japanese execute approximately 100 American POWs on Wake Island.

Oct 26, 1943—Emperor Hirohito states his country's situation is now "truly grave."

Nov 1, 1943—U.S. Marines invade Bougainville in the Solomon Islands.

Nov 2, 1943—Battle of Empress Augusta Bay.

Nov 20, 1943—U.S. troops invade Makin and Tarawa in the Gilbert Islands.

Nov 23, 1943—Japanese end resistance on Makin and Tarawa.

Dec 15, 1943—U.S. troops land on the Arawe Peninsula of New Britain in the Solomon Islands.

Dec 26, 1943—Full Allied assault on New Britain as 1st Division Marines invade Cape Gloucester.

1944

Jan 9, 1944—British and Indian troops recapture Maungdaw in Burma.

Jan 31, 1944—U.S. troops invade Kwajalein in the Marshall Islands.

Feb 1-7, 1944—U.S. troops capture Kwajalein and Majura Atolls in the Marshall Islands.

Feb 17/18—U.S. carrier-based planes destroy the Japanese naval base at Truk in the Caroline Islands.

Feb 20, 1944—U.S. carrier-based and land-based planes destroy the Japanese base at Rabaul.

Feb 23, 1944—U.S. carrier-based planes attack the Mariana Islands.

Feb 24, 1944—Merrill's Marauders begin a ground campaign in northern Burma.

March 5, 1944—Gen. Wingate's groups begin operations behind Japanese lines in Burma.

March 15, 1944—Japanese begin offensive toward Imphal and Kohima.

April 17, 1944—Japanese begin their last offensive in China, attacking U.S. air bases in eastern China.

April 22, 1944—Allies invade Aitape and Hollandia in New Guinea.

May 27, 1944—Allies invade Biak Island, New Guinea.

June 5, 1944—The first mission by B-29 Superfortress bombers occurs as 77 planes bomb Japanese railway facilities at Bangkok, Thailand.

June 15, 1944—U.S. Marines invade Saipan in the Mariana Islands.

June 15/16—The first bombing raid on Japan since the Doolittle raid of April 1942, as 47 B-29s based in Bengel, India, target the steel works at Yawata.

June 19, 1944—The "Marianas Turkey Shoot" occurs as U.S. carrier-based fighters shoot down 220 Japanese planes, while only 20 American planes are lost.

July 8, 1944—Japanese withdraw from Imphal.

July 19, 1944—U.S. Marines invade Guam in the Marianas.

July 24, 1944—U.S. Marines invade Tinian.

July 27, 1944—American troops complete the liberation of Guam.

Aug 3, 1944—U.S. and Chinese troops take Myitkyina after a two-month siege.

Aug 8, 1944—American troops complete the capture of the Mariana Islands.

Sept 15, 1944—U.S. troops invade Morotai and the Paulaus.

Oct 11, 1944—U.S. air raids against Okinawa.

Oct 18, 1944—Fourteen B-29s based on the Marianas attack the Japanese base at Truk.

Oct 20, 1944—U.S. Sixth Army invades Leyte in the Philippines.

Oct 23-26—Battle of Leyte Gulf results in a decisive U.S. Naval victory.

Oct 25, 1944—The first suicide air (Kamikaze) attacks occur against U.S. warships in Leyte Gulf. By the end of the war, Japan will have sent an estimated 2,257 aircraft. "The only weapon I feared in the war," Adm. Halsey will say later.

Nov 11, 1944—Iwo Jima bombarded by the U.S. Navy.

Nov 24, 1944—twenty-four B-29s bomb the Nakajima aircraft factory near Tokyo.

Dec 15, 1944—U.S. troops invade Mindoro in the Philippines.

Dec 17, 1944—The U.S. Army Air Force begins preparations for dropping the Atomic Bomb by establishing the 509th Composite Group to operate the B-29s that will deliver the bomb.

1945

Jan 3, 1945—Gen. MacArthur is placed in command of all U.S. ground forces and Adm. Nimitz in command of all naval forces in preparation for planned assaults against Iwo Jima, Okinawa and Japan itself.

Jan 4, 1945—British occupy Akyab in Burma.

Jan 9, 1945—U.S. Sixth Army invades Lingayen Gulf on Luzon in the Philippines.

Jan 11, 1945—Air raid against Japanese bases in Indochina by U.S. carrier-based planes.

Jan 28, 1945—The Burma road is re-opened.

Feb 3, 1945—U.S. Sixth Army attacks Japanese in Manila.

Feb 16, 1945—U.S. troops recapture Bataan in the Philippines.

Feb 19, 1945—U.S. Marines invade Iwo Jima.

March 1, 1945—A U.S. submarine sinks a Japanese merchant ship loaded with supplies for Allied POWs, resulting in a court martial for the captain of the submarine, since the ship had been granted safe passage by the U.S. government.

March 2, 1945—U.S. airborne troops recapture Corregidor in the Philippines.

March 3, 1945—U.S. and Filipino troops take Manila.

March 9/10—Fifteen square miles of Tokyo erupts in flames after it is fire bombed by 279 B29s.

March 10, 1945—U.S. Eighth Army invades Zamboanga Peninsula on Mindanao in the Philippines.

March 20, 1945—British troops liberate Mandalay, Burma.

March 27, 1945—B-29s lay mines in Japan's Shimonoseki Strait to interrupt shipping.

April 1, 1945—The final amphibious landing of the war occurs as the U.S. Tenth Army invades Okinawa.

April 7, 1945—B29s fly their first fighter-escorted mission against Japan with P-51 Mustangs based on Iwo Jima; U.S. carrier-based fighters sink the super battleship YAMATO and several escort vessels which planned to attack U.S. forces at Okinawa.

April 12, 1945—President Roosevelt dies, succeeded by Harry S. Truman.

May 8, 1945—Victory in Europe Day.

May 20, 1945—Japanese begin withdrawal from China.

May 25, 1945—U.S. Joint Chiefs of Staff approve Operation Olympic, the invasion of Japan, scheduled for November 1.

June 9, 1945—Japanese Premier Suzuki announces Japan will fight to the very end rather than accept unconditional surrender.

June 18, 1945—Japanese resistance ends on Mindanao in the Philippines.

June 22, 1945—Japanese resistance ends on Okinawa as the U.S. Tenth Army completes its capture.

June 28, 1945—MacArthur's headquarters announces the end of all Japanese resistance in the Philippines.

July 5, 1945—Liberation of Philippines declared.

July 10, 1945—1000 bomber raids against Japan begin.

July 14, 1945—The first U.S. Naval bombardment of Japanese home islands.

July 16, 1945—First Atomic Bomb is successfully tested in the U.S.

July 26, 1945—Components of the Atomic Bomb "Little Boy" are unloaded at Tinian Island in the South Pacific.

July 29, 1945—A Japanese submarine sinks the Cruiser INDIANAPOLIS resulting in the loss of 881 crewmen. The ship sinks before a radio message can be sent out leaving survivors adrift for two days.

Aug 6, 1945—First Atomic Bomb dropped on Hiroshima from a B-29 flown by Col. Paul Tibbets.

Aug 8, 1945—U.S.S.R. declares war on Japan then invades Manchuria.

Aug 9, 1945—Second Atomic Bomb is dropped on Nagasaki from a B-29 flown by Maj. Charles Sweeney—Emperor Hirohito and Japanese Prime Minister Suzuki then decide to seek an immediate peace with the Allies.

Aug 14, 1945—Japanese accept unconditional surrender; Gen. MacArthur is appointed to head the occupation forces in Japan.

Aug 16, 1945—Gen. Wainwright, a POW since May 6, 1942, is released from a POW camp in Manchuria.

Aug 27, 1945—B29s drop supplies to Allied POWs in China.

Aug 29, 1945—The Soviets shoot down a B29 dropping supplies to POWs in Korea; U.S. troops land near Tokyo to begin the occupation of Japan.

Aug 30, 1945—The British re-occupy Hong Kong.

Sept 2, 1945—Formal Japanese surrender ceremony on board the MISSOURI in Tokyo Bay as 1000 carrier-based planes fly overhead; President Truman declares VJ Day.

Sept 3, 1945—The Japanese commander in the Philippines, Gen. Yamashita, surrenders to Gen. Wainwright at Baguio.

Sept 4, 1945—Japanese troops on Wake Island surrender.

Sept 5, 1945—British land in Singapore.

Sept 8, 1945—MacArthur enters Tokyo.

Sept 9, 1945—Japanese in Korea surrender.

Sept 13, 1945—Japanese in Burma surrender.

Oct 24, 1945—United Nations is born.

WORLD WAR II CASUALTIES

Country	Military	Civilian	Total
Soviet Union*	8,668,000	16,900,000	25,568,000
China	1,324,000	10,000,000	11,324,000
Germany	3,250,000	3,810,000	7,060,000
Poland	850,000	6,000,000	6,850,000
Japan	1,506,000	300,000	1,806,000
Yugoslavia	300,000	1,400,000	1,700,000
Rumania*	520,000	465,000	985,000
France*	340,000	470,000	810,000
Hungary*			750,000
Austria	380,000	145,000	525,000
Greece*			520,000
Italy	330,000	80,000	410,000
Czechoslovakia			400,000
Great Britain	326,000	62,000	388,000
USA	295,000		295,000
Holland	14,000	236,000	250,000
Belgium	10,000	75,000	85,000
Finland	79,000		79,000
Canada	42,000		42,000
India	36,000	***	36,000
Australia	29,000		29,000
Spain**	12,000	10,000	22,000
Bulgaria	19,000	2,000	21,000
New Zealand	12,000		12,000
South Africa	9,000		9,000
Norway	5,000		5,000
Denmark	4,000		4,000

Total: c 61 million

The table above has been compiled from three sources:—

1. Alan Bullock—Hitler and Stalin: Parallel Lives pp987
2. The Times Atlas of the Second World War pp204, 205
3. Richard Overy—Russia's War pp288

The highest estimate for each country was selected during compilation—in the case of ref.3 the figures for military deaths are given as recent official figures and the civilian deaths are those estimated from a 1996 study by B V Sokolov—although the author points out that an accurate figure is difficult to calculate.

*The figures for these countries were very different in the three sources

** The military deaths for Spain, a neutral country during the war, are attributed to volunteers in the Axis (4500) and Allied (7500) armies. According to source 2, above, 10,000 Spaniards died in concentration camps. These figures may be very inaccurate and may be reviewed later.

*** This table does not take into account the 3 million Indians who died due to famine in 1943.

John Burkhalter, 2nd Lieutenant, Chaplain

D-Day at Omaha beach—Normandy, France
Courtesy John Burkhalter family

On the early morning of June 6, 1944, then 2nd Lieutenant Burkhalter landed on Omaha beach in Normandy. In one of his old trunks, a letter was found, that he wrote to his wife Mabel shortly after the invasion. In a classic wartime coincidence, a copy of the letter was wired to the Miami Daily News where a photo of John checking the identification of a dead German soldier had arrived several hours earlier. The letter and photo were printed on Sunday, August 6th, 1944:

"Dear Mable,

It is mid-afternoon here in France several weeks after D-Day. Shells from heavy artillery are humming overhead and the sounds of shells bursting are coming from all directions in the not-so-far-off distance. The regiment I'm with forms part of the front line.

I entered France on D-Day with the "Fighting First Division." This Division has well-trained, courageous and experienced men. Our officers are of the highest order, men of great courage and experience who are war-wise and have seen a lot of battle. The First Division was the first to enter France in World War I and first to enter France in this war; they were the assault troops in the American sector on D-Day. There are not many close-up photographs of the First Division on D-Day because the beach was too hot for photography in those early morning hours and also all through the afternoon. Picture taking was better in the days that followed.

When my part of the Division landed, there were impressions made on my mind that will never leave it. Just before landing we could see heavy artillery shells bursting all up and down the beach at the water's edge under well-directed fire. As I stood in line waiting to get off the LCI to a smaller craft to go into shore, I was looking toward land and saw a large shell fall right on a landing craft full of men. I had been praying quite a bit through the night as we approached the French coast but now I began praying more earnestly than ever. Danger was everywhere; death was not far off. I knew that God alone is the maker and preserver of life, who loves to hear and answer prayer. We finally landed and our assault craft was miraculously spared, for we landed with no shells hitting our boat.

Ernie Pyle came ashore the morning after the assault and after seeing the results of what took place the day before he wrote in his article for the Stars and Stripes, "Now that it's all over, it seems to me a pure miracle we ever took the beach at all."

The enemy had a long time to fix up the beach. The beach was covered with large pebbles to prevent tank movements, and mines were everywhere. The enemy was well dug in and had set up well-prepared positions for machine guns and had well chosen places for sniping. Everything was to their advantage and to our disadvantage, except one thing, the righteous cause for which we are fighting—liberation and freedom. For the moment our advantage was in the abstract and theirs was in the concrete. The beach was spotted with dead and wounded men. I passed one man whose foot had been blown completely off. Another soldier lying close by was suffering from several injuries; his foot was ripped and distorted until it didn't look much like a foot. Another I passed was lying very still, flat on his back, covered in blood. Bodies of injured men all around. Sad and horrible sights were plentiful.

In a recent write-up it is said of one of the colonels of the First Division that led his regiment in on the beach during the early morning, "This blue-eyed soldier had stood on the beach where thousands of men were pinned down by enemy fire, and in a quiet drawl said, 'Gentlemen, we are being killed here on the beaches; let's move inland and be killed there.'"

In from the beach were high hills, which we had to climb. We crawled most of the way up. As we filed by those awful scenes going up the hill and moving inland, I prayed hard for those suffering men, scattered here and there and seemingly everywhere.

We filed over the hill as shells were falling on the beach back of us, meaning deaths for others who were still coming in. Later, one of the soldiers told me that on this occasion he saw a shell land right on top of a wounded man and blow him to bits. Before going over the top of the hill we crouched for a *while close to the ground just below the top. While lying there I did most of my praying. The shells were falling all around and how I knew that God alone was able to keep them away from us. I shall never forget those moments. I am sure that during that time I was drawn very close to God.*

Later, about ten of us were crossing along the edge of a field when we heard sniper bullets whiz by. We all fell to the ground. As we lay there hugging the earth, that we might escape shrapnel from shellfire and bullets from sniper's guns, the birds were singing beautifully in the trees close by. As I lay there listening I thought of the awfulness of it all; the birds were singing and we Human Beings were trying to kill each other. We are the greatest of God's creation, made in the image of God, and here human blood was being spilt everywhere. About three minutes later and only about forty yards away we filed by one of our own boys lying by the side of the hedge, crouched over with a hole in the back of his head. His eyes were open but he was dead, hit by a sniper. We didn't have time to stop; we were pushing on inland making a new front as we went. Someone behind and hours later would move him.

On the afternoon of the second day we were quite a way inland and two of my assistants and I were out trying to locate bodies of dead soldiers. We always take care of the American dead first and then the enemy dead. This was the second day and we were still fighting our way inland, moving fast. Since we did not have any vehicles yet to send bodies back, all we could do on the move was to put the bodies in mattress covers and leave them in a marked place to be taken care of later by the rear echelons. Our business was to keep fighting on inland and pushing the enemy back. On the roadside my assistants and I saw a dead German officer. He was a tall fellow; must have been about six feet four. We turned him over and stretched him out the best we could. I looked at his face and was surprised to see how young he looked. No doubt he was in his twenties but he had the face of a boy. I thought: surely, this fellow was too young to die. It almost seemed that he had asked for it. I became conscious of an awful evil force behind it all to cause a young fellow like this to seemingly hunger and delight to kill and be killed. We slid his body into a mattress cover and left him by the side of the road.

Most of this section of France we are moving through is farming area with fields and hedges and orchards. We see cows and chickens and ducks and pigs and all that goes with farming.

On one occasion we were near some farmhouses and some large shells began to fall, so several of us near a stone barn dashed into it to get out of the way of shrapnel. Just inside was a mother hen covering her little chicks. When we hurried in she became frightened and fluffing her feathers rose up to protect her young. I looked at her and silently said, "No, mother hen, we are not trying to hurt you and your little family, we are trying to hurt each other."

Nobody can love God better than when he is looking death square in the face and talks to God and then sees God come to the rescue. As I look back through hectic days just gone by to that hellish beach I agree with Ernie Pyle, that it was a pure miracle we even took the beach at all. Yes, there were a lot of miracles on the beach that day. God was on the beach D-Day; I know He was because I was talking with Him."

Caption: Capt. John G. Burkhalter, former Miami minister and chaplain with the "Fighting First" division in France, performs a job not required of him by checking the identification of a dead German soldier just ahead of the burial squads.

(The following poem was displayed prominently in one of John's chests)

Be strong!

We are not here to play, to dream, to drift.

We have hard work to do and loads to lift.

Shun not the struggle,

face it: 'tis God's gift.

Be strong!

Say not the days are evil. Who's to blame?

And fold the hands and acquiesce, O shame!

Stand up; speak out

and bravely, in God's name.

Be strong!

It matters not how deep entrenched the wrong,

How hard the battle goes, the day is long:

Faint not, fight on!

Tomorrow comes the song.

—Maltbie D. Babcock

Col John G Burkhalter—*courtesy Burkhalter Family*

Arlington National Cemetery—*courtesy of the Burkhalter Family*

D-Day Recollections, of Jim Wilkins the Queen's Own Rifles of Canada, B Company

In spring 1941, in camp in N.B. Canada, Rfn. Wilkins is third from the left

Jim Wilkins in 1997

"In late 1942, the 3rd Canadian Infantry Division was picked to take part in the allied invasion of Normandy and began a period of intensive commando-type assault training. During all of 1943 and into the spring of '44, we spent a lot of time at sea on various types of landing craft, from what we called mother ships (where we were comfortably housed in mess decks with hammocks to sleep in, all the way down to small L.C.A. assault boats that could take just 30 men and their gear). This training was mostly done off the south coast of England except for one period when we went up to Scotland to Locke Fyne on the Duke of Argyle's estate at Invenary. Here we spent four weeks of more assault training mostly in wet weather. We were never dry.

During this same period, Hitler had ordered Field Marshall Erwin Rommel, "The Desert Fox" of the North African campaign, to erect an Atlantic Wall on the Normandy coast. He did a bang up job building huge steel reinforced concrete bunkers, pillboxes, laid barbwire, mines, artillery, machinegun nests and mortar pits. He also had deadly beach obstacles built such as steel girders and old railway tracks raised in a pyramid and hung with mines that would easily blowup an assault craft. Rommel moved new units into position including first-rate Panzer divisions and SS troops whose moral and fighting determination had become legendary. They also had superior weapons such as Panther and Tiger tanks and deadly 88mm anti-tank guns. All of this went to guarantee us a hostile reception. When Rommel addressed his generals he coined the phrase, "when they come and they will come, it will be the longest day."

In May of 1944 we went into security camps surrounded with barbwire and guards to keep us in and as we moved from camp to camp toward Southampton it became known as the sausage machine. We studied aerial photos of the beaches taken by low flying Spitfires but they still did not tell us where we were going. Then came a pay parade and we finally knew, we had been paid in brand new French francs. Eventually, we arrived in Southampton and boarded our mother ship the "SS Monowai" on the morning of June 4th and steamed off to rendezvous with the other ships. We played cards, crown & anchor or shot craps to while away the time.

Nobody seemed nervous or anxious. Tomorrow we would land in France but weather was so bad in the channel that the operation was postponed 24 hours until the 6th of June. Apparently the Navy was operating in a kind of tide timeframe and if there were any more delays the operation would have to be cancelled. Finally General Eisenhower gave the go ahead and we steamed out of Southampton, around the Isle of Wight and out into the channel headed south for Normandy. Some 7000 ships of all shapes and sizes. We went into our hammocks early because we were told it would be a very early reveille. It was, we were called around 3:30am and two men from every section were sent to the galley to get our breakfast of scrambled eggs, bacon, coffee, bread and jam. It was to be my last meal for four days.

At about 4:30 we were ordered to go on deck where sailor guides took us to our appointed stations. Our landing craft were at deck level and we could just climb in. The first section was #1 of "B" Company on the port side. They sat facing in. The next group was on the starboard side consisting of odds and sods, our platoon Sergeant, Freddy Harris who had given up a commission to be with us, the company Sergeant major Bill Wallace and company staff such as runners, stretcher bearers, combat engineers who were to somehow breach the 9 ft wall in front of us, blow up pillboxes and gun positions. Next, came my section—#2 of "B" company. We climbed in and sat on a low bench running down the center facing forward. I was at the very back. It was not a good position for us, last group in, and first group out. The waves were pretty high and as we were lowered into the water, the high seas met us with a vengeance. The marine crew had a rough time unhooking the winch lines and so off we went to rendezvous with the rest of the L.C.A. group.

Perhaps I should stop here and try to explain the makeup of the first wave. Some of you may be saying what is he talking about, what is a division, a regiment, a company or a platoon section? A division of infantry is made up of about 15,000 men, a regiment is made up of 800 men and there are 9 regiments to a division. These are broken up into three brigades of three regiments each. Each regiment has 18 platoons. The first 6 are support, consisting of a 3" mortar platoon, a bren gun carrier platoon and an anti-tank platoon. Stretcher-bearers (the band), cooks and an engineer platoon and so on. The other 12 platoons are infantry, 3 to each company of about 120 men—each platoon has bout 35 men in 3 sections plus a platoon Sergeant, an officer and a 2" motor section of 2 men. The navy finally sorted themselves out and we started to move toward the beach five miles away. At this point I must tell you how the army works. The generals always like to have reserves so they hold back one full brigade of three regiments totaling 2400 men who would come in about three-quarters to one hour later. We are down to two brigades of 6 regiments or 3200 going in. The Brigadiers of the two brigades want to hold back one regiment each for his reserve or 1600 men, so we are down to only 4 regiments to going in. Next, the Regimental colonel decides to hold back "C" and "D" company for twenty minutes as his reserve or 480 men. So who the hell is going to make the first assault? Two companies out of 4 regiments—"A" and "B" companies of the North Shore Regiment, "A" and "B" of the Queens Own Rifles, "A" and "B" from the Winnipeg Rifles and "A" and "B" from the Regina Rifles and one company from the Highland Light Infantry. Nine companies in all, plus assorted extras like engineers, medics, signalers, etc. each company has 5 boats so the total was 45 boats consisting of about 30 men each or a total of 1350 men who are to be in the first wave assault on Juno beach. We started out with 15,000—where the hell was the other 13,850?

We are told they will be along shortly, as soon as you clear the beach of pillboxes and machine gun nests. We're going to get some help from a squadron of the 1st Hussars tank regiment. They're going to land before us and take out the pillboxes and machinegun nests, but, as history proved, it didn't happen. The 45 boats start in—at about 1500 yards we can see the wall in back of the beach. It looks to be maybe 8 feet high. We are told to stand up. Beside us was a ship that fires L.C.R. rockets. The forward deck is cleared and pointing up are maybe a dozen tubes or mortars at a 45-degree angle. All of a sudden they fire a salvo, great clouds of smoke and flame engulf the boat. Ten minutes later they fire again. You can follow the rockets by eye as they curve upward. We watched one salvo go high over the beach just as a Spitfire came along. He flew right into it and blew up. That pilot never had a chance and was probably the first casualty on Juno Beach. Overhead we can hear the roar of large shells from battleships, cruisers and destroyers. Beside us is a boat with pom poms (anti-aircraft) guns shooting away at church steeples and other high buildings which had observers who where spotting for the German ground troops.

Soon we are only 500 yards from the beach and are ordered to get down. Minutes later the boat stops and begins to toss in the waves. The ramp goes down and without hesitation my section leader, Cpl. John Gibson, jumps out well over his waist in water. He only makes a few yards and is killed. We have landed dead on into a pillbox with a machine gun blazing away at us. We didn't hesitate and jumped into the water one after the other—I was last of the first row. Where was everybody? My section is only half there, some were just floating on their Mae West's.

My bren gun team of Tommy Dalrymple and Kenny Scott are just in front of me when something hit my left magazine pouch and stops me up short for a moment. The round had gone right through two magazines, entered my left side and came out my back. Kenny keeps yelling for me to come on and I tell him I'm coming. We are now up to our knees in water and you can hear a kind of buzzing sound all around as well as the sound of the machine gun itself. All of a sudden something slapped the side of my right leg and then a round caught me dead center up high on my right leg causing a compound fracture. By this time I was flat on my face in the water, I've lost my rifle, my helmet is gone and Kenny is still yelling at me to come on. He is also shot in the upper leg but has no broken bones. I yell back, I can't, my leg is broken, get the hell out of here, and away he goes and catches up to Tommy. Poor Tom, I've got ten of his bren gun magazines and they're pulling me under. I soon get rid of them and flop over onto my back and start to float to shore where I meet five other riflemen all in very bad shape. The man beside me is dead within minutes. All the while we are looking up at the machine gun firing just over our heads at the rest of our platoon and company and then our platoon Sergeant and friend of mine, who had given up a commission to be with us was killed right in front of me.

Finally I decided that this is not a good place to be and managed to slip off my pack and webbing and start to crawl backward on my back at an angle away from the gun towards the wall about 150 ft away. I finally made it and lay my back against it. In front of me I can see bodies washing back and forth in the surf. Soon, one of my friends, Willis Gambrel, a walking wounded, showed up and we each had one of my cigarettes, which surprisingly were fairly dry. Then he left to find a first aid center. A medic came along and put a bandage on my leg. I had forgotten all about the hole in my side. Then two English beach party soldiers came along carrying a 5-gallon pot of tea. "Cup of tea Canada?" and they gave me tea in a tin mug. It was hot and mixed 50/50 with rum. It was really good.

In the meantime "A" Company had gotten ashore with their share of casualties and started to take out the various gun emplacements and so did the rest of "B" Company. Presently there were 4 or 5 fellows with me. Then at last, a Sherman tank from the First Hussars finally showed up. They had come in too late to help us. All of a sudden he stopped just a few feet past us, turned toward the wall, ambles up to within ten feet of the wall and commenced to fire over the wall. There are things at the end of these gun barrels called recoil deflectors so that the muzzle blast comes out sideways. The muzzle blast came directly down where we were lying. The man beside me had a bandage around his head and eyes and he screamed every time they fired. My leg didn't like it either. Finally after much arm waving at the crew commander he finally got the message that we didn't appreciate his presence.

I had already got a shot of morphine from a medic and dozed a little. Soon the tide was almost at my boots and at long last two English stretcher-bearers came and started to evacuate us from the beach. They carried me in water up to their ankles. The fellow at my head lost his grip and said to his pal, to put me down for a second. Just then a good wave came in right over me and on the way out picked up my broken leg and through it at a right angle to the stretcher. I said "Would you mind putting my leg back on the stretcher?" "Sorry Canada", one said and grabbed my boot and put my leg back. I got back at him when they lifted me over the wall to some fellows on the top at almost 45-degree angle—all the water in the stretcher came gushing out right into his face. I was put with a group of other wounded and eventually a doctor came along and asked where I was hit. My leg is broken I said, and with that he took a look and said, you'll be okay son.

Two German POW's picked me up and carried me to a concrete air raid shelter—probably for the German defense troops, and placed me on a low bunk. Very quickly the bunks were full and people were put on the floor. A German boy was on the floor right beside me and was in bad shape. Just before it got dark a German mortar came over and landed just outside the door, blew it off and filled the bunker with dirt, smoke and chunks of gravel. Eventually a medic came in and gave the German boy a shot of morphine. I said I'd take one of those if you don't mind. Okay he said, and as darkness fell on June 6th, I was soon asleep.

By this time all that was left of my platoon of 35 men was one Lance Sergeant, one wounded Lance Corporal and six riflemen. All the rest were dead or wounded. Field Marshall Erwin Rommel had been right; it had been and will always be the longest day. Altogether, The Queen's Own Rifles lost 143 men killed or wounded. By August when the Normandy battle was over the regiment had 640 casualties including 209 killed. By May of 1945, the regiment suffered over 1000 wounded and 462 riflemen were dead.

Lest we forget."

Photos Courtesy of Jim Wilkins

Guadalcanal Journal
Guadalcanal Island

BRITISH SOLOMONS

Captured August 7, 1942

By

United States Marines

Journal Entries by Pfc. James A. Donahue (1921-1998)

The jungle is thick as hell. The Fifth regiment landed first and marched to the airport. We went straight through and then cut over to block the escape of the Japs. It took 3 days to go 6 miles. Japs took off, left surplus first day, which was done away with.

The second day was murder. All along the way were discarded packs, rifles, mess gear and everything imaginable. The second night it rained like hell and the bugs were terrible. The Second Battalion had reached the Lunga River. We had to cross four streams.

The third day we came back. The Japs had beaten us in their retreat. We took up beach defense positions. We have been bombed every day by airplanes and a submarine shells us every now and then.

Our foxholes are 4ft. deep. We go out on night patrols and it is plenty rugged. We lie in the foxholes for 13 to 14 hrs at a clip and keep firing at the Japs in the jungle. As yet there is no air support. The mosquitoes are very bad at night. The ants & fleas bother us continually. The planes strafed the beach today. A big naval battle ensued the second day we were here, which resulted in our ship, the Elliot, being sunk. All of our belongings were lost.

We raided the Jap village and now we are wearing Jap clothes. It is extremely hot. U.S.S. North Carolina sunk two cruisers and destroyers. Japs are still in the hills. We have no A.A. but use the half-tracks against the Jap airplanes. Japs landed food and ammunition by parachute. Our Lt. Colonel ambushed & bayoneted. We cleared brush from river for an expected Jap landing. The patrols are going deeper into the jungle each night. They tried to ambush us last night. We are not allowed to fire. I dreamt that C. had deserted me.

Tonight two Jap cruisers shelled us. Boy, what a noise they make! The next day three Flying Fortresses badly damaged them. The airplane scored a direct hit out of two bombs on one ship. An expected invasion kept us scurrying late last night; we got up at 4A.M. to meet the attack. But during the night the Jap convoy was blasted out of the sea. Another cruiser entered the harbor today but the bombers got it. Our beach positions have orders not to retreat.

While we were giving the one cruiser hell, the Japs landed a battalion of men on Red Beach, but we did not know about it. The next night 12 of us went on patrol & took up positions on our side of the Lunga River. About 3A.M. hell broke loose and the Japs started to cross the stream. I want to forget all about it. My buddies being shot and blown apart. I can thank God for getting out safe.

A convoy of Jap ships was sighted and tonight we prepared for a landing of 10,000. Just before dusk we got 35 more planes in and the word was passed that half our fleet was waiting for the convoy. Marine flyers knocked down 19 Japs to three losses.

Last night we were shelled with naval gunfire. The air bombings are continuing despite the fact we have planes. Guam and Wake gunners now with three defenses say this is the hottest spot of the war. The final total on the Jap landing is 1,300 Japs killed to 38 Marines.

We have had no mail as yet. When it rains here, the mud is up to our ankles. Twenty-one Jap planes came over today. They are coming over regularly. I wonder where their base is? We lose three Marines a day when not fighting. The First Battalion Fifth had the Japs in the hills at his mercy and they wound up ambushing us. Eighteen Marines killed. One supply ship came plus two destroyers and while we were unloading the supply ship, the Jap bombers sunk the destroyer.

Dysentery has swept the battalion. It started right after the battle. The score on the dead Japs is now 1,500. I am very hard hit with dysentery having had it now for 15 days. My rectum is the most painful thing on me. I can't get to sleep to the wee hours of the morning. By the time I get to sleep I am a nervous wreck. The Islands abound with rats, lizards and at night they run all around you. At night the sound is multiplied hundreds of times so you don't know whether a Jap is around or not.

Our battalion is up for some kind of cross for our action in the annihilation of the Jap Landing Party. Johnny Rivers no doubt will receive Congressional Medal of Honor. I need not fear of forgetting him for he will live in my memories.

There is some talk of us being home for Christmas. I'll trust in God. Dogfights ensue in the air each day. What a thrill to see a Jap shot out of the air! Jap airplanes raided us and hit a destroyer. It took about four minutes for it to go down. Some say it was torpedoed at the same time.

We were bombed by air last night. I don't know how they get over us without the word getting passed. One Marine got his head blown off while messing with a Jap souvenir. In their desperation to remedy dysentery, they are giving opium. They say the Japs are all hopped up when they attack.

I saw a cat right in back of our camp. I wonder where in the hell he came from? They bomb every day. Our fellows went out to the airport on working party. When air raid signal went, they went to a ravine. One of the personnel bombs landed and killed three, seriously wounded two. It was a horrible blow to us. Cameron was one of the best men in the Corps. I was going to visit him when we got home. The way men are getting killed I wonder if any of us will get back. B., one of the boys who went to hell and back with me, will be a cripple. If I get home you can be sure I will see those boys.

Bombs, bombs, one goes nuts here. I wonder when we are getting relieved? The same night we got word that the Japs were going to attack. We moved guns and ammunition to river and dug in. The burial party for our boys dug the holes. The men were lowered in wrapped in Jap blankets. Chaplain said a few words and they were gone. We are still waiting for the Japs to attack. Last night a plane flew over us and dropped flares on the airport. At first we thought it was gas. Fifteen minutes later two cruisers at Kuhum and Hell's Point shelled us.

Japs landed heavy artillery during the shelling and they opened fire. Mortars were pulled out because we did not have enough range. After guns came back, we went up to the point to cart ammo back. Early dawn our planes took off. We had three air raids today so far. Japs are using a new system. They are sending in the zero and a little while later came the bombers. Japs are sure to attack tonight. We heard machine gun fire all today. They are probably moving into position.

Two Jap seaplanes off a cruiser came in very bold like and strafed the beach defenses. We had no planes up. The fireworks began about 10:30PM when 3 battalion mortars laid down a barrage. 75mm then took it up. We shelled the Jap village all night. Jap forces are probably up the river. We hope they try to pass Hells Point.

Those two seaplanes came back this morning and we were ready for. It took about two minutes to shoot them both down. We have aircraft carrier and three cans outside the harbor. I hope. (We don't lose many pilots but the planes.) About 1800, 10 seaplanes came in and bombed and strafed the airfield. Chuck opened up with BAR.

A map found on a dead Jap officer lead us to believe they were going to hit 3rd Battalion and then come behind us, the 2nd Battalion. We got this news a day late and if the 3rd had not held last night we would all be dead. If they hit the 3rd again tonight the 2nd will move from their beach defense into position for a flank movement on the Japs.

We have had three air raids a day for the last three days. Two days ago our fighters shot down 20 Japs and lost one. The Raiders had 50% casualties when they contacted the Japs. Paratroopers lost 200 out of 300.

We get 2 meals a day and coffee for dinner. I am always hungry. I don't care what and how Cassie will cook but it will be OK with me. We have been living on Jap rice and oats for a month and our only diversion is playing cards.

The foxholes are becoming like home to us. There is a rumor that the 7th is coming in today. We have no envelopes so we can't write letters.

The four cruisers, which shelled us the other night, were sunk. Today planes off Wasp and Enterprise intercepted two waves of enemy bombers. 28 planes in the first wave and 18 in the second.

I went down to the cemetery to see Bill's grave and saw MP's burying 48 marines from our latest battle. 2100 dead Japs in front of Division Headquarters. 1400 in front of 3rd Battalion. We have been fighting every day since we got here. The strain is great. There is so much arguing amongst us. The food is getting a little better.

We have equipped the natives and they are fighting the Japs. We lost three tanks in the last skirmish. Our squad stands two-hour watches each night since three Jap officers got into Division HQ and stabbed a (TOP) Sergeant before they were killed. Our 75's fired over 4000 shells in the last big encounter. A huge naval battle ensued when our convoy carrying 7th Marines and part of the Army met a Jap convoy. We sank 20 out of 28 of their ships. We lost the Wasp. 7th Marines went back to New (Hebrides). Wish they would come.

We have mounted 11 search lights near Kuhum and have added 5" guns on the beach. Jap village was set on fire by our artillery. We made a plaque for Bill's grave today. Today the 7th pulled in to bolster defenses. USS McCauley AA guns shot down Buck Atwood, our own pilot. Raiders and paratroopers boarded ships for the states. They had about 85% casualties. They sure rate it.

We were shelled last night as a Jap planes dropped flares. The dysentery epidemic has cooled down somewhat. Our shore batteries gave the cruiser hell, which shelled us. Well, today we got the word that our battalion is going to leave the beach and protect the airport from the rear.

When I say jungle, I mean jungle. One thing though we don't have rats here. However, we can hear the alligators in the morning and night.

Harry M. was shot last…by Jap snipers. We kill the women snipers as quick as the men. We are cutting trails through the jungle in order to widen the circle around the airport. This island was pounded for 43 days by land, sea and air. Now we hope the Japs have conceded this. Every night though you hear the bullets flying. The officers can't control the men when we are on patrol. Its everyman for himself. When a Japanese patrol signals surrender, the order "cease fire" is given. We hold our fire 'till they are plainly visible in our sights and then we open up. Few are the times that a Jap will surrender.

Second Battalion 7th Marines just pushed on in front of us. These 90mm AA guns of ours are really a beautiful gun. The best Marine gunners man them. The 3rd Defense, some of which have not seen the states for 30 months. Since we have been on the island we have lived on half rations. After 8 days of peace from the air, 11 Japs came over and bombed us. The Fifth bore the brunt of the attack.

I am suffering from infected eye. Still standing two-hour watches. The Jap planes came down again today, but we shot down 12 bombers. The Japs try every trick in the bag. Trip machine gun fire, hiding grenades in rocks. I remember one calling "cease fire marines." Its no wonder to me the 3rd Battalion cracked up in this position. I think I will eventually.

I dreamed about C. last night. We were kissing a lot. Then she told me that a fellow was taking her out. His name was Bill. Well, if he is anything like the Bill I know she would be foolish to have me. Bill Cameron was the fairest, cleanest man I ever hope to know. He was willing to give his life for America. He told me this while under bombardment and we lay in the foxhole.

R. died yesterday in a US Army Hospital. Next time no one is going to talk me out of seeing my buddies who are injured. The patrol found three dead Japs, but no live ones. It's a funny thing; we will be talking at night as if it wasn't a war. Then suddenly some one hollers "Air Raid" and we dive for our holes. Once again we are in war. It happened last night three times.

We hear that the Army in the States is on a six-day maneuver without any luxuries or amusements. How perfectly horrible. We are afraid the boys might get lonesome during these long days. We Marines call McArthur "Dug-Out Doug." The Marines laugh at him. Admiral

Nimitz came around today. He awarded the Navy Cross to a few of the boys. I lost my chewing gum that I had for three days.

We all have the jitters in this position. I can understand why the 3rd Battalion needed relief. We will need it before long. We still hear we will be home for Christmas. I try not to think about it. The mail boat did not come in as expected. It just prolonged the agony. If the people back home could only realize what mail means to us. Things are getting better here. We were issued some clothing, which we needed very, very much.

A few more days have gone by now as I enter a few more facts. We have not been getting bombed in the daytime. However, the Japs come at night. Three and four times we are out of our sacks and in the shelters. We are bleary eyed. Three Jap Zero's strafed our position and all were brought down. The pilots were heavily bandaged; therefore, they were probably suicide missions. One Fortress last night crashed due to a wounded Zero going headlong. Navy construction workers are doing a bang up job building runways and bridges and roads. Now they are building a pier, which will hasten the unloading of ships. Everyone is a nice guy. We expect the Army in soon. That is if they can get them out of the USO. Our patrol captured four Jap 75's and also destroyed 2000 round of ammunition. In the larger shell was some sort of acid.

Another patrol captured two 75's approximately 2000 yds from our position. Up to this time their artillery has not worried us much. But now the situation has taken a change for the worse. There have been no Jap bombings for two days. We are supposed to have a huge Army convoy at Pago Pago in the American Samoas. This is probably a rumor. Rumors are the only thing we talk about. And it is mostly good news. It certainly keeps us thinking.

Bill Cameron's face keeps coming before me at night. He had everything in the world to go home to, of all people. Death strikes oddly.

While I am writing this, parts of the 1st, 5th, 7th regiments are engaged in a major campaign. At 10 this morning we got the word to stand by to move out. Maybe the boys were having trouble. Anyway a few hours later we were secured. The artillery has been pounding night and day. The dive-bombers and P-40's are unleashing hell on the Japs. No mercy or quarter is given. If they are wounded a few rifle shots end it all.

A few days' previous about 10 nuns were brought in. They had fled when Japan took over. Two were raped. The artillery fire continued through the night. 200 Jap prisoners so far. Well, we will need them to bury the dead Japs. Just like they did the last time.

It's noon now and we have just been given the word that an air raid is expected. Most of the boys are cleaning their rifles and bayonets for inspection. When I say hot, I mean hot. We were bombed last night by a lone duck off a cruiser. This cruiser was sunk, the other three destroyers with it escaped.

The battle at Kuhum reached its climax late yesterday. Our artillery and strafe fire murdered the Japs. There were a lot of Marine casualties but a few deaths. The General wants this island secured by the 12th of October. The First Battalion of the 7th came back to their old positions leaving only three to engage the remainder of Japs. The 3rd Battalion 1st suffered severe losses. I wonder if Waterman's all right.

The food situation has changed considerably from the time our platoon had to butcher 2 cows. We get potatoes twice a day and desert each supper. Corned beef and tongue are the only things offered in the meat line. The subjects we talk on are varied from religion to banking. As soon as it's dark the discussions begin.

I am letting my hair grow thick on the top in order to keep the sun off it. We take 4 quinine tablets a week. It's a funny thing. When we go down Kuhum on a working party to unload ships we meet a lot of our old friends. When we do we steal a couple cans of peaches and go off to a spot to eat and talk over old times. It's not unlike meeting a friend in town and going to get a couple of beers and chew the rag.

We hear that 400 planes bombed Tokyo. That makes us feel wonderful. Now they are really getting a taste of their own medicine.

Our planes went up yesterday and they had a good time. They shot down nine Zeros and sank or left sinking four Jap cruisers. This squadron expects relief. They only have two of the original ships left. 224th (pursuit) has reinforced them recently.

The Jap bombers got over us today and dropped their eggs. No damage done. Rubal had 40,000 lbs. of bombs dropped on it. The Marines believe that the Army will be in by the end of the week.

Today is Sunday and I usually celebrate it by saying three rosaries. The three thieves, Mugno, Carr and Don went down to the Division Commissary and brought back plenty of food and envelopes. It has been raining a lot lately. I hope the rainy season has not set in. I laugh at the fellows trying to roll cigarettes.

The harbor is full of dead Japs from the recent naval battles. Our planes and surface craft did a good job. Three ships of ours damaged to eight of theirs. I hear we are moving to a new position tomorrow. The Army is still not coming in. We had a slight earthquake last night. It has been the fourth one we had.

My eye is bothering me again.

The Army came in today, 3000 of them. What a reception. Three air raids today. They killed one and wounded three. This was our 89th bombing raid. This doesn't count the times our planes intercepted theirs. They sure had their eye on the airport and boy did they hit it. Nine direct times on the steel runway. Toward dusk enemy artillery opened up on us. We retaliated. At 11:30, two cruisers and one battleship shelled us for two hours. So far today we were hit by land, sea and air. A Marine Sgt. asked an Army NCO for a working party. He replied indignantly that his men were combat men. The Marine ripped his shirt open to show him bayonet wounds and asked, "What the hell do you think we are?"

The seaplanes off the cruisers bombed us four times and kept us awake till 5:30 this morning. This morning right after breakfast Condition Red was given. The Japs sure mean business.

This is the first chance I had to write. For three days and nights we have been bombarded by land, sea and air. 14-inch shells off a battleship kept punching our defenses. We have been hit by air three times in one hour. At night the Jap artillery gets started. Gas for the airplanes is very low. Situation is desperate. Our battalion pulled out of line to take up 5th's position. Army relieved us on other line.

Four transports of Jap troops unloaded. We sunk or damaged every one. We need reinforcements. The crisis is fast approaching.

All the men are in high spirits. The situation is still unchanged. We are being bombed and shelled. Our navy poured 2000 rounds into the Japs. Our planes have been dive-bombing and strafing them. We are living in the hills now. Reminds me of the cave dwellers for we live in caves that we have dug in the sides of the hills.

While 80 of our planes were landing 7seven Jap bombers and six Zeros blew up some gas drums on our beach. They were all knocked down. While test firing with our guns we spotted a Jap O.P. and we blew them to hell.

Colonel says we have a task force outside the harbor. We had an alert last night and were on the guns for two hours. We were finally secured.

My eye is clearing up.

The heat is worse in the hills than in the jungle. This position is our third and it envelops the three types of fighting. Beach, Jungle and Hills. The fellows don't think of going home for Christmas anymore. There is no use writing letters, as they can't be mailed.

We are expecting the attack any night. A few of us were down the river yesterday. First time I had a bath since three weeks ago. We have set up a Cossack Post for security of the guns. We are using three Lewis Guns. It burns me up to see the material we are using. And when America is the richest country in the world. We have the Lewis Guns but no mounts. We cut branches off trees and use them as bipods.

Three flights of Japs were intercepted today. Every man is brown as an Indian. There are still working parties. I think that even in battle we would have a working party.

Last night three Jap bombers played hell with our defenses. Dropped quite a few bombs. We had our searchlights on him and had him in the light but the AA was way off. A Jap half-track was hit by mortar shells and demolished.

The Army played smart at Hell's Point and annihilated a 30-man Jap patrol. They are a National Guard outfit from South Dakota. Seven Jap planes bombed us today killing six and wounding 43. I was very, very close. God was with me.

I finally got the story of how the Japs got through with a 10,000 man landing party. Ships carrying 250,000 Japs were heading this way. So the Navy had to let the point get through in order to get at the body.

I can't see how this division will be fit for another campaign. We certainly need to be reorganized. Every outfit has suffered heavy casualties. It is beginning to look like we will never get off this island. One thing that can be said about this place. It is the most beautiful place that I have ever seen. I am glad to say that the rats do not run around you on this position as before. Albert and I were down to Regimental Commissary on a Working Party when it was bombed. We stole plenty of fruit. I would hate to be killed with all that sin on my soul.

The fever has touched me. I feel weak all over.

One might ask, "How does it feel to kill someone?" You don't stop to think. There is a man intent on killing you, so you kill or be killed. The Jap artillery has got our position and landed some close ones. We expect mail tomorrow.

We were bombed last night again. The bombers were repulsed today. Gunner Maples brought two Japs in. They were the most emaciated people I have ever seen. One kept his hands together and prayed for mercy. The other was an imbecile. The boys had a good time kidding him. Both prisoners were treated humanely.

Again we were bombed today. The artillery pounded us all day. Our guns replied. The purpose was seen later on when the Japs tried to crash through our lines at 5th, 2nd area. We demolished seven of their tanks. Our dive-bombers raised hell with them. They hit an ammunition dump, which burnt well into the night. Our torpedo boats now have torpedoes, so we do not expect any more shelling. Most of the men have cots now except those who are in the front lines, where it would be suicide to lay above the ground. Flying shrapnel would get you.

Jungle fever is predominant here. Again today the Jap artillery pounded our front lines. We believe them to be five-inch guns, which they salvaged off their sinking transports. The Japs are very good with artillery.

They found our range and scored a direct hit on our 75mm. Our guns blazed their answer. In the last engagement 1,400 Japs dead, seven Marine casualties.

Tonight is Saturday night and our squad was on guard at the Cossack Post. It rained like hell and there was no protection from dusk till dawn in the pouring rain.

Always on the lookout for Jap infiltration. While on guard, 1st Battalion 7th shot up their respective area. I guess the Japs are feeling our line out.

I have finally procured a cot. We will probably take up a new area now. Before breakfast today Condition Red was given. Eleven Zeros and two bombers were overhead. The two bombers were shot down, one by the front lines who opened up with everything from a pistol to a 37. 20MM guns at the airport got the other one. For three hours the sky battle raged. The Zeroes came in strafing and the gunman on their tail. I saw one zero whose wing had been shot off. He bailed out and the parachute did not open. Quite a sight to see a Jap fall through space for 30,000 feet. I saw four Jap planes burst into flames and fall to the ground. We see much of this, and while this was going on, a naval battle ensued. I didn't get the news on that yet.

The Jap bombers just came over but we had a ten-plane patrol, which gave them hell. They dropped their bombs. We saw two bombers go down in flames. If you want action join the Marine Corps. I didn't believe it 'till I hit this island.

I wish I could find some ripe papaya. Our food is getting terrible again. There is a terrible strain on our men. H., R., S. and B. should be under observation.

They just (Japs) got done dive-bombing the airport. They were using Stupa dive-bombers. The story on the attack was Jap losses 20 zeros, five bombers, one cruiser, one destroyer, and a turned back task force. Japs are attacking every night. Our lines are bearing up good. This makes the 83-day mark we have been on the front lines. Guess what? We had no air raid today. However, at night two bombers came over and dropped their loads.

A squadron of Flying Fortresses from New Caldonia turned back a Jap invasion force with heavy casualties—Nine of our dive-bombers went out and dropped their load on the Nipponese. They have five six-inch guns, which they salvaged off sinking boats. We are knocking these guns off one by one. Airplanes are the only way to get them, because our guns can't reach them. The Japs on the island should be pretty well under control in another month—that is, if they don't land anymore troops.

A Jap is a vicious fighting machine. A Marine patrol the other day met another patrol, which ambushed them. They were Japs with Marine helmets and uniforms. Eight marines were killed, two Japs killed. They are sly. A friend of mine told me that I was killed the first night ashore along with 18 others when they were ambushed. Japanese are experts on camouflage.

A line of Marines withdrew off a hill they were defending. Shortly after, they were ordered to charge with fixed bayonets. They did and they recaptured the hill.

I gave a buddy a baldy. His head looked like a cue ball.

The Japs tried three bayonet charges against the Army who are in our old position. It is a very nice place for our lines. There is a huge field in front, which is strung with three aprons of barbed wire. They were let come in each consecutive time and each was broken. Result: 600 dead Japs.

I am expecting a big air raid today because of not having one yesterday. Well, the Japs have not bombed us for two days. They have something up their sleeve. A bomber came over last night and dropped his load.

The Nips attacked again last night. Again they were repulsed. This continual fighting is driving a lot of men to a nervous breakdown. They don' attack 'till the moon goes down. Last night they threw smoke bombs and shouted "Gas Attack!" But it didn't work. More Japs speak American than American speaks Jap. Regiment figures that there are 10,000 and 5,000 have been killed in this last landing of October 23, 1942. When they unloaded four transports, naval gunfire has silenced those big Jap guns. However, Whistling Pete has fired a few rounds today.

I hear the 8th Marines are coming in. We sure hope so. Last night we expected three Jap destroyers and we would think that they tried to land supplies to the Japs. However we weren't shelled, so I am hoping they did not get in.

We feel safer now that the Torpedo Boats have torpedoes. Japanese are still attacking in small numbers and are being repulsed with heavy casualties. Japs have not bombed us for four days. Fellows are getting touchy. Continual arguments. Lieutenant has punched F. on two different occasions. M. and L. had a go. S vs. M. H vs. A. A. vs. A.

I have not entered anything for eight days. Last Sunday we received orders to take up the 2nd battalion 5th who had, along with six other battalions, to take the offensive against the Japs. We went to this position, which is infested with snipers. One doesn't know when one is going to get shot. However, we are thankful that we weren't chosen for the difficult task. During this time we were bombed twice. During the day 37 Jap planes came over and dropped their loads. But only two went back. Five destroyers landed 1,500 Japs. While landing the 7th Marines 1 Bu was watching all this but they couldn't fire because the destroyers would have shelled them. The very next day two cruisers and two cons of ours shelled the honorable Nips. They fired quite a few off port side, swung around and shelled them off the starboard side. We were watching the whole procedure from the O.P. We lost one transport in the channel. Three cruisers and three cons shelled us last night 'till our torpedo boats got hot.

The rumors have it we will be home by December 20. I am getting tired hearing these rumors. Malaria is more prevalent than ever. Huck is in the hospital. We are issued four quinine pills a week. However, I maneuver another one. If four can't stop malaria, why don't they give us more? They fly the quinine in. We were given envelopes and told to write because the mail ship was leaving. I imagine we are going to get mail soon. Out of the eight days we were here, it has rained six.

I have found a stretcher here in this position and am using it for a bed. In case I am knifed in my sleep, the stretcher will come in handy. I got hold of a Reesing Gun and fired it for a test. It certainly is a swell gun. I would like to bring it home. But, who knows? Today is going to be a big day. The 105 Howitzers will fire 460 rounds followed by the 155's and the 75's will be firing constantly. The 155's have hit a Jap cruiser establishing it as a most accurate artillery piece on the island. The reason we only have seven instead of eight is due to the fact that while loading at New Hebrides, one fell into the brink. New Zealand is giving the First Division a River Bird for right shoulder. And England is giving us the (Four de Gerse) for taking back British Solomon Island(s). These paired with the fact that we will be issued new uniforms, gives us something to look for. Col. Pollack and Col. McKelvy, 2nd. and 3rd. Battalion Commanders respectively, received Congressional Medal of Honor. Reason being that their outfits have been the longest on the front line without being relieved. It has been hell, but now it makes me feel good that our commander has received recognition of the fact. We had an air raid today, which failed to materialize. Probably our planes met them far out.

Again I can thank God for letting me live. We were digging three alternate gun positions in case the Japs break through. We were not given any condition. Suddenly, Fisher spotted 30 Jap bombers just about over us. We grabbed our helmets and ran like hell. Where we were running I do not know, just trying to get out of reach of the bombers. It can't be done because no one knows where they are going to bomb. Mugno and I finally spotted a small foxhole and we dove in. Just then we heard them dropping. All the time I was repeating "Hail, Mary."

Everytime a small convoy comes here, the Japs send a mob of planes over. We now have a two-day alert. There is a 40-ship Jap convoy heading are way. This morning our ships shelled the Japs again.

It looks like we are really in for it now. We have been issued three days iron ration. Japs came over with two flights of Focke-Wielf's, 25 in each wave. Also, torpedo bombers attacked our beach. We expect heavy shelling tonight. Huge Jap convoy coming our way. We unloaded six transports this morning. The bombers did not hit anything. Our battalion received 200 replacements. They are four months out of Boot Camp—haven't seen action either.

Today we are happy. We received mail and plenty of packages. Fellows who got them shared with the unfortunates. Me. The men worked all day consolidating our positions. Tonight is probably the night. We received 30 new dive-bombers today. They help a lot. It is raining now and will be for a few days. I received two letters and it was too dark to read them. I was afraid I would get knocked off before morning and then not read the letters. I saw it happen before. I got a lot more mail. Gee, Cassie is swell.

A big Jap convoy was 300 miles out. 100,000 Japs. Boy, could they cause a lot of trouble. Our planes spotted them and then our ships got hot. Boy, the roar of the guns was terrific! Flashes illuminated the ship. We sank 11 Jap warships and we lost two. We damaged a battleship last night. It was spotted by a gunman and they sent back for dive-bombers. But the dive-bombers couldn't go into action due to clouds. They sent back for torpedo planes and they sank it. Are we glad that convoy did not get in! We are having enough trouble here already. After last night's battle, I did not think we would be molested tonight. We sank four more Jap transports. However, a heavy Jap cruiser shelled the airfield something terrific. A duck dropped flares on the field. Everytime we think the island is secure, something has happened.

It is November 14 and I have received letters dated October 7. That is real good service. A naval battle is still going on. Thirty-one Jap ships sunk and seven of ours lost. That is what Division sent to Washington. Our planes have been flying around all day. Something big is sure happening.

Another battle raged last night. Today makes 100th day we have been on the island. Four Jap transports got through our Navy and are landing at Cooley Point. All the ships have been hit. Their AA keeps firing all the while our ships are strafing. We have received 28 interceptors and nine B-26's. These will probably stop these bombings we have. According to Naval Intelligence, this war was their plan of attack. They started with a 40-ship convoy carrying approximately 100,000 troops. We were supposed to have been bombed and shelled for three days before the convoy arrived. Bombers got in one day and shelled us one night. Our task force met the convoy and 28 Jap ships had a watery grave. Out of the running, 12 were transports and the rest cruisers. Three battleships of theirs had been sunk. Then the Navy and our planes got to the remainder. They sank four transports; four had to be beached at Santa Isabel. The other four, which were beached, are landing their troops now. Our artillery is blasting them.

Jap artillery has been pounding us for two days. The situation has darkened.

Six days have gone by, and we proudly announce that the situation is well in hand, thanks to the gallant Navy. No one can appreciate it like us. We will forever show our gratitude. Had not they intercepted the Jap convoy containing 30,000 soldiers, plus the naval firepower, I daresay Guadalcanal would be another Wake Island.

We read with joy the news clippings of the Solomon Action. It is sad that a lot of the boys cannot see it, those gallant fighting men, 67-man patrol which held off 1,500 of Jap shock troops, veterans of Wake, Guam, Batan, Java. I have a flag with each of these campaigns. Yes, 67 men held them; 28 were killed, 23 wounded. Eighteen men came out alive and unhurt. By the grace of God, I was one.

I was too sick before to write the story on Hell's Point or Green Hill, as some call it. It all started about 3 A.M. in the morning. However we were warned about 11 o'clock to "Stand by your guns." Each man passed on to the other all the way down the line. Was this going to be the real test? All of a sudden our listening posts reported troops moving toward us. But somehow the word of the enemies approach got fouled up somewhere. The Japs crossed the river using coconuts as decoys. They did not expect any Marines there and their point was to assume a flanking position on the point. The point was heavily fortified. I don't mean with big guns but we had a platoon of machine gunners there and 137-men gun crew. We didn't expect 1,500 men to rush us. But we underestimated the savage Jap. A lot of the men were sleeping in their foxholes as a result of working parties during the day and patrols at night. The Japs who crossed the Lunga River caught some of these men unaware. A Jap officer stabbed Cpl. K. with his saber right thru his face. He then raised his sword and came down on the sleeping Cpl. The blow almost severed his leg. It hit him right on the knee bone. K. was very powerful and built like a barrel. By this time E.D.J., a Frenchman, had awakened and attempted to shoot him, but his safety was on and all he could do was parlay the Jap's next blow at him. E.D.J's hand was cut badly. The

Jap officer figured it was too hot for him and started to back away. C., who was about 20 feet away, shot him. The next day C. got his sword.

The Japs still came across and we kept knocking them off. Their machine guns would throw up a barrage for them but their field of fire was limited. They finally succeeded in getting a machine gun across, which was set up right below us. L.B. threw a hand grenade, which silenced it. At the point the river was terrific. The Japs could not get through. They sent a bunch of men into the ocean on rubber mats, which were to land on the left flank of the point. But the barbed wire caught them napping and they were mowed down like rats. The 37 MM gun did plenty of damage with its canister shot. The Japs brought up their field pieces and started laying them into the line and point. Following soon our 105's silenced them. Japs were using rifle grenades and mortars. After about two hours reinforcements came up. They sent two light machine guns, which were mounted between B.'s and my position and R.'s and D.'s. Within ten minutes the whole two crews were shot up. This due to the fact that they were not below the deck. At this point Sgt. M. picked up the gun and started running down the line. He would stop, fire a few good bursts and then take off to a new position. J. moved up behind M., and he and I had a BAR. He shouted if there was room for him in the foxhole. There wasn't so we had to make room. He would be killed if he stayed on the deck. A machine gun had been mounted in an abandoned alligator and they were throwing plenty of lead our way. J. crept as close as possible and made a dive for our hole. He landed okay and M. and I continued our fire. About 5 minutes later I said to B. "Why in hell doesn't he fire?" M. said slowly, "He's dead." I said, "Are you sure?" and he said, "Here is his blood. Feel for his pulse." But we couldn't determine whether he was alive. We couldn't move an inch either, for the Japs were really spraying our lines. So I reached over and felt his pulse. His face was sunken and there was no pulse. Blood began to fill the hole; so later we fixed a poncho so that the blood would stay on the other side. The next morning I saw that he had been hit in the head and chest. While our artillery was finding the Japs range they landed three in our lines so close to us that we were covered with dirt. A. and B., who had positions between B. and us, were blown apart. We thought that the next one would land square on top of us. Another Jap machine gun was set up on our side of the river. B. said, "Let's go down and get them." I said he was crazy. It was suicide to go down that bank. We had no grenades, so we called to D. to heave a pineapple. He did and another crew was wiped out. Toward morning the First Battalion started pushing them out to sea. Our mortars started to go to town. I saw the results of mortar fire. Men blown right out of clothes and shoes. A patrol closed in behind the Japs and it was tough luck for the Japs. The result was complete annihilation of the 1,500, the whole landing party. Our light tanks finished the job. They tried to use their flamethrowers on them, but machine gun fire from tanks stopped that. A few of the injured Japs took shots at our men and were they butchered! Six wounded Japs were taken prisoner and we got some information from them.

They had landed from destroyers and were crack troops. (Marines). I can tell you many tales of Jap cruelty. Sticking prisoners with bayonets. Cutting off ears. We found J.S. with his head bashed in and both ears severed. That is enough for the battle.

We haven't had an air raid for two days. We have got nine Liberators and nine B-26's. Another two days have passed. No air raids. Eight of our Fortresses bombed Rougainville. Hit all the ships in the harbor. They bombed at 12,000, which is very low in any man's language. For Thanksgiving Dinner we had four hamburgers apiece. While Major K. and I went for water in the jeep, Jap artillery let ten rounds go just as we were passing the airport. Their object was the airport. Lucky for us the shells were armor piercing as only two of the ten burst. We sure got out of there fast.

The Division had sent four Jap Officers, who have just got out of the hospital, back to the estimated 4,000 Japs. They must either surrender or die. One hundred twenty-five artillery pieces are lined up on this area and will blast them to hell if no word of surrender comes.

We finally were relieved at the advance position. We spent three weeks there. The 2nd Marines came up. We only had one section there. We were sent up because they expected trouble there. When we got back, you should have seen the tent they gave our squad. It was full of shrapnel holes.

We heard a radio report from Japan to the effect that the Marines were professional killers hired by the U.S. Government. They are merciless, cut throats. Can you imagine me a cutthroat?

We have 14 new replacements, Navy Yard Marines. The Army had a lot of casualties. They pushed on past Point Cruz. They met the Japs. The 8th Marines were sent in to soften the Japs up. The Army said that the Marines did a good job. The Marines pulled out. And by the time the Army came through, Japanese had circled behind "O" Company 182nd Mass. National Guard, and shattered the outfit. They left their machine guns and all in order to get out of the onslaught. They got word back to the rest of the boys and they charged the Japs. Japs taken off guard by this reaction set up for the (Bu rush?) In the meantime "C" turned their machine guns on the Japs. They were surrounded on all but the left flank, which led into the hills. Boy, did they take off! Our casualties were high, but theirs were worse.

For a few days everything had been running smoothly—up until last night. We were sleeping soundly when "F" who was shouting "Jap bomber" awakened us! About the time we got up (nothing flat), we heard the whistling of the coming bombs. I hit the deck as nine personnel bombs exploded. Five minutes later, "Condition Red" was given. There were 25 casualties in G Battery. Had the condition been given when it should, these men would have been under cover. Somebody was responsible for this and we blame the men on the radar. We expected two Jap transports, two cruisers, and three destroyers. So they should have been on the alert.

Japanese troops on the island who are harassing our lines are not many in number. However, they are using mortars against us, which is the most deadly infantry weapon. We now have three English bombers with us. They came in after the Gruman Wildcat gained superiority in the air.

Today I received my warrant making me a First Class Pvt. It is now November 26, Thanksgiving. I thank the Lord for many things, especially my safety.

Last night we were bombed again, we received the Condition Red long before it happened, so we were ready. I don't think there were any casualties. The 8th Marines and 2nd Bu 182nd Army have pulled back to their old defense lines. The Fifth Regiment pulled out, the first echelon; no doubt it looks like they will send the amphibious tractors back to the Florida swamps. We have not heard "Whistling Willie" for a while. We hope he is through. Gunner M. was drunk last night and he gave us the dope.

He had a 25-man combat patrol and Capt. H. had another one. The object was a Jap bivouac area. Half had Sub Tommies and half had BAR's. The ones who had BAR's carried automatic pistols. The patrols separated and were to meet at 11 hour on the two sides of the Bivouac area. However Capt. H. was late, so M. looked over the situation. The Japs were in a chow line. Just at that time a Jap sentry gave the alarm. So M. gave the word to charge. Well, it was a bloody mess. M heard Jap officer getting communications with the main body, so they pulled out. At that time Capt. H. appeared on Grassy Knoll. M. signaled H. about the situation. H wanted to go in and mop up, but M. said no. His men were out of ammo. So they withdrew. Score: two Marines dead, about 75 Jap casualties.

Jap bombers kept hitting us all night. But not last night. The El Shebra cargo vessel was hit by torpedo from a two-man Jap sub. We have lost quite a few ships out here. Lt. P. said that Gen. Marshall is on the island and he is getting the dope on bush warfare from the 5th Marines. They are standing by to board ship, talking about the battle, which is going on. They say it does not affect us. Our battalion is about four miles on the left flank…And it does not affect us! We are suffering heavy casualties. The casualties can't be brought in due to the fact that snipers are on the watch for this. I walked down to Division Army Field Hospital and I saw two big tents full of dead soldiers. They say there are plenty of dead Marines there, too. Also, Gen. Marshall said that he was trying to put a Division order refraining Marines from making slanderous remarks about Macarthur. It seems that these remarks have got to official channels.

We went on the hill with binoculars and looked at Sealark Channel. There were 15 ships, including warships. No bombing raid last night. Our planes were in the air all night.

Our three-day patrol met opposition directly in front of our lines. Nov. 30 is the date. I made a bet ($5) with C. that we wouldn't be out by Dec. 1. I will collect tonight.

C. has paid me. Lt. B. called us all together. We have tried four assaults on Japs at Kuhumbona and all have failed. They are dug in and planes have to get a direct hit to kill any. Artillery is the same way. The only way to get them is with mortars, so we are doubling up. We will take eight mortars. Everyman will have a hand grenade. 2nd Bu is the spearhead and it must push and drive. The Japs have to be killed and we got to do it. It will be a tough job. The reason given for failure of the last attempts was due to men stopping to bring their wounded buddies in. God be with us.

Japs tried to bomb us today and last night to no avail. Jap convoy of eight transports, six destroyers, and two cruisers were heading this way and our planes sunk all but four transports. God is with us. We have struck tents and are awaiting word to move out. A dive-bomber crashed at 7:15 last night right near the Bu C.P.

Today I received a beautiful card from Cassie. It rained and rained like hell. Our shack collapsed. Rifles, packs and all were soaked. It poured for an hour. Our artillery opened up and we sent a destroyer down to shell them.

The orders have been changed and temporarily we are in a bivouac area. It is the first time we have been off the front line from Aug. 7 till Dec. 2. We have been working like hell digging bomb shelters.

We had a Condition Red last night, which failed to materialize. I was scared to death, because we had no holes to jump in. Right now no one knows what is going to happen. There is a rumor that Vandergift said that the First Marine Division is through fighting in the Solomon's. We will probably go back on the lines soon. Good scuttlebutt never comes true, but the bad always comes true. I have never seen it fail.

The Chaplain has told us that L.B., who was wounded at the Tenaru Battle, died aboard a hospital ship and was buried at sea. A Jap bullet entered at the base of his spine and came out his neck. J.A. and I went down to the commissary to steal some food. The whole First Marine Regiment is now in bivouac. Report on a Jap warship was "Sighted nine enemy ships and sunk same."

We had a first lieutenant by the name of L., who made Captain. He was transferred to 3rd Battalion 1st. Well, he is being sent back to the states and has been relieved of his command. He holds the record for leading men into ambush. He lost 18 men the first time. If you can't produce in this outfit, out you go. Major F. and Major C. both got the skids. Also Lt.

W. The enlisted men who don't produce get put in galley and all other shit details.

Today is Dec. 6. We have dug our foxholes deeper in anticipation of Jap bombing raids today. All the men are hoping we bomb Japan. As we expected, we were subjected to Condition Red. Five enemy bombers came over but they were driven away. We haven't had a night raid for some time. Our artillery fired 4,000 shells into the Japs yesterday. Guess what we had today? We had noon chow. Coffee and pie.

Ships have been coming in regularly and we have been working day and night unloading them. When we have a working party at Division Commissary, we have plenty to eat and we bring lots of fruit back to our area. A two-man Jap submarine fired six torpedoes at the El Shebra. Two hit. She still has not sunk. For the last four days we have been unloading ships. The sun was quite hot. Yesterday the gallant 5th Marines left aboard three transports. It is a great outfit. Second Btu is probably the greatest fighters in the world. A Jap bomber came over last night but he left without dropping his bombs.

Flying Fortresses have been flying all around here today. The El Shebra has finally sunk. We are salvaging everything possible. I believe I got the story on the big push. It seems that Japs had dug in slit trenches and that it was impossible to dislodge them except by repeated charges. So the Army General who took over the Island after Vandergift got wind of it and he had it stopped. He said the "First Marine Division was through fighting in the Solomon's. Stand by to move out." Let's hope so. I got a few letters from home today. Letters are good morale builders.

The Jap bombers are still trying to get over but our planes are doing a wonderful job. We pray for them. With badly out-moded planes, they are doing a bang-up job.

We are going to leave Guadalcanal with 100 rounds of ammo. We landed with 220 rounds. The natives get paid six dollars a month. Two goes to the Red Cross, Two to Britain, one to their chief and they keep one. Most of them are tattooed. I heard them humming the Star Spangled Banner while they worked.

Eleven Jap Destroyers with troops were heading for this island last night and our planes were flying all night. We had a Condition Red the other day. Nothing happened. All in all, I would say we have been bombed 120 times.

Last night we were bombed again. L. and P. of our company were hurt from concussion. Three transports came in today. They unloaded 2nd Division Marines and 3rd Btu 182 Inf. Reg. The 3rd Btu. of our regiment, boarded these ships also all other Marines in the second echelon.

We arose at 3:45a.m. to unload the ships. We had chow at Div. Commissary. Boy, what chow! It is a shame the boys on the front lines don't eat this food. Fighting has halted momentarily. The artillery has not fired for several days.

We were talking to a few P-38 pilots and they said that the Jap Zero could run rings around the P-38. However, the P-38 is much faster. They have knocked down eight Zeros. Our planes have sunk all but four of those eleven destroyers. They also chased another task force away from Guadalcanal. Well, we leave for the beach tomorrow.

We are now set up on the beach and what a layout! We moved into a good tent. The cots were there for us. We found a lot of food and equipments. We also found two bottles of beer, which we drank on the spot. Boy, did they taste good. We are supposed to get an issue of two bottles per man. but as yet, it did not come.

Four Japs got through our front lines and reached the airport and blew up a P-38 and an oil truck. Two were caught. Well, we don't have to worry about them slipping through. Our worry is in a Jap landing party. The Japs are certainly sending the convoys against us. We are losing a bunch of ships, too. There is a nice place to bathe here. We are afraid to go in the ocean as we see many sharks. The boys steal alcohol from the hospital, and then add it to pineapple juice and vanilla extract. Today, S. was drinking Listerine. He is the same fellow who cried and carried on when told we are going into action.

While unloading ships yesterday, a destroyer got a two-man sub. The El Shebra is being patched up. After the working party the boys ate supper late, and later on they all got ptomaine poisoning. It burns me up to see a 10-wheel Army truck carrying about six water cans, where as a Marine has to carry it. What is the reason for this? Well, everything the Marine Corps bring ashore is combat gear. But the Army brings everything in. The Hollywood Marines, 8th Reg., are on the front lines. Japs are still trying to reinforce their garrison. But our planes are keeping them away. At Georgia Island the Japs have a small airfield, which harasses our planes. They shot down a Fortress the other day.

We are moving again today. We are scheduled to board ship in a few days. I hope we do before anything comes up.

Today is Dec. 18. We are bivouacked at the mouth of the Lunga River. For the first time since we hit the island, our machine gunners have not stood gun watch. We have found that the ship we are to board will not come closer than two miles to the shore. The captain claims there are too many subs around. As is, it will take five days to unload ship. There are bunches of Merchant Marines aboard and they do not work fast enough for us. So the First Battalion was ordered to board ship in order to unload faster. We are still standing by.

We are near the commissary and we are raiding it. The anti-tank went aboard ship, so it won't be long.

There are a few things I would like to put down. Solomon Islands are the worst place in the world for malaria. TB and Elephantitus flourish here. When it rains, the mud is up to your ankles. After it stops, a plague of flying ants eat you. Rats and lizards.

What do you think happened last night? We saw a movie, and not six miles away men were fighting for their lives. This war is pretty messed up. The 3rd Battalion 132 Inf. is really having a hot time. Three officers are dead already. Last night the Army and the Seventh captured Grassy Knowle. He who controls Grassy Knowle controls Guadalcanal. It took them 12 minutes to get to the top.

We boarded ship today—Norham and then we changed to Pres. Johnson. I now write finis to Guadalcanal.

Christmas found us at New Hebrides. We ate Christmas dinner aboard ship and we did not have any turkey. A big portion of the fleet was here. About 25 destroyers, 18 cruisers, one aircraft carrier, two tankers, 40 cargo ships, 12 tankers. Reminded me of Frisco. We are now bivouacked on Hebrides (San Esperito). It is beautiful. Colorful as hell.

From Pearl Harbor to Guadalcanal

Jack O. Phillips

1939 was an unusually hot summer in Fort Worth. I had graduated from high school in June and was living with my parents Flora and Charles W. Phillips in a small apartment in North Fort Worth.

I had looked for employment but no one was hiring. The depression was still with us.

The summer was so hot that I slept outside on a cot. One night I went down to Marine Park and spent the night sleeping on a park bench.

As I could not get a job, I decided I would go into the military if they would have me. I chose the Navy as my number one choice and passed their tests and was accepted into the Navy. The term of my enlistment was to be six years. I would have preferred four years but the Navy did not offer four-year enlistments in 1939. At my young age then, six years seemed to stretch out forever.

During my waiting period to go to boot camp Germany invaded Poland.

I was sworn into the Navy September 19, 1939, in Dallas. Our group was sent to Norfolk, Va. for boot camp. Boot camps in any service are not pleasant but at least I was now on my own (relatively speaking). I made $21.00 a month and I had food, clothing and shelter. The days at boot camp were filled with those things that turn civilians into military people. Like all boots I had the two-minute haircut and all the other humilities that boots are subject to.

\After boot camp I applied for aviation mechanics school, which was located in Pensacola, Fla…but I had to wait a month or so for a new class to be formed.

In the meantime, I served as a lifeguard at the officers' swimming pool. That was good duty.

January 29, 1940 I was increased in rating to second-class seaman and received a pay raise for having attained this lofty position.

January 31, 1940 I arrived in Pensacola and started my aviation mechanics training. This lasted until the 1st of June 1940. When I finished the school I had become a first class seaman.

In June 1940 I was assigned to Patrol Squadron 14, which was located on North Island Naval Air Station in San Diego, California. Patrol Squadron 14 (VP-14) was a PBY squadron. I was in the beaching crew. PBY's in 1940 did not have permanently attached wheels. They were strictly seaplanes. To bring the PBY up on the beach wheels had to be attached and that was the job of the beaching crew. After the wheels were attached a tractor would tow the plane up a ramp to bring it ashore.

During the time in San Diego I passed the test to become an AMM3c (Aviation Machinist Mate 3rd Class).

At that time the enlisted personnel had to withstand an old time weekly inspection. The officers wore those fore and aft hats, swords, etc. for this inspection. Remember this was then a peacetime Navy and there were no reserve officers or reserve enlisted personnel.

I was in VP-14 and San Diego almost a year. I did make a few liberties (shore leave) to San Diego, but it was like Norfolk, Va. i.e. "Sailors and dogs keep off the grass". Consequently most sailors had a rented locker ashore where they kept some civilian clothes. They changed into those when they went ashore. I had such a locker.

On May 1941 I was transferred to a "receiving ship" in San Francisco. (A receiving ship is a place where naval personal are held while being reassigned). On May 8, 1941 I was assigned to a still unfinished ship, the USS Tangier (AV8). This ship was still being modified at Moore's dry dock in Oakland.

As the ship was not ready, I was given a 30-day leave and came to Fort Worth to visit my family. As the ship was still not ready I asked for and was given another 30-day leave. The Tangier Yeoman did not record the second 30-day leave properly so I was declared to be AWOL. As I had the signed permission of our Captain (CAF Sprague), I eventually received an apology for having been declared AWOL. (Incidentally, Capt. Sprague eventually became an Admiral and distinguished himself in the battle of Leyte Gulf).

After my sixty days leave were over, the ship was still not ready so I was assigned to the Alameda Naval Air Station. There I met some of my future Tangier shipmates. At Alameda I worked in the A&R shop. This was a civilian run repair and maintenance facility for taking care of the needs of Navy planes. I was given the job of bucking rivets inside the hull of small seaplanes. Like everybody else (almost) I smoked. I could not smoke inside the seaplane hull so I got some Beach Nut Chewing tobacco to tame my nicotine craving. There was a problem with that too——you couldn't spit inside the hull so I had to swallow the juice.

Due to my robust health, youthfulness, etc, that not at all bothered me. Who needs a spittoon?

Finally our waiting was over and the Tangier was ready. The first crews on a newly commissioned ship are called "plank owners". The Tangier was built to be a Sea Plane Tender and was placed in full commission August 15, 1941. The ship was 492 feet long, 12,510 tons with a speed of 16.5 knots. With the commissioning ceremonies over and the crew assembled, the ship was ready for a shakedown cruise. That's to see if everything works before going to active duty.

We departed Oakland August 29, 1941 and the shakedown cruise lasted until October 28, 1941. During the shakedown we visited Seattle, Wash., Bremerton, Wash., San Diego and San Pedro, Calif.

We left San Pedro and headed West into the great Pacific ocean. We arrived at Pearl Harbor, TH (Territory of Hawaii) Nov. 3, 1941. We tied up at Ford Island just aft the USS Utah, an old battleship.

I went ashore a couple of times to Honolulu. One of the times a friend and I rented a box camera at the YMCA and went out to Waikiki beach. At that time there was not much development on the beach. Two hotels—one of them, The Royal Hawaiian—were the only hotels there (that I remember). Now there are dozens of hotels.

We took some pictures then and got the pictures back the following Saturday, December 6, 1941.

I was looking at the pictures on Sunday morning when general quarters sounded. The klaxon and orders for "all hands man your battle stations" was given.

I went to my battle station, which was topside on the very stern of the ship. The USS Utah was just aft of us.

When I arrived topside and started back to my battle station I was startled by a very low-lying plane right across us. I could see the pilot and I could see the rising sun insignia under each wing.

The first of the Jap planes (yes, we called them Japs) passed along our portside and then later right over us. (This is the one I saw when I first went topside). Our ship opened fire immediately and it is the impression of most that the Tangier was the first ship at Pearl to open fire at almost exactly 0800. Almost immediately, three torpedo planes came in on our starboard quarter heading south and dropped their torpedoes at the USS Utah. We could not tell if all the torpedoes hit the Utah. Two definitely did and the third, I think, went between the Tangier stern and the Utah stern. Very soon the USS Raleigh was hit causing her to sink down by the stern where she held steady. About this time the Utah sank bottom up.

Almost immediately the Arizona exploded and the smoke was dense coming over us.

All this time I was at my useless battle station on the stern. My official battle station was designated as "sky look out". It was of no value but did afford me a terrific view of the attack.

On either side of me was a 3-inch 23-caliber gun. It was manually loaded one shell at a time. About 200 rounds were fired during the attack. My ears probably have never been the same as the noise was humongous.

"Battleship Row" on the other side of Ford Island was an unbelievable disaster. All the battleships were either sunk entirely or badly damaged.

About 8:45 a submarine was sighted off our starboard bow about 300 yards out. One of our 3-inch AA guns (3"/50cal) fired six shots at it and probably hit it.

From about 8:50 on the Japanese planes made deliberate bombing attacks on the Tangier. We shot off the tail of a Jap plane just as it passed ahead and to our starboard. At about 8:55 we shot down another plane. About this time the USS Curtiss (another seaplane tender) took a direct hit by a bomb and caught fire. A destroyer came down between the Tangier and Curtiss and dropped depth charges on the submarine we had sighted earlier.

About 9:10, a third wave of about 30 or so planes came over.

At about this time we riddled another Jap plane that came up our port side. The engine caught fire, the part of the fuselage forward of the pilot burst into flame. The pilot still had some control of his plane and deliberately crashed his plane into the Curtiss, which had already taken a bomb hit.

So much was going on so fast that the mind was boggled. Up until about 9:00 we had been pretty well ignored by the Jap planes. Thick smoke from the burning Arizona was drifting across us and partially concealed us. I don't think we were primary targets until about 9:10. From about 9:10 to 9:20 five bombs from five different planes were launched at the Tangier. One bomb dropped on Ford Island off our port bow. The other four planes dropped their bombs from about 300 feet. All four fortunately were close misses. I could watch the bombs from the time of release until they missed, however, they all looked like they were going to hit us and I was surprised that they all were close misses.

The ship didn't completely escape unharmed but our damage was slight. Fragments struck only three men on deck and they were not hurt badly.

After about 9:20 no more planes came near the Tangier.

That night some of our own planes came in and we thought they were Japs. Unfortunately we shot down some of our own.

The following few days were spent getting ready to go to war. We loaded the Tangier with Marines, bombs, and ammo. radars and all manner of items.

Admiral Kimmel's last order before being relieved of his command was to send out the first Westward Naval Sally of the war.

Wake Island was under attack from Dec. 8 and was eventually overwhelmed Dec. 23, 1941.

The first Westward Naval Sally of the war was an attempt to relieve Wake Island.

Fate came close to making a possible graveyard for the Tangier. The Westward Sally of ships was designated Task Force 14. Tangier and fleet oiler Neches (as they were slow) started west one day before the rest of the Task Force. The Neches was a 1920 vessel and got a maximum of 12 knots.

The Tangier departed Pearl Harbor on Dec. 13, 1941 with a relief force of several hundred Marines of the Fourth Defense Battalion and among the items we also carried were two radars, 21,000 3-inch and 5-inch shells, three million machine gun rounds, barbed wire, etc., etc.

The day after the Tangier and Neches deported the rest of Task Force 14 left and quickly caught up with us. The Saratoga was the Task Force Aircraft Carrier.

The mission of this Task Force was to deliver supplies, reinforcements and aircraft to Wake Island.

The Saratoga was to remain out of range of the Jap planes.

The Task Force was to arrive at Wake Island On Dec. 23, 1941.

Disembarkation and unloading at Wake was going to be a huge problem at best or impossible at worst. Troops and supplies from the Tangier would have to be lightered in (taken in by boat). If the Tangier was badly damaged during the tedious process of unloading, it was ordered that the Tangier would be run aground to ensure the delivery of the vital cargo.

On Dec. 22 we were about 500 plus miles from Wake and the situation at Wake was most urgent. It was learned that enemy carriers were operating to the northwest of Wake. Admiral Fletcher felt that the fuel supply of the ships was inadequate for a fight near Wake. He ordered refueling of the ships from the Neches. The Pacific swell was rather large causing the breakage of several fuel lines. This, of course, slowed down the whole operation. Because of the shape of our Navy at that time the powers that be questioned whether to risk losing what was left of our Navy.

As a compromise measure it was decided to send the Tangier to Wake by herself. But before the Admiral could execute this hazardous decision (which would have spelled destruction for the Tangier) Wake Island garrison surrendered to the Japs. Task Force 14 was recalled to Pearl Harbor and the Tangier was not sacrificed at Wake. We were diverted to Midway instead to leave the Marines we were carrying plus the equipment that was meant for Wake. At Midway we also picked up civilians and took them back to Pearl Harbor.

In 1941 I had two Christmas eves. We were west of the 180th meridian on Dec. 24, 1941, we then returned east over the 180th meridian where again we had a Dec. 24, 1941.

On Dec. 31, 1941 we arrived back at Pearl Harbor.

We stayed in Pearl Harbor until early February 1942. We loaded aviation gasoline (250,000 gals), bombs, and torpedoes, a lot of Army gear and soldiers and civilians as passengers. Feb. 14, 1942 we put out to sea headed south. Our only escort was a tin can (destroyer) but it had left us.

We were alone making our way to somewhere in the South Pacific.

On Feb. 15, we crossed the equator. I became a "Shellback". We didn't have the traditional hazing that is common in peacetime. The war was too new.

On Feb. 18th we came into Pago Pago and stayed a day or so.

On Feb. 21, 1942 we were amongst the Fiji Islands. The scent from the islands was strong even before we anchored. This was in Suva Fiji harbor. Suva is the Capitol of Fiji. The sweet odor of vegetation was strong. As we came into the still water of the harbor there were thousands of beautifully colored jellyfish floating by the ship. Fiji was part of Colonial Great Britain. In the harbor there were only four or five ships, none of them Navy. The town was composed mainly of little white houses with red roofs. There were 3 or 4 impressive looking buildings, which were probably government buildings. The natives of Fiji are black. They were very nice and friendly. In Fiji there also are many Indians (like from the country of India). I bought some souvenirs from them. We found out that there were a lot of soldiers from New Zealand there also.

Feb. 28, 1942 we raised the anchor and departed from Suva. We hit some really rough seas. On March 2, I was seasick.

March 3, 1942 we arrived in New Caledonia (a French Colony) and Numea, it's capital.

On March 4, 1942 my old squadron from North Island San Diego came aboard the Tangier. VP-14 it was. As are we, it's on an advanced base here in New Caledonia. We are to tend the PBY's of VP-14. I saw some fellows I had known in San Diego. The squadron had moved to Hawaii to Kaneohe Naval Air Station prior to the Jap attack. They had lost some people on Dec. 7 and a lot of gear too.

This really was an advanced base. There was nothing between New Caledonia and the Jap bases to the North and west of us. We expected to see them show up at any time and we, of course, would have been destroyed had that happened. New Caledonia is rich in nickel ore and would be something the Japs needed for their war materials.

On March 5 we had a big storm. A destroyer that had just arrived was dragging anchor and almost collided with us.

March 8, 1942 was very hot. We took a PBY aboard for servicing. It was the first for us. Another PBY came in from Pearl Harbor. We hoped it would have mail but it didn't. It did bring some spark plugs though.

We were very short of many items. Most of the materials were going to the European theater. We resented that (to say the least).

March 18, A large number of soldiers have come into Numea and are setting up on the island. Their gear was piled "willy-nilly" on the docks and beaches. I don't know how order ever prevailed. We were glad the soldiers were here.

Don't forget that the Tangier and eight airplanes came here and took over the whole of New Caledonia. Had the Japs showed up we would have been an easy kill for them.

An English ship came along side. We opened our cold storage vaults to them.

We could hear broadcast from Australia. They sounded much like our stateside radio. I never got to Australia though, I sure wanted to as I heard the women were very friendly. We began to get mail a little more frequently and for us that was very important.

We began to hear (in early May, 1942) that the Japs were expected to attack somewhere east of Australia. We were east of Australia about 700 miles. I was told that a Jap Task Force was intercepted north of us. This was the Battle of Coral Sea.

May 8, 1942 we were equipped with a gas mask and a life jacket. We thought we were going to be hit but were not.

May 12 we heard that a great sea battle had been fought just to our North. The Lexington had been sunk. The beat up survivors of the Coral Sea battle headed for Numea. On May 12 seven destroyers and three cruisers came in from the battle. One of the destroyers had only 3000 gallons of fuel left. That's about half hour running time at full speed. Some of the ships were pretty beat up. We took aboard wounded from the battle and many Lexington survivors. Also our old sidekick, the oiler Neches, had been sunk. The PBY's from the Tangier conducted search and rescue missions in the area where the battle was fought.

On May 27 some Australian and American PBY's were sent out to do some patrolling and bombing of the Soloman Islands. They bombed their objective, which probably was the airstrip. However, only the Australian ship got back to Numea. Our planes ran out of gas. The Aussie PBY's had a bigger fuel capacity than ours. Two of the three US PBY's were destroyed at sea. The third was brought back and fixed.

June 16, 1942. We heard of the Battle of Midway but at that time did not know what a miraculous victory our ships and planes had won.

June 21, 1942. The Curtiss—the seaplane tender that received two hits on Dec. 7, 1941—came into Numea to relieve us. We left and went to Pearl Harbor and eventually back to Oakland and Moore's dry dock. The ship needed repairs.

We arrived in Oakland, CA. We used to say "Golden Gate in 48" but we arrived in Oakland July 15, 1942 and had liberty frequently. We took advantage of every moment because we knew we were going back.

On Sept 21, 1942 we left to a place with a code name "Button". This turned out to be Espiritu Santo, New Hebrides. We arrived in "Button" Oct. 21, 1942.

On Dec. 12, 1942 I was transferred off the Tangier to the USS Columbia, a light cruiser. I did not want to leave the Tangier but orders are orders. The Columbia was known also as "The Gem"—get it—the "gem of the ocean". It was also known as a Hollywood ship as it had several movie stars, sports figures, etc.on it.

The Columbia was a ship of the line, a fighting ship. It was very fast and maneuverable. We cruised mainly around and in the vicinity of Guadalcanal. We were in the Battle of Rennell Island in which we lost the Chicago and several destroyers.

Later I was assigned to VS-65, a scouting squadron that was operating from Funa Futi in the Ellice Islands. We were bombed a few times but mostly just a nuisance.

As I had been overseas so long I was being given a chance to come back to the States for duty. Twelve of us were chosen to come back to States. I boarded a DC-3 in Funa Futi and flew to American Samoa. I took a Liberty ship from there to San Francisco. I was given my choice of any Naval Air station for duty in the States. I chose the Naval Air Station at Grand Prairie, TX. I got married in December 1943.

I made Chief Petty Officer and was transferred to Naval Air Station, Bunker Hill, Indiana. From there I was sent back to the West Coast for redeployment over seas. Due to a physical defect in my right hand I was put in the Hospital in California and had surgery. This was in 1945. The surgery was not successful. Then came the Bomb, which ended the war.

My discharge from the Navy was past due. I went home and started TCU on the GI Bill.

Dennis M. Parker

Prologue—

It wasn't until the winter of 1992-1993 that I read completely for the first time the diaries that I had written nearly fifty years before. The journal consisted of three separate notebooks, which were sent home with the rest of my personal effects after I was reported, "missing in action." For over fifty years they remained stashed away along with the other wartime mementoes and I had just forgotten them. Other than my father, I doubt if anyone else had ever read them.

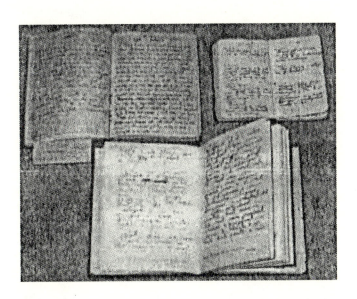

Philip D. & Dennis M. Parker Share A Laugh

DENNIS M. PARKER

DIARY AND LOG BEGINNING JANUARY 1, 1943

Aviation Cadet—Advanced Flying School Marianna, Florida—Single Engine AT-6s

Friday, January 1, 1943—Marianna, Florida
Eglin Field—Biloxi, Mississippi
1:20 Aerial gunnery AT-6
1:00 Formation

Saturday, January 2, 1943—Marianna
Eglin Field—Biloxi, Mississippi

1:50 Aerial gunnery
Ralph Parker scrapped wing—tip landing. Wrote letters.

Sunday, January 3, 1943—Marianna, Florida
1:00 Aerial gunnery
Left Eglin at 12:00 and arrived back at Marianna at 11:00. Ping Pong with Phillips and Racine.

Monday, January 4, 1943—Marianna, Florida
1:00 Link trainer
:50 Instrument flying
:55 Formations Flying
1:05 Oxygen Flight
1:00 Night transition

Tuesday, January 5, 1943—Marianna, Florida
1:00 high altitude 20,000'
1:00 Link trainer
First fatal accident—A/C Crowe killed night transition.
Wednesday, January 6, 1943—Marianna, Florida
Loafed around and played chess with Perry. Went to Auxiliary Field for night flying, but it was scratched when bad weather moved in.

Thursday, January 7, 1943—Marianna, Florida
Rain—no flying. Open post—went to Cottondale and Chipley with G. Phillips.

Friday, January 8, 1943—Marianna, Florida
Rain—no flying. Ground school in the afternoon. Stayed in and read in the evening.

Saturday, January 9, 1943—Marianna, Florida
Got my officers flying equipment at Air Force Supply. Logged 2:35 night transition.

Sunday, January 10, 1943—Marianna, Florida
Instructor and student from flight I-A killed on take off. Night transition 2:40. Night navigation 2:1 5. 1 got careless and ground-looped on landing at 0300 in the morning. Luckily, I didn't hit the wing tip, just spun around.

Monday, January 11, 1943—Marianna, Florida
Logged combat—1:05
Two ship formation—2: 1 0
Night navigation—2:25

Tuesday, January 12, 1943—Marianna, Florida
No flying. Signed discharge as aviation cadet. Signed oath of office.

Wednesday, January 13, 1943—Marianna, Florida
Graduation!!! I am now a 2nd Lt. in the Army Air Force and a potential "fighter pilot." Called Mom and Dad. Had pictures taken by George Phillips father. Logged 2:30 night navigation. Phil McCullough got lost.

Friday, January 15, 1943—Marianna, Florida
Link trainer 2:00. Jeff Hall, my neighbor from Fitchburg, was my instructor. Went to the Officers Club at night.

Saturday, January 16, 1943—Marianna, Florida
Collected $250 uniform allowance. Got discharge certificate. Signed for insurance. Logged :20 day transition. Flying all done.

Sunday, January 17, 1943—Marianna, Florida
Rain—waited for orders. Officers Club in the afternoon and evening. Played cards with Phillips, Rauch and McCullough. I lost.

Monday, January 18, 1943—Marianna, Florida
Rain—waited for orders. Read all day.

Tuesday, January 19, 1943—Marianna, Florida
Cold, windy, clear—still no orders. Went to town and spent $45 on clothes. Officers club at night.

Wednesday, January 20, 1943—Marianna, Florida
Received new assignment at 0900. After a ten-day leave I'm going to report to the 48th bomb group at Key Field, Meridian Miss. Most of the guys are going to Groton Conn. to fly P-47's. We'll be flying A-24 dive-bombers. Adams, Rauch and Phillips are also going to Key Field. Left Marianna at 23:00 by bus.

Thursday, January 21, 1943—Traveling
Arrived in Jacksonville at 0800, boarded train to New York and rode all day and night.

Friday, January 22, 1943-Traveling-Fitchburg, MA.
Arrived in New York at 10:00 and got train to Boston at 11: 00—Arrived in Boston at 16: 00 and home at 19:00. Stayed in with Mom and Dad.

Saturday, January 23, 1943—Fitchburg
Went to town and met Anne at 12:00. Went to her house in the evening.

Sunday, January 24, 1943—Fitchburg
Went to Woburn with Mom and Dad. Received telegram from Geo Phillips, I'm going to meet him in New York next Sunday.

Monday, January 25, 1943—Fitchburg
Sent telegram to George. Banged around all day. Anne and I went to movie at night.

Tuesday, January 26, 1943—Fitchburg
Visited with friends all day. Went out with Anne at night.

Wednesday, January 27, 1943—Fitchburg
Visited friends at Fitchburg Paper Co. Went to Marion's with Anne. We had to stay overnight due to snowstorm.

Friday, January 29, 1943—Fitchburg
Went to a dance at Fitchburg Teachers College with Anne. Also took in Presidents Ball.

Saturday, January 30, 1943—Fitchburg
Anne and I went to the Piccadilly Club and celebrated my last night at home.

Sunday, January 31, 1943—Traveling
Left Fitchburg at 0730 by bus to Worcester. From Worcester I took the train to New York and got there at 1430. Met George at 1500. We checked out the Astor Bar and stayed at the Governor Clinton Hotel overnight.

Monday, February 1, 1943—Travel
Left New York at 1630 on the "Southerner" bound for Meridian, Miss. Card game on train—won $30.

Tuesday, February 2, 1943—Meridian, Miss.
Arrived in Meridian at 1530 and we went directly to the field. Returned to town and spent the night at the Lamarr Hotel.

Wednesday, February 3, 1943—Meridian
Checked in at Key Field. Received my quarters and visited Finance, Personnel and Squadron Headquarters.

Thursday, February 4, 1943—Meridian
Spent the day getting adjusted and checking out the Officer's Club. I'm rooming with Jack Adams.

Friday, February 5, 1943—Meridian
Received dog tags. Collected half pay for Jan—$107.

Saturday, February 6, 1943—Meridian
Shot one round of skeet and got 8 hits, no more. Liquor at the "Club."

Sunday, February 7, 1943—Meridian
Day off. Wrote letters and played ping-pong with Don Rauch.

Monday, February 8, 1943—Meridian
Morning—ground school. Link—1:00. Got typhus shot. Sent Anne $40 money order for a hope chest.

Tuesday, February 9, 1943—Meridian
Ground school. Sex lecture. Gave $1.50 for "Group Whoop." Collected travel pay from Marianna—$26.62

Wednesday, February 10, 1943—Meridian
Ground school. Stayed in at night and read.

Thursday, February 11, 1943—Meridian
Ground school. "Group Whoop" held at Country Club. Much liquor, gambling and girls. Also went to Woodlawn.

Friday, February 12, 1943—Meridian
Day off—I needed it! Went to movie in town at night.

Saturday, February 13, 1943—Meridian
Still waiting to fly. Link trainer 1:00. Shot skeet, 18 hits.

Sunday, February 14, 1943—Meridian
Flew in the gunner's seat of an A-24. Pilot Lt. Tiemy. Played ping-pong with Rauch.

Monday, February 15, 1943—Meridian
Routine. Jack Adams and I went into town and shot pool and bowled.

Tuesday, February 16, 1943—Meridian
This place is getting on my nerves—I want to start flying. Link 1:00

Wednesday, February 17, 1943—Meridian
I spent most of the morning at Air Corp supply. Listened to lectures. Went to Country Club in the evening. Southern girls are good dancers.

Thursday, February 18, 1943—Meridian
Shot skeet in the morning, 20 hits! Took a ride in the gunner's seat of an A-24.

Friday, February 19, 1943—Meridian
Day off. George, Jack and I spent the day shooting pool and drinking beer. It's a tough war!

Saturday, February 20, 1943—Meridian
Got to fly the A-24 today! I logged 2:00 day transition. Link 1:00. George got taken for $100 at the Woodlawn Inn.

Sunday, February 21, 1943—Meridian
Started to fly but it was canceled as I was preparing for take-off. Logged: 1O. Country Club at night.

Monday, February 22, 1943—Meridian
Morning—ground school. Logged 2:05 day transition in A-24. Stayed in at night—no money.

Tuesday, February 23, 1943—Meridian
Ground school. Link 1:00. An A-20 cracked up five miles north of the field. Two bailed out and the pilot was killed.

Wednesday, February 24, 1943—Meridian
Day off—wrote letters and read. Beat Rauch at ping-pong!

Thursday, February 25, 1943—Meridian
Logged 2:10 day transition in A-24. Three accidents today! #1—A-24 pilot bailed out at 400' and lived. #2—Lt. Haynes and enlisted man killed flying too low. #3—A-24 pilot made forced landing in road. Country Club at night.

Friday, February 26, 1943—Meridian
Ground school in the morning, P.T. in the afternoon. Shot skeet, 20 hits.

Saturday, February 27, 1943—Meridian
Logged 2:05 day transition. Went to show in the evening. Borrowed $10 from Ralph Parker.

Sunday, February 28, 1943—Meridian
Went to dispensary and got treated for a cold. Rumor is that we'll be getting some P-39's soon.

Monday, March 1, 1943—Meridian
Logged 3:50 day transition in A-24. Navigation lecture. Got paid $280. Usual pay plus flight pay for half of Jan.

Tuesday, March 2, 1943—Meridian
Morning—three hour lecture on flight medicine. I've had enough schooling during the past year to qualify me for a college degree!

Wednesday, March 3, 1943—Meridian
Day off—hung around and wrote letters. Went into town in the evening with George and Jack.

Thursday, March 4, 1943—Meridian
No more ground school! Flew 2:00 day transition. Went to Country Club in the evening.

Friday, March 5, 1943—Meridian
Rain—no flying. Shot crap and lost $50. Ralph Parker got engaged. Went to movie.

Saturday, March 6, 1943—Meridian
Rain—no flying. Shot crap and won $70. Ralph Parker got disengaged.

Sunday, March 7, 1943—Meridian
Loafed around all day. Went to movie in the evening. What a way to fight a war!

Monday, March 8, 1943—Meridian
Logged 2:20 in A-24. Flew to Birmingham and had breakfast with Lt. Lee. Got cholera shot.

Tuesday, March 9, 1943—Meridian
No flying. Went to Country Club.

Wednesday, March 10, 1943—Meridian
Flew 2:00 cross country in A-24. Went into town with George and saw movie. A-36 cracked up. Pilot Lt. Shaw killed.

Thursday, March 11, 1943—Meridian
We have two A-36's in our squadron and I hope to check out in it soon. The A-36 is a P-51 Mustang modified with dive brakes for dive-bombing. Went into town with George and Don.

Friday, March 12, 1943—Meridian
Went into town and bought some summer uniforms. Jack and I went on M.P. duty in town in the evening. It was a quiet night for which I was glad. M.P. duty isn't my cup-of-tea.

Saturday, March 13, 1943—Meridian
Went into town with George and Jack. Stood retreat. Wrote letters in the evening.

Sunday, March 14, 1943—Meridian
55th squadron divided up into flights A, B, C, D and E. I will fly the A-36 as I'm in "B" flight. Went to Country Club.

Monday, March 15, 1943—Meridian
Filled out questionnaire on A-36. Shot skeet, 19 hits.

Tuesday, March 16, 1943—Meridian
Received cockpit check of A-36. Movie at night.

Wednesday, March 17, 1943—Meridian
Logged 1:00 day transition in A-36. Beautiful airplane! Country Club in the evening. Danced all night with Robin.

Thursday, March 18, 1943—Meridian
Link 1:00. Logged 1:30 day transition in A-36 and 1:10 in A-24. Country Club at night

Friday, March 19, 1943—Meridian
My birthday—23 years old. George, Jack and I went to the Country Club and had a ball. I'm glad that everyone isn't fighting the war as I am. Still, I might as well enjoy it, as I'm sure that my time will come.

Saturday, March 20, 1943—Meridian
Rain all day, no flying. Read and played cards.

Sunday, March 21, 1943—Meridian
Went on a five-ship flight to Monroe LA, Jackson Miss. and back to Key Field. Logged 4:25 in A-24. Link 1:00. Stayed in and read in the evening.

Monday, March 22, 1943—Meridian
Scheduled twice but didn't get off the ground at all, 1 got stuck in the mud when the left brake on my A-24 gave out. Country Club at night with Phillips and Lee.

Tuesday, March 23, 1943—Meridian
Flew to Birmingham for breakfast with Lt. Lee, Logged 2:30. M.P, duty in town. No more A-36's will be assigned to Key Field.

Wednesday, March 24, 1943—Meridian
No flying. Played pool and ping pong all day.

Thursday, March 25, 1943—Meridian
Shot skeet, 22 hits. Lt. Bowen of the 55th bellied up his plane today—pulled up his wheels instead of his flaps! Country Club in the evening. Stayed at the Lamarr Hotel overnight.

Friday, March 26, 1943—Meridian
Flew 1:00 formation in A-24. Pilot and gunner of the 56th squadron killed while night flying.

Saturday, March 27, 1943—Meridian
No flying. Went to dance at the Country Club and stayed at the Lamarr.

Sunday, March 28, 1943—Meridian
Flew to Montgomery Miss. and landed. New aviation cadets were impressed with the "Dauntless Dive Bomber."

Monday, March 29, 1943—Meridian
Logged 3:10 cross country in A-24.

Tuesday, March 30, 1943—Meridian
Logged 1:00 gunnery and bombing in A-24. Wrote letters in the evening.

Wednesday, March 31, 1943—Meridian
Link 1:00. Got paid $240. Played poker, won $20.

Thursday, April 1, 1943—Meridian
Logged 1:00 formation in A-24. Went into town with Lee and saw a movie.

Friday, April 2, 1943—Meridian
Flew cross-country to Jackson, Biloxi and Lacross. Logged 4:00. M.P. duty in town.

Saturday, April 3, 1943—Meridian
Link 1:00. Went to R.E. Parkers birthday party, met the I-licks girls. Stayed at the Lamarr overnight.

Sunday, April 4, 1943—Meridian
Went to Crayco Lake with R.E. and party. Link 1:00. Stayed in and read at night.

Monday, April 5, 1943—Meridian
Passed instrument flight test in A-24. Logged: 45. Played ping-pong and pool with Don Rauch.

Tuesday, April 6, 1943—Meridian
George Phillips and I went to New Orleans. I rode in the gunner's seat of Rauch's plane and George went with Adams. We ate at Antoine's and stayed overnight with George's friend. New Orleans is a fun city.

Wednesday, April 7, 1943—Meridian
Rauch and Adams picked up George and I at 11:00 and flew us back to Key Field. Logged 1:45 aerial gunnery in A-24. Pilot and gunner of the 56th squadron killed while trying to take off with the controls locked!

Thursday, April 8, 1943—Meridian
Flew to Camp Shelby and made a mock air raid. All personnel at the camp are supposed to carry their gas masks with them at all times on Thursdays. It's a real fun job to buzz the place and watch everyone run for cover. Went into town with Fred Lamer. Logged 1:45

Friday, April 9, 1943—Meridian
Went down to Pachuter bomb range as range officer. M.P. duty in town at night. Pilot from 56th squadron lost in A-36.

Saturday, April 10, 1943—Meridian
Looked for lost A-36. Don Rauch rode in my gunners seat. The plane was found 50 miles south of Selma—pilot dead.

Sunday, April 11, 1943—Meridian
Flew to Birmingham with Fred Lamer as observer. Logged 2:00. Aux tank ran dry on the way back.

Monday, April 12, 1943—Meridian
Dropped 10 bombs and shot 200 rounds of 50 caliber bullets at Pachuter range. Logged 2:00. M.P. duty in town.

Tuesday, April 13, 1943—Meridian
No flying. Stood retreat. Went into town with Fred Lamer in the evening.

Wednesday, April 14, 1943—Meridian
Lt. Lee and I flew our A-24's to Birmingham for breakfast. Logged 2:10. M.P. duty in town.

Thursday, April 15, 1943—Meridian
"Hit" Camp Shelby again in mock air raid. Logged 1:30. Fifteen pilots from 55th assigned to Baton Rouge.

Friday, April 16, 1943—Meridian
Flew cross-country to Jackson and back. Logged 1:30. Stayed in at nite and read.

Saturday, April 17, 1943—Meridian
Logged: 30 T/I 8 in A-24. Front moved in after take-off. Went into town with Lee in the evening.

Sunday, April 18, 1943—Meridian
Rain—no flying. Stayed in all day.

Monday, April 19, 1943—Meridian
Flew to Tuscaloosa and Columbus with Jack Adams on my wing. Low altitude. Logged 2:00.

Tuesday, April 20, 1943—Meridian
Morning—went to small arms lecture.
Afternoon—flew 2:00 formation in A-24.
Night—went to town with Lt. Lee.

Wednesday, April 21, 1943—Meridian
Went to Pachuter as range officer. Went into town at night.

Thursday, April 22, 1943—Meridian
Went back to Pachuter and qualified as an expert with a sub-machine gun. No flying. Link 1:00.

Friday, April 23, 1943—Meridian
No gas—No flying. Went into town in the evening with Lt. Lee. We met a "queer" and had a long talk.

Saturday, April 24, 1943—Meridian
Flew X-C to Greenville and Vicksburg. Logged 3:00. Review for new colonel of 48th bomb group.

Sunday, April 25, 1943—Meridian
Morning—2:00 x-c in A-24.
Afternoon—Logged 2:10 practicing dive-bombing. Dove once without the dive brakes open and almost got killed—pulled out at treetop level!
Night—Logged 1:45 night transition.

Monday, April 26, 1943—Meridian
Morning—Shot skeet, 20 hits.
Afternoon—Logged 2:15 dive-bombing at Pachuter. Dropped five bombs. Stayed in at night and wrote letters.

Tuesday, April 27, 1943—Meridian
Logged 2:15 dive-bombing at Pachuter. Played ping-pong and pool all afternoon with Don Rauch. Logged 2:30 night x-c

Wednesday, April 28, 1943—Meridian
Took Lee to Birmingham for breakfast. Logged 1:45.
M.P. duty in town at night.

Thursday, April 29, 1943—Meridian
Day off—played chess and wrote letters. Logged 1:30 night transition.

Friday, April 30, 1943—Meridian
Got paid $239. Flew to Mobile and landed. Logged 2:10 x-c.

Saturday, May 1, 1943—Meridian
Logged 2:20 bombing and gunnery. Went into town in the evening with Lt. Lee.

Sunday, May 2, 1943—Meridian
Filled out questionnaire on the A-25—it's a Navy plane they call the "Vultee Vengeance."
Logged 2:30 formation—unit mission.

Monday, May 3, 1943—Meridian
Logged 4:30 unit mission. Went into town at night. Remember the story about Lt. Hom buzzing the wharf at Biloxi.

Tuesday, May 4, 1943—Meridian
Logged 4:10 T/27 combat. Went into town with Lt. Lee.

Wednesday, May 5, 1943—Meridian
Logged 5:10 glide bombing and gunnery at Pachuter.
Stayed in and read at night.

Thursday, May 6, 1943—Meridian
Lt. Lee left for Biloxi. Went on A.O. duty at 11:00. Met Colonel Pratt in the evening and also called off night flying. Big stuff!

Friday, May 7, 1943—Meridian
Logged 2:15 glide bombing and gunnery, also 1:10 unit mission.
Went to Country Club to a dance in the evening, I'm glad that I'm a pretty good dancer—it helps a lot!

Saturday, May 8, 1943—Meridian
No flying. Lt. Adams, Lt. Burton and myself are scheduled to leave Tuesday for Orlando, Fla. We are going to spend a month at the "Air Force School of Applied Tactics" (AFFSAT for short). At least I'll be getting a change of scenery. I've been in Meridian too long already. Rich McNamara is in Orlando so maybe I'll get to see him.

Sunday, May 9, 1943—Meridian
Flew down to Biloxi to see Lt. Lee. Logged 4:30 x-c. Country Club in the evening.

Monday, May 10, 1943—Meridian
Stayed on base all day getting things packed for my trip to Orlando.

Tuesday, May 11, 1943—Travel
We left Key Field at 07:00 all rode all day on the train.

Wednesday, May 12, 1943—Orlando, Fla.
Arrived in Jacksonville at 08:00 and Orlando at 15:00. 1 got in touch with Rich Mac and met him in town.

Thursday, May 13, 1943—Orlando
Classes will not start here in Orlando until next Monday. So I've got the next three days off. We'll be heading to Daytona Beach tomorrow. Daytona is where WAC (Women's Army Corp) officers are trained. We've got to check it out! Went into town and saw Mac at night.

Friday, May 14, 1943—Daytona Beach
Arrived at Daytona Beach and checked into Daytona Bend Hotel. We did the beach in the afternoon and nightclubs at night. Met Lt. M. Hale (the "M" is for Muriel). She's from New York and looks like Helen O'Connell.

Saturday, May 15, 1943—Daytona Beach
Spent the day with Lt. Hale and Jack Adams and a friend of Murial's. Spent a lot of money in the evening.

Sunday, May 16, 1943—Daytona and Orlando
Jack and I headed back to Orlando at 03:00. We stayed in town until late.

Monday, May 17, 1943—Orlando
Listened to seven hours of lectures. A lot of the stuff is "restricted" and a lot of it is boring as hell. Stayed in and took it easy in the evening.

Tuesday, May 18, 1943—Orlando
Another seven hours of lectures. Stayed in and wrote letters and read.

Wednesday, May 19, 1943—Orlando
Morning—school.
Afternoon—Went to ground arms demonstration.
Evening—in town with Mac.

Thursday, May 20, 1943—Orlando
School all day. In town with Mac at night.

Friday, May 21, 1943—Orlando
School all day. It rained in the evening so I stayed in.

Saturday, May 22, 1943—Orlando
School all day. Lt. Hale came over from Daytona and we had a big time. Stayed in town overnight.

Sunday, May 23, 1943—Orlando
Stayed in town all day with Lt. Hale. She left for Daytona at 04:00.

Monday, May 24, 1943—Orlando
School all day. Met Mac in the evening and went to boxing match. I miss flying.

Tuesday, May 25, 1943—Orlando
School all day. Stayed in at night and wrote letters.

Wednesday, May 26, 1943—Orlando
School all day. Went into town and met Mac.

Thursday, May 27, 1943—Orlando
School all day. Stayed in and did laundry in the evening.

Friday, May 28, 1943—Orlando
School all day—Actor Robert Preston sat next to me. He's a nice guy. Went to officer's club with Lt. Adams in the evening.

Saturday, May 29, 1943—Orlando
No school! Muriel came over from Daytona and I met her in town. We went to the Coliseum and danced.

Sunday, May 30, 1943—Orlando
Spent the day with Muriel swimming, etc. She got a bus at 04:00 back to Daytona. Maybe I should think about getting disengaged from Ann.

Monday, May 31, 1943—Orlando
School again. Went into town in the evening with Jack Adams. Mac wasn't around.

Tuesday June 1, 1943—Orlando
School all day. Went into town. Borrowed $10 from Lt. Swan.

Wednesday June 2, 1943—Orlando
School all day. Met Mac at night and we both got a slight buzz on.

Thursday June 3, 1943—Orlando
Last day in Orlando. Went to school as usual. Good lecture from a pilot just back from New Guinea.
Left at 19:00 for Gainesville.

Friday June 4, 1943—Gainesville, Fla
Arrived in Gainesville at 01:00. Did nothing all day as everything here is screwed up.

Saturday June 5, 1943—Gainesville
Watched a couple of mock air raids, which were lousy. Went to Ocala in the evening and stayed overnight.

Sunday June 6, 1943—Gainesville
Spent the whole day at Silver Springs with Lt. Lamer and friends. Good time! Got back to Gainsville around 18:00.

Monday June 7, 1943—Gainsville
Played cards and ping-pong all day. This place is "SNAFU".

Tuesday June 8, 1943—Gainsville
Did nothing much all day. Went swimming in the afternoon.

Wednesday June 9, 1943—Gainsville
Flew 0:24 in A-24! Went swimming.

Thursday June 10, 1943—Gainsville
Hung around all day. Wrote to Lt. Hale.

Friday June 11, 1943—Gainsville
Logged 1:30 in A-24. Went swimming.

Saturday June 12, 1943—Gainsville
Flew 1:00 in a Piper Cub. Left Gainsville at 15:00 and got to Jacksonville at 18:00. Left Jacksonville at 22:00.

Sunday June 13, 1943—Travel
Arrived in Birmingham at 13:00 and left at 23:00. Saw town and a couple of movies.

Monday June 14, 1943—Meridian, Miss.
Arrived in Meridian at 03:00 and went directly to Key Field. I'm still attached to the 55th but I'm going to be assigned to a new group.

Tuesday June 15, 1943—Meridian
Went to dispensary and got three shots. Maybe I'll get overseas yet. Stayed in at night.

Wednesday June 16, 1943—Meridian
Flew 2:00 in A-24. I took Lt. Adams up with me. Ray Schiller came in from Baton Rouge in A-36 and dug up the runway. He walked away ok. While I was in Florida Fred Lamer knocked the mast off of a crash boat in Biloxi. He didn't win any points on that one!

Thursday June 17, 1943—Meridian
Had a bad cold and so I took it easy all day. Lt. Sheehan came in with a stuck throttle in his P-40. He cracked up and walked away.

Friday June 18, 1943—Meridian
Rested all day. Read and wrote letters.

Saturday June 19, 1943—Meridian
Flew 3:00 x-c in A-24.
Went into town with Adams and Lee. Met Betsy and a couple of her friends and we all went to the Country Club and danced.

Sunday June 20, 1943—Meridian
Took it easy most of the day. Went into town and went to a movie with Betsy.

Monday June 21, 1943—Meridian
Don and I flew to Birmingham and landed. Don, George and I went into town in the evening and had a good time.

Tuesday June 22, 1943—Meridian
Got transferred to 406th bomb group: 628th squadron. Don Rauch is still with me.

Wednesday June 23, 1943—Meridian
Finally checked out in a A-35. It's nothing that I want to go overseas with. Went into town with Don.

Thursday June 24, 1943—Meridian
Got Typhoid shot today.
Logged 1:30 in A-35. Stayed in and shot pool at night.

Friday June 25, 1943—Meridian
Watched a B-26 come in with one prop feathered. All ok.
Went into town and then out to the Country Club.

Saturday June 26, 1943—Meridian
Flew to Birmingham with Don—me in the gunners seat.
Went to the Country Club with Betsy and danced.

Sunday June 27, 1943—Meridian
Logged 1:20 in A-25. Logged 2:00 in A-35. Got transferred again. I'm now with the 404th group.

Monday June 28, 1943—Meridian
Checked in at the 404th group and am assigned to the 623rd squadron. Lt. Ballard is the C.O. We are leaving for South Carolina this weekend.

Tuesday June 29, 1943—Meridian
Flew to Birmingham with George as observer. Logged 2:00. Went to 404th party with Peggy Gillette. Went swimming after and George got tossed in jail after his girl friend mouthed off to the police. Peggy and I stayed in the water until everyone left. Big night!

Wednesday June 30, 1943—Meridian
Took it easy and started to pack my stuff for the trip to Carolina,

Thursday July 1, 1943—Meridian
Got my third Typhoid shot. Went into town with George Phillips. George is a great guy, we've been together ever since primary flight school.

Friday July 2, 1943—Meridian
Hung around and got things ready to leave. Jack Adams is leaving Sunday to ferry a P-51 from Georgia to California.

Saturday July 3, 1943—Travel
Left Meridian at 11:00 and flew to Birmingham. We buzzed Key Field after take-off. The weather moved in and we stayed overnight in Birmingham. Logged 1:40 in A-24.

Sunday July 4, 1943—Travel
Flew from Birmingham to Atlanta and landed. From Atlanta we flew to Congaree, South Carolina. Rough weather between Atlanta and Columbia. Logged 3:10

Monday July 5, 1943—Congaree, South Carolina
Got settled in at the base here at Congaree. Went into Columbia in the evening with Don Rauch. It's a strictly G.I. city.

Tuesday July 6, 1943—Congaree
Flew 1:10 in A-24. Went to Orangeberg and then to Shaw Field. Flew formation with some BT's.

Wednesday July 7, 1943—Congaree
Logged 3:10 x-c in A-24. Flew to Florence, Charleston and back.

Thursday July 8, 1943—Congaree
No flying. Went into Columbia with Williamson and had dinner with Fred Suehle and his wife.

Friday July 9, 1943—Congaree
Flew to Augusta Georgia and back. Logged 2:00. Stayed in at night.

Saturday July 10, 1943—Congaree
No flying. Went into Columbia with Don Rauch.

Sunday July 11, 1943—Congaree
Flew 3:30 in A-24. Stayed in and wrote letters.

Monday July 12, 1943—Congaree
Day off—no flying. Went into Columbia and did laundry and saw a movie.

Tuesday July 13, 1943—Congaree
Link 1:00
Went into town with George and Don and got tight. This place is the pits.

Wednesday July 14, 1943—Congaree
Link 1:00. Flew x-c to Augusta, Charleston and back.
Went into town at night and saw a movie.

Thursday July 15, 1943—Congaree and travel
Big day!! Seven pilots—me included—got orders at 07:00. Transferring us to the 439th fighter squadron in Tallahassee, Fla. We will be flying P-47 Thunderbolts! We had just five hours to clear the post as we left Columbia at 01:00. We spent the night in Jacksonville.

Friday July 16, 1943—Tallahassee, Fla.
We left Jacksonville at 09:00 and got to Tallahassee at 15:00. We signed in at squadron headquarters and checked out the officers club.

Saturday July 17, 1943—Tallahassee
Got settled in B.O.Q. I hope that we can get checked out in the P-47 soon. Went into town in the evening with R.E. Parker and checked out the Country Club.

Sunday July 18, 1943—Tallahassee
Listened to lecture on P-47.
Got another 6-4.
Made allotment for war bond.
Made out Power of Attorney form.

Monday July 19, 1943—Tallahassee
Listened to high altitude lecture. Lt. Diffenderfer got an emergency furlough. Went into town at night.

Tuesday July 20, 1943—Tallahassee
Went to supply and drew bedroll and other stuff.
Went into town with R.E. but came back early as he shacked up with dog from N.Y.

Wednesday July 21, 1943—Tallahassee
Went "up" in high altitude chamber—no trouble at 38,000'. Five guys had to get out.

Thursday July 22, 1943—Tallahassee
Got reassigned to the 305th squadron for training. Filled out questionnaire on P-47. R.E. Parker went to Perry.

Friday July 23, 1943—Tallahassee
Morning—watched training film and got cockpit check in P-47. Afternoon—Flew 1:00 in AT-6. Checked out in P-47 and logged 1:30. Lt. Campbell killed when he stalled out on approach.

Saturday July 24, 1943—Tallahassee
Flew 2.5 hrs transitions in P-47. Link 1:00
Stayed in at night, as I was dead tired. Don't feel good at all.

Sunday July 25, 1943—Tallahassee
Felt better today. Flew 1.8 hrs transitions in a P-47. Also 1.0 hrs instrument in AT-6. Into town with Williamson.

Monday July 26, 1943—Tallahassee
Flew 2.5 hrs in P-47 formation and acrobatics. I flew on Cap't Shooks wing and followed him thru everything in the book. Love it!

Tuesday July 27, 1943—Tallahassee
Link 2:00. Plane grounded—no gas. All other planes have gone to Tampa for two days.

Wednesday July 28, 1943—Tallahassee
Day off. Went out to the country club with Williamson in the evening.

Thursday July 29, 1943—Tallahassee
Planes all in Tampa—no flying. Went to Wakulla Springs with Williamson.

Friday July 30, 1943—Tallahassee
Flew 2:10 hrs in P-47. Stayed in and read the rest of the day.

Saturday July 31, 1943—Tallahassee
Morning—flew 1.5 hrs rat racing.
Afternoon—watched harmonizing of the P-47's guns.
Evening—went to the country club with Willie. Good Dancing!

Sunday August 1, 1943—Tallahassee
Morning—shot skeet, 21 hits. Flew 1.8 hrs formations in p-47. Went to bed early.

Monday August 2, 1943—Tallahassee
Flew 1.9 hours formation and 1.6 hours x-c. Link 1:00.
Stayed in and wrote letters.

Tuesday August 3, 1943—Tallahassee
Flew 5.4 formation and rat racing in p-47. Lt. Jost landed wheels up! Stayed in at night—tired.

Wednesday August 4, 1943—Tallahassee
I'm way ahead in flying time so I didn't fly. Went to the country club in the evening with Williamson and party.

Thursday August 5, 1943—Tallahassee
Day off. Went to Wakulla Springs with Williamson.

Friday August 6, 1943—Tallahassee
Flew 1.2 combat with Captain Shook. Broke oil line and also ran out of oxygen.
Mid-air collision in the 306th—one pilot killed and the other bailed out safely.
Went to movie on post at night.

Saturday August 7, 1943—Tallahassee
No flying. Slept all afternoon. Went to the country club in the evening and stayed in town.

Sunday August 8, 1943—Tallahassee
Flew 1.7 hrs. Aerial gunnery in P-47.
Went to a show on post in the evening.

Monday August 9, 1943—Tallahassee
Flew 1.8 hours ground gunnery with guns and camera.
Link 1:00
Two guys came in for emergency landings. One in an A-24 with wheels up and another in a P-47 with a tow target draped over his wing. Both okay.

Wednesday August 11, 1943—Tallahassee
Link 1:00
Went to the Country Club in the evening.

Thursday August 12, 1943—Tallahassee
Flew 3.0 hours x-c in P-47.
Went to movie on Post in the evening.

Friday August 13, 1943—Tallahassee
Jost got transferred. He told me that Captain Shook said that I was the hottest pilot in the group.
Went to the Country Club and stayed in town overnight.

Saturday August 14, 1943—Tallahassee
No flying.
Link 1:00
A DC-3 came in low and undershot the runway. He knocked the wheels off but was ok otherwise.

Sunday August 15, 1943—Tallahassee
Flew 2.4 hours aerial gunnery.
Stayed in and went to a movie.

Monday August 16, 1943—Tallahassee
Flew 2.00 hours formation in P-47.
Link 1:00
Stayed in and wrote letters.

Tuesday August 17, 1943—Tallahassee
Flew 1.30 hours with Captain Shook. I followed him through a double Immelman. He enjoyed it as much as I did. Got a letter from Lt. Hale. She's going to try and visit Tallahassee. Stayed in.

Wednesday August 18, 1943—Tallahassee
Flew three aerial gunnery missions and logged 2.30 hours. A P-47 ran into an AT-6 on the runway.
Pilot of AT-6 killed.
Went to Country Club and stayed in town.

Thursday August 19, 1943—Tallahassee
Day off. Stayed in town all day. Played cards in the evening and lost.

Friday August 20, 1943—Tallahassee
Flew 3.9 hours of aerial gunnery. Shot three rounds of skeet and got 16 hits every time.
Stayed in the evening.

Saturday August 21, 1943—Tallahassee
Flew 3.4 hours aerial gunnery. Did well. A 306th pilot in a P-47 took off in front of me with his rudder locked and catapulted off the runway. What a sight! He walked away okay.
Met Lt. Hale in town and we went to the Country Club and danced. Stayed in town.

Sunday August 22, 1943—Tallahassee
Went to Wakulla Springs with Murial. She left at 1500. Stayed in at night.

Monday August 23, 1943—Tallahassee
Flew 1.5 hours aerial gunnery as flight leader. Flew 1.5-night transition in P-47.
Went to movie on Post at night.

Tuesday August 24, 1943—Tallahassee
Ground school in morning. Ferried an AT-6 to Spence Field in the afternoon.
Went into town and got my laundry. Pilot from 306th stalled out on approach and was killed.

Wednesday August 25, 1943—Tallahassee
No flying.

Went to Country club in the evening. Stayed at Arlene Rogers house at night.

Thursday August 26, 1943—Tallahassee
Day off. Bought and read two books "Love at First Flight" and "Malta Spitfire".
Went to show in evening.

Friday August 27, 1943—Tallahassee
Shot skeet (22 hits) and went to P.T. in the morning. Went to review.
Met Lt. Brink tonight—old primary classmate.

Saturday August 28, 1943—Tallahassee
Flew 1.8 hours high altitude navigation. Shot skeet (18 hits).
Stayed in and read in the evening.

Sunday August 29, 1943—Tallahassee
Flew 1.4 hours high altitude combat.
Went to show in the evening.

Monday August 30, 1943—Tallahassee
No flying.
Went to Wakulla Springs with Williamson. Stayed in and read at night.

Tuesday August 31, 1943—Tallahassee
Flew 1.8 hours aerial gunnery and 2.0 hours combat with Lt. Bellemy.

Wednesday September 1, 1943—Tallahassee
Played cards (lost) and read all day.
Went to Country Club at night. Soldier killed at Joe's Spaghetti House.

Thursday September 2, 1943—Tallahassee
I was transferred back to 439th squadron today. Fifty of us P-47 jockeys are alerted for overseas. Went to "Joes".

Friday September 3, 1943—Tallahassee
Made out my "will" and also had another 6-4. Bought a lot of stuff for overseas. Went to the Forrest Inn at night.

Saturday September 4, 1943—Tallahassee
Listened to lecture on how prisoners of war are treated. Went to the country club with Williamson and Hoffman.
Met Betsy and we danced all night.

Sunday September 5, 1943—Tallahassee
Shot skeet (19 hits). Took it easy all day and night.

Monday September 6, 1943—Tallahassee
Shot 45-caliber automatic pistol. Went to town with Willie.

Tuesday September 7, 1943—Tallahassee
Took a physical fitness test and did well. Went to a movie on the post.

Wednesday September 8, 1943—Tallahassee
Listened to lectures all day. One was from an infantry officer who spent fifteen months in the South Pacific. Hope that they are not trying to tell us something. I want to go to either England or Africa—not the Pacific area.

Thursday September 9, 1943—Tallahassee
Lt. Stelle, an instructor in the 305th was killed in a mid-air collision today. The trainee who hit him cracked up upon landing but walked

away. Still waiting for orders. Took intelligence test and got a 90. Best in the West Point group 88.

Friday September 10, 1943—Tallahassee
The trainee who got into yesterday's crack-up did it again! This time both pilots parachuted to safety over the Gulf. Two mid-air collisions in as many days! Went to Joe's for spaghetti in the evening.

Saturday September 11, 1943—Tallahassee
Our shipping code came through this morning and we had busy day packing. I don't know where we're going as we're packing both jungle kits plus winter clothing. We're allowed four bags in all—barracks bag, parachute bag, val-pac and bedroll. Went to the Country Club in the evening. Met Betsy and danced till 12:00. Stayed in town.

Sunday September 12, 1943—Tallahassee
Hung around all day. We still don't know where we're going or when. Went out in the evening with Williams and Aho.

Monday September 13, 1943—Tallahassee
Listened to lecture on "How to escape if captured". Also got in a lot of sack time. Went to supply in the afternoon and drew a watch and a 45 caliber pistol with holster. Went to town in the evening with Lt. Aho.

Tuesday September 14, 1943—Tallahassee
At 13:00 we were given fifteen minutes to get ready to leave. First we went to the medics and got a "short-arm" and then collected a partial pay. Next we rode to and boarded the train. Our two cars were strictly private and we couldn't leave them. At 20:00 we got to Jacksonville. Next we headed north and spent the night on the train.

Wednesday September 15, 1943—Travel
Train arrived in Richmond VA. at 10:30 and stayed until 13:30. After we returned to the train from exploring Richmond the captain in charge of our group gave us our orders. We are on our way to Camp Patrick Henry, Lee Hall, Virginia. We arrived at Lee Hall at 16:00, signed in and did nothing. This place has more rank in it than any other place I've seen. Most of the officers are from the infantry. There are also some B-17 crews. We are the only fighter pilots. We don't know when we'll leave here or where we're going. My bet is still England. We can't get off the post and our letters are now censored. Aho, Williamson, Hoffman and I are rooming together.

Thursday September 16, 1943—Lee Hall, Virginia
Did nothing much all day. Wrote to folks and to Anne. Met Art Simpson from Fitchburg in the mess hall. He's one of about 100 B-17 pilots here waiting to go overseas. Our baggage arrived here today. There's ranker in this staging area than in the Pentagon in Washington.

Friday September 17, 1943—Lee Hall
Spent morning having teeth and gums checked—both okay. In the afternoon we drew more equipment—gun belt, magazine pouch, field bag harness, first aid packet, chemical treated hat, gloves, pants and underwear. I've now got more junk than I'll ever use. Collected $8.75 travel pay from Tallahassee. Art Simpson got a big kick out of watching us ride up to supply in a cattle truck.

Saturday September 18, 1943—Lee Hall
Bumped into Gerry Lombard and George Flathers—both from Fitchburg—in the mess hall today. They are both B17 pilots. Out of about two hundred pilots here four of us are from Fitchburg.

Sunday September 19, 1943—Lee Hall
Visited with Gerry Lombard and played horseshoes and chess with Wiliamson.

Monday September 20, 1943—Lee Hall
Played horseshoes and chess with Williamson. About 4000 GI's moved out tonight. There is also a group of high-ranking officers here who are trained to take over jobs in conquered countries. They'll probably go to Italy as they have surrendered.

Tuesday September 21, 1943—Lee Hall
Beat Williamson at chess. Rain all day. Lt. Barky came in tonight with three stitches in his lip after he got in a fight with a bomber pilot. Bomber groups got alerted.

Wednesday September 22, 1943—Lee Hall
Rain all day. Played chess with Williamson and also read. Went to a movie at night.

Thursday September 23, 1943—Lee Hall
Rain all day. About twenty B-25 and B-26 pilots arrived. Had a long talk with George Flathers and Gerry Lombard. There's a bunch of Frenchmen here and I enjoy talking to them.

Friday September 24, 1943—Lee Hall
Usual routine—chess and reading.

Saturday September 25, 1943—Lee Hall
Usual routine.

Sunday September 26, 1943—Lee Hall
It is rumored that we might be able to get a five-day pass, as we won't leave before October 5th. It's strictly "latrine" stuff.

Monday September 27, 1943—Lee Hall
Signed payroll. All of us put in applications for a five-day leave. Four of them were accepted—Jensen, Jones, Fallon and Knox. The rest of us feel as if we got screwed—and we did!

Tuesday September 28, 1943—Lee Hall
This place is beginning to fill up again as we have B-26, B-25, B-17, P-38 and P-39 pilots here now. Also a lot of new officers of high rank have come in. They're to form new military governments.

Wednesday September 29, 1943—Lee Hall
Went to a movie and saw "Lady Take a Chance" with Jean Arthur. Got paid $71.50. Received packing list and it's about the same as we came in with.

Thursday September 30, 1943—Lee Hall
Rained all day. Spent the morning packing and getting set to leave. We're to have our "B" baggage Sat. morning. We'll leave here Monday morning.

Friday October 1, 1943—Lee Hall
Spent the day packing. Bedroll, parachute bag and barracks bag will go in the hold of the ship.

Saturday October 2, 1943—Lee Hall
Got rid of "B" baggage. All that I've got left is my val-pac, field bag and blanket roll which I will carry.

Sunday October 3, 1943—Lee Hall
Took a "physical" which consisted of teeth check, chest exam, dog tag inspection and check up on our immunization record—no short-arm! Went to show in the evening. After the show, Lowry and Oxner had a drinking contest and ran out of booze after they both drank close to a quart each. Seeing that they couldn't out-do each other drinking, they decided to have a wrestling match. It was a good show and I've never seen anyone as drunk as they were.

Monday October 4,1943—Lee Hall
Got up at 06:30 and ate breakfast. After that I packed my musette bag and wrote a short note to Ann. At 11:00 we all assembled in front of the barracks with our entire field equipment and it was quite a load. Field bag, blanket roll, gun, gas mask, steel helmet, cartridge belt and val-pak. Thirty of the fifty officers in my group are going on a different ship so today was our parting. Williamson is still with me. Aho and Hoffinan are on the other boat. At 13:00 we boarded the train and rode to Newport News about one-half hour away. We boarded our ship at 15:30. It is a new "Liberty" ship. Besides the crew we have about 500 enlisted men aboard (all infantry) and fifty officers—twenty of us Air Corp and thirty infantry. It's crowded as hell as our bunks are stacked four high. As usual I managed to grab the top bunk. We're a lot better off than the enlisted men as they are 11 crowded. Five A-24's are crated on the deck. That's a surprise to me, as I didn't know that they were used at all in the European theater. I think that we're going to either Africa or Sicily as the first-mate said the trip would last about nineteen days and that's about 4000 miles. It is now 22:00 and the ship hasn't left yet. According to those who know we won't leave until 04:00. The delay is due to engine trouble. We pilots are big stuff to the infantry boys and the planes on deck give them an excuse to ask us about flying. I'm glad that I've got a lot of A-24 time, as now I really know what I'm talking about. A little while ago I went up on deck and it was really dark—no

lights anywhere. I got to thinking, for about the first time, that I might get to see some combat.

Tuesday October 5, 1943—At sea
At 23:30 last night, after I had gone to bed, we pulled out. This morning when I got up we were still in sight of land. There are about seventy ships in the convoy. It is well protected as besides the usual destroyers we have an aircraft carrier, which I haven't seen yet. Also navy blimps and PBY's are still with us. I haven't got sick although I did feel a little woozy when I stay down below. I spent most of the day looking at the water. We were informed today that we are going to Casablanca. That's better than England as far as I'm concerned. This trip is going to be rough as the food is lousy and there's nothing to do.

Wednesday October 6, 1943—At sea
The food on this ship is piss-poor and we only get two meals a day. Still I'm not bitching about it as much as the others. The aircraft carrier came into view today.

Thursday October 7, 1943—At sea
The weather was a little warmer today. I didn't wear a scarf or gloves. A couple of ships fired some practice rounds of A.A., which was interesting to watch. It rained in the evening.

Friday October 8, 1943—At sea
Fourth day at sea. Watched planes take-off and land on the carrier. Also we had a four-engined Navy Coronado floating around during the day. The food situation is really piss-poor and two meals a day isn't enough? The enlisted men can't go up on deck and—I feel sorry for them, as it's both hot and dark down below. We officers have the boat to ourselves and so we don't have to fight for a place to sit on the deck like the enlisted men.

Saturday October 9, 1943—At sea
Fifth day at sea. One of our officers cooked up a deal with the ship's steward whereby we (officers) can eat in the Navy officers mess for $2.50 a week. This is a good deal as their food is very good. I be willing to pay $20 a week if they wanted it. The water was very choppy today. Seeing that it's so hot below the captain has decided to let the enlisted men sleep on deck at night from now on. Some Dumb John will screw up the works by lighting a cigarette or something—but that's their worry not mine. The Merchant Marine guys have a pretty good deal and any guy is a sucker to be in the Army if he could be in it.

Sunday October 10, 1943—At sea
Sixth day at sea. Today was a beautiful day. Last night I slept on deck but it was too hard for comfort. The aircraft carrier hasn't been around for a day and a half. We've been paying 4 cents a pack for cigarettes and that's pretty cheap. The food is excellent in the ships officers' mess. The captain seems like a pretty good guy. The name of out ship is "C.B. Aycork". It has four gun stations, which are manned constantly by Navy gunners. It has six 20mm anti-aircraft guns and a couple larger caliber guns. Tonight I'm going to sleep in the hold even if it's hot.

Monday October 11, 1943—At sea
Seventh day at sea. New York Yankees won the World Series by beating the St. Louis Cardinals. Spent the day as usual—chess and reading. The days are getting a lot hotter and I'm beginning to get back some of the sunburn that I had before I got to Virginia. Tonight there is a full moon and it's a pretty sight on deck. We've pushed the clocks ahead two hours already and by the time we get to Africa we'll be four hours ahead of E.W.T. The Merchant Marines sailors have plenty of good stories to tell. One of them was in a convoy to Russia last year and thirty-five of the thirty-nine ships in the convoy were sunk.

Tuesday October 12, 1943—At sea
Eighth day at sea. Spent the day in the usual way. The weather is getting real warm now and I'm getting sunburned. Early this morning one of the destroyers on the other side of the convoy dropped a couple of depth charges. The sea was as smooth as glass all day and it was beautiful at night with the full moon.

Wednesday October 13, 1943—At sea
Ninth day at sea. We made slow time all day (about 5 knots) as one of the ships had engine trouble and the convoy slowed down so that it could keep up with us. Later on in the afternoon we resumed our speed of nine knots per hour. It was a beautiful day and the ocean had unusually big swells. So far I haven't seen any porpoises but I've seen some sharks and lots of flying fish. I washed all my clothes today. Every two or three days I wash what I'm wearing and so I never have my laundry pile up. Italy declared war on Germany today—or at least today was when I heard about it. In a way it bums me up to think of those bastards being our allies when just a short while ago they were our enemies. Still that's the way it goes, I guess. I feel that they should get punished more than they have. We ought to take all their spaghetti away from them. Tonight the ocean was beautiful. The moon was full and it was quite a sight.

Thursday October 14, 1943—At sea
Tenth day at sea. I spent the day as usual, playing chess, reading and laying in the sun. Tonight we had a little excitement. I was down in the hold when I heard the ships blast a couple of times and so I went up on deck to see what was going on. The destroyer that was protecting our flank dropped four depth charges just after it got dark. Things got really exciting for a while and we were expecting at any moment to see one of the ships get hit. No one got hit though so I guess the depth charges drove the sub away. Just now I heard a couple more of them go off but they sounded pretty far away.

Friday October 15, 1943—At sea
Eleventh day at sea. Usual routine—chess with Fred Suehle and Paul Jensen. It doesn't take much to start an argument here. All one has to do is start the North—South comparison and it starts. Also it gets pretty vocal when some Air Corp pilot tells an infantry officer that the infantry is a thing of the past. Sometimes it gets past the kidding stage.

Saturday October 16, 1943—At sea
Twelfth day at sea. Spent all day reading and also got in a couple of games of chess. According to the crew we should be in Casablanca by Thursday.

Sunday October 17, 1943—At sea
Thirteenth day at sea. Started reading "Paul Revere and the World He Lived In" by Esther Forbes. It's a good book. This evening before sunset some of the enlisted men put on a show. It was pretty corny but still worth seeing here.

Monday October 18, 1943—At sea
Fourteenth day at sea. We saw our first African based aircraft today. They were PBY'S. The ship in front of us—(the one with the rest of the P-47 pilots on it) dropped back for a while. We thought that they would be left behind. The convoy might slow down but it won't stop. Still reading about Paul Revere.

Tuesday October 19, 1943—At sea
Fifteenth day at sea. Usual—chess and reading. We were given three days worth of food today to be used after we get ashore. Eighteen cans of "C" ration—(three cans of stew, three of hash, three of beans, etc.) Also we got—nine packages of "D" ration. This is a very rich chocolate bar.

Wednesday October 20, 1943—At sea
Sixteenth day at sea. Today we reached the point where our convoy split up. Half of us are going to Casablanca and the rest are going on thru the Mediterranean. We are now about seventy miles out from Casa and cruising around in circles, as we have to wait until morning before we can get a pilot to guide us thru the minefields. Also we can't just lie here idle, as we'd be good targets for the submarines. The swells are really big today, kept the boat rocking.

Thursday October 21, 1943—Casablanca
We first sighted land at 12:30. Casablanca is a lot bigger than I thought as it spreads out about ten miles along the shore. We disembarked at 17:20 and rode in GI trucks out to the Casa air base. The ride out was wonderful as we saw Arabs, French, English people and soldiers. Also camels. After we received our quarters at the base we went back into town. Casablanca has a population of about 300,000 and I enjoyed walking about the city looking at the Arabs and trying to talk with the French. Most of the Frenchmen know just enough English to get by and that saves us a lot of trouble. I talked with one Limy who had been in the French Foreign Legion for nine years. He was very interesting.

Friday October 22, 1943—Casablanca
I got up at 08:30 and went down to the flight line. The airport here at Casa is not used as a training base at all so it looks as though our stay here will be short. The biggest percent of the population are the Arabs. They are interesting as they dress so differently. The men wear either cloaks or else a huge burlap-bag affair. The women are all wrapped up in a sheet. All of the unmarried women are veiled and so all you can see is their eyes. Some of the eyes looked okay but I couldn't even guess as to what the rest of them looked like. The Frenchmen here are much the same as you can find in Montreal. There isn't much to drink in Casa except wine. I did drink some champagne but it wasn't so hot. Carl

Tucker met up with an Arab pimp and the guy walked off with his wallet and wristwatch. They are expert pickpockets.

Saturday October 23, 1943—Casablanca
Went into Casa about 12:30 with Williamson. We walked around town and drank a little wine. Later we met Suehle and Jones and the four of us hired a horse and buggy and toured the city. It was very interesting. In the—evening we went to the Allied officer's club. We drank cognac and tried to talk with the Frenchmen. When we got back to the air base we were informed that we would be leaving at 08:00 in the morning for Mateur Tunisia. Eighteen of us are flying via B-17 and the rest by C-47.

Sunday October 24, 1943—Mateur, Tunisia
I got up at 06:3 0, packed and ate breakfast. Next we went down to the field and loaded our baggage in the B-17 and took off about 09:00. The weather was pretty soupy after take-off so we climbed to 17,000 ft to get above it. We flew for almost two hours up there. We were very cold and almost passing out from lack of oxygen. At 12:00 we dropped down to 4000 ft. The country was hilly all the way. At 14:00 we reached La Massa near Tunis. Here we gassed up and flew on to Mateur. The DC-3 didn't make it thru the bad weather around Casablanca so the eighteen of us in the B-17 were the only ones to get here today. The field here is pretty good and is near hill "509" which is pretty high. We are attached to the 325th fighter group, 318th squadron. Up until a couple of weeks ago this group flew P-40's but now they are switching over to P-47's. Most of the pilots that were here when we arrived are just checking out in the P-47's. The 325th has the best record in this theater of war so I'm in a good outfit. The C.O. of the 318th is Captain Garret. The whole area around here is littered with scrapped German planes, guns, etc…

Monday October 25, 1943—Mateur
Got up early and ate breakfast. After I went to the squadron orderly room and gave them my "201 file". Also filled out personnel forms. Later I went to the squadron operations area and gave them my "form 5" About noon we all assembled on the flight line as General Doolittle was supposed to come and give a couple of the pilots DFC's but he didn't show up. I'm living in a tent with Williamson, Strain and Hogg. Lt. Hogg is one the older pilots here and he has two planes to his credit. The tent is fixed up pretty good. In the evening we all watched a movie consisting of combat films taken by P-47's in England. They were good. It rained like hell tonight and so that means we won't be able to operate from this field for at least three days. I've never seen such mud in my life. Now that the rainy season has come we'll have to move out of here. We hope that we go to Italy.

Tuesday October 26, 1943—Mateur
I slept late today and so the morning was about shot when I got up. The mud is really thick around here since the rain started. All of the planes are grounded. After supper this evening Lt. Vaught came around and brought Williamson, Strain, Suehle and myself into Mateur for a shower. It was sure good to get clean again. Mateur is beat-up pretty bad from the war. There's nothing in it but Arabs. After the shower we returned and went to the Officers Club and drank a couple of "snap rolls." I think they are a mix of cognac and medical alcohol. Next we went to the movies and saw "One Thrilling Night."

Wednesday October 27, 1943—Mateur
Got up late again and shaved. Shaving is pretty rough as the water we use comes from a "belly-tank" in front of the tent and it is cold. At 10:30 we all went to the flight line and watched General Doolittle as he came in to present the DFC to three of our pilots. Wrote letters to Put Olson,

Mac, Dick Finn, Dick Vincent and George Phillips this afternoon. After supper Strain and I hit the Officers Club and had a couple "snap-rolls."

Thursday October 28, 1943—Mateur
Got up late. After dinner Willie and I went over to the "hill." Although it looks close it is almost four miles away. At the base of the hill there were a group of about fifty German prisoners working in a quarry. Only two Arabs were guarding them so I suppose that they weren't any threat of escaping. Most of them were young and wore what was left of their thin uniforms. I didn't feel too comfortable walking amongst them as none of them were smiling. We didn't see much else of interest so we came back. Stayed in the evening and read "The Merchant of Venice."

Friday October 29, 1943—Mateur
The field is still wet and so no flying. It rained off and on all day and so we played cards. In the evening I got sick all of a sudden while I was playing bridge with Suehle, Duke and Vaught. I spent the rest of the night vomiting.

Saturday October 30, 1943—Mateur
Stayed in bed all morning, as I felt lousy. This morning a fleet of about 150 B-17's flew over on their way to Italy or France. They were escorted by P-38's. Played cards all afternoon. The B-17's struggled back at 14:00. Then went to Genoa Italy. I haven't played poker since I left the U.S. of A. I'm trying to save a little money. Went to a movie in the evening.

Sunday October 31, 1943—Mateur
I still felt sick so I stayed in bed until noon. Played cards all afternoon with Willie and Strain. Got paid $59—I'm still having $100 per month sent home. Went to the movies and saw "Road to Morocco" with Crosby and Hope. Lt. Kearns who is now with the 319th got lost today and hadn't shown up even after the movie. The Arabs raided the tent of Suehle, Duke

and Vaught while we were at the movie. They took two parachute bags and one barracks bag full of equipment. They are very sneaky thieves.

Monday November 1, 1943—Mateur
Suehle, Dove, Vaught and Sergeant Crowe plus some enlisted men went out "Arab" hunting this morning. Crowe is a pretty rough boy and the Arabs don't scare him. Didn't do much all day except play volleyball and cards. In the evening Col. Basele, our group C.O., gave us "new sports" a talk. He said we're to move out of here in two or three days to a new base near Tunis. The new field has concrete runways so we should be able to get flying again. Won $2 shooting crap. Played bridge with Suehle, Duke and Vaught until 21:00 then I went over and watched the last part of the "French Show" at the hut.

Tuesday November 2, 1943—Mateur
Packed my stuff in preparation for our move to the new field. Went into Mateur and took a shower.

Wednesday November 3, 1943—Mateur
Played bridge most of the day with Suehle, Vaught and Duke.

Thursday November 4, 1943—Mateur
The group started to move today. There are not enough trucks to get us all out today so we'll have to wait until tomorrow. Our new field is about sixty miles away.

Friday November 5, 1943—Soliman, Tunisia
We broke up camp today and loaded our tent and Lt. Deckers tent in the same truck. Lt. Been who has been with Malloy and Decker asked if Williamson and I would mind swapping tents so that he could be with Hogg. We said, "okay." The ride from Mateur to Tunis was interesting as the road was very crowded all the way. Tunis is a big place and a lot like Casablanca. We arrived at our new base at 13:00 and immediately put

up our tent. Williamson and I are now with Malloy and Decker. Judging from the looks of our new tent we didn't do too well in swapping with Been. Played bridge with Suehle, Vaught and Dove.

Saturday November 6, 1943—Soliman
It rained like hell during the night and when I woke up my bed and luggage was soaking wet. The rain had seeped thru the tent—mostly in my corner. Although I'd like to stay with Williamson I moved out and went in with Suehle, Vaught and Duke. They have a good tent and also needed a fourth for bridge. Williamson also moved out and in with Murphy the Pratt and Whitney Guy and the guy from "Republic." Malloy also moved out and so Decker now has the tent all to himself—lucky fellow! This morning Williamson, Strain and I took a walk. In one of the olive groves near here the Germans had a camp and it was loaded with junk. We picked up some German helmets. Also there were some abandoned 88mm guns—a real potent looking weapon—and a load of shells. We also found a skeleton which was probably an Arab and Williamson took the skull back with him. Willie is really a character. He believes in ghosts and spooks and when he talks about his experiences with them it's funny as hell. Played cards all afternoon and evening with the guys.

Sunday November 7, 1943—Soliman
So far this month I've only spent 30 francs (60 cents). That was for a carton of cigarettes and a box of matches. Today it rained and so we played bridge all day. I'm still not too sharp at it but I'm improving. Suehle is the bridge whiz around here. We had our first casualty among the new pilots today. Lt. Quinn found an unexploded 20mm shell. He stuck it in a sand bank and fired at it with a rifle. He hit it and a piece of shrapnel flew back and hit him in the eye. There's a good possibility that he's lost his eyesight. It's a wonder no one has been killed around here.

Our tent is fixed up better than any other in the group. We've got a good floor and an oil heater.

Monday November 8, 1943—Soliman
Rain—no flying. Played bridge all morning. In the afternoon most of us pilots went into Tunis. The city is a lot like Casablanca. It's interesting to watch the local and imported characters that swarm around the city. I got a shower and a haircut and I felt a lot better. We also went to a movie and saw "Nice Girl."

Tuesday November 9, 1943—Soliman
Played bridge most of the day. Willie and I took a short walk and I nearly shot myself in the foot with my "45". Lt. Vaught, one of my tent mates, is one of the nicest guys I've met. Both he and Suehle are great and I like living with them a lot. Lt. Duke is another story.

Wednesday November 10, 1943—Soliman
Capt. Garret, our squadron C.O., gave a short talk today and told us not to expect too much flying for a while yet. Four of our pilots left today for Casablanca. They are going to ferry back some more P-47's. I wish that I were in on that deal—oh well. Played bridge in the evening with Suehle, Vaught and Capt. Lott.

Thursday November 11, 1943—Soliman
Armistice Day. Went into Tunis in the morning to try and buy a comforter for my cot but I didn't have any success. The town was crowded and I saw more good-looking girls than I have since I left the U.S. Maybe it's just that I think they look better. The French were having a good time parading around in the streets. Played bridge in the afternoon and evening. The C.O. gave Jensen a lecture—he's been goofing up ever since he got here. Lt. Quinn is still at the Third General Hospital

at Mateur. They had to remove his eye as it was badly damaged. His army flying days are over.

Friday November 12, 1943—Soliman
Flew 1:30 hrs this morning in a squadron formation. I flew #2 position in the 4th flight. I was on Major Sluder's wing after going two months without flying I was a little rusty. Still I did okay even though I forgot to watch my gas gauge. As a result I ran my aux tank dry. I just switched to the main tank in time. The rat racing was mild and I had no trouble at all. This afternoon Vaught and I felt ambitious so we went to the Gennan salvage dump and collected an odd assortment of junk. We're going to put a door on our tent and also try to rig up a gasoline stove. In the evening Vaught and I went over to the 319th to see Hoffinan and I beat him at chess—much to my surprise.

Saturday November l3, 1943—Soliman
Did nothing all morning. In the afternoon Vaught and I beat Suehle and Lott at bridge. Wrote letters in the evening.

Sunday November 14, 1943—Soliman
Vaught and I took a ride over to the salvage dump and dug up some lumber to make a door for the tent. The old French geezer in charge of the dump is a real character. Went to the movies at night and saw "Arsenic and Old—Lace."

Monday November 15, 1943—Soliman
Vaught, SueWe and I spent the morning fixing up our tent. Our door is pretty good as we even have a window in it. Lt. Walker cracked up a plane today on his first flight. He missed the runway in landing and flipped the plane over in the mud. He was unhurt although he did look like hell as he got a mud bath. This business of dragging in from three miles off on the approach is no good. Suehle, Vaught and I went into

Tunis in the afternoon. I bought a heavy GI comforter at the P.X. We played bridge in the evening.

Tuesday November 16, 1943—Soliman
Played bridge and flubbed around in the morning. In the afternoon Willie and I went into Tunis. We roamed through a lot of stores and about every salesgirl that we talked to wanted us to get something for them—mainly items which they couldn't get for themselves such as stockings, toothpaste, blue shirts, etc. Most of the girls speak just a little English so we had a lot of fun trying to figure out just what they wanted. In return for these little gifts they'd be willing to "promenade" with us. In a couple of instances I was tempted as the girls weren't too bad. I kept remembering the sex lectures they gave us back in the states and that cooled my ardor. In the evening we played bridge as usual.

Wednesday November 17, 1943—Soliman
Went into town in the afternoon with Suehle, Lott, Brown and Raper. We drank champagne and checked out the girls. Suehle and I had a good dinner at the hotel while the rest of the guys were chasing some quaff around town.—We ate with an army Lt. Colonel and he paid for the meal, which was okay.

Thursday November 18, 1943—Soliman
Didn't do much of anything in the morning. In the afternoon Vaught, Willie and I went into Tunis and poured down a lot of the so-called champagne. Later we made a big hit with one of the French girls and she invited the three of us to her house for dinner. We all had a good time, which was mostly due to the drinks as the meal was piss-poor. Vaught did very good with his French and there were some little girls who spoke pretty good English.

Friday November 19, 1943—Soliman
Vaught and a few other pilots took off on a secret mission. They'll be gone for a few days judging by the baggage they took. Stayed in the evening and had a bull session with Suehle and Jensen.

Saturday November 20, 1943—Soliman
I took a walk by myself this morning. I met a couple of GI's who had an Italian gun and a load of ammunition and I helped them get rid of it. In the afternoon Jensen and I went out and had some target practice with our 45's. In the evening Suehle, Jensen and I went to the movie and saw "Interrnetzlo." Ingrid Bergman is wonderful! Later we had another bull session. We had some medical alcohol and grapefruit juice to drink and so all had a good time.

Sunday November 21, 1943—Soliman
Eight ships from the 317th belly-landed near Oran. According to the rumors now going around the mission that our pilots went on was an escort job for a couple of DC-3's. Evidently the DC's had some VIP's aboard or else—they wouldn't have the escort especially here in Africa. Some believe that Roosevelt and Churchill are meeting with Stalin in or about Turkey. Duke and the rest of the guys got back from Casablanca.

Monday November 22, 1943—Soliman
Spent most of the day putting in another stove. It works pretty well. It's made out of half an oil drum and the smoke stack is made from a German 88mm shell cases. We have a copper coil in the stove, which leads to a wing tank outside the tent. The tank holds the 100-octane gas that we burn in the stove. It sounds crazy and I guess it is. In the evening Suehle, Jensen, Jones, Tucker and I went over to group for a war forum. Duke stayed in town overnight.

Tuesday November 23, 1943—Soliman
Spent the morning adjusting the stove. In the afternoon Suehle and I went into town and took a shower. Also we saw a couple of movies. Vaught and the other "old sports" got back today. The 325th group escorted two C-47's from Casablanca to Cairo, Egypt. In relays according to them Churchill and Roosevelt went to Cairo to meet Von Rittenkoph.

Wednesday November 24, 1943—Soliman
Flew 2:00 hrs this morning. I had to "slow time" a P-47 so I didn't get to rack it around much. I did have some fun though when I flew formation with a couple of B-17's. They seemed to get a big kick out of having a plane come in as close as I did. They kept egging me on. In the afternoon I flew another 1:30. While I was in Tunis yesterday I met Art Simpson. He's now in the 99th bomb group and already has got three missions in. Stayed in at night and wrote letters.

Thursday November 25, 1943—Soliman
Thanksgiving. We had a good dinner today. Turkey and everything else that goes with a Thanksgiving dinner. Played bridge in the afternoon and evening.

Friday November 26, 1943—Soliman
Lt. Quinn came back from the hospital today. He's going to try to get a job in the group, as they want to send him back to the states. While Lt. Bryant was out on the escort mission he had a seizure of some sort one night. That will finish his army-flying career too. Suehle and I were informed today that we are to leave tomorrow for Casablanca. We're going to pick up a couple new P-47's and fly them back to Tunis. I love it!

Saturday November 27, 1943—Soliman
Suehle and I got up at 06:00 this morning and went down to the flight line and picked up our parachutes. We left at 08:00 with Booth and Albin both from the 319th and rode to the El Armenia airport in Tunis. We were supposed to have left in a C-47 but when we got there we found out that we would have to wait until tomorrow before we can leave. Later we returned to our field and played cards the rest of the day.

Sunday November 28, 1943—Travel
Suehle and I got up at 05:30, ate breakfast and then had a GI drive us to El Armenia airport. The plane to Casablanca was canceled so we had to wait and get a C-47 to Algiers. We left Tunis at 11:00 and arrived in Algiers at 13:00. We then boarded another C-47 and flew on to Oran where we again landed. The only plane that we could get out of Oran was flying to Marakesh so we grabbed it as it was closer to Casablanca than Oran. We arrived in Marakesh at 08:30. All I know about the place is that it's about 150 miles south of Casa. After we ate supper we went to the billeting office and got a place to sleep. Tomorrow we've got to get a 06:30 plane out of here for Casablanca.

Monday November 29, 1943—Casablanca
We left Marakesh at 07:00 in a C-47 and arrived in Casa a little before 08:00. Suehle and I spent the day sight-seeing Casa. We hired a carriage and rode out to see the Sultan's Palace. We were able to walk around the—grounds outside the palace and it was great. In the evening we drank champagne and shot the shit with some Frenchmen.

Tuesday November 30, 1943—Casablanca
Went down to the flight line in the morning and checked out our ships. We have ten P-47's here in all but only eight of them are ready to go today. We intended to leave Casa at 11:30 but the weather reports weren't so hot so we didn't take off until 13:30. We have belly tanks on

the planes so we had a good three and one-half hours of gas. After we left Casa we climbed to 10,000 ft to clear the mountains. The valleys were all filled with fog. After we cleared the mountains the ground was still covered with overcast at 2000 ft so we couldn't see any of the ground. We didn't dare to let down through the stuff for fear of hitting a mountain. Finally we contacted the Oran homing station and they gave us a vector to Oran. So we landed in Oran and spent the night. Oran is a fixed base and it is set up very well. I really enjoyed sleeping on a mattress again. The town wasn't much.

Wednesday December 1, 1943—Oran
We hung around the Oran air base all day. The weather was rough so we couldn't leave. We now have ten P-47's here in all. Capt. Andrich is our head man. In the evening Suehle and I had a long chat with a couple of navy men who were headed back to the states.

Thursday December 2, 1943—Oran
The weather cleared up today. Suehle and five of the other ships took off. I was unable to leave as my planes battery was dead. Capt. Andrich, Booth and myself remained behind. Our ships should be ready to go in the morning. Went to the show in the evening with Lt. Vord a P-38 pilot that I met here.

Friday December 3, 1943—Soliman
Capt. Andrich, Booth and Myself took off at 11: 3 0. Just after take-off Booth's prop ran away so we flew to Algiers and landed. The Capt. and I gassed up and took off without Booth. We continued on to our field at Soliman. I logged 1:20 from Oran to Algiers and 1:50 from Algiers to Soliman. We arrived back at Soliman at 04:00. Half of our group has already left for Italy. We're going to go in a week or so. I didn't have any mail, which pissed me off.

Saturday December 4, 1943—Soliman
I finally got some mail! Five letters from Anne and one apiece from Mom, Hester and Dick Finn. Suehle and I went into town today and got paid. I got flight pay for November, which helped a lot. Duke, the simple shit, got a dose while he was in Casa and by the way he talks I think he's proud of it "A-la Studs Lonigan." I hope he doesn't bring that home to his wife.

Sunday December 5, 1943—Soliman
Today I had a cold and it bothered me quite a bit. Jensen and I walked to the beach and shot up a load of 45 ammunition. Hung around in the evening and wrote letters. Some of the pilots are leaving for Bizerte tomorrow where they will board a boat for Italy. The rest of us will remain here and fly up later.

Monday December 6, 1943—Soliman
All of the new pilots with the exception of Strain, Bellamy, Dowd, Jensen, Suehle and myself left today. Shortly after they left we were told that they were returning as all of us are going to Italy via air transport. Wrote letters tonight to Mom and Marion.

Tuesday December 7, 1943—Soliman
Jensen, Jones, Vaught and myself bummed into Tunis today and spent most of the afternoon touring the "Kasba." It is off limits to all U.S. troops so we had to be careful not to get caught. It was very interesting. After touring the Kasba and eating supper Vaught and I returned to the field. All of the other guys had returned from Bizerte. We had a big poker game in out tent in the evening but I didn't play. I'll stick to playing bridge for a while.

Wednesday December 8, 1943—Soliman
Took it easy most of the day as I have a cold. Also I got some of my stuff packed as we are leaving for Italy in the morning. Half of the group has already left; they're going by boat.

Thursday December 9, 1943—Foggia, Italy
Got up at 05:30, ate and got my stuff packed. All I've got to carry is my val-pac, bedroll and parachute. We were unable to take our stove and other luxuries along as we flew to Italy in a C-47. Each squadron has about ten C-47's each to carry their equipment. At 11:00 we piled in our plane and took off. Suehle and Duke went with me—Vaught flew by himself in a P-47. After leaving Tunis we flew north and passed a little west of Sicily. We hit Italy at Salerno and flew east to Foggia where we landed. There are about seven airfields in and around Foggia. We are at the main field next to town. We unloaded our tents and equipment in the middle of a plowed field. The ground was wet and we all felt lousy. By the time we got our tent and cots set up it was dark so we just crawled into our sacks and called it a day.

Friday December 10, 1943—Foggia
It was cold as hell when we woke up so we decided to spend the day trying to scrounge around for a floor and a stove for the tent. By the time that we got around to do anything it was noon so we had to eat. After dinner we found out that we had to move our tent again so we spent the afternoon doing that. We went to bed at 18:00 as we were still without a floor or stove. We are now about sixty miles behind the front lines and we can hear the big guns at night. A single German plane flew over at 2200 and dropped a couple of flares.

Saturday December 11, 1943—Foggia
Jensen and I started out this morning and rounded up a GI truck to use in our search for flooring material. We drove into Foggia and ransacked

some bombed out houses. Foggia is a mess as it's been badly damaged by the Allied bombing. We stopped first at the post office, which is in the center of town. I felt guilty about raiding the building the way we were but I figure that we need the wood as much as the Italians. Also it's tough shit for them as they were just on the wrong side. We didn't get much wood but we did get a good look at the town.

Sunday December 12, 1943—Foggia
We got hold of another GI truck today and we found a lot of lumber in a half-constructed factory that the Italians and Germans intended to use as an airplane factory. The Italians hate us American pilots and they made a big stink about our taking their lumber. "To the victor belongs the spoils"—or something like that. Suehle and Vaught got eager also and rounded up a crude stove. We'll get straightened out in time, I guess. The "Photo-Joe" came over again tonight. They will raise hell around here if they succeed in bombing the place…We've got planes all over in and around Foggia.

Monday December 13, 1943—Foggia
I spent the day putting a floor in the tent. Vaught and Suehle improved the stove and so our tent is becoming cozy again. Duke hasn't done a goddamn thing since we've got here. He's been taking pills for his "dose" so that's a good excuse for him. He's a thick shit. All of the "old sports" went on a practice mission today.

Tuesday December 14, 1943—Foggia
Our group went on its first combat mission since our arrival in Italy. None of us "new sports" got in on it as they are trying to get the "old sports" finished so that they can go back to the states. Capt. Lott now has 49 missions and so he needs just one more. The mission was a short one and so no belly tanks were used. They flew to Greece and escorted the B-17's back. Judging from the amount of airplanes that we're getting

in Italy we must be planning to bomb Germany off the map, which is a good idea. I spent most of the day fixing up our tent and stove.

Wednesday December 15, 1943—Foggia
The 325th flew its second combat mission since switching to P-47's today. Again the show was for the "old" pilots as none of us new guys went along with the exception of Strain. The mission was an escort job to Venice. It was a long trip and belly tanks were used. There were no attacks by German fighters although a few ME-109's were sighted. Suehle, Vaught and I went into Foggia and got haircuts and showers—both of which we needed badly. I received letters from Mom, Dad, Anne, Dick Finn and Dick Mac today.

Thursday December 16, 1943—Foggia
Jensen and Brown went on today's mission. No enemy fighters were seen but there was a lot of flak. Went into town in the evening and saw a movie.

Friday December 17, 1943—Foggia
Vaught and I made a new stove. No missions. Stayed in at night.

Saturday December 18, 1943—Foggia
No missions. Did nothing much all day. Played bridge in the afternoon and stayed in and wrote letters in the evening. Received three packages—a box of chocolates from Grace Parker, candy and cigarettes from Middle St. and some more candy from Elmer in California.

Sunday December 19, 1943—Foggia
I got to go on my first combat mission today! Suehle, Dowd, Fallon and I were all scheduled. Suehle got stuck in the mud before take off and was unable to go. Boy, was he pissed off! The mission was another escort job to Venice—a pretty long haul. I flew "tail-end Charley" both in the flight and squadron. Before we took off the Colonel told us that from now on

our primary job is to knock out enemy fighters and not protect the bombers as much as before. Also he put the okay on strafing on the way back. I flew in "auto-lean" all the way to the target so I conserved a lot of gas. I ran my belly tank dry over the Adriatic and dropped it. We flew at 28,000 and by the time we started I was sweating my oxygen, as it was getting low. We spotted a couple of ME-109's but they were above us and too far away to catch. After we left Venice we dropped down slowly and it was just in time as my oxygen was almost gone. About 100 miles from Foggia we spotted a flight of about thirty planes on the deck so we started after them. When we got in range we saw that they were P-40's so we felt pretty foolish. I landed with 120 gallons of gas. Logged 2:45. Stayed in and wrote letters in the evening.

Monday December 20, 1943—Foggia
Lt. Raper of our squadron operations office awoke Suehle, Vaught and myself up early this morning. Suehle and Vaught were scheduled for today's mission and I was supposed to go to Bizerte in North Africa on the B-26, which was leaving at 08:30. I had just enough time for breakfast and to get my parachute. When I got to the flight line we were informed that the trip was postponed. The group has some P-47's at Bizerte that have to be ferried to Italy. Fallon is going with me. Today's mission was a dud as the group ran into overcast about fifty miles out and had to return. They were going out on a fighter sweep. Capt. Lott, Suehle, Vaught and Duke played bridge in the afternoon while I went on a nail gathering expedition. So I spent the afternoon pulling nails out of belly tank crates. I stayed in the evening. Vaught, Duke and Suehle went to the movie.

Tuesday December 21, 1943—Foggia
I again started out for Bizerte this morning. This time the B-26 got off okay but the weather closed in when we got to Salerno so we came back. Suehle, Lott, Vaught and I played bridge in the afternoon. Vaught and I really poured it to Suehle and Lott. Stayed in the evening.

Wednesday December 22, 1943—Foggia
It rained all day so there was no flying. In the afternoon Suehle, Vaught, Jensen and I went into town and saw a movie and took a shower. Stayed in at night.

Thursday December 23, 1943—Foggia
The B-26 came in this morning and ran off the runway because of a broken hydraulic line. My parachute was still in it and got covered with hydraulic fluid. In the afternoon Vaught and I made a table and chairs for the tent. Lt's Seneften and Sayer of the 317th had a mid-air collision today. Sayer was killed when his parachute failed to open. Seneften bailed out okay but he's now very nervous and swears that he'll never fly again.

Friday December 24, 1943—Foggia
We officers each got a bottle of liquor today. They had gin, brandy, cognac and rum. I took a fifth of brandy but I wished later that I'd picked gin because the brandy was rough and we have nothing to mix it with. There were mo missions today and so we got a lot of card playing in. In the evening Vaught and I went to the "hut" and watched a movie.

Saturday December 25, 1943—Foggia
Christmas! The group had a long mission to Balzano Italy today. I flew on Vaught's wing. Balzano is in the foothills of the Italian Alps so it was a long haul for the bombers. The B-17's hit the marshalling yards and we gave then withdrawal escort. We didn't run into any German fighters but we sure did have a lot of flak thrown up at us. Those black puffs seem so harmless when in reality they are loaded with shrapnel. The weather was getting rough on the return trip and the group was pretty well split up. Joey Muller, Slattery and Watkins all failed to return. They were all in the same flight. It is now 22:00 and still no word has been heard from them. I sure hope they didn't go down in the Adriatic. In the afternoon we had a turkey dinner with all the fixings. After dinner

Jensen, Vaught and I got into the Christmas spirit and rounded up all the candy, cigarettes and anything else we could and brought it to some Italians in town. Both Jensen and Vaught feel about God and religion much the same as I do—which isn't much compared to the majority of people. Still none of the good churchgoers wanted to help us with our little mission of Christmas goodwill. I think that I'll continue my agnostic belief for some time. We also went to see the Ella Logan show while we were in town. She was terrific! Lt. Queen of the 317th was killed yesterday. He got into overcast and got mixed up. He went into the ground at a 30-degree angle upside down!

Sunday December 26, 1943—Foggia
Today was both cold and rainy. I spent the day reading and playing bridge. Still no word from Muller, Slattery and Watkins.

Monday December 27, 1943—Foggia
No missions—rain. Played cards and read all day. Still no word on Muller, Slattery and Watkins.

Tuesday December 28, 1943—Foggia
Suehle and Vaught went on today's mission to Rimini Italy. It was an escort mission and the bombers hit the marshalling yards at Rimini in northern Italy on the Adriatic. No enemy fighters were seen. Word came in today that both Slattery and Watkins planes were found in the mountains north of here. Both planes burned after they hit and so there wasn't much left of the bodies. Watkins plane was about four miles from Slattery's. Evidently they let down through the overcast thinking that they were over the Adriatic. Still no word on Joey Muller. I spent most of the day reading short stories from Jensen's book "Stories for Men."

Wednesday December 29, 1943—Foggia
Today the 325th flew escort for the bombers as they hit the airfield at Reggio Rimilia in northern Italy. Vaught was the only one from our tent to go. No German fighters were seen. Doc Reynolds got into a crack-up

today and washed out the P-47. All he got out of it was a scratch on the nose. He collided with an Italian tri-motored plane on the approach leg. All the guys in the tri-motor got out okay but the plane burned up after they got out. Our group is really goofing up. We've had seven accidents in just a short period. Five pilots have been killed and not a shot has been fired during this time. There was a big fire in Foggia tonight but I haven't heard what was burning. It must have been a gasoline fire because a couple of times it looked like tank cars were exploding. We expect to be moving to a new field soon but we don't know when. This field is over-crowded now.

Thursday December 30, 1943—Foggia
Our whole group moved from "Foggia main" to Foggia # 1. We are now located about seven miles north of Foggia. I made the trip to #1 via P-47 and logged 0:30 minutes. The field here is much better than the one we left as it has a better runway and the ground is good and solid. We couldn't take the tent floor and other "goodies" that we had at the main field so we will be starting from scratch again as far as tent fixing up goes. Joey Muller's plane was found today cracked up on a hillside. By the looks of the plane he must have gone straight in. I'm glad that Joey was found because I figure it's better to know just what happened to him.

Friday December 31, 1943—Foggia #1
Vaught and I spent the morning looking over the field. Until we got here the English had the place pretty well filled up with "Spitfires", A-20's and English "Maryland's." Today the 325th flew withdrawal support for the bombers, which hit the marshalling yards at Verona Italy. The 319th squadron jumped a dozen ME-109's, which were on the deck and got three of them. Boy, I wish that I could run into something like that. New Years Eve! Cripes what a dull evening. Jensen, Jones, Suehle, Vaught and I spent the time drinking and throwing the bull. Oh yeah,

Carl Tucker was here too. We went to bed at 23:00 but I stayed awake until after twelve.

Saturday January 1, 1944—Foggia #1
1944 came in with a bang as it was really storming when I awoke at six. I was afraid that our tent was going to blow away. I got up and went out and drove in some more tent stakes. I got soaking wet and miserable. Just after I got through fixing our tent Captain Garret's tent blew down. It was quite a sight watching Lott, Garret and Raper running around in all the wind and rain in their PJ's. We spent most of the day huddled around the fire hoping that the tent would stay up. The wind died down in the late afternoon and so we went into Foggia and saw a movie.

Sunday January 2, 1944—Foggia #1
After nearly having our tent blown away yesterday we decided to spend the day fixing it up. First we laid a floor using heavy glass and cement slabs that we "liberated" from a factory in Foggia. We are proud of our new glass floor. Today's mission was a fighter sweep to the Rome area. Vaught was the only one from my tent to go. No enemy fighters were seen but the flak was heavy. Stayed in and read at night.

Monday January 3, 1944—Foggia #1
Today was a beautiful day as it was both clear and warm. Today's mission was an escort to Turin where the target was the marshalling yards. No one from my tent went. I spent the morning building a shelf and chair for the tent. In the afternoon Suehle, Vaught and I went into Foggia and took a shower. Stayed in the evening and wrote letters. Jones and Tucker spent the evening with us.

Tuesday January 4, 1944—Foggia #1
We had another super-duper rain and windstorm today. This time it came in from the north. Our tent held up well and so we were okay. Lt. Strain's tent was ripped to shreds by the wind and finally blew down. I

stayed in all day and read "The Robe" by Lloyd C. Douglas. Went to the movie with Dove and Jensen at Foggia main in the evening.

Wednesday January 5, 1944—Foggia #1
It was very cold today and there were no missions. I spent another day reading. Went to the show in the evening with Major Garett, Captain Lott, Suehle and Vaught.

Thursday January 6, 1944—Foggia #1
The weather was bad again today and so no missions were scheduled. It even snowed this morning. Read all day and wrote letters in the evening.

Friday January 7, 1944—Foggia #1
Suehle started out on today's mission but he didn't take off as he had a 100-drop on the left magneto. Later he got to go on another mission. While he was over the target his motor started to cut out as he had carburetor icing. He didn't think of closing his intercooler doors so he had trouble all the way back and was scared stiff. Major Toner took over as C.O. of the 318th today. Wrote two letters—one to Zip Romano and one to Elmer. Went into Foggia in the evening and took in a movie.

Saturday January 8, 1944—Foggia #1
Vaught was the only one from our tent to go on today's mission. It was a milk run to Reggio Emilia. Got a box of candy today from George R. Wallace. Stayed in, in the evening.

Sunday January 9, 1944—Foggia #1
Today we had an escort mission to Fiume and I got to go. The target was an assembly plant and the bombers did a good job. Major Sluder was supposed to have lead the squadron with Fallon, Lowry and I in the same flight. Sluder was unable to take off so Lowry and I flew as a two-man flight. On the way out we had overcast at 20,000 ft. so we went up to 28,000 before we came out of it. My engine was cutting out at 30

inches of manifold pressure, which made me very uncomfortable. Although a large number of German and Italian fighters are supposed to be based near Fiume none of them showed up. I logged 3:00 hours. This afternoon General Atchinson came and presented the DFC to Duke and Capt. Lott and some others got the Air Medal. The Soldiers Medal was also presented to quite a few enlisted men.

Monday January 10, 1944—Foggia #1
Today's target for the bombers was Sofia Bulgaria. The 325th provided cover both going and coming. Suehle and I spent most of the day in the control tower. Bev. Miller of the 319th went into the Adriatic just off the coast of Yugoslavia after his motor quit. None of his flight saw him go in and so they spent a lot of time looking for him without success. All he had to keep him afloat was his "Mae West." I don't see how he could live long in the water, as it's very cold. Miller called his flight just before he hit the water and told them that he was "kind of nervous" because it was a long swim to the coast. That was putting it mildly, I figure. Today I found out that there are a couple of enlisted men in the 318th who live near Fitchburg. One of the fellows named Sontag comes from Clinton and the other is from Gardner.

Tuesday January 11, 1944—Foggia #1
I started out on a "fighter sweep" mission to Yugoslavia today flying #2 position on Lt. Rapers wing. Just after we left the coast the weather closed and we had to abort the mission. I logged 1:15. Lt. Miller is still missing and so I guess that he'll never be found, as he couldn't have lived long in that water. We went into Foggia in the evening and saw a movie.

Wednesday January 12, 1944—Foggia #1
This morning twelve planes from the 318th flew a training flight at 30,000 ft. I was on Lt. Kitchen's wing in the #2 position. Suehle flew #. 4 in Major Toners flight. Logged 2:15. In the afternoon we had a fighter

sweep mission over the "front lines." I flew #2 position on Major Sluder's wing. Suehle and Duke both had to return—Suehle with engine problems and Duke had a problem with his oxygen. The flak was very accurate and our flight seemed to get the most of it. We were at 20,000 ft and the stuff was puffing all around us. Major Sluder got hit in his wing but not much damage was done. It was really exciting for a while. Logged 2:15 hours.

Thursday January 13, 1944—Foggia #1
The group went on a lulu of a mission today but I didn't get to go. It was a fighter sweep to the Rome area. A bunch of ME-109's and Foche-Wolf 190's were met at 25,000 ft over Rome. Major Toner and Lt. Forrest of the 319th both got a victory. Jack Fallon got hit by flak and failed to return. He was heard getting a heading from "Big Fence" so he may get back yet. Plummer got in a spin over Rome and went down 10,000 ft before pulling out. Cripes, I wish that I'd been there! This afternoon I ferried a P-47 over to the 57th group and logged 0:30. Went into town and saw a movie in the evening. We still have no lights in our tent and there are no candles.

Friday January 14, 1944—Foggia #1
We escorted the bombers to Moster Yugoslavia today. They hit a German fighter field. We expected to see some action but no enemy planes were seen. I flew #2 position on Major Toners wing. The B-17's did a hell of a job of bombing and I enjoyed it. The flak was light. Logged 2:45 hours. Jack Fallon got back this afternoon. He got shot up pretty bad during yesterdays show over Rome and he had to land at Naples. According to Jack flak didn't hit him. Instead, he said, it was another P-47 that blasted him. Lt. Lynch also said that he saw a P-47 shooting the shit out of another P-47. Boy, I figure it's bad enough having to worry about enemy planes so when you also have to watch your own guys that's a little too much. I went into town with Suehle, Duke and Jensen and took a shower.

Saturday January 15, 1944—Foggia #1
We had a long mission today to the Florence area. Malloy and I went along as spares but we completed the mission as Major Toner and his wingman aborted the mission over Rome and we took their place. Besides the regular gas we carried one belly tank (75 gallons) and two wing tanks (165 gallons each). This brought the total weight up to about eight tons—which is plenty heavy for a fighter. Over Rome we had a lot of flak thrown up at us. We rendezvoused with the B-17's off the coast of Corsica and escorted them to Florence where they bombed the enemy airfields. On the way back we got into some more flak and Bellemy got hit but was okay. Logged 3:30 hours.

Tuesday January 18, 1944—Foggia #1
Today Fallon, Dowd, Reynold, Wirth and I managed to get a jeep and drove 50 miles down the coast to Bari. We picked up some comforters and other junk. Major Garret, Captain Lott and Lt. Raper were all sitting around in Bari as they have completed their tours in Italy and are headed back to the U.S. of A. Suehle and Duke went on today's mission. Duke landed at Naples as his canopy was covered with oil. He didn't really have to land there but he wanted to see the place. Suehle also said that he saw a couple of JU-88's but Duke wouldn't go after them. Stayed in, in the evening.

Wednesday January 19, 1944—Foggia #1
Half of our group went on an escort mission to the Rome area today. I flew #2 position on Lt. Kitchen's wing. We rendezvoused with the B-17's over Capri and flew on up the coast. The targets were three airfields in the Rome area and the B-17's did a good job. A few enemy fighters were seen but our flight didn't get near any. Today's assault on the Rome area was an "all-out" affair as besides our P-47's there were B-25's, P-38's, Spitfires, A-36's, B-24's and A-20's in the area. The flak was very thick over Rome but none of us got hit. I got a Christmas package from Anne

today—cigarettes, candy, razor blades, soap and her love were included. Stayed in, in the evening.

Thursday January 20, 1944—Foggia #1
We flew an escort mission to Yugoslavia today and I flew #2 position on Duke's wing while he was leading the squadron. We provided cover for eight Italian transport planes that dropped a lot of supplies to a partisan group near Sarajevo. The drop area was marked with a cross-made of fires. We flew fairly low—10,000 ft—most of the way. It was a fun mission. I logged 3:45 hrs and it was my seventh mission.

Friday January 21, 1944—Foggia #1
The 325th flew two missions today. One was a short range (belly tank) fighter sweep to the Rome area. The other was a long range (wing tanks) to Florence. I went on the long job. There were a few F-W-190's over the area but the 318th didn't get a crack at them as we were at 25,000 feet. The 319th ran smack into three F.W.'s and shot them down. I logged 3:35 for the mission. The sweep to Rome was uneventful as there were no enemy fighters in the air. Lt. Hussey of the 318th had engine trouble over enemy territory and said that he was going to bail out but no one saw him do it. I sure hope he makes out okay. Judging by the way that the Air Force has been cleaning out the area around Rome seems to indicate that an invasion force will land there soon. Also there is a large fleet of ships at Naples

Saturday January 22, 1944—Foggia #1
Suehle and I were "alerted" at 07:00 this morning. The Americans started their invasion of the Rome area. They landed on the coast near Anzio south of Rome. We didn't get a mission until afternoon and I couldn't go as my P-47 was having engine trouble. I was pissed off. The fighters were having a field day strafing the retreating Germans. Our group got over the beachhead about 04:00 in the afternoon. As usual the 318th was flying top-cover at 15,000 ft and so they didn't see much. Spot

Collins got two ME-109's; Barky and Elliot each got one. Lt's Legg, Deanne and Brumfield all from the 319th failed to return. Cripes, I wish I could get in on a deal like that! Still no word from Lt. Hussey. In the evening Suehle, Jensen, Vaught, Dove and I went to Sansivaao and had a good spaghetti dinner.

Sunday January 23, 1944—Foggia #1
The 325th flew three missions today. Two fighter sweeps to the Rome area and a long-range escort job to Florence. The bombers hit marshalling yards in both Siena and Poggibonsi. I went on the long mission. I flew #2 position on Whitesides wing. All of central Italy was covered by overcast and no enemy fighters were sighted. I logged 4 hours. Lt. Rogers got a ME-109 over Rome today. Legg and Brumfield of the 319th are still missing from yesterdays mission. Also Lt. Hussey of the 318th is still among the missing. In the evening Jensen and I went into Foggia. I met Jerry Lombard at the Officer's Red Cross and we had a long chat. Jerry told me that Art Simpson is missing from a raid over southern France.

Monday January 24, 1944—Foggia #1
Today we had a long escort mission to South Bulgaria. I started off flying #2 position on Major Toners wing. When we got out over the Adriatic our element leader and his wingman aborted and then the Major himself returned. I was left by myself but I finally joined up with Been's flight. The bombers overshot the Sofia target as there was a solid overcast over both Yugoslavia and Bulgaria. We flew 450 miles out. I dropped my empty wing tanks over the target and set my gas on auto-lean—I didn't want to run out of gas. We had a hundred mile an hour headwind on the way back. Everyone was sweating out their gas supply. I logged 5:30 for the mission!

Tuesday January 25, 1944—Foggia #1
The group had the day off today. We needed it after that red-ass ride we had yesterday. The P-38's and B-17's also had a rough time getting back yesterday. A few of them had to "belly" it in the Adriatic.

Wednesday January 26, 1944—Foggia #1
The weather was bad today and so there were no missions scheduled. Stayed in and read and wrote letters.

Thursday January 27, 1944—Foggia #1
The 325th flew two missions today. One was a fighter sweep to the Rome area and the other was a fighter sweep to the Florence area. I didn't go on either mission as I've now got ten missions and that's more than most of the pilots have. In the afternoon I "slow-timed" a new D-16 and I had a good time flying formation with some B-17's and "dog fighting" with some P-38's. Stayed in at night and read.

Friday January 28, 1944—Foggia #1
I ferried one of our older P-47's over to the 57th group today but it wasn't in very good shape when I left it. My engine quit at 1700 ft near the 2nd bomb group's field. At first I thought that I could make a 180-degree turn and land on the runway. But once that prop stopped turning the plane dropped like a rock. So I headed for a plowed field at the end of the runway. I had to stretch my glide over a ditch and I stalled in from about twenty feet. I was lucky as I only got a slight cut on my knee. I really felt like shit, as it was my first airplane accident. Oh well, "c'est la guerre."

Saturday January 29, 1944—Foggia #1
I went over to the 57th group today to see if I could find out what made the plane's engine cut out yesterday. The engineering officer couldn't tell much but he figured that the gas line was clogged up. Tonight I was called in the C.O.'s tent for a secret briefing on tomorrows mission. The German airfields in the Udine area have been filling up lately. These planes have been hitting both coming and going on their way to targets.

So the 325th is going to pull a sneak "fighter-sweep" of the area. We're going to fly all the way up the Adriatic on the "deck." We've got to stay below fifty feet'to avoid radar detection. We'll get to the area before the bombers and hopefully the enemy fighters will be just taking off. The mission is voluntary and strict radio silence will be essential. It should be a good show.

Sunday January 30, 1944—Foggia #1
What a day! We pulled the sneak attack on Udine and it worked to perfection. I flew #2 position on Col. Sluders wing. We flew on the deck all the way up the Adriatic. About 50 miles off the coast we broke the radio silence and started climbing. There was a low thin overcast over the water and it was quite a sight seeing all the planes appearing out of the haze. I stayed with Col. Sluder as we were flying top-cover. We didn't get into the action, as it was all going on down low. The group got 36 planes in all. Whiteside, Hogg and Kitchen each got two planes apiece. Capt. Green of the 319th got five. General Twining was on hand when we returned and presented Col. Basseler the Silver Star on the spot. Lowry and Jack Fallon both failed to return.

Monday January 31, 1944—Foggia #1
The 325th went on another escort mission to the Udine area. I wasn't scheduled so I spent the morning on the flight line helping Norbutus clean and service my plane. Lt. Been of the 318th got a victory today. Our group is the talk of Italy and everywhere else because of yesterday's rape of the Udine airfields. Suehle told me that he's going to be the group's new duty officer. It's a good deal for him. Stayed in for the evening and played bridge.

Tuesday February 1, 1944—Foggia #1
The group had the day off today. I went into Foggia with Suehle and Duke and picked up my laundry and dry cleaning. In the afternoon I went back into town and spent a couple of hours with Jerry Lombard in

the Red Cross officer's club. In the evening Major Toner got all of the pilots together and gave us an outline of his new program. He also informed us that he didn't join the Air Corps to make friends. (?)

Wednesday February 2, 1944-Foggia #1
We got briefed today for a mission to Vienna Austria. The mission was scratched just after take-off. I was flying on Major Toners wing and I logged 1:15 for the aborted flight. I was glad that today's mission was scratched as I'm coming down with a cold. Hung around all afternoon and evening.

Thursday February 3, 1944—Foggia #1
Today's mission was a fighter sweep to the area north. I didn't go as my cold is pretty bad. Took it easy all day.

Friday February 4, 1944—Foggia #1
No missions today. Played bridge and read all day. Went to a "flak" lecture in the evening.

Saturday February 5, 1944-Foggia #1
Today was rainy, windy and cold and so no missions were scheduled. I read and wrote letters all day. Went into town in the evening and saw a movie.

Sunday February 6, 1944—Foggia #1
Today's weather was the same as yesterday and so no missions. Went and took in a movie in the evening.

Monday February 7, 1944—Foggia #1
Still lousy weather and still no missions. Played bridge and read all day. Went to Aprecini in the evening with Jensen, Vaught and Suehle. We had a pretty good spaghetti dinner.

Tuesday February 8, 1944—Foggia #1
We had an escort mission to Verona Italy today and I went along in Bellemy's place as he had a cold. I flew #4 position in Gonda's flight.

Whiteside was leading the 318th. On the way up the Adriatic we climbed through a couple of layers of overcast and the squadron got broken up a little. We were at about 20,000 ft and still with Whitesides flight. There was a lone contrail above us and nothing to be concerned about. Suddenly someone hollered, "Bogey at one o'clock." Whiteside started to turn and went into a spin. He spun from 20,000 ft down through the overcast and that was the last we saw of him. It was an awful sight. Hank Southern, Whitesides wingman also spun but he pulled out of it! The rest of the mission was uneventful. Tucson left today as he had completed his fifty missions. Plummer and Steffler both left too as their nerves are getting the best of them.

Wednesday February 9, 1944—Foggia #1
The weather was rough today and so no missions. Received letters today from Hester, Mom and Anne. According to reports the German fighter strength is increasing in the Rome area. We should be seeing some action there soon. Still no word from Whiteside.

Thursday February 10, 1944—Foggia #1
The group had an early fighter sweep mission over the beachhead today. They ran into a lot of flak and that's all. I was alerted for a mission later in the day but it was scrubbed. Went into town in the evening and saw a movie.

Friday February 11, 1944—Foggia #1
No missions—rain. Hung around all day and took it easy. A lot of heavy fighting going on at the beachhead.

Saturday February 12, 1944—Foggia #1
The weather was lousy again today. We were scheduled for an escort mission to Yugoslavia but it was canceled. A bunch of transports were going to bring over supplies to the partisans. I went into town and saw Jerry Lombard and George Flathers in the afternoon. Stayed in and read in the evening.

Sunday February 13, 1944—Foggia #1, Italy
I was alerted for a mission today but we didn't go, as the weather was bad. I hung around all day and read. The 318th got three new pilots today—McDonald, Emmet and Crookem. Went into town in the evening and listened to the 301st bomb group's "Melody Five"

Monday February 14, 1944—Foggia #1
We had a super-duper mission today. The group went out in full Strength on an escort mission to Verona (home of Romeo and Juliet). I flew in Vaught's flight as element leader. We were supposed to arrive at the target five minutes before the bombers but we were a little late. We arrived with the B-17's. We were at 25,000 feet providing top cover for the bombers when a whole shitload of ME-109's came in above us dragging con-trails. It was a beautiful sight! The 109 have started down through the bomber formation. Vaught and I latched on to one of them but we couldn't catch him as he headed for the deck. One ME-109 ran smack into a B-17 and they both went down in a cloud of smoke. Six ME-109's were shot down and four guys from the 319th are missing. Clinch from the 317th came back with his plane full of holes. We sweated out the weather and gas on the way home. Logged 4:15 hrs. Collected my shot of booze in the evening and went to bed.

Tuesday February 15, 1944—Foggia #1
The weather was bad today and so no missions were scheduled. I hung around all day and read.

Wednesday February 16, 1944—Foggia #1
Bad weather—no flying. Took it easy and read all day. In the evening Jensen and I went over and paid a visit to the RAF lads in the 322nd wing. They are a "bloody" nice bunch of fellows and their Scotch whiskey is very good. Springer, Robst and Davis all great. I'll get a pair of English flying boots yet!

Thursday February 17, 1944—Foggia #1
Again—no flying. Played 10-cent poker all day. Went to a movie in town in the evening.

Friday February 18, 1944—Foggia #1
No flying. Played bridge and read all day. Wrote letters in the evening.

Saturday February 19, 1944—Foggia #1
We were briefed early for another escort mission to Yugoslavia where the Italian transport planes drop supplies to the Partisans. Later the mission was scratched. In the evening Jensen, Duke and I went into town to the Red Cross officers club. There was a dance with the 301st band playing. George Flathers was there and we had a long talk. George told me that Jerry Lombard got shot down over the beachhead the other day. He and his crew got out okay.

Sunday February 20, 1944—Foggia #1
We started out on a long-range escort mission to the Brenner Pass (in the Alps) today but the weather closed in after take-off and it was scratched. I logged 1:50 for the aborted mission. Stayed in and played bridge most of the day.

Monday February 21, 1944—Foggia #1
We were briefed for a fighter sweep and an escort mission to the Viterbo airfield but it was later scratched because of bad weather. According to S-2 there are now over 200 German and Italian fighter planes in the Rome area. Played bridge and read all day.

Tuesday February 22, 1944—Foggia #1
Today we had the first combined attack by both the 15th A.F. in Italy and the 8th A.F. in England. The target was an aircraft factory at Regensburg, Austria. Our group escorted the bombers as far as the Brenner Pass in the Alps. Other B-17's from the 15th A.F. attacked targets in northern Yugoslavia and so drew a lot of enemy fighters away from the main target—Regensburg. I didn't go on today's mission and so I went to the

flight line and helped Norbutus—my crew chief—clean up the plane. Lt. Sopper of the 319th was lost on today's mission.

Wednesday February 23, 1944—Foggia #1
We had another long-range escort mission today. The target was a ball bearing factory at Steyer, Austria. The weather closed in after take-off and the mission was aborted. I flew Reynolds plane as mine is out. I flew in Rogers flight as element leader. Today's mission was to be another combined effort of both English and Italian based bombers. This combined bombing is the start of a new air offensive to destroy aircraft production of the German Reich. The long awaited second front will probably be starting. Logged 1:30 hrs and played bridge in the evening.

Thursday February 24, 1944—Foggia #1
Today's mission was the same as yesterdays only we went all the way. We provided withdrawal support for the bombers. I flew Been's ship as nine is still out with brake trouble. I flew in Malloy's flight as element leader. We didn't see any enemy fighters although there were plenty around. Lt. Forrest of the 318th had engine trouble over the target and he went down to 13,000 ft with a dead engine. Eight ME-109's jumped him and two of them collided when he turned into them. His engine then restarted and he came home. At least he found out where the enemy fighters were. Jensen and I went into town in the evening and saw a movie.

Friday February 25, 1944—Foggia #1
The weather wasn't very good today but the group still got in a couple of missions. Suehle and I didn't go as our ships were out. Everyone got back okay and there wasn't much excitement other than sweating out the weather.

Saturday February 26, 1944—Foggia #1
No missions. I went into town and picked up my dry cleaning. Neither Gerry nor George was around at the officers club. Played bridge in the evening with Maj. Toner, Vaught and Suehle.

Sunday February 27, 1944—Foggia #1
No mission. I went into town in the afternoon with Jensen. I met George Flathers at the officers club. George's plane got shot up pretty bad on the mission to Regensburg. A bunch of ME-109's after he turned back early jumped him. Still he got the plane back with no casualties.

Monday February 28, 1944—Foggia #1
No mission. Hung around all day and read. Also helped Norbutus sandpaper the plane.

Tuesday February 29, 1944—Foggia #1
No mission—lousy weather. Stayed in and read "Young Man with a Home."

Wednesday March 1, 1944—Foggia #1
The group was briefed for a mission to the beachhead today but it was scratched, as the weather was bad over the target area. The beachhead at Anzio isn't doing too well right now. Played football all afternoon.

Thursday March 2, 1944—Foggia #1
This morning we got up at 5:30 for briefing. The mission was the same as yesterday—fighter sweep and escort over the beachhead. I flew my own ship in #2 position on Colonel Sluders wing. There were no enemy planes around and the bomber dropped frag bombs all over the place. The beachhead is a beautiful sight from 20,000 ft as the water is filled with boats. Norbutus went to the hospital today with malaria. Went over to the English squadron with Jensen in the evening. I finally managed to latch on to a pair of English flying boots. Logged 2:30 hrs.

Friday March 3, 1944—Foggia #1
Today I am very lucky to be able to write in this diary as I should be dead instead. We escorted B-24's to the Viterbo airdrome north of Rome. I flew #2 on Kitchen's wing. We got into a big dogfight and we had only 14 ships from the 318th. About a dozen ME-109's came down

from above us and headed for the bombers. Gus Kitchen and I latched onto a couple of the M.E.'s. Gus took the one on our left and I took off after the other. I followed him all the way down to 5000'—firing at him all the time. I know that I hit him and at 5000 ft he did a "split s" and headed for the deck. I wasn't about to follow him as I was going to fast. I climbed up to 20000 ft again. There were a couple of fighters in the distance, which I couldn't identify so I headed toward them. I broke one of a fighter pilots cardinal rule by flying straight and level and not checking behind me. An F.W. 190 flew up behind me and blasted me with everything he had. Tracer bullets were going by me so fast that at first I thought my own guns were firing. In about one second I realized what was happening and I broke to the right and watched him as he headed for the deck. I really sweated out the ride home as my plane was shaking like a leaf and I had been hit in the right leg. I called in and asked for an emergency landing, as my hydraulic system was about gone. All of the field's emergency equipment was ready when I came in. I blew a tire on landing and ran off the runway. Luckily I stopped just short of a Limy tent. The doc gave me a shot of whiskey and stitched up my leg. Been, Ridgeway and Walker all got shot down so I guess that I was lucky. Deakins got two ME's, Brown and Vaught each got one.

Saturday March 4, 1944—Foggia #1
No missions. I am now grounded for a few days on account of my leg. My plane caused a lot of commotion at the flight line as nobody has ever seen a fighter come back shot up as much as mine was. I had about twenty hits in it in all. My right elevator got hit with a 20mm explosive shell, which did a lot of damage. One of the propeller blades had a hole through it. The slug that grazed my leg was a 15mm armor-piercing incendiary. It ended up in the bottom of the cockpit still burning. I'm saving it as a memento of my stupidity. I feel silly for receiving a Purple Heart for such a slight wound. Still I sweated out the ride home so maybe it's okay.

Sunday March 5, 1944—Foggia #1
No missions. Hung around all day and played bridge.

Monday March 6, 1944—Foggia #1
No missions. I'm still grounded but the doc says I can fly tomorrow if there's a mission. Went into town with Fred Suehle in the evening.

Tuesday March 7, 1944—Foggia #1
Today the group had another escort mission to the Rome area. Gus Kitchen led the group and I flew #2 position on his wing. The 318th was the low squadron at 22,000 ft. Four ME-109's attacked the bombers and our flight went after them. They headed down through the low overcast and so we lost them. Logged 3:25 hrs. I felt lousy as hell at altitude today as I have a slight cold. Major Tonor and Major Chick both got their Lt. Colonel leafs today.

Wednesday March 8, 1944—Foggia #1
No missions. Hung around all day and took it easy as I still have a cold.

Thursday March 9, 1944—Foggia #1
No missions—bad weather. Lt. Rugby left for home today. His nerves have been getting the best of him for some time so I guess that it's best for all of us that he goes. Chet Hill also left as he completed his fifty missions. I went into town in the evening and saw "Shadow of a Doubt" with Teresa Wright and Joseph Cotton.

Friday March 10, 1944—Foggia #1
No mission—rain. Hung around all day and read "The Soviet Power" by Hewlett Johnson, Dean of Canterbury.

Saturday March 11, 1944—Foggia #1
We had an escort mission to Padua, Italy today. Lt. Hogg led the 318th and I was his wingman. The enemy fighter strength in the Venice area is getting stronger all the time. There were a lot of ME-109's and FW 190's making their one pass down through the bomber formations. No

enemy fighters came near our flight though. I saw two B-17's go down in a stream of smoke. No 318th pilots were lost although Williamson got his ass shot at. I think that he was sorry that he didn't get hit himself, as he wants a Purple Heart in the worst way. The 319th C.O. Colonel Chick was shot down. Also Lt. Jones got shot down by one of his own pilots—Lt. Hudson. It was Hudson's first mission and he got nervous and confused in all the action. My job was to stay with Hogg and that's what I did. Logged 3:3 0 hrs. Vaught and I went into Foggia in the afternoon and took a shower.

Sunday March 12, 1944—Foggia #1
Rain—no missions. I hung around all day, read and played bridge. In the evening Jensen and I went to the English squadron and shot the shit.

Monday March 13, 1944—Foggia #1
Rain—no missions. I went into town in the afternoon and met Gerry Lombard in the officers club. Gerry was very pessimistic about his chances of getting through this war alive. Still that's Gerry—always looking at the dark side. He's a wonderful guy though and I'm sure we'll see a lot of each other in Fitchburg after the war.

Tuesday March 14, 1944—Foggia #1
Rain—no missions. Read and played bridge all day.

Wednesday March 15, 1944—Foggia #1
Today the weather was good and so the whole 15th Air Force went out in full strength and pounded the hell out of Cassino on the 5th Army front in an attempt to break the stalemate there. Our group flew two missions to Vitterbo above Rome to keep the enemy fighters away from Cassino. Still no fighters showed up so it was a dull day. I went into town in the evening with Williamson and saw a movie.

Thursday March 16, 1944—Foggia #1
Rain—no missions. Played bridge and read all day.

Friday March 17, 1944—Foggia #1
The bombers made a raid on the ME-109 factory at Fischamend Market near Vienna, Austria. We met the bombers on their withdrawal and escorted them back. I lead Malloy's element. No enemy fighters showed up and we all got back safely. I logged 3:40 for the mission.

Saturday March 18, 1944—Foggia #1
Today's targets for the bombers were the enemy airfields in the Udine area. We flew across the Adriatic on the deck and climbed up over the coast of Yugoslavia below Fiume. I flew on Lt. Ring's wing in Kitchens flight. Just as we met the bombers a flight of about 30 NE-109's came in high above us dragging con-trails. We kept the NE's away from the bombers and had a real scrap doing it. I stuck close to Lt. Ring, as he couldn't get rid of his fight wing tank. My carburetor / air temperature gauge went out and I was sweating out icing. I watched four ME-109's go down and saw only one parachute. The 317th lost Davis and Malloy in the flight. The group got eight ME-109's. I logged 3:15 hrs.

Sunday March 19, 1944—Foggia #1
Today is my 24th birthday! Today's target for the bombers was a ball-bearing factory at Styer, Austria. We picked the bombers up over Yugoslavia and flew escort almost to the target. No enemy planes were met. I flew in Vaught's flight as element leader. Logged 4:00 hrs. I found out today that Gerry Lombard was lost on yesterdays raid on Udine. Some bombers that unloaded above him hit his plane. Gerry may have got down okay as they say that he still had some control of his plane. I sure hope that he was able to walk away from it. Better to be a P.O.W. than dead.

Monday March 20, 1944—Foggia #1
No missions. I hung around and played volleyball. Also I read, "Heaven is my Destination" by Thornton Wilder.

Tuesday March 21, 1944—Foggia #1
No mission. I went into Foggia in the afternoon. I tried to find some of the guys from Gerry Lombard's squadron to see if I could find more information about what happened to him but none of them were around.

Wednesday March 22, 1944—Foggia #1
The 325th had an escort mission to Yugoslavia today. Lt. Kitchen led the squadron and I led his element. I had to return short of the target as my plane was cutting out at high altitude. Jensen came back with me. On the way back we buzzed a couple of islands off the coast near Pescara. Jensen hit a wire that was strung between two of the islands and brought back about fifty feet of the stuff with him. Logged 3:40 hrs for the mission.

Thursday March 23, 1944—Foggia #1
We started out on another mission to Steyer, Austria today but the weather closed in when we hit the coast and the mission was scratched. Logged 0:45 hrs. I guess the bombers didn't do a very good job on Steyer on the last raid so it will have to be hit again. Went into town in the evening. Still no word on Gerry Lombard's status.

Friday March 24, 1944—Foggia #1

We started out for Steyer again today. This time we got a little bit further before we had to return. I flew in Gonda's flight as element leader. Just after takeoff we went into a big-ass cloud and all four of us were headed into the ground when we came out of it. Emmet was on Gonda's wing and he never did rejoin the formation. We had to turn around over the coast of Yugoslavia because of bad weather. I logged 0:45 in "41".

Saturday March 25, 1944—Foggia #1
No missions. I hung around all day and read "McSorleys Wonderful Saloon" by Joe Mitchell. Our group is now starting to move to a new field up the coast near Lesina. Foggia #1 is getting crowded, as a couple

of bomb groups are moving in. Our new field at Lesina is supposed to be very good.

Sunday March 26, 1944-Foggia #1
Today's mission was another attempt to hit the ball-bearing factory at Steyer Austria. It was unsuccessful again as all of upper Yugoslavia and Austria was covered with a heavy overcast. I flew in Hogg's flight as element leader. We met the bombers over the coast of Yugoslavia and returned. No enemy fighters were seen. I logged 4:15 hrs. I went into Foggia in the evening and stayed at the Red Cross Officer's Club. It was quiet. I got a package from home today. Mom sent my camera and some candy. Also a couple of books. Ann sent me a fountain pen.

Monday March 27, 1944—Foggia #1
No mission. I hung around all morning reading. The group is now on the move again so things are kind of screwed up. I went into town in the afternoon with Kitchen and McDonald and played ping-pong. George Flathers wasn't around. I haven't seen him since Gerry Lombard was lost. Stayed in this evening and read "God is my Co-pilot" by Scott.

Tuesday March 28, 1944—Foggia #1
We had another super mission today. The target was Verona and we escorted the B-17's all the way. Colonel Sluder led the group and I flew as his element leader. There were a shitload of ME-109's in the area. A flight of ME's headed for the bombers and our flight went after them. I latched on to one of the 109's and fired a couple of real long bursts at him. I know that he got hit before he rolled over and headed for the deck. It was a good scrap and I enjoyed it. Emmet my wingman stayed with me but we became separated from Sluder. We later met four more ME-I09's. Both Emmet and I got shots off at them but there were no signs of damage. Capt. Rynne, the C.O. of the 319th, was lost as were Lt's Jones and Hudson. Hudson was the pilot who shot down Lt. Jim Jones on March 11th. I liked both Jones and Hudson so I hope that they will

make it okay. Colonel Sluder got a victory for the ME that he went after. Tomorrow we are moving. I logged 3:35 for today's mission.

Wednesday March 29, 1944—Lesina, Italy
Today was one of the roughest days that I've put in. I got up at 06:30 and packed all my stuff to be moved to our new field at Lesina. At 08: 00 we were briefed for an escort mission to Tourin Italy where both the B-17's and B-24's leveled the marshalling yards. A few enemy fighters showed up but none of them was in our area. The 319th ran into some FW 190's and Henry Green and Lt. Forrest both got victories. After we left Tourin we flew to Corsica and landed. Lt. Komunicki of the 318th cracked up his plane in landing. We gassed up at Corsica and flew back. We landed at our new field at Lesina. Our tent was up but that's all. I went all day without eating and I sure was glad to get back and eat. Today's mission was the longest yet. I logged 6:35 hrs. We had a good look at Mount Vesuvius on the way home. It was smoking like hell.

Thursday March 30, 1944—Lesina
We got up at 06:30 today for a 07:00 briefing. We missed breakfast and I was starving. The mission was to Sofia Bulgaria but I was unable to go as my plane hadn't been gassed up and also the oil and oxygen hadn't been taken care of We really shouldn't have been scheduled today because the pilots are tired and the crew chiefs didn't have the time and men to service the ships last night. We are now without a floor for our tent so I guess we'll be living rough until we can scrounge a new one. C'est la guerre. Suehle is now living with Gus Kitchen so Winnie Vaught and I have the tent; such as it is, to us. We'll get it fixed up soon. I doubt whether we will have a mission tomorrow. Our new field isn't too bad but it sure is out in the sticks.

Friday March 31, 1944—Lesina
The 325th had the day off today and everyone needed it. Winnie Vaught and I got eager and spent the day building a floor for our tent. It's a good one and so we should be living in style again soon. Got paid $122.

Saturday April 1, 1944—Lesina
Today was cloudy and windy. We were briefed for another "on the deck" mission to Udine but it was later scratched. Winnie and I worked all day on our tent and we've got it fixed up pretty good. I get a big kick out of listening to "Axis Sally" on the radio in the evening. Sally dished out German propaganda and it's funny. Last night she said that the Checkertail group in Italy was going to be bombed.

Sunday April 2, 1944—Lesina
The 15th Air Force made another try at Steyer and they finally hit it. We escorted the bombers on the way in. It was a screwed up affair. There were a few ME-109's around and the 317th got three of them. Winnie Vaught led the 318th and I lead his element. "Sally" said tonight that she knew that the checkertail group moved to a new field. Big deal!

Monday April 3, 1944—Lesina
We had a real long haul for today's mission. The bombers went to Budapest Hungary and we gave them cover as far as we could. I flew #57. Winnie Vaught led the group and I was his element leader. My tachometer went out near the target and it scared the piss out of me. Tomorrow some general is coming to Lesina to dish out some medals. I've got to stay around and receive my Purple Heart.

Tuesday April 4, 1944—Lesina
The 325th escorted the bombers to Bucherest, Romania today. I didn't go as a general was supposed to show up and dish out some medals. Still the general didn't show so I hung around all day. I miss not being able to whip into Foggia like we did at Foggia #1. The weather was good for the bombers and so they were able to cream the marshalling yards at Bucherest. Both of the attacks on Steyer and Bucherest were successful. In the evening I got eager and did some weight lifting with George Sontag.

Wednesday April 5, 1944—Lesina
The group had another long escort job over the Balkans again today. The target was the marshalling yards at Polesti, Romania. Polesti is only 150 miles from the Russian front, Col Sluder led the group and I lead his element with Emmet on my wing. It was a dull mission, as we didn't see any enemy action. I dropped my wing tanks over the Danube River. It was a beautiful sight from 30,000 feet. I logged 4:20 hrs in "57".

Thursday April 6, 1944—Lesina
Today the bombers hit Zagreb in northern Yugoslavia. Vaught lead the squadron and I was his element leader. The bombers had three groups of P-38's and the 325th group of P-47's as escorts. A bunch of ME-109's came in high above us—as usual. Most of the action was in the areas of the bomber formation where our flight wasn't. Still the 317th and the 319th squadrons were able to knock down a total of 10 enemy planes. The three groups of P-38's didn't get a one. Vaught and I with our wingmen chased a couple of ME's almost to Udine but they disappeared into the overcast. I logged 3:25 in number "57". Played poker in the evening.

Friday April 7, 1944—Lesina
Today we went on another "on-the-deck" mission to the Udine area. Col. Sluder led the group and I was his element leader with Crookham on my wing. By rights we should have had a lot of action but we didn't see any enemy fighters. We arrived at the target about twenty minutes before the bombers but all was quiet. No hits, no runs, no errors. I logged 3:25 in number 64.

Saturday April 8, 1944—Lesina
We were briefed for an escort mission to Weinemeustat, which is near Vienna Austria. Later the mission was scratched. Colonel Toner, Suehle, Hogg, Vaught and I took a ride to the beach today. The water of the Adriatic was very cold. Three new pilots came in tonight. Now we'll get a little more rest.

Sunday April 9, 1944—Lesina
Easter Sunday. George Sontag got us all out today and had us take a physical fitness test. I did very well as Lt. Adams was the only one who scored better than me. In the afternoon General Twining came around and we had a formation where he presented our medals. I received the Purple Heart and Kitchen and Hogg both received DFC'S. I played poker in the evening and won $370!!

Monday April 10, 1944—Lesina
Bad weather—no missions. Five new pilots came in last night. Mumford, Fitch, Harper, Johnson and Lauren. Winnie Vaught went to Bari yesterday and didn't come back so I let Harper sleep in his sack, as he'll be living in our tent. I flew a training mission for some of the "new sports" in the afternoon. I lead one flight and Suehle led the other.

Tuesday April 11, 1944—Lesina
The weather was good locally but not so good up north so there was no mission. In the afternoon I test hopped my ship "41" at altitude. It still "cuts out" at 28,500 ft, which pisses me off. I got into a mock dogfight with P-38's and a P-51 on my way down. Logged 1:20 hrs. Wrote letters at night.

Epilogue—
On April 12th 1944 I was forced to "bail-out" of my P-47 Thunderbolt over the small town of Gumbach, Austria. It was an escort mission to Weiner Neustat Austria and I had trouble over the target, as I couldn't release my right wing-tank. In an attempt to take evasive action from a couple of approaching ME-109's I flipped over into an inverted flat spin. I spun from 22,000 feet down to about 5000 feet before I was able to recover. As I pulled out of it my canopy—became covered with oil and my oil pressure gauge was at zero. I was traveling too fast to bailout safely so I pulled up into a loop to slow down and at the top I opened the canopy, unbuckled my safety belt and dropped out of the airplane…And so I began my thirteen months as a prisoner of war in Germany. It wasn't

long before I was reunited with some old friends including Phil McCullough, Jerry Lombard, Jack Fallon, Paul Kenny and Ken Douglas.

BATAAN DEATH MARCH

Allen L. Laurence

I was a member of "A" Troop, 124th Cavalry (horses), Texas National Guard when the unit was mobilized in November 1940, and attached to the 1st Cavalry Division. We were sent to Ft. Bliss, Texas for about 4 months; then to Ft. Brown, Brownsville, Texas for about 4 months; then back to Ft. Bliss. During that time I was a member of the Troop's Training Cadre, training draftees as they were assigned to our unit.

In August 1941, I transferred to the Army Air Force and was sent to Jefferson Barracks, in Missouri. In October a group of us was assigned to the 91st Bombardment Squadron, 27th Bombardment Group (L) stationed at Savannah, Ga. We arrived in time to help pack for a train trip to San Francisco, Calif. We arrived there about the middle of October and were stationed on Angel Island pending our departure to the Philippine Islands. We embarked on 1 November 1941 aboard the President Coolidge. After leaving Hawaii, we were escorted by a Navy light cruiser which went at flank speed, gun turrets at the ready whenever a ship appeared on the horizon. We arrived in Manila, Philippines on November 21, 1941 and were stationed at Ft. McKinley near Manila. Since we were supposed to be sent to another island (other than Luzon) we lived in tents at Ft. McKinley. After the war started I spent most of my time guarding Nielson Field, which was several miles away. Our planes, Douglas A24's, never arrived, they were diverted to Australia.

About midnight on Christmas Eve, most of the Air Force personnel at Ft. McKinley and other military personnel in Manila were loaded on small vessels bound for Mariveles, Bataan. We arrived about dawn Christmas day and started walking up the peninsula. We had no food other than what we could scrounge along the road, and we had to watch out for attacks by Japanese dive bombers, which were rather frequent. The Air Force units, which had arrived in November, were designated as provisional infantry and were used to support front line troops and/or give them temporary relief.

About the middle of February after the regular infantry had lost more than half of their strength and the front line had retreated to the middle of the Bataan Peninsula, we became part of the front line positioned just east of Mt. Sumat.

When the Japanese broke the line at Mt. Sumat things got a little messy and muddled. After some difficulty along the way, I arrived at a site where I encountered several members of my unit; this site was in the mountains just above Mariveles. That night there was a pretty good earthquake, which I thought was ammunition dumps being destroyed. I arrived at another site where my unit was located late in the evening of the 9th of April after we heard General King had surrendered Bataan. The formal surrender was the 9th of April in the morning. On the 9th we walked down the mountainous road from near Cabcaben to a site near Mariveles. We started the Death March the morning of the 10th. From Christmas day food rations had gone from little to none by April. Men lived on what they could obtain from the area, mostly sugar cane and that was very little. All of us had lost a lot of weight and many were sick with malaria and/or dysentery. And what did we find at our rendezvous but a mountain of food of all kinds brought over from Corregidor. But we didn't get to eat any of it; early on the morning of the 10th the Japanese started us on the March known as the Bataan Death March.

And a Death March it was, thousands dying from brutality, disease, lack of food and water, and many just too weak to continue; the Japanese shot many at roadside. I made the march with several of my buddies in five days and four nights with one ball of rice and a canteen of water and a little food and water from brave Filipinos along the way; they risked big trouble by their help. At San Fernando we were herded into an open, fenced area with several hundred other prisoners; a man was lucky if he could find a spot to lie down. There was no food or water and men were relieving their dysentery pains where they lay; malaria victims were moaning; it was most unpleasant. From San Fernando to Capas by packed railroad cars and then on foot for a few miles to Camp O'Donnell—a real hellhole; many more died there.

Twenty of us volunteered for a Japanese work detail shortly after arriving at O'Donnell. We figured it was unlikely that anything could be worse than conditions at O'Donnell. We were divided into groups of 10 and told that if one escaped the other nine would be shot. The group I was in was assigned to a truck transport company; with them I traveled to quite a few cities and towns around the Linguyan Gulf. I was slapped around several times but not hurt too much—physically that is. In November 1942, the Japanese delivered us to Cabanatuan POW Camp No.1, they were going to the Soloman Islands, they heard.

At Cabanatuan the people in each barracks were divided into groups of 10 for security and accountability; if one escaped the other nine would be shot. Conditions at Cabanatuan were not too good; the number of bodies being buried about every other day was still quite high. We did get two Red Cross packages—one around Christmas and another in early spring. Most of the enlisted men worked most days on the farm, wood detail, or taking care of some brahma cattle the Japanese had gotten.

In September 1943, several hundred of the most healthy POW's left Cabanatuan for Bilibid Prison, Manila, where we stayed for several days. On the 19th we were marched to the dock area and loaded on an unmarked transport vessel (I later read that about 400 were put in the forward hold and 400 in the aft hold. The ship was named Corral Maru or Taga Maru, one of the hell-ships). We were bound for Japan. We stopped in a port on the south end of Formosa for three or four days. As we left port I happened to be on deck for a few minutes—many ships had been sunk—and we came under attack by an American sub. Shortly after I got below, a dud torpedo struck us. In about seven to 10 days we arrived in Moji, a city on the north end of Kyushu; we immediately disembarked and were put on a train for our assigned work sites. During the night we stopped and about half of the men got off. The rest of us rode all night and arrived in Niigata early the next morning. There about 200 were assigned to the coal (Rinko) detail and 200 to the regular dock (Maritso) area. I was in the coal gang. Conditions were quite bad there too, especially in winter of 1943. Conditions got better in '44-'45. The body lice were as bad as were the bedbugs in Cabanatuan.

We learned the war was over in August '45 when we awoke and found the guards had left during the night. B-29s dropped food to us until we left the camp about Sept. 5, 1945. We went by rail to Yokohama or near there, and then to Atsugi airport. Some of us boarded a plane for Okinawa where we arrived that night. After about three or four days we flew to Manila and a replacement depot where we stayed until mid-September. A troop transport took us to San Francisco and Letterman General Hospital in the Presidio. After two or three weeks I boarded a plane for Biggs Air Force Base and then on to Kelly AFB in San Antonio. I stayed at Fort Sam Houston General Hospital for about one year, and was discharged 1 August 1946.

It was a unique experience to say the least, but I wouldn't want to do it again. I guess at time of this writing—1993—about 80 percent of those who were on Bataan are dead; all of us have had serious physical problems—and I guess mental problems too—during the years since we were freed.

CAMP O'DONNELL

This was a real hellhole. We got there about April 15, 1942. The Japanese had not anticipated capturing such a large number of prisoners—Americans and Filipinos. There were no provisions for water or cooking, latrines, and hospital area. Camp O'Donnell was originally a Filipino army training camp, made up of large, airy barracks made of bamboo and nipa grass. Each end was open and they had dirt floors with bunks—upper and lower—on both sides. Bamboo and grass windows could be opened to let in air. When we arrived there was no order, we went to any barrack that was unoccupied in the American section—the Americans and Filipinos were separated.

As I recall, there was only one water faucet in the American sector and we had to wait many hours in line to fill our canteens or water containers. The sick men were scattered in the barracks and they defecated and urinated where they were lying. Since we had little if anything to eat or drink the volume of waste was not large. We got a ball of rice on the second day we were there. Also, some Americans were trying to get things organized, but there was little headway; the Japanese were not helping much at that time. Shortly after we arrived, the Japanese Camp Commander made a very angry and hostile speech to us. We were prisoners and they would show us no mercy. The days on Bataan and the Death March were quite evident on the condition of the men—many having malaria and/or dysentery. Many of them were dying. Conditions were so terrible several of my buddies and members of the 27th decided we should take a chance and get on a Japanese work detail as soon as possible. We got selected the second day. The unknown couldn't be any worse than the known and it might be better.

As I remember, there were four of us from the 91st on the truck detail that went to Cabanatuan—John Poncio, Jack Bradley, Freddie Ball and myself.

WORK DETAIL:

During this period of approximately seven or eight months, I lived and worked with the men of a Japanese Motor Transport unit to which we had been assigned. Ten of us were assigned to what I guess was a Company, and then we were divided into groups of three or four and assigned to a platoon or similar unit. The Japanese unit to which I and John Poncio, (we lost one man who got sick), were assigned was stationed at a school in Cabanatuan for about two months. John and I were assigned to help the three Japanese who were the cooks for the unit. We were well treated and fortunately for us, we gained back some of the weight and strength we had lost while on Bataan. This unit serviced the central part of Luzon, primarily the areas around the Lingayen Gulf, the City of Cabanatuan and areas north and east of it, and up into the mountains to Bagio.

John and I used the same facilities and ate the same food, as did the Japanese. Freddy Ball was assigned to a small unit that was stationed at Baler, a village on the far east coast of Luzon. His unit came to Cabanatuan several times and I saw him then, on other trips to Cabanatuan he didn't get to come but he sent me notes (one of them—the last one—is in my service issue Bible). If any of us got sick the POW did not get any medical treatment and if he did not get well on his own he was sent back to the prison camp—O'Donnell, or later on, Cabanatuan. The only clothing given to us was a couple of breechcloths and some thongs or gators as they called them. Some of the places we were stationed during this time are Dagupan, Lingayen, and Camp 3 on the road to Bagio, Bagio (Camp Hays), Binalonon, Rosales, and San Carlos. While with this group one of the Japanese cook was named Ota. He and I became quite friendly and he saved me from getting slapped around by soldiers in other units several times. He was very good to me.

Notes

After his last visit to the school in Cabanatuan, I never saw Freddy Ball again. For some reason he didn't return to the Cabanatuan POW Camp with the rest of us.

Until we were returned to the POW camp all of us on the work detail were reported to be Missing in action.

Henry Vara was in the cavalry with me; he was in the group that transferred to the Army AF and sent to Jefferson Barracks, St. Louis; he was sent to Savannah to join the 27th Bomb Gp. (l) which was preparing to go overseas; he was in the 91st with me, I met him again in the POW camp and then we were shipped in the same group that went to Niigata, Japan. He was in the Maritsu Gang (dock work) and I was in the Rinko Gang (loading coal off ships and into train cars).

When we were assigned to the Motor Transport Company, the 10 of us in my group were given Japanese Samurai names—I think in jest. John Poncio, who was a Staff Sergeant, was named Zerocho, the head of the gang; I was named Omasa who was supposed to be big and strong; and Freddy Ball was named Comasa.

I heard that Freddy was on the Arisan Maru, which left the Philippines in late 1944 and was sunk by an American sub. There were only a few survivors; he was not one of them.

Sgt. Jack Bradley was with John and me at the Cabanatuan school at first, but his beriberi got so bad his legs split open and the Japanese took him to O'Donnell. He did survive and I talked to him after the war and we returned home.

CABANATUAN POW CAMP No. 1.

It was a large camp near the city of Cabanatuan, in central Luzon. It was an old military training camp and our area was enclosed by barbed wire. The individual barracks were about 20 feet wide and 50-60 feet long. They were made of bamboo and grass. There was an aisle down the length of the building and on each side was an upper and lower level divided into bays where about three men lived and slept. Flooring in the bays—upper and lower—was made of split bamboo laced into place with grass or bamboo, with a space between each slat for air circulation. The sides opened out for ventilation.

There were about three or four barracks lined up end-to-end and spaced about 10 yards apart. Set at a right angle from the end of about each three rows of barracks and about 20 yards distance was a similar building, which served as the kitchen. On the other end of the three rows was the latrine. The rows of barracks were about 20 yards apart-I don't know how many barracks there were in the Army section of the camp but there must have been 15 or 20. The Navy and civilian sections were smaller. There was a Headquarters building and a stage used for camp meetings and church services in the center of our portion of the camp. A road ran the length of the camp on the outside of the row of kitchens, and on the other side of this road were several other buildings. One of these was for the so-called hospital and morgue; others were for the Japanese troops and storage. The camp bordered a road leading to Cabanatuan (I think the road was on the north side). On the south side of the camp and outside the wire was a large area for the "farm" where vegetables were grown for the Japanese. We got the tops or vine of a plant similar to a sweet potato; this vine was used for our soup or as greens with the rice.

We were assigned to a specific barrack and then into groups of 10 for accountability, security, and work assignments. We were told that if one escaped the other nine in the group would be shot. Those physically able were assigned for work on the "farm," to duty on the ranch area (they kept about 50-100 head of Brahma cattle for meat; we never got any however) to burial detail; to wood detail, which we liked because it gave us a chance to get some mangos or other food. I was on several burial details which buried 10 to 20 bodies in mass graves; most of the time the hole was filled with water so that the bodies had to be held down so that soil could be thrown over the bodies. Earlier details had buried 100 or more bodies at times. The death rate slowed down about November 1942.

While at Cabanatuan I had wet beriberi, dysentery, dengue fever (I think), and suffered from more malnutrition and weight loss. Insofar as I know there was no medicine for use by medical personnel. We had no toothbrushes or razors; we used grass, or anything else after defecating (those with bad diarrhea used nothing in most cases). Bedbugs lived by the thousands on the bamboo slats of the sleeping platform and ate on us at night. One's hand would be covered with blood after rubbing his body and/or the bamboo-sleeping platform at night. To kill them we took the platforms out in the sunlight, which killed them, we mashed those remaining if we could find them. Of course, we had no way to kill the eggs, which were in the grass or bamboo ties.

Our diet consisted of boiled rice and greens most of the time. Occasionally, we would get a little dried, wormy fish or soybean curd for our soup. We got half of a Red Cross package about Christmas of 1942 and a whole one another time before I left in September 1943. I can't recall any clothing being distributed while I was in Cabanatuan; I wore what I came in with. I imagine that some clothing was given to those that needed it most. Most of our daily contacts were with Americans but Japanese guards were in charge.

In 1943 Lt. Thompson, of the 91st, arranged contact with an underground group, which smuggled in some money with which we could buy a little extra food. It helped but it was dangerous.

Along with several hundred other of the most able-bodied POWs, I left Cabanatuan POW Camp No.1 about the middle of September 1943. We marched or walked the six or seven miles to the City of Cabanatuan where we boarded the train for Manila and Bilibid Prison.

One of the memorable events I experienced while I was at Camp No. 1 was the Xmas night mass held in 1942 at midnight.

John and I were assigned to separate areas at the POW camp and I never saw him again until we came back to the States. He visited me while I was at Ft. Sam Hospital.

BILIBID PRISON (MANILA)

I can't recall much about the conditions at Bilibid; I was there only about two days. It was primarily for the confinement of civilians. I recall it being crowded where we were and the rooms or hall where we slept were about 20 feet wide and 50-60 feet long with high, steeply pitched roofs like churches. We slept on the floor and if you were lucky you had a grass mat. We could go to 2 or 3 of these rooms where others from Cabanatuan were billeted. The food was about like that at Cabanatuan. I recall conversations with some POWs who had been there for some time who said the death rate had been pretty high and that most of the civilians were undernourished, sick and skinny like us.

As I recall we marched to the dock on September 19, 1943. September 19 was Dess's birthday.

TRANSPORT SHIP TO JAPAN

During the middle of September 1943, several hundred of the most able-bodied POW's were assigned for travel to Japan. We walked to the city of Cabanatuan where we were put on train cars and rode to Manila, where we walked to Bilibid Prison. There were other POWs who were also going to Japan; I read that there were about 850 us in total. About two days were spent at Bilibid. We walked to the port area—Pier 7—where 400 of us were put in the aft or rear hold and 450 were put in the forward hold. The ship was an unmarked transport named Corral Maru or Taga Maru. Platforms—upper and lower—had been built around the walls of the hold. It was rather crowded There were buckets in the middle of the bay areas for urinals or other emergencies. A jerry built outhouse with two holes was built so as to hang over the edge. We boarded the ship September 19, Dess's birthday, and left the next day. It was rather warm and close most of the trip, but since they had selected the healthiest POWs there wasn't as much diarrhea as there had been at Camp 1. Also we were more fortunate than most on Hell Ships, the captain and Japanese guards let those who wanted to go on deck to wash our mess kits or dishes and to defecate. Only two or three at a time though. We made it to Takao, a port at the southern tip of Formosa, in two or three days. We stayed there about two days but did not disembark. An American Corpsman while there performed an emergency appendectomy on Joe Quintero—Joe recovered.

I happened to be on deck as we cleared the harbor and I could see that our Navy had been rather active; there were several mast tops sticking out of the water. We had also picked up two small, wooden sub-chasers who were quite busy and I knew we were under attack by an American submarine.

I was immediately chased below deck and returned to my bay, which was on the port side. I noted that the sea was very rough, our ship and the small sub-chasers were rolling and pitching a lot. Navy people later told me the China Sea was always very rough. Shortly after I had reached my bay, a very loud and heavy blow hit amidships close to my bay. I'm quite sure a torpedo—fortunately a dud, hit us. After the war I read that the Navy was experiencing many misfires of torpedoes at that time. They were apparently made in peacetime and had been in storage a long time. The sea continued to be very rough and many of the fellows became seasick with unpleasant consequences. Results of the seasickness in conjunction with the diarrhea and unwashed bodies made conditions in the hold quite unpleasant the rest of the trip. We arrived in Moji, at the northern tip of Kyusho Island, late in the day and shortly disembarked and put on a train for our trip to the camps, which we had been assigned. A tunnel connected Kyushu and Honshu Islands. The time was about the lst of October.

Niigata POW Camp 5B

Late in the day the train stopped in Omata, a small town west of Tokyo. I read later, where about 450 POWs got off who were assigned to Prison Camp Hirohata. The rest of us rode the train all night and arrived at Niigata early in morning. I must say that what I saw of Japan that morning was very pretty. We walked from the train to the first site of Camp 5B. The first site was located in some concrete buildings near the coal yard and the dock area where the coal ships came in to unload. The buildings were about 20 feet wide and about 40 feet long with concrete floors on which we slept. They gave each of a grass mat to sleep on. They also issued each of us Japanese winter clothing, including an overcoat and a grass raincoat, shoes, and a couple of blankets. We were not used to the cold weather, especially coming from the tropics. We generally slept in our clothes to keep warm. The food was rice and dicon or radish soup; rarely we were given some soup with dried fish in it—what a treat! Latrines were outside of course.

While at this site the work gang to which I was assigned worked the night shift—normally 10—12 hours including the short walk to and from the work site. Many times we worked in the rain and those grass raincoats didn't do much good after a while. We would just lie down and try to sleep in our wet clothes in an effort to stay warm. After about two months at the first site we moved to another site farther away from the coal yard and docks. We moved to this new site the latter part of December '43 or January '44. It was located at the edge of Niigata, several miles from the dock area where we worked. More docks were farther down the channel. Niigata was on the northwestern side of Honshu across from Korea. The channel or river ran southeast from the coast. The basin for the docks we worked at was cut on the northeast side of the channel and was about a mile from the channel entrance. We could see the ships before they entered the channel. We walked to the new site in the snow, and when we entered there were three POWs tied to posts with no shirts on. They were being punished for some infraction; they later died from exposure. There were three large wooden buildings for the work gangs. One was for the Maritsu gang and the other two were for Rinko (coal) and other gangs. There were several smaller buildings for cooking, bathing, camp headquarters and the Japanese guard detail. Latrines were at the end of each work gang building. A wooden fence about eight feet tall surrounded all of the camp. At this site we slept on grass mats also, but we slept on raised wood platforms in each of the upper and lower bays. There was a barrel stove in the center of the POW barracks; coal was burned in them.

We got to bathe and wash our clothes on weekends. Body lice were terrible and we never got rid of them. We couldn't kill the nits in the lining or seams of our clothes; and the lice were in our blankets too; we didn't get to wash them. I forgot to mention that when we arrived at this site there were quite a few Canadians there. One of them was a medical corpsman that was called the camp doctor. He had little if any medicine. I had many sprains and bruises, one of which became inflamed and swollen; it was on my knee and this guy lanced it—no medicine. I did get to stay in camp a couple of days since it was difficult to walk. I guess that was the time I came to nearly not caring if I made it or not;

laying there feeling the body lice on me and watching them crawl around on the blankets, with my knee throbbing, and not getting anything to eat at lunch. I wondered if dying wouldn't be easier than living or existing as we were. The feeling soon wore off though.

Rinko encompassed about 10 acres, laid out alongside a dock on which two or three huge unloading vehicles ran on rails running the length of the docking area. These vehicles had long chain-operated devices like escalators with big buckets for carrying coal from the holds of the ships to the top of the trestle. The trestle was about 12-15 feet high, built upon large posts like telephone posts. The trestle ran in circles, one around the perimeter and smaller diameter ones inside. Rail tracks were placed in the center of the supports and plank walkways were between the tracks and extended about three feet on each side of the track. There were switches that permitted the one-man coal cars to be guided to the area where the coal would be dumped alongside train tracks below. These coal cars were four-wheeled, with a triangular body capable of carrying about a ton of coal. Each car was about five feet wide at the top and about four and a half feet deep. The body pivoted on steel beams along each side and had a pin used to keep the body from turning over and spilling the coal. A man would push the car under the unloading buckets running into the ship and get a load. Then the car would be pushed around the tracks to the site where the coal would be dumped. Two men—dumpers—would be stationed at the site and the man pushing the car would pull the locking pin and the men would tip the car to one side. There was an area opposite the ship dock where barges could be placed for loading or unloading. Oh yes, the steel beams carrying the car bucket extended about 2 feet in front and back of the car so that the pusher could be protected when two cars ran together. Of course when you were stretched out, pushing hard, your legs could still be hit from behind. When this happened you had to hold on to your car and be dragged along until the cars slowed down so you could get on your feet. A lot of bruises and strains from this situation.

When we weren't unloading ships, we loaded railway coal cars and/or barges. To load the coal cars we used coolie baskets on each end of a strong wooden stick balanced on your shoulder. Each basket carried about 20-25 pounds. Planks 2 by 12 would be angled up to planks running the length of the coal car. People with shovels on the ground would load your baskets and you would go up the planks to the planks in the coal car, empty your baskets, walk down the planks to the ground and get another load. You had to develop a rhythm to be able to carry these loaded baskets. You also quickly developed an enlarged shoulder muscle on each side where the stick was balanced. It was pretty hard and tiring for us since our diet was inadequate and we had not much strength. We used shovels to load or unload the barges. A steam crane with a net was used to carry the coal from barge to shore or the other way. Working on the trestle was difficult in the winter; the winds and rain and snow came in from the sea and it was very cold and wet. Occasionally when a ship wasn't in and our ground tasks were completed we were taken to covered warehouses on the other side of the ship basin to work, it was more pleasant.

About the end of 1944, we began seeing high flying reconnaissance planes overhead; they became more frequent as time went on. We couldn't tell what they were because they were mere specks in the sky. But we soon learned what they were from the two nice guys who operated the crane in the barge area—they were B-NiJu ku's or B-29's. In about April or May, the planes started coming over at about 11 o'clock at night, once a week at first and then more frequently. They were so low we could see into the open, lighted bomb bays. We didn't know why they were coming over so frequently and so low at first but we soon learned. On the way to work we began to see mines that had missed their targets—the Americans were mining the entrance to the channel as well as the harbor. We watched from the trestle as mines at the entrance sank several freighters to the channel—it was a grand sight and of course we quietly cheered each time. I was amazed at the toughness of these mines—one of them hit a rail that the huge vehicles used to unload the ship ran on and the rail was bent up from each end in a U shape; I had to see it to believe it. Needless to say, there weren't many ships coming in for either work gang to unload. We could tell from the way the guards acted and what some of them said that the war wasn't going well for them.

We learned when President Roosevelt died; the guards were eager to tell us. Occasionally we would see a Japanese newspaper that apparently was printed especially for it and us contained information as to the great number of ships and planes the Americans were losing—this really told us how the war was going. In July as we were working in the barge area, Navy fighter planes attacked a Japanese destroyer which was anchored in the channel. They strafed it pretty good but unfortunately one fighter had a wing blown off at the root. The pilot never got out. About the same time period, we were at the barracks when a Navy torpedo bomber came over our camp very low and we all began waving and cheering. He made a turn and came back very low, about 40-50 feet, and the crew threw all the smokes they had out. We knew the war was nearly over.

About the middle of August, we woke up and no guards were there; we knew it was over. The next day or so, B-29's flew over and dropped food and clothing in a field adjoining the camp. This food was placed in 55 gallon barrels, with a parachute tied on and pushed out the bays. It was very dangerous to be near the drop area; sometimes the parachute would snap off and the barrels would come down like bombs. Too, the drops would miss the target area quite frequently. One man was killed when he ran out to the target and was hit. Another barrel came through one of our barracks but we were all outside.

In the latter part of August 1945, Navy Commander Harold Stassen came to our camp with information as to what was going on. He told us to say there until they could arrange transportation to take us out of Japan. A few of the fellows left immediately on their own. Most of us stayed near camp—we did do some sight seeing around the area—and got word a train would be at a certain rail yard to pick us up and on to Tokyo. We left the camp on Sept. 5, 1945.

The war was over on 16 Aug. '45. We stayed at Camp 5B Niigata until 5 Sept 45 (before, Commander Harold Stassen came to our camp and told us a train would be available soon to take us to Tokyo) when we boarded the train for Tokyo and Yokohama. We arrived in Yokohama late in the afternoon. We were trucked to Atsugi AFB where we boarded a plane late that evening for Okinawa. We arrived late at night on the fifth. We stayed there for about seven days and then flew to Nichols AFB in Manila where we stayed about 10 days and then boarded a troop ship for San Francisco and home. We arrived in SF about the 4th of October. I was taken to Letterman Gen. Hosp. in the Presidio. Stayed there 2 weeks. Flown to San Antonio, Ft. Sam General Hospital.

GOING HOME
Discharged 1 August 1946

We had made it! We were going home—most of us had dreamed about it for a long time. After nearly four years of hell, starvation, sickness, and being deprived of our freedom, we were free and going home.

As stated previously, we left Camp 5B, (Niigata, early in the morning of September 5, 1945. About two or three o'clock that afternoon we entered what remained of Tokyo. I was astounded, there were only a few masonry buildings standing, most of the city had been burned as far as we could see. We passed through Tokyo and stopped near Yokohama. Then we were transported by bus to Atsugi Airport where we were told to hang around until aircraft would be available to take us out of Japan.

We boarded a C-54 aircraft shortly before dusk and were told we were going to Okinawa. At first there was a lot of talking but soon things became rather quite, I guess everybody was tired and become reflective. It was dark when I got up to walk up towards the cockpit; I looked in and the pilot was alone. He spoke to me and asked if I would like to sit in the co-pilot's seat for a while. That thrilled me and we chatted for a few minutes. It was pitch-dark and I knew he was flying by instruments so I went back to my seat. The plane landed in the dark and we were picked up and taken to tents. When we got off the plane and before getting on the vehicles we were to discard all our clothes in a building and we got new Army clothing. I hated to give up an old mess kit, which I had carried during and after Bataan. It had markings—names and insignia—from WW1.

We stayed in Okinawa about four or five days; the kitchen was open to us 24 hours a day. I don't recall us doing anything but laying and walking around the area and eating. Tom Huffman and I became separated at Okinawa; I never saw him again.

Thomas Huffman and I were buddies in Japan—we shared the same bay, were on the same work crew, and talked to each other during those hard times. He was very outgoing, liked to talk and tell jokes and stories about his home and his girlfriend, whom he married when he got home.

About the 13th of September, we were flown to Manila to a big reception and replacement area. As I recall, POW's were billeted in one general area. While there we were examined, questioned about our experiences, Japanese guards who mistreated us, given additional clothing, and had an open kitchen 24 hours a day. We were gaining weight back rapidly. We did not get to go out of the depot and see Manila or Fort McKinley. I guess we still looked rather bad and the Army didn't want the public to see us or talk to us. We embarked on a troop transport at the old pier on about September 21. It took us 14 days to arrive in San Francisco about October 4. Nobody met us at the dock but buses from Letterman Gen Hosp. In fact we got off the ship separately—from the aft. I stayed at Letterman about three weeks. I was examined a few times while there, never saw a psychologist and received no treatment; all the doctors were trying to get out of service and go home. Finally, towards the end of October we were taken to an Air Force base northeast of San Francisco, Travis Air Force Base, where we boarded DC-3s for the trip to Biggs AFB at El Paso, where we stayed overnight. The next day we flew to Kelly AFB in San Antonio and Fort Sam Houston General Hospital. I was met at Kelly by Dess, Aunt Pearl, Uncle Wheeler, Edna, Mary and Leroy and Gardene. It was good to get back home. I stayed a year at Ft. Sam General Hospital, getting leaves quite frequently to go home to Ft. Worth or to stay at Aunt Pearl's.

REPORT ON AMERICAN PRISONERS OF WAR INTERNED BY THE JAPANESE IN THE PHILIPPINES

Prepared by OFFICE OF THE PROVOST MARSHAL GENERAL
19 November 1945

CAMP O'DONNELL

(Following the Bataan Death March)

Once arrived on the area at San Fernando, the prisoners were crowded into boxcars and taken to Camp O'Donnell, located at Capas, in North Central Luzon. Here they were housed in Nips shacks that had formerly been used by the Filipino Army training units. About 1500 American and 22,000 Filipino prisoners of war died at Camp O'Donnell from starvation, disease and the brutal treatment they received at the hands of their captors.

On June 6, 1942 the American prisoners at Camp O'Donnell were evacuated in small groups to another camp at Cabanatuan, approximately 8 kilometers west of the town of the same name. Only a few small medical and civilian units were left at Camp O'Donnell. These units—500 men and 50 officers—were organized into labor battalions of about 100 men each, which were later assigned to camps in adjacent airfields and to road building projects under the direction of the Japanese War Prisoners' Administration. After the Americans were removed from the camp it was turned into a rehabilitation center for Filipino prisoners of war.

Many of the Americans who surrendered at Bataan died enroute to their final destination at Camp O'Donnell, and the health of those who survived was so undermined that they perished at the rate of 50 a day on the starvation diet in that unsavory place of internment. More than 2000 Americans in all died there of disease and undernourishment before the others were finally moved to Cabanatuan in July 1942.

Corporal Arthur A. Chenowith, an American prisoner of war at Camp O'Donnell, describes conditions there as follows:

From 10 April 1942 to 5 May 1942 (6 weeks) nearly 1600 Americans and 26,768 Filipinos died from lack of quinine and food, [although] the Japanese Army had plenty of food and medicine on hand.

Captain Mark M. Wohfeld has this to say about the maltreatment of American prisoners of war at Camp O'Donnell:

Lacked water. Cooking water taken from a murky creek 2 miles away in empty oil drums carried on bamboo poles. For drinking water the prisoners had to stand in long lines in front of 3 spigots in the center of the camp for the greater part of the day.

3rd week. Salt, sweet potatoes and squash added to rice diet. Plenty to eat as most of sick could not force the rice down due to malaria and dysentery. So-called hospital had patients lined in two rows on the floor, which was saturated with feces, blood, vomit, all of which was covered with flies.

The G.H.Q. Weekly Summary No. 104 of 29 October 1943, too, carried a summary of a statement made by Major William E. Dyess, another American officer who was imprisoned at Camp O'Donnell, concerning the insufferable conditions there. Major Dyess reported:

Treatment of American and Filipino prisoners was brutal in the extreme. When captured, prisoners were searched and beheaded if found with Japanese money and tokens in their possession. They were marched with no food and little water for several days, made to sit without cover in the boiling sun, continually beaten by Japanese troops, [and] not permitted to lie down at night.

Prisoners too weak to continue, many of them sick and delirious, were killed if they fell out of line. Three Filipinos and 3 Americans were buried alive. An American colonel attempting to help some soldiers who had fallen out was severely horsewhipped. A Japanese officer struck another who asked for food for the prisoners on the head with a can of salmon. Continual efforts were made to terrorize and dehumanize the prisoners. In six days Maj. Dyess marched 135 kilometers and was fed one mess kit of rice.

[Major Dyess] was brought to Camp O'Donnell and remained there two months with thousands of other Americans and Filipinos. The Japanese camp commander made a speech informing them not to expect treatment as prisoners of war but as captives, as they were enemies of Japan. The conditions under which American prisoners lived [Maj. Dyess declares] were well known to high Japanese military and civil authorities, which made frequent visits.

Principal diet in all camps was rice, with occasionally about a tablespoon of camote, the native sweet potato, often rotten. The Japs issued meat twice in two months, in portions too small to give even a fourth of the men a piece one inch square. [According to Maj. Dyess] abundant food supplies were available in the countryside, and the Japs deliberately held prisoners on a starvation diet.

Many of the prisoners at O'Donnell had no shelter. The death rate among Americans from malnutrition and disease increased rapidly from 20 daily during the first week to 50 daily after the second week. The death rate among Filipinos was six times greater. Hospital and sanitary facilities did not in any real sense exist. Medicines were promised but never supplied. Prisoners lived in filth, and died in large numbers of malaria, dysentery and beriberi.

The Japanese nevertheless constantly insisted on work details. By 1 May 1942 only about 20 out of every company of 200 were able to work. [Maj. Dyess states] that 2,200 Americans and 27,000 Filipinos died at O'Donnell Prison Camp.

About 1 May 1942, all full colonels and generals were moved to Capas, Tarlac, and were later sent to Formosa or Japan.

Corporal William W. Duncan, another American prisoner of war at Camp O'Donnell, testifies:

> The Japanese captured me at the time of the surrender on Bataan, Luzon Philippine Islands. After my capture, I was held on Bataan for about one day and was then taken to Camp O'Donnell. During the trip from Bataan to O'Donnell, about the second day of the trip, as we marched along the road near the Barrio of Balanga, Japanese soldiers standing along side of the road beat us with clubs and sticks as we passed. During this trip we were not given any food except on the last day, at which

time the Japanese gave us a small portion of rice, about one handful of cooked rice. The trip took approximately 6 days and I arrived at O'Donnell about April 15th or 16th, 1942. I am not certain of the exact date.

I remained at Camp O'Donnell, Luzon, Philippine Islands from about April 15th or 16th, 1942 until about June 1, 1942. At O'Donnell the food was very poor and there was little medicine to treat the sick. During this time I had dysentery. At Camp O'Donnell about 25 men from my company died. I recall the following:

Sergeant William T. Wooten died from wet beriberi.

PFC Coleman died probably from malaria.

Sergeant Backman died probably from malnutrition and malaria.

Lieutenant Brown died probably from malaria.

Finding a sufficient number of able-bodied men among the prisoners to bury the dead was not the least of the problems with which the camp authorities were confronted. It was not unusual to have several of the burial detail drop dead from exhaustion and overwork in the midst of their duties, and be thrown into the common grave, which they were digging for their dead comrades. Not infrequently men who had collapsed from exhaustion were even buried before they were actually dead.

William Collins—USS Indianapolis

Sanders: "You were born February 5th, 1919. Who was the first President that you remember?"

Collins: "Calvin Coolidge."

Sanders: "What do you remember about him?"

Collins: "Well, he was the President and a powerful man. This was the late twenties. "Silent Cal", they called him. He was my impression of what a President should be, a man I respected.

Sanders: "Where were you born exactly?"

Collins: "Fort Worth."

Sanders: "Tell me about your father. What was his background?"

Collins: "My father was a merchant here and his father before him. My grandfather came to Fort Worth in 1881. My father was born in 1892, and I was born in 1919, so I was the third generation. All three of us were merchants. Over the years I went

	to high school in Fort Worth and then a year to prep school in Dallas and finally to College."
Sanders:	"How old were you at the time of the Wall Street Crash and the depression that followed?"
Collins:	"Really, my teenage years were during the depression. When the Crash came in 1929, I was ten years old."
Sanders:	"Did it have an impact on your family?"
Collins:	"I was very fortunate. My father was an excellent businessman, and during the depression he did quite well financially. That set up the situation where my sister and I each went to a fine eastern college."
Sanders:	"After high school, what college did you choose?"
Collins:	"William's College in Massachusetts."
Sanders:	"Why did you choose William's College?"
Collins:	"My family selected it for me. My mother was born is Rochester, New York, called upstate New York, a very conservative part of the state. Many of the men from that area went to William's College, one of the oldest colleges in the country, being established in 1793. It is a very fine liberal arts college."
Sanders:	"Did you know what you wanted to do when you went to college?"

Collins:	"No, not exactly. I knew I wanted to be in business. I didn't want to be an artist or a professional musician."
Sanders:	"What was your first year in college?"
Collins:	"1937, and I graduated in 1941."
Sanders:	"During the latter part of your college years, were you aware of what was going on in Europe?"
Collins:	"Yes, we were acutely aware of it. In 1939 and 1940, this country was getting into the battle of the Atlantic, by loaning destroyers to Great Britain. Most people who could read and who had any kind of education knew what was going on, especially we felt we were going to be directly involved."
Sanders:	"The attack on Pearl Harbor happened just shortly after you graduated in 1941?"
Collins:	"Yes, December following my graduation, which was in June, of 1941. I had a BA degree."
Sanders:	"What were your thoughts during this time? Were you more concerned about going to war or starting a family and a business?"
Collins:	"There was too much going on for me to think about starting a family. I was mainly interested in getting started in business. Fortunately, I had a family business to go into that was doing reasonably well. My aspiration at that time was to be

	the third generation in the family business that had been in Fort Worth since 1888."
Sanders:	"What feelings did your father impart to you about the world situation?"
Collins:	"We were more like brothers than we were father and son. He knew that he was not going to be involved in a war because of his age, and I knew I was,"
Sanders:	"Did you believe it was only a matter of time before we were in the war?"
Collins:	"I didn't know we would be at war, but it looked so threatening, that in my senior year in college I volunteered for two services, one of which took me. Later I received my papers to join the Navy V-7 program. I was asked to go to the Naval Academy at Annapolis. They wanted graduate engineers, but more importantly, graduates. I knew very little about engineering, but I had a couple of year's math and physics. They were desperate to get men whom could be qualified as engineers rather than having an engineering degree. I thought that I was going to one of the deck officer's schools, but I knew because of my education I would be going to an engineering school"
Sanders:	"What were your views of Roosevelt at this time since he had been President for almost ten years?"

Collins: "I knew that most businessmen didn't care for Roosevelt and his policies. They thought they were too liberal, especially in using public funds for unnecessary projects."

Sanders: "How did you feel about Roosevelt as a war leader and your Commander in Chief?"

Collins: "I never gave it a great deal of thought. I simply believed that since he was the Commander in Chief of the Armed Forces, that it was no point dwelling on whether I liked it or not. I will say this though, I think it was very fortunate he was President of the United States, when we were getting involved in this tremendous war."

Sanders: "On December 7th, the attack on Pearl Harbor. Does that change everything for you?"

Collins: "No, but I was surprised at the attack, as everybody was."

Sanders: "Were you aware of the location of Pearl Harbor and it proximity to the West Coast?"

Collins: "No, I didn't pay too much attention, since I was being sent to training school, and I had no idea where. As soon as Pearl Harbor was attacked, I got orders, sending me to the Naval Academy on January 1st, 1942."

Sanders: "In the spring of 1941 you had first volunteered with your college friend Pete Richards?"

Collins: "Many college students who were graduating in the very near future decided to volunteer. We felt

	war was inevitable. At that time we had already given 50 destroyers to England to offset the inroads of the German U-boat program."
Sanders:	"What were your feelings about Europe at this time? Did Lindbergh's isolationism have any effect?"
Collins:	"My feeling was, and the people I knew felt the same way, that the United States would inevitably be pulled in. After Pearl Harbor, Roosevelt used the attack to galvanize the United States to action. Before Pearl Harbor the Midwest, especially, was isolationist. The attack by the Japanese changed it."
Sanders:	"You and Pete decided pre-Pearl Harbor to volunteer for the Marines. He ended up going. You ended up going in the Navy. Why did you initially want to be in the Marines?"
Collins:	"I thought that it was the toughest service, and I was pretty convinced that I was tough. I had a few athletic accomplishments in my life, but the Marines turned me down because of my flat feet, and accepted Pete."
Sanders:	"What happened to Pete Richards?"
Collins:	"On the landing of Guadalcanal, he was sent with one of the Marine regiments, over to the nearby island of Tulagi and on the landing he was killed."

Sanders: "When you left home to go to Annapolis, were you afraid of what was ahead?"

Collins: "No, I was ready. I had graduated from college, and I felt I had all the education I needed or wanted. I was going to Annapolis for training, but when I got there I realized that most of my training would be along the lines of engineering. I knew very little. I remember saying at the time that I didn't know the difference between a radio and a boiler, which I didn't. I had a few scientific courses in college, but I felt capable of learning the work. One thing that I did enjoy was the Naval Academy for the first time developed a squash team. I had been on the varsity squash team, which was a winter sport, at William's, and had played in the National Championship's. So, for recreation, I played on the Navy squash team. Since the Navy was just beginning, they welcomed a "reserve"."

Sanders: "Tell me about your training, how did it start?"

Collins: "On the 1st of January, which was a cold day, we switched from civvies to military clothes, and were billeted, and made our formations. I remember it being a cold, cold day on that field there in Annapolis."

Sanders: "Did the reality set in immediately of the scope of what you were doing, and what was ahead?"

Collins: "We didn't know what was ahead, but we were quite confident. Most of us didn't feel that any nationalities were as good as we were, and that was the basis of our confidence."

Sanders: " How long were you at Annapolis and give me an example of a typical day during training?"

Collins: "I was there from the 1st of January until the end of April, 1942, a total of four months. We got up at 6'o clock in the morning to reveille, and I think there were three or four of us to a room and one lavatory. The Naval Academy at night had strict rules and regulations about "lights out". Early in the morning we would hurry and get dressed and go out onto the parade ground, which was really a muster. Then we would go into the huge dining room of the Naval Academy for breakfast. After that we started our classes. My classes included, steam engineering, electrical engineering, and mathematics, as well as every other kind of engineering course there was."

Sanders: "At the end of April, the Navy offered you additional courses, what did you do?"

Collins: "I had just had four years of college at William's, and that was not an easy college from which to graduate, at least for me. Then I went to Annapolis and took all these engineering courses, in something I didn't know a thing about, but I learned pretty quickly. A youthful mind at that age is very receptive. But by the end of April, I had just had enough of studying.

We were offered new courses such as diesel school, local defense, and coast guard. My reaction then was I am just fed up with studying, and somebody should to the Pacific and fight the Japanese. That really was my thinking, and so, I volunteered for "combat duty" in the Pacific. I knew I was jumping right into the middle of it, but I felt confident nothing was going to happen to me."

Sanders: "Did you get any leave time after completion of training in April?"

Collins: "I was told to report to the USS Indianapolis in San Francisco on the 1st of June. So, I had 30 days leave in Fort Worth, and I visited one or two other places. I visited my sister and met my wife in Chicago. It was the first time I met her, and was introduced to her by my sister. I then came back to Fort Worth, then flew back to Chicago. Most of the transportation I had was on military aircraft. For instance, I flew from Chicago to Fort Worth, and then I went from Fort Worth to San Francisco on a Navy dive bomber."

Sanders: "Did the grim atmosphere of war and the possibility that you might not return affect your mental outlook?"

Collins: "I realized that I was 24, and what I really wanted to do, knowing I was going to war, and knowing this would be a long thing, I would like to get married but I really wasn't that interested. I wanted to have a son on the way, or have a child. That's what I thought about, because I wasn't sure I would be coming back. In fact, the odds were about fifty fifty."

Sanders: "Did you ever feel that fate had played a cruel joke on you, throwing you into a war in the prime of your life?"

Collins: "No, we felt the war was inevitable, even though we had nothing to do with bringing it on, but we knew our country was going to get into it. During the summer of 1941, prior to my training, which was a free summer for me, we all knew this was coming and we made all kinds of preparations whenever we could. This took the form of getting our affairs in order, or setting up a job when we came back, things of that sort. It was dead serious, there wasn't any question as to whether we were going into war."

(Photo courtesy of W.W. Collins)

Sanders: "Did your time in the service have a time limit or was it for the duration?"

Collins: "The duration."

Sanders: "You arrived in San Francisco and boarded the USS Louisville. Basically you took the Louisville as a transit ship to meet up with the USS Indianapolis that was in the Aleutians at this time. In doing so, you inadvertently became a participant in the Battle of Midway before you even arrived to your ship. Tell me about this?"

Collins: "At the Battle of Midway, we had three carriers, and we lost one. We had some cruisers there, and some destroyers. The USS Louisville, which I was aboard, was headed up to the Aleutians, where the Indianapolis, Raleigh, and I think it was the Nashville was located, as well as some destroyers. They were cruising up there to offset this huge, Japanese second fleet stationed at Attu. At that time, while we were in transit, and just before the Battle of Midway, the principal part of the Japanese fleet was coming towards Midway. These are things we didn't know at that time. The idea being that once they took Midway that the large second fleet there would come right down the Aleutian chain of islands and probably would strike Seattle. I had left San Francisco June 1st of 1942, and the Battle of Midway occurred June 4th through the 7th. We steamed Northeast of Admiral Spruance and his task force, not knowing this was all brewing."

Sanders: "Did you have any information being fed to you during the battle of the magnitude, or scope of the operation?"

Collins: "We got the information after the fact. During the Battle of Midway, Admiral Spruance had radio silence. The Japanese did not know where he was. As a result of that, Spruance was north-

	west of Hawaii, while the Japanese and their huge fleet was coming in. I think that they had six carriers and I believe they lost four during the Battle of Midway. That was really a devastating blow for the Japanese. It was in World War II, obviously that carriers came into their own."
Sanders:	"Was there ever a ship to ship engagement in the Battle of Midway?"
Collins:	"No, it was all done by airplanes from the carriers."
Sanders:	"During battle, what were your duties?"
Collins:	"We all had battle stations. My battle stations varied. My first battle station was in the forward engine room, where I was the Officer in Charge. There were two huge engine rooms on a heavy cruiser. Later on in the war, another battle station was damage control. I was Officer in Charge of damage control, and my battle station was on the main deck, which was below the working deck. The main deck was defined primarily by metal about six inches thick, all the way across for protection against damage. The job of damage control in case of casualties or getting hit was to put the fires out or whatever was needed."

(Collins sitting on upper bunk)

Sanders: "Were you allowed fire arms during battle?"

Collins: "Oh yes. During battle stations I always carried a sidearm."

Sanders: "What issue was that?"

Collins: "A Colt .45, and I will tell you, that Colt .45 would really stop anybody."

Sanders: "After the Battle of Midway, where did the Louisville go?"

Collins: "It then went on to Kodiak, Alaska. The USS Indianapolis was there refueling and I was transferred to this ship. Kodiak was about 500 miles out the Aleutian chain from Anchorage. We came into a place called 'Woman's Bay', and I remember that the sporting girls up there got rich. They owned the taxi cabs, everything. In Kodiak, we would go ashore to the Officer's Club for relaxation."

Sanders: "What were your impressions of Alaska?"

Collins: "It was the first time I had ever been there, but it turned out I was stationed out on that Aleutian chain off and on for fourteen months, which was long enough. We cruised Dutch Harbor, Kiska, and Attu, which is way out on the Aleutian chain. We sank a Japanese ship off of Attu, I remember watching that, using the 16-inch guns. It was a merchant ship bringing supplies to the Japanese at Attu and he never got through."

Sanders: "What was the weather like that far north?"

Collins: "The weather was terrible. I remember we were going up 'Alley Oop" pass, which was a pass up into the Bering Sea. We hit this tremendous weather up there, and the ship was rolling incredibly. It felt like if you even moved this huge ship would turn over. It would heel about 23 degrees, and that's a lot for a ship that size, especially. If I recall correctly, we lost a destroyer or two, through the bad weather. The waves were less like swells, more like mountains."

Admiral Nimitz and Admiral Spruance, Saipan 1944—photo taken by Sedivi, USS Indianapolis' (Courtesy of W.W. Collins)

Sanders: "What was your first impression upon finally being on the Indianapolis?"

Collins: "I was glad to get to my destination. It wasn't just another ship, it was *my* ship. I had been on somebody else's ship for three months and now I was where I was supposed to be. Keep in mind I had been near the Battle of Midway, and three months at sea and before that the naval academy, and still I wasn't at my station. So I was glad to be aboard at my station."

Sanders: "Which divisions were you trained for as an officer at this time?"

Collins: "A Division, which was auxiliary, B Division, which was boiler, and M Division, which was machinery. Over three years I was the division officer of all three, finally becoming the Assistant Engineer of the complete department"

Sanders: "How many men were you responsible for at a given time?"

Collins: "We had four divisions. I was never officer of E Division, which was electrical. But the three I was in charge of, a couple of hundred men. The Engineering department comprised of four divisions"

Sanders: "Tell me about your roommate on the Indianapolis, Sageser, who flew for the Navy Air Force."

Collins: "Yes, he was in the Air Force. What he did, he flew SOC's, which are scout observation planes. We had two of these planes on the ship, and he flew one of them. We were bombarding Kiska, and the ship needed his plane to fly over Kiska, and help direct our gunfire. We were in a very dangerous area, infiltrated by Japanese submarines, which, of course one got to the Indianapolis at the end of the war. He was flying the SOC, and one of the great things about the SOC, was that it could turn on a dime, and gives you nine cents change. The Japanese Zero, on the other hand, is so fast; it would go right on by. Unfortunately, though, he was no match for a zero, which could just stand off and shoot him down. So, he was last seen trying to get away from two Zeroes in the cloud formations over Kiska. We never heard from him again. What a great guy! What a loss."

Sanders: "Was this the first real casualty that you experienced?"

Collins: "Yes, the first real casualty. When he left room "JJ", I remember seeing him leave; he was all dressed in warm clothing. As he left he said 'see you later boys', and went right off. He was trained to do what he did, and it didn't bother him that he was being called to do this, even though it was very dangerous in bad weather areas."

Sanders: "After he failed to return, was the feeling sadness, or a 'that's the breaks' attitude?"

Collins: "Well, both. No one deliberately loses a friend. He was a greatly dedicated fellow. That's war. We didn't know for instance, that three years later when the Indianapolis was torpedoed, it was torpedoed right under the room I was living in before I was detached. The three men who occupied that room were never seen again after the attack. So, the loss of Sageser was the first real contact with death and it came very early in 1942. Many more contacts followed."

Sanders: "Then you were able to go ashore on the island of Tarawa during that battle."

Collins: "The ship was on the landings, when the 1st Marine Division went in. Throughout the war, they alternated between the 1st, 2nd, and 3rd Divisions in the invasion of different parts of the Pacific."

Sanders: "What did the battle look like from the ship during an attack on an island?"

Collins: "It was terrible. Mostly you saw the flame-throwers. The flame-throwers would go in and just incinerate the Japanese, in the caves and so forth. Meanwhile, they were shooting at the Marines trying to land. There was much loss of life of the Marines landing. Admiral Sprunace, who was the Commander of the 5th Fleet, came aboard during this time. The naval ships bombarded the islands. It was called "creeping bombarded", which meant just moving forward and bombing inch by inch. So, here we have Admiral Spruance on board, in charge of the whole theater of operation, and my ship's rudder gets stuck in one position. Our ship was the Flagship, and being the A Division Officer, it fell upon me to have that rudder stick during battle. That damn ship kept going around in a circle, about a one mile radius during the landings."

Sanders: "What were you doing as the man responsible to get the ship righted?"

Collins: "Fortunately, I had a machinists mate who knew all about the system and its' operation. This machinist knew all about this. He was from another division, but I got him down there because he knew what to do. It was never a question of which division, it was, get somebody down there and fix this thing. He did, after about a couple of hours, but I think I lost ten pounds just sweating this situation out."

Sanders: "After this dilemma was finished, you went ashore on the island of Tarawa."

Collins: "I remember going ashore and the stench of the bodies. The Marines had huge stacks, thirty or forty feet high, of just Japanese bodies, I believe six or seven thousand, and then they would pour gasoline over them and dispose of them that way. That was something of a battlefield procedure. I was witnessing all this and smelling all that, I was glad to get the hell away from that island and back on my ship."

Sanders: "What interaction did you have with the other Marines after the battle?"

Collins: "The repartee was very good. I would go up to a Marine and say 'this was a pretty bad affair', and he would say, 'yea, it sure was'. There was never a feeling of what service I was in or he was in, we were all in this together. We had to take Tarawa.

The only difference was I was on ship, and I was glad of that. Although, I tried to get in the Marines, but my flat feet kept me out of that service. The Marines were a vital part of that war in the Pacific, no question about it. The Marines and the carriers worked hand in hand. So there was no rivalry, everyone just wanted to get the job done,"

Sanders: "How long was Admiral Spruance on board from this point on?"

Collins: "I believe this was his first engagement, which was 1943, and he left the ship in 1945, so a couple of years. Admiral Halsey had the 3rd Fleet, and Admiral Spruance commanded the 5th Fleet. Since we were his Flagship, we were involved in all the operations."

Sanders: "At this time, who was the Captain of the Indianapolis?"

Collins: "I believe it was Captain Johnson. I had about five skippers. The navy rotated them. They transferred them to wherever they thought they were most needed. The theory was, if a man is a Captain, he ought to be able to run a ship, any ship."

Sanders: "What was the longest time you were ever out in sea during the war?"

Collins: "I was on ship from May to October and didn't touch land once. That was the longest time. Prior and following that, it was usually two months or so."

Sanders: "Did you feel that you were more at risk being the Flagship?"

Collins: "No, we didn't have that feeling at all. We felt that we were very special because Admiral Spruance was on our ship. Consequently, we went to many places that others did not"

Sanders: "How many men were on the Indianapolis on a given time?"

Collins: "A thousand to twelve hundred."

Sanders: "What was the next battle you faced aboard the Indianapolis after Tarawa?"

Collins: "That was the Marshall Islands, in late 1943 and early 1944. Enewetok and Kwajalein; but we didn't run into massive Japanese resistance there."

Sanders: "Tell me about what is called the "turkey shoot" in the Mariannas in 1944, and what led up to it?

Collins: "We still needed to take Saipan, Timian, and Guam from the Japanese, and about this time, the Japanese fleet made a sortie, out of the Philippines. We found out about the sortie from one of our submarines near the Philippines. The submarine had spotted the whole Japanese fleet coming down, and looked like it was headed to the Mariannas. So, Admiral Spruance immediately gathered the 5th Fleet, which was in the

Saipan area and set sail to meet the Japanese head on."

Sanders: "How many ships were involved in this potential engagement?"

Collins: "I am not sure of the number. It was the major part of our Pacific Fleet and what was left of the Japanese Fleet."

Sanders: "This had the potential to be the second biggest naval battle in the war?"

Collins: "It could have been. But the Japanese veered off, and would not contact us ship for ship. But they sent about 400 planes in to attack, what they did was fly over our ships and land on Guam, load up with torpedoes and bombs again, and then make the run back to their carriers. I remember being the Senior Engineer Officer of the Watch, and I kept thinking to myself, "don't screw up this one". We were the lead cruiser, because of Admiral Sprunace aboard. Behind us were these huge battleships, about four or five, and with them were about six aircraft carriers, all them twice the size of us. We were the lead ship of this massive force, headed like the shape of an arrow, towards the Japanese Fleet, hoping to engage. We all knew what was ahead, and we were all excited."

Sanders: "Excited because that was one of the few times you knew what you were headed for."

Collins: "We knew what we were headed for, but what happened was the Japanese decided not to engage ship to ship. They were trying to save the Mariannas, and they were hoping their Fleet would come down and do something about it. So, both Fleets were headed towards each other, and the Japanese made it about half way down the Philippines, before turning north to Japan. They would not engage. But they sent about four hundred planes to attack, and we were shooting at them from the ships. But most of the fighting came from the carriers and their pilots; and they had a major triumph in this battle. We only lost ten or fifteen planes, and the Japs lost around four hundred, that's why it is called the "turkey shoot"."

Sanders: "Now at this time you had been on a ship over two and half years?"

Collins: "Yes, at this time I was an old salty dog. My favorite gear was my cap. It got all salted up; the brim was a leather brim and had salted up. My officer insignia was getting worn a little bit. I wouldn't let anyone touch that cap. All these kids coming on board were wearing crisp, new gear, and I had this cap that had seen it all."

Sanders: "Now as 1945 approached and a whole new crop of islands had to be taken, such as Guam, Iwo Jima, and Okinawa, you began to witness first hand the horror of the Kamikaze. Had you heard about them before you actually were attacked by them?"

Collins: "Oh yes, we knew about them for a long time. We also knew the further west we went, we were going to start running into more and more. After the landing of the Philippines, the Kamikaze began to be more and more prevalent. It became a big thing in Japan. They persuaded all these thirteen, fourteen, fifteen-year-old kids that it would be heroic to die for their emperor.

The whole Kamikaze operation was partly religious, and partly for their emperor. Where I ran into it, with great severity, was off of Okinawa the day before "D-Day". A Kamikaze began this 10,000-foot plummet towards our ship. One of our men was on the 20mm, and he began to shoot at this plane, and follow him down the entire way. The plane hit about 20 feet from him. That plane was coming straight on down on top of this fellow, and he was strapped into his gun, and all he could do was keep firing as it must have looked until the last second to be coming straight for him. Afterwards the talk of the ship was what this man's drawers must have looked like. That must have been a terrifying thing. This was on the last day of March 1945. As for myself personally, this attack was a very near miss. I was the Officer in Charge of the early morning watch. We had been bombarding Okinawa for the landing.

The landing of Okinawa was unopposed. The Marines didn't run into trouble until they were inland. We were laying down these creeping barrages, and I had been the Officer of the Watch the night before, from twelve until four. When I was through I had gone to my room, which was the forward part of the ship. The Chief of the Watch went to his room at the back of the ship. The sailors went to a compartment, where they had hammocks one above the other. Well, every one of those that had gone back to their compartments were killed during the Kamikaze attack. The only two that weren't killed from that engine room watch were the Chief and myself, because of where our rooms were located. We lost nineteen on that attack.

Most of those deaths occurred by drowning in fuel oil. The outboard tanks of the compartment were where the fuel was stored, and when the plane hit it ruptured these oil tanks. It also ruined two of our four propeller shafts. We managed to limp our way to an anchorage called Karama Retto, and that was where more Kamikaze's were coming in. If I saw one, I must have seen fifty. The Admiral at this time was transferred from our ship to one of the nearby battleships. We stayed there as long as we could."

Sanders: "How were you feeling at this time?"

Collins: "Well, how many more of these was I going to be able to take before my number came up? I will say that was a very, very intense situation. This was also the same time the Captain suddenly called up the ship at seven a.m. and said a Marine had been found knocked out at his lookout post. It could have been a guy on board who didn't like him, you never know, but the Japanese had been improvising a new thing with a suicide swimmer. They had these very small and fast vessels where they could go out to a ship and climb the boat boom, and blow themselves and as much as they could with them. So, we passed out firearms and went on a search of the ship very carefully."

Sanders: "Was the value of human life different in the midst of war?"

Collins: "The closer you got to the battlefront the less value was placed on human life and more value in a jeep. I have heard of instances where the enemy caught two or three men because they lost their jeep, stolen by some of their friends. The value of human life seemed to grow very small the closer you got to battle."

Sanders: "World War II is portrayed in movies as very romantic, did you find it that way?"

Collins: "When you get into a war it is nothing, that I found, very romantic, adventurous, or macho. All I was ever thinking was getting through this alive, get home, and get my life started. I didn't get back until I was twenty-eight years old. I had given those productive years to my country."

Sanders: "What did you do during your spare time?"

Collins: "In the Officer's Ward Room we played our games. Acey Ducey, which is the same as backgammon was most popular. We also had bridge tournaments. Down in the engine room, it was against navy regulations, but the sailors indulged in a few crap games in different parts of the ship. If I wanted to do my guys a favor, after eight o'clock, just don't go down. The Officer in Charge is supposed to go to the boiler room for a ship's inspection. I rarely went down there at night; I wanted those guys to enjoy a little recreation"

Sanders: "It's been reported that Nixon helped finance his first congressional campaign from his war winnings at poker."

Collins: "He might have. Many officers played poker. The big game was Acey Ducey in the Ward Room, played between two people and there was some betting going on. Then at certain times we had movies. One thing about war that many people who have never been in it don't realize is that there is a lot of quiet time. We would sail month on end and nothing ever happen. It makes for some tense moments because you know something is coming eventually."

Sanders: "Now you were being finally transferred from the Indianapolis at the exact same time they were loading the Atomic Bomb onto the Indianapolis?"

Collins: "We were docked in San Francisco, I had thirty days leave before going to my next assignment. I was a little sad at leaving the Indianapolis. They knew I was being detached to go to a new light cruiser under construction before we docked in San Francisco, so they brought in another officer. They asked me to revise or rewrite the damage control book. I did that, but as you know, in the end, it didn't do any good."

Sanders: "Tell me what you saw when you left the Indianapolis in San Francisco?"

Collins: "They were loading these huge wooden crates. They were 10 feet by 10 feet by 10 feet. Just huge! Nobody knew what was going on. There were FBI agents everywhere, a lot of secrecy and security. The Atomic Bombs were being loaded onto the Indianapolis. A week after I was detached I heard the ship was on a high speed run, the fastest any heavy cruiser had made it from San Francisco to Pearl Harbor. They only stopped long enough to fill the tanks and onto Tinian."

Sanders: "Your orders took you to New York to your new ship?"

Collins: "Yes, it was being put into commission, the USS Juno. I was in New York when the Atomic Bomb was dropped. My thoughts at that second, were well, the war is over. It was about be over anyway, and this seals it. My hope now was that we would not have to land on Japan, because that would have been a very bloody affair."

Sanders: "Tell me about those days around August 6th, 1945."

Collins: "Well, the bomb was dropped August 6th, my son was born August 7th, and the Russians entered the war against Japan August 8th. During this same time, the first week or two in August, I was staying in a hotel in New York, and I got a New York Times paper to read, and there on the front page was a picture of the Indianapolis, and how it had been sunk. I looked at that and said, what is this, I was just in shock. I couldn't believe it. We had gone through the whole war! Then I thought to myself, how lucky can I be, for I had just got off that ship. My main question at this second was, who survived?"

Sanders: "Where did you go to try to gather information?"

Collins: "I went to the Navy Headquarters there in New York, 90 Church St., and tried to get information, but none was available. The Navy was very close mouthed about it. One little anecdote to this that had a large impact on my future happened, was that in 1945 I knew the war would most likely not last into the next year.

I wrote to a friend of mine who was a roommate on board ship, who had been aboard the Indianapolis with me. Six months before I was detached, he had been detached and sent to Princeton, University to train for Government service in the terms of capitulated countries. I wrote him, Frank Fisk, who died last year, and told him if he ever got down to Washington, go to the Cruiser desk and tell them I have been on this ship three years. What I really wanted was to get shore leave and see my wife, and after three years, it seemed more than enough. I told him to check it out and see if they can detach me, and I thought my time was due for a transfer.

At the minimum, I wanted at least thirty days leave. Frank actually went down there, and it turned out an old ship mate was at the Cruiser desk, and Frank told him I was still on the Indianapolis, and he said, he's been on there too long. Frank said, 'why don't you get some papers together and send him to new construction, he's been on the Indianapolis the whole war'. So, the guy sure enough did this, and I got my papers just three weeks before she was sunk. It all started with me writing a letter to my friend, and him taking the initiative to follow through by going to Washington on my behalf; that saved me from going down with the Indianapolis. Where my room was located on the ship is where one of the torpedoes hit, so I would have never survived. I saw my wife and child, who was already two months old, at LaGuardia Airport. He was sitting there in his basket and she said, 'here you take him'. It was all diapers from that point on. I began looking around for someone to write up orders back to the ship. I was twenty-eight years old and ready to live my life."

Admirals Spruance and Nimitz (courtesy of W.W. Collins)

244 • Heroes to Remember

Admiral Spruance (courtesy of WW Collins)

PFC Mason Herrin 134th Infantry 35 Division Company A General Patton's 3rd Army

August 28, 1944

Somewhere in France

"Dearest Sweetheart, wife and baby. How does my sweet darling today? Fine, I hope. As for me, I am still ok. Darling, do you still love me like you used to? Sure honey, I know you do, and I love you too, sweetheart, just as much as I ever did, and more too, for since I have been so far away from my darling I have found out that you mean more to me than anything in the world.

Darling, when I get home again you will hardly know me, for I will be so different from the husband that went away that night at Butner.

Honey, I was just a kid that had never been shown just how tough life could be and how hard it could be to live on a beautiful day as a cloudy one. Yes, honey, you will only know me by sight, for even though I may look the same, I will be and I am a different man.

Honey, I love you a thousand times more if that is possible, than I did when I last saw you. Now, don't get me wrong, darling, I loved you then more than anything in the world, but I have learned a lot since I have been over here. I have learned that you mean more than all the money in the world, or anything else in the world to me.

Honey, why shouldn't I be proud of the sweetest and most beautiful girl in the world? The sweet, beautiful girl that is the mother of my sweet little baby daughter and will be the mother of our little son soon.

I hope it will be a little boy. For we have a little girl for you to teach all about housework and to teach how to make some man a good wife. Now, I want a son to be with me out in the fields and woods, to teach the ways of the farm and how to fish, hunt, and so on.

Well, Darling, I guess I will have to close for this time, as I want to write to mother and dad. So be sweet just for me and love me forever, as I love you, for I do love you Honey.

Tell Mom, Pop, Bo, Maud, and the Kiddies all hello for me and kiss our baby for me. Bye for now sweet angel,

Your loving Husband and Father, forever,

Mason

I Love You Sweetheart."

Mason Herrin was killed September 21, 1944 near Nancy, France.

WORLD WAR II MEDAL OF HONOR RECIPIENTS

* Constitutes honor given posthumously

ADAMS, LUCIAN

Rank and organization: Staff Sergeant, U.S. Army, 30th Infantry, 3d Infantry Division. Place and date: Near St. Die, France, 28 October 1944. Entered service at: Port Arthur, Tex. Birth: Port Arthur, Tex. G.O. No.: 20, 29 March 1945. Citation: For conspicuous gallantry and intrepidity at risk of life above and beyond the call of duty on 28 October 1944, near St. Die, France. When his company was stopped in its effort to drive through the Mortagne Forest to reopen the supply line to the isolated third battalion, S/Sgt. Adams braved the concentrated fire of machineguns in a lone assault on a force of German troops. Although his company had progressed less than 10 yards and had lost 3 killed and 6 wounded, S/Sgt. Adams charged forward dodging from tree to tree firing a borrowed BAR from the hip. Despite intense machinegun fire which the enemy directed at him and rifle grenades which struck the trees over his head showering him with broken twigs and branches, S/Sgt. Adams made his way to within 10 yards of the closest machinegun and killed the gunner with a hand grenade. An enemy soldier threw hand grenades at him from a position only 10 yards distant; however, S/Sgt. Adams dispatched him with a single burst of BAR fire. Charging into the vortex of the enemy fire, he killed another machine gunner at

15 yards range with a hand grenade and forced the surrender of 2 supporting infantrymen. Although the remainder of the German group concentrated the full force of its automatic weapons fire in a desperate effort to knock him out, he proceeded through the woods to find and exterminate 5 more of the enemy. Finally, when the third German machinegun opened up on him at a range of 20 yards, S/Sgt. Adams killed the gunner with BAR fire. In the course of the action, he personally killed 9 Germans, eliminated 3 enemy machineguns, vanquished a specialized force which was armed with automatic weapons and grenade launchers, cleared the woods of hostile elements, and reopened the severed supply lines to the assault companies of his battalion.

*AGERHOLM, HAROLD CHRIST

Rank and organization: Private First Class, U.S. Marine Corps Reserve. Born: 29 January 1925, Racine, Wis. Accredited to: Wisconsin. Citation: For conspicuous gallantry and intrepidity at the risk of his life above and beyond the call of duty while serving with the 4th Battalion, 10th Marines, 2d Marine Division, in action against enemy Japanese forces on Saipan, Marianas Islands, 7 July 1944. When the enemy launched a fierce, determined counterattack against our positions and overran a neighboring artillery battalion, Pfc. Agerholm immediately volunteered to assist in the efforts to check the hostile attack and evacuate our wounded. Locating and appropriating an abandoned ambulance jeep, he repeatedly made extremely perilous trips under heavy rifle and mortar fire and single-handedly loaded and evacuated approximately 45 casualties, working tirelessly and with utter disregard for his own safety during a grueling period of more than 3 hours. Despite intense, persistent enemy fire, he ran out to aid 2 men whom he believed to be wounded marines but was himself mortally wounded by a Japanese sniper while carrying out his hazardous mission. Pfc. Agerholm's brilliant initiative, great personal valor and self-sacrificing efforts in the face of almost certain death reflect the highest credit upon himself and the U.S. Naval Service. He gallantly gave his life for his country.

ANDERSON, BEAUFORT T.

Rank and organization: Technical Sergeant, U.S. Army, 381st Infantry, 96th Infantry Division. Place and date: Okinawa, 13 April 1945. Entered service at: Soldiers Grove, Wis. Birth: Eagle, Wis. G.O. No.: 63, 27 June 1946. Citation: He displayed conspicuous gallantry and intrepidity above and beyond the call of duty. When a powerfully conducted predawn Japanese counterattack struck his unit's flank, he ordered his men to take cover in an old tomb, and then, armed only with a carbine, faced the onslaught alone. After emptying 1 magazine at pointblank range into the screaming attackers, he seized an enemy mortar dud and threw it back among the charging Japs, killing several as it burst. Securing a box of mortar shells, he extracted the safety pins, banged the bases upon a rock to arm them and proceeded alternately to hurl shells and fire his piece among the fanatical foe, finally forcing them to withdraw. Despite the protests of his comrades, and bleeding profusely from a severe shrapnel wound, he made his way to his company commander to report the action. T/Sgt. Anderson's intrepid conduct in the face of overwhelming odds accounted for 25 enemy killed and several machineguns and knee mortars destroyed, thus single-handedly removing a serious threat to the company's flank.

*ANDERSON, RICHARD BEATTY

Rank and organization: Private First Class, U.S. Marine Corps. Born: 26 June 1921, Tacoma, Wash. Accredited to: Washington. Citation: For conspicuous gallantry and intrepidity at the risk of his life above and beyond the call of duty while serving with the 4th Marine Division during action against enemy Japanese forces on Roi Island, Kwajalein Atoll, Marshall Islands, 1 February 1944. Entering a shell crater occupied by 3 other marines, Pfc. Anderson was preparing to throw a grenade at an enemy position when it slipped from his hands and rolled toward the men at the bottom of the hole. With insufficient time to retrieve the armed weapon and throw it, Pfc. Anderson fearlessly chose to sacrifice himself and save his companions by hurling his body upon the grenade and taking the full impact of the explosion. His personal valor and exceptional spirit of loyalty in the face of almost certain death were in keeping with the highest traditions of the U.S. Naval Service. He gallantly gave his life for his country.

*ANTOLAK, SYLVESTER

Rank and organization: Sergeant, U.S. Army, Company B, 15th Infantry, 3d Infantry Division. Place and date: Near Cisterna di Littoria, Italy, 24 May 1944. Entered service at: St. Clairsville, Ohio. Birth: St. Clairsville, Ohio. G.O. No.: 89, 19 October 1945. Citation: Near Cisterna di Littoria, Italy, he charged 200 yards over flat, coverless terrain to destroy an enemy machinegun nest during the second day of the offensive which broke through the German cordon of steel around the Anzio beachhead. Fully 30 yards in advance of his squad, he ran into withering enemy machinegun, machine-pistol and rifle fire. Three times he was struck by bullets and knocked to the ground, but each time he struggled to his feet to continue his relentless advance. With one shoulder deeply gashed and his right arm shattered, he continued to rush directly into the enemy fire concentration with his submachinegun wedged under his uninjured arm until within 15 yards of the enemy strong point, where he opened fire at deadly close range, killing 2 Germans and forcing the remaining 10 to surrender. He reorganized his men and, refusing to seek medical attention so badly needed, chose to lead the way toward another strong point 100 yards distant. Utterly disregarding the hail of bullets concentrated upon him, he had stormed ahead nearly three-fourths of the space between strong points when he was instantly killed by hostile enemy fire. Inspired by his example, his squad went on to overwhelm the enemy troops. By his supreme sacrifice, superb fighting courage, and heroic devotion to the attack, Sgt. Antolak was directly responsible for eliminating 20 Germans, capturing an enemy machinegun, and clearing the path for his company to advance.

ANTRIM, RICHARD NOTT

Rank and organization: Commander, U.S. Navy. Place and date: Makassar, Celebes, Netherlands East Indies, April 1942. Entered service at: Indiana. Born: 17 December 1907, Peru, Ind. Citation: For conspicuous gallantry and intrepidity at the risk of his life above and beyond the call of duty while interned as a prisoner of war of the enemy Japanese in the city of Makassar, Celebes, Netherlands East Indies, in April 1942. Acting instantly on behalf of a naval officer who was subjected to a vicious clubbing by a frenzied Japanese guard venting his insane wrath upon the helpless prisoner, Comdr. (then Lt.) Antrim boldly intervened, attempting to quiet the guard and finally persuading him to discuss the charges against the officer. With the entire Japanese force assembled and making extraordinary preparations for the threatened beating, and with the tension heightened by 2,700 Allied prisoners rapidly closing in, Comdr. Antrim courageously appealed to the fanatic enemy, risking his own life in a desperate effort to mitigate the punishment. When the other had been beaten unconscious by 15 blows of a hawser and was repeatedly kicked by 3 soldiers to a point beyond which he could not survive, Comdr. Antrim gallantly stepped forward and indicated to the perplexed guards that he would take the remainder of the punishment, throwing the Japanese completely off balance in their amazement and eliciting a roar of acclaim from the suddenly inspired Allied prisoners. By his fearless leadership and valiant concern for the welfare of another, he not only saved the life of a fellow officer and stunned the Japanese into sparing his own life but also brought about a new respect for American officers and men and a great improvement in camp living conditions. His heroic conduct throughout reflects the highest credit upon Comdr. Antrim and the U.S. Naval Service.

ATKINS, THOMAS E.

Rank and organization: Private First Class, U.S. Army, Company A, 127th Infantry, 32d Infantry Division. Place and date: Villa Verde Trail, Luzon, Philippine Islands, 10 March 1945. Entered service at: Campobello, S.C. Birth: Campobello, S.C. G.O. No.: 95, 30 October 1945. Citation: He fought gallantly on the Villa Verde Trail, Luzon, Philippine Islands. With 2 companions he occupied a position on a ridge outside the perimeter defense established by the 1st Platoon on a high hill. At about 3 a.m., 2 companies of Japanese attacked with rifle and machinegun fire, grenades, TNT charges, and land mines, severely wounding Pfc. Atkins and killing his 2 companions. Despite the intense hostile fire and pain from his deep wound, he held his ground and returned heavy fire. After the attack was repulsed, he remained in his precarious position to repel any subsequent assaults instead of returning to the American lines for medical treatment. An enemy machinegun, set up within 20 yards of his foxhole, vainly attempted to drive him off or silence his gun. The Japanese repeatedly made fierce attacks, but for 4 hours, Pfc. Atkins determinedly remained in his fox hole, bearing the brunt of each assault and maintaining steady and accurate fire until each charge was repulsed. At 7 a.m., 13 enemy dead lay in front of his position; he had fired 400 rounds, all he and his 2 dead companions possessed, and had used 3 rifles until each had jammed too badly for further operation. He withdrew during a lull to secure a rifle and more ammunition, and was persuaded to remain for medical treatment. While waiting, he saw a Japanese within the perimeter and, seizing a nearby rifle, killed him. A few minutes later, while lying on a litter, he discovered an enemy group moving up behind the platoon's lines. Despite his severe wound, he sat up, delivered heavy rifle fire against the group and forced them to withdraw. Pfc. Atkins' superb bravery and his fearless determination to hold his post against the main force of repeated enemy attacks, even though painfully wounded, were major factors in enabling his comrades to maintain their lines against a numerically superior enemy force.

*BAILEY, KENNETH D.

Rank and organization: Major, U.S. Marine Corps. Born: 21 October 1910, Pawnee, Okla. Appointed from: Illinois. Other Navy awards: Silver Star Medal. Citation: For extraordinary courage and heroic conduct above and beyond the call of duty as Commanding Officer of Company C, 1st Marine Raider Battalion, during the enemy Japanese attack on Henderson Field, Guadalcanal, Solomon Islands, on 12-13 September 1942. Completely reorganized following the severe engagement of the night before, Maj. Bailey's company, within an hour after taking its assigned position as reserve battalion between the main line and the coveted airport, was threatened on the right flank by the penetration of the enemy into a gap in the main line. In addition to repulsing this threat, while steadily improving his own desperately held position, he used every weapon at his command to cover the forced withdrawal of the main line before a hammering assault by superior enemy forces. After rendering invaluable service to the battalion commander in stemming the retreat, reorganizing the troops and extending the reverse position to the left, Maj. Bailey, despite a severe head wound, repeatedly led his troops in fierce hand-to-hand combat for a period of 10 hours. His great personal valor while exposed to constant and merciless enemy fire, and his indomitable fighting spirit inspired his troops to heights of heroic endeavor which enabled them to repulse the enemy and hold Henderson Field. He gallantly gave his life in the service of his country.

*BAKER, ADDISON E. (Air Mission)

Rank and organization: Lieutenant Colonel, U.S. Army Air Corps, 93d Heavy Bombardment Group. Place and date: Ploesti Raid, Rumania, 1 August 1943. Entered service at: Akron, Ohio. Born: 1 January 1907, Chicago, Ill. G.O. No.: 20, 11 March 1944. Citation: For conspicuous gallantry and intrepidity above and beyond the call of duty in action with the enemy on 1 August 1943. On this date he led his command, the 93d Heavy Bombardment Group, on a daring low-level attack against enemy oil refineries and installations at Ploesti, Rumania. Approaching the target, his aircraft was hit by a large caliber antiaircraft shell, seriously damaged and set on fire. Ignoring the fact he was flying over terrain suitable for safe landing, he refused to jeopardize the mission by breaking up the lead formation and continued unswervingly to lead his group to the target upon which he dropped his bombs with devastating effect. Only then did he leave formation, but his valiant attempts to gain sufficient altitude for the crew to escape by parachute were unavailing and his aircraft crashed in flames after his successful efforts to avoid other planes in formation. By extraordinary flying skill, gallant leadership and intrepidity, Lt. Col. Baker rendered outstanding, distinguished, and valorous service to our Nation.

*BAKER, THOMAS A.

Rank and organization: Sergeant, U.S. Army, Company A, 105th Infantry, 27th Infantry Division. Place and date: Saipan, Mariana Islands, 19 June to 7 July 1944. Entered service at: Troy, N.Y. Birth: Troy, N.Y. G.O. No.: 35, 9 May 1945. Citation: For conspicuous gallantry and intrepidity at the risk of his life above and beyond the call of duty at Saipan, Mariana Islands, 19 June to 7 July 1944. When his entire company was held up by fire from automatic weapons and small-arms fire from strongly fortified enemy positions that commanded the view of the company, Sgt. (then Pvt.) Baker voluntarily took a bazooka and dashed alone to within 100 yards of the enemy. Through heavy rifle and machinegun fire that was directed at him by the enemy, he knocked out the strong point, enabling his company to assault the ridge. Some days later while his company advanced across the open field flanked with obstructions and places of concealment for the enemy, Sgt. Baker again voluntarily took up a position in the rear to protect the company against surprise attack and came upon 2 heavily fortified enemy pockets manned by 2 officers and 10 enlisted men which had been bypassed. Without regard for such superior numbers, he unhesitatingly attacked and killed all of them. Five hundred yards farther, he discovered 6 men of the enemy who had concealed themselves behind our lines and destroyed all of them. On 7 July 1944, the perimeter of which Sgt. Baker was a part was attacked from 3 sides by from 3,000 to 5,000 Japanese. During the early stages of this attack, Sgt. Baker was seriously wounded but he insisted on remaining in the line and fired at the enemy at ranges sometimes as close as 5 yards until his ammunition ran out. Without ammunition and with his own weapon battered to uselessness from hand-to-hand combat, he was carried about 50 yards to the rear by a comrade, who was then himself wounded. At this point Sgt. Baker refused to be moved any farther stating that he preferred to be left to die rather than risk the lives of any more of his friends. A short time later, at his request, he was placed in a sitting position against a small tree . Another comrade, withdrawing, offered assistance. Sgt. Baker refused, insisting that he be left alone and be given a soldier's pistol with its remaining 8 rounds of ammunition. When last seen alive, Sgt. Baker was propped against a tree, pistol in hand, calmly facing the foe. Later Sgt. Baker's body was found in the same position, gun empty, with 8 Japanese lying dead before him. His deeds were in keeping with the highest traditions of the U.S. Army.

BARFOOT, VAN T.

Rank and organization: Second Lieutenant, U.S. Army, 157th Infantry, 45th Infantry Division. Place and date: Near Carano, Italy, 23 May 1944. Entered service at: Carthage, Miss. Birth: Edinburg, Miss. G.O. No.: 79, 4 October 1944. Citation: For conspicuous gallantry and intrepidity at the risk of life above and beyond the call of duty on 23 May 1944, near Carano, Italy. With his platoon heavily engaged during an assault against forces well entrenched on commanding ground, 2d Lt. Barfoot (then

Tech. Sgt.) moved off alone upon the enemy left flank. He crawled to the proximity of 1 machinegun nest and made a direct hit on it with a hand grenade, killing 2 and wounding 3 Germans. He continued along the German defense line to another machinegun emplacement, and with his tommygun killed 2 and captured 3 soldiers. Members of another enemy machinegun crew then abandoned their position and gave themselves up to Sgt. Barfoot. Leaving the prisoners for his support squad to pick up, he proceeded to mop up positions in the immediate area, capturing more prisoners and bringing his total count to 17. Later that day, after he had reorganized his men and consolidated the newly captured ground, the enemy launched a fierce armored counterattack directly at his platoon positions. Securing a bazooka, Sgt. Barfoot took up an exposed position directly in front of 3 advancing Mark VI tanks. From a distance of 75 yards his first shot destroyed the track of the leading tank, effectively disabling it, while the other 2 changed direction toward the flank. As the crew of the disabled tank dismounted, Sgt. Barfoot killed 3 of them with his tommygun. He continued onward into enemy terrain and destroyed a recently abandoned German fieldpiece with a demolition charge placed in the breech. While returning to his platoon position, Sgt. Barfoot, though greatly fatigued by his Herculean efforts, assisted 2 of his seriously wounded men 1,700 yards to a position of safety. Sgt. Barfoot's extraordinary heroism, demonstration of magnificent valor, and aggressive determination in the face of pointblank fire are a perpetual inspiration to his fellow soldiers.

BARRETT, CARLTON W.

Rank and organization: Private, U.S. Army, 18th Infantry, 1st Infantry Division. Place and date: Near St. Laurent-sur-Mer, France, 6 June 1944. Entered service at: Albany, N.Y. Birth: Fulton, N.Y. G.O. No.: 78, 2 October 1944. Citation: For gallantry and intrepidity at the risk of his life above and beyond the call of duty on 6 June 1944, in the vicinity of St. Laurent-sur-Mer, France. On the morning of D-day Pvt. Barrett, landing in the face of extremely heavy enemy fire, was forced to wade ashore through neck-deep water. Disregarding the personal danger, he returned to the surf again and again to assist his floundering comrades and save them from drowning. Refusing to remain pinned down by the intense barrage of small-arms and mortar fire poured at the landing points, Pvt. Barrett, working with fierce determination, saved many lives by carrying casualties to an evacuation boat lying offshore. In addition to his assigned mission as guide, he carried dispatches the length of the fire-swept beach; he assisted the wounded; he calmed the shocked; he arose as a leader in the stress of the occasion. His coolness and his dauntless daring courage while constantly risking his life during a period of many hours had an inestimable effect on his comrades and is in keeping with the highest traditions of the U.S. Army.

BASILONE, JOHN

Rank and organization: Sergeant, U.S. Marine Corps. Born: 4 November 1916, Buffalo, N.Y. Accredited to: New Jersey. Other Navy award: Navy Cross. Citation: For extraordinary heroism and conspicuous gallantry in action against enemy Japanese forces, above and beyond the call of duty, while serving with the 1st Battalion, 7th Marines, 1st Marine Division in the Lunga Area. Guadalcanal, Solomon Islands, on 24 and 25 October 1942. While the enemy was hammering at the Marines' defensive positions, Sgt. Basilone, in charge of 2 sections of heavy machineguns, fought valiantly to check the savage and determined assault. In a fierce frontal attack with the Japanese blasting his guns with grenades and mortar fire, one of Sgt. Basilone's sections, with its guncrews, was put out of action, leaving only 2 men able to carry on. Moving an extra gun into position, he placed it in action, then, under continual fire, repaired another and personally manned it, gallantly holding his line until replacements arrived. A little later, with ammunition critically low and the supply lines cut off, Sgt. Basilone, at great risk of his life and in the face of continued enemy attack, battled his way through hostile lines with urgently needed shells for his gunners, thereby contributing in large measure to the virtual annihilation of a Japanese regiment. His great personal valor and courageous initiative were in keeping with the highest traditions of the U.S. Naval Service.

*BAUER, HAROLD WILLIAM

Rank and organization: Lieutenant Colonel, U.S. Marine Corps. Born: 20 November 1908. Woodruff, Kans. Appointed from: Nebraska. Citation: For extraordinary heroism and conspicuous courage as Squadron Commander of Marine Fighting Squadron 212 in the South Pacific Area during the period 10 May to 14 November 1942. Volunteering to pilot a fighter plane in defense of our positions on Guadalcanal, Lt. Col. Bauer participated in 2 air battles against enemy bombers and fighters outnumbering our force more than 2 to 1, boldly engaged the enemy and destroyed 1 Japanese bomber in the engagement of 28 September and shot down 4 enemy fighter planes in flames on 3 October, leaving a fifth smoking badly. After successfully leading 26 planes on an over-water ferry flight of more than 600 miles on 16 October, Lt. Col. Bauer, while circling to land, sighted a squadron of enemy planes attacking the U.S.S. McFarland. Undaunted by the formidable opposition and with valor above and beyond the call of duty, he engaged the entire squadron and, although alone and his fuel supply nearly exhausted, fought his plane so brilliantly that 4 of the Japanese planes were destroyed before he was forced down by lack of fuel. His intrepid fighting spirit and distinctive ability as a leader and an airman, exemplified in his splendid record of combat achievement, were vital factors in the successful operations in the South Pacific Area.

*BAUSELL, LEWIS KENNETH

Rank and organization: Corporal, U.S. Marine Corps. Born: 17 April 1924, Pulaski, Va. Accredited to: District of Columbia. Citation: For conspicuous gallantry and intrepidity at the risk of his life above and beyond the call of duty while serving with the 1st Battalion, 5th Marines, 1st Marine Division, during action against enemy Japanese forces on Peleliu Island, Palau Group, 15 September 1944. Valiantly placing himself at the head of his squad, Cpl. Bausell led the charge forward against a hostile pillbox which was covering a vital sector of the beach and, as the first to reach the emplacement, immediately started firing his automatic into the aperture while the remainder of his men closed in on the enemy. Swift to act, as a Japanese grenade was hurled into their midst, Cpl. Bausell threw himself on the deadly weapon, taking the full blast of the explosion and sacrificing his own life to save his men. His unwavering loyalty and inspiring courage reflect the highest credit upon Cpl. Bausell and the U.S. Naval Service. He gallantly gave his life for his country.

*BEAUDOIN, RAYMOND O.

Rank and organization: First Lieutenant, U.S. Army, Company F, 119th Infantry, 30th Infantry Division. Place and date: Hamelin, Germany, 6 April 1945. Entered service at: Holyoke, Mass. Birth: Holyoke, Mass. G.O. No.: 9, 25 January 1946. Citation: He was leading the 2d Platoon of Company F over flat, open terrain to Hamelin, Germany, when the enemy went into action with machineguns and automatic weapons, laying down a devastating curtain of fire which pinned his unit to the ground. By rotating men in firing positions he made it possible for his entire platoon to dig in, defying all the while the murderous enemy fire to encourage his men and to distribute ammunition. He then dug in himself at the most advanced position, where he kept up a steady fire, killing 6 hostile soldiers, and directing his men in inflicting heavy casualties on the numerically superior opposing force. Despite these defensive measures, however, the position of the platoon became more precarious, for the enemy had brought up strong reinforcements and was preparing a counterattack. Three men, sent back at intervals to obtain ammunition and reinforcements, were killed by sniper fire. To relieve his command from the desperate situation, 1st Lt. Beaudoin decided to make a 1-man attack on the most damaging enemy sniper nest 90 yards to the right flank, and thereby divert attention from the runner who would attempt to pierce the enemy's barrier of bullets and secure help. Crawling over completely exposed ground, he relentlessly advanced, undeterred by 8 rounds of bazooka fire which threw mud and stones over him or by rifle fire which ripped his uniform. Ten yards from the enemy position he stood up and charged. At point-blank range he shot and killed 2 occupants of the nest; a third, who tried to bayonet him, he overpowered and killed with the butt of his carbine; and the fourth adversary was cut down by the platoon's rifle fire as he attempted to flee. He continued his attack by running toward a dugout, but there he was struck and killed by a burst from a machinegun. By his intrepidity, great fighting skill, and supreme devotion to his responsibility for the well-being of his platoon, 1st Lt. Beaudoin single-handedly accomplished a mission that enabled a messenger to secure help which saved the stricken unit and made possible the decisive defeat of the German forces.

BELL, BERNARD P.

Rank and organization: Technical Sergeant, U.S. Army, Company I, 142d Infantry, 36th Infantry Division. Place and date: Mittelwihr, France, 18 December 1944. Entered service at: New York, N.Y. Birth: Grantsville, W. Va. G.O. No.: 73, 30 August 1945. Citation: For fighting gallantly at Mittelwihr, France. On the morning of 18 December 1944, he led a squad against a schoolhouse held by enemy troops. While his men covered him, he dashed toward the building, surprised 2 guards at the door and took them prisoner without firing a shot. He found that other Germans were in the cellar. These he threatened with hand grenades, forcing 26 in all to emerge and surrender. His squad then occupied the building and prepared to defend it against powerful enemy action. The next day, the enemy poured artillery and mortar barrages into the position, disrupting communications which T/Sgt. Bell repeatedly repaired under heavy small-arms fire as he crossed dangerous terrain to keep his company commander informed of the squad's situation. During the day, several prisoners were taken and other Germans killed when hostile forces were attracted to the schoolhouse by the sound of captured German weapons fired by the Americans. At dawn the next day the enemy prepared to assault the building. A German tank fired round after round into the structure, partially demolishing the upper stories. Despite this heavy fire, T/Sgt. Bell climbed to the second floor and directed artillery fire which forced the hostile tank to withdraw. He then adjusted mortar fire on large forces of enemy foot soldiers attempting to reach the American position and, when this force broke and attempted to retire, he directed deadly machinegun and rifle fire into their disorganized ranks. Calling for armored support to blast out the German troops hidden behind a wall, he unhesitatingly exposed himself to heavy small-arms fire to stand beside a friendly tank and tell its occupants where to rip holes in walls protecting approaches to the school building. He then trained machineguns on the gaps and mowed down all hostile troops attempting to cross the openings to get closer to the school building. By his intrepidity and bold, aggressive leadership, T/Sgt. Bell enabled his 8-man squad to drive back approximately 150 of the enemy, killing at least 87 and capturing 42. Personally, he killed more than 20 and captured 33 prisoners.

BENDER, STANLEY

Rank and organization: Staff Sergeant, U.S. Army, Company E, 7th Infantry, 3d Infantry Division. Place and date: Near La Lande, France, 17 August 1944. Entered service at: Chicago, 111. Born: 31 October 1909, Carlisle, W. Va. G.O. No.: 7, 1 February 1945. Citation: For conspicuous gallantry and intrepidity at risk of life above and beyond the call of duty. On 17 August 1944, near La Lande, France, he climbed on top of a knocked-out tank, in the face of withering machinegun fire which had halted the advance of his company, in an effort to locate the source of this fire. Although bullets ricocheted off the turret at his feet, he nevertheless remained standing upright in full view of the enemy for over 2 minutes. Locating the enemy machineguns on a knoll 200 yards away, he ordered 2 squads to cover him and led his men down an irrigation ditch, running a gauntlet of intense machinegun fire, which completely blanketed 50 yards of his advance and wounded 4 of his men. While the Germans hurled hand grenades at the ditch, he stood his ground until his squad caught up with him, then advanced alone, in a wide flanking approach, to the rear of the knoll. He walked deliberately a distance of 40 yards, without cover, in full view of the Germans and under a hail of both enemy and friendly fire, to the first machinegun and knocked it out with a single short burst. Then he made his way through the strong point, despite bursting hand grenades, toward the second machinegun, 25 yards distant, whose 2-man crew swung the machinegun around and fired two bursts at him, but he walked calmly through the fire and, reaching the edge of the emplacement, dispatched the crew. Signaling his men to rush the rifle pits, he then walked 35 yards further to kill an enemy rifleman and returned to lead his squad in the destruction of the 8 remaining Germans in the strong point. His audacity so inspired the remainder of the assault company that the men charged out of their positions, shouting and yelling, to overpower the enemy roadblock and sweep into town, knocking out 2 antitank guns, killing 37 Germans and capturing 26 others. He had sparked and led the assault company in an attack which overwhelmed the enemy, destroying a roadblock, taking a town, seizing intact 3 bridges over the Maravenne River, and capturing commanding terrain which dominated the area.

*BENJAMIN, GEORGE, JR.

Rank and organization: Private First Class, U.S. Army, Company A, 306th Infantry, 77th Infantry Division. Place and date: Leyte, Philippine Islands, 21 December 1944. Entered service at: Carney's Point, N.J.

Birth: Philadelphia, Pa. G.O. No.: 49, 28 June 1945. Citation: He was a radio operator, advancing in the rear of his company as it engaged a well-defended Japanese strong point holding up the progress of the entire battalion. When a rifle platoon supporting a light tank hesitated in its advance, he voluntarily and with utter disregard for personal safety left his comparatively secure position and ran across bullet-whipped terrain to the tank, waving and shouting to the men of the platoon to follow. Carrying his bulky radio and armed only with a pistol, he fearlessly penetrated intense machinegun and rifle fire to the enemy position, where he killed 1 of the enemy in a foxhole and moved on to annihilate the crew of a light machinegun. Heedless of the terrific fire now concentrated on him, he continued to spearhead the assault, killing 2 more of the enemy and exhorting the other men to advance, until he fell mortally wounded. After being evacuated to an aid station, his first thought was still of the American advance. Overcoming great pain he called for the battalion operations officer to report the location of enemy weapons and valuable tactical information he had secured in his heroic charge. The unwavering courage, the unswerving devotion to the task at hand, the aggressive leadership of Pfc. Benjamin were a source of great and lasting inspiration to his comrades and were to a great extent responsible for the success of the battalion's mission.

BENNETT, EDWARD A.

Rank and organization: Corporal, U.S. Army, Company B, 358th Infantry, 90th Infantry Division. Place and date: Heckhuscheid, Germany, February 1945. Entered service at: Middleport, Ohio. Birth: Middleport, Ohio. G.O. No.: 95, 30 October 1945. Citation: He was advancing with Company B across open ground to assault Heckhuscheid, Germany, just after dark when vicious enemy machinegun fire from a house on the outskirts of the town pinned down the group and caused several casualties. He began crawling to the edge of the field in an effort to flank the house, persisting in this maneuver even when the hostile machinegunners located him by the light of burning buildings and attempted to cut him down as he made for the protection of some trees. Reaching safety, he stealthily made his way by a circuitous route to the rear of the building occupied by the German gunners. With his trench knife he killed a sentry on guard there and then charged into the darkened house. In a furious hand-to-hand struggle he stormed about a single room which harbored 7 Germans. Three he killed with rifle fire, another he clubbed to death with the butt of his gun, and the 3 others he dispatched with his .45 caliber pistol. The fearless initiative, stalwart combat ability, and outstanding gallantry of Cpl. Bennett eliminated the enemy fire which was decimating his company's ranks and made it possible for the Americans to sweep all resistance from the town.

*BENNION, MERVYN SHARP

Rank and organization: Captain, U.S. Navy. Born: 5 May 1887, Vernon, Utah. Appointed from: Utah. Citation: For conspicuous devotion to duty, extraordinary courage, and complete disregard of his own life, above and beyond the call of duty, during the attack on the Fleet in Pearl Harbor, by Japanese forces on 7 December 1941. As Commanding Officer of the U.S.S. West Virginia, after being mortally wounded, Capt. Bennion evidenced apparent concern only in fighting and saving his ship, and strongly protested against being carried from the bridge.

*BERRY, CHARLES JOSEPH

Rank and organization: Corporal, U.S. Marine Corps. Born: 10 July 1923, Lorain, Ohio. Accredited to: Ohio. Citation: For conspicuous gallantry and intrepidity at the risk of his life above and beyond the call of duty as member of a machinegun crew, serving with the 1st Battalion, 26th Marines, 5th Marine Division, in action against enemy Japanese forces during the seizure of Iwo Jima in the Volcano Islands, on 3 March 1945. Stationed in the front lines, Cpl. Berry manned his weapon with alert readiness as he maintained a constant vigil with other members of his guncrew during the hazardous night hours. When infiltrating Japanese soldiers launched a surprise attack shortly after midnight in an attempt to overrun his position, he engaged in a pitched hand grenade duel, returning the dangerous weapons with prompt and deadly accuracy until an enemy grenade landed in the foxhole. Determined to save his comrades, he unhesitatingly chose to sacrifice himself and immediately dived on the deadly missile, absorbing the shattering violence of the exploding charge in his own body and protecting the others from serious injury. Stouthearted and indomitable, Cpl. Berry fearlessly yielded his own life that his fellow marines might carry on the relentless battle against a ruthless enemy and his superb valor and unfaltering devotion to duty in the face of certain death reflect the highest credit upon himself and upon the U.S. Naval Service. He gallantly gave his life for his country.

BERTOLDO, VITO R.

Rank and organization: Master Sergeant, U.S. Army, Company A, 242d Infantry, 42d Infantry Division. Place and date: Hatten, France, 9-10 January 1945. Entered service at: Decatur, 111. Born: 1 December 1916, Decatur, 111. G.O. No.: 5, 10 January 1946. Citation: He fought with extreme gallantry while guarding 2 command posts against the assault of powerful infantry and armored forces which had overrun the battalion's main line of resistance. On the close approach of enemy soldiers, he left the protection of the building he defended and set up his gun in the street, there to remain for almost 12 hours driving back attacks while in full view of his adversaries and completely exposed to 88-mm., machinegun and small-arms fire. He moved back inside the command post, strapped his machinegun to a table and covered the main approach to the building by firing through a window, remaining steadfast even in the face of 88-mm. fire from tanks only 75 yards away. One shell blasted him across the room, but he returned to his weapon. When 2 enemy personnel carriers led by a tank moved toward his position, he calmly waited for the troops to dismount and then, with the tank firing directly at him, leaned out of the window and mowed down the entire group of more than 20 Germans. Some time later, removal of the command post to another building was ordered. M/Sgt. Bertoldo voluntarily remained behind, covering the withdrawal of his comrades and maintaining his stand all night. In the morning he carried his machinegun to an adjacent building used as the command post of another battalion and began a daylong defense of that position. He broke up a heavy attack, launched by a self-propelled 88-mm. gun covered by a tank and about 15 infantrymen. Soon afterward another 88-mm. weapon moved up to within a few feet of his position, and, placing the muzzle of its gun almost inside the building, fired into the room, knocking him down and seriously wounding others. An American bazooka team set the German weapon afire, and M/Sgt. Bertoldo went back to his machinegun dazed as he was and killed several of the hostile troops as they attempted to withdraw. It was decided to evacuate the command post under the cover of darkness, but before the plan could be put into operation the enemy began an intensive assault supported by fire from their tanks and heavy guns. Disregarding the devastating barrage, he remained at his post and hurled white phosphorous grenades into the advancing enemy troops until they broke and retreated. A tank less than 50 yards away fired at his stronghold, destroyed the machinegun and blew him across the room again but he once more returned to the bitter fight and, with a rifle, single-handedly covered the withdrawal of his fellow soldiers when the post was finally abandoned. With inspiring bravery and intrepidity M/Sgt. Bertoldo withstood the attack of vastly superior forces for more than 48 hours without rest or relief, time after time escaping death only by the slightest margin while killing at least 40 hostile soldiers and wounding many more during his grim battle against the enemy hordes.

BEYER, ARTHUR O.

Rank and organization: Corporal, U.S. Army, Company C, 603d Tank Destroyer Battalion. Place and date: Near Arloncourt, Belgium, 15 January 1945. Entered service at: St. Ansgar, Iowa. Born: 20 May 1909, Rock Township, Mitchell County, Iowa. G.O. No.: 73, 30 August 1945. Citation: He displayed conspicuous gallantry in action. His platoon, in which he was a tank-destroyer gunner, was held up by antitank, machinegun, and rifle fire from enemy troops dug in along a ridge about 200 yards to the front. Noting a machinegun position in this defense line, he fired upon it with his 76-mm. gun killing 1 man and silencing the weapon. He dismounted from his vehicle and, under direct enemy observation, crossed open ground to capture the 2 remaining members of the crew. Another machinegun, about 250 yards to the left, continued to fire on him. Through withering fire, he advanced on the position. Throwing a grenade into the emplacement, he killed 1 crewmember and again captured the 2 survivors. He was subjected to concentrated small-arms fire but, with great bravery, he worked his way a quarter mile along the ridge, attacking hostile soldiers in their foxholes with his carbine and grenades. When he had completed his self-imposed mission against powerful German forces, he had destroyed 2 machinegun positions, killed 8 of the enemy and captured 18 prisoners, including 2 bazooka teams. Cpl. Beyer's intrepid action and unflinching determination to close with and destroy the enemy eliminated the German defense line and enabled his task force to gain its objective.

*BIANCHI, WILLIBALD C.

Rank and organization: First Lieutenant, U.S. Army, 45th Infantry, Philippine Scouts. Place and date: Near Bagac, Bataan Province, Philippine Islands, 3 February 1942. Entered service at: New Ulm, Minn. Birth: New Ulm, Minn. G.O. No.: 11, 5 March 1942. Citation: For conspicuous gallantry and intrepidity above and beyond the call of duty in action with the enemy on 3 February 1942, near Bagac, Province of Bataan, Philippine Islands. When the rifle platoon of another company was ordered to wipe out 2 strong enemy machinegun nests, 1st Lt. Bianchi voluntarily and of his own initiative, advanced with the platoon leading part of the men. When wounded early in the action by 2 bullets through the left hand, he did not stop for first aid but discarded his rifle and began firing a pistol. He located a machinegun nest and personally silenced it with grenades. When wounded the second time by 2 machinegun bullets through the chest muscles, 1st Lt. Bianchi climbed to the top of an American tank, manned its antiaircraft machinegun, and fired into strongly held enemy position until knocked completely off the tank by a third severe wound.

BIDDLE, MELVIN E.

Rank and organization: Private First Class, U.S. Army, Company B, 517th Parachute Infantry Regiment. Place and date: Near Soy, Belgium, 23-24 December 1944. Entered service at: Anderson, Ind. Birth: Daleville, Ind. G.O. No.. 95, 30 October 1945. Citation: He displayed conspicuous gallantry and intrepidity in action against the enemy near Soy, Belgium, on 23 and 24 December 1944. Serving as lead scout during an attack to relieve the enemy-encircled town of Hotton, he aggressively penetrated a densely wooded area, advanced 400 yards until he came within range of intense enemy rifle fire, and within 20 yards of enemy positions killed 3 snipers with unerring marksmanship. Courageously continuing his advance an additional 200 yards, he discovered a hostile machinegun position and dispatched its 2 occupants. He then located the approximate position of a well-concealed enemy machinegun nest, and crawling forward threw hand grenades which killed two Germans and fatally wounded a third. After signaling his company to advance, he entered a determined line of enemy defense, coolly and deliberately shifted his position, and shot 3 more enemy soldiers. Undaunted by enemy fire, he crawled within 20 yards of a machinegun nest, tossed his last hand grenade into the position, and after the explosion charged the emplacement firing his rifle. When night fell, he scouted enemy positions alone for several hours and returned with valuable information which enabled our attacking infantry and armor to knock out 2 enemy tanks. At daybreak he again led the advance and, when flanking elements were pinned down by enemy fire, without hesitation made his way toward a hostile machinegun position and from a distance of 50 yards killed the crew and 2 supporting riflemen. The remainder of the enemy, finding themselves without automatic weapon support, fled panic stricken. Pfc. Biddle's intrepid courage and superb daring during his 20-hour action enabled his battalion to break the enemy grasp on Hotton with a minimum of casualties.

*BIGELOW, ELMER CHARLES

Rank and organization: Watertender First Class, U.S. Naval Reserve. Born: 12 July 1920, Hebron, 111. Accredited to. Illinois. Citation: For conspicuous gallantry and intrepidity at the risk of his life above and beyond the call of duty while serving on board the U.S.S. Fletcher during action against enemy Japanese forces off Corregidor Island in the Philippines, 14 February 1945. Standing topside when an enemy shell struck the Fletcher, Bigelow, acting instantly as the deadly projectile exploded into fragments which penetrated the No. 1 gun magazine and set fire to several powder cases, picked up a pair of fire extinguishers and rushed below in a resolute attempt to quell the raging flames. Refusing to waste the precious time required to don rescue-breathing apparatus, he plunged through the blinding smoke billowing out of the magazine hatch and dropped into the blazing compartment. Despite the acrid, burning powder smoke which seared his lungs with every agonizing breath, he worked rapidly and with instinctive sureness and succeeded in quickly extinguishing the fires and in cooling the cases and bulkheads, thereby preventing further damage to the stricken ship.

Although he succumbed to his injuries on the following day, Bigelow, by his dauntless valor, unfaltering skill and prompt action in the critical emergency, had averted a magazine explosion which undoubtedly would have left his ship wallowing at the mercy of the furiously pounding Japanese guns on Corregidor, and his heroic spirit of self-sacrifice in the face of almost certain death enhanced and sustained the highest traditions of the U.S. Naval Service. He gallantly gave his life in the service of his country.

BJORKLUND, ARNOLD L.

Rank and organization: First Lieutenant, U.S. Army, 36th Infantry Division. Place and date: Near Altavilla, Italy, 13 September 1943. Entered service at: Seattle, Wash. Birth: Clinton, Wash. G.O. No.: 73, 6 September 1944. Citation: For conspicuous gallantry and intrepidity at the risk of life above and beyond the call of duty in action with the enemy near Altavilla, Italy, 13 September 1943. When his company attacked a German position on Hill 424, the first platoon, led by 1st Lt. Bjorklund, moved forward on the right flank to the slope of the hill where it was pinned down by a heavy concentration of machinegun and rifle fire. Ordering his men to give covering fire, with only 3 hand grenades, he crept and crawled forward to a German machinegun position located on a terrace along the forward slope. Approaching within a few yards of the position, and while continuously exposed to enemy fire, he hurled 1 grenade into the nest, destroyed the gun and killed 3 Germans. Discovering a second machinegun 20 yards to the right on a higher terrace, he moved under intense enemy fire to a point within a few yards and threw a second grenade into this position, destroying it and killing 2 more Germans. The first platoon was then able to advance 150 yards further up the slope to the crest of the hill, but was again stopped by the fire from a heavy enemy mortar on the reverse slope. 1st Lt. Bjorklund located the mortar and worked his way under little cover to within 10 yards of its position and threw his third grenade, destroying the mortar, killing 2 of the Germans, and forcing the remaining 3 to flee. His actions permitted the platoon to take its objective .

BLOCH, ORVILLE EMIL

Rank and organization: First Lieutenant, U.S. Army, Company E, 338th Infantry, 85th Infantry Division. Place and date: Near Firenzuola, Italy, 22 September 1944. Entered service at: Streeter, N. Dak. Birth: Big Falls, Wis. G.O. No.: 9, 10 February 1945. Citation: For conspicuous gallantry and intrepidity at risk of life above and beyond the call of duty. 1st Lt. Bloch undertook the task of wiping out 5 enemy machinegun nests that had held up the advance in that particular sector for 1 day. Gathering 3 volunteers from his platoon, the patrol snaked their way to a big rock, behind which a group of 3 buildings and 5 machinegun nests were located. Leaving the 3 men behind the rock, he attacked the first machinegun nest alone charging into furious automatic fire, kicking over the machinegun, and capturing the machinegun crew of 5. Pulling the pin from a grenade, he held it ready in his hand and dashed into the face of withering automatic fire toward this second enemy machinegun nest located at the corner of an adjacent building 15 yards distant. When within 20 feet of the machinegun he hurled the grenade, wounding the machinegunner, the other 2 members of the crew fleeing into a door of the house. Calling one of his volunteer group to accompany him, they advanced to the opposite end of the house, there contacting a machinegun crew of 5 running toward this house. 1st Lt Bloch and his men opened fire on the enemy crew, forcing them to abandon this machinegun and ammunition and flee into the same house. Without a moment's hesitation, 1st Lt. Bloch, unassisted, rushed through the door into a hail of small-arms fire, firing his carbine from the hip, and captured the 7 occupants, wounding 3 of them. 1st Lt. Bloch with his men then proceeded to a third house where they discovered an abandoned enemy machinegun and detected another enemy machinegun nest at the next corner of the building. The crew of 6 spotted 1st Lt. Bloch the instant he saw them. Without a moment's hesitation he dashed toward them. The enemy fired pistols wildly in his direction and vanished through a door of the house, 1st Lt. Bloch following them through the door, firing his carbine from the hip, wounding 2 of the enemy and capturing 6. Altogether 1st Lt. Bloch had single-handedly captured 19 prisoners, wounding 6 of them and eliminating a total of 5 enemy machinegun nests. His gallant and heroic actions saved his company many casualties and permitted them to continue the attack with new inspiration and vigor.

BOLDEN, PAUL L.

Rank and organization: Staff Sergeant, U.S. Army, Company 1, 120th Infantry, 30th Infantry Division. Place and date: Petit-Coo, Belgium, 23 December 1944. Entered service at: Madison, Ala. Birth: Hobbes Island, Iowa. G.O. No.: 73, 30 August 1945-. Citation: He voluntarily attacked a formidable enemy strong point in Petit-Coo, Belgium, on 23 December, 1944, when his company was pinned down by extremely heavy automatic and small-arms fire coming from a house 200 yards to the front. Mortar and tank artillery shells pounded the unit, when S/Sgt. Bolden and a comrade, on their own initiative, moved forward into a hail of bullets to eliminate the ever-increasing fire from the German position. Crawling ahead to close with what they knew was a powerfully armed, vastly superior force, the pair reached the house and took up assault positions, S/Sgt. Bolden under a window, his comrade across the street where he could deliver covering fire. In rapid succession, S/Sgt. Bolden hurled a fragmentation grenade and a white phosphorous grenade into the building; and then, fully realizing that he faced tremendous odds, rushed to the door, threw it open and fired into 35 SS troopers who were trying to reorganize themselves after the havoc wrought by the grenades. Twenty Germans died under fire of his submachinegun before he was struck in the shoulder, chest, and stomach by part of a burst which killed his comrade across the street. He withdrew from the house, waiting for the surviving Germans to come out and surrender. When none appeared in the doorway, he summoned his ebbing strength, overcame the extreme pain he suffered and boldly walked back into the house, firing as he went. He had killed the remaining 15 enemy soldiers when his ammunition ran out. S/Sgt. Bolden's heroic advance against great odds, his fearless assault, and his magnificent display of courage in reentering the building where he had been severely wounded cleared the path for his company and insured the success of its mission.

BOLTON, CECIL H.

Rank and organization: First Lieutenant, U.S. Army, Company E, 413th Infantry, 104th Infantry Division. Place and date: Mark River, Holland, 2 November 1944. Entered service at: Huntsville, Ala. Birth: Crawfordsville, Fla. G.O. No.: 74, 1 September 1945. Citation: As leader of the weapons platoon of Company E, 413th Infantry, on the night of 2 November 1944, he fought gallantly in a pitched battle which followed the crossing of the Mark River in Holland. When 2 machineguns pinned down his company, he tried to eliminate, with mortar fire, their grazing fire which was inflicting serious casualties and preventing the company's advance from an area rocked by artillery shelling. In the moonlight it was impossible for him to locate accurately the enemy's camouflaged positions; but he continued to direct fire until wounded severely in the legs and rendered unconscious by a German shell. When he recovered consciousness he instructed his unit and then crawled to the forward rifle platoon positions. Taking a two-man bazooka team on his voluntary mission, he advanced chest deep in chilling water along a canal toward 1 enemy machinegun. While the bazooka team covered him, he approached alone to within 15 yards of the hostile emplacement in a house. He charged the remaining distance and killed the 2 gunners with hand grenades. Returning to his men he led them through intense fire over open ground to assault the second German machinegun. An enemy sniper who tried to block the way was dispatched, and the trio pressed on. When discovered by the machinegun crew and subjected to direct fire, 1st Lt. Bolton killed 1 of the 3 gunners with carbine fire, and his 2 comrades shot the others. Continuing to disregard his wounds, he led the bazooka team toward an 88-mm. artillery piece which was having telling effect on the American ranks, and approached once more through icy canal water until he could dimly make out the gun's silhouette. Under his fire direction, the two soldiers knocked out the enemy weapon with rockets. On the way back to his own lines he was again wounded. To prevent his men being longer subjected to deadly fire, he refused aid and ordered them back to safety, painfully crawling after them until he reached his lines, where he collapsed. 1st Lt. Bolton's heroic assaults in the face of vicious fire, his inspiring leadership, and continued aggressiveness even through suffering from serious wounds, contributed in large measure to overcoming strong enemy resistance and made it possible for his battalion to reach its objective.

BONG, RICHARD I. (Air Mission)

Rank and organization: Major, U.S. Army Air Corps. Place and date: Over Borneo and Leyte, 10 October to 15 November 1944. Entered service at: Poplar, Wis. Birth: Poplar, Wis. G.O. No.: 90, 8 December 1944. Citation: For conspicuous gallantry and intrepidity in action above and beyond the call of duty in the Southwest Pacific area from 10 October to 15 November 1944. Though assigned to duty as gunnery instructor and neither required nor expected to perform combat duty, Maj. Bong voluntarily and at his own urgent request engaged in repeated combat missions, including unusually hazardous sorties over Balikpapan, Borneo, and in the Leyte area of the Philippines. His aggressiveness and daring resulted in his shooting down 8 enemy airplanes during this period.

*BONNYMAN, ALEXANDER, JR.

Rank and organization: First Lieutenant, U.S. Marine Corps Reserves. Born: 2 May 1910, Atlanta, Ga. Accredited to: New Mexico. Citation: For conspicuous gallantry and intrepidity at the risk of his life above and beyond the call of duty as Executive Officer of the 2d Battalion Shore Party, 8th Marines, 2d Marine Division, during the assault against enemy Japanese-held Tarawa in the Gilbert Islands, 20-22 November 1943. Acting on his own initiative when assault troops were pinned down at the far end of Betio Pier by the overwhelming fire of Japanese shore batteries, 1st Lt. Bonnyman repeatedly defied the blasting fury of the enemy bombardment to organize and lead the besieged men over the long, open pier to the beach and then, voluntarily obtaining flame throwers and demolitions, organized his pioneer shore party into assault demolitionists and directed the blowing of several hostile installations before the close of D-day. Determined to effect an opening in the enemy's strongly organized defense line the following day, he voluntarily crawled approximately 40 yards forward of our lines and placed demolitions in the entrance of a large Japanese emplacement as the initial move in his planned attack against the heavily garrisoned, bombproof installation which was stubbornly resisting despite the destruction early in the action of a large number of Japanese who had been inflicting heavy casualties on our forces and holding up our advance. Withdrawing only to replenish his ammunition, he led his men in a renewed assault, fearlessly exposing himself to the merciless slash of hostile fire as he stormed the formidable bastion, directed the placement of demolition charges in both entrances and seized the top of the bombproof position, flushing more than 100 of the enemy who were instantly cut down, and effecting the annihilation of approximately 150 troops inside the emplacement. Assailed by additional Japanese after he had gained his objective, he made a heroic stand on the edge of the structure, defending his strategic position with indomitable determination in the face of the desperate charge and killing 3 of the enemy before he fell, mortally wounded. By his dauntless fighting spirit, unrelenting aggressiveness and forceful leadership throughout 3 days of unremitting, violent battle, 1st Lt. Bonnyman had inspired his men to heroic effort, enabling them to beat off the counterattack and break the back of hostile resistance in that sector for an immediate gain of 400 yards with no further casualties to our forces in this zone. He gallantly gave his life for his country.

*BOOKER, ROBERT D.

Rank and organization: Private, U.S. Army, 34th Infantry Division. Place and date: Near Fondouk, Tunisia, 9 April 1943. Entered service at: Callaway, Nebr. Born: 11 July 1920, Callaway, Nebr. G.O. No.: 34, 25 April 1944. Citation: For conspicuous gallantry and intrepidity at risk of life above and beyond the call of duty in action. On 9 April 1943 in the vicinity of Fondouk, Tunisia, Pvt. Booker, while engaged in action against the enemy, carried a light machinegun and a box of ammunition over 200 yards of open ground. He continued to advance despite the fact that 2 enemy machineguns and several mortars were using him as an individual target. Although enemy artillery also began to register on him, upon reaching his objective he immediately commenced firing. After being wounded he silenced 1 enemy machinegun and was beginning to fire at the other when he received a second mortal wound. With his last remaining strength he encouraged the members of his squad and directed their fire. Pvt. Booker acted without regard for his own safety. His initiative and courage against insurmountable odds are an example of the highest standard of self-sacrifice and fidelity to duty.

*BORDELON, WILLIAM JAMES

Rank and organization: Staff Sergeant, U.S. Marine Corps. Born: 25 December 1920, San Antonio, Tex. Accredited to: Texas. Citation: For valorous and gallant conduct above and beyond the call of duty as a member of an assault engineer platoon of the 1st Battalion, 18th

Marines, tactically attached to the 2d Marine Division, in action against the Japanese-held atoll of Tarawa in the Gilbert Islands on 20 November 1943. Landing in the assault waves under withering enemy fire which killed all but 4 of the men in his tractor, S/Sgt. Bordelon hurriedly made demolition charges and personally put 2 pillboxes out of action. Hit by enemy machinegun fire just as a charge exploded in his hand while assaulting a third position, he courageously remained in action and, although out of demolition, provided himself with a rifle and furnished fire coverage for a group of men scaling the seawall. Disregarding his own serious condition, he unhesitatingly went to the aid of one of his demolition men, wounded and calling for help in the water, rescuing this man and another who had been hit by enemy fire while attempting to make the rescue. Still refusing first aid for himself, he again made up demolition charges and single-handedly assaulted a fourth Japanese machinegun position but was instantly killed when caught in a final burst of fire from the enemy. S/Sgt. Bordelon's great personal valor during a critical phase of securing the limited beachhead was a contributing factor in the ultimate occupation of the island, and his heroic determination throughout 3 days of violent battle reflects the highest credit upon the U.S. Naval Service. He gallantly gave his life for his country.

*BOYCE, GEORGE W. G., JR.

Rank and organization: Second Lieutenant, U.S. Army, 112th Cavalry Regimental Combat Team. Place and date. Near Afua, New Guinea, 23 July 1944. Entered service at: Town of Cornwall, Orange County, N.Y. Birth: New York City, N.Y. G.O. No.: 25, 7 April 1945. Citation: For conspicuous gallantry and intrepidity at risk of his life above and beyond the call of duty near Afua, New Guinea, on 23 July 1944. 2d Lt. Boyce's troop, having been ordered to the relief of another unit surrounded by superior enemy forces, moved out, and upon gaining contact with the enemy, the two leading platoons deployed and built up a firing line. 2d

Lt. Boyce was ordered to attack with his platoon and make the main effort on the right of the troop. He launched his attack but after a short advance encountered such intense rifle, machinegun, and mortar fire that the forward movement of his platoon was temporarily halted. A shallow depression offered a route of advance and he worked his squad up this avenue of approach in order to close with the enemy. He was promptly met by a volley of hand grenades, 1 falling between himself and the men immediately following. Realizing at once that the explosion would kill or wound several of his men, he promptly threw himself upon the grenade and smothered the blast with his own body. By thus deliberately sacrificing his life to save those of his men, this officer exemplified the highest traditions of the U.S. Armed Forces.

BOYINGTON, GREGORY

Rank and organization: Major, U.S. Marine Corps Reserve, Marine Squadron 214. Place and date: Central Solomons area, from 12 September 1943 to 3 January 1944. Entered service at: Washington. Born: 4 December 1912, Coeur D'Alene, Idaho. Other Navy award: Navy Cross. Citation: For extraordinary heroism and valiant devotion to duty as commanding officer of Marine Fighting Squadron 214 in action against enemy Japanese forces in the Central Solomons area from 12 September 1943 to 3 January 1944. Consistently outnumbered throughout successive hazardous flights over heavily defended hostile territory, Maj. Boyington struck at the enemy with daring and courageous persistence, leading his squadron into combat with devastating results to Japanese shipping, shore installations, and aerial forces. Resolute in his efforts to inflict crippling damage on the enemy, Maj. Boyington led a formation of 24 fighters over Kahili on 17 October and, persistently circling the airdrome where 60 hostile aircraft were grounded, boldly challenged the Japanese to send up planes. Under his brilliant command, our fighters shot down 20 enemy craft in the ensuing action without the loss of a single ship. A superb airman and determined fighter against overwhelming odds, Maj. Boyington personally destroyed 26 of the many Japanese planes shot down by his squadron and, by his forceful leadership, developed the combat readiness in his command which was a distinctive factor in the Allied aerial achievements in this vitally strategic area.

BRILES, HERSCHEL F.

Rank and organization: Staff Sergeant, U.S. Army, Co. C, 899th Tank Destroyer Battalion. Place and date: Near Scherpenseel, Germany, 20 November 1944. Entered service at: Fort Des Moines, Iowa. Birth: Colfax, Iowa. G.O. No.: 77, 10 September 1945. Citation: He was leading a platoon of destroyers across an exposed slope near Scherpenseel, Germany, on 20 November 1944, when they came under heavy enemy artillery fire. A direct hit was scored on 1 of the vehicles, killing 1 man, seriously wounding 2 others, and setting the destroyer afire. With a comrade, S/Sgt. Briles left the cover of his own armor and raced across ground raked by artillery and small-arms fire to the rescue of the men in the shattered destroyer. Without hesitation, he lowered himself into the burning turret, removed the wounded and then extinguished the fire. From a position he assumed the next morning, he observed hostile infantrymen advancing. With his machinegun, he poured such deadly fire into the enemy ranks that an entire pocket of 55 Germans surrendered, clearing the way for a junction between American units which had been held up for 2 days. Later that day, when another of his destroyers was hit by a concealed enemy tank, he again left protection to give assistance. With the help of another soldier, he evacuated two wounded under heavy fire and, returning to the burning vehicle, braved death from exploding ammunition to put out the flames. By his heroic initiative and complete disregard for personal safety, S/Sgt. Briles was largely responsible for causing heavy enemy casualties, forcing the surrender of 55 Germans, making possible the salvage of our vehicles, and saving the lives of wounded comrades.

BRITT, MAURICE L.

Rank and organization: Captain (then Lieutenant), U.S. Army, 3d Infantry Division. Place and date: North of Mignano, Italy, 10 November 1943. Entered service at: Lonoke, Ark. Born: 29 June 1919, Carlisle, Ark. G.O. No.: 23, 24 March 1944. Citation: For conspicuous gallantry and intrepidity at the risk of his life above and beyond the call of duty. Disdaining enemy hand grenades and close-range machine pistol, machinegun, and rifle, Lt. Britt inspired and led a handful of his men in repelling a bitter counterattack by approximately 100 Germans against his company positions north of Mignano, Italy, the morning of 10 November 1943. During the intense fire fight, Lt. Britt's canteen and field glasses were shattered; a bullet pierced his side; his chest, face, and hands were covered with grenade wounds. Despite his wounds, for which he refused to accept medical attention until ordered to do so by his battalion commander following the battle, he personally killed 5 and wounded an unknown number of Germans, wiped out one enemy machinegun crew, fired 5 clips of carbine and an undetermined amount of M1 rifle ammunition, and threw 32 fragmentation grenades. His bold, aggressive actions, utterly disregarding superior enemy numbers, resulted in capture of 4 Germans, 2 of them wounded, and enabled several captured Americans to escape. Lt. Britt's undaunted courage and prowess in arms were largely responsible for repulsing a German counterattack which, if successful, would have isolated his battalion and destroyed his company.

*BROSTROM, LEONARD C.

Rank and organization: Private First Class, U.S. Army, Company F, 17th Infantry, 7th Infantry Division. Place and date: Near Dagami, Leyte, Philippine Islands, 28 October 1944. Entered service at: Preston, Idaho. Birth: Preston, Idaho. G.O. No.: 104, 15 November 1945. Citation: He was a rifleman with an assault platoon which ran into powerful resistance near Dagami, Leyte, Philippine Islands, on 28 October 1944. From pillboxes, trenches, and spider holes, so well camouflaged that they could be detected at no more than 20 yards, the enemy poured machinegun and rifle fire, causing severe casualties in the platoon. Realizing that a key pillbox in the center of the strong point would have to be knocked out if the company were to advance, Pfc. Bostrom, without orders and completely ignoring his own safety, ran forward to attack the pillbox with grenades. He immediately became the prime target for all the riflemen in the area, as he rushed to the rear of the pillbox and tossed grenades through the entrance. Six enemy soldiers left a trench in a bayonet charge against the heroic American, but he killed 1 and drove the others off with rifle fire. As he threw more grenades from his completely exposed position he was wounded several times in the abdomen and knocked to the ground. Although suffering intense pain and rapidly weakening from loss of blood, he slowly rose to his feet and once more hurled his deadly missiles at the pillbox. As he collapsed, the enemy began fleeing from the fortification and were killed by riflemen of his platoon. Pfc. Brostrom died while being carried from the battlefield, but his intrepidity and unhesitating willingness to sacrifice himself in a 1-man attack against overwhelming odds enabled his company to reorganize against attack, and annihilate the entire enemy position.

BROWN, BOBBIE E.

Rank and organization: Captain, U S. Army, Company C, 18th Infantry, 1st Infantry Division. Place and date: Crucifix Hill, Aachen, Germany, 8 October 1944. Entered service at: Atlanta, Ga. Born: 2 September 1903, Dublin, Ga. G.O. No.: 74, 1 September 1945. Citation: He commanded Company C, 18th Infantry Regiment, on 8 October 1944, when it, with the Ranger Platoon of the 1st Battalion, attacked Crucifix Hill, a key point in the enemy's defense of Aachen, Germany. As the leading rifle platoon assaulted the first of many pillboxes studding the rising ground, heavy fire from a flanking emplacement raked it. An intense artillery barrage fell on the American troops which had been pinned down in an exposed position. Seeing that the pillboxes must be neutralized to prevent the slaughter of his men, Capt. Brown obtained a pole charge and started forward alone toward the first pillbox, about 100 yards away. Hugging the ground while enemy bullets whipped around him, he crawled and then ran toward the aperture of the fortification, rammed his explosive inside and jumped back as the pillbox and its occupants were blown up. He rejoined the assault platoon, secured another pole charge, and led the way toward the next pillbox under continuous artillery mortar, automatic, and small-arms fire. He again ran forward and placed his charge in the enemy fortification, knocking it out. He then found that fire from a third pillbox was pinning down his company; so he returned to his men, secured another charge, and began to creep and crawl toward the hostile emplacement. With heroic bravery he disregarded opposing fire and worked ahead in the face of bullets streaming from the pillbox. Finally reaching his objective, he stood up and inserted his explosive, silencing the enemy. He was wounded by a mortar shell but refused medical attention and, despite heavy hostile fire, moved swiftly among his troops exhorting and instructing them in subduing powerful opposition. Later, realizing the need for information of enemy activity beyond the hill, Capt. Brown went out alone to reconnoiter. He observed possible routes of enemy approach and several times deliberately drew enemy fire to locate gun emplacements. Twice more, on this self-imposed mission, he was wounded; but he succeeded in securing information which led to the destruction of several enemy guns and enabled his company to throw back 2 powerful counterattacks with heavy losses. Only when Company C's position was completely secure did he permit treatment of his 3 wounds. By his indomitable courage, fearless leadership, and outstanding skill as a soldier, Capt. Brown contributed in great measure to the taking of Crucifix Hill, a vital link in the American line encircling Aachen.

BULKELEY, JOHN DUNCAN

Rank and organization: Lieutenant Commander, Commander of Motor Torpedo Boat Squadron 3, U.S. Navy. Place and date: Philippine waters, 7 December 1941 to 10 April 1942. Entered service at: Texas. Born: 19 August 1911, New York, N.Y. Other awards: Navy Cross, Distinguished Service Cross, Silver Star, Legion of Merit. Citation: For extraordinary heroism, distinguished service, and conspicuous gallantry above and beyond the call of duty as commander of Motor Torpedo Boat Squadron 3, in Philippine waters during the period 7 December 1941 to 10 April 1942. The remarkable achievement of Lt. Comdr. Bulkeley's command in damaging or destroying a notable number of Japanese enemy planes, surface combatant and merchant ships, and in dispersing landing parties and land-based enemy forces during the 4 months and 8 days of operation without benefit of repairs, overhaul, or maintenance facilities for his squadron, is believed to be without precedent in this type of warfare. His dynamic forcefulness and daring in offensive action, his brilliantly planned and skillfully executed attacks, supplemented by a unique resourcefulness and ingenuity, characterize him as an outstanding leader of men and a gallant and intrepid seaman. These qualities coupled with a complete disregard for his own personal safety reflect great credit upon him and the Naval Service .

BURKE, FRANK (also known as FRANCIS X. BURKE)

Rank and organization: First Lieutenant, U.S. Army, 15th Infantry, 3d Infantry Division. Place and date: Nuremberg, Germany, 17 April 1945. Entered service at: Jersey City, N.J. Born: 29 September 1918, New York, N.Y. G.O. No.: 4, 9 January 1946. Citation: He fought with extreme gallantry in the streets of war-torn Nuremberg, Germany, where the 1st Battalion, 15th Infantry, was engaged in rooting out fanatical defenders of the citadel of Nazism. As battalion transportation officer he had gone forward to select a motor-pool site, when, in a desire to perform more than his assigned duties and participate in the fight, he advanced beyond the lines of the forward riflemen. Detecting a group of about 10 Germans making preparations for a local counterattack, he rushed back to a nearby American company, secured a light machinegun with ammunition, and daringly opened fire on this superior force, which deployed and returned his fire with machine pistols, rifles, and rocket launchers. From another angle a German machinegun tried to blast him from his emplacement, but 1st Lt. Burke killed this guncrew and drove off the survivors of the unit he had originally attacked. Giving his next attention to enemy infantrymen in ruined buildings, he picked up a rifle dashed more than 100 yards through intense fire and engaged the Germans from behind an abandoned tank. A sniper nearly hit him from a cellar only 20 yards away, but he dispatched this adversary by running directly to the basement window, firing a full clip into it and then plunging through the darkened aperture to complete the job. He withdrew from the fight only long enough to replace his jammed rifle and secure grenades, then re-engaged the Germans. Finding his shots ineffective, he pulled the pins from 2 grenades, and, holding 1 in each hand, rushed the enemy-held building, hurling his missiles just as the enemy threw a potato masher grenade at him. In the triple explosion the Germans were wiped out and 1st Lt. Burke was dazed; but he emerged from the shower of debris that engulfed him, recovered his rifle, and went on to kill 3 more Germans and meet the charge of a machine pistolman, whom he cut down with 3 calmly delivered shots. He then retired toward the American lines and there assisted a platoon in a raging, 30-minute fight against formidable armed hostile forces. This enemy group was repulsed, and the intrepid fighter moved to another friendly group which broke the power of a German unit armed with a 20-mm. gun in a fierce fire fight. In 4 hours of heroic action, 1st Lt. Burke single-handedly killed 11 and wounded 3 enemy soldiers and took a leading role in engagements in which an additional 29 enemy were killed or wounded. His extraordinary bravery and superb fighting skill were an inspiration to his comrades, and his entirely voluntary mission into extremely dangerous territory hastened the fall of Nuremberg, in his battalion's sector.

*BURR, ELMER J.

Rank and organization: First Sergeant, U.S. Army, Company 1, 127th Infantry, 32d Infantry Division. Place and date: Buna, New Guinea, 24 December 1942. Entered service at: Menasha, Wis. Birth: Neenah, Wis. G.O. No.: 66, 11 Oct. 1943. Citation: For conspicuous gallantry and intrepidity in action above and beyond the call of duty. During an attack near Buna, New Guinea, on 24 December 1942, 1st Sgt. Burr saw an enemy grenade strike near his company commander. Instantly and with heroic self-sacrifice he threw himself upon it, smothering the explosion with his body. 1st Sgt. Burr thus gave his life in saving that of his commander.

BURR, HERBERT H.

Rank and organization: Staff Sergeant, U.S. Army, Company C, 41st Tank Battalion, 11th Armored Division. Place and date: Near Dorrmoschel, Germany, 19 March 1945. Entered service at: Kansas City, Mo. Birth: St. Joseph, Mo. G.O. No.: 73, 30 August 1945. Citation: He displayed conspicuous gallantry during action when the tank in which he was bow gunner was hit by an enemy rocket, which severely wounded the platoon sergeant and forced the remainder of the crew to abandon the vehicle. Deafened, but otherwise unhurt, S/Sgt. Burr immediately climbed into the driver's seat and continued on the mission of entering the town to reconnoiter road conditions. As he rounded a turn he encountered an 88-mm. antitank gun at pointblank range. Realizing that he had no crew, no one to man the tank's guns, he heroically chose to disregard his personal safety in a direct charge on the German weapon. At considerable speed he headed straight for the loaded gun, which was fully manned by enemy troops who had only to pull the lanyard to send a shell into his vehicle. So unexpected and daring was his assault that he was able to drive his tank completely over the gun, demolishing it and causing its crew to flee in confusion. He then skillfully sideswiped a large truck, overturned it, and wheeling his lumbering vehicle, returned to his company. When medical personnel who had been summoned to treat the wounded sergeant could not locate him, the valiant soldier ran through a hail of sniper fire to direct them to his stricken comrade. The bold, fearless determination of S/Sgt. Burr, his skill and courageous devotion to duty, resulted in the completion of his mission in the face of seemingly impossible odds.

BURT, JAMES M.

Rank and organization: Captain, U.S. Army, Company B, 66th Armored Regiment, 2d Armored Division. Place and date: Near Wurselen, Germany, 13 October 1944. Entered service at: Lee, Mass. Birth: Hinsdale, Mass. G.O. No.: 95, 30 October 1945. Citation: Capt. James M. Burt was in command of Company B, 66th Armored Regiment on the western outskirts of Wurselen, Germany, on 13 October 1944, when his organization participated in a coordinated infantry-tank attack destined to isolate the large German garrison which was tenaciously defending the city of Aachen. In the first day's action, when infantrymen ran into murderous small-arms and mortar fire, Capt. Burt dismounted from his tank about 200 yards to the rear and moved forward on foot beyond the infantry positions, where, as the enemy concentrated a tremendous volume of fire upon him, he calmly motioned his tanks into good firing positions. As our attack gained momentum, he climbed aboard his tank and directed the action from the rear deck, exposed to hostile volleys which finally wounded him painfully in the face and neck. He maintained his dangerous post despite pointblank self-propelled gunfire until friendly artillery knocked out these enemy weapons, and then proceeded to the advanced infantry scouts' positions to deploy his tanks for the defense of the gains which had been made.

The next day, when the enemy counterattacked, he left cover and went 75 yards through heavy fire to assist the infantry battalion commander who was seriously wounded. For the next 8 days, through rainy, miserable weather and under constant, heavy shelling, Capt. Burt held the combined forces together, dominating and controlling the critical situation through the sheer force of his heroic example. To direct artillery fire, on 15 October, he took his tank 300 yards into the enemy lines, where he dismounted and remained for 1 hour giving accurate data to friendly gunners. Twice more that day he went into enemy territory under deadly fire on reconnaissance. In succeeding days he never faltered in his determination to defeat the strong German forces opposing him. Twice the tank in which he was riding was knocked out by enemy action, and each time he climbed aboard another vehicle and continued the fight. He took great risks to rescue wounded comrades and inflicted prodigious destruction on enemy personnel and materiel even though suffering from the wounds he received in the battle's opening phase. Capt. Burt's intrepidity and disregard of personal safety were so complete that his own men and the infantry who attached themselves to him were inspired to overcome the wretched and extremely hazardous conditions which accompanied one of the most bitter local actions of the war. The victory achieved closed the Aachen gap.

BUSH, RICHARD EARL

Rank and organization: Corporal, U.S. Marine Corps Reserve, 1st Battalion, 4th Marines, 6th Marine Division. Place and date: Mount Yaetake on Okinawa, Ryukyu Islands, 16 April 1945. Entered service at: Kentucky. Born: 23 December 1923, Glasgow, Ky. Citation: For conspicuous gallantry and intrepidity at the risk of his life above and beyond the call of duty as a squad leader serving with the 1st Battalion, 4th Marines, 6th Marine Division, in action against enemy Japanese forces, during the final assault against Mount Yaetake on Okinawa, Ryukyu Islands, 16 April 1945. Rallying his men forward with indomitable determination, Cpl. Bush boldly defied the slashing fury of concentrated Japanese artillery fire pouring down from the gun-studded mountain fortress to lead his squad up the face of the rocky precipice, sweep over the ridge, and drive the defending troops from their deeply entrenched position. With his unit, the first to break through to the inner defense of Mount Yaetake, he fought relentlessly in the forefront of the action until seriously wounded and evacuated with others under protecting rocks. Although prostrate under medical treatment when a Japanese hand grenade landed in the midst of the group, Cpl. Bush, alert and courageous in extremity as in battle, unhesitatingly pulled the deadly missile to himself and absorbed the shattering violence of the exploding charge in his body, thereby saving his fellow marines from severe injury or death despite the certain peril to his own life. By his valiant leadership and aggressive tactics in the face of savage opposition, Cpl. Bush contributed materially to the success of the sustained drive toward the conquest of this fiercely defended outpost of the Japanese Empire. His constant concern for the welfare of his men, his resolute spirit of self-sacrifice, and his unwavering devotion to duty throughout the bitter conflict enhance and sustain the highest traditions of the U.S. Naval Service.

BUSH, ROBERT EUGENE

Rank and organization: Hospital Apprentice First Class, U.S. Naval Reserve, serving as Medical Corpsman with a rifle company, 2d Battalion, 5th Marines, 1st Marine Division. Place and date: Okinawa Jima, Ryukyu Islands, 2 May 1945. Entered service at: Washington. Born: 4 October 1926, Tacoma, Wash. Citation: For conspicuous gallantry and intrepidity at the risk of his life above and beyond the call of duty while serving as Medical Corpsman with a rifle company, in action against enemy Japanese forces on Okinawa Jima, Ryukyu Islands, 2 May 1945. Fearlessly braving the fury of artillery, mortar, and machinegun fire from strongly entrenched hostile positions, Bush constantly and unhesitatingly moved from 1 casualty to another to attend the wounded falling under the enemy's murderous barrages. As the attack passed over a ridge top, Bush was advancing to administer blood plasma to a marine officer lying wounded on the skyline when the Japanese launched a savage counterattack. In this perilously exposed position, he resolutely maintained the flow of life-giving plasma. With the bottle held high in 1 hand, Bush drew his pistol with the other and fired into the enemy's ranks until his ammunition was expended. Quickly seizing a discarded carbine, he trained his fire on the Japanese charging pointblank over the hill, accounting for 6 of the enemy despite his own serious wounds and the loss of 1 eye suffered during his desperate battle in defense of the helpless man. With the hostile force finally routed, he calmly disregarded his own critical condition to complete his mission, valiantly refusing medical treatment for himself until his officer patient had been evacuated, and collapsing only after attempting to walk to the battle aid station. His daring initiative, great personal valor, and heroic spirit of self-sacrifice in service of others reflect great credit upon Bush and enhance the finest traditions of the U.S. Naval Service.

*BUTTS, JOHN E.

Rank and organization: Second Lieutenant, U.S. Army, Co. E, 60th Infantry, 9th Infantry Division. Place and date: Normandy, France, 14, 16, and 23 June 1944. Entered service at: Buffalo, N.Y. Birth: Medina, N.Y. G.O. No.: 58, 19 July 1945. Citation: Heroically led his platoon against the enemy in Normandy, France, on 14, 16, and 23 June 1944. Although painfully wounded on the 14th near Orglandes and again on the 16th while spearheading an attack to establish a bridgehead across the Douve River, he refused medical aid and remained with his platoon. A week later, near Flottemanville Hague, he led an assault on a tactically important and stubbornly defended hill studded with tanks, antitank guns, pillboxes, and machinegun emplacements, and protected by concentrated artillery and mortar fire. As the attack was launched, 2d Lt.

Butts, at the head of his platoon, was critically wounded by German machinegun fire. Although weakened by his injuries, he rallied his men and directed 1 squad to make a flanking movement while he alone made a frontal assault to draw the hostile fire upon himself. Once more he was struck, but by grim determination and sheer courage continued to crawl ahead. When within 10 yards of his objective, he was killed by direct fire. By his superb courage, unflinching valor and inspiring actions, 2d Lt. Butts enabled his platoon to take a formidable strong point and contributed greatly to the success of his battalion's mission.

*CADDY, WILLIAM ROBERT

Rank and organization: Private First Class, U.S. Marine Corps Reserve. Born: 8 August 1925, Quincy, Mass. Accredited to: Massachusetts. Citation: For conspicuous gallantry and intrepidity at the risk of his life above and beyond the call of duty while serving as a rifleman with Company 1, 3d Battalion, 26th Marines, 5th Marine Division, in action against enemy Japanese forces during the seizure of Iwo Jima in the Volcano Islands, 3 March 1945. Consistently aggressive, Pfc. Caddy boldly defied shattering Japanese machinegun and small arms fire to move forward with his platoon leader and another marine during the determined advance of his company through an isolated sector and, gaining the comparative safety of a shell hole, took temporary cover with his comrades. Immediately pinned down by deadly sniper fire from a well-concealed position, he made several unsuccessful attempts to again move forward and then, joined by his platoon leader, engaged the enemy in a fierce exchange of hand grenades until a Japanese grenade fell beyond reach in the shell hole. Fearlessly disregarding all personal danger, Pfc. Caddy instantly dived on the deadly missile, absorbing the exploding charge in his own body and protecting the others from serious injury. Stouthearted and indomitable, he unhesitatingly yielded his own life that his fellow marines might carry on the relentless battle against a fanatic enemy. His dauntless courage and valiant spirit of self-sacrifice in the face of certain death reflect the highest credit upon Pfc. Caddy and upon the U.S. Naval Service. He gallantly gave his life for his comrades.

*CALLAGHAN, DANIEL JUDSON

Rank and organization: Rear Admiral, U.S. Navy. Born: 26 July 1892, San Francisco, Calif. Appointed from: California. Entered service at: Oakland, Calif. Other Navy award: Distinguished Service Medal. Citation: For extraordinary heroism and conspicuous intrepidity above and beyond the call of duty during action against enemy Japanese forces off Savo Island on the night of 12-13 November 1942. Although out-balanced in strength and numbers by a desperate and determined enemy, Rear Adm. Callaghan, with ingenious tactical skill and superb coordination of the units under his command, led his forces into battle against tremendous odds, thereby contributing decisively to the rout of a powerful invasion fleet, and to the consequent frustration of a formidable Japanese offensive. While faithfully directing close-range operations in the face of furious bombardment by superior enemy fire power, he was killed on the bridge of his flagship. His courageous initiative, inspiring leadership, and judicious foresight in a crisis of grave responsibility were in keeping with the finest traditions of the U.S. Naval Service. He gallantly gave his life in the defense of his country.

CALUGAS, JOSE

Rank and organization: Sergeant, U.S. Army, Battery B, 88th Field Artillery, Philippine Scouts. Place and date: At Culis, Bataan Province, Philippine Islands, 16 January 1942. Entered service at: Fort Stotsenburg, Philippine Islands. Born: 29 December 1907, Barrio Tagsing, Leon, %Iloilo, Philippine Islands. G.O. No.: 10, 24 February 1942. Citation: The action for which the award was made took place near Culis, Bataan Province, Philippine Islands, on 16 January 1942. A battery gun position was bombed and shelled by the enemy until 1 gun was put out of commission and all the cannoneers were killed or wounded. Sgt. Calugas, a mess sergeant of another battery, voluntarily and without orders ran 1,000 yards across the shell-swept area to the gun position. There he organized a volunteer squad which placed the gun back in commission and fired effectively against the enemy, although the position remained under constant and heavy Japanese artillery fire.

*CANNON, GEORGE HAM

Rank and organization: First Lieutenant, U.S. Marine Corps. Born: S November 1915, Webster Groves, Mo. Entered service at: Michigan. Citation: For distinguished conduct in the line of his profession, extraordinary courage and disregard of his own condition during the bombardment of Sand Island, Midway Islands, by Japanese forces on 7 December 1941. 1st Lt. Cannon, Battery Commander of Battery H, 6th Defense Battalion, Fleet Marine Force, U.S. Marine Corps, was at his command post when he was mortally wounded by enemy shellfire. He refused to be evacuated from his post until after his men who had been wounded by the same shell were evacuated, and directed the reorganization of his command post until forcibly removed. As a result of his utter disregard of his own condition he died from loss of blood.

*CAREY, ALVIN P.

Rank and organization: Staff Sergeant, U.S. Army, 38th Infantry, 2-t Infantry Division. Place and date: Near Plougastel, Brittany, France, 23 August 1944. Entered service at: Laughlinstown, Pa. Born: 16 August 1916, Lycippus, Pa. G.O. No.: 37, 11 May 1945. Citation: For conspicuous gallantry and intrepidity at the risk of his life, above and beyond the call of duty, on 23 August 1944. S/Sgt. Carey, leader of a machinegun section, was advancing with his company in the attack on the strongly held enemy hill 154, near Plougastel, Brittany, France. The advance was held up when the attacking units were pinned down by intense enemy machinegun fire from a pillbox 200 yards up the hill. From his position covering the right flank, S/Sgt. Carey displaced his guns to an advanced position and then, upon his own initiative, armed himself with as many hand grenades as he could carry and without regard for his personal safety started alone up the hill toward the pillbox. Crawling forward under its withering fire, he proceeded 150 yards when he met a German rifleman whom he killed with his carbine. Continuing his steady forward movement until he reached grenade-throwing distance, he hurled his grenades at the pillbox opening in the face of intense enemy fire which wounded him mortally. Undaunted, he gathered his strength and continued his grenade attack until one entered and exploded within the pillbox, killing the occupants and putting their guns out of action. Inspired by S/Sgt. Carey's heroic act, the riflemen quickly occupied the position and overpowered the remaining enemy resistance in the vicinity.

*CAREY, CHARLES F., JR.

Rank and organization: Technical Sergeant, U.S. Army, 379th Infantry, 100th Infantry Division. Place and date: Rimling, France, 8-9 January 1945. Entered service at: Cheyenne, Wyo. Birth: Canadian, Okla. G.O. No.: 53, July 1945. Citation: He was in command of an antitank platoon when about 200 enemy infantrymen and 12 tanks attacked his battalion, overrunning part of its position. After losing his guns, T/Sgt. Carey, acting entirely on his own initiative, organized a patrol and rescued 2 of his squads from a threatened sector, evacuating those who had been wounded. He organized a second patrol and advanced against an enemy-held house from which vicious fire issued, preventing the free movement of our troops. Covered by fire from his patrol, he approached the house, killed 2 snipers with his rifle, and threw a grenade in the door. He entered alone and a few minutes later emerged with 16 prisoners. Acting on information he furnished, the American forces were able to capture an additional 41 Germans in adjacent houses. He assembled another patrol, and, under covering fire, moved to within a few yards of an enemy tank and damaged it with a rocket. As the crew attempted to leave their burning vehicle, he calmly shot them with his rifle, killing 3 and wounding a fourth. Early in the morning of 9 January, German infantry moved into the western part of the town and encircled a house in which T/Sgt. Carey had previously posted a squad. Four of the group escaped to the attic. By maneuvering an old staircase against the building, T/Sgt. Carey was able to rescue these men. Later that day, when attempting to reach an outpost, he was struck down by sniper fire. The fearless and aggressive leadership of T/Sgt. Carey, his courage in the face of heavy fire from superior enemy forces, provided an inspiring example for his comrades and materially helped his battalion to withstand the German onslaught.

CARR, CHRIS (name legally changed from CHRISTOS H.

KARABERIS, under which name the medal was awarded)

Rank and organization: Sergeant, U.S. Army, Company L, 337th Infantry, 85th Infantry Division. Place and date: Near Guignola, Italy, 1-2 October 1944. Entered service at: Manchester, N.H. Birth: Manchester, N.H. G.O. No.: 97, 1 November 1945. Citation Leading a squad of Company L, he gallantly cleared the way for his company's approach along a ridge toward its objective, the Casoni di Remagna. When his platoon was pinned down by heavy fire from enemy mortars, machineguns, machine pistols, and rifles, he climbed in advance of his squad on a maneuver around the left flank to locate and eliminate the enemy gun positions. Undeterred by deadly fire that ricocheted off the barren rocky hillside, he crept to the rear of the first machinegun and charged, firing his submachinegun. In this surprise attack he captured 8 prisoners and turned them over to his squad before striking out alone for a second machinegun. Discovered in his advance and subjected to direct fire from the hostile weapon, he leaped to his feet and ran forward, weaving and crouching, pouring automatic fire into the emplacement that killed 4 of its defenders and forced the surrender of a lone survivor. He again moved forward through heavy fire to attack a third machinegun. When close to the emplacement, he closed with a nerve-shattering shout and burst of fire. Paralyzed by his whirlwind attack, all 4 gunners immediately surrendered. Once more advancing aggressively in the face of a thoroughly alerted enemy, he approached a point of high ground occupied by 2 machineguns which were firing on his company on the slope below. Charging the first of these weapons, he killed 4 of the crew and captured 3 more. The 6 defenders of the adjacent position, cowed by the savagery of his assault, immediately gave up. By his l-man attack, heroically and voluntarily undertaken in the face of tremendous risks, Sgt. Karaberis captured 5 enemy machinegun positions, killed 8 Germans, took 22 prisoners, cleared the ridge leading to his company's objective, and drove a deep wedge into the enemy line, making it possible for his battalion to occupy important, commanding ground.

*CARSWELL, HORACE S., JR. (Air Mission)

Rank and organization: Major, 308th Bombardment Group, U.S. Army Air Corps. Place and date: Over South China Sea, 26 October 1944. Entered service at: San Angelo, Tex. Birth: Fort Worth, Tex. G.O. No.: 14, 4 February 1946. Citation: He piloted a B-24 bomber in a one-plane strike against a Japanese convoy in the South China Sea on the night of 26 October 1944. Taking the enemy force of 12 ships escorted by at least 2 destroyers by surprise, he made 1 bombing run at 600 feet, scoring a near miss on 1 warship and escaping without drawing fire. He circled. and fully realizing that the convoy was thoroughly alerted and would meet his next attack with a barrage of antiaircraft fire, began a second low-level run which culminated in 2 direct hits on a large tanker. A hail of steel from Japanese guns, riddled the bomber, knocking out 2 engines, damaging a third, crippling the hydraulic system, puncturing 1 gasoline tank, ripping uncounted holes in the aircraft, and wounding the copilot; but by magnificent display of flying skill, Maj. Carswell controlled the plane's plunge toward the sea and carefully forced it into a halting climb in the direction of the China shore. On reaching land, where it would have been possible to abandon the staggering bomber, one of the crew discovered that his parachute had been ripped by flak and rendered useless; the pilot, hoping to cross mountainous terrain and reach a base. continued onward until the third engine failed. He ordered the crew to bail out while he struggled to maintain altitude. and, refusing to save himself, chose to remain with his comrade and attempt a crash landing. He died when the airplane struck a mountainside and burned. With consummate gallantry and intrepidity, Maj. Carswell gave his life in a supreme effort to save all members of his crew. His sacrifice. far beyond that required of him, was in keeping with the traditional bravery of America's war heroes.

CASAMENTO, ANTHONY

Rank and organization: Corporal, Company D, First Battalion, Fifth Marines, First Marine Division. Place and date: Guadalcanal, Solomon Islands. Entered service at: Brooklyn, New York. Date and place of birth: 16 November 1920, Brooklyn, New York. For conspicuous gallantry and intrepidity at the risk of his life above and beyond the call of duty while serving with Company D, 1st Battalion, 5th Marines, 1st Marine Division on Guadalcanal, British Solomon Islands, in action against the enemy Japanese forces on 1 November 1942. Serving as a leader of a machine gun section, Corporal Casamento directed his unit to advance along a ridge near the Matanikau River where they engaged the enemy. He positioned his section to provide covering fire for two flanking units and to provide direct support for the main force of his company which was behind him. During the course of this engagement, all members of his section were either killed or severely wounded and he himself suffered multiple, grievous wounds. Nonetheless, Corporal Casamento continued to provide critical supporting fire for the attack and in defense of his position. Following the loss of all effective personnel, he set up, loaded, and manned his unit's machine gun. tenaciously holding the enemy forces at bay. Corporal Casamento single-handedly engaged and destroyed one machine gun emplacement to his front and took under fire the other emplacement on the flank. Despite the heat and ferocity of the engagement, he continued to man his weapon and repeatedly repulsed multiple assaults by the enemy forces, thereby protecting the flanks of the adjoining companies and holding his position until the arrival of his main attacking force. Corporal Casamento's courageous fighting spirit, heroic conduct, and unwavering dedication to duty reflected great credit upon himself and were in keeping with the highest traditions of the Marine Corps and the United States Naval Service.

*CASTLE, FREDERICK W. (Air Mission)

Rank and organization: Brigadier General. Assistant Commander, 4th Bomber Wing, U.S. Army Air Corps. Place and date: Germany, 24 December 1944. Entered service at: Mountain Lake, N.J. Born: 14 October 1908, Manila P.I. G.O. No. 22, 28 February 1947. Citation: He was air commander and leader of more than 2,000 heavy bombers in a strike against German airfields on 24 December 1944. En route to the target, the failure of 1 engine forced him to relinquish his place at the head of the formation. In order not to endanger friendly troops on the ground below, he refused to jettison his bombs to gain speed maneuverability. His lagging, unescorted aircraft became the target of numerous enemy fighters which ripped the left wing with cannon shells. set the oxygen system afire, and wounded 2 members of the crew. Repeated attacks started fires in 2 engines, leaving the Flying Fortress in imminent danger of exploding. Realizing the hopelessness of the situation, the bail-out order was given. Without regard for his personal safety he gallantly remained alone at the controls to afford all other crewmembers an opportunity to escape. Still another attack exploded gasoline tanks in the right wing, and the bomber plunged earthward. carrying Gen. Castle to his death. His intrepidity and willing sacrifice of his life to save members of the crew were in keeping with the highest traditions of the military service.

CHAMBERS, JUSTICE M.

Rank and organization: Colonel. U.S. Marine Corps Reserve, 3rd Assault Battalion Landing Team. 25th Marines, 4th Marine Division. Place and date: On Iwo Jima, Volcano Islands. from 19 to 22 February 1945. Entered service at: Washington, D.C. Born: 2 February 1908, Huntington, W. Va. Citation: For conspicuous gallantry and intrepidity at the risk of his life above and beyond the call of duty as commanding officer of the 3d Assault Battalion Landing Team, 25th Marines, 4th Marine Division, in action against enemy Japanese forces on Iwo Jima, Volcano Islands, from 19 to 22 February 1945. Under a furious barrage of enemy machinegun and small-arms fire from the commanding cliffs on the right, Col. Chambers (then Lt. Col.) landed immediately after the initial assault waves of his battalion on D-day to find the momentum of the assault threatened by heavy casualties from withering Japanese artillery, mortar rocket, machinegun, and rifle fire. Exposed to relentless hostile fire, he coolly reorganized his battle-weary men, inspiring them to heroic efforts by his own valor and leading them in an attack on the critical, impregnable high ground from which the enemy was pouring an increasing volume of fire directly onto troops ashore as well as amphibious craft in succeeding waves. Constantly in the front lines encouraging his men to push forward against the enemy's savage resistance, Col. Chambers led the 8-hour battle to carry the flanking ridge top and reduce the enemy's fields of aimed fire, thus protecting the vital foothold gained. In constant defiance of hostile fire while reconnoitering the entire regimental combat team zone of action, he maintained contact with adjacent units and forwarded vital information to the regimental commander. His zealous fighting spirit undiminished despite terrific casualties and the loss of most of his key officers, he again reorganized his troops for renewed attack against the enemy's main line of resistance and was directing the fire of the rocket platoon when he fell, critically wounded. Evacuated under heavy Japanese fire, Col. Chambers, by forceful leadership, courage, and fortitude in the face of staggering odds, was directly instrumental in insuring the success of subsequent operations of the 5th Amphibious Corps on Iwo Jima, thereby sustaining and enhancing the finest traditions of the U.S. Naval Service.

*CHELI, RALPH (Air Mission)

Rank and organization: Major, U.S. Army Air Corps. Place and date: Near Wewak, New Guinea, 18 August 1943. Entered service at: Brooklyn, N.Y. Birth: San Francisco, Calif. G.O. No.: 72, 28 October 1943. Citation: For conspicuous gallantry and intrepidity above and beyond the call of duty in action with the enemy. While Maj. Cheli was leading his squadron in a dive to attack the heavily defended Dagua Airdrome, intercepting enemy aircraft centered their fire on his plane, causing it to burst into flames while still 2 miles from the objective. His speed would have enabled him to gain necessary altitude to parachute to safety, but this action would have resulted in his formation becoming disorganized and exposed to the enemy. Although a crash was inevitable, he courageously elected to continue leading the attack in his blazing plane. From a minimum altitude, the squadron made a devastating bombing and strafing attack on the target. The mission completed, Maj. Cheli instructed his wingman to lead the formation and crashed into the sea.

CHILDERS, ERNEST

Rank and organization: Second Lieutenant, U.S. Army, 45th Infantry Division. Place and date: At Oliveto, Italy, 22 September 1943. Entered service at: Tulsa, Okla. Birth: Broken Arrow, Okla. G.O. No.: 30, 8 April 1944. Citation: For conspicuous gallantry and intrepidity at risk of life above and beyond the call of duty in action on 22 September 1943, at

Oliveto, Italy. Although 2d Lt. Childers previously had just suffered a fractured instep he, with 8 enlisted men, advanced up a hill toward enemy machinegun nests. The group advanced to a rock wall overlooking a cornfield and 2d Lt. Childers ordered a base of fire laid across the field so that he could advance. When he was fired upon by 2 enemy snipers from a nearby house he killed both of them. He moved behind the machinegun nests and killed all occupants of the nearer one. He continued toward the second one and threw rocks into it. When the 2 occupants of the nest raised up, he shot 1. The other was killed by 1 of the 8 enlisted men. 2d Lt. Childers continued his advance toward a house farther up the hill, and single-handed, captured an enemy mortar observer. The exceptional leadership, initiative, calmness under fire, and conspicuous gallantry displayed by 2d Lt. Childers were an inspiration to his men.

CHOATE, CLYDE L.

Rank and organization: Staff Sergeant, U.S. Army, Company C, 601st Tank Destroyer Battalion. Place and date: Near Bruyeres, France, 25 October 1944. Entered service at: Anna, 111. Born: 28 June 1920, West Frankfurt, 111. G.O. No.: 75, 5 September 1945. Citation: He commanded a tank destroyer near Bruyeres, France, on 25 October 1944. Our infantry occupied a position on a wooded hill when, at dusk, an enemy Mark IV tank and a company of infantry attacked, threatening to overrun the American position and capture a command post 400 yards to the rear. S/Sgt. Choate's tank destroyer, the only weapon available to oppose the German armor, was set afire by 2 hits. Ordering his men to abandon the destroyer, S/Sgt. Choate reached comparative safety. He returned to the burning destroyer to search for comrades possibly trapped in the vehicle risking instant death in an explosion which was imminent and braving enemy fire which ripped his jacket and tore the helmet from his head. Completing the search and seeing the tank and its supporting infantry overrunning our infantry in their shallow foxholes, he secured a bazooka and ran after the tank, dodging from tree to tree and passing through the enemy's loose skirmish line. He fired a rocket from a distance of 20 yards, immobilizing the tank but leaving it able to spray the area with cannon and machinegun fire. Running back to our infantry through vicious fire, he secured another rocket, and, advancing against a hail of machinegun and small-arms fire reached a position 10 yards from the tank. His second shot shattered the turret. With his pistol he killed 2 of the crew as they emerged from the tank; and then running to the crippled Mark IV while enemy infantry sniped at him, he dropped a grenade inside the tank and completed its destruction. With their armor gone, the enemy infantry became disorganized and was driven back. S/Sgt. Choate's great daring in assaulting an enemy tank single-handed, his determination to follow the vehicle after it had passed his position, and his skill and crushing thoroughness in the attack prevented the enemy from capturing a battalion command post and turned a probable defeat into a tactical success.

*CHRISTENSEN, DALE ELDON

Rank and organization: Second Lieutenant, U.S. Army, Troop E, 112th Cavalry Regiment. Place and date: Driniumor River, New Guinea, 16-19 July 1944. Entered service at: Gray, Iowa. Birth: Cameron Township, Iowa. G.O. No.: 36, 10 May 1945. Citation: For conspicuous gallantry and intrepidity at the risk of his life above and beyond the call of duty along the Driniumor River, New Guinea, from 16-19 July 1944. 2d Lt. Christensen repeatedly distinguished himself by conspicuous gallantry above and beyond the call of duty in the continuous heavy fighting which occurred in this area from 16-19 July. On 16 July, his platoon engaged in a savage fire fight in which much damage was caused by 1 enemy machinegun effectively placed. 2d Lt. Christensen ordered his men to remain under cover, crept forward under fire, and at a range of 15 yards put the gun out of action with hand grenades. Again, on 19 July, while attacking an enemy position strong in mortars and machineguns, his platoon was pinned to the ground by intense fire. Ordering his men to remain under cover, he crept forward alone to locate definitely the enemy automatic weapons and the best direction from which to attack. Although his rifle was struck by enemy fire and knocked from his hands he continued his reconnaissance, located 5 enemy machineguns, destroyed 1 with hand grenades, and rejoined his platoon. He then led his men to the point selected for launching the attack and, calling encouragement, led the charge. This assault was successful and the enemy was driven from the positions with a loss of 4 mortars and 10 machineguns and leaving many dead on the field. On 4 August 1944, near Afua, Dutch New Guinea, 2d Lt. Christensen was killed in action about 2 yards from his objective while leading his platoon in an attack on an enemy machinegun position. 2d Lt. Christensen's leadership, intrepidity, and repeatedly demonstrated gallantry in action at the risk of his life, above and beyond the call of duty, exemplify the highest traditions of the U.S. Armed Forces.

*CHRISTIAN, HERBERT F.

Rank and organization: Private, U.S. Army, 15th Infantry, 3d Infantry Division. Place and date: Near Valmontone, Italy, 2-3 June 1944. Entered service at: Steubenville, Ohio. Birth: Byersville, Ohio. G.O. No.: 43, 30 May 1945. Citation: For conspicuous gallantry and intrepidity at risk of life above and beyond the call of duty. On 2-3 June 1944, at 1 a.m., Pvt. Christian elected to sacrifice his life in order that his comrades might extricate themselves from an ambush. Braving massed fire of about 60 riflemen, 3 machineguns, and 3 tanks from positions only 30 yards distant, he stood erect and signaled to the patrol to withdraw. The whole area was brightly illuminated by enemy flares. Although his right leg was severed above the knee by cannon fire, Pvt. Christian advanced on his left knee and the bloody stump of his right thigh, firing his submachinegun. Despite excruciating pain, Pvt. Christian continued on his self-assigned mission. He succeeded in distracting the enemy and enabled his 12 comrades to escape. He killed 3 enemy soldiers almost at once. Leaving a trail of blood behind him, he made his way forward 20 yards, halted at a point within 10 yards of the enemy, and despite intense fire killed a machine-pistol man. Reloading his weapon, he fired directly into the enemy position. The enemy appeared enraged at the success of his ruse, concentrated 20-mm. machinegun, machine-pistol and rifle fire on him, yet he refused to seek cover. Maintaining his erect position, Pvt. Christian fired his weapon to the very last. Just as he emptied his submachinegun, the enemy bullets found their mark and Pvt. Christian slumped forward dead. The courage and spirit of self-sacrifice displayed by this soldier were an inspiration to his comrades and are in keeping with the highest traditions of the armed forces.

*CICCHETTI, JOSEPH J.

Rank and organization: Private First Class, U.S. Army, Company A, 148th Infantry, 37th Infantry Division. Place and date: South Manila, Luzon, Philippine Islands, 9 February 1945. Entered service at: Waynesburg, Ohio. Birth: Waynesburg, Ohio. G.O. No.: 115, 8 December 1945. Citation: He was with troops assaulting the first important line of enemy defenses. The Japanese had converted the partially destroyed Manila Gas Works and adjacent buildings into a formidable system of mutually supporting strongpoints from which they were concentrating machinegun, mortar, and heavy artillery fire on the American forces. Casualties rapidly mounted, and the medical aid men, finding it increasingly difficult to evacuate the wounded, called for volunteer litter bearers. Pfc. Cicchetti immediately responded, organized a litter team and skillfully led it for more than 4 hours in rescuing 14 wounded men, constantly passing back and forth over a 400-yard route which was the impact area for a tremendous volume of the most intense enemy fire. On 1 return trip the path was blocked by machinegun fire, but Pfc. Cicchetti deliberately exposed himself to draw the automatic fire which he neutralized with his own rifle while ordering the rest of the team to rush past to safety with the wounded.

While gallantly continuing his work, he noticed a group of wounded and helpless soldiers some distance away and ran to their rescue although the enemy fire had increased to new fury. As he approached the casualties, he was struck in the head by a shell fragment, but with complete disregard for his gaping wound he continued to his comrades, lifted 1 and carried him on his shoulders 50 yards to safety. He then collapsed and died. By his skilled leadership, indomitable will, and dauntless courage, Pfc. Cicchetti saved the lives of many of his fellow soldiers at the cost of his own.

CLARK, FRANCIS J.

Rank and organization: Technical Sergeant, U.S. Army, Company K, 109th Infantry, 28th Infantry Division. Place and date: Near Kalborn, Luxembourg, 12 September 1944; near Sevenig, Germany, 17 September 1944. Entered service at: Salem, N.Y. Birth: Whitehall, N.Y. G.O. No.: 77, 10 September 1945. Citation: He fought gallantly in Luxembourg and Germany. On 12 September 1944, Company K began fording the Our River near Kalborn, Luxembourg, to take high ground on the opposite bank. Covered by early morning fog, the 3d Platoon, in which T/Sgt. Clark was squad leader, successfully negotiated the crossing; but when the 2d Platoon reached the shore, withering automatic and small-arms fire ripped into it, eliminating the platoon leader and platoon sergeant and pinning down the troops in the open. From his comparatively safe position, T/Sgt. Clark crawled alone across a field through a hail of bullets to the stricken troops. He led the platoon to safety and then unhesitatingly returned into the fire-swept area to rescue a wounded soldier, carrying him to the American line while hostile gunners tried to cut him down. Later, he led his squad and men of the 2d Platoon in dangerous sorties against strong enemy positions to weaken them by lightning-like jabs. He assaulted an enemy machine-gun with hand grenades, killing 2 Germans. He roamed the front and flanks, dashing toward hostile weapons, killing and wounding an undetermined number of the enemy, scattering German patrols and, eventually, forcing the withdrawal of a full company of Germans heavily armed with automatic weapons. On 17 September, near Sevenig, Germany, he advanced alone against an enemy machinegun, killed the gunner and forced the assistant to flee. The Germans counterattacked, and heavy casualties were suffered by Company K. Seeing that 2 platoons lacked leadership, T/Sgt. Clark took over their command and moved among the men to give encouragement. Although wounded on the morning of 18 September, he refused to be evacuated and took up a position in a pillbox when night came. Emerging at daybreak, he killed a German soldier setting up a machinegun not more than 5 yards away. When he located another enemy gun, he moved up unobserved and killed 2 Germans with rifle fire. Later that day he voluntarily braved small-arms fire to take food and water to members of an isolated platoon. T/Sgt. Clark's actions in assuming command when leadership was desperately needed, in launching attacks and beating off counterattacks, in aiding his stranded comrades, and in fearlessly facing powerful enemy fire, were strikingly heroic examples and put fighting heart into the hard-pressed men of Company K.

COLALILLO, MIKE

Rank and organization: Private First Class, U.S. Army, Company C, 398th Infantry, 100th Infantry Division. Place and date: Near Untergriesheim, Germany, 7 April 1945. Entered service at. Duluth, Minn. Birth: Hibbing, Minn. G.O. No.: 4, 9 January 1946. Citation: He was pinned down with other members of his company during an attack against strong enemy positions in the vicinity of Untergriesheim, Germany. Heavy artillery, mortar, and machinegun fire made any move hazardous when he stood up, shouted to the company to follow, and ran forward in the wake of a supporting tank, firing his machine pistol. Inspired by his example, his comrades advanced in the face of savage enemy fire. When his weapon was struck by shrapnel and rendered useless, he climbed to the deck of a friendly tank, manned an exposed machinegun on the turret of the vehicle, and, while bullets rattled about him, fired at an enemy emplacement with such devastating accuracy that he killed or wounded at least 10 hostile soldiers and destroyed their machinegun. Maintaining his extremely dangerous post as the tank forged ahead, he blasted 3 more positions, destroyed another machinegun emplacement and silenced all resistance in his area, killing at least 3 and wounding an undetermined number of riflemen as they fled. His machinegun eventually jammed; so he secured a submachinegun from the tank crew to continue his attack on foot. When our armored forces exhausted their ammunition and the order to withdraw was given, he remained behind to help a seriously wounded comrade over several hundred yards of open terrain rocked by an intense enemy artillery and mortar barrage. By his intrepidity and inspiring courage Pfc. Colallilo gave tremendous impetus to his company's attack, killed or wounded 25 of the enemy in bitter fighting, and assisted a wounded soldier in reaching the American lines at great risk of his own life.

*COLE, DARRELL SAMUEL

Rank and organization: Sergeant, U.S. Marine Corps Reserve. Born: 20 July 1920, Flat River, Mo. Entered service at. Esther, Mo. other Navy award: Bronze Star Medal. Citation: For conspicuous gallantry and intrepidity at the risk of his life above and beyond the call of duty while serving as leader of a Machinegun Section of Company B, 1st Battalion, 23d Marines, 4th Marine Division, in action against enemy Japanese forces during the assault on Iwo Jima in the Volcano Islands, 19 February 1945. Assailed by a tremendous volume of small-arms, mortar and artillery fire as he advanced with 1 squad of his section in the initial assault wave, Sgt. Cole boldly led his men up the sloping beach toward Airfield No. 1 despite the blanketing curtain of flying shrapnel and, personally destroying with hand grenades 2 hostile emplacements which menaced the progress of his unit, continued to move forward until a merciless barrage of fire emanating from 3 Japanese pillboxes halted the advance. Instantly placing his 1 remaining machinegun in action, he delivered a shattering fusillade and succeeded in silencing the nearest and most threatening emplacement before his weapon jammed and the enemy, reopening fire with knee mortars and grenades, pinned down his unit for the second time. Shrewdly gauging the tactical situation and evolving a daring plan of counterattack, Sgt. Cole, armed solely with a pistol and 1 grenade, coolly advanced alone to the hostile pillboxes. Hurling his 1 grenade at the enemy in sudden, swift attack, he quickly withdrew, returned to his own lines for additional grenades and again advanced, attacked, and withdrew. With enemy guns still active, he ran the gauntlet of slashing fire a third time to complete the total destruction of the Japanese strong point and the annihilation of the defending garrison in this final assault. Although instantly killed by an enemy grenade as he returned to his squad, Sgt. Cole had eliminated a formidable Japanese position, thereby enabling his company to storm the remaining fortifications, continue the advance, and seize the objective. By his dauntless initiative, unfaltering courage, and indomitable determination during a critical period of action, Sgt. Cole served as an inspiration to his comrades, and his stouthearted leadership in the face of almost certain death sustained and enhanced the highest tradition of the U.S. Naval Service. He gallantly gave his life for his country.

*COLE, ROBERT G.

Rank and organization: Lieutenant Colonel, U.S. Army, 101st Airborne Division. Place and date: Near Carentan, France, 11 June 1944. Entered service at: San Antonio, Tex. Birth: Fort Sam Houston, Tex. G.O. No.: 79, 4 October 1944. Citation: For gallantry and intrepidity at the risk of his own life, above and beyond the call of duty on 11 June 1944, in France. Lt. Col. Cole was personally leading his battalion in forcing the last 4 bridges on the road to Carentan when his entire unit was suddenly pinned to the ground by intense and withering enemy rifle, machinegun, mortar, and artillery fire placed upon them from well-prepared and heavily fortified positions within 150 yards of the foremost elements. After the devastating and unceasing enemy fire had for over 1 hour prevented any move and inflicted numerous casualties, Lt. Col. Cole, observing this almost hopeless situation, courageously issued orders to assault the enemy positions with fixed bayonets. With utter disregard for his own safety and completely ignoring the enemy fire, he rose to his feet in front of his battalion and with drawn pistol shouted to his men to follow him in the assault. Catching up a fallen man's rifle and bayonet, he charged on and led the remnants of his battalion across the bullet-swept open ground and into the enemy position. His heroic and valiant action in so inspiring his men resulted in the complete establishment of our bridgehead across the Douve River. The cool fearlessness, personal bravery, and outstanding leadership displayed by Lt. Col. Cole reflect great credit upon himself and are worthy of the highest praise in the military service.

CONNOR, JAMES P.

Rank and organization: Sergeant, U.S. Army, 7th Infantry, 3d Infantry Division. Place and date: Cape Cavalaire, southern France, 15 August 1944. Entered service at: Wilmington, Del. Birth: Wilmington, Del. G.O. No.: 18, 15 March 1945. Citation: For conspicuous gallantry and intrepidity at risk of life above and beyond the call of duty. On 15 August 1944, Sgt. Connor, through sheer grit and determination, led his platoon in clearing an enemy vastly superior in numbers and firepower from strongly entrenched positions on Cape Cavalaire, removing a grave enemy threat to his division during the amphibious landing in southern France, and thereby insured safe and uninterrupted landings for the huge volume of men and materiel which followed. His battle patrol landed on "Red Beach" with the mission of destroying the strongly fortified enemy positions on Cape Cavalaire with utmost speed. From the peninsula the enemy had commanding observation and seriously menaced the vast landing operations taking place.

Though knocked down and seriously wounded in the neck by a hanging mine which killed his platoon lieutenant, Sgt. Connor refused medical aid and with his driving spirit practically carried the platoon across several thousand yards of mine-saturated beach through intense fire from mortars, 20-mm. flak guns, machineguns, and snipers. En route to the Cape he personally shot and killed 2 snipers. The platoon sergeant was killed and Sgt. Connor became platoon leader. Receiving a second wound, which lacerated his shoulder and back, he again refused evacuation, expressing determination to carry on until physically unable to continue. He reassured and prodded the hesitating men of his decimated platoon forward through almost impregnable mortar concentrations. Again emphasizing the prevalent urgency of their mission, he impelled his men toward a group of buildings honeycombed with enemy snipers and machineguns. Here he received his third grave wound, this time in the leg, felling him in his tracks. Still resolved to carry on, he relinquished command only after his attempts proved that it was physically impossible to stand. Nevertheless, from his prone position, he gave the orders and directed his men in assaulting the enemy. Infused with Sgt. Connor's dogged determination, the platoon, though reduced to less than one-third of its original 36 men, outflanked and rushed the enemy with such furiousness that they killed 7, captured 40, seized 3 machineguns and considerable other materiel, and took all their assigned objectives, successfully completing their mission. By his repeated examples of tenaciousness and indomitable spirit Sgt Connor transmitted his heroism to his men until they became a fighting team which could not be stopped.

COOLEY, RAYMOND H.

Rank and organization: Staff Sergeant, U.S. Army, Company B, 27th Infantry, 25th Infantry Division. Place and date: Near Lumboy, Luzon, Philippine Islands, 24 February 1945. Entered service at: Richard City, Tenn. Born: 7 May 1914, Dunlap, Tenn. G.O. No.: 77, 10 September

1945. Citation: He was a platoon guide in an assault on a camouflaged entrenchment defended by machineguns, rifles, and mortars. When his men were pinned down by 2 enemy machineguns, he voluntarily advanced under heavy fire to within 20 yards of 1 of the guns and attacked it with a hand grenade. The enemy, however, threw the grenade back at him before it could explode. Arming a second grenade, he held it for several seconds of the safe period and then hurled it into the enemy position, where it exploded instantaneously, destroying the gun and crew. He then moved toward the remaining gun, throwing grenades into enemy foxholes as he advanced. Inspired by his actions, 1 squad of his platoon joined him. After he had armed another grenade and was preparing to throw it into the second machinegun position, 6 enemy soldiers rushed at him. Knowing he could not dispose of the armed grenade without injuring his comrades, because of the intermingling in close combat of the men of his platoon and the enemy in the melee which ensued, he deliberately covered the grenade with his body and was severely wounded as it exploded. By his heroic actions, S/Sgt. Cooley not only silenced a machinegun and so inspired his fellow soldiers that they pressed the attack and destroyed the remaining enemy emplacements, but also, in complete disregard of his own safety, accepted certain injury and possible loss of life to avoid wounding his comrades.

COOLIDGE, CHARLES H.

Rank and organization: Technical Sergeant, U.S. Army, Company M, 141st Infantry, 36th Infantry Division. Place and date: East of Belmont sur Buttant, France, 2427 October 1944. Entered service at: Signal Mountain, Tenn. Birth: Signal Mountain, Tenn. G.O. No.: 53, July 1945. Citation: Leading a section of heavy machineguns supported by 1 platoon of Company K, he took a position near Hill 623, east of Belmont sur Buttant, France, on 24 October 1944, with the mission of covering the right flank of the 3d Battalion and supporting its action. T/Sgt. Coolidge went forward with a sergeant of Company K to reconnoiter positions for coordinating the fires of the light and heavy machineguns. They ran into an enemy force in the woods estimated to be an infantry company. T/Sgt. Coolidge, attempting to bluff the Germans by a show of assurance and boldness called upon them to surrender, whereupon the enemy opened fire. With his carbine, T/Sgt. Coolidge wounded 2 of them. There being no officer present with the force, T/Sgt. Coolidge at once assumed command. Many of the men were replacements recently arrived; this was their first experience under fire. T/Sgt. Coolidge, unmindful of the enemy fire delivered at close range, walked along the position, calming and encouraging his men and directing their fire. The attack was thrown back. Through 25 and 26 October the enemy launched repeated attacks against the position of this combat group but each was repulsed due to T/Sgt. Coolidge's able leadership. On 27 October, German infantry, supported by 2 tanks, made a determined attack on the position. The area was swept by enemy small arms, machinegun, and tank fire. T/Sgt. Coolidge armed himself with a bazooka and advanced to within 25 yards of the tanks. His bazooka failed to function and he threw it aside. Securing all the hand grenades he could carry, he crawled forward and inflicted heavy casualties on the advancing enemy. Finally it became apparent that the enemy, in greatly superior force, supported by tanks, would overrun the position. T/Sgt. Coolidge, displaying great coolness and courage, directed and conducted an orderly withdrawal, being himself the last to leave the position. As a result of T/Sgt. Coolidge's heroic and superior leadership, the mission of this combat group was accomplished throughout 4 days of continuous fighting against numerically superior enemy troops in rain and cold and amid dense woods.

*COURTNEY, HENRY ALEXIUS, JR.

Rank and organization: Major, U.S. Marine Corps Reserve. Born: 6 January 1916, Duluth, Minn. Appointed from: Minnesota. Citation: For conspicuous gallantry and intrepidity at the risk of his life above and beyond the call of duty as Executive Officer of the 2d Battalion, 22d Marines, 6th Marine Division, in action against enemy Japanese forces on Okinawa Shima in the Ryukyu Islands, 14 and 15 May 1945. Ordered to hold for the night in static defense behind Sugar Loaf Hill after leading the forward elements of his command in a prolonged fire fight, Maj. Courtney weighed the effect of a hostile night counterattack against the tactical value of an immediate marine assault, resolved to initiate the assault, and promptly obtained permission to advance and seize the forward slope of the hill. Quickly explaining the situation to his small remaining force, he declared his personal intention of moving forward and then proceeded on his way, boldly blasting nearby cave positions and neutralizing enemy guns as he went. Inspired by his courage, every man followed without hesitation, and together the intrepid marines braved a terrific concentration of Japanese gunfire to skirt the hill on the right and reach the reverse slope. Temporarily halting, Maj. Courtney sent guides to the rear for more ammunition and possible replacements. Subsequently reinforced by 26 men and an LVT load of grenades, he determined to storm the crest of the hill and crush any planned counterattack before it could gain sufficient momentum to effect a breakthrough. Leading his men by example rather than by command, he pushed ahead with unrelenting aggressiveness, hurling grenades into cave openings on the slope with devastating effect. Upon reaching the crest and observing large numbers of Japanese forming for action less than 100 yards away, he instantly attacked, waged a furious battle and succeeded in killing many of the enemy and in forcing the remainder to take cover in the caves. Determined to hold, he ordered his men to dig in and, coolly disregarding the continuous hail of flying enemy shrapnel to rally his weary troops, tirelessly aided casualties and assigned his men to more advantageous positions. Although instantly killed by a hostile mortar burst while moving among his men, Maj. Courtney, by his astute military acumen, indomitable leadership and decisive action in the face of overwhelming odds, had contributed essentially to the success of the Okinawa campaign. His great personal valor throughout sustained and enhanced the highest traditions of the U.S. Naval Service. He gallantly gave his life for his country.

*COWAN, RICHARD ELLER

Rank and organization: Private First Class, U.S. Army, Company M, 23d Infantry, 2d Infantry Division. Place and date: Near Krinkelter Wald, Belgium, 17 December 1944. Entered service at: Wichita, Kans. Birth: Lincoln, Nebr. G.O. No.: 48, 23 June 1945. Citation: He was a heavy machinegunner in a section attached to Company I in the vicinity of Krinkelter Wald, Belgium, 17 December 1944, when that company was attacked by a numerically superior force of German infantry and tanks. The first 6 waves of hostile infantrymen were repulsed with heavy casualties, but a seventh drive with tanks killed or wounded all but 3 of his section, leaving Pvt. Cowan to man his gun, supported by only 15 to 20 riflemen of Company I. He maintained his position, holding off the Germans until the rest of the shattered force had set up a new line along a firebreak. Then, unaided, he moved his machinegun and ammunition to the second position. At the approach of a Royal Tiger tank, he held his fire until about 80 enemy infantrymen supporting the tank appeared at a distance of about 150 yards. His first burst killed or wounded about half of these infantrymen. His position was rocked by an 88mm. shell when the tank opened fire, but he continued to man his gun, pouring deadly fire into the Germans when they again advanced. He was barely missed by another shell. Fire from three machineguns and innumerable small arms struck all about him; an enemy rocket shook him badly, but did not drive him from his gun. Infiltration by the enemy had by this time made the position untenable, and the order was given to withdraw. Pvt. Cowan was the last man to leave, voluntarily covering the withdrawal of his remaining comrades. His heroic actions were entirely responsible for allowing the remaining men to retire successfully from the scene of their last-ditch stand.

CRAFT, CLARENCE B.

Rank and organization: Private, First Class, U.S. Army, Company G, 382d Infantry, 96th Infantry Division. Place and date: Hen Hill, Okinawa, Ryukyu Islands, 31 May 1945. Entered service at: Santa Ana, Calif. Birth: San Bernardino, Calif. G.O. No.: 97, 1 November 1945. Citation: He was a rifleman when his platoon spearheaded an attack on Hen Hill, the tactical position on which the entire Naha-Shuri-Yonaburu line of Japanese defense on Okinawa, Ryukyu Islands, was hinged. For 12 days our forces had been stalled, and repeated, heavy assaults by 1 battalion and then another had been thrown back by the enemy with serious casualties. With 5 comrades, Pfc. Craft was dispatched in advance of Company G to feel out the enemy resistance. The group had proceeded only a short distance up the slope when rifle and machinegun fire, coupled with a terrific barrage of grenades, wounded 3 and pinned down the others. Against odds that appeared suicidal, Pfc. Craft launched a remarkable 1-man attack. He stood up in full view of the enemy and began shooting with deadly marksmanship wherever he saw a hostile movement. He steadily advanced up the hill, killing Japanese soldiers with rapid fire, driving others to cover in their strongly disposed trenches, unhesitatingly facing alone the strength that had previously beaten back attacks in battalion strength. He reached the crest of the hill, where he stood silhouetted against the sky while quickly throwing grenades at extremely short range into the enemy positions. His extraordinary assault lifted the pressure from his company for the moment, allowing members of his platoon to comply with his motions to advance and pass him more grenades. With a chain of his comrades supplying him while he stood atop the hill, he furiously hurled a total of 2 cases of grenades into a main trench and other positions on the reverse slope of Hen Hill, meanwhile directing the aim of his fellow soldiers who threw grenades from the slope below him. He left his position, where grenades from both sides were passing over his head and bursting on either slope, to attack the main enemy trench as confusion and panic seized the defenders. Straddling the excavation, he pumped rifle fire into the Japanese at pointblank range, killing many and causing the others to flee down the trench. Pursuing them, he came upon a heavy machinegun which was still creating havoc in the American ranks. With rifle fire and a grenade he wiped out this position. By this time the Japanese were in complete rout and American forces were swarming over the hill. Pfc. Craft continued down the central trench to the mouth of a cave where many of the enemy had taken cover. A satchel charge was brought to him, and he tossed it into the cave. It failed to explode. With great daring, the intrepid fighter retrieved the charge from the cave, relighted the fuse and threw it back, sealing up the Japs in a tomb. In the local action, against tremendously superior forces heavily armed with rifles, machineguns, mortars, and grenades, Pfc. Craft killed at least 25 of the enemy; but his contribution to the campaign on Okinawa was of much more far-reaching consequence for Hen Hill was the key to the entire defense line, which rapidly crumbled after his utterly fearless and heroic attack.

*CRAIG, ROBERT

Rank and organization: Second Lieutenant, U.S. Army, 15th Infantry, 3d Infantry Division. Place and date: Near Favoratta, Sicily, 11 July 1943. Entered service at: Toledo, Ohio. Birth: Scotland. G.O. No.: 41, 26 May 1944. Citation: For conspicuous gallantry and intrepidity at the risk of life, above and beyond the call of duty, on 11 July 1943 at Favoratta, Sicily. 2d Lt. Craig voluntarily undertook the perilous task of locating and destroying a hidden enemy machinegun which had halted the advance of his company. Attempts by 3 other officers to locate the weapon had resulted in failure, with each officer receiving wounds. 2d Lt. Craig located the gun and snaked his way to a point within 35 yards of the hostile position before being discovered. Charging headlong into the furious automatic fire, he reached the gun, stood over it, and killed the 3 crew members with his carbine. With this obstacle removed, his company continued its advance. Shortly thereafter while advancing down the forward slope of a ridge, 2d Lt. Craig and his platoon, in a position devoid of cover and concealment, encountered the fire of approximately 100 enemy soldiers. Electing to sacrifice himself so that his platoon might carry on the battle, he ordered his men to withdraw to the cover of the crest while he drew the enemy fire to himself. With no hope of survival, he charged toward the enemy until he was within 25 yards of them. Assuming a kneeling position, he killed 5 and wounded 3 enemy soldiers. While the hostile force concentrated fire on him, his platoon reached the cover of the crest. 2d Lt. Craig was killed by enemy fire, but his intrepid action so inspired his men that they drove the enemy from the area, inflicting heavy casualties on the hostile force.

*CRAIN, MORRIS E.

Rank and organization: Technical Sergeant, U.S. Army, Company E, 141st Infantry, 36th Infantry Division. Place and date: Haguenau, France, 13 March 1945. Entered service at: Paducah, Ky. Birth: Bandana, Ky. G.O. No.: 18, 13 February 1946. Citation: He led his platoon against powerful German forces during the struggle to enlarge the bridgehead across the Moder River. With great daring and aggressiveness he spearheaded the platoon in killing 10 enemy soldiers, capturing 12 more and securing its objective near an important road junction. Although heavy concentrations of artillery, mortar, and self-propelled gunfire raked the area, he moved about among his men during the day, exhorting them to great efforts and encouraging them to stand firm. He carried ammunition and maintained contact with the company command post, exposing himself to deadly enemy fire. At nightfall the enemy barrage became more intense and tanks entered the fray to cover foot troops while they bombarded our positions with grenades and rockets. As buildings were blasted by the Germans, the Americans fell back from house to house. T/Sgt. Crain deployed another platoon which had been sent to his support and then rushed through murderous tank and small-arms fire to the foremost house, which was being defended by 5 of his men. With the enemy attacking from an adjoining room and a tank firing pointblank at the house, he ordered the men to withdraw while he remained in the face of almost certain death to hold the position. Although shells were crashing through the walls and bullets were hitting all around him, he held his ground and with accurate fire from his submachinegun killed 3 Germans. He was killed when the building was destroyed by the enemy. T/Sgt. Crain's outstanding valor and intrepid leadership enabled his platoon to organize a new defense, repel the attack and preserve the hard-won bridgehead.

*CRAW, DEMAS T.

Rank and organization: Colonel, U.S. Army Air Corps. Place and date. Near Port Lyautey, French Morocco, 8 November 1942. Entered service at: Michigan. Born: 9 April 1900, Traverse City, Mich. G.O. No.: 11, 4 March 1943. Citation: For conspicuous gallantry and intrepidity in action above and beyond the call of duty. On 8 November 1942, near Port Lyautey, French Morocco, Col. Craw volunteered to accompany the leading wave of assault boats to the shore and pass through the enemy lines to locate the French commander with a view to suspending hostilities. This request was first refused as being too dangerous but upon the officer's ins1stence that he was qualified to undertake and accomplish the mission he was allowed to go. Encountering heavy fire while in the landing boat and unable to dock in the river because of shell fire from shore batteries, Col. Craw, accompanied by 1 officer and 1 soldier, succeeded in landing on the beach at Mehdia Plage under constant low-level strafing from 3 enemy planes. Riding in a bantam truck toward French headquarters, progress of the party was hindered by fire from our own naval guns. Nearing Port Lyautey, Col. Craw was instantly killed by a sustained burst of machinegun fire at pointblank range from a concealed position near the road.

CRAWFORD, WILLIAM J.

Rank and organization: Private, U.S. Army, 36th Infantry Division. Place and date: Near Altavilla, Italy, 13 September 1943. Entered service at: Pueblo, Colo. Birth: Pueblo, Colo. G.O. No.: 57, 20 July 1944. Citation: For conspicuous gallantry and intrepidity at risk of life above and beyond the call of duty in action with the enemy near Altavilla, Italy, 13 September 1943. When Company I attacked an enemy-held position on Hill 424, the 3d Platoon, in which Pvt. Crawford was a squad scout, attacked as base platoon for the company. After reaching the crest of the hill, the platoon was pinned down by intense enemy machinegun and small-arms fire. Locating 1 of these guns, which was dug in on a terrace on his immediate front, Pvt. Crawford, without orders and on his own initiative, moved over the hill under enemy fire to a point within a few yards of the gun emplacement and single-handedly destroyed the machinegun and killed 3 of the crew with a hand grenade, thus enabling his platoon to continue its advance. When the platoon, after reaching the crest, was once more delayed by enemy fire, Pvt. Crawford again, in the face of intense fire, advanced directly to the front midway between 2 hostile machinegun nests located on a higher terrace and emplaced in a small ravine. Moving first to the left, with a hand grenade he destroyed 1 gun emplacement and killed the crew; he then worked his way, under continuous fire, to the other and with 1 grenade and the use of his rifle, killed 1 enemy and forced the remainder to flee. Seizing the enemy machinegun, he fired on the withdrawing Germans and facilitated his company's advance.

CREWS, JOHN R.

Rank and organization: Staff Sergeant, U.S. Army, Company F, 253d Infantry, 63d Infantry Division. Place and date: Near Lobenbacherhof, Germany, 8 April 1945. Entered service at: Bowlegs, Okla. Birth: Golden, Okla. Citation: He displayed conspicuous gallantry and intrepidity at the risk of his life above and beyond the call of duty on 8 April 1945 near Lobenbacherhof, Germany. As his company was advancing toward the village under heavy fire, an enemy machinegun and automatic rifle with rifle support opened upon it from a hill on the right flank. Seeing that his platoon leader had been wounded by their fire, S/Sgt. Crews, acting on his own initiative, rushed the strongpoint with 2 men of his platoon. Despite the fact that 1 of these men was killed and the other was badly wounded, he continued his advance up the hill in the face of terrific enemy fire. Storming the well-dug-in position singlehandedly, he killed 2 of the crew of the machinegun at pointblank range with his M 1 rifle and wrested the gun from the hands of the German whom he had already wounded. He then with his rifle charged the strongly emplaced automatic rifle. Although badly wounded in the thigh by crossfire from the remaining enemy, he kept on and silenced the entire position with his accurate and deadly rifle fire. His actions so unnerved the remaining enemy soldiers that 7 of them surrendered and the others fled. His heroism caused the enemy to concentrate on him and permitted the company to move forward into the village.

*CROMWELL, JOHN PHILIP

Rank and organization: Captain, U.S. Navy. Born: 11 September 1901, Henry, Ill. Appointed from: Illinois. Other Navy award: Legion of Merit. Citation: For conspicuous gallantry and intrepidity at the risk of his life above and beyond the call of duty as Commander of a Submarine Coordinated Attack Group with Flag in the U.S.S. Sculpin, during the 9th War Patrol of that vessel in enemy-controlled waters off Truk Island,

19 November 1943. Undertaking this patrol prior to the launching of our first large-scale offensive in the Pacific, Capt. Cromwell, alone of the entire Task Group, possessed secret intelligence information of our submarine strategy and tactics, scheduled Fleet movements and specific attack plans. Constantly vigilant and precise in carrying out his secret orders, he moved his underseas flotilla inexorably forward despite savage opposition and established a line of submarines to southeastward of the main Japanese stronghold at Truk. Cool and undaunted as the submarine, rocked and battered by Japanese depth charges, sustained terrific battle damage and sank to an excessive depth, he authorized the Sculpin to surface and engage the enemy in a gunfight, thereby providing an opportunity for the crew to abandon ship. Determined to sacrifice himself rather than risk capture and subsequent danger of revealing plans under Japanese torture or use of drugs, he stoically remained aboard the mortally wounded vessel as she plunged to her death. Preserving the security of his mission, at the cost of his own life, he had served his country as he had served the Navy, with deep integrity and an uncompromising devotion to duty. His great moral courage in the face of certain death adds new luster to the traditions of the U.S. Naval Service. He gallantly gave his life for his country.

CURREY, FRANCIS S.

Rank and organization: Sergeant, U.S. Army, Company K, 120th Infantry, 30th Infantry Division. Place and date: Malmedy, Belgium, 21 December 1944. Entered service at: Hurleyville, N.Y. Birth: Loch Sheldrake, N.Y. G.O. No.: 69, 17 August 1945. Citation: He was an automatic rifleman with the 3d Platoon defending a strong point near Malmedy, Belgium, on 21 December 1944, when the enemy launched a powerful attack. Overrunning tank destroyers and antitank guns located near the strong point, German tanks advanced to the 3d Platoon's position, and, after prolonged fighting, forced the withdrawal of this group to a nearby factory. Sgt. Currey found a bazooka in the building and crossed the street to secure rockets meanwhile enduring intense fire from enemy tanks and hostile infantrymen who had taken up a position at a house a short distance away. In the face of small-arms, machinegun, and artillery fire, he, with a companion, knocked out a tank with 1 shot. Moving to another position, he observed 3 Germans in the doorway of an enemy-held house. He killed or wounded all 3 with his automatic rifle. He emerged from cover and advanced alone to within 50 yards of the house, intent on wrecking it with rockets. Covered by friendly fire, he stood erect, and fired a shot which knocked down half of 1 wall. While in this forward position, he observed 5 Americans who had been pinned down for hours by fire from the house and 3 tanks. Realizing that they could not escape until the enemy tank and infantry guns had been silenced, Sgt. Currey crossed the street to a vehicle, where he procured an armful of antitank grenades. These he launched while under heavy enemy fire, driving the tankmen from the vehicles into the house. He then climbed onto a half-track in full view of the Germans and fired a machinegun at the house. Once again changing his position, he manned another machinegun whose crew had been killed; under his covering fire the 5 soldiers were able to retire to safety. Deprived of tanks and with heavy infantry casualties, the enemy was forced to withdraw. Through his extensive knowledge of weapons and by his heroic and repeated braving of murderous enemy fire, Sgt. Currey was greatly responsible for inflicting heavy losses in men and material on the enemy, for rescuing 5 comrades, 2 of whom were wounded, and for stemming an attack which threatened to flank his battalion's position.

DAHLGREN, EDWARD C.

Rank and organization: Second Lieutenant (then Sergeant), U.S. Army, Company E, 142d Infantry, 36th Infantry Division. Place and date: Oberhoffen, France, 11 February 1945. Entered service at: Portland, Maine. Birth: Perham, Maine. G.O. No.: 77, 10 September 1945.

Citation: He led the 3d Platoon to the rescue of a similar unit which had been surrounded in an enemy counterattack at Oberhoffen, France. As he advanced along a street, he observed several Germans crossing a field about 100 yards away. Running into a barn, he took up a position in a window and swept the hostile troops with submachine gun fire, killing 6, wounding others, and completely disorganizing the group. His platoon then moved forward through intermittent sniper fire and made contact with the besieged Americans. When the 2 platoons had been reorganized, Sgt. Dahlgren continued to advance along the street until he drew fire from an enemy-held house. In the face of machine pistol and rifle fire, he ran toward the building, hurled a grenade through the door, and blasted his way inside with his gun. This aggressive attack so rattled the Germans that all 8 men who held the strongpoint immediately surrendered. As Sgt. Dahlgren started toward the next house, hostile machinegun fire drove him to cover. He secured rifle grenades, stepped to an exposed position, and calmly launched his missiles from a difficult angle until he had destroyed the machinegun and killed its 2 operators. He moved to the rear of the house and suddenly came under the fire of a machinegun emplaced in a barn. Throwing a grenade into the structure, he rushed the position, firing his weapon as he ran; within, he overwhelmed 5 Germans. After reorganizing his unit he advanced to clear hostile riflemen from the building where he had destroyed the machinegun. He entered the house by a window and trapped the Germans in the cellar, where he tossed grenades into their midst, wounding several and forcing 10 more to surrender. While reconnoitering another street with a comrade, he heard German voices in a house. An attack with rifle grenades drove the hostile troops to the cellar. Sgt. Dahlgren entered the building, kicked open the cellar door, and, firing several bursts down the stairway, called for the trapped enemy to surrender. Sixteen soldiers filed out with their hands in the air. The bold leadership and magnificent courage displayed by Sgt. Dahlgren in his heroic attacks were in a large measure responsible for repulsing an enemy counterattack and saving an American platoon from great danger.

DALESSONDRO, PETER J.

Rank and organization: Technical Sergeant, U.S. Army, Company E, 39th Infantry, 9th Infantry Division. Place and date: Near Kalterherberg, Germany, 22 December 1944. Entered service at: Watervliet, N.Y. Born: 19 May 1918, Watervliet, N.Y. G.O. No.: 73, 30 August, 1945. Citation: He was with the 1st Platoon holding an important road junction on high ground near Kalterherberg, Germany, on 22 December 1944. In the early morning hours, the enemy after laying down an intense artillery and mortar barrage, followed through with an all-out attack that threatened to overwhelm the position. T/Sgt. Dalessondro, seeing that his men were becoming disorganized, braved the intense fire to move among them with words of encouragement. Advancing to a fully exposed observation post, he adjusted mortar fire upon the attackers, meanwhile firing upon them with his rifle and encouraging his men in halting and repulsing the attack. Later in the day the enemy launched a second determined attack. Once again, T/Sgt. Dalessondro, in the face of imminent death, rushed to his forward position and immediately called for mortar fire. After exhausting his rifle ammunition, he crawled 30 yards over exposed ground to secure a light machinegun, returned to his position, and fired upon the enemy at almost pointblank range until the gun jammed. He managed to get the gun to fire 1 more burst, which used up his last round, but with these bullets he killed 4 German soldiers who were on the verge of murdering an aid man and 2 wounded soldiers in a nearby foxhole. When the enemy had almost surrounded him, he remained alone, steadfastly facing almost certain death or capture, hurling grenades and calling for mortar fire closer and closer to his outpost as he covered the withdrawal of his platoon to a second line of defense. As the German hordes swarmed about him, he was last heard calling for a barrage, saying, "OK, mortars, let me have it—right in this position!" The gallantry and intrepidity shown by T/Sgt. Dalessondro against an overwhelming enemy attack saved his company from complete rout.

DALY, MICHAEL J.

Rank and organization: Captain (then Lieutenant), U.S. Army, Company A, 15th Infantry, 3d Infantry Division. Place and date: Nuremberg, Germany, 18 April 1945. Entered service at: Southport, Conn. Born: 15 September 1924, New York, N.Y. G.O. No.: 77, 10 September 1945. Citation: Early in the morning of 18 April 1945, he led his company through the shell-battered, sniper-infested wreckage of Nuremberg, Germany. When blistering machinegun fire caught his unit in an exposed position, he ordered his men to take cover, dashed forward alone, and, as bullets whined about him, shot the 3-man guncrew with his carbine. Continuing the advance at the head of his company, he located an enemy patrol armed with rocket launchers which threatened friendly armor. He again went forward alone, secured a vantage point and opened fire on the Germans. Immediately he became the target for concentrated machine pistol and rocket fire, which blasted the rubble about him. Calmly, he continued to shoot at the patrol until he had killed all 6 enemy infantrymen. Continuing boldly far in front of his company, he entered a park, where as his men advanced, a German machinegun opened up on them without warning. With his carbine, he killed the gunner; and then, from a completely exposed position, he directed machinegun fire on the remainder of the crew until all were dead. In a final duel, he wiped out a third machinegun emplacement with rifle fire at a range of 10 yards. By fearlessly engaging in 4 single-handed fire fights with a desperate, powerfully armed enemy, Lt. Daly, voluntarily taking all major risks himself and protecting his men at every opportunity, killed 15 Germans, silenced 3 enemy machineguns and wiped out an entire enemy patrol. His heroism during the lone bitter struggle with fanatical enemy forces was an inspiration to the valiant Americans who took Nuremberg.

*DAMATO, ANTHONY PETER

Rank and organization: Corporal, U.S. Marine Corps. Born: 28 March 1922, Shenandoah, Pa. Accredited to: Pennsylvania. Citation: For conspicuous gallantry and intrepidity at the risk of his life above and beyond the call of duty while serving with an assault company in action against enemy Japanese forces on Engebi Island, Eniwetok Atoll, Marshall Islands, on the night of 1920 February 1944. Highly vulnerable to sudden attack by small, fanatical groups of Japanese still at large despite the efficient and determined efforts of our forces to clear the area, Cpl. Damato lay with 2 comrades in a large foxhole in his company's defense perimeter which had been dangerously thinned by the forced withdrawal of nearly half of the available men. When 1 of the enemy approached the foxhole undetected and threw in a hand grenade, Cpl. Damato desperately groped for it in the darkness. Realizing the imminent peril to all 3 and fully aware of the consequences of his act, he unhesitatingly flung himself on the grenade and, although instantly killed as his body absorbed the explosion, saved the lives of his 2 companions. Cpl. Damato's splendid initiative, fearless conduct and valiant sacrifice reflect great credit upon himself and the U.S. Naval Service. He gallantly gave his life for his comrades.

*DAVID, ALBERT LEROY

Rank and organization: Lieutenant, Junior Grade, U.S. Navy. Born: 18 July 1902, Maryville, Mo. Accredited to: Missouri. Other Navy award: Navy Cross with gold star. Citation: For conspicuous gallantry and intrepidity at the risk of his life above and beyond the call of duty while attached to the U.S.S. Pillsbury during the capture of an enemy German submarine off French West Africa, 4 June 1944. Taking a vigorous part in the skillfully coordinated attack on the German U-505 which climaxed a prolonged search by the Task Group, Lt. (then Lt. j.g.) David boldly led a party from the Pillsbury in boarding the hostile submarine as it circled erratically at 5 or 6 knots on the surface. Fully aware that the U-boat might momentarily sink or be blown up by exploding demolition and scuttling charges, he braved the added danger of enemy gunfire to plunge through the conning tower hatch and, with his small party, exerted every effort to keep the ship afloat and to ass1st the succeeding and more fully equipped salvage parties in making the U-505 seaworthy for the long tow across the Atlantic to a U.S. port. By his valiant service during the first successful boarding and capture of an enemy man-o-war on the high seas by the U.S. Navy since 1815, Lt. David contributed materially to the effectiveness of our Battle of the Atlantic and upheld the highest traditions of the U.S. Naval Service.

DAVIS, CHARLES W.

Rank and organization: Major, U.S. Army, 25th Infantry Division. Place and date: Guadalcanal Island, 12 January 1943. Entered service at: Montgomery, Ala. Birth: Gordo, Ala. G.O. No.: 40, 17 July 1943. Citation: For d1stinguishing himself conspicuously by gallantry and intrepidity at the risk of his life above and beyond the call of duty in action with the enemy on Guadalcanal Island. On 12 January 1943, Maj. Davis (then Capt.), executive officer of an infantry battalion, volunteered to carry instructions to the leading companies of his battalion which had been caught in crossfire from Japanese machineguns. With complete disregard for his own safety, he made his way to the trapped units, delivered the instructions, supervised their execution, and remained overnight in this exposed position. On the following day, Maj. Davis again volunteered to lead an assault on the Japanese position which was holding up the advance. When his rifle jammed at its first shot, he drew his pistol and, waving his men on, led the assault over the top of the hill. Electrified by this action, another body of soldiers followed and seized the hill. The capture of this position broke Japanese resistance and the battalion was then able to proceed and secure the corps objective. The courage and leadership displayed by Maj. Davis inspired the entire battalion and unquestionably led to the success of its attack.

*DAVIS, GEORGE FLEMING

Rank and organization: Commander, U.S. Navy. Born: 23 March 1911, Manila, Philippine Islands. Accredited to: Philippine Islands. Other Navy awards: Silver Star Medal, Legion of Merit. Citation: For conspicuous gallantry and intrepidity at the risk of his life and beyond the call of duty as Commanding Officer of the U.S.S. Walke engaged in a detached mission in support of minesweeping operations to clear the waters for entry of our heavy surface and amphibious forces preparatory to the invasion of Lingayen Gulf, Luzon, Philippine Islands, 6 January 1945. Operating without gun support of other surface ships when 4 Japanese suicide planes were detected flying low overland to attack simultaneously, Comdr. Davis boldly took his position in the exposed wings of the bridge and directed control to pick up the leading plane and open fire. Alert and fearless as the Walke's deadly fire sent the first target crashing into the water and caught the second as it passed close over the bridge to plunge into the sea of portside, he remained steadfast in the path of the third plane plunging swiftly to crash the after end of the bridge structure. Seriously wounded when the craft struck, drenched with gasoline and immediately enveloped in flames, he conned the Walke in the midst of the wreckage; he rallied his command to heroic efforts; he exhorted his officers and men to save the ship and, still on his feet, saw the barrage from his guns destroy the fourth suicide bomber. With the fires under control and the safety of the ship assured, he consented to be carried below. Succumbing several hours later, Comdr. Davis by his example of valor and his unhesitating self-sacrifice, steeled the fighting spirit of his command into unyielding purpose in completing a vital mission. He gallantly gave his life in the service of his country.

*DEALEY, SAMUEL DAVID

Rank and organization: Commander, U.S. Navy. Born: 13 September 1906, Dallas, Tex. Appointed from: Texas. Other Navy awards: Navy Cross with 3 Gold Stars, Silver Star Medal. Citation: For conspicuous gallantry and intrepidity at the risk of his life above and beyond the call of duty as Commanding Officer of the U.S.S. Harder during her 5th War Patrol in Japanese-controlled waters. Floodlighted by a bright moon and disclosed to an enemy destroyer escort which bore down with intent to attack, Comdr. Dealey quickly dived to periscope depth and waited for the pursuer to close range, then opened fire, sending the target and all aboard down in flames with his third torpedo. Plunging deep to avoid fierce depth charges, he again surfaced and, within 9 minutes after sighting another destroyer, had sent the enemy down tail first with a hit directly amidship. Evading detection, he penetrated the confined waters off Tawi Tawi with the Japanese Fleet base 6 miles away and scored death blows on 2 patrolling destroyers in quick succession. With his ship heeled over by concussion from the first exploding target and the second vessel nose-diving in a blinding detonation, he cleared the area at high speed. Sighted by a large hostile fleet force on the following day, he swung his bow toward the lead destroyer for another "down-the-throat" shot, fired 3 bow tubes and promptly crash-dived to be terrifically rocked seconds later by the exploding ship as the Harder passed beneath. This remarkable record of 5 vital Japanese destroyers sunk in 5 short-range torpedo attacks attests the valiant fighting spirit of Comdr. Dealey and his indomitable command.

DEBLANC, JEFFERSON JOSEPH

Rank and Organization: Captain, U.S. Marine Corps Reserve, Marine Fighting Squadron 112. Place and date: Off Kolombangara Island in the

Solomons group, 31 January 1943. Entered service at: Louisiana. Born: 15 February 1921, Lockport, La. Citation: For conspicuous gallantry and intrepidity at the risk of his life above and beyond the call of duty as leader of a section of 6 fighter planes in Marine Fighting Squadron 112, during aerial operations against enemy Japanese forces off Kolombangara Island in the Solomons group, 31 January 1943. Taking off with his section as escort for a strike force of dive bombers and torpedo planes ordered to attack Japanese surface vessels, 1st Lt. DeBlanc led his flight directly to the target area where, at 14,000 feet, our strike force encountered a large number of Japanese Zeros protecting the enemy's surface craft. In company with the other fighters, 1st Lt. DeBlanc instantly engaged the hostile planes and aggressively countered their repeated attempts to drive off our bombers, persevering in his efforts to protect the diving planes and waging fierce combat until, picking up a call for assistance from the dive bombers, under attack by enemy float planes at 1,000 feet, he broke off his engagement with the Zeros, plunged into the formation of float planes and disrupted the savage attack, enabling our dive bombers and torpedo planes to complete their runs on the Japanese surface disposition and withdraw without further incident. Although his escort mission was fulfilled upon the safe retirement of the bombers, 1st Lt. DeBlanc courageously remained on the scene despite a rapidly diminishing fuel supply and, boldly challenging the enemy's superior number of float planes, fought a valiant battle against terrific odds, seizing the tactical advantage and striking repeatedly to destroy 3 of the hostile aircraft and to disperse the remainder. Prepared to maneuver his damaged plane back to base, he had climbed aloft and set his course when he discovered 2 Zeros closing in behind. Undaunted, he opened fire and blasted both Zeros from the sky in a short, bitterly fought action which resulted in such hopeless damage to his own plane that he was forced to bail out at a perilously low altitude atop the trees on enemy-held Kolombangara. A gallant officer, a superb airman, and an indomitable fighter, 1st Lt. DeBlanc had rendered decisive assistance during a critical stage of operations, and his unwavering fortitude in the face of overwhelming opposition reflects the highest credit upon himself and adds new luster to the traditions of the U.S. Naval Service.

*DEFRANZO, ARTHUR F.

Rank and organization: Staff Sergeant, U.S. Army, 1st Infantry Division. Place and date: Near Vaubadon, France, 10 June 1944. Entered service at: Saugus, Mass. Birth: Saugus, Mass. G.O. No.: 1, 4 January 1945. Citation: For conspicuous gallantry and intrepidity at the risk of his life, above and beyond the call of duty, on 10 June 1944, near Vaubadon, France. As scouts were advancing across an open field, the enemy suddenly opened fire with several machineguns and hit 1 of the men. S/Sgt. DeFranzo courageously moved out in the open to the aid of the wounded scout and was himself wounded but brought the man to safety. Refusing aid, S/Sgt. DeFranzo reentered the open field and led the advance upon the enemy. There were always at least 2 machineguns bringing unrelenting fire upon him, but S/Sgt. DeFranzo kept going forward, firing into the enemy and 1 by 1 the enemy emplacements became silent. While advancing he was again wounded, but continued on until he was within 100 yards of the enemy position and even as he fell, he kept firing his rifle and waving his men forward. When his company came up behind him, S/Sgt. DeFranzo, despite his many severe wounds, suddenly raised himself and once more moved forward in the lead of his men until he was again hit by enemy fire. In a final gesture of indomitable courage, he threw several grenades at the enemy machinegun position and completely destroyed the gun. In this action, S/Sgt. DeFranzo lost his life, but by bearing the brunt of the enemy fire in leading the attack, he prevented a delay in the assault which would have been of considerable benefit to the foe, and he made possible his company's advance with a minimum of casualties. The extraordinary heroism and magnificent devotion to duty displayed by S/Sgt. DeFranzo was a great inspiration to all about him, and is in keeping with the highest traditions of the armed forces.

*DEGLOPPER, CHARLES N.

Rank and organization: Private First Class, U.S. Army, Co. C, 325th Glider Infantry, 82d Airborne Division. Place and date: Merderet River at la Fiere, France, 9 June 1944. Entered service at: Grand Island, N.Y. Birth: Grand Island, N.Y. G.O. No.: 22, 28 February 1946. Citation: He was a member of Company C, 325th Glider Infantry, on 9 June 1944 advancing with the forward platoon to secure a bridgehead across the Merderet River at La Fiere, France. At dawn the platoon had penetrated an outer line of machineguns and riflemen, but in so doing had become cut off from the rest of the company. Vastly superior forces began a decimation of the stricken unit and put in motion a flanking maneuver which would have completely exposed the American platoon in a shallow roadside ditch where it had taken cover. Detecting this danger, Pfc. DeGlopper volunteered to support his comrades by fire from his automatic rifle while they attempted a withdrawal through a break in a hedgerow 40 yards to the rear. Scorning a concentration of enemy automatic weapons and rifle fire, he walked from the ditch onto the road in full view of the Germans, and sprayed the hostile positions with assault fire. He was wounded, but he continued firing. Struck again, he started to fall; and yet his grim determination and valiant fighting spirit could not be broken. Kneeling in the roadway, weakened by his grievous wounds, he leveled his heavy weapon against the enemy and fired burst after burst until killed outright. He was successful in drawing the enemy action away from his fellow soldiers, who continued the fight from a more advantageous position and established the first bridgehead over the Merderet. In the area where he made his intrepid stand his comrades later found the ground strewn with dead Germans and many machineguns and automatic weapons which he had knocked out of action. Pfc. DeGlopper's gallant sacrifice and unflinching heroism while facing unsurmountable odds were in great measure responsible for a highly important tactical victory in the Normandy Campaign.

*DELEAU, EMILE, JR.

Rank and organization: Sergeant, U.S. Army, Company A, 142d Infantry, 36th Infantry Division. Place and date: Oberhoffen, France, 12 February 1945. Entered service at: Blaine, Ohio. Birth: Lansing, Ohio. G.O. No.: 60, 25 July 1945. Citation: He led a squad in the night attack on Oberhoffen, France, where fierce house-to-house fighting took place. After clearing 1 building of opposition, he moved his men toward a second house from which heavy machinegun fire came. He courageously exposed himself to hostile bullets and, firing his submachine gun as he went, advanced steadily toward the enemy position until close enough to hurl grenades through a window, killing 3 Germans and wrecking their gun. His progress was stopped by heavy rifle and machinegun fire from another house. Sgt. Deleau dashed through the door with his gun blazing. Within, he captured 10 Germans. The squad then took up a position for the night and awaited daylight to resume the attack. At dawn of 2 February Sgt. Deleau pressed forward with his unit, killing 2 snipers as he advanced to a point where machinegun fire from a house barred the way. Despite vicious small-arms fire, Sgt. Deleau ran across an open area to reach the rear of the building, where he destroyed 1 machinegun and killed its 2 operators with a grenade. He worked to the front of the structure and located a second machinegun. Finding it impossible to toss a grenade into the house from his protected position, he fearlessly moved away from the building and was about to hurl his explosive when he was instantly killed by a burst from the gun he sought to knock out. With magnificent courage and daring aggressiveness, Sgt. Deleau cleared 4 well-defended houses of Germans, inflicted severe losses on the enemy and at the sacrifice of his own life aided his battalion to reach its objective with a minimum of casualties.

DERVISHIAN, ERNEST H.

Rank and organization: Second Lieutenant, U.S. Army, 34th Infantry Division. Place and date: Near Cisterna, Italy, 23 May 1944. Entered service at: Richmond, Va. Birth: Richmond, Va. G.O. No.: 3, 8 January 1945. Citation: For conspicuous gallantry and intrepidity at risk of life above and beyond the call of duty on 23 May 1944, in the vicinity of Cisterna, Italy. 2d Lt. Dervishian (then Tech. Sgt.) and 4 members of his platoon found themselves far ahead of their company after an aggressive advance in the face of enemy artillery and sniper fire. Approaching a railroad embankment, they observed a force of German soldiers hiding in dugouts. 2d Lt. Dervishian, directing his men to cover him, boldly moved forward and firing his carbine forced 10 Germans to surrender. His men then advanced and captured 15 more Germans occupying adjacent dugouts. The prisoners were returned to the rear to be picked up by advancing units. From the railroad embankment, 2d Lt. Dervishian and his men then observed 9 Germans who were fleeing across a ridge. He and his men opened fire and 3 of the enemy were wounded. As his men were firing, 2d Lt. Dervishian, unnoticed, fearlessly dashed forward alone and captured all of the fleeing enemy before his companions joined him on the ridge. At this point 4 other men joined 2d Lt. Dervishian's group. An attempt was made to send the 4 newly arrived men along the left flank of a large, dense vineyard that lay ahead, but murderous machinegun fire forced them back. Deploying his men, 2d Lt. Dervishian moved to the front of his group and led the advance into the vineyard. He and his men suddenly became pinned down by a machinegun firing at them at a distance of 15 yards. Feigning death while the hostile weapon blazed away at him, 2d Lt. Dervishian assaulted the position during a halt in the firing, using a hand grenade and carbine fire, and forced the 4 German crewmembers to surrender. The 4 men on the left flank were now ordered to enter the vineyard but encountered machinegun fire which killed 1 soldier and wounded another. At this moment the enemy intensified the fight by throwing potato-masher grenades at the valiant band of American soldiers within the vineyard. 2d Lt. Dervishian ordered his men to withdraw; but instead of following, jumped into the machinegun position he had just captured and opened fire with the enemy weapon in the direction of the second hostile machinegun nest. Observing movement in a dugout 2 or 3 yards to the rear, 2d Lt. Dervishian seized a machine pistol. Simultaneously blazing away at the entrance to the dugout to prevent its occupants from firing and firing his machinegun at the other German nest, he forced 5 Germans in each position to surrender. Determined to rid the area of all Germans, 2d Lt. Dervishian continued his advance alone. Noticing another machinegun position beside a house, he picked up an abandoned machine pistol and forced 6 more Germans to surrender by spraying their position with fire. Unable to locate additional targets in the vicinity, 2d Lt. Dervishian conducted these prisoners to the rear. The prodigious courage and combat skill exhibited by 2d Lt. Dervishian are exemplary of the finest traditions of the U.S. Armed Forces.

*DIAMOND, JAMES H.

Rank and organization: Private First Class, U.S. Army, Company D, 21st Infantry, 24th Infantry Division. Place and date: Mintal, Mindanao, Philippine Islands, 814 May 1945. Entered service at: Gulfport, Miss. Birth: New Orleans, La. G.O. No.: 23, 6 March 1946. Citation: As a member of the machinegun section, he displayed extreme gallantry and intrepidity above and beyond the call of duty. When a Japanese sniper rose from his foxhole to throw a grenade into their midst, this valiant soldier charged and killed the enemy with a burst from his submachine gun; then, by delivering sustained fire from his personal arm and simultaneously directing the fire of 105mm. and .50 caliber weapons upon the enemy pillboxes immobilizing this and another machinegun section, he enabled them to put their guns into action. When 2 infantry companies established a bridgehead, he voluntarily assisted in evacuating the wounded under heavy fire; and then, securing an abandoned vehicle, transported casualties to the rear through mortar and artillery fire so intense as to render the vehicle inoperative and despite the fact he was suffering from a painful wound. The following day he again volunteered, this time for the hazardous job of repairing a bridge under heavy enemy fire. On 14 May 1945, when leading a patrol to evacuate casualties from his battalion, which was cut off, he ran through a virtual hail of Japanese fire to secure an abandoned machine gun. Though mortally wounded as he reached the gun, he succeeded in drawing sufficient fire upon himself so that the remaining members of the patrol could reach safety. Pfc. Diamond's indomitable spirit, constant disregard of danger, and eagerness to assist his comrades, will ever remain a symbol of selflessness and heroic sacrifice to those for whom he gave his life.

*DIETZ, ROBERT H.

Rank and organization: Staff Sergeant, U.S. Army, Company A, 38th Armored Infantry Battalion, 7th Armored Division. Place and date: Kirchain, Germany, 29 March 1945. Entered service at: Kingston, N.Y. Birth: Kingston, N.Y. G.O. No.: 119, 17 December 1945. Citation: He was a squad leader when the task force to which his unit was attached encountered resistance in its advance on Kirchain, Germany. Between the town's outlying buildings 300 yards distant, and the stalled armored column were a minefield and 2 bridges defended by German rocket-launching teams and riflemen. From the town itself came heavy small-arms fire. Moving forward with his men to protect engineers while they removed the minefield and the demolition charges attached to the bridges, S/Sgt. Dietz came under intense fire. On his own initiative he advanced alone, scorning the bullets which struck all around him, until he was able to kill the bazooka team defending the first bridge. He continued ahead and had killed another bazooka team, bayoneted an enemy soldier armed with a panzerfaust and shot 2 Germans when he was knocked to the ground by another blast of another panzerfaust. He quickly recovered, killed the man who had fired at him and then jumped into waist-deep water under the second bridge to disconnect the demolition charges. His work was completed; but as he stood up to signal that the route was clear, he was killed by another enemy volley from the left flank. S/Sgt. Dietz by his intrepidity and valiant effort on his self-imposed mission, single-handedly opened the road for the capture of Kirchain and left with his comrades an inspiring example of gallantry in the face of formidable odds.

DOOLITTLE, JAMES H. (Air Mission)

Rank and organization: Brigadier General, U.S. Army. Air Corps. Place and date: Over Japan. Entered service at: Berkeley, Calif. Birth: Alameda, Calif. G.O. No.: 29, 9 June 1942. Citation: For conspicuous leadership above the call of duty, involving personal valor and intrepidity at an extreme hazard to life. With the apparent certainty of being forced to land in enemy territory or to perish at sea, Gen. Doolittle personally led a squadron of Army bombers, manned by volunteer crews, in a highly destructive raid on the Japanese mainland.

DOSS, DESMOND T.

Rank and organization: Private First Class, U.S. Army, Medical Detachment, 307th Infantry, 77th Infantry Division. Place and date: Near Urasoe Mura, Okinawa, Ryukyu Islands, 29 April-21 May 1945. Entered service at: Lynchburg, Va. Birth: Lynchburg, Va. G.O. No.: 97, 1 November 1945. Citation: He was a company aid man when the 1st Battalion assaulted a jagged escarpment 400 feet high As our troops gained the summit, a heavy concentration of artillery, mortar and machinegun fire crashed into them, inflicting approximately 75 casualties and driving the others back. Pfc. Doss refused to seek cover and remained in the fire-swept area with the many stricken, carrying them 1 by 1 to the edge of the escarpment and there lowering them on a rope-supported litter down the face of a cliff to friendly hands. On 2 May, he exposed himself to heavy rifle and mortar fire in rescuing a wounded man 200 yards forward of the lines on the same escarpment; and 2 days later he treated 4 men who had been cut down while assaulting a strongly defended cave, advancing through a shower of grenades to within 8 yards of enemy forces in a cave's mouth, where he dressed his comrades' wounds before making 4 separate trips under fire to evacuate them to safety. On 5 May, he unhesitatingly braved enemy shelling and small arms fire to assist an artillery officer. He applied bandages, moved his patient to a spot that offered protection from small arms fire and, while artillery and mortar shells fell close by, painstakingly administered plasma. Later that day, when an American was severely wounded by fire from a cave, Pfc. Doss crawled to him where he had fallen 25 feet from the enemy position, rendered aid, and carried him 100 yards to safety while continually exposed to enemy fire. On 21 May, in a night attack on high ground near Shuri, he remained in exposed territory while the rest of his company took cover, fearlessly risking the chance that he would be mistaken for an infiltrating Japanese and giving aid to the injured until he was himself seriously wounded in the legs by the explosion of a grenade. Rather than call another aid man from cover, he cared for his own injuries and waited 5 hours before litter bearers reached him and started carrying him to cover. The trio was caught in an enemy tank attack and Pfc. Doss, seeing a more critically wounded man nearby, crawled off the litter; and directed the bearers to give their first attention to the other man. Awaiting the litter bearers' return, he was again struck, this time suffering a compound fracture of 1 arm. With magnificent fortitude he bound a rifle stock to his shattered arm as a splint and then crawled 300 yards over rough terrain to the aid station. Through his outstanding bravery and unflinching determination in the face of desperately dangerous conditions Pfc. Doss saved the lives of many soldiers. His name became a symbol throughout the 77th Infantry Division for outstanding gallantry far above and beyond the call of duty.

DROWLEY, JESSE R.

Rank and organization: Staff Sergeant, U.S. Army, Americal Infantry Division. Place and date: Bougainville, Solomon Islands, 30 January 1944. Entered service at: Spokane, Wash. Birth: St. Charles, Mich. G.O. No.: 73, 6 September 1944. Citation: For gallantry and intrepidity at the risk of his life above and beyond the call of duty in action with the enemy at Bougainville, Solomon Islands, 30 January 1944. S/Sgt. Drowley, a squad leader in a platoon whose mission during an attack was to remain under cover while holding the perimeter defense and acting as a reserve for assaulting echelon, saw 3 members of the assault company fall badly wounded. When intense hostile fire prevented aid from reaching the casualties, he fearlessly rushed forward to carry the wounded to cover. After rescuing 2 men, S/Sgt. Drowley discovered an enemy pillbox undetected by assaulting tanks that was inflicting heavy casualties upon the attacking force and was a chief obstacle to the success of the advance. Delegating the rescue of the third man to an assistant, he ran across open terrain to 1 of the tanks. Signaling to the crew, he climbed to the turret, exchanged his weapon for a submachine gun and voluntarily rode the deck of the tank directing it toward the pillbox by tracer fire. The tank, under constant heavy enemy fire, continued to within 20 feet of the pillbox where S/Sgt. Drowley received a severe bullet wound in the chest. Refusing to return for medical treatment, he remained on the tank and continued to direct its progress until the enemy box was definitely located by the crew. At this point he again was wounded by small arms fire, losing his left eye and falling to the ground. He remained alongside the tank until the pillbox had been completely demolished and another directly behind the first destroyed. S/Sgt. Drowley, his voluntary mission successfully accomplished, returned alone for medical treatment.

DUNHAM, RUSSELL E.

Rank and organization: Technical Sergeant, U.S. Army, Company I, 30th Infantry, 3d Infantry Division. Place and date: Near Kayserberg, France, 8 January 1945. Entered service at: Brighton Ill. Born: 23 February 1920, East Carondelet, Ill. G.O. No.: 37, 11 May 1945. Citation: For conspicuous gallantry and intrepidity at risk of life above and beyond the call of duty. At about 1430 hours on 8 January 1945, during an attack on Hill 616, near Kayserberg, France, T/Sgt. Dunham single-handedly assaulted 3 enemy machineguns. Wearing a white robe made of a mattress cover, carrying 12 carbine magazines and with a dozen hand grenades snagged in his belt, suspenders, and buttonholes, T/Sgt. Dunham advanced in the attack up a snow-covered hill under fire from 2 machineguns and supporting riflemen. His platoon 35 yards behind him, T/Sgt. Dunham crawled 75 yards under heavy direct fire toward the timbered emplacement shielding the left machinegun. As he jumped to his feet 10 yards from the gun and charged forward, machinegun fire tore through his camouflage robe and a rifle bullet seared a 10-inch gash across his back sending him spinning 15 yards down hill into the snow. When the indomitable sergeant sprang to his feet to renew his 1-man assault, a German egg grenade landed beside him. He kicked it aside, and as it exploded 5 yards away, shot and killed the German machinegunner and assistant gunner. His carbine empty, he jumped into the emplacement and hauled out the third member of the gun crew by the collar. Although his back wound was causing him excruciating pain and blood was seeping through his white coat, T/Sgt. Dunham proceeded 50 yards through a storm of automatic and rifle fire to attack the second machinegun. Twenty-five yards from the emplacement he hurled 2 grenades, destroying the gun and its crew; then fired down into the supporting foxholes with his carbine dispatching and dispersing the enemy riflemen. Although his coat was so thoroughly blood-soaked that he was a conspicuous target against the white landscape, T/Sgt. Dunham again advanced ahead of his platoon in an assault on enemy positions farther up the hill. Coming under machinegun fire from 65 yards to his front, while rifle grenades exploded 10 yards from his position, he hit the ground and crawled forward. At 15 yards range, he jumped to his feet, staggered a few paces toward the timbered machinegun emplacement and killed the crew with hand grenades. An enemy rifleman fired at pointblank range, but missed him. After killing the rifleman, T/Sgt. Dunham drove others from their foxholes with grenades and carbine fire. Killing 9 Germans—wounding 7 and capturing 2—firing about 175 rounds of carbine ammunition, and expending 11 grenades, T/Sgt. Dunham, despite a painful wound, spearheaded a spectacular and successful diversionary attack.

DUNLAP, ROBERT. HUGO

Rank and organization: Captain, U.S. Marine Corps Reserve, Company C, 1st Battalion, 26th Marines, 5th Marine Division. Place and date: On Iwo Jima, Volcano Islands, 20 and 21 February 1945. Entered service at: Illinois. Born: 19 October 1920, Abingdon, Ill. Citation: For conspicuous gallantry and intrepidity at the risk of his life above and beyond the call of duty as commanding officer of Company C, 1st Battalion, 26th Marines, 5th Marine Division, in action against enemy Japanese forces during the seizure of Iwo Jima in the Volcano Islands, on 20 and 21 February, 1945. Defying uninterrupted blasts of Japanese artillery. mortar, rifle and machinegun fire, Capt. Dunlap led his troops in a determined advance from low ground uphill toward the steep cliffs from which the enemy poured a devastating rain of shrapnel and bullets, steadily inching forward until the tremendous volume of enemy fire from the caves located high to his front temporarily halted his progress. Determined not to yield, he crawled alone approximately 200 yards forward of his front lines, took observation at the base of the cliff 50 yards from Japanese lines, located the enemy gun positions and returned to his own lines where he relayed the vital information to supporting artillery and naval gunfire units. Persistently disregarding his own personal safety, he then placed himself in an exposed vantage point to direct more accurately the supporting fire and, working without respite for 2 days and 2 nights under constant enemy fire, skillfully directed a smashing bombardment against the almost impregnable Japanese positions despite numerous obstacles and heavy marine casualties. A brilliant leader, Capt. Dunlap inspired his men to heroic efforts during this critical phase of the battle and by his cool decision, indomitable fighting spirit, and daring tactics in the face of fanatic opposition greatly accelerated the final decisive defeat of Japanese countermeasures in his sector and materially furthered the continued advance of his company. His great personal valor and gallant spirit of self-sacrifice throughout the bitter hostilities reflect the highest credit upon Capt. Dunlap and the U.S. Naval Service.

*DUTKO, JOHN W.

Rank and organization: Private First Class, U.S. Army, 3d Infantry Division. Place and date: Near Ponte Rotto, Italy, 23 May 1944. Entered service at: Riverside, N.J. Birth: Dilltown, Pa. G.O. No.: 80, 5 October 1944. citation: For conspicuous gallantry and intrepidity at risk of life above and beyond the call of duty, on 23 May 1944, near Ponte Rotto, Italy. Pfc. Dutko left the cover of an abandoned enemy trench at the height of an artillery concentration in a single-handed attack upon 3 machineguns and an 88mm. mobile gun. Despite the intense fire of these 4 weapons which were aimed directly at him, Pfc. Dutko ran 10.0 yards through the impact area, paused momentarily in a shell crater, and then continued his 1-man assault. Although machinegun bullets kicked up the dirt at his heels, and 88mm. shells exploded within 30 yards of him, Pfc. Dutko nevertheless made his way to a point within 30 yards of the first enemy machinegun and killed both gunners with a hand grenade. Although the second machinegun wounded him, knocking him to the ground, Pfc. Dutko regained his feet and advanced on the

88mm. gun, firing his Browning automatic rifle from the hip. When he came within 10 yards of this weapon he killed its 5-man crew with 1 long burst of fire. Wheeling on the machinegun which had wounded him, Pfc. Dutko killed the gunner and his assistant. The third German machinegun fired on Pfc. Dutko from a position 20 yards distant wounding him a second time as he proceeded toward the enemy weapon in a half run. He killed both members of its crew with a single burst from his Browning automatic rifle, continued toward the gun and died, his body falling across the dead German crew.

*DYESS, AQUILLA JAMES

Rank and organization: Lieutenant Colonel, U.S. Marine Corps Reserve. Born: 11 January 1909, Augusta, Ga. Appointed from: Georgia. Citation: For conspicuous gallantry and intrepidity at the risk of his life above and beyond the call of duty as Commanding Officer of the 1st Battalion, 24th Marines (Rein), 4th Marine Division, in action against enemy Japanese forces during the assault on Namur Island, Kwajalein Atoll, Marshall Islands, 1 and 2 February 1944. Undaunted by severe fire from automatic Japanese weapons, Lt. Col. Dyess launched a powerful final attack on the second day of the assault, unhesitatingly posting himself between the opposing lines to point out objectives and avenues of approach and personally leading the advancing troops. Alert, and determined to quicken the pace of the offensive against increased enemy fire, he was constantly at the head of advance units, inspiring his men to push forward until the Japanese had been driven back to a small center of resistance and victory assured. While standing on the parapet of an antitank trench directing a group of infantry in a flanking attack against the last enemy position, Lt. Col. Dyess was killed by a burst of enemy machinegun fire. His daring and forceful leadership and his valiant fighting spirit in the face of terrific opposition were in keeping with the highest traditions of the U.S. Naval Service. He gallantly gave his life for his country.

EDSON, MERRITT AUSTIN

Rank and organization: Colonel, U.S. Marine Corps. Born: 25 April 1897, Rutland, Vt. Appointed from: Vermont. Other Navy awards: Navy Cross with Gold Star, Silver Star Medal, Legion of Merit with Gold Star. Citation: For extraordinary heroism and conspicuous intrepidity above and beyond the call of duty as Commanding Officer of the 1st Marine Raider Battalion, with Parachute Battalion attached, during action against enemy Japanese forces in the Solomon Islands on the night of 1314 September 1942. After the airfield on Guadalcanal had been seized from the enemy on 8 August, Col. Edson, with a force of 800 men, was assigned to the occupation and defense of a ridge dominating the jungle on either side of the airport. Facing a formidable Japanese attack which, augmented by infiltration, had crashed through our front lines, he, by skillful handling of his troops, successfully withdrew his forward units to a reserve line with minimum casualties. When the enemy, in a subsequent series of violent assaults, engaged our force in desperate hand-to-hand combat with bayonets, rifles, pistols, grenades, and knives, Col. Edson, although continuously exposed to hostile fire throughout the night, personally directed defense of the reserve position against a fanatical foe of greatly superior numbers. By his astute leadership and gallant devotion to duty, he enabled his men, despite severe losses, to cling tenaciously to their position on the vital ridge, thereby retaining command not only of the Guadalcanal airfield, but also of the 1st Division's entire offensive installations in the surrounding area.

EHLERS, WALTER D.

Rank and organization: Staff Sergeant, U.S. Army, 18th Infantry, 1st Infantry Division. Place and dare: Near Goville, France, 9-10 June 1944. Entered service at: Manhattan, Kans. Birth: Junction City, Kans. G.O. No.: 91, 19 December 1944. Citation: For conspicuous gallantry and intrepidity at the risk of his life above and beyond the call of duty on 9-10 June

1944, near Goville, France. S/Sgt. Ehlers, always acting as the spearhead of the attack, repeatedly led his men against heavily defended enemy strong points exposing himself to deadly hostile fire whenever the situation required heroic and courageous leadership. Without waiting for an order, S/Sgt. Ehlers, far ahead of his men, led his squad against a strongly defended enemy strong point, personally killing 4 of an enemy patrol who attacked him en route. Then crawling forward under withering machinegun fire, he pounced upon the guncrew and put it out of action. Turning his attention to 2 mortars protected by the crossfire of 2 machineguns, S/Sgt. Ehlers led his men through this hail of bullets to kill or put to flight the enemy of the mortar section, killing 3 men himself. After mopping up the mortar positions, he again advanced on a machinegun, his progress effectively covered by his squad. When he was almost on top of the gun he leaped to his feet and, although greatly outnumbered, he knocked out the position single-handed. The next day, having advanced deep into enemy territory, the platoon of which S/Sgt. Ehlers was a member, finding itself in an untenable position as the enemy brought increased mortar, machinegun, and small arms fire to bear on it, was ordered to withdraw. S/Sgt. Ehlers, after his squad had covered the withdrawal of the remainder of the platoon, stood up and by continuous fire at the semicircle of enemy placements, diverted the bulk of the heavy hostile fire on himself, thus permitting the members of his own squad to withdraw. At this point, though wounded himself, he carried his wounded automatic rifleman to safety and then returned fearlessly over the shell-swept field to retrieve the automatic rifle which he was unable to carry previously. After having his wound treated, he refused to be evacuated, and returned to lead his squad. The intrepid leadership, indomitable courage, and fearless aggressiveness displayed by S/Sgt. Ehlers in the face of overwhelming enemy forces serve as an inspiration to others.

*ELROD, HENRY TALMAGE

Rank and organization: Captain, U.S. Marine Corps. Born: 27 September 1905, Rebecca, Ga. Entered service at: Ashburn, Ga. Citation: For conspicuous gallantry and intrepidity at the risk of his life above and beyond the call of duty while attached to Marine Fighting Squadron 211, during action against enemy Japanese land, surface and aerial units at Wake Island, 8 to 23 December 1941. Engaging vastly superior forces of enemy bombers and warships on 9 and 12 December, Capt. Elrod shot down 2 of a flight of 22 hostile planes and, executing repeated bombing and strafing runs at extremely low altitude and close range, succeeded in inflicting deadly damage upon a large Japanese vessel, thereby sinking the first major warship to be destroyed by small caliber bombs delivered from a fighter-type aircraft. When his plane was disabled by hostile fire and no other ships were operative, Capt. Elrod assumed command of 1 flank of the line set up in defiance of the enemy landing and, conducting a brilliant defense, enabled his men to hold their positions and repulse intense hostile fusillades to provide covering fire for unarmed ammunition carriers. Capturing an automatic weapon during 1 enemy rush in force, he gave his own firearm to 1 of his men and fought on vigorously against the Japanese. Responsible in a large measure for the strength of his sector's gallant resistance, on 23 December, Capt. Elrod led his men with bold aggressiveness until he fell, mortally wounded. His superb skill as a pilot, daring leadership and unswerving devotion to duty distinguished him among the defenders of Wake Island, and his valiant conduct reflects the highest credit upon himself and the U.S. Naval Service. He gallantly gave his life for his country.

*ENDL, GERALD L.

Rank and organization: Staff Sergeant, U S. Army, 32d Infantry Division. Place and date: Near Anamo, New Guinea, 11 July 1944. Entered service at: Janesville, Wis. Birth: Ft. Atkinson, Wis. G.O. No.: 17,

13 March 1945. Citation: For conspicuous gallantry and intrepidity at the risk of his life above and beyond the call of duty near Anamo, New Guinea, on 11 July 1944. S/Sgt. Endl was at the head of the leading platoon of his company advancing along a jungle trail when enemy troops were encountered and a fire fight developed. The enemy attacked in force under heavy rifle, machinegun, and grenade fire. His platoon leader wounded, S/Sgt. Endl immediately assumed command and deployed his platoon on a firing line at the fork in the trail toward which the enemy attack was directed. The dense jungle terrain greatly restricted vision and movement, and he endeavored to penetrate down the trail toward an open clearing of Kunai grass. As he advanced, he detected the enemy, supported by at least 6 light and 2 heavy machineguns, attempting an enveloping movement around both flanks. His commanding officer sent a second platoon to move up on the left flank of the position, but the enemy closed in rapidly, placing our force in imminent danger of being isolated and annihilated. Twelve members of his platoon were wounded, 7 being cut off by the enemy. Realizing that if his platoon were forced farther back, these 7 men would be hopelessly trapped and at the mercy of a vicious enemy, he resolved to advance at all cost, knowing it meant almost certain death, in an effort to rescue his comrades. In the face of extremely heavy fire he went forward alone and for a period of approximately 10 minutes engaged the enemy in a heroic close-range fight, holding them off while his men crawled forward under cover to evacuate the wounded and to withdraw. Courageously refusing to abandon 4 more wounded men who were lying along the trail, 1 by 1 he brought them back to safety. As he was carrying the last man in his arms he was struck by a heavy burst of automatic fire and was killed. By his persistent and daring self-sacrifice and on behalf of his comrades, S/Sgt. Endl made possible the successful evacuation of all but 1 man, and enabled the 2 platoons to withdraw with their wounded and to reorganize with the rest of the company.

*EPPERSON, HAROLD GLENN

Rank and organization: Private First Class, U.S. Marine Corps Reserve. Born: 14 July 1923, Akron, Ohio. Accredited to: Ohio. Citation: For conspicuous gallantry and intrepidity at the risk of his life above and beyond the call of duty while serving with the 1st Battalion, 6th Marines, 2d Marine Division, in action against enemy Japanese forces on the Island of Saipan in the Marianas, on 25 June 1944. With his machine-gun emplacement bearing the full brunt of a fanatic assault initiated by the Japanese under cover of predawn darkness, Pfc. Epperson manned his weapon with determined aggressiveness, fighting furiously in the defense of his battalion's position and maintaining a steady stream of devastating fire against rapidly infiltrating hostile troops to aid materially in annihilating several of the enemy and in breaking the abortive attack. Suddenly a Japanese soldier, assumed to be dead, sprang up and hurled a powerful hand grenade into the emplacement. Determined to save his comrades, Pfc. Epperson unhesitatingly chose to sacrifice himself and, diving upon the deadly missile, absorbed the shattering violence of the exploding charge in his own body. Stouthearted and indomitable in the face of certain death, Pfc. Epperson fearlessly yielded his own life that his able comrades might carry on the relentless battle against a ruthless enemy. His superb valor and unfaltering devotion to duty throughout reflect the highest credit upon himself and upon the U.S. Naval Service. He gallantly gave his life for his country.

ERWIN, HENRY E. (Air Mission)

Rank and organization: Staff Sergeant, U.S. Army Air Corps, 52d Bombardment Squadron, 29th Bombardment Group, 20th Air Force. Place and date: Koriyama, Japan, 12 April 1945. Entered service at: Bessemer, Ala. Born: 8 May 1921, Adamsville, Ala. G.O. No.: 44, 6 June 1945. Citation: He was the radio operator of a B-29 airplane leading a group formation to attack Koriyama, Japan. He was charged with the additional duty of dropping phosphoresce smoke bombs to aid in assembling the group when the launching point was reached. Upon entering the assembly area, aircraft fire and enemy fighter opposition was encountered. Among the phosphoresce bombs launched by S/Sgt. Erwin, 1 proved faulty, exploding in the launching chute, and shot back into the interior of the aircraft, striking him in the face. The burning phosphoresce obliterated his nose and completely blinded him. Smoke filled the plane, obscuring the vision of the pilot. S/Sgt. Erwin realized that the aircraft and crew would be lost if the burning bomb remained in the plane. Without regard for his own safety, he picked it up and feeling his way, instinctively, crawled around the gun turret and headed for the copilot's window. He found the navigator's table obstructing his passage. Grasping the burning bomb between his forearm and body, he unleashed the spring lock and raised the table. Struggling through the narrow passage he stumbled forward into the smoke-filled pilot's compartment. Groping with his burning hands, he located the window and threw the bomb out. Completely aflame, he fell back upon the floor. The smoke cleared, the pilot, at 300 feet, pulled the plane out of its dive. S/Sgt. Erwin's gallantry and heroism above and beyond the call of duty saved the lives of his comrades.

*EUBANKS, RAY E.

Rank and organization: Sergeant, U.S. Army, Company D, 503d Parachute Infantry. Place and date: At Noemfoor Island, Dutch New Guinea, 23 July 1944. Entered service at: LaGrange, N.C. Born: 6 February 1922, Snow Hill, N.C. G.O. No.: 20, 29 March 1945. Citation: For conspicuous gallantry and intrepidity at the risk of his life above and beyond the call of duty at Noemfoor Island, Dutch New Guinea, 23 July 1944. While moving to the relief of a platoon isolated by the enemy, his company encountered a strong enemy position supported by machinegun, rifle, and mortar fire. Sgt. Eubanks was ordered to make an attack with 1 squad to neutralize the enemy by fire in order to assist the advance of his company. He maneuvered his squad to within 30 yards of the enemy where heavy fire checked his advance. Directing his men to maintain their fire, he and 2 scouts worked their way forward up a shallow depression to within 25 yards of the enemy. Directing the scouts to remain in place, Sgt. Eubanks armed himself with an automatic rifle and worked himself forward over terrain swept by intense fire to within 15 yards of the enemy position when he opened fire with telling effect. The enemy, having located his position, concentrated their fire with the result that he was wounded and a bullet rendered his rifle useless. In spite of his painful wounds he immediately charged the enemy and using his weapon as a club killed 4 of the enemy before he was himself again hit and killed. Sgt. Eubanks' heroic action, courage, and example in leadership so inspired his men that their advance was successful. They killed 45 of the enemy and drove the remainder from the position, thus effecting the relief of our beleaguered troops.

*EVANS, ERNEST EDWIN

Rank and organization: Commander, U.S. Navy. Born: 13 August 1908, Pawnee, Okla. Accredited to: Oklahoma. Other Navy awards: Navy Cross, Bronze Star Medal. Citation: For conspicuous gallantry and intrepidity at the risk of his life above and beyond the call of duty as commanding officer of the U.S.S. Johnston in action against major units of the enemy Japanese fleet during the battle off Samar on 25 October 1944. The first to lay a smokescreen and to open fire as an enemy task force, vastly superior in number, firepower and armor, rapidly approached. Comdr. Evans gallantly diverted the powerful blasts of hostile guns from the lightly armed and armored carriers under his protection, launching the first torpedo attack when the Johnston came under straddling Japanese shellfire. Undaunted by damage sustained under the terrific volume of fire, he unhesitatingly joined others of his group to provide fire support during subsequent torpedo attacks against the Japanese and, outshooting and outmaneuvering the enemy as he consistently interposed his vessel between the hostile fleet units and our carriers despite the crippling loss of engine power and communications with steering aft, shifted command to the fantail, shouted steering orders through an open hatch to men turning the rudder by hand and battled furiously until the Johnston, burning and shuddering from a mortal blow, lay dead in the water after 3 hours of fierce combat. Seriously wounded early in the engagement, Comdr. Evans, by his indomitable courage and brilliant professional skill, aided materially in turning back the enemy during a critical phase of the action. His valiant fighting spirit throughout this historic battle will venture as an inspiration to all who served with him.

EVERHART, FORREST E.

Rank and organization: Technical Sergeant, U.S. Army, Company H, 359th Infantry, 90th Infantry Division. Place and date: Near Kerling, France, 12 November 1944. Entered service at: Texas City, Tex. Birth: Bainbridge, Ohio. G.O. No.: 77, 10 September 1945. Citation: He commanded a platoon that bore the brunt of a desperate enemy counterattack near Korling, France, before dawn on 12 November 1944. When German tanks and self-propelled guns penetrated his left flank and overwhelming infantry forces threatened to overrun the 1 remaining machinegun in that section, he ran 400 yards through woods churned by artillery and mortar concentrations to strengthen the defense. With the 1 remaining gunner, he directed furious fire into the advancing hordes until they swarmed close to the position. He left the gun, boldly charged the attackers and, after a 15-minute exchange of hand grenades, forced them to withdraw leaving 30 dead behind. He recrossed the fire-swept terrain to his then threatened right flank, exhorted his men and directed murderous fire from the single machinegun at that position. There, in the light of bursting mortar shells, he again closed with the enemy in a hand grenade duel and, after a fierce 30-minute battle, forced the Germans to withdraw leaving another 20 dead. The gallantry and intrepidity of T/Sgt. Everhart in rallying his men and refusing to fall back in the face of terrible odds were highly instrumental in repelling the fanatical enemy counterattack directed at the American bridgehead across the Moselle River.

*FARDY, JOHN PETER

Rank and organization: Corporal, U.S Marine Corps. Born: 8 August 1922, Chicago, Ill. Accredited to: Illinois. Citation: For conspicuous gallantry and intrepidity at the risk of his life above and beyond the call of duty as a squad leader, serving with Company C, 1st Battalion, 1st Marines, 1st Marine Division, in action against enemy Japanese forces on Okinawa Shima in the Ryukyu Islands, 7 May 1945. When his squad was suddenly assailed by extremely heavy small arms fire from the front during a determined advance against strongly fortified, fiercely defended Japanese positions, Cpl. Fardy temporarily deployed his men along a nearby drainage ditch. Shortly thereafter, an enemy grenade fell among the marines in the ditch. Instantly throwing himself upon the deadly missile, Cpl. Fardy absorbed the exploding blast in his own body, thereby protecting his comrades from certain and perhaps fatal injuries. Concerned solely for the welfare of his men, he willingly relinquished his own hope of survival that his fellow marines might live to carry on the fight against a fanatic enemy. A stouthearted leader and indomitable fighter, Cpl. Fardy, by his prompt decision and resolute spirit of self-sacrifice in the face of certain death, had rendered valiant service, and his conduct throughout reflects the highest credit upon himself and the U.S. Naval Service. He gallantly gave his life for his country.

*FEMOYER, ROBERT E. (Air Mission)

Rank and organization: Second Lieutenant, 711th Bombing Squadron, 447th Bomber Group, U.S. Army Air Corps. Place and date: Over Merseburg, Germany, 2 November 1944. Entered service at: Jacksonville, Fla. Born: 31 October 1921, Huntington, W. Va. G.O. No.: 35, 9 May

1945. Citation: For conspicuous gallantry and intrepidity at the risk of his life above and beyond the call of duty near Merseburg, Germany, on 2 November 1944. While on a mission, the bomber, of which 2d Lt. Femoyer was the navigator, was struck by 3 enemy antiaircraft shells. The plane suffered serious damage and 2d Lt. Femoyer was severely wounded in the side and back by shell fragments which penetrated his body. In spite of extreme pain and great loss of blood he refused an offered injection of morphine. He was determined to keep his mental faculties clear in order that he might direct his plane out of danger and so save his comrades. Not being able to arise from the floor, he asked to be propped up in order to enable him to see his charts and instruments. He successfully directed the navigation of his lone bomber for 2 1/2 hours so well it avoided enemy flak and returned to the field without further damage. Only when the plane had arrived in the safe area over the English Channel did he feel that he had accomplished his objective; then, and only then, he permitted an injection of a sedative. He died shortly after being removed from the plane. The heroism and self-sacrifice of 2d Lt. Femoyer are in keeping with the highest traditions of the U.S. Army.

FIELDS, JAMES H.

Rank and organization: First Lieutenant, U.S. Army, 10th Armored Infantry, 4th Armored Division. Place and date: Rechicourt, France, 27 September 1944. Entered service at: Houston, Tex. Birth: Caddo, Tex. G.O. No.: 13, 27 February 1945. Citation: For conspicuous gallantry and intrepidity at risk of life above and beyond the call of duty, at Rechicourt, France. On 27 September 1944, during a sharp action with the enemy infantry and tank forces, 1st Lt. Fields personally led his platoon in a counterattack on the enemy position. Although his platoon had been seriously depleted, the zeal and fervor of his leadership was such as to inspire his small force to accomplish their mission in the face of overwhelming enemy opposition. Seeing that 1 of the men had been wounded, he left his slit trench and with complete disregard for his personal safety attended the wounded man and administered first aid. While returning to his slit trench he was seriously wounded by a shell burst, the fragments of which cut through his face and head, tearing his teeth, gums, and nasal passage. Although rendered speechless by his wounds, 1st Lt. Fields refused to be evacuated and continued to lead his platoon by the use of hand signals. On 1 occasion, when 2 enemy machineguns had a portion of his unit under deadly crossfire, he left his hole, wounded as he was, ran to a light machinegun, whose crew had been knocked out, picked up the gun, and fired it from his hip with such deadly accuracy that both the enemy gun positions were silenced. His action so impressed his men that they found new courage to take up the fire fight, increasing their firepower, and exposing themselves more than ever to harass the enemy with additional bazooka and machinegun fire. Only when his objective had been taken and the enemy scattered did 1st Lt. Fields consent to be evacuated to the battalion command post. At this point he refused to move further back until he had explained to his battalion commander by drawing on paper the position of his men and the disposition of the enemy forces. The dauntless and gallant heroism displayed by 1st Lt. Fields were largely responsible for the repulse of the enemy forces and contributed in a large measure to the successful capture of his battalion objective during this action. His eagerness and determination to close with the enemy and to destroy him was an inspiration to the entire command, and are in the highest traditions of the U.S. Armed Forces.

FINN, JOHN WILLIAM

Rank and organization: Lieutenant, U.S. Navy. Place and date: Naval Air Station, Kaneohe Bay, Territory of Hawaii, 7 December 1941. Entered service at: California. Born: 23 July 1909, Los Angeles, Calif. Citation: For extraordinary heroism distinguished service, and devotion above and beyond the call of duty. During the first attack by Japanese airplanes on the Naval Air Station, Kaneohe Bay, on 7 December 1941, Lt. Finn promptly secured and manned a .50-caliber machinegun mounted on an instruction stand in a completely exposed section of the parking ramp, which was under heavy enemy machinegun strafing fire. Although painfully wounded many times, he continued to man this gun and to return the enemy's fire vigorously and with telling effect throughout the enemy strafing and bombing attacks and with complete disregard for his own personal safety. It was only by specific orders that he was persuaded to leave his post to seek medical attention. Following first aid treatment, although obviously suffering much pain and moving with great difficulty, he returned to the squadron area and actively supervised the rearming of returning planes. His extraordinary heroism and conduct in this action were in keeping with the highest traditions of the U.S. Naval Service.

FISHER, ALMOND E.

Rank and organization: Second Lieutenant, U.S. Army, Company E, 157th Infantry, 45th Infantry Division. Place and date: Near Grammont, France, 12-13 September 1944. Entered service at: Brooklyn, N.Y. Birth: Hume, N.Y. G.O. No: 32, 23 April 1945. Citation: For conspicuous gallantry and intrepidity at the risk of his life above and beyond the call of duty on the night of 1213 September 1944, near Grammont, France. In the darkness of early morning, 2d Lt. Fisher was leading a platoon of Company E, 157th Infantry, in single column to the attack of a strongly defended hill position. At 2:30 A.M., the forward elements were brought under enemy machinegun fire from a distance of not more than 20 yards. Working his way alone to within 20 feet of the gun emplacement, he opened fire with his carbine and killed the entire guncrew. A few minutes after the advance was resumed, heavy machinegun fire was encountered from the left flank. Again crawling forward alone under withering fire, he blasted the gun and crew from their positions with hand grenades. After a halt to replenish ammunition, the advance was again resumed and continued for 1 hour before being stopped by intense machinegun and rifle fire. Through the courageous and skillful leadership of 2d Lt. Fisher, the pocket of determined enemy resistance was rapidly obliterated. Spotting an emplaced machine pistol a short time later, with 1 of his men he moved forward and destroyed the position. As the advance continued the fire fight became more intense. When a bypassed German climbed from his foxhole and attempted to tear an Ml rifle from the hands of 1 of his men, 2d Lt. Fisher whirled and killed the enemy with a burst from his carbine. About 30 minutes later the platoon came under the heavy fire of machineguns from across an open field. 2d Lt. Fisher, disregarding the terrific fire, moved across the field with no cover or concealment to within range, knocked the gun from the position and killed or wounded the crew. Still under heavy fire he returned to his platoon and continued the advance. Once again heavy fire was encountered from a machinegun directly in front. Calling for hand grenades, he found only 2 remaining in the entire platoon. Pulling the pins and carrying a grenade in each hand, he crawled toward the gun emplacement, moving across areas devoid of cover and under intense fire to within 15 yards when he threw the grenades, demolished the gun and killed the guncrew. With ammunition low and daybreak near, he ordered his men to dig in and hold the ground already won. Under constant fire from the front and from both flanks, he moved among them directing the preparations for the defense. Shortly after the ammunition supply was replenished, the Germans launched a last determined effort against the depleted group. Attacked by superior numbers from the front, right, and left flank, and even from the rear, the platoon, in bitter hand-to-hand engagements drove back the enemy at every point. Wounded in both feet by close-range machine pistol fire early in the battle, 2d Lt. Fisher refused medical attention. Unable to walk, he crawled from man to man encouraging them and checking each position. Only after the fighting had subsided did 2d Lt. Fisher crawl 300 yards to the aid station from which he was evacuated. His extraordinary heroism, magnificent valor, and aggressive determination in the face of pointblank enemy fire is an inspiration to his organization and reflects the finest traditions of the U.S. Armed Forces.

*FLAHERTY, FRANCIS C.

Rank and organization: Ensign, U.S. Naval Reserve. Born: 15 March 1919, Charlotte, Mich. Accredited to: Michigan. Citation: For conspicuous devotion to duty and extraordinary courage and complete disregard of his own life, above and beyond the call of duty, during the attack on the Fleet in Pearl Harbor, by Japanese forces on 7 December 1941. When it was seen that the U.S.S. Oklahoma was going to capsize and the order was given to abandon ship, Ens. Flaherty remained in a turret, holding a flashlight so the remainder of the turret crew could see to escape, thereby sacrificing his own life.

*FLEMING, RICHARD E.

Rank and organization: Captain, U.S. Marine Corps Reserve. Born: 2 November 1917, St. Paul, Minn. Appointed from: Minnesota. Citation: For extraordinary heroism and conspicuous intrepidity above and beyond the call of duty as Flight Officer, Marine Scout Bombing Squadron 241, during action against enemy Japanese forces in the battle of Midway on 4 and 5 June 1942. When his Squadron Commander was shot down during the initial attack upon an enemy aircraft carrier, Capt. Fleming led the remainder of the division with such fearless determination that he dived his own plane to the perilously low altitude of 400 feet before releasing his bomb. Although his craft was riddled by 179 hits in the blistering hail of fire that burst upon him from Japanese fighter guns and antiaircraft batteries, he pulled out with only 2 minor wounds inflicted upon himself. On the night of 4 June, when the squadron commander lost his way and became separated from the others, Capt. Fleming brought his own plane in for a safe landing at its base despite hazardous weather conditions and total darkness. The following day, after less than 4 hours' sleep, he led the second division of his squadron in a coordinated glide-bombing and dive-bombing assault upon a Japanese battleship. Undeterred by a fateful approach glide, during which his ship was struck and set afire, he grimly pressed home his attack to an altitude of 500 feet, released his bomb to score a near miss on the stern of his target, then crashed to the sea in flames. His dauntless perseverance and unyielding devotion to duty were in keeping with the highest traditions of the U.S. Naval Service.

FLUCKEY, EUGENE BENNETT

Rank and organization: Commander, U.S. Navy, Commanding U.S.S. Barb. Place and date: Along coast of China, 19 December 1944 to 15 February 1945. Entered service at: Illinois. Born: S October 1913, Washington, D.C. Other Navy award: Navy Cross with 3 Gold Stars. Citation: For conspicuous gallantry and intrepidity at the risk of his life above and beyond the call of duty as commanding officer of the U.S.S. Barb during her 11th war patrol along the east coast of China from 19 December 1944 to 15 February 1945. After sinking a large enemy ammunition ship and damaging additional tonnage during a running 2-hour night battle on 8 January, Comdr. Fluckey, in an exceptional feat of brilliant deduction and bold tracking on 25 January, located a concentration of more than 30 enemy ships in the lower reaches of Nankuan Chiang (Mamkwan Harbor). Fully aware that a safe retirement would necessitate an hour's run at full speed through the uncharted, mined, and rock-obstructed waters, he bravely ordered, "Battle station—torpedoes!" In a daring penetration of the heavy enemy screen, and riding in 5 fathoms of water, he launched the Barb's last forward torpedoes at 3,000-yard range. Quickly bringing the ship's stern tubes to bear, he turned loose 4 more torpedoes into the enemy, obtaining 8 direct hits on 6 of the main targets to explode a large ammunition ship and cause inestimable damage by the resultant flying shells and other pyrotechnics. Clearing the treacherous area at high speed, he brought the Barb through to safety and 4 days later sank a large Japanese freighter to complete a record of heroic combat achievement, reflecting the highest credit upon Comdr. Fluckey, his gallant officers and men, and the U.S. Naval Service.

FOSS, JOSEPH JACOB

Rank and organization: Captain, U.S. Marine Corps Reserve, Marine Fighting Squadron 121, 1st Marine Aircraft Wing. Place and date: Over Guadalcanal, 9 October to 19 November 1942, 15 and 23 January 1943. Entered service at: South Dakota. Born: 17 April 1 915, Sioux Falls, S. Dak. Citation: For outstanding heroism and courage above and beyond the call of duty as executive officer of Marine Fighting Squadron 121, 1st Marine Aircraft Wing, at Guadalcanal. Engaging in almost daily combat with the enemy from 9 October to 19 November 1942, Capt. Foss personally shot down 23 Japanese planes and damaged others so severely that their destruction was extremely probable. In addition, during this period, he successfully led a large number of escort missions, skillfully covering reconnaissance, bombing, and photographic planes as well as surface craft. On 15 January 1943, he added 3 more enemy planes to his already brilliant successes for a record of aerial combat achievement unsurpassed in this war. Boldly searching out an approaching enemy force on 25 January, Capt. Foss led his 8 F-4F Marine planes and 4 Army P-38's into action and, undaunted by tremendously superior numbers, intercepted and struck with such force that 4 Japanese fighters were shot down and the bombers were turned back without releasing a single bomb. His remarkable flying skill, inspiring leadership, and indomitable fighting spirit were distinctive factors in the defense of strategic American positions on Guadalcanal.

*FOSTER, WILLIAM ADELBERT

Rank and organization: Private First Class, U.S. Marine Corps Reserve. Born: 17 February 1915, Cleveland, Ohio. Accredited to: Ohio. Citation: For conspicuous gallantry and intrepidity at the risk of his life above and beyond the call of duty while serving as a rifleman with the 3d Battalion, 1st Marines, 1st Marine Division, in action against enemy Japanese forces on Okinawa Shima in the Ryukyu Chain 2 May 1945. Dug in with another marine on the point of the perimeter defense after waging a furious assault against a strongly fortified Japanese position, Pfc. Foster and his comrade engaged in a fierce hand grenade duel with infiltrating enemy soldiers. Suddenly an enemy grenade landed beyond reach in the foxhole. Instantly diving on the deadly missile, Pfc. Foster absorbed the exploding charge in his own body, thereby protecting the other marine from serious injury. Although mortally wounded as a result of his heroic action, he quickly rallied, handed his own remaining 2 grenades to his comrade and said, "Make them count." Stouthearted and indomitable, he had unhesitatingly relinquished his own chance of survival that his fellow marine might carry on the relentless fight against a fanatic enemy, and his dauntless determination, cool decision and valiant spirit of self-sacrifice in the face of certain death reflect the highest credit upon Pfc. Foster and upon the U.S. Naval Service. He gallantly gave his life in the service of his country.

*FOURNIER, WILLIAM G.

Rank and organization: Sergeant, U.S. Army, Company M, 35th Infantry, 25th Infantry Division. Place and date: Mount Austen, Guadalcanal, Solomon Islands, 10 January 1943. Entered service at: Winterport, Maine. Birth: Norwich, Conn. G.O. No.: 28, 5 June 1943. Citation: For gallantry and intrepidity above and beyond the call of duty. As leader of a machinegun section charged with the protection of other battalion units, his group was attacked by a superior number of Japanese, his gunner killed, his assistant gunner wounded, and an adjoining guncrew put out of action. Ordered to withdraw from this hazardous position, Sgt. Fournier refused to retire but rushed forward to the idle gun and, with the aid of another soldier who joined him, held up the machinegun by the tripod to increase its field action. They opened fire and inflicted heavy casualties upon the enemy. While so engaged both these gallant soldiers were killed, but their sturdy defensive was a decisive factor in the following success of the attacking battalion .

*FOWLER, THOMAS W.

Rank and organization: Second Lieutenant, U.S. Army, 1st Armored Division. Place and date: Near Carano, Italy, 23 May 1944. Entered service at: Wichita Falls, Tex. Birth: Wichita Falls, Tex. G.O. No.: 84, 28 October, 1944. Citation: For conspicuous gallantry and intrepidity at risk of life above and beyond the call of duty, on 23 May 1944, in the vicinity of Carano, Italy. In the midst of a full-scale armored-infantry attack, 2d Lt. Fowler, while on foot, came upon 2 completely disorganized infantry platoons held up in their advance by an enemy minefield. Although a tank officer, he immediately reorganized the infantry. He then made a personal reconnaissance through the minefield, clearing a path as he went, by lifting the antipersonnel mines out of the ground with his hands. After he had gone through the 75-yard belt of deadly explosives, he returned to the infantry and led them through the minefield, a squad at a time. As they deployed, 2d Lt. Fowler, despite small arms fire and the constant danger of antipersonnel mines, made a reconnaissance into enemy territory in search of a route to continue the advance. He then returned through the minefield and, on foot, he led the tanks through the mines into a position from which they could best support the infantry. Acting as scout 300 yards in front of the infantry, he led the 2 platoons forward until he had gained his objective, where he came upon several dug-in enemy infantrymen. Having taken them by surprise, 2d Lt. Fowler dragged them out of their foxholes and sent them to the rear; twice, when they resisted, he threw hand grenades into their dugouts. Realizing that a dangerous gap existed between his company and the unit to his right, 2d Lt. Fowler decided to continue his advance until the gap was filled. He reconnoitered to his front, brought the infantry into position where they dug in and, under heavy mortar and small arms fire, brought his tanks forward. A few minutes later, the enemy began an armored counterattack. Several Mark VI tanks fired their cannons directly on 2d Lt. Fowler's position. One of his tanks was set afire. With utter disregard for his own life, with shells bursting near him, he ran directly into the enemy tank fire to reach the burning vehicle. For a half-hour, under intense strafing from the advancing tanks, although all other elements had withdrawn, he remained in his forward position, attempting to save the lives of the wounded tank crew. Only when the enemy tanks had almost overrun him, did he withdraw a short distance where he personally rendered first aid to 9 wounded infantrymen in the midst of the relentless incoming fire. 2d Lt. Fowler's courage, his ability to estimate the situation and to recognize his full responsibility as an officer in the Army of the United States, exemplify the high traditions of the military service for which he later gave his life.

*FRYAR, ELMER E.

Rank and organization: Private, U.S. Army, Company E, 511th Parachute Infantry, 11th Airborne Division. Place and date: Leyte, Philippine Islands, 8 December 1944. Entered service at: Denver, Colo. Birth: Denver, Colo. G.O. No.: 35, 9 May 1945. Citation: For conspicuous gallantry and intrepidity at the risk of his life above and beyond the call of duty. Pvt. Fryar's battalion encountered the enemy strongly entrenched in a position supported by mortars and automatic weapons. The battalion attacked, but in spite of repeated efforts was unable to take the position. Pvt. Fryar's company was ordered to cover the battalion's withdrawal to a more suitable point from which to attack, but the enemy launched a strong counterattack which threatened to cut off the company. Seeing an enemy platoon moving to outflank his company, he moved to higher ground and opened heavy and accurate fire. He was hit, and wounded, but continuing his attack he drove the enemy back with a loss of 27 killed. While withdrawing to overtake his squad, he found a seriously wounded comrade, helped him to the rear, and soon overtook his platoon leader, who was assisting another wounded. While these 4 were moving to rejoin their platoon, an enemy sniper appeared and aimed his weapon at the platoon leader. Pvt. Fryar instantly sprang forward, received the full burst of automatic fire in his own body and fell mortally wounded. With his remaining strength he threw a hand grenade and killed the sniper. Pvt. Fryar's indomitable fighting spirit and extraordinary gallantry above and beyond the call of duty contributed outstandingly to the success of the battalion's withdrawal and its subsequent attack and defeat of the enemy. His heroic action in unhesitatingly giving his own life for his comrade in arms exemplifies the highest tradition of the U.S. Armed Forces.

FUNK, LEONARD A., JR.

Rank and organization: First Sergeant, U.S. Army, Company C, 508th Parachute Infantry, 82d Airborne Division. Place and date: Holzheim, Belgium, 29 January 1945. Entered service at: Wilkinsburg, Pa. Birth: Braddock Township, Pa. G.O. No.: 75, 5 September 1945. Citation: He distinguished himself by gallant, intrepid actions against the enemy. After advancing 15 miles in a driving snowstorm, the American force prepared to attack through waist-deep drifts. The company executive officer became a casualty, and 1st Sgt. Funk immediately assumed his duties, forming headquarters soldiers into a combat unit for an assault in the face of direct artillery shelling and harassing fire from the right flank. Under his skillful and courageous leadership, this miscellaneous group and the 3d Platoon attacked 15 houses, cleared them, and took 30 prisoners without suffering a casualty. The fierce drive of Company C quickly overran Holzheim, netting some 80 prisoners, who were placed under a 4-man guard, all that could be spared, while the rest of the understrength unit went about mopping up isolated points of resistance. An enemy patrol, by means of a ruse, succeeded in capturing the guards and freeing the prisoners, and had begun preparations to attack

Company C from the rear when 1st Sgt. Funk walked around the building and into their midst. He was ordered to surrender by a German officer who pushed a machine pistol into his stomach. Although overwhelmingly outnumbered and facing almost certain death, 1st Sgt. Funk, pretending to comply with the order, began slowly to unsling his submachine gun from his shoulder and then, with lightning motion, brought the muzzle into line and riddled the German officer. He turned upon the other Germans, firing and shouting to the other Americans to seize the enemy's weapons. In the ensuing fight 21 Germans were killed, many wounded, and the remainder captured. 1st Sgt. Funk's bold action and heroic disregard for his own safety were directly responsible for the recapture of a vastly superior enemy force, which, if allowed to remain free, could have taken the widespread units of Company C by surprise and endangered the entire attack plan.

FUQUA, SAMUEL GLENN

Rank and organization: Captain, U.S. Navy, U.S.S. Arizona. Place and date: Pearl Harbor, Territory of Hawaii, 7 December 1941. Entered service at: Laddonia, Mo. Born: 15 October 1899, Laddonia Mo. Citation: For distinguished conduct in action, outstanding heroism, and utter disregard of his own safety above and beyond the call of duty during the attack on the Fleet in Pearl Harbor, by Japanese forces on 7 December 1941. Upon the commencement of the attack, Lt. Comdr. Fuqua rushed to the quarterdeck of the U.S.S. Arizona to which he was attached where he was stunned and knocked down by the explosion of a large bomb which hit the guarterdeck, penetrated several decks, and started a severe fire. Upon regaining consciousness, he began to direct the fighting of the fire and the rescue of wounded and injured personnel. Almost immediately there was a tremendous explosion forward, which made the ship appear to rise out of the water, shudder, and settle down by the bow rapidly. The whole forward part of the ship was enveloped in flames which were spreading rapidly, and wounded and burned men were pouring out of the ship to the quarterdeck. Despite these conditions, his harrowing experience, and severe enemy bombing and strafing, at the time, Lt. Comdr. Fuqua continued to direct the fighting of fires in order to check them while the wounded and burned could be taken from the ship and supervised the rescue of these men in such an amazingly calm and cool manner and with such excellent judgment that it inspired everyone who saw him and undoubtedly resulted in the saving of many lives. After realizing the ship could not be saved and that he was the senior surviving officer aboard, he directed it to be abandoned, but continued to remain on the quarterdeck and directed abandoning ship and rescue of personnel until satisfied that all personnel that could be had been saved, after which he left his ship with the boatload. The conduct of Lt. Comdr. Fuqua was not only in keeping with the highest traditions of the naval service but characterizes him as an outstanding leader of men.

GALER, ROBERT EDWARD

Rank and organization: Major, U.S. Marine Corps, Marine Fighter Sqdn. 244. Place: Solomon Islands Area. Entered service at: Washington. Born: 23 October 1913, Seattle, Wash. Other Navy awards: Navy Cross, Distinguished Flying Cross. Citation: For conspicuous heroism and courage above and beyond the call of duty as leader of a marine fighter squadron in aerial combat with enemy Japanese forces in the Solomon Islands area. Leading his squadron repeatedly in daring and aggressive raids against Japanese aerial forces, vastly superior in numbers, Maj. Galer availed himself of every favorable attack opportunity, individually shooting down 11 enemy bomber and fighter aircraft over a period of 29 days. Though suffering the extreme physical strain attendant upon protracted fighter operations at an altitude above 25,000 feet, the squadron under his zealous and inspiring leadership shot down a total of 27 Japanese planes. His superb airmanship, his outstanding skill and personal valor reflect great credit upon Maj. Galer's gallant fighting spirit and upon the U.S. Naval Service.

*GALT, WILLIAM WYLIE

Rank and organization: Captain, U.S. Army, 168th Infantry, 34th Infantry Division. Place and date: At Villa Crocetta, Italy, 29 May 1944. Entered service at: Stanford, Mont. Birth: Geyser, Mont. G.O. No.: 1, 1 February 1945. Citation: For conspicuous gallantry and intrepidity above and beyond the call of duty. Capt. Galt, Battalion S3, at a particularly critical period following 2 unsuccessful attacks by his battalion, of his own volition went forward and ascertained just how critical the situation was. He volunteered, at the risk of his life, personally to lead the battalion against the objective. When the lone remaining tank destroyer refused to go forward, Capt. Galt jumped on the tank destroyer and ordered it to precede the attack. As the tank destroyer moved forward, followed by a company of riflemen, Capt. Galt manned the .30-caliber machinegun in the turret of the tank destroyer, located and directed fire on an enemy 77mm. anti-tank gun, and destroyed it. Nearing the enemy positions, Capt. Galt stood fully exposed in the turret, ceaselessly firing his machinegun and tossing hand grenades into the enemy zigzag series of trenches despite the hail of sniper and machinegun bullets ricocheting off the tank destroyer. As the tank destroyer moved, Capt. Galt so maneuvered it that 40 of the enemy were trapped in one trench. When they refused to surrender, Capt. Galt pressed the trigger of the machinegun and dispatched every one of them. A few minutes later an 88mm shell struck the tank destroyer and Capt. Galt fell mortally wounded across his machinegun. He had personally killed 40 Germans and wounded many more. Capt. Galt pitted his judgment and superb courage against overwhelming odds, exemplifying the highest measure of devotion to his country and the finest traditions of the U.S. Army.

*GAMMON, ARCHER T.

Rank and organization: Staff Sergeant, U.S. Army, Company A, 9th Armored Infantry Battalion, 6th Armored Division. Place and date: Near Bastogne, Belgium, 11 January 1945. Entered service at: Roanoke, Va. Born: 11 September 1918, Chatham, Va. G.O. No.: 18, 13 February 1946. Citation: He charged 30 yards through hip-deep snow to knock out a machinegun and its 3-man crew with grenades, saving his platoon from being decimated and allowing it to continue its advance from an open field into some nearby woods. The platoon's advance through the woods had only begun when a machinegun supported by riflemen opened fire and a Tiger Royal tank sent 88mm. shells screaming at the unit from the left flank. S/Sgt. Gammon, disregarding all thoughts of personal safety, rushed forward, then cut to the left, crossing the width of the platoon's skirmish line in an attempt to get within grenade range of the tank and its protecting foot troops. Intense fire was concentrated on him by riflemen and the machinegun emplaced near the tank. He charged the automatic weapon, wiped out its crew of 4 with grenades, and, with supreme daring, advanced to within 25 yards of the armored vehicle, killing 2 hostile infantrymen with rifle fire as he moved forward. The tank had started to withdraw, backing a short distance, then firing, backing some more, and then stopping to blast out another round, when the man whose single-handed relentless attack had put the ponderous machine on the defensive was struck and instantly killed by a direct hit from the Tiger Royal's heavy gun. By his intrepidity and extreme devotion to the task of driving the enemy back no matter what the odds, S/Sgt. Gammon cleared the woods of German forces, for the tank continued to withdraw, leaving open the path for the gallant squad leader's platoon.

GARCIA, MARCARIO

Rank and organization: Staff Sergeant, U.S. Army, Company B, 22d Infantry, 4th Infantry Division. Place and date: Near Grosshau, Germany,

27 November 1944. Entered service at: Sugarland, Tex. Born: 20 January 1920, Villa de Castano, Mexico. G.O. No.: 74, 1 September 1945. Citation: While an acting squad leader of Company B, 22d Infantry, on 27 November 1944, near Grosshau, Germany, he single-handedly assaulted 2 enemy machinegun emplacements. Attacking prepared positions on a wooded hill, which could be approached only through meager cover, his company was pinned down by intense machinegun fire and subjected to a concentrated artillery and mortar barrage. Although painfully wounded, he refused to be evacuated and on his own initiative crawled forward alone until he reached a position near an enemy emplacement. Hurling grenades, he boldly assaulted the position, destroyed the gun, and with his rifle killed 3 of the enemy who attempted to escape. When he rejoined his company, a second machinegun opened fire and again the intrepid soldier went forward, utterly disregarding his own safety. He stormed the position and destroyed the gun, killed 3 more Germans, and captured 4 prisoners. He fought on with his unit until the objective was taken and only then did he permit himself to be removed for medical care. S/Sgt. (then private) Garcia's conspicuous heroism, his inspiring, courageous conduct, and his complete disregard for his personal safety wiped out 2 enemy emplacements and enabled his company to advance and secure its objective.

GARMAN, HAROLD A.

Rank and organization: Private, U.S. Army, Company B, 5th Medical Battalion, 5th Infantry Division. Place and date: Near Montereau, France, 25 August 1944. Entered service at: Albion, Ill. Born: 26 February 1918, Fairfield, Ill. G.O. No.: 20, 29 March 1945. Citation: For conspicuous gallantry and intrepidity at the risk of his life above and beyond the call of duty. On 25 August 1944, in the vicinity of Montereau, France, the enemy was sharply contesting any enlargement of the bridgehead which our forces had established on the northern bank of the Seine River in this sector. Casualties were being evacuated to the southern shore in assault boats paddled by litter bearers from a medical battalion. Pvt. Garman, also a litter bearer in this battalion, was working on the friendly shore carrying the wounded from the boats to waiting ambulances. As 1 boatload of wounded reached midstream, a German machinegun suddenly opened fire upon it from a commanding position on the northern bank 100 yards away. All of the men in the boat immediately took to the water except 1 man who was so badly wounded he could not rise from his litter. Two other patients who were unable to swim because of their wounds clung to the sides of the boat. Seeing the extreme danger of these patients, Pvt. Garman without a moment's hesitation plunged into the Seine. Swimming directly into a hail of machinegun bullets, he rapidly reached the assault boat and then while still under accurately aimed fire towed the boat with great effort to the southern shore. This soldier's moving heroism not only saved the lives of the three patients but so inspired his comrades that additional assault boats were immediately procured and the evacuation of the wounded resumed. Pvt. Garman's great courage and his heroic devotion to the highest tenets of the Medical Corps may be written with great pride in the annals of the corps.

GARY, DONALD ARTHUR

Rank and organization: Lieutenant, Junior Grade, U.S. Navy, U.S.S. Franklin. Place and date: Japanese Home Islands near Kobe, Japan, 19 March 1945. Entered service at: Ohio. Born: 23 July 1903, Findlay, Ohio. Citation: For conspicuous gallantry and intrepidity at the risk of his life above and beyond the call of duty as an engineering officer attached to the U.S.S. Franklin when that vessel was fiercely attacked by enemy aircraft during the operations against the Japanese Home Islands near Kobe, Japan, 19 March 1945. Stationed on the third deck when the ship was rocked by a series of violent explosions set off in her own ready bombs, rockets, and ammunition by the hostile attack, Lt. (j.g.) Gary unhesitatingly risked his life to assist several hundred men trapped in a messing compartment filled with smoke, and with no apparent egress. As the imperiled men below decks became increasingly panic stricken under the raging fury of incessant explosions, he confidently assured them he would find a means of effecting their release and, groping through the dark, debris-filled corridors, ultimately discovered an escapeway. Stanchly determined, he struggled back to the messing compartment 3 times despite menacing flames, flooding water, and the ominous threat of sudden additional explosions, on each occasion calmly leading his men through the blanketing pall of smoke until the last one had been saved. Selfless in his concern for his ship and his fellows, he constantly rallied others about him, repeatedly organized and led fire-fighting parties into the blazing inferno on the flight deck and, when firerooms 1 and 2 were found to be inoperable, entered the No. 3 fireroom and directed the raising of steam in 1 boiler in the face of extreme difficulty and hazard. An inspiring and courageous leader, Lt. (j.g.) Gary rendered self-sacrificing service under the most perilous conditions and, by his heroic initiative, fortitude, and valor, was responsible for the saving of several hundred lives. His conduct throughout reflects the highest credit upon himself and upon the U.S. Naval Service.

GERSTUNG, ROBERT E.

Rank and organization: Technical Sergeant, U.S. Army, Company H, 313th Infantry, 79th Infantry Division. Place and date: Siegfried Line near Berg, Germany, 19 December 1944. Entered service at: Chicago, Ill. Born: 6 August 1915, Chicago, Ill. G.O. No.: 75, 5 September 1945. Citation: On 19 December 1944 he was ordered with his heavy machinegun squad to the support of an infantry company attacking the outer defense of the Siegfried Line near Berg, Germany. For 8 hours he maintained a position made almost untenable by the density of artillery and mortar fire concentrated upon it and the proximity of enemy troops who threw hand grenades into the emplacement. While all other members of his squad became casualties, he remained at his gun. When he ran out of ammunition, he fearlessly dashed across bullet-swept, open terrain to secure a new supply from a disabled friendly tank. A fierce barrage pierced the water jacket of his gun, but he continued to fire until the weapon overheated and jammed. Instead of withdrawing, he crawled 50 yards across coverless ground to another of his company's machineguns which had been silenced when its entire crew was killed. He continued to man this gun, giving support vitally needed by the infantry. At one time he came under direct fire from a hostile tank, which shot the glove from his hand with an armor-piercing shell but could not drive him from his position or stop his shooting. When the American forces were ordered to retire to their original positions, he remained at his gun, giving the only covering fire. Finally withdrawing, he cradled the heavy weapon in his left arm, slung a belt of ammunition over his shoulder, and walked to the rear, loosing small bursts at the enemy as he went. One hundred yards from safety, he was struck in the leg by a mortar shell; but, with a supreme effort, he crawled the remaining distance, dragging along the gun which had served him and his comrades so well. By his remarkable perseverance, indomitable courage, and heroic devotion to his task in the face of devastating fire, T/Sgt. Gerstung gave his fellow soldiers powerful support in their encounter with formidable enemy forces.

*GIBSON, ERIC G.

Rank and organization. Technician Fifth Grade, U.S. Army, 3d Infantry Division. Place and date: Near Isola Bella, Italy, 28 January 1944. Entered service at: Chicago, Ill. Birth: Nysund, Sweden. G.O. No.: 74, 11 September 1944. Citation: For conspicuous gallantry and intrepidity at risk of life above and beyond the call of duty. On 28 January 1944, near Isola Bella, Italy, Tech. 5th Grade Gibson, company cook, led a squad of replacements through their initial baptism of fire, destroyed four enemy positions, killed 5 and captured 2 German soldiers, and secured the left flank of his company during an attack on a strongpoint. Placing himself 50 yards in front of his new men, Gibson advanced down the wide stream ditch known as the Fossa Femminamorta, keeping pace with the advance of his company. An enemy soldier allowed Tech. 5th Grade Gibson to come within 20 yards of his concealed position and then opened fire on him with a machine pistol. Despite the stream of automatic fire which barely missed him, Gibson charged the position, firing his submachine gun every few steps. Reaching the position, Gibson fired pointblank at his opponent, killing him. An artillery concentration fell in and around the ditch; the concussion from one shell knocked him flat. As he got to his feet Gibson was fired on by two soldiers armed with a machine pistol and a rifle from a position only 75 yards distant. Gibson immediately raced toward the foe. Halfway to the position a machinegun opened fire on him. Bullets came within inches of his body, yet Gibson never paused in his forward movement. He killed one and captured the other soldier. Shortly after, when he was fired upon by a heavy machinegun 200 yards down the ditch, Gibson crawled back to his squad and ordered it to lay down a base of fire while he flanked the emplacement. Despite all warning, Gibson crawled 125 yards through an artillery concentration and the cross fire of 2 machineguns which showered dirt over his body, threw 2 hand grenades into the emplacement and charged it with his submachine gun, killing 2 of the enemy and capturing a third. Before leading his men around a bend in the stream ditch, Gibson went forward alone to reconnoiter. Hearing an exchange of machine pistol and submachine gun fire, Gibson's squad went forward to find that its leader had run 35 yards toward an outpost, killed the machine pistol man, and had himself been killed while firing at the Germans.

*GILMORE, HOWARD WALTER

Rank and organization: Commander, U.S. Navy. Born: 29 September 1902, Selma, Ala. Appointed from: Louisiana. Other Navy award: Navy

Cross with one gold star. Citation: For distinguished gallantry and valor above and beyond the call of duty as commanding officer of the U.S.S. Growler during her Fourth War Patrol in the Southwest Pacific from 10 January to 7 February 1943. Boldly striking at the enemy in spite of continuous hostile air and antisubmarine patrols, Comdr. Gilmore sank one Japanese freighter and damaged another by torpedo fire, successfully evading severe depth charges following each attack. In the darkness of night on 7 February, an enemy gunboat closed range and prepared to ram the Growler. Comdr. Gilmore daringly maneuvered to avoid the crash and rammed the attacker instead, ripping into her port side at 11 knots and bursting wide her plates. In the terrific fire of the sinking gunboat's heavy machineguns, Comdr. Gilmore calmly gave the order to clear the bridge, and refusing safety for himself, remained on deck while his men preceded him below. Struck down by the fusillade of bullets and having done his utmost against the enemy, in his final living moments, Comdr. Gilmore gave his last order to the officer of the deck, "Take her down." The Growler dived; seriously damaged but under control, she was brought safely to port by her well-trained crew inspired by the courageous fighting spirit of their dead captain.

*GONSALVES, HAROLD

Rank and organization: Private First Class, U.S. Marine Corps Reserve. Born: 28 January 1926, Alameda, Calif. Accredited to: California. Citation: For conspicuous gallantry and intrepidity at the risk of his life above and beyond the call of duty while serving as Acting Scout Sergeant with the 4th Battalion, 15th Marines, 6th Marine Division, during action against enemy Japanese forces on Okinawa Shima in the Ryukyu Chain, 15 April 1945. Undaunted by the powerfully organized opposition encountered on Motobu Peninsula during the fierce assault waged by his battalion against the Japanese stronghold at Mount Yaetake, Pfc. Gonsalves repeatedly braved the terrific enemy bombardment to aid his forward observation team in directing well-placed artillery fire. When his commanding officer determined to move into the front lines in order to register a more effective bombardment in the enemy's defensive position, he unhesitatingly advanced uphill with the officer and another Marine despite a slashing barrage of enemy mortar and rifle fire. As they reached the front and a Japanese grenade fell close within the group, instantly Pfc. Gonsalves dived on the deadly missile, absorbing the exploding charge in his own body and thereby protecting the others from serious and perhaps fatal wounds. Stouthearted and indomitable, Pfc. Gonsalves readily yielded his own chances of survival that his fellow marines might carry on the relentless battle against a fanatic enemy and his cool decision, prompt action and valiant spirit of self-sacrifice in the face of certain death reflect the highest credit upon himself and upon the U.S. Naval Service.

*GONZALES, DAVID M.

Rank and organization: Private First Class, U.S. Army, Company A, 127th Infantry, 32d Infantry Division. Place and date: Villa Verde Trail, Luzon, Philippine Islands, 25 April 1945. Entered service at: Pacoima, Calif. Birth: Pacoima, Calif. G.O. No.: 115, 8 December 1945. Citation: He was pinned down with his company. As enemy fire swept the area, making any movement extremely hazardous, a 500-pound bomb smashed into the company's perimeter, burying 5 men with its explosion. Pfc. Gonzales, without hesitation, seized an entrenching tool and under a hail of fire crawled 15 yards to his entombed comrades, where his commanding officer, who had also rushed forward, was beginning to dig the men out. Nearing his goal, he saw the officer struck and instantly killed by machinegun fire. Undismayed, he set to work swiftly and surely with his hands and the entrenching tool while enemy sniper and machinegun bullets struck all about him. He succeeded in digging one of the men out of the pile of rock and sand. To dig faster he stood up regardless of the greater danger from so exposing himself. He extricated a second man, and then another. As he completed the liberation of the third, he was hit and mortally wounded, but the comrades for whom he so gallantly gave his life were safely evacuated. Pfc. Gonzales' valiant and intrepid conduct exemplifies the highest tradition of the military service.

GORDON, NATHAN GREEN

Rank and organization: Lieutenant, U.S. Navy, commander of Catalina patrol plane. Place and date: Bismarck Sea, 15 February 1944. Entered service at: Arkansas. Born: 4 September 1916, Morrilton, Ark. Citation: For extraordinary heroism above and beyond the call of duty as commander of a Catalina patrol plane in rescuing personnel of the U.S. Army 5th Air Force shot down in combat over Kavieng Harbor in the Bismarck Sea, 15 February 1944. On air alert in the vicinity of Vitu Islands, Lt. (then Lt. j.g.) Gordon unhesitatingly responded to a report of the crash and flew boldly into the harbor, defying close-range fire from enemy shore guns to make 3 separate landings in full view of the Japanese and pick up 9 men, several of them injured. With his cumbersome flying boat dangerously overloaded, he made a brilliant takeoff despite heavy swells and almost total absence of wind and set a course for base, only to receive the report of another group stranded in a rubber life raft 600 yards from the enemy shore. Promptly turning back, he again risked his life to set his plane down under direct fire of the heaviest defenses of Kavieng and take aboard 6 more survivors, coolly making his fourth dexterous takeoff with 15 rescued officers and men. By his exceptional daring, personal valor, and incomparable airmanship under most perilous conditions, Lt. Gordon prevented certain death or capture of our airmen by the Japanese.

*GOTT, DONALD J. (Air Mission)

Rank and organization: First Lieutenant, U.S. Army Air Corps, 729th Bomber Squadron, 452d Bombardment Group. Place and date: Saarbrucken, Germany, 9 November 1944. Entered service at: Arnett,

Okla. Born: 3 June 1923, Arnett, Okla. G.O. No.: 38, 16 May 1945. Citation: On a bombing run upon the marshaling yards at Saarbrucken a B-17 aircraft piloted by 1st. Lt. Gott was seriously damaged by antiaircraft fire. Three of the aircraft's engines were damaged beyond control and on fire; dangerous flames from the No. 4 engine were leaping back as far as the tail assembly. Flares in the cockpit were ignited and a fire raged therein, which was further increased by free-flowing fluid from damaged hydraulic lines. The interphone system was rendered useless. In addition to these serious mechanical difficulties the engineer was wounded in the leg and the radio operator's arm was severed below the elbow. Suffering from intense pain, despite the application of a tourniquet, the radio operator fell unconscious. Faced with the imminent explosion of his aircraft, and death to his entire crew, mere seconds before bombs away on the target, 1st. Lt. Gott and his copilot conferred. Something had to be done immediately to save the life of the wounded radio operator. The lack of a static line and the thought that his unconscious body striking the ground in unknown territory would not bring immediate medical attention forced a quick decision. 1st. Lt. Gott and his copilot decided to fly the flaming aircraft to friendly territory and then attempt to crash land. Bombs were released on the target and the crippled aircraft proceeded alone to Allied-controlled territory. When that had been reached, 1st. Lt. Gott had the copilot personally inform all crewmembers to bail out. The copilot chose to remain with 1st. Lt. Gott in order to assist in landing the bomber. With only one normally functioning engine, and with the danger of explosion much greater, the aircraft banked into an open field, and when it was at an altitude of 100 feet it exploded, crashed, exploded again and then disintegrated. All 3 crewmembers were instantly killed. 1st. Lt. Gott's loyalty to his crew, his determination to accomplish the task set forth to him, and his deed of knowingly performing what may have been his last service to his country was an example of valor at its highest.

*GRABIARZ, WILLIAM J.

Rank and organization: Private First Class, U.S. Army. Troop E, 5th Cavalry, 1st Cavalry Division. Place and date: Manila, Luzon, Philippine Islands, 23 February 1945. Entered service at: Buffalo, N.Y. Birth: Buffalo, N.Y. G.O. No.: 115, 8 December 1945. Citation: He was a scout when the unit advanced with tanks along a street in Manila, Luzon, Philippine Islands. Without warning, enemy machinegun and rifle fire from concealed positions in the Customs building swept the street, striking down the troop commander and driving his men to cover. As the officer lay in the open road, unable to move and completely exposed to the pointblank enemy fire, Pfc. Grabiarz voluntarily ran from behind a tank to carry him to safety, but was himself wounded in the shoulder. Ignoring both the pain in his injured useless arm and his comrades' shouts to seek the cover which was only a few yards distant, the valiant rescuer continued his efforts to drag his commander out of range. Finding this impossible, he rejected the opportunity to save himself and deliberately covered the officer with his own body to form a human shield, calling as he did so for a tank to maneuver into position between him and the hostile emplacement. The enemy riddled him with concentrated fire before the tank could interpose itself. Our troops found that he had been successful in preventing bullets from striking his leader, who survived. Through his magnificent sacrifice in gallantly giving his life to save that of his commander, Pfc. Grabiarz provided an outstanding and lasting inspiration to his fellow soldiers.

*GRAY, ROSS FRANKLIN

Rank and organization: Sergeant, U.S. Marine Corps Reserve. Born: August 1920, Marvel Valley, Ala. Accredited to: Alabama. Citation: For conspicuous gallantry and intrepidity at the risk of his life above and beyond the call of duty as a Platoon Sergeant attached to Company A, 1st Battalion, 25th Marines, 4th Marine Division, in action against enemy Japanese forces on Iwo Jima, Volcano Islands, 21 February 1945. Shrewdly gauging the tactical situation when his platoon was held up by a sudden barrage of hostile grenades while advancing toward the high ground northeast of Airfield No. 1, Sgt. Gray promptly organized the withdrawal of his men from enemy grenade range, quickly moved forward alone to reconnoiter and discovered a heavily mined area extending along the front of a strong network of emplacements joined by covered trenches. Although assailed by furious gunfire, he cleared a path leading through the minefield to one of the fortifications, then returned to the platoon position and, informing his leader of the serious situation, volunteered to initiate an attack under cover of 3 fellow marines. Alone and unarmed but carrying a huge satchel charge, he crept up on the Japanese emplacement, boldly hurled the short-fused explosive and sealed the entrance. Instantly taken under machinegun fire from a second entrance to the same position, he unhesitatingly braved the increasingly vicious fusillades to crawl back for another charge, returned to his objective and blasted the second opening, thereby demolishing the position. Repeatedly covering the ground between the savagely defended enemy fortifications and his platoon area, he systematically approached, attacked and withdrew under blanketing fire to destroy a total of 6 Japanese positions, more than 25 troops and a quantity of vital ordnance gear and ammunition. Stouthearted and indomitable, Sgt. Gray had single-handedly overcome a strong enemy garrison and had completely disarmed a large minefield before finally rejoining his unit. By his great personal valor, daring tactics and tenacious perseverance in the face of extreme peril, he had contributed materially to the fulfillment of his company mission. His gallant conduct throughout enhanced and sustained the highest traditions of the U.S. Naval Service.

GREGG, STEPHEN R.

Rank and organization: Second Lieutenant, U.S. Army, 143d Infantry, 36th Infantry Division. Place and date: Near Montelimar, France, 27 August 1944. Entered service at: Bayonne, N.J. Birth: New York, N.Y. G.O. No.: 31, 17 April 1945. Citation: For conspicuous gallantry and intrepidity at risk of life above and beyond the call of duty on 27 August 1944, in the vicinity of Montelimar, France. As his platoon advanced upon the enemy positions; the leading scout was fired upon and 2d Lt. Gregg (then a Tech. Sgt.) immediately put his machineguns into action to cover the advance of the riflemen. The Germans, who were at close range, threw hand grenades at the riflemen, killing some and wounding 7. Each time a medical aid man attempted to reach the wounded, the Germans fired at him. Realizing the seriousness of the situation, 2d Lt. Gregg took 1 of the light .30-caliber machineguns, and firing from the hip, started boldly up the hill with the medical aid man following him. Although the enemy was throwing hand grenades at him, 2d Lt. Gregg remained and fired into the enemy positions while the medical aid man removed the 7 wounded men to safety. When 2d Lt. Gregg had expended all his ammunition, he was covered by 4 Germans who ordered him to surrender. Since the attention of most of the Germans had been diverted by watching this action, friendly riflemen were able to maneuver into firing positions. One, seeing 2d Lt. Gregg's situation, opened fire on his captors. The 4 Germans hit the ground and thereupon 2d Lt. Gregg recovered a machine pistol from one of the Germans and managed to escape to his other machinegun positions. He manned a gun, firing at his captors, killed 1 of them and wounded the other. This action so discouraged the Germans that the platoon was able to continue its advance up the hill to achieve its objective. The following morning, just prior to daybreak, the Germans launched a strong attack, supported by tanks, in an attempt to drive Company L from the hill. As these tanks moved along the valley and their foot troops advanced up the hill, 2d Lt. Gregg immediately ordered his mortars into action. During the day by careful observation, he was able to direct effective fire on the enemy, inflicting heavy casualties. By late afternoon he had directed 600 rounds when his communication to the mortars was knocked out. Without hesitation he started checking his wires, although the area was under heavy enemy small arms and artillery fire. When he was within 100 yards of his mortar position, 1 of his men informed him that the section had been captured and the Germans were using the mortars to fire on the company. 2d Lt. Gregg with this man and another nearby rifleman started for the gun position where he could see 5 Germans firing his mortars. He ordered the 2 men to cover him, crawled up, threw a hand grenade into the position, and then charged it. The hand grenade killed 1, injured 2, 2d Lt. Gregg took the other 2 prisoners, and put his mortars back into action.

*GRUENNERT, KENNETH E.

Rank and organization: Sergeant, U.S. Army, Company L, 127th Infantry, 32d Infantry Division. Place and date: Near Buna, New Guinea, 24 December 1942. Entered service at: Helenville, Wis. Birth: Helenville, Wis. G.O. No.: 66, 11 October 1943. Citation: For conspicuous gallantry and intrepidity in action above and beyond the call of duty. On 24 December 1942, near Buna, New Guinea, Sgt. Gruennert was second in command of a platoon with a mission to drive through the enemy lines to the beach 600 yards ahead. Within 150 yards of the objective, the platoon encountered 2 hostile pillboxes. Sgt. Gruennert advanced alone on the first and put it out of action with hand grenades and rifle fire, killing 3 of the enemy. Seriously wounded in the shoulder, he bandaged his wound under cover of the pillbox, refusing to withdraw to the aid station and leave his men. He then, with undiminished daring, and under extremely heavy fire, attacked the second pillbox. As he neared it he threw grenades which forced the enemy out where they were easy targets for his platoon. Before the leading elements of his platoon could reach him he was shot by enemy snipers. His inspiring valor cleared the way for his platoon which was the first to attain the beach in this successful effort to split the enemy position.

*GURKE, HENRY

Rank and organization: Private First Class, U.S. Marine Corps. Born: 6 November 1922, Neche, N. Dak. Accredited to: North Dakota. Citation: For extraordinary heroism and courage above and beyond the call of duty while attached to the 3d Marine Raider Battalion during action against enemy Japanese forces in the Solomon Islands area on 9 November 1943. While his platoon was engaged in the defense of a vital road block near Empress Augusta Bay on Bougainville Island. Pfc. Gurke, in company with another Marine, was delivering a fierce stream of fire against the main vanguard of the Japanese. Concluding from the increasing ferocity of grenade barrages that the enemy was determined to annihilate their small, 2-man foxhole, he resorted to a bold and desperate measure for holding out despite the torrential hail of shells. When a Japanese grenade dropped squarely into the foxhole, Pfc. Gurke, mindful that his companion manned an automatic weapon of superior fire power and therefore could provide more effective resistance, thrust him roughly aside and flung his own body over the missile to smother the explosion. With unswerving devotion to duty and superb valor, Pfc. Gurke sacrificed himself in order that his comrade might live to carry on the fight. He gallantly gave his life in the service of his country.

HALL, GEORGE J.

Rank and organization: Staff Sergeant, U.S. Army, 135th Infantry, 34th Infantry Division. Place and date: Near Anzio, Italy, 23 May 1944. Entered service at: Boston, Mass. Born: 9 January 1921, Stoneham, Mass. G.O. No.: 24, 6 April 1945. Citation: For conspicuous gallantry and intrepidity at risk of life above and beyond the call of duty. Attacking across flat, open terrain under direct enemy observation, S/Sgt. Hall's company was pinned down by grazing fire from 3 enemy machineguns and harassing sniper fire. S/Sgt. Hall volunteered to eliminate these obstacles in the path of advance. Crawling along a plowed furrow through furious machinegun fire, he made his way to a point within hand grenade range of 1 of the enemy positions. He pounded the enemy with 4 hand grenades, and when the smoke had died away, S/Sgt. Hall and 2 dead Germans occupied the position, while 4 of the enemy were crawling back to our lines as prisoners. Discovering a quantity of German potato-masher grenades in the position, S/Sgt. Hall engaged the second enemy nest in a deadly exchange of grenades. Each time he exposed himself to throw a grenade the Germans fired machinegun bursts at him. The vicious duel finally ended in S/Sgt. Hall's favor with 5 of the enemy surrendered and 5 others lay dead. Turning his attention to the third machinegun, S/Sgt. Hall left his position and crawled along a furrow, the enemy firing frantically in an effort to halt him. As he neared his final objective, an enemy artillery concentration fell on the area, and S/Sgt. Hall's right leg was severed by a shellburst. With 2 enemy machineguns eliminated, his company was able to flank the third and continue its advance without incurring excessive casualties. S/Sgt. Hall's fearlessness, his determined fighting spirit, and his prodigious combat skill exemplify the heroic tradition of the American Infantryman.

*HALL, LEWIS

Rank and organization: Technician Fifth Grade, U.S. Army, Company M, 35th Infantry, 25th Infantry Division. Place and date: Mount Austen, Guadalcanal, Solomon Islands, 10 January 1943. Entered service at: Obetz, Rural Station 7, Columbus, Ohio. Born: 1895, Bloom, Ohio. G.O. No.: 28, 5 June 1943. Citation: For gallantry and intrepidity above and beyond the call of duty. As leader of a machinegun squad charged with the protection of other battalion units, his group was attacked by a superior number of Japanese, his gunner killed, his assistant gunner wounded, and an adjoining guncrew put out of action. Ordered to withdraw from his hazardous position, he refused to retire but rushed forward to the idle gun and with the aid of another soldier who joined him and held up the machinegun by the tripod to increase its field of action he opened fire and inflicted heavy casualties upon the enemy. While so engaged both these gallant soldiers were killed, but their sturdy defense was a decisive factor in the following success of the attacking battalion.

HALL, WILLIAM E.

Rank and organization: Lieutenant, Junior Grade, U.S. Naval Reserve. Place and date: Coral Sea, 7 and 8 May 1942. Entered service at: Utah. Born: 31 October 1913, Storrs, Utah. Citation: For extreme courage and conspicuous heroism in combat above and beyond the call of duty as pilot of a scouting plane in action against enemy Japanese forces in the Coral Sea on 7 and 8 May 1942. In a resolute and determined attack on 7 May, Lt. (j.g.) Hall dived his plane at an enemy Japanese aircraft carrier, contributing materially to the destruction of that vessel. On 8 May, facing heavy and fierce fighter opposition, he again displayed extraordinary skill as an airman and the aggressive spirit of a fighter in repeated and effectively executed counterattacks against a superior number of enemy planes in which 3 enemy aircraft were destroyed. Though seriously wounded in this engagement, Lt. (j.g.) Hall, maintaining the fearless and indomitable tactics pursued throughout these actions, succeeded in landing his plane safe.

*HALLMAN, SHERWOOD H.

Rank and organization: Staff Sergeant, U.S. Army, 175th Infantry, 29th Infantry Division. Place and date: Brest, Brittany, France, 13 September 1944. Entered service at: Spring City, Pa. Birth: Spring City, Pa. G.O.

No.: 31, 17 April 1945. Citation: For conspicuous gallantry and intrepidity at risk of his life above and beyond the call of duty. On 13 September 1944, in Brittany, France, the 2d Battalion in its attack on the fortified city of Brest was held up by a strongly defended enemy position which had prevented its advance despite repeated attacks extending over a 3-day period. Finally, Company F advanced to within several hundred yards of the enemy position but was again halted by intense fire. Realizing that the position must be neutralized without delay, S/Sgt. Hallman ordered his squad to cover his movements with fire while he advanced alone to a point from which he could make the assault. Without hesitating, S/Sgt. Hallman leaped over a hedgerow into a sunken road, the central point of the German defenses which was known to contain an enemy machinegun position and at least 30 enemy riflemen. Firing his carbine and hurling grenades, S/Sgt. Hallman, unassisted, killed or wounded 4 of the enemy, then ordered the remainder to surrender. Immediately, 12 of the enemy surrendered and the position was shortly secured by the remainder of his company. Seeing the surrender of this position, about 75 of the enemy in the vicinity surrendered, yielding a defensive organization which the battalion with heavy supporting fires had been unable to take. This single heroic act on the part of S/Sgt. Hallman resulted in the immediate advance of the entire battalion for a distance of 2,000 yards to a position from which Fort Keranroux was captured later the same day. S/Sgt. Hallman's fighting determination and intrepidity in battle exemplify the highest tradition of the U.S. Armed Forces.

*HALYBURTON, WILLIAM DAVID, JR.

Rank and organization: Pharmacist's Mate Second Class, U.S. Naval Reserve. Born: 2 August 1924, Canton, N.C. Accredited to: North Carolina. Citation: For conspicuous gallantry and intrepidity at the risk of his life above and beyond the call of duty while serving with a Marine Rifle Company in the 2d Battalion, 5th Marines, 1st Marine Division, during action against enemy Japanese forces on Okinawa Shima in the Ryukyu Chain, 10 May 1945. Undaunted by the deadly accuracy of Japanese counterfire as his unit pushed the attack through a strategically important draw, Halyburton unhesitatingly dashed across the draw and up the hill into an open fire-swept field where the company advance squad was suddenly pinned down under a terrific concentration of mortar, machinegun and sniper fire with resultant severe casualties. Moving steadily forward despite the enemy's merciless barrage, he reached the wounded marine who lay farthest away and was rendering first aid when his patient was struck for the second time by a Japanese bullet. Instantly placing himself in the direct line of fire, he shielded the fallen fighter with his own body and staunchly continued his ministrations although constantly menaced by the slashing fury of shrapnel and bullets falling on all sides. Alert, determined and completely unselfish in his concern for the helpless marine, he persevered in his efforts until he himself sustained mortal wounds and collapsed, heroically sacrificing himself that his comrade might live. By his outstanding valor and unwavering devotion to duty in the face of tremendous odds, Halyburton sustained and enhanced the highest traditions of the U.S. Naval Service. He gallantly gave his life in the service of his country.

HAMILTON, PIERPONT M.

Rank and organization: Major, U.S. Army Air Corps. Place and date: Near Port Lyautey, French Morocco, 8 November 1942. Entered service at: New York, N.Y. Born: 3 August 1898, Tuxedo Park, N.Y. G.O. No.: 4, 23 January 1943. Citation: For conspicuous gallantry and intrepidity in action above and beyond the call of duty. On 8 November 1942, near Port Lyautey, French Morocco, Lt. Col. Hamilton volunteered to accompany Col. Demas Craw on a dangerous mission to the French commander, designed to bring about a cessation of hostilities. Driven away from the mouth of the Sebou River by heavy shelling from all sides, the landing boat was finally beached at Mehdia Plage despite continuous machinegun fire from 3 low-flying hostile planes. Driven in a light truck toward French headquarters, this courageous mission encountered intermittent firing, and as it neared Port Lyautey a heavy burst of machinegun fire was delivered upon the truck from pointblank range, killing Col. Craw instantly. Although captured immediately, after this incident, Lt. Col. Hamilton completed the mission .

*HAMMERBERG, OWEN FRANCIS PATRICK

Rank and organization: Boatswain's Mate Second Class, U.S. Navy. Born: 31 May 1920, Daggett, Mich. Accredited to: Michigan. Citation: For conspicuous gallantry and intrepidity at the risk of his life above and beyond the call of duty as a diver engaged in rescue operations at West Loch, Pearl Harbor, 17 February 1945. Aware of the danger when 2 fellow divers were hopelessly trapped in a cave-in of steel wreckage while tunneling with jet nozzles under an LST sunk in 40 feet of water and 20 feet of mud. Hammerberg unhesitatingly went overboard in a valiant attempt to effect their rescue despite the certain hazard of additional cave-ins and the risk of fouling his lifeline on jagged pieces of steel imbedded in the shifting mud. Washing a passage through the original excavation, he reached the first of the trapped men, freed him from the wreckage and, working desperately in pitch-black darkness, finally effected his release from fouled lines, thereby enabling him to reach the surface. Wearied but undaunted after several hours of arduous labor, Hammerberg resolved to continue his struggle to wash through the oozing submarine, subterranean mud in a determined effort to save the second diver. Venturing still farther under the buried hulk, he held tenaciously to his purpose, reaching a place immediately above the other man just as another cave-in occurred and a heavy piece of steel pinned him crosswise over his shipmate in a position which protected the man beneath from further injury while placing the full brunt of terrific pressure on himself. Although he succumbed in agony 18 hours after he had gone to the aid of his fellow divers, Hammerberg, by his cool judgment, unfaltering professional skill and consistent disregard of all personal danger in the face of tremendous odds, had contributed effectively to the saving of his 2 comrades. His heroic spirit of self-sacrifice throughout enhanced and sustained the highest traditions of the U.S. Naval Service. He gallantly gave his life in the service of his country.

*HANSEN, DALE MERLIN

Rank and organization: Private, U.S. Marine Corps. Born: 13 December 1922, Wisner, Nebr. Accredited to: Nebraska. Citation: For conspicuous gallantry and intrepidity at the risk of his life above and beyond the call of duty while serving with Company E, 2d Battalion, 1st Marines, 1st Marine Division, in action against enemy Japanese forces on Okinawa Shima in the Ryukyu Chain, 7 May 1945. Cool and courageous in combat, Pvt. Hansen unhesitatingly took the initiative during a critical stage of the action and, armed with a rocket launcher, crawled to an exposed position where he attacked and destroyed a strategically located hostile pillbox. With his weapon subsequently destroyed by enemy fire, he seized a rifle and continued his 1-man assault. Reaching the crest of a ridge, he leaped across, opened fire on 6 Japanese and killed 4 before his rifle jammed. Attacked by the remaining 2 Japanese, he beat them off with the butt of his rifle and then climbed back to cover. Promptly returning with another weapon and supply of grenades, he fearlessly advanced, destroyed a strong mortar position and annihilated 8 more of the enemy. In the forefront of battle throughout this bitterly waged engagement, Pvt. Hansen, by his indomitable determination, bold tactics and complete disregard of all personal danger, contributed essentially to the success of his company's mission and to the ultimate capture of this fiercely defended outpost of the Japanese Empire. His great personal valor in the face of extreme peril reflects the highest credit upon himself and the U.S. Naval Service.

*HANSON, ROBERT MURRAY

Rank and organization: First Lieutenant, U.S. Marine Corps Reserve. Born: 4 February 1920, Lucknow, India. Accredited to: Massachusetts. Other Navy awards: Navy Cross, Air Medal. Citation: For conspicuous gallantry and intrepidity at the risk of his life and above and beyond the call of duty as fighter pilot attached to Marine Fighting Squadron 215 in action against enemy Japanese forces at Bougainville Island, 1 November 1943; and New Britain Island, 24 January 1944. Undeterred by fierce opposition, and fearless in the face of overwhelming odds, 1st Lt. Hanson fought the Japanese boldly and with daring aggressiveness. On 1 November, while flying cover for our landing operations at Empress Augusta Bay, he dauntlessly attacked 6 enemy torpedo bombers, forcing them to jettison their bombs and destroying 1 Japanese plane during the action. Cut off from his division while deep in enemy territory during a high cover flight over Simpson Harbor on 24 January, 1st Lt. Hanson waged a lone and gallant battle against hostile interceptors as they were orbiting to attack our bombers and, striking with devastating fury, brought down 4 Zeroes and probably a fifth. Handling his plane superbly in both pursuit and attack measures, he was a master of individual air combat, accounting for a total of 25 Japanese aircraft in this theater of war. His great personal valor and invincible fighting spirit were in keeping with the highest traditions of the U.S. Naval Service.

*HARMON, ROY W.

Rank and organization: Sergeant, U.S. Army, Company C, 362d Infantry, 91st Infantry Division. Place and date: Near Casaglia, Italy, 12 July 1944. Entered service at: Pixley, Calif. Birth: Talala, Okla. G.O. No.: 83, 2 October 1945. Citation: He was an acting squad leader when heavy machinegun fire from enemy positions, well dug in on commanding ground and camouflaged by haystacks, stopped his company's advance and pinned down 1 platoon where it was exposed to almost certain annihilation. Ordered to rescue the beleaguered platoon by neutralizing the German automatic fire, he led his squad forward along a draw to the right of the trapped unit against 3 key positions which poured murderous fire into his helpless comrades. When within range, his squad fired tracer bullets in an attempt to set fire to the 3 haystacks which were strung out in a loose line directly to the front, 75, 150, and 250 yards away. Realizing that this attack was ineffective, Sgt. Harmon ordered his squad to hold their position and voluntarily began a 1-man assault. Carrying white phosphorus grenades and a submachine gun, he skillfully took advantage of what little cover the terrain afforded and crept to within 25 yards of the first position. He set the haystack afire with a grenade, and when 2 of the enemy attempted to flee from the inferno, he killed them with his submachine gun. Crawling toward the second machinegun emplacement, he attracted fire and was wounded; but he continued to advance and destroyed the position with hand grenades, killing the occupants. He then attacked the third machinegun, running to a small knoll, then crawling over ground which offered no concealment or cover. About halfway to his objective, he was again wounded. But he struggled ahead until within 20 yards of the machinegun nest, where he raised himself to his knees to throw a grenade. He was knocked down by direct enemy fire. With a final, magnificent effort, he again arose, hurled the grenade and fell dead, riddled by bullets. His missile fired the third position, destroying it. Sgt. Harmon's extraordinary heroism, gallantry, and self-sacrifice saved a platoon from being wiped out, and made it possible for his company to advance against powerful enemy resistance.

*HARR, HARRY R.

Rank and organization: Corporal, U.S. Army, Company D, 124th Infantry, 31st Infantry Division. Place and date: Near Maglamin, Mindanao, Philippine Islands, 5 June 1945. Entered service at: East Freedom, Pa. Birth: Pine Croft, Pa. G.O. No.: 28, 28 March 1946.

Citation: He displayed conspicuous gallantry and intrepidity. In a fierce counterattack, the Japanese closed in on his machinegun emplacement, hurling hand grenades, 1 of which exploded under the gun, putting it out of action and wounding 2 of the crew. While the remaining gunners were desperately attempting to repair their weapon another grenade landed squarely in the emplacement. Quickly realizing he could not safely throw the unexploded missile from the crowded position, Cpl. Harr unhesitatingly covered it with his body to smother the blast. His supremely courageous act, which cost him his life, saved 4 of his comrades and enabled them to continue their mission.

HARRELL, WILLIAM GEORGE

Rank and organization: Sergeant, U.S. Marine Corps, 1st Battalion, 28th Marines, 5th Marine Division. Place and date: Iwo Jima, Volcano Islands, 3 March 1945. Entered service at: Mercedes, Tex. Born: 26 June 1922, Rio Grande City, Tex. Citation: For conspicuous gallantry and intrepidity at the risk of his life above and beyond the call of duty as leader of an assault group attached to the 1st Battalion, 28th Marines, 5th Marine Division during hand-to-hand combat with enemy Japanese at Iwo Jima, Volcano Islands, on 3 March 1945. Standing watch alternately with another marine in a terrain studded with caves and ravines, Sgt. Harrell was holding a position in a perimeter defense around the company command post when Japanese troops infiltrated our lines in the early hours of dawn. Awakened by a sudden attack, he quickly opened fire with his carbine and killed 2 of the enemy as they emerged from a ravine in the light of a star shellburst. Unmindful of his danger as hostile grenades fell closer, he waged a fierce lone battle until an exploding missile tore off his left hand and fractured his thigh. He was vainly attempting to reload the carbine when his companion returned from the command post with another weapon. Wounded again by a Japanese who rushed the foxhole wielding a saber in the darkness, Sgt. Harrell succeeded in drawing his pistol and killing his opponent and then ordered his wounded companion to a place of safety. Exhausted by profuse bleeding but still unbeaten, he fearlessly met the challenge of 2 more enemy troops who charged his position and placed a grenade near his head. Killing 1 man with his pistol, he grasped the sputtering grenade with his good right hand, and, pushing it painfully toward the crouching soldier, saw his remaining assailant destroyed but his own hand severed in the explosion. At dawn Sgt. Harrell was evacuated from a position hedged by the bodies of 12 dead Japanese, at least 5 of whom he had personally destroyed in his self-sacrificing defense of the command post. His grim fortitude, exceptional valor, and indomitable fighting spirit against almost insurmountable odds reflect the highest credit upon himself and enhance the finest traditions of the U.S. Naval Service.

*HARRIS, JAMES L.

Rank and organization: Second Lieutenant, U.S. Army, 756th Tank Battalion. Place and date: At Vagney, France, 7 October 1944. Entered service at: Hillsboro, Tex. Birth: Hillsboro, Tex. G.O. No.: 32, 23 April 1945. Citation: For conspicuous gallantry and intrepidity at risk of life above and beyond the call of duty on 7 October 1944, in Vagney, France. At 9 p.m. an enemy raiding party, comprising a tank and 2 platoons of infantry, infiltrated through the lines under cover of mist and darkness and attacked an infantry battalion command post with hand grenades, retiring a short distance to an ambush position on hearing the approach of the M-4 tank commanded by 2d Lt. Harris. Realizing the need for bold aggressive action, 2d Lt. Harris ordered his tank to halt while he proceeded on foot, fully 10 yards ahead of his 6-man patrol and armed only with a service pistol, to probe the darkness for the enemy. Although struck down and mortally wounded by machinegun bullets which penetrated his solar plexus, he crawled back to his tank, leaving a trail of blood behind him, and, too weak to climb inside it, issued fire orders while lying on the road between the 2 contending armored vehicles. Although the tank which he commanded was destroyed in the course of the fire fight, he stood the enemy off until friendly tanks, preparing to come to his aid, caused the enemy to withdraw and thereby lose an opportunity to kill or capture the entire battalion command personnel. Suffering a second wound, which severed his leg at the hip, in the course of this tank duel, 2d Lt. Harris refused aid until after a wounded member of his crew had been carried to safety. He died before he could be given medical attention.

*HASTINGS, JOE R.

Rank and organization: Private First Class, U.S. Army, Company C, 386th Infantry, 97th Infantry Division. Place and date: Drabenderhohe, Germany, 12 April 1945. Entered service at: Magnolia, Ohio. Birth: Malvern, Ohio. G.O. No.: 101, 8 November 1945. Citation: He fought gallantly during an attack against strong enemy forces defending Drabenderhohe, Germany, from the dug-in positions on commanding ground. As squad leader of a light machinegun section supporting the advance of the 1st and 3d Platoons, he braved direct rifle, machinegun, 20mm., and mortar fire, some of which repeatedly missed him only by inches, and rushed forward over 350 yards of open, rolling fields to reach a position from which he could fire on the enemy troops. From this vantage point he killed the crews of a 20mm. gun and a machinegun, drove several enemy riflemen from their positions, and so successfully shielded the 1st Platoon, that it had time to reorganize and remove its wounded to safety. Observing that the 3d Platoon to his right was being met by very heavy 40mm. and machinegun fire, he ran 150 yards with his gun to the leading elements of that unit, where he killed the crew of the 40mm. gun. As spearhead of the 3d Platoon's attack, he advanced, firing his gun held at hip height, disregarding the bullets that whipped past him, until the assault had carried 175 yards to the objective. In this charge he and the riflemen he led killed or wounded many of the fanatical enemy and put 2 machineguns out of action. Pfc.

Hastings, by his intrepidity, outstanding leadership, and unrelenting determination to wipe out the formidable German opposition, cleared the path for his company's advance into Drabenderhohe. He was killed 4 days later while again supporting the 3d Platoon.

*HAUGE, LOUIS JAMES, JR.

Rank and organization: Corporal, U.S. Marine Corps Reserve. Born: 12 December 1924, Ada, Minn. Accredited to: Minnesota. Citation: For conspicuous gallantry and intrepidity at the risk of his life above and beyond the call of duty as leader of a machinegun squad serving with Company C, 1st Battalion, 1st Marines, 1st Marine Division, in action against enemy Japanese forces on Okinawa Shima in the Ryukyu Chain on 14 May 1945. Alert and aggressive during a determined assault against a strongly fortified Japanese hill position, Cpl. Hauge boldly took the initiative when his company's left flank was pinned down under a heavy machinegun and mortar barrage with resultant severe casualties and, quickly locating the 2 machineguns which were delivering the uninterrupted stream of enfilade fire, ordered his squad to maintain a covering barrage as he rushed across an exposed area toward the furiously blazing enemy weapons. Although painfully wounded as he charged the first machinegun, he launched a vigorous single-handed grenade attack, destroyed the entire hostile gun position and moved relentlessly forward toward the other emplacement despite his wounds and the increasingly heavy Japanese fire. Undaunted by the savage opposition, he again hurled his deadly grenades with unerring aim and succeeded in demolishing the second enemy gun before he fell under the slashing fury of Japanese sniper fire. By his ready grasp of the critical situation and his heroic 1-man assault tactics, Cpl. Hauge had eliminated 2 strategically placed enemy weapons, thereby releasing the besieged troops from an overwhelming volume of hostile fire and enabling his company to advance. His indomitable fighting spirit and decisive valor in the face of almost certain death reflect the highest credit upon Cpl. Hauge and the U.S. Naval Service. He gallantly gave his life in the service of his country.

HAWK, JOHN D.

Rank and organization: Sergeant, U.S. Army, Company E, 359th Infantry, 90th Infantry Division. Place and date: Near Chambois, France, 20 August 1944. Entered service at: Bremerton, Wash. Birth: San Francisco, Calif. G.O. No.: 55, 13 July 1945. Citation: He manned a light machinegun on 20 August 1944, near Chambois, France, a key point in the encirclement which created the Falaise Pocket. During an enemy counterattack, his position was menaced by a strong force of tanks and infantry. His fire forced the infantry to withdraw, but an artillery shell knocked out his gun and wounded him in the right thigh. Securing a bazooka, he and another man stalked the tanks and forced them to retire to a wooded section. In the lull which followed, Sgt. Hawk reorganized 2 machinegun squads and, in the face of intense enemy fire, directed the assembly of 1 workable weapon from 2 damaged guns. When another enemy assault developed, he was forced to pull back from the pressure of spearheading armor. Two of our tank destroyers were brought up. Their shots were ineffective because of the terrain until Sgt. Hawk, despite his wound, boldly climbed to an exposed position on a knoll where, unmoved by fusillades from the enemy, he became a human aiming stake for the destroyers. Realizing that his shouted fire directions could not be heard above the noise of battle, he ran back to the destroyers through a concentration of bullets and shrapnel to correct the range. He returned to his exposed position, repeating this performance until 2 of the tanks were knocked out and a third driven off. Still at great risk, he continued to direct the destroyers' fire into the Germans' wooded position until the enemy came out and surrendered. Sgt. Hawk's fearless initiative and heroic conduct, even while suffering from a painful wound, was in large measure responsible for crushing 2 desperate attempts of the enemy to escape from the Falaise Picket and for taking more than 500 prisoners.

*HAWKINS, WILLIAM DEAN

Rank and organization: First Lieutenant, U.S. Marine Corps. Born: 19 April 1914, Fort Scott, Kans. Appointed from: El Paso, Tex. Citation: For valorous and gallant conduct above and beyond the call of duty as commanding officer of a Scout Sniper Platoon attached to the Assault Regiment in action against Japanese-held Tarawa in the Gilbert Island, 20 and 21 November 1943. The first to disembark from the jeep lighter, 1st Lt. Hawkins unhesitatingly moved forward under heavy enemy fire at the end of the Betio Pier, neutralizing emplacements in coverage of troops assaulting the main beach positions. Fearlessly leading his men on to join the forces fighting desperately to gain a beachhead, he repeatedly risked his life throughout the day and night to direct and lead attacks on pillboxes and installations with grenades and demolitions. At dawn on the following day, 1st Lt. Hawkins resumed the dangerous mission of clearing the limited beachhead of Japanese resistance, personally initiating an assault on a hostile position fortified by S enemy machineguns, and, crawling forward in the face of withering fire, boldly fired pointblank into the loopholes and completed the destruction with grenades. Refusing to withdraw after being seriously wounded in the chest during this skirmish, 1st Lt. Hawkins steadfastly carried the fight to the enemy, destroying 3 more pillboxes before he was caught in a burst of Japanese shellfire and mortally wounded. His relentless fighting spirit in the face of formidable opposition and his exceptionally daring tactics served as an inspiration to his comrades during the most crucial phase of the battle and reflect the highest credit upon the U.S. Naval Service. He gallantly gave his life for his country.

HAWKS, LLOYD C.

Rank and organization: Private First Class, U.S. Army, Medical Detachment, 30th Infantry, 3d Infantry Division. Place and date: Near Carano, Italy, 30 January 1944. Entered service at: Park Rapids, Minn. Born: 13 January 1911, Becker, Minn. G.O. No.: 5, 15 January 1945. Citation: For gallantry and intrepidity at risk of life above and beyond the call of duty. On 30 January 1944, at 3 p.m., near Carano, Italy, Pfc. Hawks braved an enemy counterattack in order to rescue 2 wounded men who, unable to move, were lying in an exposed position within 30 yards of the enemy. Two riflemen, attempting the rescue, had been forced to return to their fighting holes by extremely severe enemy machinegun fire, after crawling only 10 yards toward the casualties. An aid man, whom the enemy could plainly identify as such, had been critically wounded in a similar attempt. Pfc. Hawks, nevertheless, crawled 50 yards through a veritable hail of machinegun bullets and flying mortar fragments to a small ditch, administered first aid to his fellow aid man who had sought cover therein, and continued toward the 2 wounded men 50 yards distant. An enemy machinegun bullet penetrated his helmet, knocking it from his head, momentarily stunning him. Thirteen bullets passed through his helmet as it lay on the ground within 6 inches of his body. Pfc. Hawks, crawled to the casualties, administered first aid to the more seriously wounded man and dragged him to a covered position 25 yards distant. Despite continuous automatic fire from positions only 30 yards away and shells which exploded within 25 yards, Pfc. Hawks returned to the second man and administered first aid to him. As he raised himself to obtain bandages from his medical kit his right hip was shattered by a burst of machinegun fire and a second burst splintered his left forearm. Displaying dogged determination and extreme self-control, Pfc. Hawks, despite severe pain and his dangling left arm, completed the task of bandaging the remaining casualty and with superhuman effort dragged him to the same depression to which he had brought the first man. Finding insufficient cover for 3 men at this point, Pfc. Hawks crawled 75 yards in an effort to regain his company, reaching the ditch in which his fellow aid man was lying.

*HEDRICK, CLINTON M.

Rank and organization: Technical Sergeant, U.S. Army, Company I, 194th Glider Infantry, 17th Airborne Division. Place and date: Near Lembeck, Germany, 27-28 March 1945. Entered service at: Riverton, W. Va. Birth: Cherrygrove, W. Va. G.O. No.: 89, 19 October 1945. Citation: He displayed extraordinary heroism and gallantry in action on 2728 March 1945, in Germany. Following an airborne landing near Wesel, his unit was assigned as the assault platoon for the assault on Lembeck. Three times the landing elements were pinned down by intense automatic weapons fire from strongly defended positions. Each time, T/Sgt. Hedrick fearlessly charged through heavy fire, shooting his automatic rifle from his hip. His courageous action so inspired his men that they reduced the enemy positions in rapid succession. When 6 of the enemy attempted a surprise, flanking movement, he quickly turned and killed the entire party with a burst of fire. Later, the enemy withdrew across a moat into Lembeck Castle. T/Sgt. Hedrick, with utter disregard for his own safety, plunged across the drawbridge alone in pursuit. When a German soldier, with hands upraised, declared the garrison wished to surrender, he entered the castle yard with 4 of his men to accept the capitulation. The group moved through a sally port, and was met by fire from a German self-propelled gun. Although mortally wounded, T/Sgt. Hedrick fired at the enemy gun and covered the withdrawal of his comrades. He died while being evacuated after the castle was taken. His great personal courage and heroic leadership contributed in large measure to the speedy capture of Lembeck and provided an inspiring example to his comrades.

HENDRIX, JAMES R.

Rank and organization: Private, U.S. Army, Company C, 53d Armored Infantry Battalion, 4th Armored Division. Place and date: Near Assenois, Belgium, 26 December 1944. Entered service at: Lepanto, Ark. Birth: Lepanto, Ark. G.O. No.: 74, 1 September 1945. Citation: On the night of 26 December 1944, near Assenois, Belgium, he was with the leading element engaged in the final thrust to break through to the besieged garrison at Bastogne when halted by a fierce combination of artillery and small arms fire. He dismounted from his half-track and advanced against two 88mm. guns, and, by the ferocity of his rifle fire, compelled the guncrews to take cover and then to surrender. Later in the attack he again left his vehicle, voluntarily, to aid 2 wounded soldiers, helpless and exposed to intense machinegun fire. Effectively silencing 2 hostile machineguns, he held off the enemy by his own fire until the wounded men were evacuated. Pvt. Hendrix again distinguished himself when he hastened to the aid of still another soldier who was trapped in a burning half-track. Braving enemy sniper fire and exploding mines and ammunition in the vehicle, he extricated the wounded man and extinguished his flaming clothing, thereby saving the life of his fellow soldier. Pvt. Hendrix, by his superb courage and heroism, exemplified the highest traditions of the military service.

*HENRY, ROBERT T.

Rank and organization: Private, U.S. Army, 16th Infantry, 1st Infantry Division. Place and date: Luchem, Germany, 3 December 1944. Entered service at: Greenville, Miss. Birth: Greenville, Miss. G.O. No.: 45, 12 June 1945. Citation: Near Luchem, Germany, he volunteered to attempt the destruction of a nest of 5 enemy machineguns located in a bunker 150 yards to the flank which had stopped the advance of his platoon. Stripping off his pack, overshoes, helmet, and overcoat, he sprinted alone with his rifle and hand grenades across the open terrain toward the enemy emplacement. Before he had gone half the distance he was hit by a burst of machinegun fire. Dropping his rifle, he continued to stagger forward until he fell mortally wounded only 10 yards from the enemy emplacement. His single-handed attack forced the enemy to leave the machineguns. During this break in hostile fire the platoon moved forward and overran the position. Pvt. Henry, by his gallantry and intrepidity and utter disregard for his own life, enabled his company to reach its objective, capturing this key defense and 70 German prisoners.

HERRERA, SILVESTRE S.

Rank and organization: Private First Class, U.S. Army, Company E, 142d Infantry, 36th Infantry Division. Place and date: Near Mertzwiller, France, 15 March 1945. Entered service at: Phoenix, Ariz. Birth: El Paso, Tex. G.O. No.: 75, 5 September 1945. Citation: He advanced with a platoon along a wooded road until stopped by heavy enemy machinegun fire. As the rest of the unit took cover, he made a 1-man frontal assault on a strongpoint and captured 8 enemy soldiers. When the platoon resumed its advance and was subjected to fire from a second emplacement beyond an extensive minefield, Pvt. Herrera again moved forward, disregarding the danger of exploding mines, to attack the position. He stepped on a mine and had both feet severed but, despite intense pain and unchecked loss of blood, he pinned down the enemy with accurate rifle fire while a friendly squad captured the enemy gun by skirting the minefield and rushing in from the flank. The magnificent courage, extraordinary heroism, and willing self-sacrifice displayed by Pvt. Herrera resulted in the capture of 2 enemy strongpoints and the taking of 8 prisoners.

HERRING, RUFUS G.

Rank and organization: Lieutenant, U.S. Naval Reserve, LCI (G) 449. Place and date: Iwo Jima, 17 February 1945. Entered service at: North

Carolina. Born: 11 June 1921, Roseboro, N.C. Citation: For conspicuous gallantry and intrepidity at the risk of his life above and beyond the call of duty as commanding officer of LCI (G) 449 operating as a unit of LCI (G) Group 8, during the preinvasion attack on Iwo Jima on 17 February 1945. Boldly closing the strongly fortified shores under the devastating fire of Japanese coastal defense guns, Lt. (then Lt. (j.g.)) Herring directed shattering barrages of 40mm. and 20mm. gunfire against hostile beaches until struck down by the enemy's savage counterfire which blasted the 449's heavy guns and whipped her decks into sheets of flame. Regaining consciousness despite profuse bleeding he was again critically wounded when a Japanese mortar crashed the conning station, instantly killing or fatally wounding most of the officers and leaving the ship wallowing without navigational control. Upon recovering the second time, Lt. Herring resolutely climbed down to the pilothouse and, fighting against his rapidly waning strength, took over the helm, established communication with the engineroom, and carried on valiantly until relief could be obtained. When no longer able to stand, he propped himself against empty shell cases and rallied his men to the aid of the wounded; he maintained position in the firing line with his 20mm. guns in action in the face of sustained enemy fire, and conned his crippled ship to safety. His unwavering fortitude, aggressive perseverance, and indomitable spirit against terrific odds reflect the highest credit upon Lt. Herring and uphold the highest traditions of the U.S. Naval Service.

*HILL, EDWIN JOSEPH

Rank and organization: Chief Boatswain, U.S. Navy. Born: 4 October 1894, Philadelphia, Pa. Accredited to: Pennsylvania. Citation: For distinguished conduct in the line of his profession, extraordinary courage, and disregard of his own safety during the attack on the Fleet in Pearl Harbor, by Japanese forces on 7 December 1941. During the height of the strafing and bombing, Chief Boatswain Hill led his men of the linehandling details of the U.S.S. Nevada to the quays, cast off the lines and swam back to his ship. Later, while on the forecastle, attempting to let go the anchors, he was blown overboard and killed by the explosion of several bombs.

HORNER, FREEMAN V.

Rank and organization: Staff Sergeant, U.S. Army, Company K, 119th Infantry, 30th Infantry Division. Place and date: Wurselen, Germany, 16 November 1944. Entered service at: Shamokin, Pa. Birth: Mount Carmel, Pa. G.O. No.: 95, 30 October 1945. Citation: S/Sgt. Horner and other members of his company were attacking Wurselen, Germany, against stubborn resistance on 16 November 1944, when machinegun fire from houses on the edge of the town pinned the attackers in flat, open terrain 100 yards from their objective. As they lay in the field, enemy artillery observers directed fire upon them, causing serious casualties. Realizing that the machineguns must be eliminated in order to permit the company to advance from its precarious position, S/Sgt. Horner voluntarily stood up with his submachine gun and rushed into the teeth of concentrated fire, burdened by a heavy load of ammunition and hand grenades. Just as he reached a position of seeming safety, he was fired on by a machinegun which had remained silent up until that time. He coolly wheeled in his fully exposed position while bullets barely missed him and killed 2 hostile gunners with a single, devastating burst. He turned to face the fire of the other 2 machineguns, and dodging fire as he ran, charged the 2 positions 50 yards away. Demoralized by their inability to hit the intrepid infantryman, the enemy abandoned their guns and took cover in the cellar of the house they occupied. S/Sgt. Horner burst into the building, hurled 2 grenades down the cellar stairs, and called for the Germans to surrender. Four men gave up to him. By his extraordinary courage, S/Sgt. Horner destroyed 3 enemy machinegun positions, killed or captured 7 enemy, and cleared the path for his company's successful assault on Wurselen.

HOWARD, JAMES H. (Air Mission)

Rank and organization: Lieutenant Colonel, U.S. Army Air Corps. Place and date: Over Oschersleben, Germany, 11 January 1944. Entered service at: St. Louis, Mo. Birth: Canton, China. G.O. No.: 45, 5 June 1944. Citation: For conspicuous gallantry and intrepidity above and beyond the call of duty in action with the enemy near Oschersleben, Germany, on 11 January 1944. On that day Col. Howard was the leader of a group of P51 aircraft providing support for a heavy bomber formation on a long-range mission deep in enemy territory. As Col. Howard's group met the bombers in the target area the bomber force was attacked by numerous enemy fighters. Col. Howard, with his group, and at once engaged the enemy and himself destroyed a German ME. 110. As a result of this attack Col. Howard lost contact with his group, and at once returned to the level of the bomber formation. He then saw that the bombers were being heavily attacked by enemy airplanes and that no other friendly fighters were at hand. While Col. Howard could have waited to attempt to assemble his group before engaging the enemy, he chose instead to attack single-handed a formation of more than 30 German airplanes. With utter disregard for his own safety he immediately pressed home determined attacks for some 30 minutes, during which time he destroyed 3 enemy airplanes and probably destroyed and damaged others. Toward the end of this engagement 3 of his guns went out of action and his fuel supply was becoming dangerously low. Despite these handicaps and the almost insuperable odds against him, Col. Howard continued his aggressive action in an attempt to protect the bombers from the numerous fighters. His skill, courage, and intrepidity on this occasion set an example of heroism which will be an inspiration to the U.S. Armed Forces.

HUFF, PAUL B.

Rank and organization: Corporal, U.S. Army, 509th Parachute Infantry Battalion. Place and date: Near Carano, Italy, 8 February 1944. Entered service at: Cleveland, Tenn. Birth: Cleveland, Tenn. G.O. No.: 41, 26 May 1944. Citation: For conspicuous gallantry and intrepidity at risk of life above and beyond the call of duty, in action on 8 February 1944, near Carano, Italy. Cpl. Huff volunteered to lead a 6-man patrol with the mission of determining the location and strength of an enemy unit which was delivering fire on the exposed right flank of his company. The terrain over which he had to travel consisted of exposed, rolling ground, affording the enemy excellent visibility. As the patrol advanced, its members were subjected to small arms and machinegun fire and a concentration of mortar fire, shells bursting within 5 to 10 yards of them and bullets striking the ground at their feet. Moving ahead of his patrol, Cpl. Huff drew fire from 3 enemy machineguns and a 20mm. weapon. Realizing the danger confronting his patrol, he advanced alone under deadly fire through a minefield and arrived at a point within 75 yards of the nearest machinegun position. Under direct fire from the rear machinegun, he crawled the remaining 75 yards to the closest emplacement, killed the crew with his submachine gun and destroyed the gun. During this act he fired from a kneeling position which drew fire from other positions, enabling him to estimate correctly the strength and location of the enemy. Still under concentrated fire, he returned to his patrol and led his men to safety. As a result of the information he gained, a patrol in strength sent out that afternoon, 1 group under the leadership of Cpl. Huff, succeeded in routing an enemy company of 125 men, killing 27 Germans and capturing 21 others, with a loss of only 3 patrol members. Cpl. Huff's intrepid leadership and daring combat skill reflect the finest traditions of the American infantryman.

*HUGHES, LLOYD H. (Air Mission)

Rank and organization: Second Lieutenant, U.S. Army Air Corps, 564th Bomber Squadron, 389th Bomber Group, 9th Air Force. Place and date: Ploesti Raid, Rumania, 1 August 1943. Entered service at: San Antonio, Tex. Born: 12 July 1921, Alexandria, La. G.O. No.: 17, 26 February 1944. Citation: For conspicuous gallantry in action and intrepidity at the risk of his life above and beyond the call of duty. On August 1943, 2d Lt. Hughes served in the capacity of pilot of a heavy bombardment aircraft participating in a long and hazardous minimum-altitude attack against the Axis oil refineries of Ploesti, Rumania, launched from the northern shores of Africa. Flying in the last formation to attack the target, he arrived in the target area after previous flights had thoroughly alerted the enemy defenses. Approaching the target through intense and accurate antiaircraft fire and dense balloon barrages at dangerously low altitude, his plane received several direct hits from both large and small caliber antiaircraft guns which seriously damaged his aircraft, causing sheets of escaping gasoline to stream from the bomb bay and from the left wing. This damage was inflicted at a time prior to reaching the target when 2d Lt. Hughes could have made a forced landing in any of the grain fields readily available at that time. The target area was blazing with burning oil tanks and damaged refinery installations from which flames leaped high above the bombing level of the formation. With full knowledge of the consequences of entering this blazing inferno when his airplane was profusely leaking gasoline in two separate locations, 2d Lt. Hughes, motivated only by his high conception of duty which called for the destruction of his assigned target at any cost, did not elect to make a forced landing or turn back from the attack. Instead, rather than jeopardize the formation and the success of the attack, he unhesitatingly entered the blazing area and dropped his bomb load with great precision. After successfully bombing the objective, his aircraft emerged from the conflagration with the left wing aflame. Only then did he attempt a forced landing, but because of the advanced stage of the fire enveloping his aircraft the plane crashed and was consumed. By 2d Lt. Hughes' heroic decision to complete his mission regardless of the consequences in utter disregard of his own life, and by his gallant and valorous execution of this decision, he has rendered a service to our country in the defeat of our enemies which will everlastingly be outstanding in the annals of our Nation's history.

*HUTCHINS, JOHNNIE DAVID

Rank and organization: Seaman First Class, U.S. Naval Reserve. Born: 4 August 1922, Weimer, Tex. Accredited to: Texas. Citation: For extraordinary heroism and conspicuous valor above and beyond the call of duty while serving on board a Landing Ship, Tank, during the assault on Lae, New Guinea, 4 September 1943. As the ship on which Hutchins was stationed approached the enemy-occupied beach under a veritable hail of fire from Japanese shore batteries and aerial bombardment, a hostile torpedo pierced the surf and bore down upon the vessel with deadly accuracy. In the tense split seconds before the helmsman could steer clear of the threatening missile, a bomb struck the pilot house, dislodged him from his station, and left the stricken ship helplessly exposed. Fully aware of the dire peril of the situation, Hutchins, although mortally wounded by the shattering explosion, quickly grasped the wheel and exhausted the last of his strength in maneuvering the vessel clear of the advancing torpedo. Still clinging to the helm, he eventually succumbed to his injuries, his final thoughts concerned only with the safety of his ship, his final efforts expended toward the security of his mission. He gallantly gave his life in the service of his country.

*JACHMAN, ISADORE S.

Rank and organization: Staff Sergeant, U.S. Army, Company B, 513th Parachute Infantry Regiment. Place and date: Flamierge, Belgium, 4 January 1945. Entered service at: Baltimore, Md. Birth: Berlin,

Germany. G.O. No.: 25, 9 June 1950. Citation: For conspicuous gallantry and intrepidity above and beyond the call of duty at Flamierge, Belgium, on 4 January 1945, when his company was pinned down by enemy artillery, mortar, and small arms fire, 2 hostile tanks attacked the unit, inflicting heavy. casualties. S/Sgt. Jachman, seeing the desperate plight of his comrades, left his place of cover and with total disregard for his own safety dashed across open ground through a hail of fire and seizing a bazooka from a fallen comrade advanced on the tanks, which concentrated their fire on him. Firing the weapon alone, he damaged one and forced both to retire. S/Sgt. Jachman's heroic action, in which he suffered fatal wounds, disrupted the entire enemy attack, reflecting the highest credit upon himself and the parachute infantry.

JACKSON, ARTHUR J.

Rank and organization: Private First Class, U.S. Marine Corps, 3d Battalion, 7th Marines, 1st Marine Division. Place and date: Island of Peleliu in the Palau group, 18 September 1944. Entered service at: Oregon. Born: 18 October 1924, Cleveland Ohio. Citation: For conspicuous gallantry and intrepidity at the risk of his life above and beyond the call of duty while serving with the 3d Battalion, 7th Marines, 1st Marine Division, in action against enemy Japanese forces on the Island of Peleliu in the Palau group, 18 September 1944. Boldly taking the initiative when his platoon's left flank advance was held up by the fire of Japanese troops concealed in strongly fortified positions, Pfc. Jackson unhesitatingly proceeded forward of our lines and, courageously defying the heavy barrages, charged a large pillbox housing approximately 35 enemy soldiers. Pouring his automatic fire into the opening of the fixed installation to trap the occupying troops, he hurled white phosphorus grenades and explosive charges brought up by a fellow marine, demolishing the pillbox and killing all of the enemy. Advancing alone under the continuous fire from other hostile emplacements, he employed similar means to smash 2 smaller positions in the immediate vicinity. Determined to crush the entire pocket of resistance although harassed on all sides by the shattering blasts of Japanese weapons and covered only by small rifle parties, he stormed 1 gun position after another, dealing death and destruction to the savagely fighting enemy in his inexorable drive against the remaining defenses, and succeeded in wiping out a total of 12 pillboxes and 50 Japanese soldiers. Stouthearted and indomitable despite the terrific odds. Pfc. Jackson resolutely maintained control of the platoon's left flank movement throughout his valiant 1-man assault and, by his cool decision and relentless fighting spirit during a critical situation, contributed essentially to the complete annihilation of the enemy in the southern sector of the island. His gallant initiative and heroic conduct in the face of extreme peril reflect the highest credit upon Pfc. Jackson and the U.S. Naval Service.

JACOBSON, DOUGLAS THOMAS

Rank and organization: Private First Class, U.S. Marine Corps Reserve, 3d Battalion, 23d Marines, 4th Marine Division. Place and date: Iwo Jima, Volcano Islands, 26 February 1945. Entered service at: New York. Born: 25 November 1925, Rochester, N.Y. Citation: For conspicuous gallantry and intrepidity at the risk of his life above and beyond the call of duty while serving with the 3d Battalion, 23d Marines, 4th Marine Division, in combat against enemy Japanese forces during the seizure of Iwo Jima in the Volcano Island, 26 February 1945. Promptly destroying a stubborn 20mm. antiaircraft gun and its crew after assuming the duties of a bazooka man who had been killed, Pfc. Jacobson waged a relentless battle as his unit fought desperately toward the summit of Hill 382 in an effort to penetrate the heart of Japanese cross-island defense. Employing his weapon with ready accuracy when his platoon was halted by overwhelming enemy fire on 26 February, he first destroyed 2 hostile machinegun positions, then attacked a large blockhouse, completely neutralizing the fortification before dispatching the 5-man crew of a second pillbox and exploding the installation with a terrific demolitions blast. Moving steadily forward, he wiped out an earth-covered rifle emplacement and, confronted by a cluster of similar emplacements which constituted the perimeter of enemy defenses in his assigned sector, fearlessly advanced, quickly reduced all 6 positions to a shambles, killed 10 of the enemy, and enabled our forces to occupy the strong point. Determined to widen the breach thus forced, he volunteered his services to an adjacent assault company, neutralized a pillbox holding up its advance, opened fire on a Japanese tank pouring a steady stream of bullets on 1 of our supporting tanks, and smashed the enemy tank's gun turret in a brief but furious action culminating in a single-handed assault against still another blockhouse and the subsequent neutralization of its firepower. By his dauntless skill and valor, Pfc. Jacobson destroyed a total of 16 enemy positions and annihilated approximately 75 Japanese, thereby contributing essentially to the success of his division's operations against this fanatically defended outpost of the Japanese Empire. His gallant conduct in the face of tremendous odds enhanced and sustained the highest traditions of the U.S. Naval Service.

*JERSTAD, JOHN L. (Air Mission)

Rank and organization: Major, U.S. Army Air Corps, 9th Air Force. Place and date: Ploesti Raid, Rumania, 1 August 1943. Entered service at: Racine, Wis. Born: 12 February 1918, Racine, Wis. G.O. No.: 72, 28 October 1943. Citation: For conspicuous gallantry and intrepidity above and beyond the call of duty. On 1 August 1943, he served as pilot of the lead aircraft in his group in a daring low-level attack against enemy oil refineries and installations at Ploesti, Rumania. Although he had completed more than his share of missions and was no longer connected with this group, so high was his conception of duty that he volunteered to lead the formation in the correct belief that his participation would contribute materially to success in this attack. Maj. Jerstad led the formation into attack with full realization of the extreme hazards involved and despite withering fire from heavy and light antiaircraft guns. Three miles from the target his airplane was hit, badly damaged, and set on fire. Ignoring the fact that he was flying over a field suitable for a forced landing, he kept on the course. After the bombs of his aircraft were released on the target, the fire in his ship became so intense as to make further progress impossible and he crashed into the target area. By his voluntary acceptance of a mission he knew was extremely hazardous, and his assumption of an intrepid course of action at the risk of life over and above the call of duty, Maj. Jerstad set an example of heroism which will be an inspiration to the U.S. Armed Forces.

*JOHNSON, ELDEN H.

Rank and organization: Private, U.S. Army, 15th Infantry, 3d Infantry Division. Place and date: Near Valmontone, Italy, 3 June 1944. Entered service at: East Weymouth, Mass. Birth: Bivalue, N.J. G.O. No.: 38, 16 May 1945. Citation: For conspicuous gallantry and intrepidity at risk of life above and beyond the call of duty. Pvt. Johnson elected to sacrifice his life in order that his comrades might extricate themselves from an ambush. Braving the massed fire of about 60 riflemen, 3 machineguns, and 3 tanks from positions only 25 yards distant, he stood erect and signaled his patrol leader to withdraw. The whole area was brightly illuminated by enemy flares. Then, despite 20mm. machineguns, machine pistol, and rifle fire directed at him, Pvt. Johnson advanced beyond the enemy in a slow deliberate walk. Firing his automatic rifle from the hip, he succeeded in distracting the enemy and enabled his 12 comrades to escape. Advancing to within 5 yards of a machinegun, emptying his weapon, Pvt. Johnson killed its crew. Standing in full view of the enemy he reloaded and turned on the riflemen to the left, firing directly into their positions. He either killed or wounded 4 of them. A burst of machinegun fire tore into Pvt. Johnson and he dropped to his knees. Fighting to the very last, he steadied himself on his knees and sent a final burst of fire crashing into another German. With that he slumped forward dead. Pvt. Johnson had willingly given his life in order that his comrades might live. These acts on the part of Pvt. Johnson were an inspiration to the entire command and are in keeping with the highest traditions of the armed forces.

JOHNSON, LEON W. (Air Mission)

Rank and organization: Colonel, U.S. Army Air Corps, 44th Bomber Group, 9th Air Force. Place and date: Ploesti Raid, Rumania, 1 August 1943. Entered service at: Moline, Kans. Born: 13 September 1904, Columbia, Mo. G.O. No.: 54, 7 September 1943. Citation: For conspicuous gallantry in action and intrepidity at the risk of his life above and beyond the call of duty on 1 August 1943. Col. Johnson, as commanding officer of a heavy bombardment group, let the formation of the aircraft of his organization constituting the fourth element of the mass low-level bombing attack of the 9th U.S. Air Force against the vitally important enemy target of the Ploesti oil refineries. While proceeding to the target on this 2,400-mile flight, his element became separated from the leading elements of the mass formation in maintaining the formation of the unit while avoiding dangerous cumulous cloud conditions encountered over mountainous territory. Though temporarily lost, he reestablished contact with the third element and continued on the mission with this reduced force to the prearranged point of attack, where it was discovered that the target assigned to Col. Johnson's group had been attacked and damaged by a preceding element. Though having lost the element of surprise upon which the safety and success of such a daring form of mission in heavy bombardment aircraft so strongly depended, Col. Johnson elected to carry out his planned low-level attack despite the thoroughly alerted defenses, the destructive anti-aircraft fire, enemy fighter airplanes, the imminent danger of exploding delayed action bombs from the previous element, of oil fires and explosions, and of intense smoke obscuring the target. By his gallant courage, brilliant leadership, and superior flying skill, Col. Johnson so led his formation as to destroy totally the important refining plants and installations which were the object of his mission. Col. Johnson's personal contribution to the success of this historic raid, and the conspicuous gallantry in action, and intrepidity at the risk of his life above and beyond the call of duty demonstrated by him on this occasion constitute such deeds of valor and distinguished service as have during our Nation's history formed the finest traditions of our Armed Forces.

*JOHNSON, LEROY

Rank and organization: Sergeant, U.S. Army, Company K, 126th Infantry, 32d Infantry Division. Place and date: Near Limon, Leyte, Philippine Islands, 15 December 1944. Entered service at: Oakdale, La. Birth: Caney Creek, La. G.O. No.: 83, 2 October 1945. Citation: He was squad leader of a 9-man patrol sent to reconnoiter a ridge held by a well-entrenched enemy force. Seeing an enemy machinegun position, he ordered his men to remain behind while he crawled to within 6 yards of the gun. One of the enemy crew jumped up and prepared to man the weapon. Quickly withdrawing, Sgt. Johnson rejoined his patrol and reported the situation to his commanding officer. Ordered to destroy the gun, which covered the approaches to several other enemy positions, he chose 3 other men, armed them with hand grenades, and led them to a point near the objective. After taking partial cover behind a log, the men had knocked out the gun and begun an assault when hostile troops on the flank hurled several grenades. As he started for cover, Sgt. Johnson saw 2 unexploded grenades which had fallen near his men. Knowing that his comrades would be wounded or killed by the explosion, he deliberately threw himself on the grenades and received their full charge in his body. Fatally wounded by the blast, he died soon afterward. Through his outstanding gallantry in sacrificing his life for his comrades, Sgt. Johnson provided a shining example of the highest traditions of the U.S. Army.

JOHNSON, OSCAR G.

Rank and organization: Sergeant, U.S. Army, Company B, 363d Infantry, 91st Infantry Division. Place and date: Near Scarperia, Italy, 16 18 September 1944. Entered service at: Foster City, Mich. Birth: Foster City, Mich. G.O. No.: 58, 19 July 1945. Citation: (then Pfc.) He practically single-handed protected the left flank of his company's position in the offensive to break the German's gothic line. Company B was the extreme left assault unit of the corps. The advance was stopped by heavy fire from Monticelli Ridge, and the company took cover behind an embankment. Sgt. Johnson, a mortar gunner, having expended his ammunition, assumed the duties of a rifleman. As leader of a squad of 7 men he was ordered to establish a combat post 50 yards to the left of the company to cover its exposed flank. Repeated enemy counterattacks, supported by artillery, mortar, and machinegun fire from the high ground to his front, had by the afternoon of 16 September killed or wounded all his men. Collecting weapons and ammunition from his fallen comrades, in the face of hostile fire, he held his exposed position and inflicted heavy casualties upon the enemy, who several times came close enough to throw hand grenades. On the night of 16 17 September, the enemy launched his heaviest attack on Company B, putting his greatest pressure against the lone defender of the left flank. In spite of mortar fire which crashed about him and machinegun bullets which whipped the crest of his shallow trench, Sgt. Johnson stood erect and repulsed the attack with grenades and small arms fire. He remained awake and on the alert throughout the night, frustrating all attempts at infiltration. On 17 September, 25 German soldiers surrendered to him. Two men, sent to reinforce him that afternoon, were caught in a devastating mortar and artillery barrage. With no thought of his own safety, Sgt. Johnson rushed to the shell hole where they lay half buried and seriously wounded, covered their position by his fire, and assisted a Medical Corpsman in rendering aid. That night he secured their removal to the rear and remained on watch until his company was relieved. Five companies of a German paratroop regiment had been repeatedly committed to the attack on Company B without success. Twenty dead Germans were found in front of his position. By his heroic stand and utter disregard for personal safety, Sgt. Johnson was in a large measure responsible for defeating the enemy's attempts to turn the exposed left flank.

JOHNSTON, WILLIAM J.

Rank and organization: Private First Class, U.S. Army, Company G, 180th Infantry, 45th Infantry Division. Place and date: Near Padiglione, Italy, 17 19 February 1944. Entered service at: Colchester, Conn. Birth: Trenton, N.J. G.O. No.: 73, 6 September 1944. Citation: For conspicuous gallantry and intrepidity at risk of life above and beyond the call of duty in action against the enemy. On 17 February 1944, near Padiglione, Italy, he observed and fired upon an attacking force of approximately 80 Germans, causing at least 25 casualties and forcing withdrawal of the remainder. All that day he manned his gun without relief, subject to mortar, artillery, and sniper fire. Two Germans individually worked so close to his position that his machinegun was ineffective, whereupon he killed 1 with his pistol, the second with a rifle taken from another soldier. When a rifleman protecting his gun position was killed by a sniper, he immediately moved the body and relocated the machinegun in that spot in order to obtain a better field of fire. He volunteered to cover the platoon's withdrawal and was the last man to leave that night. In his new position he maintained an all-night vigil, the next day causing 7 German casualties. On the afternoon of the 18th, the organization on the left flank having been forced to withdraw, he again covered the withdrawal of his own organization. Shortly thereafter, he was seriously wounded over the heart, and a passing soldier saw him trying to crawl up the embankment. The soldier aided him to resume his position behind the machinegun which was soon heard in action for about 10 minutes. Though reported killed, Pfc. Johnston was seen returning to the American lines on the morning of 19 February slowly and painfully working his way back from his overrun position through enemy lines. He gave valuable information of new enemy dispositions. His heroic determination to destroy the enemy and his disregard of his own safety aided immeasurably in halting a strong enemy attack, caused an enormous amount of enemy casualties, and so inspired his fellow soldiers that they fought for and held a vitally important position against greatly superior forces.

*JONES, HERBERT CHARPOIT

Rank and organization: Ensign, U.S. Naval Reserve. Born: 1 December 1918, Los Angeles, Calif. Accredited to: California. Citation: For conspicuous devotion to duty, extraordinary courage, and complete disregard of his own life, above and beyond the call of duty, during the attack on the Fleet in Pearl Harbor, by Japanese forces on 7 December 1941. Ens. Jones organized and led a party, which was supplying ammunition to the antiaircraft battery of the U.S.S. California after the mechanical hoists were put out of action when he was fatally wounded by a bomb explosion. When 2 men attempted to take him from the area which was on fire, he refused to let them do so, saying in words to the effect, "Leave me alone! I am done for. Get out of here before the magazines go off."

*JULIAN, JOSEPH RODOLPH

Rank and organization: Platoon Sergeant, U.S. Marine Corps Reserve. Born: 3 April 1918, Sturbridge, Mass. Accredited to: Massachusetts. Citation: For conspicuous gallantry and intrepidity at the risk of his life above and beyond the call of duty as a P/Sgt. serving with the 1st Battalion, 27th Marines, 5th Marine Division, in action against enemy Japanese forces during the seizure of Iwo Jima in the Volcano Islands, 9 March 1945. Determined to force a breakthrough when Japanese troops occupying trenches and fortified positions on the left front laid down a terrific machinegun and mortar barrage in a desperate effort to halt his company's advance, P/Sgt. Julian quickly established his platoon's guns in strategic supporting positions, and then, acting on his own initiative, fearlessly moved forward to execute a 1-man assault on the nearest pillbox. Advancing alone, he hurled deadly demolition and white phosphorus grenades into the emplacement, killing 2 of the enemy and driving the remaining 5 out into the adjoining trench system. Seizing a discarded rifle, he jumped into the trench and dispatched the 5 before they could make an escape. Intent on wiping out all resistance, he obtained more explosives and, accompanied by another marine, again charged the hostile fortifications and knocked out 2 more cave positions. Immediately thereafter, he launched a bazooka attack unassisted, firing 4 rounds into the 1 remaining pillbox and completely destroying it before he fell, mortally wounded by a vicious burst of enemy fire. Stouthearted and indomitable, P/Sgt. Julian consistently disregarded all personal danger and, by his bold decision, daring tactics, and relentless fighting spirit during a critical phase of the battle, contributed materially to the continued advance of his company and to the success of his division's operations in the sustained drive toward the conquest of this fiercely defended outpost of the Japanese Empire. His outstanding valor and unfaltering spirit of self-sacrifice throughout the bitter conflict sustained and enhanced the highest traditions of the U.S. Naval Service. He gallantly gave his life for his country.

*KANDLE, VICTOR L.

Rank and organization: First Lieutenant, U.S. Army, 15th Infantry, 3d Infantry Division. Place and date: Near La Forge, France, 9 October 1944. Entered service at: Redwood City, Calif. Birth: Roy, Wash. G.O. No.: 37, 11 May 1945. Citation: For conspicuous gallantry and intrepidity at risk of his life above and beyond the call of duty. On 9 October 1944, at about noon, near La Forge, France, 1st Lt. Kandle, while leading a reconnaissance patrol into enemy territory, engaged in a duel at pointblank range with a German field officer and killed him. Having already taken 5 enemy prisoners that morning, he led a skeleton platoon of 16 men, reinforced with a light machinegun squad, through fog and over precipitous mountain terrain to fall on the rear of a German quarry stronghold which had checked the advance of an infantry battalion for 2 days. Rushing forward, several yards ahead of his assault elements, 1st Lt. Kandle fought his way into the heart of the enemy strongpoint, and, by his boldness and audacity, forced the Germans to surrender. Harassed by machinegun fire from a position which he had bypassed in the dense fog, he moved to within 15 yards of the enemy, killed a German machinegunner with accurate rifle fire and led his men in the destruction of another machinegun crew and its rifle security elements. Finally, he led his small force against a fortified house held by 2 German officers and 30 enlisted men. After establishing a base of fire, he rushed forward alone through an open clearing in full view of the enemy, smashed through a barricaded door, and forced all 32 Germans to surrender. His intrepidity and bold leadership resulted in the capture or killing of 3 enemy officers and 54 enlisted men, the destruction of 3 enemy strongpoints, and the seizure of enemy positions which had halted a battalion attack.

KANE, JOHN R. (Air Mission)

Rank and organization: Colonel, U.S. Army Air Corps, 9th Air Force. Place and date: Ploetsi Raid, Rumania, 1 August 1943. Entered service at: Shreveport, La. Birth: McGregor, Tex. G.O. No.: 54, 9 August 1943. Citation: For conspicuous gallantry in action and intrepidity at the risk of his life above and beyond the call of duty on 1 August 1943. On this date he led the third element of heavy bombardment aircraft in a mass low-level bombing attack against the vitally important enemy target of the Ploesti oil refineries. En route to the target, which necessitated a round-trip flight of over 2,400 miles, Col. Kane's element became separated from the leading portion of the massed formation in avoiding dense and dangerous cumulous cloud conditions over mountainous terrain. Rather than turn back from such a vital mission he elected to proceed to his target. Upon arrival at the target area it was discovered that another group had apparently missed its target and had previously attacked ??and damaged the target assigned to Col. Kane's element. Despite the thoroughly warned defenses, the intensive antiaircraft fire, enemy fighter airplanes, extreme hazards on a low-level attack of exploding delayed action bombs from the previous element, of oil fires and explosions and dense smoke over the target area, Col. Kane elected to lead his formation into the attack. By his gallant courage, brilliant leadership, and superior flying skill, he and the formation under his command successfully attacked this vast refinery so essential to our enemies' war effort. Through his conspicuous gallantry in this most hazardous action against the enemy, and by his intrepidity at the risk of his life above and beyond the call of duty, Col. Kane personally contributed vitally to the success of this daring mission and thereby rendered most distinguished service in the furtherance of the defeat of our enemies.

KEARBY, NEEL E. (Air Mission)

Rank and organization: Colonel, U.S. Army Air Corps. Place and date: Near Wewak, New Guinea, 11 October 1943. Entered service at: Dallas, Tex. Birth: Wichita Falls, Tex. G.O. No.: 3, 6 January 1944. Citation: For conspicuous gallantry and intrepidity above and beyond the call of duty in action with the enemy, Col. Kearby volunteered to lead a flight of 4 fighters to reconnoiter the strongly defended enemy base at Wewak. Having observed enemy installations and reinforcements at 4 airfields, and secured important tactical information, he saw an enemy fighter below him, made a diving attack and shot it down in flames. The small formation then sighted approximately 12 enemy bombers accompanied by 36 fighters. Although his mission had been completed, his fuel was running low, and the numerical odds were 12 to 1, he gave the signal to attack. Diving into the midst of the enemy airplanes he shot down 3 in quick succession. Observing 1 of his comrades with 2 enemy fighters in pursuit, he destroyed both enemy aircraft. The enemy broke off in large numbers to make a multiple attack on his airplane but despite his peril he made one more pass before seeking cloud protection. Coming into the clear, he called his flight together and led them to a friendly base. Col. Kearby brought down 6 enemy aircraft in this action, undertaken with superb daring after his mission was completed.

*KEATHLEY, GEORGE D.

Rank and organization: Staff Sergeant, U.S. Army, 85th Infantry Division. Place and date: Mt. Altuzzo, Italy, 14 September 1944. Entered service at: Lamesa, Tex. Birth: Olney, Tex. G.O. No.: 20, 29 March 1945. Citation: For conspicuous gallantry and intrepidity at risk of life above and beyond the call of duty, in action on the western ridge of Mount Altuzzo, Italy. After bitter fighting his company had advanced to within 50 yards of the objective, where it was held up due to intense enemy sniper, automatic, small arms, and mortar fire. The enemy launched 3 desperate counterattacks in an effort to regain their former positions, but all 3 were repulsed with heavy casualties on both sides. All officers and noncommissioned officers of the 2d and 3d platoons of Company B had become casualties, and S/Sgt. Keathley, guide of the 1st platoon, moved up and assumed command of both the 2d and 3d platoons, reduced to 20 men. The remnants of the 2 platoons were dangerously low on ammunition, so S/Sgt. Keathley, under deadly small arms and mortar fire, crawled from 1 casualty to another, collecting their ammunition and administering first aid. He then visited each man of his 2 platoons, issuing the precious ammunition he had collected from the dead and wounded, and giving them words of encouragement. The enemy now delivered their fourth counterattack, which was approximately 2 companies in strength. In a furious charge they attacked from the front and both flanks, throwing hand grenades, firing automatic weapons, and assisted by a terrific mortar barrage. So strong was the enemy counterattack that the company was given up for lost. The remnants of the 2d and 3d platoons of Company B were now looking to S/Sgt. Keathley for leadership. He shouted his orders precisely and with determination and the men responded with all that was in them. Time after time the enemy tried to drive a wedge into S/Sgt. Keathley's position and each time they were driven back, suffering huge casualties. Suddenly an enemy hand grenade hit and exploded near S/Sgt. Keathley, inflicting a mortal wound in his left side. However, hurling defiance at the enemy, he rose to his feet. Taking his left hand away from his wound and using it to steady his rifle, he fired and killed an attacking enemy soldier, and continued shouting orders to his men. His heroic and intrepid action so inspired his men that they fought with incomparable determination and viciousness. For 15 minutes S/Sgt. Keathley continued leading his men and effectively firing his rifle. He could have sought a sheltered spot and perhaps saved his life, but instead he elected to set an example for his men and make every possible effort to hold his position. Finally, friendly artillery fire helped to force the enemy to withdraw, leaving behind many of their number either dead or seriously wounded. S/Sgt. Keathley died a few moments later. Had it not been for his indomitable courage and incomparable heroism, the remnants of 3 rifle platoons of Company B might well have been annihilated by the overwhelming enemy attacking force. His actions were in keeping with the highest traditions of the military service.

*KEFURT, GUS

Rank and organization: Staff Sergeant, U.S. Army, Company K, 15th Infantry, 3d Infantry Division. Place and date: Near Bennwihr, France, 2324 December 1944. Entered service at: Youngstown, Ohio. Birth: Greenville, Pa. Citation: He distinguished himself by conspicuous gallantry and intrepidity above and beyond the call of duty on 23 and 24 December 1944, near Bennwihr, France. Early in the attack S/Sgt. Kefurt jumped through an opening in a wall to be confronted by about 15 Germans. Although outnumbered he opened fire, killing 10 and capturing the others. During a seesaw battle which developed he effectively adjusted artillery fire on an enemy tank close to his position although exposed to small arms fire. When night fell he maintained a 3-man outpost in the center of the town in the middle of the German positions and successfully fought off several hostile patrols attempting to penetrate our lines. Assuming command of his platoon the following morning he led it in hand-to-hand fighting through the town until blocked by a tank. Using rifle grenades he forced surrender of its crew and some supporting infantry. He then continued his attack from house to house against heavy machinegun and rifle fire. Advancing against a strongpoint that was holding up the company, his platoon was subjected to a strong counterattack and infiltration to its rear. Suffering heavy casualties in their exposed position the men remained there due to S/Sgt. Kefurt's personal example of bravery, determination and leadership. He constantly exposed himself to fire by going from man to man to direct fire. During this time he killed approximately 15 of the enemy at close range. Although severely wounded in the leg he refused first aid and immediately resumed fighting. When the forces to his rear were pushed back 3 hours later, he refused to be evacuated, but, during several more counterattacks moved painfully about under intense small arms and mortar fire, stiffening the resistance of his platoon by encouraging individual men and by his own fire until he was killed. As a result of S/Sgt. Kefurt's gallantry the position was maintained.

*KELLEY, JONAH E.

Rank and organization: Staff Sergeant, U.S. Army, 311th Infantry, 78th Infantry Division. Place and date: Kesternich, Germany, 3031 January 1945. Entered service at: Keyser, W. Va. Birth: Roda, W. Va. G.O. No.: 77, 10 September 1945. Citation: In charge of the leading squad of Company E, he heroically spearheaded the attack in furious house-to-house fighting. Early on 30 January, he led his men through intense mortar and small arms fire in repeated assaults on barricaded houses. Although twice wounded, once when struck in the back, the second time when a mortar shell fragment passed through his left hand and rendered it practically useless, he refused to withdraw and continued to lead his squad after hasty dressings had been applied. His serious wounds forced him to fire his rifle with 1 hand, resting it on rubble or over his left forearm. To blast his way forward with hand grenades, he set aside his rifle to pull the pins with his teeth while grasping the missiles with his good hand. Despite these handicaps, he created tremendous havoc in the enemy ranks. He rushed 1 house, killing 3 of the enemy and clearing the way for his squad to advance. On approaching the next house, he was fired upon from an upstairs window. He killed the sniper with a single shot and similarly accounted for another enemy soldier who ran from the cellar of the house. As darkness came, he assigned his men to defensive positions, never leaving them to seek medical attention. At dawn the next day, the squad resumed the attack, advancing to a point where heavy automatic and small arms fire stalled them. Despite his wounds, S/Sgt. Kelley moved out alone, located an enemy gunner dug in under a haystack and killed him with rifle fire. He returned to his men and found that a German machinegun, from a well-protected position in a neighboring house, still held up the advance. Ordering the squad to remain in comparatively safe positions, he valiantly dashed into the open and attacked the position single-handedly through a hail of bullets. He was hit several times and fell to his knees when within 25 yards of his objective; but he summoned his waning strength and emptied his rifle into the machinegun nest, silencing the weapon before he died. The superb courage, aggressiveness, and utter disregard for his own safety displayed by S/Sgt. Kelley inspired the men he led and enabled them to penetrate the last line of defense held by the enemy in the village of Kesternich .

*KELLEY, OVA A.

Rank and organization: Private, U.S. Army, Company A, 382d Infantry, 96th Infantry Division. Place and date: Leyte, Philippine Islands, 8 December 1944. Entered service at: Norwood, Mo. Birth: Norwood, Mo. G.O. No.: 89 19 October 1945. Citation: For conspicuous gallantry and intrepidity at the risk of his life above and beyond the call of duty. Before dawn, near the edge of the enemy-held Buri airstrip, the company was immobilized by heavy, accurate rifle and machinegun fire from hostile troops entrenched in bomb craters and a ditch less than 100 yards distant. The company commander ordered a mortar concentration which destroyed 1 machinegun but failed to dislodge the main body of the enemy. At this critical moment Pvt. Kelley, on his own initiative, left his shallow foxhole with an armload of hand grenades and began a 1-man assault on the foe. Throwing his missiles with great accuracy, he moved forward, killed or wounded 5 men, and forced the remainder to flee in a disorganized route. He picked up a M-1 rifle and emptied its clip at the running Japanese, killing 3. Discarding this weapon, he took a carbine and killed 3 more of the enemy. Inspired by his example, his comrades followed him in a charge which destroyed the entire enemy force of 34 enlisted men and 2 officers and captured 2 heavy and 1 light machineguns. Pvt. Kelley continued to press the attack on to an airstrip, where sniper fire wounded him so grievously that he died 2 days later. His outstanding courage, aggressiveness, and initiative in the face of grave danger was an inspiration to his entire company and led to the success of the attack.

KELLY, CHARLES E.

Rank and organization: Corporal, U.S. Army, Company L, 143d Infantry, 36th Infantry Division. Place and date: Near Altavilla, Italy, 13 September 1943. Entered service at: Pittsburgh, Pa. Birth: Pittsburgh, Pa. G.O. No.: 13, 18 February 1944. Citation: For conspicuous gallantry and intrepidity at risk of life above and beyond the call of duty. On 13 September 1943, near Altavilla, Italy, Cpl. Kelly voluntarily joined a patrol which located and neutralized enemy machinegun positions. After this hazardous duty he volunteered to establish contact with a battalion of U.S. infantry which was believed to be located on Hill 315, a mile distant. He traveled over a route commanded by enemy observation and under sniper, mortar, and artillery fire; and later he returned with the correct information that the enemy occupied Hill 315 in organized positions. Immediately thereafter Cpl. Kelly, again a volunteer patrol member, assisted materially in the destruction of 2 enemy machinegun nests under conditions requiring great skill and courage. Having effectively fired his weapon until all the ammunition was exhausted, he secured permission to obtain more at an ammunition dump. Arriving at the dump, which was located near a storehouse on the extreme flank of his regiment's position, Cpl. Kelly found that the Germans were attacking ferociously at this point. He obtained his ammunition and was given the mission of protecting the rear of the storehouse. He held his position throughout the night. The following morning the enemy attack was resumed. Cpl. Kelly took a position at an open window of the storehouse. One machine gunner had been killed at this position and several other soldiers wounded. Cpl. Kelly delivered continuous aimed and effective fire upon the enemy with his automatic rifle until the weapon locked from overheating. Finding another automatic rifle, he again directed effective fire upon the enemy until this weapon also locked. At this critical point, with the enemy threatening to overrun the position, Cpl. Kelly picked up 60mm. mortar shells, pulled the safety pins, and used the shells as grenades, killing at least 5 of the enemy. When it became imperative that the house be evacuated, Cpl. Kelly, despite his sergeant's injunctions, volunteered to hold the position until the remainder of the detachment could withdraw. As the detachment moved out, Cpl. Kelly was observed deliberately loading and firing a rocket launcher from the window. He was successful in covering the withdrawal of the unit, and later in joining his own organization. Cpl. Kelly's fighting determination and intrepidity in battle exemplify the highest traditions of the U.S. Armed Forces.

*KELLY, JOHN D.

Rank and organization: Technical Sergeant (then Corporal), U.S. Army, Company E, 314th Infantry, 79th Infantry Division. Place and date: Fort du Roule, Cherbourg, France, 25 June 1944. Entered service at: Cambridge Springs, Pa. Birth: Venango Township, Pa. G.O. No.: 6, 24 January 1945. Citation: For conspicuous gallantry and intrepidity at the risk of his life above and beyond the call of duty. On 25 June 1944, in the vicinity of Fort du Roule, Cherbourg, France, when Cpl. Kelly's unit was pinned down by heavy enemy machinegun fire emanating from a deeply entrenched strongpoint on the slope leading up to the fort, Cpl. Kelly volunteered to attempt to neutralize the strongpoint. Arming himself with a pole charge about 10 feet long and with 15 pounds of explosive affixed, he climbed the slope under a withering blast of machinegun fire and placed the charge at the strongpoint's base. The subsequent blast was ineffective, and again, alone and unhesitatingly, he braved the slope to repeat the operation. This second blast blew off the ends of the enemy guns. Cpl. Kelly then climbed the slope a third time to place a pole charge at the strongpoint's rear entrance. When this had been blown open he hurled hand grenades inside the position, forcing survivors of the enemy guncrews to come out and surrender The gallantry, tenacity of purpose, and utter disregard for personal safety displayed by Cpl. Kelly were an incentive to his comrades and worthy of emulation by all.

KELLY, THOMAS J.

Rank and organization: Corporal, U.S. Army, Medical Detachment, 48th Armored Infantry Battalion, 7th Armored Division. Place and date: Alemert, Germany, 5 April 1945. Entered service at: Brooklyn, N.Y.

Birth: Brooklyn, N.Y. G.O. No.: 97, 1 November 1945. Citation: He was an aid man with the 1st Platoon of Company C during an attack on the town of Alemert, Germany. The platoon, committed in a flanking maneuver, had advanced down a small, open valley overlooked by wooded slopes hiding enemy machineguns and tanks, when the attack was stopped by murderous fire that inflicted heavy casualties in the American ranks. Ordered to withdraw, Cpl. Kelly reached safety with uninjured remnants of the unit, but, on realizing the extent of casualties suffered by the platoon, voluntarily retraced his steps and began evacuating his comrades under direct machinegun fire. He was forced to crawl, dragging the injured behind him for most of the 300 yards separating the exposed area from a place of comparative safety. Two other volunteers who attempted to negotiate the hazardous route with him were mortally wounded, but he kept on with his herculean task after dressing their wounds and carrying them to friendly hands. In all, he made 10 separate trips through the brutal fire, each time bringing out a man from the death trap. Seven more casualties who were able to crawl by themselves he guided and encouraged in escaping from the hail of fire. After he had completed his heroic, self-imposed task and was near collapse from fatigue, he refused to leave his platoon until the attack had been resumed and the objective taken. Cpl. Kelly's gallantry and intrepidity in the face of seemingly certain death saved the lives of many of his fellow soldiers and was an example of bravery under fire.

*KEPPLER, REINHARDT JOHN

Rank and organization: Boatswain's Mate First Class, U.S. Navy. Born: 22 January 1918, Ralston, Wash. Accredited to: Washington. Other Navy award: Navy Cross. Citation: For extraordinary heroism and distinguished courage above and beyond the call of duty while serving aboard the U.S.S. San Francisco during action against enemy Japanese forces in the Solomon Islands, 1213 November 1942. When a hostile torpedo plane, during a daylight air raid, crashed on the after machine-gun platform,

Keppler promptly assisted in removal of the dead and, by his capable supervision of the wounded, undoubtedly helped save the lives of several shipmates who otherwise might have perished. That night, when the ship's hangar was set afire during the great battle off Savo Island, he bravely led a hose into the starboard side of the stricken area and there, without assistance and despite frequent hits from terrific enemy bombardment, eventually brought the fire under control. Later, although mortally wounded, he labored valiantly in the midst of bursting shells, persistently directing fire-fighting operations and administering to wounded personnel until he finally collapsed from loss of blood. His great personal valor, maintained with utter disregard of personal safety, was in keeping with the highest traditions of the U.S. Naval Service. He gallantly gave his life for his country.

KERSTETTER, DEXTER J.

Rank and organization: Private First Class, U.S. Army, Company C, 130th Infantry, 33d Infantry Division. Place and date: Near Galiano, Luzon, Philippine Islands, 13 April 1945. Entered service at: Centralia, Wash. Birth: Centralia, Wash. G.O. No.: 97, 1 November 1945. Citation: He was with his unit in a dawn attack against hill positions approachable only along a narrow ridge paralleled on each side by steep cliffs which were heavily defended by enemy mortars, machineguns, and rifles in well-camouflaged spider holes and tunnels leading to caves. When the leading element was halted by intense fire that inflicted 5 casualties, Pfc. Kerstetter passed through the American line with his squad. Placing himself well in advance of his men, he grimly worked his way up the narrow steep hogback, meeting the brunt of enemy action. With well-aimed shots and rifle-grenade fire, he forced the Japs to take cover. He left the trail and moving down a cliff that offered only precarious footholds, dropped among 4 Japs at the entrance to a cave, fired his rifle from his hip and killed them all. Climbing back to the trail, he advanced against heavy enemy machinegun, rifle, and mortar fire to silence a heavy machinegun by killing its crew of 4 with rifle fire and grenades. He expended his remaining ammunition and grenades on a group of approximately 20 Japs, scattering them, and returned to his squad for more ammunition and first aid for his left hand, which had been blistered by the heat from his rifle. Resupplied, he guided a fresh platoon into a position from which a concerted attack could be launched, killing 3 hostile soldiers on the way. In all, he dispatched 16 Japs that day. The hill was taken and held against the enemy's counterattacks, which continued for 3 days. Pfc. Kerstetter's dauntless and gallant heroism was largely responsible for the capture of this key enemy position, and his fearless attack in the face of great odds was an inspiration to his comrades in their dangerous task.

*KESSLER, PATRICK L.

Rank and organization: Private First Class, U.S. Army, Company K, 30th Infantry, 3d Infantry Division. Place and date: Near Ponte Rotto, Italy, 23 May 1944. Entered service at: Middletown, Ohio. Birth: Middletown, Ohio. G.O. No.: 1, 4 January 1945. Citation: For conspicuous gallantry and intrepidity at risk of life above and beyond the call of duty. Pfc. Kessler, acting without orders, raced 50 yards through a hail of machinegun fire, which had killed 5 of his comrades and halted the advance of his company, in order to form an assault group to destroy the machinegun. Ordering 3 men to act as a base of fire, he left the cover of a ditch and snaked his way to a point within 50 yards of the enemy machinegun before he was discovered, whereupon he plunged headlong into the furious chain of automatic fire. Reaching a spot within 6 feet of the emplacement he stood over it and killed both the gunner and his assistant, jumped into the gun position, overpowered and captured a third German after a short struggle. The remaining member of the crew escaped, but Pfc. Kessler wounded him as he ran. While taking his prisoner to the rear, this soldier saw 2 of his comrades killed as they assaulted an enemy strongpoint, fire from which had already killed 10 men in the company. Turning his prisoner over to another man, Pfc.

Kessler crawled 35 yards to the side of 1 of the casualties, relieved him of his BAR and ammunition and continued on toward the strongpoint, 125 yards distant. Although 2 machineguns concentrated their fire directly on him and shells exploded within 10 yards, bowling him over, Pfc. Kessler crawled 75 yards, passing through an antipersonnel minefield to a point within 50 yards of the enemy and engaged the machineguns in a duel. When an artillery shell burst within a few feet of him, he left the cover of a ditch and advanced upon the position in a slow walk, firing his BAR from the hip. Although the enemy poured heavy machinegun and small arms fire at him, Pfc. Kessler succeeded in reaching the edge of their position, killed the gunners, and captured 13 Germans. Then, despite continuous shelling, he started to the rear. After going 25 yards, Pfc. Kessler was fired upon by 2 snipers only 100 yards away. Several of his prisoners took advantage of this opportunity and attempted to escape; however, Pfc. Kessler hit the ground, fired on either flank of his prisoners, forcing them to cover, and then engaged the 2 snipers in a fire fight, and captured them. With this last threat removed, Company K continued its advance, capturing its objective without further opposition. Pfc. Kessler was killed in a subsequent action.

*KIDD, ISAAC CAMPBELL

Rank and organization: Rear Admiral, U.S. Navy. Born: 26 March 1884, Cleveland, Ohio. Appointed from: Ohio. Citation: For conspicuous devotion to duty, extraordinary courage and complete disregard of his own life, during the attack on the Fleet in Pearl Harbor, by Japanese forces on 7 December 1941. Rear Adm. Kidd immediately went to the bridge and, as Commander Battleship Division One, courageously discharged his duties as Senior Officer Present Afloat until the U.S.S. Arizona, his Flagship, blew up from magazine explosions and a direct bomb hit on the bridge which resulted in the loss of his life.

*KIMBRO, TRUMAN

Rank and organization: Technician Fourth Grade, U.S. Army, Company C, 2d Engineer Combat Battalion, 2d Infantry Division. Place and date: Near Rocherath, Belgium, 19 December 1944. Entered service at: Houston, Tex. Birth: Madisonville, Tex. G.O. No.: 42, 24 May 1945. Citation: On 19 December 1944, as scout, he led a squad assigned to the mission of mining a vital crossroads near Rocherath, Belgium. At the first attempt to reach the objective, he discovered it was occupied by an enemy tank and at least 20 infantrymen. Driven back by withering fire, Technician 4th Grade Kimbro made 2 more attempts to lead his squad to the crossroads but all approaches were covered by intense enemy fire. Although warned by our own infantrymen of the great danger involved, he left his squad in a protected place and, laden with mines, crawled alone toward the crossroads. When nearing his objective he was severely wounded, but he continued to drag himself forward and laid his mines across the road. As he tried to crawl from the objective his body was riddled with rifle and machinegun fire. The mines laid by his act of indomitable courage delayed the advance of enemy armor and prevented the rear of our withdrawing columns from being attacked by the enemy.

*KINER, HAROLD G.

Rank and organization: Private, U.S. Army, Company F, 117th Infantry, 30th Infantry Division. Place and date: Near Palenberg, Germany, 2 October 1944. Entered service at: Enid, Okla. Birth: Aline, Okla. G.O. No.: 48, 23 June 1945. With 4 other men, he was leading in a frontal assault 2 October 1944, on a Siegfried Line pillbox near Palenberg, Germany. Machinegun fire from the strongly defended enemy position 25 yards away pinned down the attackers. The Germans threw hand grenades, 1 of which dropped between Pvt. Kiner and 2 other men. With no hesitation, Private Kiner hurled himself upon the grenade, smothering the explosion. By his gallant action and voluntary sacrifice of his own life, he saved his 2 comrades from serious injury or death.

*KINGSLEY, DAVID R. (Air Mission)

Rank and organization: Second Lieutenant, U.S. Army Air Corps, 97th Bombardment Group, 15th Air Force. Place and date: Ploesti Raid, Rumania, 23 June 1944. Entered service at. Portland, Oreg. Birth: Oregon. G.O. No.: 26, 9 April 1945. Citation: For conspicuous gallantry and intrepidity in action at the risk of life above and beyond the call of duty, 23 June 1944 near Ploesti, Rumania, while flying as bombardier of a B17 type aircraft. On the bomb run 2d Lt. Kingsley's aircraft was severely damaged by intense flak and forced to drop out of formation but the pilot proceeded over the target and 2d Lt. Kingsley successfully dropped his bombs, causing severe damage to vital installations. The damaged aircraft, forced to lose altitude and to lag behind the formation, was aggressively attacked by 3 ME-109 aircraft, causing more damage to the aircraft and severely wounding the tail gunner in the upper arm. The radio operator and engineer notified 2d Lt. Kingsley that the tail gunner had been wounded and that assistance was needed to check the bleeding. 2d Lt. Kingsley made his way back to the radio room, skillfully applied first aid to the wound, and succeeded in checking the bleeding. The tail gunner's parachute harness and heavy clothes were removed and he was covered with blankets, making him as comfortable as possible. Eight ME-109 aircraft again aggressively attacked 2d Lt. Kingsley's aircraft and the ball turret gunner was wounded by 20mm. shell fragments. He went forward to the radio room to have 2d Lt. Kingsley administer first aid. A few minutes later when the pilot gave the order to prepare to bail out, 2d Lt. Kingsley immediately began to assist the wounded gunners in putting on their parachute harness. In the confusion the tail gunner's harness, believed to have been damaged, could not be located in the bundle of blankets and flying clothes which had been removed from the wounded men. With utter disregard for his own means of escape, 2d Lt. Kingsley unhesitatingly removed his parachute harness and adjusted it to the wounded tail gunner. Due to the extensive damage caused by the accurate and concentrated 20mm. fire by the enemy aircraft the pilot gave the order to bail out, as it appeared that the aircraft would disintegrate at any moment. 2d Lt. Kingsley aided the wounded men in bailing out and when last seen by the crewmembers he was standing on the bomb bay catwalk. The aircraft continued to fly on automatic pilot for a short distance, then crashed and burned. His body was later found in the wreckage. 2d Lt. Kingsley by his gallant heroic action was directly responsible for saving the life of the wounded gunner.

*KINSER, ELBERT LUTHER

Rank and organization: Sergeant, U.S. Marine Corps Reserve. Born: 21 October 1922, Greeneville, Tenn. Accredited to: Tennessee. Citation: For conspicuous gallantry and intrepidity at the risk of his life above and beyond the call of duty while acting as leader of a Rifle Platoon, serving with Company I, 3d Battalion, 1st Marines, 1st Marine Division, in action against Japanese forces on Okinawa Shima in the Ryukyu Chain, 4 May 1945. Taken under sudden, close attack by hostile troops entrenched on the reverse slope while moving up a strategic ridge along which his platoon was holding newly won positions, Sgt. Kinser engaged the enemy in a fierce hand grenade battle. Quick to act when a Japanese grenade landed in the immediate vicinity, Sgt. Kinser unhesitatingly threw himself on the deadly missile, absorbing the full charge of the shattering explosion in his own body and thereby protecting his men from serious injury and possible death. Stouthearted and indomitable, he had yielded his own chance of survival that his comrades might live to carry on the relentless battle against a fanatic enemy. His courage, cool decision and valiant spirit of self-sacrifice in the face of certain death sustained and enhanced the highest traditions of the U.S. Naval Service. He gallantly gave his life for his country.

KISTERS, GERRY H.

Rank and organization: Second Lieutenant (then Sergeant), U.S. Army, 2d Armored Division. Place and date: Near Gagliano, Sicily, 31 July 1943. Entered service at: Bloomington, Ind. Birth: Salt Lake City, Utah. G.O. No.: 13, 18 February 1944. Citation: On 31 July 1943, near Gagliano, Sicily, a detachment of 1 officer and 9 enlisted men, including Sgt. Kisters, advancing ahead of the leading elements of U.S. troops to fill a large crater in the only available vehicle route through Gagliano, was taken under fire by 2 enemy machineguns. Sgt. Kisters and the officer, unaided and in the face of intense small arms fire, advanced on the nearest machinegun emplacement and succeeded in capturing the gun and its crew of 4. Although the greater part of the remaining small arms fire was now directed on the captured machinegun position, Sgt. Kisters voluntarily advanced alone toward the second gun emplacement. While creeping forward, he was struck 5 times by enemy bullets, receiving wounds in both legs and his right arm. Despite the wounds, he continued to advance on the enemy, and captured the second machinegun after killing 3 of its crew and forcing the fourth member to flee. The courage of this soldier and his unhesitating willingness to sacrifice his life, if necessary, served as an inspiration to the command.

KNAPPENBERGER, ALTON W.

Rank and organization: Private First Class, U.S. Army, 3d Infantry Division. Place and date: Near Cisterna di Littoria, Italy, 1 February 1944. Entered service at: Spring Mount, Pa. Birth: Cooperstown, Pa. G.O. No.: 41, 26 May 1944. Citation: For conspicuous gallantry and intrepidity at the risk of his life above and beyond the call of duty in action involving actual conflict with the enemy, on 1 February 1944 near Cisterna di Littoria, Italy. When a heavy German counterattack was launched against his battalion, Pfc. Knappenberger crawled to an exposed knoll and went into position with his automatic rifle. An enemy machinegun 85 yards away opened fire, and bullets struck within 6 inches of him. Rising to a kneeling position, Pfc. Knappenberger opened fire on the hostile crew, knocked out the gun, killed 2 members of the crew, and wounded the third. While he fired at this hostile position, 2 Germans crawled to a point within 20 yards of the knoll and threw potato-masher grenades at him, but Pfc. Knappenberger killed them both with 1 burst from his automatic rifle. Later, a second machinegun opened fire upon his exposed position from a distance of 100 yards, and this weapon also was silenced by his well-aimed shots. Shortly thereafter, an enemy 20mm. antiaircraft gun directed fire at him, and again Pfc. Knappenberger returned fire to wound 1 member of the hostile crew. Under tank and artillery shellfire, with shells bursting within 15 yards of him, he held his precarious position and fired at all enemy infantrymen armed with machine pistols and machineguns which he could locate. When his ammunition supply became exhausted, he crawled 15 yards forward through steady machinegun fire, removed rifle clips from the belt of a casualty, returned to his position and resumed firing to repel an assaulting German platoon armed with automatic weapons. Finally, his ammunition supply being completely exhausted, he rejoined his company. Pfc. Knappenberger's intrepid action disrupted the enemy attack for over 2 hours.

*KNIGHT, JACK L.

Rank and organization: First Lieutenant, U.S. Army, 124th Cavalry Regiment, Mars Task Force. Place and date: Near LoiKang, Burma, 2 February 1945. Entered service at: Weatherford, Tex. Birth: Garner, Tex. G.O. No.: 44, 6 June 1945. Citation: He led his cavalry troop against heavy concentrations of enemy mortar, artillery, and small arms fire. After taking the troop's objective and while making preparations for a defense, he discovered a nest of Japanese pillboxes and foxholes to the right front. Preceding his men by at least 10 feet, he immediately led an attack Single-handedly he knocked out 2 enemy pillboxes and killed the occupants of several foxholes. While attempting to knock out a third pillbox, he was struck and blinded by an enemy grenade. Although unable to see, he rallied his platoon and continued forward in the assault on the remaining pillboxes. Before the task was completed he fell mortally wounded. 1st Lt. Knight's gallantry and intrepidity were responsible for the successful elimination of most of the Jap positions and served as an inspiration to officers and men of his troop.

*KNIGHT, RAYMOND L. (Air Mission)

Rank and organization: First Lieutenant, U.S. Army Air Corps. Place and date: In Northern Po Valley, Italy, 2425 April 1945. Entered service at: Houston, Tex. Birth: Texas. G.O. No.: 81, 24 September 1945. Citation: He piloted a fighter-bomber aircraft in a series of low-level strafing missions, destroying 14 grounded enemy aircraft and leading attacks which wrecked 10 others during a critical period of the Allied drive in northern Italy. On the morning of 24 April, he volunteered to lead 2 other aircraft against the strongly defended enemy airdrome at Ghedi. Ordering his fellow pilots to remain aloft, he skimmed the ground through a deadly curtain of antiaircraft fire to reconnoiter the field, locating 8 German aircraft hidden beneath heavy camouflage. He rejoined his flight, briefed them by radio, and then led them with consummate skill through the hail of enemy fire in a low-level attack, destroying 5 aircraft, while his flight accounted for 2 others. Returning to his base, he volunteered to lead 3 other aircraft in reconnaissance of Bergamo airfield, an enemy base near Ghedi and 1 known to be equally well defended. Again ordering his flight to remain out of range of antiaircraft fire, 1st Lt. Knight flew through an exceptionally intense barrage, which heavily damaged his Thunderbolt, to observe the field at minimum altitude. He discovered a squadron of enemy aircraft under heavy camouflage and led his flight to the assault. Returning alone after this strafing, he made 10 deliberate passes against the field despite being hit by antiaircraft fire twice more, destroying 6 fully loaded enemy twin-engine aircraft and 2 fighters. His skillfully led attack enabled his flight to destroy 4 other twin-engine aircraft and a fighter plane. He then returned to his base in his seriously damaged plane. Early the next morning, when he again attacked Bergamo, he sighted an enemy plane on the runway. Again he led 3 other American pilots in a blistering low-level sweep through vicious antiaircraft fire that damaged his plane so severely that it was virtually nonflyable. Three of the few remaining enemy twin-engine aircraft at that base were destroyed. Realizing the critical need for aircraft in his unit, he declined to parachute to safety over friendly territory and unhesitatingly attempted to return his shattered plane to his home field. With great skill and strength, he flew homeward until caught by treacherous air conditions in the Appennines Mountains, where he crashed and was killed. The gallant action of 1st Lt. Knight eliminated the German aircraft which were poised to wreak havoc on Allied forces pressing to establish the first firm bridgehead across the Po River; his fearless daring and voluntary self-sacrifice averted possible heavy casualties among ground forces and the resultant slowing on the German drive culminated in the collapse of enemy resistance in Italy.

*KRAUS, RICHARD EDWARD

Rank and organization: Private First Class, U.S. Marine Corps Reserve. Born: 24 November 1925, Chicago, Ill. Accredited to: Minnesota. Citation: For conspicuous gallantry and intrepidity at the risk of his life above and beyond the call of duty while serving with the 8th Amphibious Tractor Battalion, Fleet Marine Force, in action against enemy Japanese forces on Peleliu, Palau Islands, on 5 October 1944. Unhesitatingly volunteering for the extremely hazardous mission of evacuating a wounded comrade from the front lines, Pfc. Kraus and 3 companions courageously made their way forward and successfully penetrated the lines for some distance before the enemy opened with an intense, devastating barrage of hand grenades which forced the stretcher party to take cover and subsequently abandon the mission. While returning to the rear, they observed 2 men approaching who appeared to be marines and immediately demanded the password. When, instead of answering, 1 of the 2 Japanese threw a hand grenade into the midst of the group, Pfc. Kraus heroically flung himself upon the grenade and, covering it with his body, absorbed the full impact of the explosion and was instantly killed. By his prompt action and great personal valor in the face of almost certain death, he saved the lives of his 3 companions, and his loyal spirit of self-sacrifice reflects the highest credit upon himself and the U.S. Naval Service. He gallantly gave his life for his comrades.

*KROTIAK, ANTHONY L.

Rank and organization: Private First Class, U.S. Army, Company I, 148th Infantry, 37th Infantry Division. Place and date: Balete Pass, Luzon, Philippine Islands, 8 May 1945. Entered service at: Chicago, Ill. Born: 15 August 1915, Chicago, Ill. G.O. No.: 18, 13 February 1946. Citation: He was an acting squad leader, directing his men in consolidating a newly won position on Hill B when the enemy concentrated small arms fire and grenades upon him and 4 others, driving them to cover in an abandoned Japanese trench. A grenade thrown from above landed in the center of the group. Instantly pushing his comrades aside and jamming the grenade into the earth with his rifle butt, he threw himself over it, making a shield of his body to protect the other men. The grenade exploded under him, and he died a few minutes later. By his extraordinary heroism in deliberately giving his life to save those of his comrades, Pfc. Krotiak set an inspiring example of utter devotion and self-sacrifice which reflects the highest traditions of the military service.

*LA BELLE, JAMES DENNIS

Rank and organization: Private First Class, U.S. Marine Corps Reserve. Born: 22 November 1925, Columbia Heights, Minn. Accredited to:

Minnesota. Citation: For conspicuous gallantry and intrepidity at the risk of his life above and beyond the call of duty while attached to the 27th Marines, 5th Marine Division, in action against enemy Japanese forces during the seizure of Iwo Jima in the Volcano Islands, 8 March 1945. Filling a gap in the front lines during a critical phase of the battle, Pfc. LaBelle had dug into a foxhole with 2 other marines and, grimly aware of the enemy's persistent attempts to blast a way through our lines with hand grenades, applied himself with steady concentration to maintaining a sharply vigilant watch during the hazardous night hours. Suddenly a hostile grenade landed beyond reach in his foxhole. Quickly estimating the situation, he determined to save the others if possible, shouted a warning, and instantly dived on the deadly missile, absorbing the exploding charge in his own body and thereby protecting his comrades from serious injury. Stouthearted and indomitable, he had unhesitatingly relinquished his own chance of survival that his fellow marines might carry on the relentless fight against a fanatic enemy His dauntless courage, cool decision and valiant spirit of self-sacrifice in the face of certain death reflect the highest credit upon Pfc. LaBelle and upon the U.S. Naval Service. He gallantly gave his life in the service of his country.

LAWLEY, WILLIAM R., JR. (Air Mission)

Rank and organization: First Lieutenant, U.S. Army Air Corps, 364th Bomber Squadron, 305th Bomber Group. Place and date: Over Europe, 20 February 1944. Entered service at: Birmingham, Ala. Born: 23 August 1920, Leeds, Ala. G.O. No.: 64, 8 August 1944. Citation: For conspicuous gallantry and intrepidity in action above and beyond the call of duty, 20 February 1944, while serving as pilot of a B-17 aircraft on a heavy bombardment mission over enemy-occupied continental Europe. Coming off the target he was attacked by approximately 20 enemy fighters, shot out of formation, and his plane severely crippled. Eight crewmembers were wounded, the copilot was killed by a 20-mm. shell. One engine was on fire, the controls shot away, and 1st Lt. Lawley seriously and painfully wounded about the face. Forcing the copilot's body off the controls, he brought the plane out of a steep dive, flying with his left hand only. Blood covered the instruments and windshield and visibility was impossible. With a full bomb load the plane was difficult to maneuver and bombs could not be released because the racks were frozen. After the order to bail out had been given, 1 of the waist gunners informed the pilot that 2 crewmembers were so severely wounded that it would be impossible for them to bail out. With the fire in the engine spreading, the danger of an explosion was imminent. Because of the helpless condition of his wounded crewmembers 1st Lt. Lawley elected to remain with the ship and bring them to safety if it was humanly possible, giving the other crewmembers the option of bailing out. Enemy fighters again attacked but by using masterful evasive action he managed to lose them. One engine again caught on fire and was extinguished by skillful flying. 1st Lt. Lawley remained at his post, refusing first aid until he collapsed from sheer exhaustion caused by loss of blood, shock, and the energy he had expended in keeping control of his plane. He was revived by the bombardier and again took over the controls. Coming over the English coast 1 engine ran out of gasoline and had to be feathered. Another engine started to burn and continued to do so until a successful crash landing was made on a small fighter base. Through his heroism and exceptional flying skill, 1st Lt. Lawley rendered outstanding distinguished and valorous service to our Nation.

LAWS, ROBERT E.

Rank and organization: Staff Sergeant, U.S. Army, Company G, 169th Infantry, 43d Infantry Division. Place and date: Pangasinan Province, Luzon, Philippine Islands, 12 January 1945. Entered service at: Altoona, Pa. Birth: Altoona, Pa. G.O. No.: 77, 10 September 1945. Citation: He led the assault squad when Company G attacked enemy hill positions. The enemy force, estimated to be a reinforced infantry company, was well supplied with machineguns, ammunition, grenades, and blocks of TNT and could be attacked only across a narrow ridge 70 yards long. At the end of this ridge an enemy pillbox and rifle positions were set in rising ground. Covered by his squad, S/Sgt Laws traversed the hogback through vicious enemy fire until close to the pillbox, where he hurled grenades at the fortification. Enemy grenades wounded him, but he persisted in his assault until 1 of his missiles found its mark and knocked out the pillbox. With more grenades, passed to him by members of his squad who had joined him, he led the attack on the entrenched riflemen. In the advance up the hill, he suffered additional wounds in both arms and legs, about the body and in the head, as grenades and TNT charges exploded near him. Three Japs rushed him with fixed bayonets, and he emptied the magazine of his machine pistol at them, killing 2. He closed in hand-to-hand combat with the third, seizing the Jap's rifle as he met the onslaught. The 2 fell to the ground and rolled some 50 or 60 feet down a bank. When the dust cleared the Jap lay dead and the valiant American was climbing up the hill with a large gash across the head. He was given first aid and evacuated from the area while his squad completed the destruction of the enemy position. S/Sgt. Laws' heroic actions provided great inspiration to his comrades, and his courageous determination, in the face of formidable odds and while suffering from multiple wounds, enabled them to secure an important objective with minimum casualties.

LEE, DANIEL W.

Rank and organization: First Lieutenant, U.S. Army, Troop A, 117th Cavalry Reconnaissance Squadron. Place and date: Montreval, France, 2 September 1944. Entered service at: Alma, Ga. Born: 23 June 1919, Alma, Ga. G.O. No.: 14, 4 February 1946. Citation: 1st Lt. (then 2d Lt.) Daniel W. Lee was leader of Headquarters Platoon, Troop A, 117th Cavalry Reconnaissance Squadron, Mechanized, at Montreval, France, on 2 September 1944, when the Germans mounted a strong counterattack, isolating the town and engaging its outnumbered defenders in a pitched battle. After the fight had raged for hours and our forces had withstood heavy shelling and armor-supported infantry attacks, 2d Lt. Lee organized a patrol to knock out mortars which were inflicting heavy casualties on the beleaguered reconnaissance troops. He led the small group to the edge of the town, sweeping enemy riflemen out of position on a ridge from which he observed 7 Germans manning 2 large mortars near an armored half-track about 100 yards down the reverse slope. Armed with a rifle and grenades, he left his men on the high ground and crawled to within 30 yards of the mortars, where the enemy discovered him and unleashed machine-pistol fire which shattered his right thigh. Scorning retreat, bleeding and suffering intense pain, he dragged himself relentlessly forward He killed 5 of the enemy with rifle fire and the others fled before he reached their position. Fired on by an armored car, he took cover behind the German half-track and there found a panzerfaust with which to neutralize this threat. Despite his wounds, he inched his way toward the car through withering machinegun fire, maneuvering into range, and blasted the vehicle with a round from the rocket launcher, forcing it to withdraw. Having cleared the slope of hostile troops, he struggle back to his men, where he collapsed from pain and loss of blood. 2d Lt. Lee's outstanding gallantry, willing risk of life, and extreme tenacity of purpose in coming to grips with the enemy, although suffering from grievous wounds, set an example of bravery and devotion to duty in keeping with the highest traditions of the military service.

LEIMS, JOHN HAROLD

Rank and organization: Second Lieutenant, U.S. marine Corps Reserve, Company B, 1st Battalion, 9th Marines, 3d Marine Division. Place and date: Iwo Jima, Volcano Islands, 7 march 1945. Entered service at: Chicago, Ill. Born: 8 June 1921, Chicago, Ill. Citation: For conspicuous gallantry and intrepidity at the risk of his life above and beyond the call of duty as commanding officer of Company B, 1st Battalion, 9th

Marines, 3d Marine Division, in action against enemy Japanese forces on Iwo Jima in the Volcano Islands, 7 march 1945. Launching a surprise attack against the rock-imbedded fortification of a dominating Japanese hill position, 2d Lt. Leims spurred his company forward with indomitable determination and, skillfully directing his assault platoons against the cave-emplaced enemy troops and heavily fortified pillboxes, succeeded in capturing the objective in later afternoon. When it became apparent that his assault platoons were cut off in this newly won position, approximately 400 yards forward of adjacent units and lacked all communication with the command post, he personally advanced and laid telephone lines across the isolating expanse of open fire-swept terrain. Ordered to withdraw his command after he had joined his forward platoons, he immediately complied, adroitly effecting the withdrawal of his troops without incident. Upon arriving at the rear, he was informed that several casualties had been left at the abandoned ridge position beyond the frontlines. Although suffering acutely from the strain and exhausting of battle, he instantly went forward despite darkness and the slashing fury of hostile machinegun fire, located and carried to safety 1 seriously wounded marine and then, running the gauntlet of enemy fire for the third time that night, again made his tortuous way into the bullet-riddled deathtrap and rescued another of his wounded men. A dauntless leader, concerned at all time for the welfare of his men, 2d Lt. Leims soundly maintained the coordinated strength of his battle-wearied company under extremely difficult conditions and, by his bold tactics, sustained aggressiveness, and heroic disregard for all personal danger, contributed essentially to the success of his division's operations against this vital Japanese base. His valiant conduct in the face of fanatic opposition sustains and enhances the highest traditions of the U.S. Naval Service.

*LEONARD, TURNEY W.

Rank and organization: First Lieutenant, U.S. Army, Company C, 893d Tank Destroyer Battalion. Place and date: Kommerscheidt, Germany, 46 November 1944. Entered service at: Dallas, Tex. Birth: Dallas, Tex. G.O. No.: 74, 1 September 1945. Citation: He displayed extraordinary heroism while commanding a platoon of mobile weapons at Kommerscheidt, Germany, on 4, 5, and 6 November 1944. During the fierce 3-day engagement, he repeatedly braved overwhelming enemy fire in advance of his platoon to direct the fire of his tank destroyer from exposed, dismounted positions. He went on lone reconnaissance missions to discover what opposition his men faced, and on 1 occasion, when fired upon by a hostile machinegun, advanced alone and eliminated the enemy emplacement with a hand grenade. When a strong German attack threatened to overrun friendly positions, he moved through withering artillery, mortar, and small arms fire, reorganized confused infantry units whose leaders had become casualties, and exhorted them to hold firm. Although wounded early in battle, he continued to direct fire from his advanced position until he was disabled by a high-explosive shell which shattered his arm, forcing him to withdraw. He was last seen at a medical aid station which was subsequently captured by the enemy. By his superb courage, inspiring leadership, and indomitable fighting spirit, 1st Lt. Leonard enabled our forces to hold off the enemy attack and was personally responsible for the direction of fire which destroyed 6 German tanks.

*LESTER, FRED FAULKNER

Rank and organization: Hospital Apprentice First Class, U.S. Navy. Born: 29 April 1926, Downers Grove, Ill. Accredited to: Illinois. Citation: For conspicuous gallantry and intrepidity at the risk of his life above and beyond the call of duty while serving as a Medical Corpsman with an Assault Rifle Platoon, attached to the 1st Battalion, 22d Marines,

6th Marine Division, during action against enemy Japanese forces on Okinawa Shima in the Ryukyu Chain, 8 June 1945. Quick to spot a wounded marine lying in an open field beyond the front lines following the relentless assault against a strategic Japanese hill position, Lester unhesitatingly crawled toward the casualty under a concentrated barrage from hostile machineguns, rifles, and grenades. Torn by enemy rifle bullets as he inched forward, he stoically disregarded the mounting fury of Japanese fire and his own pain to pull the wounded man toward a covered position. Struck by enemy fire a second time before he reached cover, he exerted tremendous effort and succeeded in pulling his comrade to safety where, too seriously wounded himself to administer aid, he instructed 2 of his squad in proper medical treatment of the rescued marine. Realizing that his own wounds were fatal, he staunchly refused medical attention for himself and, gathering his fast-waning strength with calm determination, coolly and expertly directed his men in the treatment of 2 other wounded marines, succumbing shortly thereafter. Completely selfless in his concern for the welfare of his fighting comrades, Lester, by his indomitable spirit, outstanding valor, and competent direction of others, had saved the life of 1 who otherwise must have perished and had contributed to the safety of countless others. Lester's fortitude in the face of certain death sustains and enhances the highest traditions of the U.S. Naval Service. He gallantly gave his life for his country.

*LINDSEY, DARRELL R. (Air Mission)

Rank and organization: Captain, U.S. Army Air Corps. Place and date: L'Isle Adam railroad bridge over the Seine in occupied France, 9 August 1944. Entered service at: Storm Lake, Iowa. Birth: Jefferson, Iowa. G.O. No.: 43, 30 May 1945. Citation: On 9 August 1944, Capt. Lindsey led a formation of 30 B-26 medium bombers in a hazardous mission to destroy the strategic enemy held L'Isle Adam railroad bridge over the Seine in occupied France. With most of the bridges over the Seine destroyed, the heavily fortified L'Isle Adam bridge was of inestimable value to the enemy in moving troops, supplies, and equipment to Paris. Capt. Lindsey was fully aware of the fierce resistance that would be encountered. Shortly after reaching enemy territory the formation was buffeted with heavy and accurate antiaircraft fire. By skillful evasive action, Capt. Lindsey was able to elude much of the enemy flak, but just before entering the bombing run his B-26 was peppered with holes. During the bombing run the enemy fire was even more intense, and Capt. Lindsey's right engine received a direct hit and burst into flames. Despite the fact that his ship was hurled out of formation by the violence of the concussion, Capt. Lindsey brilliantly maneuvered back into the lead position without disrupting the flight. Fully aware that the gasoline tanks might explode at any moment, Capt. Lindsey gallantly elected to continue the perilous bombing run. With fire streaming from his right engine and his right wing half enveloped in flames, he led his formation over the target upon which the bombs were dropped with telling effect. Immediately after the objective was attacked, Capt. Lindsey gave the order for the crew to parachute from the doomed aircraft. With magnificent coolness and superb pilotage, and without regard for his own life, he held the swiftly descending airplane in a steady glide until the members of the crew could jump to safety. With the right wing completely enveloped in flames and an explosion of the gasoline tank imminent, Capt. Lindsey still remained unperturbed. The last man to leave the stricken plane was the bombardier, who offered to lower the wheels so that Capt. Lindsey might escape from the nose. Realizing that this might throw the aircraft into an uncontrollable spin and jeopardize the bombardier's chances to escape, Capt. Lindsey refused the offer. Immediately after the bombardier had bailed out, and before Capt. Lindsey was able to follow, the right gasoline tank exploded. The aircraft sheathed in fire, went into a steep dive and was seen to explode as it crashed. All who are living today from this plane owe their lives to the fact that Capt. Lindsey remained cool and showed supreme courage in this emergency.

LINDSEY, JAKE W.

Rank and organization: Technical Sergeant, U.S. Army, 16th Infantry, 1st Infantry Division. Place and date: Near Hamich, Germany, 16 November 1944. Entered service at: Lucedale, Miss. Birth: Isney, Ala. G.O. No.: 43, 30 May 1945. Citation: For gallantry and intrepidity at the risk of his life above and beyond the call of duty on 16 November 1944, in Germany. T/Sgt. Lindsey assumed a position about 10 yards to the front of his platoon during an intense enemy infantry-tank counterattack, and by his unerringly accurate fire destroyed 2 enemy machinegun nests, forced the withdrawal of 2 tanks, and effectively halted enemy flanking patrols. Later, although painfully wounded, he engaged 8 Germans, who were reestablishing machinegun positions, in hand-to-hand combat, killing 3, capturing 3, and causing the other 2 to flee. By his gallantry, T/Sgt. Lindsey secured his unit's position, and reflected great credit upon himself and the U.S. Army.

*LINDSTROM, FLOYD K.

Rank and organization: Private First Class, U.S. Army, 3d Infantry Division. Place and date: Near Mignano, Italy, 11 November 1943. Entered service at: Colorado Springs, Colo. Birth: Holdredge, Nebr. G.O. No.: 32, 20 April 1944. Citation: For conspicuous gallantry and intrepidity at risk of life above and beyond the call of duty. On 11 November 1943, this soldier's platoon was furnishing machinegun support for a rifle company attacking a hill near Mignano, Italy, when the enemy counterattacked, forcing the riflemen and half the machinegun platoon to retire to a defensive position. Pfc. Lindstrom saw that his small section was alone and outnumbered 5 to 1, yet he immediately deployed the few remaining men into position and opened fire with his single gun. The enemy centered fire on him with machinegun, machine pistols, and grenades. Unable to knock out the enemy nest from his original position, Pfc. Lindstrom picked up his own heavy machinegun and staggered 15 yards up the barren, rocky hillside to a new position, completely ignoring enemy small arms fire which was striking all around him. From this new site, only 10 yards from the enemy machinegun, he engaged it in an intense duel. Realizing that he could not hit the hostile gunners because they were behind a large rock, he charged uphill under a steady stream of fire, killed both gunners with his pistol and dragged their gun down to his own men, directing them to employ it against the enemy. Disregarding heavy rifle fire, he returned to the enemy machinegun nest for 2 boxes of ammunition, came back and resumed withering fire from his own gun. His spectacular performance completely broke up the German counterattack. Pfc. Lindstrom demonstrated aggressive spirit and complete fearlessness in the face of almost certain death.

*LLOYD, EDGAR H.

Rank and organization: First Lieutenant, U.S. Army, Company E, 319th Infantry, 80th Infantry Division. Place and date: Near Pompey, France, 14 September 1944. Entered service at: Blytheville, Ark. Birth: Blytheville, Ark. G.O. No.: 25, 7 April 1945. Citation: For conspicuous gallantry and intrepidity at the risk of his life above and beyond the call of duty. On 14 September 1944, Company E, 319th Infantry, with which 1st Lt. Lloyd was serving as a rifle platoon leader, was assigned the mission of expelling an estimated enemy force of 200 men from a heavily fortified position near Pompey, France. As the attack progressed, 1st Lt. Lloyd's platoon advanced to within 50 yards of the enemy position where they were caught in a withering machinegun and rifle crossfire which inflicted heavy casualties and momentarily disorganized the platoon. With complete disregard for his own safety, 1st Lt. Lloyd leaped to his feet and led his men on a run into the raking fire, shouting encouragement to them. He jumped into the first enemy machinegun position, knocked out the gunner with his fist, dropped a grenade, and jumped out before it exploded. Still shouting encouragement he went from 1 machinegun nest to another, pinning the enemy down with submachine gun fire until he was within throwing distance, and then destroyed them with hand grenades. He personally destroyed 5 machineguns and many of the enemy, and by his daring leadership and conspicuous bravery inspired his men to overrun the enemy positions and accomplish the objective in the face of seemingly insurmountable odds. His audacious determination and courageous devotion to duty exemplify the highest traditions of the military forces of the United States.

*LOBAUGH, DONALD R.

Rank and organization: Private, U.S. Army, 127th Infantry, 32d Infantry Division. Place and date: Near Afua, New Guinea, 22 July 1944. Entered service at: Freeport, Pa. Birth: Freeport, Pa. G.O. No.: 31, 17 April 1945. Citation: For conspicuous gallantry and intrepidity at the risk of his life above and beyond the call of duty near Afua, New Guinea, on 22 July 1944. While Pvt. Lobaugh's company was withdrawing from its position on 21 July, the enemy attacked and cut off approximately 1 platoon of our troops. The platoon immediately occupied, organized, and defended a position, which it held throughout the night. Early on 22 July, an attempt was made to effect its withdrawal, but during the preparation therefor, the enemy emplaced a machinegun, protected by the fire of rifles and automatic weapons, which blocked the only route over which the platoon could move. Knowing that it was the key to the enemy position, Pfc. Lobaugh volunteered to attempt to destroy this weapon, even though in order to reach it he would be forced to work his way about 30 yards over ground devoid of cover. When part way across this open space he threw a hand grenade, but exposed himself in the act and was wounded. Heedless of his wound, he boldly rushed the emplacement, firing as he advanced. The enemy concentrated their fire on him, and he was struck repeatedly, but he continued his attack and killed 2 more before he was himself slain. Pfc. Lobaugh's heroic actions inspired his comrades to press the attack, and to drive the enemy from the position with heavy losses. His fighting determination and intrepidity in battle exemplify the highest traditions of the U.S. Armed Forces.

LOGAN, JAMES M.

Rank and organization: Sergeant, U.S. Army, 36th Infantry Division. Place and date: Near Salerno, Italy, 9 September 1943. Entered service at: Luling, Tex. Birth: McNeil, Tex. G.O. No.: 54, 5 July 1944. Citation: For conspicuous gallantry and intrepidity at risk of life above and beyond the call of duty in action involving actual conflict on 9 September 1943 in the vicinity of Salerno, Italy. As a rifleman of an infantry company, Sgt. Logan landed with the first wave of the assault echelon on the beaches of the Gulf of Salerno, and after his company had advanced 800 yards inland and taken positions along the forward bank of an irrigation canal, the enemy began a serious counterattack from positions along a rock wall which ran parallel with the canal about 200 yards further inland. Voluntarily exposing himself to the fire of a machinegun located along the rock wall, which sprayed the ground so close to him that he was splattered with dirt and rock splinters from the impact of the bullets, Sgt. Logan killed the first 3 Germans as they came through a gap in the wall. He then attacked the machinegun. As he dashed across the 200 yards of exposed terrain a withering stream of fire followed his advance. Reaching the wall, he crawled along the base, within easy reach of the enemy crouched along the opposite side, until he reached the gun. Jumping up, he shot the 2 gunners down, hurdled the wall, and seized the gun. Swinging it around, he immediately opened fire on the enemy with the remaining ammunition, raking their flight and inflicting further casualties on them as they fled. After smashing the machinegun over the rocks, Sgt. Logan captured an enemy officer and private who were attempting to sneak away. Later in the morning, Sgt. Loan went after a sniper hidden in a house about 150 yards from the company. Again the intrepid Sgt. ran a gauntlet of fire to reach his objective. Shooting the lock off the door, Sgt. Loan kicked it in and shot the sniper who had just reached the bottom of the stairs. The conspicuous gallantry and intrepidity which characterized Sgt. Logan's exploits proved a constant inspiration to all the men of his company, and aided materially in insuring the success of the beachhead at Salerno.

LOPEZ, JOSE M.

Rank and organization: Sergeant, U.S. Army, 23d Infantry, 2d Infantry Division. Place and date: Near Krinkelt, Belgium, 17 December 1944. Entered service at: Brownsville, Tex. Birth: Mission, Tex. G.O. No.: 47, 18 June 1945. Citation: On his own initiative, he carried his heavy machinegun from Company K's right flank to its left, in order to protect that flank which was in danger of being overrun by advancing enemy infantry supported by tanks. Occupying a shallow hole offering no protection above his waist, he cut down a group of 10 Germans. Ignoring enemy fire from an advancing tank, he held his position and cut down 25 more enemy infantry attempting to turn his flank. Glancing to his right, he saw a large number of infantry swarming in from the front. Although dazed and shaken from enemy artillery fire which had crashed into the ground only a few yards away, he realized that his position soon would be outflanked. Again, alone, he carried his machinegun to a position to the right rear of the sector; enemy tanks and infantry were forcing a withdrawal. Blown over backward by the concussion of enemy fire, he immediately reset his gun and continued his fire. Single-handed he held off the German horde until he was satisfied his company had effected its retirement. Again he loaded his gun on his back and in a hail of small arms fire he ran to a point where a few of his comrades were attempting to set up another defense against the onrushing enemy. He fired from this position until his ammunition was exhausted. Still carrying his gun, he fell back with his small group to

Krinkelt. Sgt. Lopez's gallantry and intrepidity, on seemingly suicidal missions in which he killed at least 100 of the enemy, were almost solely responsible for allowing Company K to avoid being enveloped, to withdraw successfully and to give other forces coming up in support time to build a line which repelled the enemy drive.

LUCAS, JACKLYN HAROLD

Rank and organization: Private First Class, U.S. Marine Corps Reserve, 1st Battalion, 26th Marines, 5th Marine Division. Place and date: Iwo Jima, Volcano Islands, 20 February 1945. Entered service at: Norfolk, Va. Born: 14 February 1928, Plymouth, N.C. Citation: For conspicuous gallantry and intrepidity at the risk of his life above and beyond the call of duty while serving with the 1st Battalion, 26th Marines, 5th Marine Division, during action against enemy Japanese forces on Iwo Jima, Volcano Islands, 20 February 1945. While creeping through a treacherous, twisting ravine which ran in close proximity to a fluid and uncertain frontline on D-plus-1 day, Pfc. Lucas and 3 other men were suddenly ambushed by a hostile patrol which savagely attacked with rifle fire and grenades. Quick to act when the lives of the small group were endangered by 2 grenades which landed directly in front of them, Pfc. Lucas unhesitatingly hurled himself over his comrades upon 1 grenade and pulled the other under him, absorbing the whole blasting forces of the explosions in his own body in order to shield his companions from the concussion and murderous flying fragments. By his inspiring action and valiant spirit of self-sacrifice, he not only protected his comrades from certain injury or possible death but also enabled them to rout the Japanese patrol and continue the advance. His exceptionally courageous initiative and loyalty reflect the highest credit upon Pfc. Lucas and the U.S. Naval Service.

*LUMMUS, JACK

Rank and organization: First Lieutenant, U.S. Marine Corps Reserve. Born: 22 October 1915, Ennie, Tex. Appointed from: Texas. Citation: For conspicuous gallantry and intrepidity at the risk of his life above and beyond the call of duty as leader of a Rifle Platoon attached to the 2d Battalion, 27th Marines, 5th Marine Division, in action against enemy Japanese forces on Iwo Jima in the Volcano Islands, 8 March 1945. Resuming his assault tactics with bold decision after fighting without respite for 2 days and nights, 1st Lt. Lummus slowly advanced his platoon against an enemy deeply entrenched in a network of mutually supporting positions. Suddenly halted by a terrific concentration of hostile fire, he unhesitatingly moved forward of his front lines in an effort to neutralize the Japanese position. Although knocked to the ground when an enemy grenade exploded close by, he immediately recovered himself and, again moving forward despite the intensified barrage, quickly located, attacked, and destroyed the occupied emplacement. Instantly taken under fire by the garrison of a supporting pillbox and further assailed by the slashing fury of hostile rifle fire, he fell under the impact of a second enemy grenade but, courageously disregarding painful shoulder wounds, staunchly continued his heroic 1-man assault and charged the second pillbox, annihilating all the occupants. Subsequently returning to his platoon position, he fearlessly traversed his lines under fire, encouraging his men to advance and directing the fire of supporting tanks against other stubbornly holding Japanese emplacements. Held up again by a devastating barrage, he again moved into the open, rushed a third heavily fortified installation and killed the defending troops. Determined to crush all resistance, he led his men indomitably, personally attacking foxholes and spider traps with his carbine and systematically reducing the fanatic opposition until, stepping on a land mine, he sustained fatal wounds. By his outstanding valor, skilled tactics, and tenacious perseverance in the face of overwhelming odds, 1st Lt.

Lummus had inspired his stouthearted marines to continue the relentless drive northward, thereby contributing materially to the success of his regimental mission. His dauntless leadership and unwavering devotion to duty throughout sustain and enhance the highest traditions of the U.S. Naval Service. He gallantly gave his life in the service of his country.

MABRY, GEORGE L., JR.

Rank and organization: Lieutenant Colonel, U.S. Army, 2d Battalion, 8th Infantry, 4th Infantry Division Place and date: Hurtgen Forest near Schevenhutte, Germany, 20 November 1944. Entered service at: Sumter, S.C. Birth: Sumter, SC G.O. No.: 77, September 1945. Citation: He was commanding the 2d Battalion, 8th Infantry, in an attack through the Hurtgen Forest near Schevenhutte, Germany, on 20 November 1944. During the early phases of the assault, the leading elements of his battalion were halted by a minefield and immobilized by heavy hostile fire. Advancing alone into the mined area, Col. Mabry established a safe route of passage. He then moved ahead of the foremost scouts, personally leading the attack, until confronted by a boobytrapped double concertina obstacle. With the assistance of the scouts, he disconnected the explosives and cut a path through the wire. Upon moving through the opening, he observed 3 enemy in foxholes whom he captured at bayonet point. Driving steadily forward he paced the assault against 3 log bunkers which housed mutually supported automatic weapons. Racing up a slope ahead of his men, he found the initial bunker deserted, then pushed on to the second where he was suddenly confronted by 9 onrushing enemy. Using the butt of his rifle, he felled 1 adversary and bayoneted a second, before his scouts came to his aid and assisted him in overcoming the others in hand-to-hand combat. Accompanied by the riflemen, he charged the third bunker under pointblank small arms fire and led the way into the fortification from which he prodded 6 enemy at bayonet point. Following the consolidation of this area, he led his battalion across 300 yards of fire-swept terrain to seize elevated ground upon which he established a defensive position which menaced the enemy on both flanks, and provided his regiment a firm foothold on the approach to the Cologne Plain. Col. Mabry's superlative courage, daring, and leadership in an operation of major importance exemplify the finest characteristics of the military service.

MacARTHUR, DOUGLAS

Rank and organization: General, U.S. Army, commanding U.S. Army Forces in the Far East. Place and date: Bataan Peninsula, Philippine Islands. Entered service at: Ashland, Wis. Birth: Little Rock, Ark. G.O. No.: 16, 1 April 1942. Citation: For conspicuous leadership in preparing the Philippine Islands to resist conquest, for gallantry and intrepidity above and beyond the call of duty in action against invading Japanese forces, and for the heroic conduct of defensive and offensive operations on the Bataan Peninsula. He mobilized, trained, and led an army which has received world acclaim for its gallant defense against a tremendous superiority of enemy forces in men and arms. His utter disregard of personal danger under heavy fire and aerial bombardment, his calm judgment in each crisis, inspired his troops, galvanized the spirit of resistance of the Filipino people, and confirmed the faith of the American people in their Armed Forces.

MacGILLIVARY, CHARLES A.

Rank and organization: Sergeant, U.S. Army, Company I, 71st Infantry, 44th Infantry Division. Place and date: Near Woelfling, France, 1 January 1945. Entered service at: Boston, Mass. Birth: Charlottetown, Prince Edward Island, Canada. G.O. No.: 77, 10 September 1945. Citation: He led a squad when his unit moved forward in darkness to meet the threat of a breakthrough by elements of the 17th German Panzer Grenadier Division. Assigned to protect the left flank, he discovered hostile troops digging in. As he reported this information, several

German machineguns opened fire, stopping the American advance. Knowing the position of the enemy, Sgt. MacGillivary volunteered to knock out 1 of the guns while another company closed in from the right to assault the remaining strong points. He circled from the left through woods and snow, carefully worked his way to the emplacement and shot the 2 camouflaged gunners at a range of 3 feet as other enemy forces withdrew. Early in the afternoon of the same day, Sgt. MacGillivary was dispatched on reconnaissance and found that Company I was being opposed by about 6 machineguns reinforcing a company of fanatically fighting Germans. His unit began an attack but was pinned down by furious automatic and small arms fire. With a clear idea of where the enemy guns were placed, he voluntarily embarked on a lone combat patrol. Skillfully taking advantage of all available cover, he stalked the enemy, reached a hostile machinegun and blasted its crew with a grenade. He picked up a submachine gun from the battlefield and pressed on to within 10 yards of another machinegun, where the enemy crew discovered him and feverishly tried to swing their weapon into line to cut him down. He charged ahead, jumped into the midst of the Germans and killed them with several bursts. Without hesitation, he moved on to still another machinegun, creeping, crawling, and rushing from tree to tree, until close enough to toss a grenade into the emplacement and close with its defenders. He dispatched this crew also, but was himself seriously wounded. Through his indomitable fighting spirit, great initiative, and utter disregard for personal safety in the face of powerful enemy resistance, Sgt. MacGillivary destroyed four hostile machineguns and immeasurably helped his company to continue on its mission with minimum casualties.

*MAGRATH, JOHN D.

Rank and organization: Private First Class, U.S. Army, Company G, 85th Infantry, 10th Mountain Division. Place and date: Near Castel d'Aiano, Italy, 14 April 1945. Entered service at: East Norwalk, Conn. Birth: East

Norwalk, Conn. G.O. No.: 71, 17 July 1946. Citation: He displayed conspicuous gallantry and intrepidity above and beyond the call of duty when his company was pinned down by heavy artillery, mortar, and small arms fire, near Castel d'Aiano, Italy. Volunteering to act as a scout, armed with only a rifle, he charged headlong into withering fire, killing 2 Germans and wounding 3 in order to capture a machinegun. Carrying this enemy weapon across an open field through heavy fire, he neutralized 2 more machinegun nests; he then circled behind 4 other Germans, killing them with a burst as they were firing on his company. Spotting another dangerous enemy position to this right, he knelt with the machinegun in his arms and exchanged fire with the Germans until he had killed 2 and wounded 3. The enemy now poured increased mortar and artillery fire on the company's newly won position. Pfc. Magrath fearlessly volunteered again to brave the shelling in order to collect a report of casualties. Heroically carrying out this task, he made the supreme sacrifice—a climax to the valor and courage that are in keeping with highest traditions of the military service.

*MANN, JOE E.

Rank and organization: Private First Class, U.S. Army, Company H, 502d Parachute Infantry, 101st Airborne Division. Place and date: Best, Holland, 18 September 1944. Entered service at: Seattle, Wash. Birth: Rearden, Wash. G.O. No.: 73, 30 August 1945. Citation: He distinguished himself by conspicuous gallantry above and beyond the call of duty. On 18 September 1944, in the vicinity of Best., Holland, his platoon, attempting to seize the bridge across the Wilhelmina Canal, was surrounded and isolated by an enemy force greatly superior in personnel and firepower. Acting as lead scout, Pfc. Mann boldly crept to within rocket-launcher range of an enemy artillery position and, in the face of heavy enemy fire, destroyed an 88mm. gun and an ammunition dump. Completely disregarding the great danger involved, he remained in his exposed position, and, with his M-1 rifle, killed the enemy one by one until he was wounded 4 times. Taken to a covered position, he insisted on returning to a forward position to stand guard during the night. On the following morning the enemy launched a concerted attack and advanced to within a few yards of the position, throwing hand grenades as they approached. One of these landed within a few feet of Pfc. Mann. Unable to raise his arms, which were bandaged to his body, he yelled "grenade" and threw his body over the grenade, and as it exploded, died. His outstanding gallantry above and beyond the call of duty and his magnificent conduct were an everlasting inspiration to his comrades for whom he gave his life.

*MARTIN, HARRY LINN

Rank and organization: First Lieutenant, U.S. Marine Corps Reserve. Born: 4 January 1911, Bucyrus, Ohio. Appointed from. Ohio. Citation: For conspicuous gallantry and intrepidity at the risk of his life above and beyond the call of duty as platoon leader attached to Company C, 5th Pioneer Battalion, 5th Marine Division, in action against enemy Japanese forces on Iwo Jima, Volcano Islands, 26 March 1945. With his sector of the 5th Pioneer Battalion bivouac area penetrated by a concentrated enemy attack launched a few minutes before dawn, 1st Lt. Martin instantly organized a firing line with the marines nearest his foxhole and succeeded in checking momentarily the headlong rush of the Japanese. Determined to rescue several of his men trapped in positions overrun by the enemy, he defied intense hostile fire to work his way through the Japanese to the surrounded marines. Although sustaining 2 severe wounds, he blasted the Japanese who attempted to intercept him, located his beleaguered men and directed them to their own lines. When 4 of the infiltrating enemy took possession of an abandoned machinegun pit and subjected his sector to a barrage of hand grenades, 1st Lt. Martin, alone and armed only with a pistol, boldly charged the hostile position and killed all of its occupants. Realizing that his few remaining comrades could not repulse another organized attack, he called to his men to follow and then charged into the midst of the strong enemy force, firing his weapon and scattering them until he fell, mortally wounded by a grenade. By his outstanding valor, indomitable fighting spirit and tenacious determination in the face of overwhelming odds, 1st Lt. Martin permanently disrupted a coordinated Japanese attack and prevented a greater loss of life in his own and adjacent platoons. His inspiring leadership and unswerving devotion to duty reflect the highest credit upon himself and the U.S. Naval Service. He gallantly gave his life in the service of his country.

*MARTINEZ, JOE P.

Rank and organization: Private, U.S. Army, Company K, 32d Infantry, 7th Infantry Division. Place and date: On Attu, Aleutians, 26 May 1943. Entered service at: Ault, Colo. Birth: Taos, N. Mex. G.O. No.: 71, 27 October 1943. Citation: For conspicuous gallantry and intrepidity above and beyond the call of duty in action with the enemy. Over a period of several days, repeated efforts to drive the enemy from a key defensive position high in the snow-covered precipitous mountains between East Arm Holtz Bay and Chichagof Harbor had failed. On 26 May 1943, troop dispositions were readjusted and a trial coordinated attack on this position by a reinforced battalion was launched. Initially successful, the attack hesitated. In the face of severe hostile machinegun, rifle, and mortar fire, Pvt. Martinez, an automatic rifleman, rose to his feet and resumed his advance. Occasionally he stopped to urge his comrades on. His example inspired others to follow. After a most difficult climb, Pvt. Martinez eliminated resistance from part of the enemy position by BAR fire and hand grenades, thus assisting the advance of other attacking elements. This success only partially completed the action. The main Holtz-Chichagof Pass rose about 150 feet higher, flanked by steep rocky ridges and reached by a snow-filled defile. Passage was barred by enemy fire from either flank and from tiers of snow trenches in front. Despite these obstacles, and knowing of their existence, Pvt. Martinez again led the troops on and up, personally silencing several trenches with BAR fire and ultimately reaching the pass itself. Here, just below the knifelike rim of the pass, Pvt. Martinez encountered a final enemy-occupied trench and as he was engaged in firing into it he was mortally wounded. The pass, however, was taken, and its capture was an important preliminary to the end of organized hostile resistance on the island.

*MASON, LEONARD FOSTER

Rank and organization: Private First Class, U.S. Marine Corps. Born: 2 February 1920, Middleborough, Ky. Accredited to: Ohio. Citation: For conspicuous gallantry and intrepidity at the risk of his life above and beyond the call of duty as an automatic rifleman serving with the 2d Battalion, 3d Marines, 3d Marine Division, in action against enemy Japanese forces on the Asan-Adelup Beachhead, Guam, Marianas Islands on 22 July 1944. Suddenly taken under fire by 2 enemy machineguns not more than 15 yards away while clearing out hostile positions holding up the advance of his platoon through a narrow gully, Pfc. Mason, alone and entirely on his own initiative, climbed out of the gully and moved parallel to it toward the rear of the enemy position. Although fired upon immediately by hostile riflemen from a higher position and wounded repeatedly in the arm and shoulder, Pfc. Mason grimly pressed forward and had just reached his objective when hit again by a burst of enemy machinegun fire, causing a critical wound to which he later succumbed. With valiant disregard for his own peril, he persevered, clearing out the hostile position, killing 5 Japanese, wounding another and then rejoining his platoon to report the results of his action before consenting to be evacuated. His exceptionally heroic act in the face of almost certain death enabled his platoon to accomplish its mission and reflects the highest credit upon Pfc. Mason and the U.S. Naval Service. He gallantly gave his life for his country.

*MATHIES, ARCHIBALD (Air Mission)

Rank and organization: Sergeant, U.S. Army Air Corps, 510th Bomber Squadron, 351st Bomber Group. Place and date: Over Europe, 20 February 1944. Entered service at: Pittsburgh, Pa. Born: 3 June 1918, Scotland. G.O. No.: 52, 22 June 1944. Citation: For conspicuous gallantry and intrepidity at risk of life above and beyond the call of duty in action against the enemy in connection with a bombing mission over enemy-occupied Europe on 20 February 1944. The aircraft on which Sgt. Mathies was serving as engineer and ball turret gunner was attacked by a squadron of enemy fighters with the result that the copilot was killed outright, the pilot wounded and rendered unconscious, the radio operator wounded and the plane severely damaged. Nevertheless, Sgt. Mathies and other members of the crew managed to right the plane and fly it back to their home station, where they contacted the control tower and reported the situation. Sgt. Mathies and the navigator volunteered to attempt to land the plane. Other members of the crew were ordered to jump, leaving Sgt. Mathies and the navigator aboard. After observing the distressed aircraft from another plane, Sgt. Mathies' commanding officer decided the damaged plane could not be landed by the inexperienced crew and ordered them to abandon it and parachute to safety. Demonstrating unsurpassed courage and heroism, Sgt. Mathies and the navigator replied that the pilot was still alive but could not be moved and they would not desert him. They were then told to attempt a landing. After two unsuccessful efforts, the plane crashed into an open field in a third attempt to land. Sgt. Mathies, the navigator, and the wounded pilot were killed.

*MATHIS, JACK W. (Air Mission)

Rank and organization: First Lieutenant, U.S. Army Air Corps, 359th Bomber Squadron, 303d Bomber Group. Place and date: Over Vegesack, Germany, 18 March 1943. Entered service at: San Angelo, Tex.

Born: 25 September 1921, San Angelo, Tex. G.O. No.: 38, 12 July 1943. Citation: For conspicuous gallantry and intrepidity above and beyond the call of duty in action with the enemy over Vegesack, Germany, on 18 March 1943. 1st Lt. Mathis, as leading bombardier of his squadron, flying through intense and accurate antiaircraft fire, was just starting his bomb run, upon which the entire squadron depended for accurate bombing, when he was hit by the enemy antiaircraft fire. His right arm was shattered above the elbow, a large wound was torn in his side and abdomen, and he was knocked from his bomb sight to the rear of the bombardier's compartment. Realizing that the success of the mission depended upon him, 1st Lt. Mathis, by sheer determination and willpower, though mortally wounded, dragged himself back to his sights, released his bombs, then died at his post of duty. As the result of this action the airplanes of his bombardment squadron placed their bombs directly upon the assigned target for a perfect attack against the enemy. 1st Lt. Mathis' undaunted bravery has been a great inspiration to the officers and men of his unit.

MAXWELL, ROBERT D.

Rank and organization: Technician Fifth Grade, U.S. Army, 7th Infantry, 3d Infantry Division. Place and date: Near Besancon, France, 7 September 1944. Entered service at: Larimer County, Colo. Birth: Boise, Idaho. G.O. No.: 24, 6 April 1945. Citation: For conspicuous gallantry and intrepidity at risk of life above and beyond the call of duty on 7 September 1944, near Besancon, France. Technician 5th Grade Maxwell and 3 other soldiers, armed only with .45 caliber automatic pistols, defended the battalion observation post against an overwhelming onslaught by enemy infantrymen in approximately platoon strength, supported by 20mm. flak and machinegun fire, who had infiltrated through the battalion's forward companies and were attacking the observation post with machinegun, machine pistol, and grenade fire at ranges as close as 10 yards. Despite a hail of fire from automatic weapons and grenade launchers, Technician 5th Grade Maxwell aggressively fought off advancing enemy elements and, by his calmness, tenacity, and fortitude, inspired his fellows to continue the unequal struggle. When an enemy hand grenade was thrown in the midst of his squad, Technician 5th Grade Maxwell unhesitatingly hurled himself squarely upon it, using his blanket and his unprotected body to absorb the full force of the explosion. This act of instantaneous heroism permanently maimed Technician 5th Grade Maxwell, but saved the lives of his comrades in arms and facilitated maintenance of vital military communications during the temporary withdrawal of the battalion's forward headquarters.

*MAY, MARTIN O.

Rank and organization: Private First Class, U.S. Army, 307th Infantry, 77th Infantry Division. Place and date: Iegusuku-Yama, Ie Shima, Ryukyu Islands, 1921 April 1945. Entered service at: Phillipsburg, N.J. Birth: Phillipsburg, N.J. G.O. No: 9, 25 January 1946. Citation: He gallantly maintained a 3-day stand in the face of terrible odds when American troops fought for possession of the rugged slopes of Iegusuku-Yama on Ie Shima, Ryukyu Islands. After placing his heavy machinegun in an advantageous yet vulnerable position on a ridge to support riflemen, he became the target of fierce mortar and small arms fire from counterattacking Japanese. He repulsed this assault by sweeping the enemy with accurate bursts while explosions and ricocheting bullets threw blinding dust and dirt about him. He broke up a second counterattack by hurling grenades into the midst of the enemy forces, and then refused to withdraw, volunteering to maintain his post and cover the movement of American riflemen as they reorganized to meet any further hostile action. The major effort of the enemy did not develop until the morning of 21 April. It found Pfc. May still supporting the rifle company in the face of devastating rifle, machinegun, and mortar fire. While many of the friendly troops about him became casualties, he continued to fire his machinegun until he was severely wounded and his gun rendered useless by the burst of a mortar shell. Refusing to withdraw from the violent action, he blasted fanatical Japanese troops with hand grenades until wounded again, this time mortally. By his intrepidity and the extreme tenacity with which he held firm until death against overwhelming forces, Pfc. May killed at least 16 Japanese, was largely responsible for maintaining the American lines, and inspired his comrades to efforts which later resulted in complete victory and seizure of the mountain stronghold.

MAYFIELD, MELVIN

Rank and organization: Corporal, U.S. Army, Company D, 20th Infantry, 6th Infantry Division. Place and date: Cordillera Mountains, Luzon, Philippine Islands, 29 July 1945. Entered service at: Nashport, Ohio. Birth: Salem, W. Va. G.O. No.: 49, 31 May 1946. Citation: He displayed conspicuous gallantry and intrepidity above and beyond the call of duty while fighting in the Cordillera Mountains of Luzon, Philippine Islands. When 2 Filipino companies were pinned down under a torrent of enemy fire that converged on them from a circular ridge commanding their position, Cpl. Mayfield, in a gallant single-handed effort to aid them, rushed from shell hole to shell hole until he reached 4 enemy caves atop the barren fire-swept hill. With grenades and his carbine, he assaulted each of the caves while enemy fire pounded about him. However, before he annihilated the last hostile redoubt, a machinegun bullet destroyed his weapon and slashed his left hand. Disregarding his wound, he secured more grenades and dauntlessly charged again into the face of pointblank fire to help destroy a hostile observation post. By his gallant determination and heroic leadership, Cpl. Mayfield inspired the men to eliminate all remaining pockets of resistance in the area and to press the advance against the enemy.

McCALL, THOMAS E.

Rank and organization: Staff Sergeant, U.S. Army, Company F, 143d Infantry, 36th Infantry Division. Place and date: Near San Angelo, Italy, 22 January 1944. Entered service at: Veedersburg, Ind. Birth: Burton, Kans. G.O. No.: 31, 17 April 1945. Citation: For conspicuous gallantry and intrepidity at risk of life above and beyond the call of duty. On 22 January 1944, Company F had the mission of crossing the Rapido River in the vicinity of San Angelo, Italy, and attacking the well-prepared German positions to the west. For the defense of these positions the enemy had prepared a network of machinegun positions covering the terrain to the front with a pattern of withering machinegun fire, and mortar and artillery positions zeroed in on the defilade areas. S/Sgt. McCall commanded a machinegun section that was to provide added fire support for the riflemen. Under cover of darkness, Company F advanced to the river crossing site and under intense enemy mortar, artillery, and machinegun fire crossed an ice-covered bridge which was continually the target for enemy fire. Many casualties occurred on reaching the west side of the river and reorganization was imperative. Exposing himself to the deadly enemy machinegun and small arms fire that swept over the flat terrain, S/Sgt. McCall, with unusual calmness, encouraged and welded his men into an effective fighting unit. He then led them forward across the muddy, exposed terrain. Skillfully he guided his men through a barbed-wire entanglement to reach a road where he personally placed the weapons of his two squads into positions of vantage, covering the battalion's front. A shell landed near one of the positions, wounding the gunner, killing the assistant gunner, and destroying the weapon. Even though enemy shells were falling dangerously near, S/Sgt. McCall crawled across the treacherous terrain and rendered first aid to the wounded man, dragging him into a position of cover with the help of another man. The gunners of the second machinegun had been wounded from the fragments of an enemy shell, leaving S/Sgt. McCall the only remaining member of his machinegun section. Displaying outstanding aggressiveness, he ran forward with the weapon on his hip, reaching a point 30 yards from the enemy, where he fired 2 bursts of fire into the nest, killing or wounding all of the crew and putting the gun out of action. A second machinegun now opened fire upon him and he rushed its position, firing his weapon from the hip, killing 4 of the guncrew. A third machinegun, 50 yards in rear of the first two, was delivering a tremendous volume of fire upon our troops. S/Sgt. McCall spotted its position and valiantly went toward it in the face of overwhelming enemy fire. He was last seen courageously moving forward on the enemy position, firing his machinegun from his hip. S/Sgt. McCall's intrepidity and unhesitating willingness to sacrifice his life exemplify the highest traditions of the Armed Forces.

McCAMPBELL, DAVID

Rank and organization: Commander, U.S. Navy, Air Group 15. Place and date: First and second battles of the Philippine Sea, 19 June 1944. Entered service at: Florida. Born: 16 January 1 910, Bessemer, Ala. Other Navy awards: Navy Cross, Silver Star, Legion of Merit, Distinguished Flying Cross with 2 Gold Stars, Air Medal. Citation: For conspicuous gallantry and intrepidity at the risk of his life above and beyond the call of duty as commander, Air Group 15, during combat against enemy Japanese aerial forces in the first and second battles of the Philippine Sea. An inspiring leader, fighting boldly in the face of terrific odds, Comdr. McCampbell led his fighter planes against a force of 80 Japanese carrier-based aircraft bearing down on our fleet on 19 June 1944. Striking fiercely in valiant defense of our surface force, he personally destroyed 7 hostile planes during this single engagement in which the outnumbering attack force was utterly routed and virtually annihilated. During a major fleet engagement with the enemy on 24 October, Comdr. McCampbell, assisted by but 1 plane, intercepted and daringly attacked a formation of 60 hostile land-based craft approaching our forces. Fighting desperately but with superb skill against such overwhelming airpower, he shot down 9 Japanese planes and, completely disorganizing the enemy group, forced the remainder to abandon the attack before a single aircraft could reach the fleet. His great personal valor and indomitable spirit of aggression under extremely perilous combat conditions reflect the highest credit upon Comdr. McCampbell and the U.S. Naval Service.

McCANDLESS, BRUCE

Rank and organization: Commander, U.S. Navy, U.S.S. San Francisco. Place and date: Battle off Savo Island, 1213 November 1942. Entered service at: Colorado. Born: 12 August 1911, Washington, D.C. Other Navy award: Silver Star. Citation: For conspicuous gallantry and exceptionally distinguished service above and beyond the call of duty as communication officer of the U.S.S. San Francisco in combat with enemy Japanese forces in the battle off Savo Island, 1213 November 1942. In the midst of a violent night engagement, the fire of a determined and desperate enemy seriously wounded Lt. Comdr. McCandless and rendered him unconscious, killed or wounded the admiral in command, his staff, the captain of the ship, the navigator, and all other personnel on the navigating and signal bridges. Faced with the lack of superior command upon his recovery, and displaying superb initiative, he promptly assumed command of the ship and ordered her course and gunfire against an overwhelmingly powerful force. With his superiors in other vessels unaware of the loss of their admiral, and challenged by his great responsibility, Lt. Comdr. McCandless boldly continued to engage the enemy and to lead our column of following vessels to a great victory. Largely through his brilliant seamanship and great courage, the San Francisco was brought back to port, saved to fight again in the service of her country.

*McCARD, ROBERT HOWARD

Rank and organization: Gunnery Sergeant, U.S. Marine Corps. Born: 25 November 1918, Syracuse, N.Y. Accredited to: New York. Citation: For conspicuous gallantry and intrepidity at the risk of his life above and beyond the call of duty while serving as platoon sergeant of Company A, 4th Tank Battalion, 4th Marine Division, during the battle for enemy Japanese-held Saipan, Marianas Islands, on 16 June 1944. Cut off from the other units of his platoon when his tank was put out of action by a battery of enemy 77mm. guns, G/Sgt. McCard carried on resolutely, bringing all the tank's weapons to bear on the enemy, until the severity of hostile fire caused him to order his crew out of the escape hatch while he courageously exposed himself to enemy guns by hurling hand grenades, in order to cover the evacuation of his men. Seriously wounded during this action and with his supply of grenades exhausted, G/Sgt. McCard then dismantled one of the tank's machineguns and faced the Japanese for the second time to deliver vigorous fire into their positions, destroying 16 of the enemy but sacrificing himself to insure the safety of his crew. His valiant fighting spirit and supreme loyalty in the face of almost certain death reflect the highest credit upon G/Sgt. McCard and the U.S. Naval Service. He gallantly gave his life for his country.

McCARTER, LLOYD G.

Rank and organization: Private, U.S. Army, 503d Parachute Infantry Regiment. Place and date: Corregidor, Philippine Islands, 16 19 February 1945. Entered service at: Tacoma, Wash. Born: 11 May 1917, St. Maries, Idaho. G.O. No.: 77, 10 September 1945. Citation: He was a scout with the regiment which seized the fortress of Corregidor, Philippine Islands. Shortly after the initial parachute assault on 16 February 1945, he crossed 30 yards of open ground under intense enemy fire, and at pointblank range silenced a machinegun with hand grenades. On the afternoon of 18 February he killed 6 snipers. That evening, when a large force attempted to bypass his company, he voluntarily moved to an exposed area and opened fire. The enemy attacked his position repeatedly throughout the night and was each time repulsed. By 2 o'clock in the morning, all the men about him had been wounded; but shouting encouragement to his comrades and defiance at the enemy, he continued to bear the brunt of the attack, fearlessly exposing himself to locate enemy soldiers and then pouring heavy fire on them. He repeatedly crawled back to the American line to secure more ammunition. When his submachine gun would no longer operate, he seized an automatic rifle and continued to inflict heavy casualties. This weapon, in turn, became too hot to use and, discarding it, he continued with an M-l rifle. At dawn the enemy attacked with renewed intensity. Completely exposing himself to hostile fire, he stood erect to locate the most dangerous enemy positions. He was seriously wounded; but, though he had already killed more than 30 of the enemy, he refused to evacuate until he had pointed out immediate objectives for attack. Through his sustained and outstanding heroism in the face of grave and obvious danger, Pvt. McCarter made outstanding contributions to the success of his company and to the recapture of Corregidor.

McCARTHY, JOSEPH JEREMIAH

Rank and organization: Captain, U.S. Marine Corps Reserve, 2d Battalion, 24th Marines, 4th Marine Division. Place and date: Iwo Jima, Volcano Islands, 21 February 1945. Entered service at: Illinois. Born: 10 August 1911, Chicago, Ill. Citation: For conspicuous gallantry and intrepidity at the risk of his life above and beyond the call of duty as commanding officer of a rifle company attached to the 2d Battalion, 24th Marines, 4th Marine Division, in action against enemy Japanese forces during the seizure of Iwo Jima, Volcano Islands, on 21 February 1945. Determined to break through the enemy's cross-island defenses, Capt. McCarthy acted on his own initiative when his company advance was held up by uninterrupted Japanese rifle, machinegun, and high-velocity

47mm. fire during the approach to Motoyama Airfield No. 2. Quickly organizing a demolitions and flamethrower team to accompany his picked rifle squad, he fearlessly led the way across 75 yards of fire-swept ground, charged a heavily fortified pillbox on the ridge of the front and, personally hurling hand grenades into the emplacement as he directed the combined operations of his small assault group, completely destroyed the hostile installation. Spotting 2 Japanese soldiers attempting an escape from the shattered pillbox, he boldly stood upright in full view of the enemy and dispatched both troops before advancing to a second emplacement under greatly intensified fire and then blasted the strong fortifications with a well-planned demolitions attack. Subsequently entering the ruins, he found a Japanese taking aim at 1 of our men and, with alert presence of mind, jumped the enemy, disarmed and shot him with his own weapon. Then, intent on smashing through the narrow breach, he rallied the remainder of his company and pressed a full attack with furious aggressiveness until he had neutralized all resistance and captured the ridge. An inspiring leader and indomitable fighter, Capt. McCarthy consistently disregarded all personal danger during the fierce conflict and, by his brilliant professional skill, daring tactics, and tenacious perseverance in the face of overwhelming odds, contributed materially to the success of his division's operations against this savagely defended outpost of the Japanese Empire. His cool decision and outstanding valor reflect the highest credit upon Capt. McCarthy and enhance the finest traditions of the U.S. Naval Service.

McCOOL, RICHARD MILES,

Rank and organization: Lieutenant, U.S. Navy, U.S.S. LSC(L)(3) 122. Place and date: Off Okinawa, 10 and 11 June 1945. Entered service at: Oklahoma. Born: 4 January 1922, Tishomingo, Okla. Citation: For conspicuous gallantry and intrepidity at the risk of his life above and beyond the call of duty as commanding officer of the U.S.S. LSC(L)(3) 122 during operations against enemy Japanese forces in the Ryukyu chain, 10 and 11 June 1945. Sharply vigilant during hostile air raids against Allied ships on radar picket duty off Okinawa on 10 June, Lt. McCool aided materially in evacuating all survivors from a sinking destroyer which had sustained mortal damage under the devastating attacks. When his own craft was attacked simultaneously by 2 of the enemy's suicide squadron early in the evening of 11 June, he instantly hurled the full power of his gun batteries against the plunging aircraft, shooting down the first and damaging the second before it crashed his station in the conning tower and engulfed the immediate area in a mass of flames. Although suffering from shrapnel wounds and painful burns, he rallied his concussion-shocked crew and initiated vigorous firefighting measures and then proceeded to the rescue of several trapped in a blazing compartment, subsequently carrying 1 man to safety despite the excruciating pain of additional severe burns. Unmindful of all personal danger, he continued his efforts without respite until aid arrived from other ships and he was evacuated. By his staunch leadership, capable direction, and indomitable determination throughout the crisis, Lt. McCool saved the lives of many who otherwise might have perished and contributed materially to the saving of his ship for further combat service. His valiant spirit of self-sacrifice in the face of extreme peril sustains and enhances the highest traditions of the U.S. Naval Service.

McGAHA, CHARLES L.

Rank and organization: Master Sergeant, U.S. Army, Company G, 35th Infantry, 25th Infantry Division. Place and date: Near Lupao, Luzon, Philippine Islands, 7 February 1945. Entered service at: Crosby, Tenn. Birth: Crosby, Tenn. G.O. No.: 30, 2 April 1946. Citation: He displayed conspicuous gallantry and intrepidity. His platoon and 1 other from Company G were pinned down in a roadside ditch by heavy fire from 5 Japanese tanks supported by 10 machineguns and a platoon of riflemen. When 1 of his men fell wounded 40 yards away, he unhesitatingly crossed the road under a hail of bullets and moved the man 75 yards to safety. Although he had suffered a deep arm wound, he returned to his post. Finding the platoon leader seriously wounded, he assumed command and rallied his men. Once more he braved the enemy fire to go to the aid of a litter party removing another wounded soldier. A shell exploded in their midst, wounding him in the shoulder and killing 2 of the party. He picked up the remaining man, carried him to cover, and then moved out in front deliberately to draw the enemy fire while the American forces, thus protected, withdrew to safety. When the last man had gained the new position, he rejoined his command and there collapsed from loss of blood and exhaustion. M/Sgt. McGaha set an example of courage and leadership in keeping with the highest traditions of the service.

McGARITY, VERNON

Rank and organization: Technical Sergeant, U.S. Army, Company L, 393d Infantry, 99th Infantry Division. Place and date: Near Krinkelt, Belgium, 16 December 1944. Entered service at: Model, Tenn. Born: 1 December 1921, Right, Tenn. G.O. No.: 6, 11 January 1946. Citation: He was painfully wounded in an artillery barrage that preceded the powerful counteroffensive launched by the Germans near Krinkelt, Belgium, on the morning of 16 December 1944. He made his way to an aid station, received treatment, and then refused to be evacuated, choosing to return to his hard-pressed men instead. The fury of the enemy's great Western Front offensive swirled about the position held by T/Sgt. McGarity's small force, but so tenaciously did these men fight on orders to stand firm at all costs that they could not be dislodged despite murderous enemy fire and the breakdown of their communications. During the day the heroic squad leader rescued 1 of his friends who had been wounded in a forward position, and throughout the night he exhorted his comrades to repulse the enemy's attempts at infiltration. When morning came and the Germans attacked with tanks and infantry, he braved heavy fire to run to an advantageous position where he immobilized the enemy's lead tank with a round from a rocket launcher. Fire from his squad drove the attacking infantrymen back, and 3 supporting tanks withdrew. He rescued, under heavy fire, another wounded American, and then directed devastating fire on a light cannon which had been brought up by the hostile troops to clear resistance from the area. When ammunition began to run low, T/Sgt. McGarity, remembering an old ammunition hole about 100 yards distant in the general direction of the enemy, braved a concentration of hostile fire to replenish his unit's supply. By circuitous route the enemy managed to emplace a machinegun to the rear and flank of the squad's position, cutting off the only escape route. Unhesitatingly, the gallant soldier took it upon himself to destroy this menace single-handedly. He left cover, and while under steady fire from the enemy, killed or wounded all the hostile gunners with deadly accurate rifle fire and prevented all attempts to reman the gun. Only when the squad's last round had been fired was the enemy able to advance and capture the intrepid leader and his men. The extraordinary bravery and extreme devotion to duty of T/Sgt. McGarity supported a remarkable delaying action which provided the time necessary for assembling reserves and forming a line against which the German striking power was shattered.

*McGEE, WILLIAM D.

Rank and organization: Private, U.S. Army, Medical Detachment, 304th Infantry, 76th Infantry Division. Place and date: Near Mulheim, Germany, 18 March 1945. Entered service at: Indianapolis, Ind. Birth: Indianapolis, Ind. G.O. No.: 21, 26 February 1946. Citation: A medical aid man, he made a night crossing of the Moselle River with troops endeavoring to capture the town of Mulheim. The enemy had retreated in the sector where the assault boats landed, but had left the shore heavily strewn with antipersonnel mines. Two men of the first wave attempting to work their way forward detonated mines which wounded them seriously, leaving them bleeding and in great pain beyond the reach of their comrades. Entirely on his own initiative, Pvt. McGee entered the minefield, brought out 1 of the injured to comparative safety, and had returned to rescue the second victim when he stepped on a mine and was severely wounded in the resulting explosion. Although suffering intensely and bleeding profusely, he shouted orders that none of his comrades was to risk his life by entering the death-sown field to render first aid that might have saved his life. In making the supreme sacrifice, Pvt. demonstrated a concern for the well-being of his fellow soldiers that transcended all considerations for his own safety and a gallantry in keeping with the highest traditions of the military service.

*McGILL, TROY A.

Rank and organization: Sergeant, U.S. Army, Troop G, 5th Cavalry Regiment, 1st Cavalry Division. Place and date: Los Negros Islands, Admiralty Group, 4 March 1944. Entered service at: Ada, Okla. Birth: Knoxville, Tenn. G.O. No.: 74, 11 September 1944. Citation: For conspicuous gallantry and intrepidity above and beyond the call of duty in action with the enemy at Los Negros Island, Admiralty Group, on 4 March 1944. In the early morning hours Sgt. McGill, with a squad of 8 men, occupied a revetment which bore the brunt of a furious attack by approximately 200 drinkcrazed enemy troops. Although covered by crossfire from machineguns on the right and left flank he could receive no support from the remainder of our troops stationed at his rear. All members of the squad were killed or wounded except Sgt. McGill and another man, whom he ordered to return to the next revetment. Courageously resolved to hold his position at all cost, he fired his weapon until it ceased to function. Then, with the enemy only 5 yards away, he charged from his foxhole in the face of certain death and clubbed the enemy with his rifle in handtohand combat until he was killed. At dawn 105 enemy dead were found around his position. Sgt. McGill's intrepid stand was an inspiration to his comrades and a decisive factor in the defeat of a fanatical enemy.

*McGRAW, FRANCIS X.

Rank and organization: Private First Class, U.S. Army, Company H, 26th Infantry, 1st Infantry Division. Place and date: Near Schevenhutte, Germany, 19 November 1944. Entered service at: Camden. N.J. Birth: Philadelphia, Pa. G.O. No.: 92, 25 October 1945. Citation: He manned a heavy machinegun emplaced in a foxhole near Schevenhutte, Germany, on 19 November 1944, when the enemy launched a fierce counterattack. Braving an intense hour-long preparatory barrage, he maintained his stand and poured deadly accurate fire into the advancing foot troops until they faltered and came to a halt. The hostile forces brought up a machinegun in an effort to dislodge him but were frustrated when he lifted his gun to an exposed but advantageous position atop a log, courageously stood up in his foxhole and knocked out the enemy weapon. A rocket blasted his gun from position, but he retrieved it and continued firing. He silenced a second machinegun and then made repeated trips over fire-swept terrain to replenish his ammunition supply. Wounded painfully in this dangerous task, he disregarded his injury and hurried back to his post, where his weapon was showered with mud when another rocket barely missed him. In the midst of the battle, with enemy troops taking advantage of his predicament to press forward, he calmly cleaned his gun, put it back into action and drove off the attackers. He continued to fire until his ammunition was expended, when, with a fierce desire to close with the enemy, he picked up a carbine, killed 1 enemy soldier, wounded another and engaged in a desperate firefight with a third until he was mortally wounded by a burst from a machine pistol. The extraordinary heroism and intrepidity displayed by Pvt. McGraw inspired his comrades to great efforts and was a major factor in repulsing the enemy attack.

*McGUIRE, THOMAS B., JR. (Air Mission)

Rank and organization: Major, U.S. Army Air Corps, 13th Air Force. Place and date: Over Luzon, Philippine Islands, 2526 December 1944. Entered service at: Sebring, Fla.. Birth: Ridgewood, N.J. G.O. No.: 24, 7 March 1946. Citation: He fought with conspicuous gallantry and intrepidity over Luzon, Philippine Islands. Voluntarily, he led a squadron of 15 P-38's as top cover for heavy bombers striking Mabalacat Airdrome, where his formation was attacked by 20 aggressive Japanese fighters. In the ensuing action he repeatedly flew to the aid of embattled comrades, driving off enemy assaults while himself under attack and at times outnumbered 3 to 1, and even after his guns jammed, continuing the fight by forcing a hostile plane into his wingman's line of fire. Before he started back to his base he had shot down 3 Zeros. The next day he again volunteered to lead escort fighters on a mission to strongly defended Clark Field. During the resultant engagement he again exposed himself to attacks so that he might rescue a crippled bomber. In rapid succession he shot down 1 aircraft, parried the attack of 4 enemy fighters, 1 of which he shot down, single-handedly engaged 3 more Japanese, destroying 1, and then shot down still another, his 38th victory in aerial combat. On 7 January 1945, while leading a voluntary fighter sweep over Los Negros Island, he risked an extremely hazardous maneuver at low altitude in an attempt to save a fellow flyer from attack, crashed, and was reported missing in action. With gallant initiative, deep and unselfish concern for the safety of others, and heroic determination to destroy the enemy at all costs, Maj. McGuire set an inspiring example in keeping with the highest traditions of the military service.

McKINNEY, JOHN R.

Rank and organization: Sergeant (then Private), U.S. Army, Company A, 123d Infantry, 33d Infantry Division. Place and date: Tayabas Province, Luzon, Philippine Islands, 11 May 1945. Entered service at:

Woodcliff, Ga. Birth: Woodcliff, Ga. G.O. No.: 14, 4 February 1946. Citation: He fought with extreme gallantry to defend the outpost which had been established near Dingalan Bay. Just before daybreak approximately 100 Japanese stealthily attacked the perimeter defense, concentrating on a light machinegun position manned by 3 Americans. Having completed a long tour of duty at this gun, Pvt. McKinney was resting a few paces away when an enemy soldier dealt him a glancing blow on the head with a saber. Although dazed by the stroke, he seized his rifle, bludgeoned his attacker, and then shot another assailant who was charging him. Meanwhile, 1 of his comrades at the machinegun had been wounded and his other companion withdrew carrying the injured man to safety. Alone, Pvt. McKinney was confronted by 10 infantrymen who had captured the machinegun with the evident intent of reversing it to fire into the perimeter. Leaping into the emplacement, he shot 7 of them at pointblank range and killed 3 more with his rifle butt. In the melee the machinegun was rendered inoperative, leaving him only his rifle with which to meet the advancing Japanese, who hurled grenades and directed knee mortar shells into the perimeter. He warily changed position, secured more ammunition, and reloading repeatedly, cut down waves of the fanatical enemy with devastating fire or clubbed them to death in hand-to-hand combat. When assistance arrived, he had thwarted the assault and was in complete control of the area. Thirty-eight dead Japanese around the machinegun and 2 more at the side of a mortar 45 yards distant was the amazing toll he had exacted single-handedly. By his indomitable spirit, extraordinary fighting ability, and unwavering courage in the face of tremendous odds, Pvt. McKinley saved his company from possible annihilation and set an example of unsurpassed intrepidity.

*McTUREOUS, ROBERT MILLER, JR.

Rank and organization: Private, U.S. Marine Corps. Born: 26 March 1924, Altoona, Fla. Accredited to: Florida. Citation: For conspicuous gallantry and intrepidity at the risk of his life above and beyond the call of duty, while serving with the 3d Battalion, 29th Marines, 6th Marine Division, during action against enemy Japanese forces on Okinawa in the Ryukyu Chain, 7 June 1945. Alert and ready for any hostile counteraction following his company's seizure of an important hill objective, Pvt. McTureous was quick to observe the plight of company stretcher bearers who were suddenly assailed by slashing machinegun fire as they attempted to evacuate wounded at the rear of the newly won position. Determined to prevent further casualties, he quickly filled his jacket with hand grenades and charged the enemy-occupied caves from which the concentrated barrage was emanating. Coolly disregarding all personal danger as he waged his furious 1-man assault, he smashed grenades into the cave entrances, thereby diverting the heaviest fire from the stretcher bearers to his own person and, resolutely returning to his own lines under a blanketing hail of rifle and machinegun fire to replenish his supply of grenades, dauntlessly continued his systematic reduction of Japanese strength until he himself sustained serious wounds after silencing a large number of the hostile guns. Aware of his own critical condition and unwilling to further endanger the lives of his comrades, he stoically crawled a distance of 200 yards to a sheltered position within friendly lines before calling for aid. By his fearless initiative and bold tactics, Pvt. McTureous had succeeded in neutralizing the enemy fire, killing 6 Japanese troops and effectively disorganizing the remainder of the savagely defending garrison. His outstanding valor and heroic spirit of self-sacrifice during a critical stage of operations reflect the highest credit upon himself and the U.S. Naval Service.

*McVEIGH, JOHN J.

Rank and organization: Sergeant, U.S. Army, Company H, 23d Infantry, 2d Infantry Division. Place and date: Near Brest, France, 29 August 1944. Entered service at: Philadelphia, Pa. Birth: Philadelphia, Pa. G.O. No.: 24, 6 April 1945. Citation: For conspicuous gallantry and intrepidity at risk of his life above and beyond the call of duty near Brest, France, on 29 August 1944. Shortly after dusk an enemy counterattack of platoon strength was launched against 1 platoon of Company G, 23d Infantry. Since the Company G platoon was not dug in and had just begun to assume defensive positions along a hedge, part of the line sagged momentarily under heavy fire from small arms and 2 flak guns, leaving a section of heavy machineguns holding a wide frontage without rifle protection. The enemy drive moved so swiftly that German riflemen were soon almost on top of 1 machinegun position. Sgt. McVeigh, heedless of a tremendous amount of small arms and flak fire directed toward him, stood up in full view of the enemy and directed the fire of his squad on the attacking Germans until his position was almost overrun. He then drew his trench knife. and single-handed charged several of the enemy. In a savage hand-to-hand struggle, Sgt. McVeigh killed 1 German with the knife, his only weapon, and was advancing on 3 more of the enemy when he was shot down and killed with small arms fire at pointblank range. Sgt. McVeigh's heroic act allowed the 2 remaining men in his squad to concentrate their machinegun fire on the attacking enemy and then turn their weapons on the 3 Germans in the road, killing all 3. Fire from this machinegun and the other gun of the section was almost entirely responsible for stopping this enemy assault, and allowed the rifle platoon to which it was attached time to reorganize, assume positions on and hold the high ground gained during the day.

*McWHORTER, WILLIAM A.

Rank and organization: Private First Class, U.S. Army, Company M, 126th Infantry, 32d Infantry Division. Place and date: Leyte, Philippine Islands, 5 December 1944. Entered service at: Liberty, S.C. Birth: Liberty, S.C. G.O. No.: 82, 27 September 1945. Citation: He displayed gallantry and intrepidity at the risk of his life above and beyond the call of duty while engaged in operations against the enemy. Pfc. McWhorter, a machine gunner, was emplaced in a defensive position with 1 assistant when the enemy launched a heavy attack. Manning the gun and opening fire, he killed several members of an advancing demolition squad, when 1 of the enemy succeeded in throwing a fused demolition charge in the entrenchment. Without hesitation and with complete disregard for his own safety, Pfc. McWhorter picked up the improvised grenade and deliberately held it close to his body, bending over and turning away from his companion. The charge exploded, killing him instantly, but leaving his assistant unharmed. Pfc. McWhorter's outstanding heroism and supreme sacrifice in shielding a comrade reflect the highest traditions of the military service.

MEAGHER, JOHN

Rank and organization: Technical Sergeant, U.S. Army, Company E, 305th Infantry, 77th Infantry Division. Place and date: Near Ozato, Okinawa, 19 June 1945. Entered service at: Jersey City, N.J. Birth: Jersey City, N.J. G.O. No.: 60, 26 June 1946. Citation: He displayed conspicuous gallantry and intrepidity above and beyond the call of duty. In the heat of the fight, he mounted an assault tank, and, with bullets splattering about him, designated targets to the gunner. Seeing an enemy soldier carrying an explosive charge dash for the tank treads, he shouted fire orders to the gunner, leaped from the tank, and bayoneted the charging soldier. Knocked unconscious and his rifle destroyed, he regained consciousness, secured a machinegun from the tank, and began a furious 1-man assault on the enemy. Firing from his hip, moving through vicious crossfire that ripped through his clothing, he charged the nearest pillbox, killing 6. Going on amid the hail of bullets and grenades, he dashed for a second enemy gun, running out of ammunition just as he reached the position. He grasped his empty gun by the barrel and in a violent onslaught killed the crew. By his fearless assaults T/Sgt. Meagher single-handedly broke the enemy resistance, enabling his platoon to take its objective and continue the advance.

MERLI, GINO J.

Rank and organization: Private First Class, U.S. Army, 18th Infantry, 1st Infantry Division. Place and date: Near Sars la Bruyere, Belgium, 45 September 1944. Entered service at: Peckville, Pa. Birth: Scranton, Pa. G.O. No.: 64, 4 August 1945. Citation: He was serving as a machine gunner in the vicinity of Sars la Bruyere, Belgium, on the night of 45 September 1944, when his company was attacked by a superior German force Its position was overrun and he was surrounded when our troops were driven back by overwhelming numbers and firepower. Disregarding the fury of the enemy fire concentrated on him he maintained his position, covering the withdrawal of our riflemen and breaking the force of the enemy pressure. His assistant machine gunner was killed and the position captured; the other 8 members of the section were forced to surrender. Pfc. Merli slumped down beside the dead assistant gunner and feigned death. No sooner had the enemy group withdrawn then he was up and firing in all directions. Once more his position was taken and the captors found 2 apparently lifeless bodies. Throughout the night Pfc. Merli stayed at his weapon. By daybreak the enemy had suffered heavy losses, and as our troops launched an assault, asked for a truce. Our negotiating party, who accepted the German surrender, found Pfc. Merli still at his gun. On the battlefield lay 52 enemy dead, 19 of whom were directly in front of the gun. Pfc. Merli's gallantry and courage, and the losses and confusion that he caused the enemy, contributed materially to our victory .

*MERRELL, JOSEPH F.

Rank and organization: Private, U.S. Army, Company I, 15th Infantry, 3d Infantry Division. Place and date: Near Lohe, Germany, 18 April 1945. Entered service at: Staten Island, N.Y. Birth: Staten Island, N.Y. G.O. No.: 21, 26 February 1946. Citation: He made a gallant, 1-man attack against vastly superior enemy forces near Lohe, Germany. His unit, attempting a quick conquest of hostile hill positions that would open the route to Nuremberg before the enemy could organize his defense of that city, was pinned down by brutal fire from rifles, machine pistols, and 2 heavy machineguns. Entirely on his own initiative, Pvt. Merrell began a single-handed assault. He ran 100 yards through concentrated fire, barely escaping death at each stride, and at pointblank range engaged 4 German machine pistolmen with his rifle, killing all of them while their bullets ripped his uniform. As he started forward again, his rifle was smashed by a sniper's bullet, leaving him armed only with 3 grenades. But he did not hesitate. He zigzagged 200 yards through a hail of bullets to within 10 yards of the first machinegun, where he hurled 2 grenades and then rushed the position ready to fight with his bare hands if necessary. In the emplacement he seized a Luger pistol and killed what Germans had survived the grenade blast. Rearmed, he crawled toward the second machinegun located 30 yards away, killing 4 Germans in camouflaged foxholes on the way, but himself receiving a critical wound in the abdomen. And yet he went on, staggering, bleeding, disregarding bullets which tore through the folds of his clothing and glanced off his helmet. He threw his last grenade into the machinegun nest and stumbled on to wipe out the crew. He had completed this self-appointed task when a machine pistol burst killed him instantly. In his spectacular 1-man attack Pvt. Merrell killed 6 Germans in the first machinegun emplacement, 7 in the next, and an additional 10 infantrymen who were astride his path to the weapons which would have decimated his unit had he not assumed the burden of the assault and stormed the enemy positions with utter fearlessness, intrepidity of the highest order, and a willingness to sacrifice his own life so that his comrades could go on to victory.

*MESSERSCHMIDT, HAROLD O.

Rank and organization: Sergeant, U.S. Army, Company L, 30th Infantry, 3d Infantry Division. Place and date: Near Radden, France, 17

September 1944. Entered service at: Chester, Pa. Birth: Grier City, Pa. G.O. No.: 71, 17 July 1946. Citation: He displayed conspicuous gallantry and intrepidity above and beyond the call of duty. Braving machinegun, machine pistol, and rifle fire, he moved fearlessly and calmly from man to man along his 40-yard squad front, encouraging each to hold against the overwhelming assault of a fanatical foe surging up the hillside. Knocked to the ground by a burst from an enemy automatic weapon, he immediately jumped to his feet, and ignoring his grave wounds, fired his submachine gun at the enemy that was now upon them, killing 5 and wounding many others before his ammunition was spent. Virtually surrounded by a frenzied foe and all of his squad now casualties, he elected to fight alone, using his empty submachine gun as a bludgeon against his assailants. Spotting 1 of the enemy about to kill a wounded comrade, he felled the German with a blow of his weapon. Seeing friendly reinforcements running up the hill, he continued furiously to wield his empty gun against the foe in a new attack, and it was thus that he made the supreme sacrifice. Sgt. Messerschmidt's sustained heroism in hand-to-hand combat with superior enemy forces was in keeping with the highest traditions of the military service .

*METZGER, WILLIAM E., JR. (Air Mission)

Rank and organization: Second Lieutenant, U.S. Army Air Corps, 729th Bomber Squadron 452d Bombardment Group. Place and date: Saarbrucken, Germany, 9 November 1944. Entered service at: Lima, Ohio. Born: 9 February 1922, Lima, Ohio. G.O. No.: 38, 16 May 1945. Citation: On a bombing run upon the marshaling yards at Saarbrucken, Germany, on 9 November 1944, a B17 aircraft on which 2d Lt. Metzger was serving as copilot was seriously damaged by antiaircraft fire. Three of the aircraft's engines were damaged beyond control and on fire; dangerous flames from the No. 4 engine were leaping back as far as the tail assembly. Flares in the cockpit were ignited and a fire roared therein which was further increased by free-flowing fluid from damaged hydraulic lines. The interphone system was rendered useless. In addition to these serious mechanical difficulties the engineer was wounded in the leg and the radio operator's arm was severed below the elbow. Suffering from intense pain, despite the application of a tourniquet, the radio operator fell unconscious. Faced with the imminent explosion of his aircraft and death to his entire crew, mere seconds before bombs away on the target, 2d Lt. Metzger and his pilot conferred. Something had to be done immediately to save the life of the wounded radio operator. The lack of a static line and the thought that his unconscious body striking the ground in unknown territory would not bring immediate medical attention forced a quick decision. 2d Lt. Metzger and his pilot decided to fly the flaming aircraft to friendly territory and then attempt to crash land. Bombs were released on the target and the crippled aircraft proceeded along to Allied-controlled territory. When that had been reached 2d Lt. Metzger personally informed all crewmembers to bail out upon the suggestion of the pilot. 2d Lt. Metzger chose to remain with the pilot for the crash landing in order to assist him in this emergency. With only 1 normally functioning engine and with the danger of explosion much greater, the aircraft banked into an open field, and when it was at an altitude of 100 feet it exploded, crashed, exploded again, and then disintegrated. All 3 crewmembers were instantly killed. 2d Lt. Metzger's loyalty to his crew, his determination to accomplish the task set forth to him, and his deed of knowingly performing what may have been his last service to his country was an example of valor at its highest.

MICHAEL, EDWARD S. (Air Mission)

Rank and organization: First Lieutenant, U.S. Army Air Corps, 364th Bomber Squadron, 305th Bomber Group. Place and date: Over Germany, 11 April 1944. Entered service at: Chicago, Ill. Born: 2 May 1918, Chicago, Ill. G.O. No.: 5, 15 January 1945. Citation: For conspicuous gallantry and intrepidity above and beyond the call of duty while serving as pilot of a B17 aircraft on a heavy-bombardment mission to Germany, 11 April 1944. The group in which 1st Lt. Michael was flying was attacked by a swarm of fighters. His plane was singled out and the fighters pressed their attacks home recklessly, completely disregarding the Allied fighter escort and their own intense flak. His plane was riddled from nose to tail with exploding cannon shells and knocked out of formation, with a large number of fighters following it down, blasting it with cannon fire as it descended. A cannon shell exploded in the cockpit, wounded the copilot, wrecked the instruments, and blew out the side window. 1st Lt. Michael was seriously and painfully wounded in the right thigh. Hydraulic fluid filmed over the windshield making visibility impossible, and smoke filled the cockpit. The controls failed to respond and 3,000 feet were lost before he succeeded in leveling off. The radio operator informed him that the whole bomb bay was in flames as a result of the explosion of 3 cannon shells, which had ignited the incendiaries. With a full load of incendiaries in the bomb bay and a considerable gas load in the tanks, the danger of fire enveloping the plane and the tanks exploding seemed imminent. When the emergency release lever failed to function, 1st Lt. Michael at once gave the order to bail out and 7 of the crew left the plane. Seeing the bombardier firing the navigator's gun at the enemy planes, 1st Lt. Michael ordered him to bail out as the plane was liable to explode any minute. When the bombardier looked for his parachute he found that it had been riddled with 20mm. fragments and was useless. 1st Lt. Michael, seeing the ruined parachute, realized that if the plane was abandoned the bombardier would perish and decided that the only chance would be a crash landing. Completely disregarding his own painful and profusely bleeding wounds, but thinking only of the safety of the remaining crewmembers, he gallantly evaded the enemy, using violent evasive action despite the battered condition of his plane. After the plane had been under sustained enemy attack for fully 45 minutes, 1st Lt. Michael finally lost the persistent fighters in a cloud bank. Upon emerging, an accurate barrage of flak caused him to come down to treetop level where flak towers poured a continuous rain of fire on the plane. He continued into France, realizing that at any moment a crash landing might have to be attempted, but trying to get as far as possible to increase the escape possibilities if a safe landing could be achieved. 1st Lt. Michael flew the plane until he became exhausted from the loss of blood, which had formed on the floor in pools, and he lost consciousness. The copilot succeeded in reaching England and sighted an RAF field near the coast. 1st Lt. Michael finally regained consciousness and insisted upon taking over the controls to land the plane. The undercarriage was useless; the bomb bay doors were jammed open; the hydraulic system and altimeter were shot out. In addition, there was no airspeed indicator, the ball turret was jammed with the guns pointing downward, and the flaps would not respond. Despite these apparently insurmountable obstacles, he landed the plane without mishap.

*MICHAEL, HARRY J.

Rank and organization: Second Lieutenant, U.S. Army, Company L, 318th Infantry, 80th Infantry Division. Place and date: Near Neiderzerf, Germany, 14 March 1945. Entered service at: Milford, Ind. Birth: Milford, Ind. G.O. No.: 18, 13 February 1946. Citation: He was serving as a rifle platoon leader when his company began an assault on a wooded ridge northeast of the village of Neiderzerf, Germany, early on 13 March 1945. A short distance up the side of the hill, 2d Lt. Michael, at the head of his platoon, heard the click of an enemy machinegun bolt. Quietly halting the company, he silently moved off into the woods and discovered 2 enemy machineguns and crews. Executing a sudden charge, he completely surprised the enemy and captured the guns and crews. At daybreak, enemy voices were heard in the thick woods ahead. Leading his platoon in a flanking movement, they charged the enemy with hand grenades and, after a bitter fight, captured 25 members of an SS mountain division, 3 artillery pieces, and 20 horses. While his company was establishing its position, 2d Lt. Michael made 2 personal reconnaissance missions of the wood on his left flank. On his first mission he killed 2, wounded 4, and captured 6 enemy soldiers single-handedly. On the second mission he captured 7 prisoners. During the afternoon he led his platoon on a frontal assault of a line of enemy pillboxes, successfully capturing the objective, killing 10 and capturing 30 prisoners. The following morning the company was subjected to sniper fire and 2d Lt. Michael, in an attempt to find the hidden sniper, was shot and killed. The inspiring leadership and heroic aggressiveness displayed by 2d Lt. Michael upheld the highest traditions of the military service.

*MILLER, ANDREW

Rank and organization: Staff Sergeant, U.S. Army, Company G, 377th Infantry, 95th Infantry Division. Place and date: From Woippy, France, through Metz to Kerprich Hemmersdorf, Germany, 1629 November 1944. Entered service at: Two Rivers, Wis. Birth: Manitowoc, Wis. G.O. No.: 74, 1 September 1945. Citation: For performing a series of heroic deeds from 1629 November 1944, during his company's relentless drive from Woippy, France, through Metz to Kerprich Hemmersdorf, Germany. As he led a rifle squad on 16 November at Woippy, a crossfire from enemy machineguns pinned down his unit. Ordering his men to remain under cover, he went forward alone, entered a building housing 1 of the guns and forced S Germans to surrender at bayonet point. He then took the second gun single-handedly by hurling grenades into the enemy position, killing 2, wounding 3 more, and taking 2 additional prisoners. At the outskirts of Metz the next day, when his platoon, confused by heavy explosions and the withdrawal of friendly tanks, retired, he fearlessly remained behind armed with an automatic rifle and exchanged bursts with a German machinegun until he silenced the enemy weapon. His quick action in covering his comrades gave the platoon time to regroup and carry on the fight. On 19 November S/Sgt. Miller led an attack on large enemy barracks. Covered by his squad, he crawled to a barracks window, climbed in and captured 6 riflemen occupying the room. His men, and then the entire company, followed through the window, scoured the building, and took 75 prisoners. S/Sgt. Miller volunteered, with 3 comrades, to capture Gestapo officers who were preventing the surrender of German troops in another building. He ran a gauntlet of machinegun fire and was lifted through a window. Inside, he found himself covered by a machine pistol, but he persuaded the 4 Gestapo agents confronting him to surrender. Early the next morning, when strong hostile forces punished his company with heavy fire, S/Sgt. Miller assumed the task of destroying a well-placed machinegun. He was knocked down by a rifle grenade as he climbed an open stairway in a house, but pressed on with a bazooka to find an advantageous spot from which to launch his rocket. He discovered that he could fire only from the roof, a position where he would draw tremendous enemy fire. Facing the risk, he moved into the open, coolly took aim and scored a direct hit on the hostile emplacement, wreaking such havoc that the enemy troops became completely demoralized and began surrendering by the score. The following day, in Metz, he captured 12 more prisoners and silenced an enemy machinegun after volunteering for a hazardous mission in advance of his company's position. On 29 November, as Company G climbed a hill overlooking Kerprich Hemmersdorf, enemy fire pinned the unit to the ground. S/Sgt. Miller, on his own initiative, pressed ahead with his squad past the company's leading element to meet the surprise resistance. His men stood up and advanced deliberately, firing as they went. Inspired by S/Sgt. Miller's leadership, the platoon followed, and then another platoon arose and grimly closed with the Germans. The enemy action was smothered, but at the cost of S/Sgt. Miller's life. His tenacious devotion to the attack, his gallant choice to expose himself to enemy action rather than endanger his men, his limitless bravery, assured the success of Company G.

MILLS, JAMES H.

Rank and organization: Private, U.S. Army, Company F, 15th Infantry, 3d Infantry Division. Place and date: Near Cisterna di Littoria, Italy, 24 May 1944. Entered service at: Fort Meade, Fla. Birth: Fort Meade, Fla. G.O. No.: 87, 14 November 1944. Citation: For conspicuous gallantry and intrepidity at risk of life above and beyond the call of duty. Pvt. Mills, undergoing his baptism of fire, preceded his platoon down a draw to reach a position from which an attack could be launched against a heavily fortified strongpoint. After advancing about 300 yards, Pvt. Mills was fired on by a machinegun only S yards distant. He killed the gunner with 1 shot and forced the surrender of the assistant gunner. Continuing his advance, he saw a German soldier in a camouflaged position behind a large bush pulling the pin of a potato-masher grenade. Covering the German with his rifle, Pvt. Mills forced him to drop the grenade and captured him. When another enemy soldier attempted to throw a hand grenade into the draw, Pvt. Mills killed him with 1 shot. Brought under fire by a machinegun, 2 machine pistols, and 3 rifles at a range of only 50 feet, he charged headlong into the furious chain of automatic fire shooting his M 1 from the hip. The enemy was completely demoralized by Pvt. Mills' daring charge, and when he reached a point within 10 feet of their position, all 6 surrendered. As he neared the end of the draw, Pvt. Mills was brought under fire by a machinegunner 20 yards distant. Despite the fact that he had absolutely no cover, Pvt. Mills killed the gunner with 1 shot. Two enemy soldiers near the machinegunner fired wildly at Pvt. Mills and then fled. Pvt. Mills fired twice, killing 1 of the enemy. Continuing on to the position, he captured a fourth soldier. When it became apparent that an assault on the strongpoint would in all probability cause heavy casualties on the platoon, Pvt. Mills volunteered to cover the advance down a shallow ditch to a point within 50 yards of the objective. Standing on the bank in full view of the enemy less than 100 yards away, he shouted and fired his rifle directly into the position. His ruse worked exactly as planned. The enemy centered his fire on Pvt. Mills. Tracers passed within inches of his body, rifle and machine pistol bullets ricocheted off the rocks at his feet. Yet he stood there firing until his rifle was empty. Intent on covering the movement of his platoon, Pvt. Mills jumped into the draw, reloaded his weapon, climbed out again, and continued to lay down a base of fire. Repeating this action 4 times, he enabled his platoon to reach the designated spot undiscovered, from which position it assaulted and overwhelmed the enemy, capturing 22 Germans and taking the objective without casualties.

*MINICK, JOHN W.

Rank and organization: Staff Sergeant, U.S. Army, Company I, 121st Infantry, 8th Infantry Division. Place and date: Near Hurtgen, Germany, 21 November 1944. Entered service at: Carlisle, Pa. Birth: Wall, Pa. Citation: He displayed conspicuous gallantry and intrepidity at the risk of his own life, above and beyond the call of duty, in action involving actual conflict with the enemy on 21 November 1944, near Hurtgen, Germany. S/Sgt. Minick's battalion was halted in its advance by extensive minefields, exposing troops to heavy concentrations of enemy artillery and mortar fire. Further delay in the advance would result in numerous casualties and a movement through the minefield was essential. Voluntarily, S/Sgt. Minick led 4 men through hazardous barbed wire and debris, finally making his way through the minefield for a distance of 300 yards. When an enemy machinegun opened fire, he signaled his men to take covered positions, edged his way alone toward the flank of the weapon and opened fire, killing 2 members of the guncrew and capturing 3 others. Moving forward again, he encountered and engaged single-handedly an entire company killing 20 Germans and capturing 20, and enabling his platoon to capture the remainder of the hostile group. Again moving ahead and spearheading his battalion's advance, he again encountered machinegun fire. Crawling forward toward the weapon, he reached a point from which he knocked the weapon out of action. Still another minefield had to be crossed. Undeterred, S/Sgt. Minick advanced forward alone through constant enemy fire and while thus moving, detonated a mine and was instantly killed.

*MINUE, NICHOLAS

Rank and organization: Private, U.S. Army, Company A, 6th Armored Infantry, 1st Armored Division. Place and date: Near MedjezelBab, Tunisia, 28 April 1943. Entered service at: Carteret, N.J. Birth: Sedden, Poland. G.O. No.: 24, 25 March 1944. Citation: For distinguishing himself conspicuously by gallantry and intrepidity at the loss of his life above and beyond the call of duty in action with the enemy on 28 April 1943, in the vicinity of MedjezelBab, Tunisia. When the advance of the assault elements of Company A was held up by flanking fire from an enemy machinegun nest, Pvt. Minue voluntarily, alone, and unhesitatingly, with complete disregard of his own welfare, charged the enemy entrenched position with fixed bayonet. Pvt. Minue assaulted the enemy under a withering machinegun and rifle fire, killing approximately 10 enemy machinegunners and riflemen. After completely destroying this position, Pvt. Minue continued forward, routing enemy riflemen from dugout positions until he was fatally wounded. The courage, fearlessness and aggressiveness displayed by Pvt. Minue in the face of inevitable death was unquestionably the factor that gave his company the offensive spirit that was necessary for advancing and driving the enemy from the entire sector.

*MONTEITH, JIMMIE W., JR.

Rank and organization: First Lieutenant, U.S. Army, 16th Infantry, 1st Infantry Division. Place and date: Near Colleville-sur-Mer, France, 6 June 1944. Entered service at: Richmond, Va. Born: 1 July 1917, Low Moor, Va. G.O. No.: 20, 29 March 1945. Citation: For conspicuous gallantry and intrepidity above and beyond the call of duty on 6 June 1944, near Colleville-sur-Mer, France. 1st Lt. Monteith landed with the initial assault waves on the coast of France under heavy enemy fire. Without regard to his own personal safety he continually moved up and down the beach reorganizing men for further assault. He then led the assault over a narrow protective ledge and across the flat, exposed terrain to the comparative safety of a cliff. Retracing his steps across the field to the beach, he moved over to where 2 tanks were buttoned up and blind under violent enemy artillery and machinegun fire. Completely exposed to the intense fire, 1st Lt. Monteith led the tanks on foot through a minefield and into firing positions. Under his direction several enemy positions were destroyed. He then rejoined his company and under his leadership his men captured an advantageous position on the hill. Supervising the defense of his newly won position against repeated vicious counterattacks, he continued to ignore his own personal safety, repeatedly crossing the 200 or 300 yards of open terrain under heavy fire to strengthen links in his defensive chain. When the enemy succeeded in completely surrounding 1st Lt. Monteith and his unit and while leading the fight out of the situation, 1st Lt. Monteith was killed by enemy fire. The courage, gallantry, and intrepid leadership displayed by 1st Lt. Monteith is worthy of emulation.

MONTGOMERY, JACK C.

Rank and organization: First Lieutenant, U.S. Army, 45th Infantry Division. Place and date: Near, Padiglione, Italy, 22 February 1944. Entered service at: Sallisaw, Okla. Birth: Long, Okla. G.O. No.: 5, 15 January 1945. Citation: For conspicuous gallantry and intrepidity at risk of life above and beyond the call of duty on 22 February 1944, near Padiglione, Italy. Two hours before daybreak a strong force of enemy infantry established themselves in 3 echelons at 50 yards, 100 yards, and 300 yards, respectively, in front of the rifle platoons commanded by 1st Lt. Montgomery. The closest position, consisting of 4 machineguns and

1 mortar, threatened the immediate security of the platoon position. Seizing an Ml rifle and several hand grenades, 1st Lt. Montgomery crawled up a ditch to within hand grenade range of the enemy. Then climbing boldly onto a little mound, he fired his rifle and threw his grenades so accurately that he killed 8 of the enemy and captured the remaining 4. Returning to his platoon, he called for artillery fire on a house, in and around which he suspected that the majority of the enemy had entrenched themselves. Arming himself with a carbine, he proceeded along the shallow ditch, as withering fire from the riflemen and machinegunners in the second position was concentrated on him. He attacked this position with such fury that 7 of the enemy surrendered to him, and both machineguns were silenced. Three German dead were found in the vicinity later that morning. 1st Lt. Montgomery continued boldly toward the house, 300 yards from his platoon position. It was now daylight, and the enemy observation was excellent across the flat open terrain which led to 1st Lt. Montgomery's objective. When the artillery barrage had lifted, 1st Lt. Montgomery ran fearlessly toward the strongly defended position. As the enemy started streaming out of the house, 1st Lt. Montgomery, unafraid of treacherous snipers, exposed himself daringly to assemble the surrendering enemy and send them to the rear. His fearless, aggressive, and intrepid actions that morning, accounted for a total of 11 enemy dead, 32 prisoners, and an unknown number of wounded. That night, while aiding an adjacent unit to repulse a counterattack, he was struck by mortar fragments and seriously wounded. The selflessness and courage exhibited by 1st Lt. Montgomery in alone attacking 3 strong enemy positions inspired his men to a degree beyond estimation.

*MOON, HAROLD H., JR.

Rank and organization: Private, U.S. Army, Company G, 34th Infantry, 24th Infantry Division. Place and date: Pawig, Leyte, Philippine Islands, 21 October 1944. Entered service at: Gardena, Calif. Birth: Albuquerque,

N. Mex. G.O. No.: 104, 15 November 1945. Citation: He fought with conspicuous gallantry and intrepidity when powerful Japanese counterblows were being struck in a desperate effort to annihilate a newly won beachhead. In a forward position, armed with a submachinegun, he met the brunt of a strong, well-supported night attack which quickly enveloped his platoon's flanks. Many men in nearby positions were killed or injured, and Pvt. Moon was wounded as his foxhole became the immediate object of a concentration of mortar and machinegun fire. Nevertheless, he maintained his stand, poured deadly fire into the enemy, daringly exposed himself to hostile fire time after time to exhort and inspire what American troops were left in the immediate area. A Japanese officer, covered by machinegun fire and hidden by an embankment, attempted to knock out his position with grenades, but Pvt. Moon, after protracted and skillful maneuvering, killed him. When the enemy advanced a light machinegun to within 20 yards of the shattered perimeter and fired with telling effects on the remnants of the platoon, he stood up to locate the gun and remained exposed while calling back range corrections to friendly mortars which knocked out the weapon. A little later he killed 2 Japanese as they charged an aid man. By dawn his position, the focal point of the attack for more than 4 hours, was virtually surrounded. In a fanatical effort to reduce it and kill its defender, an entire platoon charged with fixed bayonets. Firing from a sitting position, Pvt. Moon calmly emptied his magazine into the advancing horde, killing 18 and repulsing the attack. In a final display of bravery, he stood up to throw a grenade at a machinegun which had opened fire on the right flank. He was hit and instantly killed, falling in the position from which he had not been driven by the fiercest enemy action. Nearly 200 dead Japanese were found within 100 yards of his foxhole. The continued tenacity, combat sagacity, and magnificent heroism with which Pvt. Moon fought on against overwhelming odds contributed in a large measure to breaking up a powerful enemy threat and did much to insure our initial successes during a most important operation.

MORGAN, JOHN C. (Air Mission)

Rank and organization: Second Lieutenant, U.S. Army Air Corps, 326th Bomber Squadron, 92d Bomber Group. Place and date: Over Europe, 28 July 1943. Entered service at: London, England. Born: 24 August 1914, Vernon, Tex. G.O. No.: 85, 17 December 1943. Citation: For conspicuous gallantry and intrepidity above and beyond the call of duty, while participating on a bombing mission over enemy-occupied continental Europe, 28 July 1943. Prior to reaching the German coast on the way to the target, the B17 airplane in which 2d Lt. Morgan was serving as copilot was attacked by a large force of enemy fighters, during which the oxygen system to the tail, waist, and radio gun positions was knocked out. A frontal attack placed a cannon shell through the windshield, totally shattering it, and the pilot's skull was split open by a .303 caliber shell, leaving him in a crazed condition. The pilot fell over the steering wheel, tightly clamping his arms around it. 2d Lt. Morgan at once grasped the controls from his side and, by sheer strength, pulled the airplane back into formation despite the frantic struggles of the semiconscious pilot. The interphone had been destroyed, rendering it impossible to call for help. At this time the top turret gunner fell to the floor and down through the hatch with his arm shot off at the shoulder and a gaping wound in his side. The waist, tail, and radio gunners had lost consciousness from lack of oxygen and, hearing no fire from their guns, the copilot believed they had bailed out. The wounded pilot still offered desperate resistance in his crazed attempts to fly the airplane. There remained the prospect of flying to and over the target and back to a friendly base wholly unassisted. In the face of this desperate situation, 2d Lt. Officer Morgan made his decision to continue the flight and protect any members of the crew who might still be in the ship and for 2 hours he flew in formation with one hand at the controls and the other holding off the struggling pilot before the navigator entered the steering compartment and relieved the situation. The miraculous and heroic performance of 2d Lt. Morgan on this occasion resulted in the successful completion of a vital bombing mission and the safe return of his airplane and crew.

*MOSKALA, EDWARD J.

Rank and organization: Private First Class, U.S. Army, Company C, 383d Infantry, 96th Infantry Division. Place and date: Kakazu Ridge, Okinawa, Ryukyu Islands, 9 April 1945. Entered service at: Chicago, Ill. Born: 6 November 1921, Chicago, Ill. G.O. No.: 21, 26 February 1946. Citation: He was the leading element when grenade explosions and concentrated machinegun and mortar fire halted the unit's attack on Kakazu Ridge, Okinawa, Ryukyu Islands. With utter disregard for his personal safety, he charged 40 yards through withering, grazing fire and wiped out 2 machinegun nests with well-aimed grenades and deadly accurate fire from his automatic rifle. When strong counterattacks and fierce enemy resistance from other positions forced his company to withdraw, he voluntarily remained behind with 8 others to cover the maneuver. Fighting from a critically dangerous position for 3 hours, he killed more than 25 Japanese before following his surviving companions through screening smoke down the face of the ridge to a gorge where it was discovered that one of the group had been left behind, wounded. Unhesitatingly, Pvt. Moskala climbed the bullet-swept slope to assist in the rescue, and, returning to lower ground, volunteered to protect other wounded while the bulk of the troops quickly took up more favorable positions. He had saved another casualty and killed 4 enemy infiltrators when he was struck and mortally wounded himself while aiding still another disabled soldier. With gallant initiative, unfaltering courage, and heroic determination to destroy the enemy, Pvt. Moskala gave his life in his complete devotion to his company's mission and his comrades' well-being. His intrepid conduct provided a lasting inspiration for those with whom he served.

*MOWER, CHARLES E.

Rank and organization: Sergeant, U.S. Army, Company A, 34th Infantry, 24th Infantry Division. Place and date: Near Capoocan, Leyte. Philippine Islands, 3 November 1944. Entered service at: Chippewa Falls, Wis. Birth: Chippewa Falls, Wis. G.O. No.: 17, 11 February 1946. Citation: He was an assistant squad leader in an attack against strongly defended enemy positions on both sides of a stream running through a wooded gulch. As the squad advanced through concentrated fire, the leader was killed and Sgt. Mower assumed command. In order to bring direct fire upon the enemy, he had started to lead his men across the stream, which by this time was churned by machinegun and rifle fire, but he was severely wounded before reaching the opposite bank. After signaling his unit to halt, he realized his own exposed position was the most advantageous point from which to direct the attack, and stood fast. Half submerged, gravely wounded, but refusing to seek shelter or accept aid of any kind, he continued to shout and signal to his squad as he directed it in the destruction of 2 enemy machineguns and numerous riflemen. Discovering that the intrepid man in the stream was largely responsible for the successful action being taken against them, the remaining Japanese concentrated the full force of their firepower upon him, and he was killed while still urging his men on. Sgt. Mower's gallant initiative and heroic determination aided materially in the successful completion of his squad's mission. His magnificent leadership was an inspiration to those with whom he served.

*MULLER, JOSEPH E.

Rank and organization: Sergeant, U.S. Army, Company B, 305th Infantry, 77th Infantry Division. Place and date: Near Ishimmi, Okinawa, Ryukyu Islands, 15-16 May 1945. Entered service at: New York, N.Y. Birth: Holyoke, Mass. G.O. No.: 71, 17 July 1946. Citation: He displayed conspicuous gallantry and intrepidity above and beyond the call of duty. When his platoon was stopped by deadly fire from a strongly defended ridge, he directed men to points where they could cover his attack. Then through the vicious machinegun and automatic fire, crawling forward alone, he suddenly jumped up, hurled his grenades, charged the enemy, and drove them into the open where his squad shot them down. Seeing enemy survivors about to man a machinegun, He fired his rifle at point-blank range, hurled himself upon them, and killed the remaining 4. Before dawn the next day, the enemy counterattacked fiercely to retake the position. Sgt. Muller crawled forward through the flying bullets and explosives, then leaping to his feet, hurling grenades and firing his rifle, he charged the Japs and routed them. As he moved into his foxhole shared with 2 other men, a lone enemy, who had been feigning death, threw a grenade. Quickly seeing the danger to his companions, Sgt. Muller threw himself over it and smothered the blast with his body. Heroically sacrificing his life to save his comrades, he upheld the highest traditions of the military service.

*MUNEMORI, SADAO S.

Rank and organization: Private First Class, U.S. Army, Company A,

100th Infantry Battalion, 442d Combat Team. Place and date: Near Seravezza, Italy, 5 April 1945. Entered service at: Los Angeles, Calif Birth: Los Angeles, Calif. G.O. No.. 24, 7 March 1946. Citation: He fought with great gallantry and intrepidity near Seravezza, Italy. When his unit was pinned down by grazing fire from the enemy's strong mountain defense and command of the squad devolved on him with the wounding of its regular leader, he made frontal, l-man attacks through direct fire and knocked out 2 machineguns with grenades Withdrawing under murderous fire and showers of grenades from other enemy emplacements, he had nearly reached a shell crater occupied by 2 of his men when an unexploded grenade bounced on his helmet and rolled toward his helpless comrades. He arose into the withering fire, dived for the missile and smothered its blast with his body. By his swift, supremely heroic action Pfc. Munemori saved 2 of his men at the cost of his own life and did much to clear the path for his company's victorious advance.

*MUNRO, DOUGLAS ALBERT

Rank and organization: Signalman First Class, U.S. Coast Guard Born: 11 October 1919, Vancouver, British Columbia. Accredited to Washington. Citation: For extraordinary heroism and conspicuous gallantry m action above and beyond the call of duty as Petty Officer in Charge of a group of 24 Higgins boats, engaged in the evacuation of a battalion of marines trapped by enemy Japanese forces at Point Cruz Guadalcanal, on 27 September 1942. After making preliminary plans for the evacuation of nearly 500 beleaguered marines, Munro, under constant strafing by enemy machineguns on the island, and at great risk of his life, daringly led 5 of his small craft toward the shore. As he closed the beach, he signaled the others to land, and then in order to draw the enemy's fire and protect the heavily loaded boats, he valiantly placed his craft with its 2 small guns as a shield between the beachhead and the Japanese. When the perilous task of evacuation was nearly completed, Munro was instantly killed by enemy fire, but his crew, 2 of whom were wounded, carried on until the last boat had loaded and cleared the beach. By his outstanding leadership, expert planning, and dauntless devotion to duty, he and his courageous comrades undoubtedly saved the lives of many who otherwise would have perished. He gallantly gave his life for his country.

MURPHY, AUDIE L.

Rank and organization: Second Lieutenant, U.S. Army, Company B 1 5th Infantry, 3d Infantry Division. Place and date: Near Holtzwihr France, 26 January 1945. Entered service at: Dallas, Tex. Birth: Hunt County, near Kingston, Tex. G.O. No.. 65, 9 August 1945. Citation 2d Lt. Murphy commanded Company B, which was attacked by 6 tanks and waves of infantry. 2d Lt. Murphy ordered his men to withdraw to prepared positions in a woods, while he remained forward at his command post and continued to give fire directions to the artillery by telephone. Behind him, to his right, 1 of our tank destroyers received a direct hit and began to burn. Its crew withdrew to the woods. 2d Lt. Murphy continued to direct artillery fire which killed large numbers of the advancing enemy infantry. With the enemy tanks abreast of his position, 2d Lt. Murphy climbed on the burning tank destroyer, which was in danger of blowing up at any moment, and employed its .50 caliber machinegun against the enemy. He was alone and exposed to German fire from 3 sides, but his deadly fire killed dozens of Germans and caused their infantry attack to waver. The enemy tanks, losing infantry support, began to fall back. For an hour the Germans tried every available weapon to eliminate 2d Lt. Murphy, but he continued to hold his position and wiped out a squad which was trying to creep up unnoticed on his right flank. Germans reached as close as 10 yards, only to be mowed down by his fire. He received a leg wound, but ignored it and continued the single-handed fight until his ammunition was exhausted. He then made his way to his company, refused medical attention, and organized the company in a counterattack which forced the Germans to withdraw. His directing of artillery fire wiped out many of the enemy; he killed or wounded about 50. 2d Lt. Murphy's indomitable courage and his refusal to give an inch of ground saved his company from possible encirclement and destruction, and enabled it to hold the woods which had been the enemy's objective.

*MURPHY, FREDERICK C.

Rank and organization: Private First Class, U.S. Army, Medical Detachment, 259th Infantry, 65th Infantry Division. Place and date: Siegfried Line at Saarlautern, Germany, 18 March 1945. Entered service at: Weymouth, Mass. Birth: Boston, Mass. G.O. No.: 21, 26 February 1946. Citation: An aid man, he was wounded in the right shoulder soon after his comrades had jumped off in a dawn attack 18 March 1945, against the Siegfried Line at Saarlautern, Germany. He refused to withdraw for treatment and continued forward, administering first aid under heavy machinegun, mortar, and artillery fire. When the company ran into a thickly sown antipersonnel minefield and began to suffer more and more casualties, he continued to disregard his own wound and unhesitatingly braved the danger of exploding mines, moving about through heavy fire and helping the injured until he stepped on a mine which severed one of his feet. In spite of his grievous wounds, he struggled on with his work, refusing to be evacuated and crawling from man to man administering to them while in great pain and bleeding profusely. He was killed by the blast of another mine which he had dragged himself across in an effort to reach still another casualty. With indomitable courage, and unquenchable spirit of self-sacrifice and supreme devotion to duty which made it possible for him to continue performing his tasks while barely able to move, Pfc. Murphy saved many of his fellow soldiers at the cost of his own life.

MURRAY, CHARLES P., JR.

Rank and organization: First Lieutenant, U.S. Army, Company C, 30th Infantry, 3d Infantry Division. Place and date: Near Kaysersberg, France, 16 December 1944. Entered service at: Wilmington, N.C. Birth: Baltimore, Md. G.O. No.: 63, 1 August 1945. Citation: For commanding Company C, 30th Infantry, displaying supreme courage and heroic initiative near Kaysersberg, France, on 16 December 1944, while leading a reinforced platoon into enemy territory. Descending into a valley beneath hilltop positions held by our troops, he observed a force of 200 Germans pouring deadly mortar, bazooka, machinegun, and small arms fire into an American battalion occupying the crest of the ridge. The enemy's position in a sunken road, though hidden from the ridge, was open to a flank attack by 1st Lt. Murray's patrol but he hesitated to commit so small a force to battle with the superior and strongly disposed enemy. Crawling out ahead of his troops to a vantage point, he called by radio for artillery fire. His shells bracketed the German force, but when he was about to correct the range his radio went dead. He returned to his patrol, secured grenades and a rifle to launch them and went back to his self-appointed outpost. His first shots disclosed his position; the enemy directed heavy fire against him as he methodically fired his missiles into the narrow defile. Again he returned to his patrol. With an automatic rifle and ammunition, he once more moved to his exposed position. Burst after burst he fired into the enemy, killing 20, wounding many others, and completely disorganizing its ranks, which began to withdraw. He prevented the removal of 3 German mortars by knocking out a truck. By that time a mortar had been brought to his support. 1st Lt. Murray directed fire of this weapon, causing further casualties and confusion in the German ranks. Calling on his patrol to follow, he then moved out toward his original objective, possession of a bridge and construction of a roadblock. He captured 10 Germans in foxholes. An eleventh, while pretending to surrender, threw a grenade which knocked him to the ground, inflicting 8 wounds. Though suffering and bleeding profusely, he refused to return to the rear until he had chosen the spot for the block and had seen his men correctly deployed. By his single-handed attack on an overwhelming force and by his intrepid and heroic fighting, 1st Lt. Murray stopped a counterattack, established an advance position against formidable odds, and provided an inspiring example for the men of his command.

*NELSON, WILLIAM L.

Rank and organization: Sergeant, U.S. Army, 60th Infantry, 9th Infantry Division. Place and date: At Djebel Dardys, Northwest of Sedjenane, Tunisia, 24 April 1943. Entered service at: Middletown, Del. Birth: Dover, Del. G.O. No.: 85, 17 December 1943. Citation: For conspicuous gallantry and intrepidity at risk of life, above and beyond the call of duty in action involving actual conflict. On the morning of 24 April

1943, Sgt. Nelson led his section of heavy mortars to a forward position where he placed his guns and men. Under intense enemy artillery, mortar, and small-arms fire, he advanced alone to a chosen observation position from which he directed the laying of a concentrated mortar barrage which successfully halted an initial enemy counterattack. Although mortally wounded in the accomplishment of his mission, and with his duty clearly completed, Sgt. Nelson crawled to a still more advanced observation point and continued to direct the fire of his section. Dying of handgrenade wounds and only 50 yards from the enemy, Sgt. Nelson encouraged his section to continue their fire and by doing so they took a heavy toll of enemy lives. The skill which Sgt. Nelson displayed in this engagement, his courage, and self-sacrificing devotion to duty and heroism resulting in the loss of his life, was a priceless inspiration to our Armed Forces and were in keeping with the highest tradition of the U.S. Army.

NEPPEL, RALPH G.

Rank and organization: Sergeant, U.S. Army, Company M, 329th Infantry, 83d Infantry Division. Place and date: Birgel, Germany, 14 December 1944. Entered service at: Glidden, Iowa. Birth: Willey, Iowa. G.O. No.: 77, 10 September 1945. Citation: He was leader of a machine-gun squad defending an approach to the village of Birgel, Germany, on 14 December 1944, when an enemy tank, supported by 20 infantrymen, counterattacked. He held his fire until the Germans were within 100 yards and then raked the foot soldiers beside the tank killing several of them. The enemy armor continued to press forward and, at the point-blank range of 30 yards, fired a high-velocity shell into the American emplacement, wounding the entire squad. Sgt. Neppel, blown 10 yards from his gun, had 1 leg severed below the knee and suffered other wounds. Despite his injuries and the danger from the onrushing tank and infantry, he dragged himself back to his position on his elbows, remounted his gun and killed the remaining enemy riflemen. Stripped of its infantry protection, the tank was forced to withdraw. By his superb courage and indomitable fighting spirit, Sgt. Neppel inflicted heavy casualties on the enemy and broke a determined counterattack.

NETT, ROBERT P.

Rank and organization: Captain (then Lieutenant), U.S. Army, Company E, 305th Infantry, 77th Infantry Division. Place and date: Near Cognon, Leyte, Philippine Islands, 14 December 1944. Entered service at: Lynchburg, Va. Birth: New Haven, Conn. G.O. No.: 16, 8 February 1946. Citation: He commanded Company E in an attack against a reinforced enemy battalion which had held up the American advance for 2 days from its entrenched positions around a 3-story concrete building. With another infantry company and armored vehicles, Company E advanced against heavy machinegun and other automatic weapons fire with Lt. Nett spearheading the assault against the strongpoint. During the fierce hand-to-hand encounter which ensued, he killed 7 deeply entrenched Japanese with his rifle and bayonet and, although seriously wounded, gallantly continued to lead his men forward, refusing to relinquish his command. Again he was severely wounded, but, still unwilling to retire, pressed ahead with his troops to assure the capture of the objective. Wounded once more in the final assault, he calmly made all arrangements for the resumption of the advance, turned over his command to another officer, and then walked unaided to the rear for medical treatment. By his remarkable courage in continuing forward through sheer determination despite successive wounds, Lt. Nett provided an inspiring example for his men and was instrumental in the capture of a vital strongpoint.

*NEW, JOHN DURY

Rank and organization: Private First Class, U.S. Marine Corps. Born: 12 August 1924, Mobile, Ala. Accredited to: Alabama. Citation: For conspicuous gallantry and intrepidity at the risk of his life above and beyond the call of duty while serving with the 2d Battalion, 7th Marines, 1st Marine Division, in action against enemy Japanese forces on Peleliu Island, Palau Group, 25 September 1944. When a Japanese soldier emerged from a cave in a cliff directly below an observation post and suddenly hurled a grenade into the position from which 2 of our men were directing mortar fire against enemy emplacements, Pfc. New instantly perceived the dire peril to the other marines and, with utter disregard for his own safety, unhesitatingly flung himself upon the grenade and absorbed the full impact of the explosion, thus saving the lives of the 2 observers. Pfc. New's great personal valor and selfless conduct in the face of almost certain death reflect the highest credit upon himself and the U.S. Naval Service. He gallantly gave his life for his country.

NEWMAN, BERYL R.

Rank and organization: First Lieutenant, U.S. Army, 133d Infantry, 34th Infantry Division. Place and date: Near Cisterna, Italy, 26 May 1944. Entered service at: Baraboo, Wis. Birth: Baraboo, Wis. G.O. No.: 5, 15 January 1945. Citation: For conspicuous gallantry and intrepidity above and beyond the call of duty on 26 May 1944. Attacking the strongly held German Anzio-Nettuno defense line near Cisterna, Italy, 1st Lt. Newman, in the lead of his platoon, was suddenly fired upon by 2 enemy machineguns located on the crest of a hill about 100 yards to his front. The 4 scouts with him immediately hit the ground, but 1st Lt. Newman remained standing in order to see the enemy positions and his platoon then about 100 yards behind. Locating the enemy nests, 1st Lt. Newman called back to his platoon and ordered 1 squad to advance to him and the other to flank the enemy to the right. Then, still standing upright in the face of the enemy machinegun fire, 1st Lt. Newman opened up with his tommygun on the enemy nests. From this range, his fire was not effective in covering the advance of his squads, and 1 squad was pinned down by the enemy fire. Seeing that his squad was unable to advance, 1st Lt. Newman, in full view of the enemy gunners and in the face of their continuous fire, advanced alone on the enemy nests. He returned their fire with his tommygun and succeeded in wounding a German in each of the nests. The remaining 2 Germans fled from the position into a nearby house. Three more enemy soldiers then came out of the house and ran toward a third machinegun. 1st Lt. Newman, still relentlessly advancing toward them, killed 1 before he reached the gun, the second before he could fire it. The third fled for his life back into the house. Covering his assault by firing into the doors and windows of the house, 1st Lt. Newman, boldly attacking by himself, called for the occupants to surrender to him. Gaining the house, he kicked in the door and went inside. Although armed with rifles and machine pistols, the 11 Germans there, apparently intimidated, surrendered to the lieutenant without further resistance, 1st Lt. Newman, single-handed, had silenced 3 enemy machineguns, wounded 2 Germans, killed 2 more, and took 11 prisoners. This demonstration of sheer courage, bravery, and willingness to close with the enemy even in the face of such heavy odds, instilled into these green troops the confidence of veterans and reflects the highest traditions of the U.S. Armed Forces.

*NININGER, ALEXANDER R., JR.

Rank and organization: Second Lieutenant, U.S. Army, 57th Infantry, Philippine Scouts. Place and date: Near Abucay, Bataan, Philippine Islands, 12 January 1942. Entered service at: Fort Lauderdale, Fla. Birth: Gainesville, Ga. G.O. No.: 9, 5 February 1942. Citation: For conspicuous gallantry and intrepidity above and beyond the call of duty in action with the enemy near Abucay, Bataan, Philippine Islands, on 12 January 1942. This officer, though assigned to another company not then engaged in combat, voluntarily attached himself to Company K, same regiment, while that unit was being attacked by enemy force superior in firepower. Enemy snipers in trees and foxholes had stopped a counterattack to regain part of position. In hand-to-hand fighting which followed,

2d Lt. Nininger repeatedly forced his way to and into the hostile position. Though exposed to heavy enemy fire, he continued to attack with rifle and handgrenades and succeeded in destroying several enemy groups in foxholes and enemy snipers. Although wounded 3 times, he continued his attacks until he was killed after pushing alone far within the enemy position. When his body was found after recapture of the position, 1 enemy officer and 2 enemy soldiers lay dead around him.

*O'BRIEN, WILLIAM J.

Rank and organization: Lieutenant Colonel, U.S. Army, 1st Battalion, 105th Infantry, 27th Infantry Division. Place and date: At Saipan, Marianas Islands, 20 June through 7 July 1944. Entered service at: Troy, N.Y. Birth: Troy, N.Y. G.O. No.: 35, 9 May 1945. Citation: For conspicuous gallantry and intrepidity at the risk of his life above and beyond the call of duty at Saipan, Marianas Islands, from 20 June through 7 July 1944. When assault elements of his platoon were held up by intense enemy fire, Lt. Col. O'Brien ordered 3 tanks to precede the assault companies in an attempt to knock out the strongpoint. Due to direct enemy fire the tanks' turrets were closed, causing the tanks to lose direction and to fire into our own troops. Lt. Col. O'Brien, with complete disregard for his own safety, dashed into full view of the enemy and ran to the leader's tank, and pounded on the tank with his pistol butt to attract 2 of the tank's crew and, mounting the tank fully exposed to enemy fire, Lt. Col. O'Brien personally directed the assault until the enemy strongpoint had been liquidated. On 28 June 1944, while his platoon was attempting to take a bitterly defended high ridge in the vicinity of Donnay, Lt. Col. O'Brien arranged to capture the ridge by a double envelopment movement of 2 large combat battalions. He personally took control of the maneuver. Lt. Col. O'Brien crossed 1,200 yards of sniper-infested underbrush alone to arrive at a point where 1 of his platoons was being held up by the enemy. Leaving some men to contain the enemy he personally led 4 men into a narrow ravine behind, and killed or drove off all the Japanese manning that strongpoint. In this action he captured S machineguns and one 77-mm. fieldpiece. Lt. Col. O'Brien then organized the 2 platoons for night defense and against repeated counterattacks directed them. Meanwhile he managed to hold ground. On 7 July 1944 his battalion and another battalion were attacked by an overwhelming enemy force estimated at between 3,000 and 5,000 Japanese. With bloody hand-to-hand fighting in progress everywhere, their forward positions were finally overrun by the sheer weight of the enemy numbers. With many casualties and ammunition running low, Lt. Col. O'Brien refused to leave the front lines. Striding up and down the lines, he fired at the enemy with a pistol in each hand and his presence there bolstered the spirits of the men, encouraged them in their fight and sustained them in their heroic stand. Even after he was seriously wounded, Lt. Col. O'Brien refused to be evacuated and after his pistol ammunition was exhausted, he manned a .50 caliber machinegun, mounted on a jeep, and continued firing. When last seen alive he was standing upright firing into the Jap hordes that were then enveloping him. Some time later his body was found surrounded by enemy he had killed His valor was consistent with the highest traditions of the service.

O'CALLAHAN, JOSEPH TIMOTHY

Rank and organization: Commander (Chaplain Corps), U.S. Naval Reserve, U.S.S. Franklin. Place and date: Near Kobe, Japan, 19 March 1945. Entered service at: Massachusetts. Born: 14 May 1904, Boston, Mass. Citation: For conspicuous gallantry and intrepidity at the risk of his life above and beyond the call of duty while serving as chaplain on board the U.S.S. Franklin when that vessel was fiercely attacked by enemy Japanese aircraft during offensive operations near Kobe, Japan, on 19 March 1945. A valiant and forceful leader, calmly braving the perilous barriers of flame and twisted metal to aid his men and his ship, Lt. Comdr. O'Callahan groped his way through smoke-filled corridors to the open flight deck and into the midst of violently exploding bombs, shells, rockets, and other armament. With the ship rocked by incessant explosions, with debris and fragments raining down and fires raging in ever-increasing fury, he ministered to the wounded and dying, comforting and encouraging men of all faiths; he organized and led firefighting crews into the blazing inferno on the flight deck; he directed the jettisoning of live ammunition and the flooding of the magazine; he manned a hose to cool hot, armed bombs rolling dangerously on the listing deck, continuing his efforts, despite searing, suffocating smoke which forced men to fall back gasping and imperiled others who replaced them. Serving with courage, fortitude, and deep spiritual strength, Lt. Comdr. O'Callahan inspired the gallant officers and men of the Franklin to fight heroically and with profound faith in the face of almost certain death and to return their stricken ship to port.

OGDEN, CARLOS C.

Rank and organization: First Lieutenant, U.S. Army, Company K, 314th Infantry, 79th Infantry Division. Place and date: Near Fort du Roule, France, 25 June 1944. Entered service at: Fairmont, Ill. Born: 19 May 1917, Borton, Ill. G.O. No.: 49, 28 June 1945. Citation: On the morning of 25 June 1944, near Fort du Roule, guarding the approaches to Cherbourg, France, 1st Lt. Ogden's company was pinned down by fire from a German 88-mm. gun and 2 machineguns. Arming himself with an M-1 rifle, a grenade launcher, and a number of rifle and handgrenades, he left his company in position and advanced alone, under fire, up the slope toward the enemy emplacements. Struck on the head and knocked down by a glancing machinegun bullet, 1st Lt. Ogden, in spite of his painful wound and enemy fire from close range, continued up the hill. Reaching a vantage point, he silenced the 88mm. gun with a well-placed rifle grenade and then, with handgrenades, knocked out the 2 machineguns, again being painfully wounded. 1st Lt. Ogden's heroic leadership and indomitable courage in alone silencing these enemy weapons inspired his men to greater effort and cleared the way for the company to continue the advance and reach its objectives.

O'HARE, EDWARD HENRY

Rank and organization: Lieutenant, U.S. Navy. Born: 13 March 1914, St. Louis, Mo. Entered service at: St. Louis, Mo. Other Navy awards: Navy Cross, Distinguished Flying Cross with 1 gold star. Citation: For conspicuous gallantry and intrepidity in aerial combat, at grave risk of his life above and beyond the call of duty, as section leader and pilot of Fighting Squadron 3 on 20 February 1942. Having lost the assistance of his teammates, Lt. O'Hare interposed his plane between his ship and an advancing enemy formation of 9 attacking twin-engine heavy bombers. Without hesitation, alone and unaided, he repeatedly attacked this enemy formation, at close range in the face of intense combined machinegun and cannon fire. Despite this concentrated opposition, Lt. O'Hare, by his gallant and courageous action, his extremely skillful marksmanship in making the most of every shot of his limited amount of ammunition, shot down 5 enemy bombers and severely damaged a sixth before they reached the bomb release point. As a result of his gallant action—one of the most daring, if not the most daring, single action in the history of combat aviation—he undoubtedly saved his carrier from serious damage.

O'KANE, RICHARD HETHERINGTON

Rank and organization: Commander, U.S. Navy, commanding U.S.S. Tang. Place and date: Vicinity Philippine Islands, 23 and 24 October 1944. Entered service at: New Hampshire. Born: 2 February 1911, Dover, N.H. Citation: For conspicuous gallantry and intrepidity at the risk of his life above and beyond the call of duty as commanding officer of the U.S.S. Tang operating against 2 enemy Japanese convoys on 23 and 24 October 1944, during her fifth and last war patrol. Boldly maneuvering on the surface into the midst of a heavily escorted convoy,

Comdr. O'Kane stood in the fusillade of bullets and shells from all directions to launch smashing hits on 3 tankers, coolly swung his ship to fire at a freighter and, in a split-second decision, shot out of the path of an onrushing transport, missing it by inches. Boxed in by blazing tankers, a freighter, transport, and several destroyers, he blasted 2 of the targets with his remaining torpedoes and, with pyrotechnics bursting on all sides, cleared the area. Twenty-four hours later, he again made contact with a heavily escorted convoy steaming to support the Leyte campaign with reinforcements and supplies and with crated planes piled high on each unit. In defiance of the enemy's relentless fire, he closed the concentration of ship and in quick succession sent 2 torpedoes each into the first and second transports and an adjacent tanker, finding his mark with each torpedo in a series of violent explosions at less than 1,000-yard range. With ships bearing down from all sides, he charged the enemy at high speed, exploding the tanker in a burst of flame, smashing the transport dead in the water, and blasting the destroyer with a mighty roar which rocked the Tang from stem to stern. Expending his last 2 torpedoes into the remnants of a once powerful convoy before his own ship went down, Comdr. O'Kane, aided by his gallant command, achieved an illustrious record of heroism in combat, enhancing the finest traditions of the U.S. Naval Service.

*OLSON, ARLO L.

Rank and organization: Captain, U.S. Army, 1 5th Infantry, 3d Infantry Division. Place and date: Crossing of the Volturno River, Italy, 13 October 1943. Entered service at: Toronto, S. Dak. Birth: Greenville, lowa. G.O. No.: 71, 31 August 1944. Citation: For conspicuous gallantry and intrepidity at the risk of his life above and beyond the call of duty. On 13 October 1943, when the drive across the Volturno River began, Capt. Olson and his company spearheaded the advance of the regiment through 30 miles of mountainous enemy territory in 13 days. Placing himself at the head of his men, Capt. Olson waded into the chest-deep water of the raging Volturno River and despite pointblank machine-gun fire aimed directly at him made his way to the opposite bank and threw 2 handgrenades into the gun position, killing the crew. When an enemy machinegun 150 yards distant opened fire on his company, Capt. Olson advanced upon the position in a slow, deliberate walk. Although 5 German soldiers threw handgrenades at him from a range of 5 yards, Capt. Olson dispatched them all, picked up a machine pistol and continued toward the enemy. Advancing to within 15 yards of the position he shot it out with the foe, killing 9 and seizing the post. Throughout the next 13 days Capt. Olson led combat patrols, acted as company No. 1 scout and maintained unbroken contact with the enemy. On 27 October 1943, Capt. Olson conducted a platoon in attack on a strongpoint, crawling to within 25 yards of the enemy and then charging the position. Despite continuous machinegun fire which barely missed him, Capt. Olson made his way to the gun and killed the crew with his pistol. When the men saw their leader make this desperate attack they followed him and overran the position. Continuing the advance, Capt. Olson led his company to the next objective at the summit of Monte San Nicola. Although the company to his right was forced to take cover from the furious automatic and small arms fire, which was directed upon him and his men with equal intensity, Capt. Olson waved his company into a skirmish line and despite the fire of a machinegun which singled him out as its sole target led the assault which drove the enemy away. While making a reconnaissance for defensive positions, Capt. Olson was fatally wounded. Ignoring his severe pain, this intrepid officer completed his reconnaissance, Supervised the location of his men in the best defense positions, refused medical aid until all of his men had been cared for, and died as he was being carried down the mountain.

*OLSON, TRUMAN O.

Rank and organization: Sergeant, U.S. Army, Company B, 7th Infantry, 3d Infantry Division. Place and date: Near Cisterna di Littoria, Italy,

30-31 January 1944. Entered service at: Cambridge, Wis. Birth: Christiana, Wis. G.O. No.: 6, 24 January 1945. Citation: For conspicuous gallantry and intrepidity above and beyond the call of duty. Sgt. Olson, a light machine gunner, elected to sacrifice his life to save his company from annihilation. On the night of 30 January 1944, after a 16-hour assault on entrenched enemy positions in the course of which over one-third of Company B became casualties, the survivors dug in behind a horseshoe elevation, placing Sgt. Olson and his crew, with the 1 available machinegun, forward of their lines and in an exposed position to bear the brunt of the expected German counterattack. Although he had been fighting without respite, Sgt. Olson stuck grimly to his post all night while his guncrew was cut down, 1 by 1, by accurate and overwhelming enemy fire. Weary from over 24 hours of continuous battle and suffering from an arm wound, received during the night engagement, Sgt. Olson manned his gun alone, meeting the full force of an all-out enemy assault by approximately 200 men supported by mortar and machinegun fire which the Germans launched at daybreak on the morning of 31 January. After 30 minutes of fighting, Sgt. Olson was mortally wounded, yet, knowing that only his weapons stood between his company and complete destruction, he refused evacuation. For an hour and a half after receiving his second and fatal wound he continued to fire his machinegun, killing at least 20 of the enemy, wounding many more, and forcing the assaulting German elements to withdraw.

ORESKO, NICHOLAS

Rank and organization: Master Sergeant, U.S. Army, Company C, 302d Infantry, 94th Infantry Division. Place and date: Near Tettington, Germany, 23 January 1945. Entered service at: Bayonne, N.J. Birth: Bayonne, N.J. G.O. No.: 95, 30 October 1945. Citation: M/Sgt. Oresko was a platoon leader with Company C, in an attack against strong enemy positions. Deadly automatic fire from the flanks pinned down his unit.

Realizing that a machinegun in a nearby bunker must be eliminated, he swiftly worked ahead alone, braving bullets which struck about him, until close enough to throw a grenade into the German position. He rushed the bunker and, with pointblank rifle fire, killed all the hostile occupants who survived the grenade blast. Another machinegun opened up on him, knocking him down and seriously wounding him in the hip. Refusing to withdraw from the battle, he placed himself at the head of his platoon to continue the assault. As withering machinegun and rifle fire swept the area, he struck out alone in advance of his men to a second bunker. With a grenade, he crippled the dug-in machinegun defending this position and then wiped out the troops manning it with his rifle, completing his second self-imposed, 1-man attack. Although weak from loss of blood, he refused to be evacuated until assured the mission was successfully accomplished. Through quick thinking, indomitable courage, and unswerving devotion to the attack in the face of bitter resistance and while wounded, M /Sgt. Oresko killed 12 Germans, prevented a delay in the assault, and made it possible for Company C to obtain its objective with minimum casualties.

*OWENS, ROBERT ALLEN

Rank and organization: Sergeant, U.S. Marine Corps. Born: 13 September 1920, Greenville, S.C. Accredited to: South Carolina. Citation: For conspicuous gallantry and intrepidity at the risk of his life above and beyond the call of duty while serving with a marine division, in action against enemy Japanese forces during extremely hazardous landing operations at Cape Torokina, Bougainville, Solomon Islands, on 1 November 1943. Forced to pass within disastrous range of a strongly protected, well-camouflaged Japanese 75-mm. regimental gun strategically located on the beach, our landing units were suffering heavy losses in casualties and boats while attempting to approach the beach, and the success of the operations was seriously threatened. Observing the ineffectiveness of marine rifle and grenade attacks against the incessant, devastating fire of the enemy weapon and aware of the urgent need for prompt action, Sgt. Owens unhesitatingly determined to charge the gun bunker from the front and, calling on 4 of his comrades to assist him, carefully placed them to cover the fire of the 2 adjacent hostile bunkers. Choosing a moment that provided a fair opportunity for passing these bunkers, he immediately charged into the mouth of the steadily firing cannon and entered the emplacement through the fire port, driving the guncrew out of the rear door and insuring their destruction before he himself was wounded. Indomitable and aggressive in the face of almost certain death, Sgt. Owens silenced a powerful gun which was of inestimable value to the Japanese defense and, by his brilliant initiative and heroic spirit of self-sacrifice, contributed immeasurably to the success of the vital landing operations. His valiant conduct throughout reflects the highest credit upon himself and the U.S. Naval Service.

*OZBOURN, JOSEPH WILLIAM

Rank and organization: Private, U.S. Marine Corps. Born: 24 October 1919, Herrin, Ill. Accredited to: Illinois. Citation: For conspicuous gallantry and intrepidity at the risk of his life above and beyond the call of duty as a Browning Automatic Rifleman serving with the 1st Battalion, 23d Marines, 4th Marine Division, during the battle for enemy Japanese-held Tinian Island, Marianas Islands, 30 July 1944. As a member of a platoon assigned the mission of clearing the remaining Japanese troops from dugouts and pillboxes along a tree line, Pvt. Ozbourn, flanked by 2 men on either side, was moving forward to throw an armed handgrenade into a dugout when a terrific blast from the entrance severely wounded the 4 men and himself. Unable to throw the grenade into the dugout and with no place to hurl it without endangering the other men, Pvt. Ozbourn unhesitatingly grasped it close to his body and fell upon it, sacrificing his own life to absorb the full impact of the explosion, but saving his comrades. His great personal valor and unwavering loyalty reflect the highest credit upon Pvt. Ozbourn and the U.S. Naval Service. He gallantly gave his life for his country.

PAIGE, MITCHELL

Rank and organization: Platoon Sergeant, U.S. Marine Corps. Place and date: Solomon Islands, 26 October 1942. Entered service at: Pennsylvania. Born: 31 August 1918, Charleroi, Pa. Citation: For extraordinary heroism and conspicuous gallantry in action above and beyond the call of duty while serving with a company of marines in combat against enemy Japanese forces in the Solomon Islands on 26 October 1942. When the enemy broke through the line directly in front of his position, P/Sgt. Paige, commanding a machinegun section with fearless determination, continued to direct the fire of his gunners until all his men were either killed or wounded. Alone, against the deadly hail of Japanese shells, he fought with his gun and when it was destroyed, took over another, moving from gun to gun, never ceasing his withering fire against the advancing hordes until reinforcements finally arrived. Then, forming a new line, he dauntlessly and aggressively led a bayonet charge, driving the enemy back and preventing a breakthrough in our lines. His great personal valor and unyielding devotion to duty were in keeping with the highest traditions of the U.S. Naval Service.

*PARLE, JOHN JOSEPH

Rank and organization: Ensign, U.S. Naval Reserve. Born: 26 May 1920, Omaha, Nebr. Accredited to: Nebraska. Citation: For valor and courage above and beyond the call of duty as Officer-in-Charge of Small Boats in the U.S.S. LST 375 during the amphibious assault on the island of Sicily, 9-10 July 1943. Realizing that a detonation of explosives would prematurely disclose to the enemy the assault about to be carried out, and with full knowledge of the peril involved, Ens. Parle unhesitatingly risked his life to extinguish a smoke pot accidentally ignited in a boat carrying charges of high explosives, detonating fuses and ammunition. Undaunted by fire and blinding smoke, he entered the craft, quickly snuffed out a burning fuse, and after failing in his desperate efforts to extinguish the fire pot, finally seized it with both hands and threw it over the side. Although he succumbed a week later from smoke and fumes inhaled, Ens. Parle's heroic self-sacrifice prevented grave damage to the ship and personnel and insured the security of a vital mission. He gallantly gave his life in the service of his country.

*PARRISH, LAVERNE

Rank and organization: Technician 4th Grade, U.S. Army, Medical Detachment, 161st Infantry, 25th Infantry Division . Place and date: Binalonan, Luzon, Philippine Islands, 18-24 January 1945. Entered service at: Ronan, Mont. Birth: Knox City, Mo. G.O. No.: 55, 13 July 1945. Citation: He was medical aid man with Company C during the fighting in Binalonan, Luzon, Philippine Islands. On the 18th, he observed 2 wounded men under enemy fire and immediately went to their rescue. After moving 1 to cover, he crossed 25 yards of open ground to administer aid to the second. In the early hours of the 24th, his company, crossing an open field near San Manuel, encountered intense enemy fire and was ordered to withdraw to the cover of a ditch. While treating the casualties, Technician Parrish observed 2 wounded still in the field. Without hesitation he left the ditch, crawled forward under enemy fire, and in 2 successive trips brought both men to safety. He next administered aid to 12 casualties in the same field, crossing and re-crossing the open area raked by hostile fire. Making successive trips, he then brought 3 wounded in to cover. After treating nearly all of the 37 casualties suffered by his company, he was mortally wounded by mortar fire, and shortly after was killed. The indomitable spirit, intrepidity, and gallantry of Technician Parrish saved many lives at the cost of his own.

*PEASE, HARL, JR. (Air Mission)

Rank and organization: Captain, U.S. Army Air Corps, Heavy Bombardment Squadron. Place and date: Near Rabaul, New Britain, 6-7 August 1942. Entered service at: Plymouth, N.H. Birth: Plymouth, N.H. G.O. No.: 59, 4 November 1942. Citation: For conspicuous gallantry and intrepidity above and beyond the call of duty in action with the enemy on 6-7 August 1942. When 1 engine of the bombardment airplane of which he was pilot failed during a bombing mission over New Guinea, Capt. Pease was forced to return to a base in Australia. Knowing that all available airplanes of his group were to participate the next day in an attack on an enemy-held airdrome near Rabaul, New Britain, although he was not scheduled to take part in this mission, Capt. Pease selected the most serviceable airplane at this base and prepared it for combat, knowing that it had been found and declared unserviceable for combat missions. With the members of his combat crew, who volunteered to accompany him, he rejoined his squadron at Port Moresby, New Guinea, at 1 a.m. on 7 August, after having flown almost continuously since early the preceding morning. With only 3 hours' rest, he took off with his squadron for the attack. Throughout the long flight to Rabaul, New Britain, he managed by skillful flying of his unserviceable airplane to maintain his position in the group. When the formation was intercepted by about 30 enemy fighter airplanes before reaching the target, Capt. Pease, on the wing which bore the brunt of the hostile attack, by gallant action and the accurate shooting by his crew, succeeded in destroying several Zeros before dropping his bombs on the hostile base as planned, this in spite of continuous enemy attacks. The fight with the enemy pursuit lasted 25 minutes until the group dived into cloud cover. After leaving the target, Capt. Pease's aircraft fell behind the balance of the group due to unknown difficulties as a result of the combat, and was unable to reach this cover before the enemy pursuit succeeded in igniting 1 of his bomb bay tanks. He was seen to drop the flaming tank. It is believed that Capt. Pease's airplane and crew were subsequently shot down in flames, as they did not return to their base. In ??voluntarily performing this mission Capt. Pease contributed materially to the success of the group, and displayed high devotion to duty, valor, and complete contempt for personal danger. His undaunted bravery has been a great insplration to the officers and men of his unit.

*PEDEN, FORREST E.

Rank and organization: Technician 5th Grade, U.S. Army, Battery C, 10th Field Artillery Battalion, 3d Infantry Division. Place and date: Near Biesheim, France, 3 February 1945. Entered service at: Wathena, Kans. Birth: St. Joseph, Mo. G.O. No.: 18, 13 February 1946. Citation: He was a forward artillery observer when the group of about 45 infantrymen with whom he was advancing was ambushed in the uncertain light of a waning moon. Enemy forces outnumbering the Americans by 4 to 1 poured withering artillery, mortar, machinegun, and small-arms fire into the stricken unit from the flanks, forcing our men to seek the cover of a ditch which they found already occupied by enemy foot troops. As the opposing infantrymen struggled in hand-to-hand combat, Technician Peden courageously went to the assistance of 2 wounded soldiers and rendered first aid under heavy fire. With radio communications inoperative, he realized that the unit would be wiped out unless help could be secured from the rear. On his own initiative, he ran 800 yards to the battalion command post through a hail of bullets which pierced his jacket and there secured 2 light tanks to go to the relief of his hard-pressed comrades. Knowing the terrible risk involved, he climbed upon the hull of the lead tank and guided it into battle. Through a murderous concentration of fire the tank lumbered onward, bullets and shell fragments ricocheting from its steel armor within inches of the completely exposed rider, until it reached the ditch. As it was about to go into action it was turned into a flaming pyre by a direct hit which killed Technician Peden. However, his intrepidity and gallant sacrifice was not in vain. Attracted by the light from the burning tank, reinforcements found the beleaguered Americans and drove off the enemy.

*PENDLETON, JACK J.

Rank and organization: Staff Sergeant, U.S. Army, Company I, 120th Infantry, 30th Infantry Division. Place and date: Bardenberg, Germany, 12 October 1944. Entered service at: Yakima, Wash. Birth: Sentinel Butte, N. Dak. G.O. No.: 24, 6 April 1945. Citation: For conspicuous gallantry and intrepidity at the risk of his life above and beyond the call of duty on 12 October 1944. When Company I was advancing on the town of Bardenberg, Germany, they reached a point approximately two-thirds of the distance through the town when they were pinned down by fire from a nest of enemy machineguns. This enemy strong point was protected by a lone machinegun strategically placed at an intersection and firing down a street which offered little or no cover or concealment for the advancing troops. The elimination of this protecting machinegun was imperative in order that the stronger position it protected could be neutralized. After repeated and unsuccessful attempts had been made to knock out this position, S/Sgt. Pendleton volunteered to lead his squad in an attempt to neutralize this strongpoint. S/Sgt. Pendleton started his squad slowly forward, crawling about 10 yards in front of his men in the advance toward the enemy gun. After advancing approximately 130 yards under the withering fire, S/Sgt. Pendleton was seriously wounded in the leg by a burst from the gun he was assaulting. Disregarding his grievous wound, he ordered his men to remain where they were, and with a supply of handgrenades he slowly and painfully worked his way forward alone. With no hope of surviving the veritable hail of machinegun fire which he deliberately drew onto himself, he succeeded in advancing to within 10 yards of the enemy position when he was instantly killed by a burst from the enemy gun. By deliberately diverting the attention of the enemy machine gunners upon himself, a second squad was able to advance, undetected, and with the help of S/Sgt. Pendleton's squad, neutralized the lone machinegun, while another platoon of his company advanced up the intersecting street and knocked out the machinegun nest which the first gun had been covering. S/Sgt. Pendleton's sacrifice enabled the entire company to continue the advance and complete their mission at a critical phase of the action.

*PEREGORY, FRANK D.

Rank and organization: Technical Sergeant, U.S. Army, Company K 116th Infantry, 29th Infantry Division. Place and date: Grandcampe France, 8 June 1944. Entered service at: Charlottesville, Va. Born. 10 April 1915, Esmont, Va. G.O. No.: 43, 30 May 1945. Citation: On 8 June 1944, the 3d Battalion of the 116th Infantry was advancing on the strongly held German defenses at Grandcampe, France, when the leading elements were suddenly halted by decimating machinegun fire from a firmly entrenched enemy force on the high ground overlooking the town. After numerous attempts to neutralize the enemy position by supporting artillery and tank fire had proved ineffective, T/Sgt. Peregory, on his own initiative, advanced up the hill under withering fire, and worked his way to the crest where he discovered an entrenchment leading to the main enemy fortifications 200 yards away. Without hesitating, he leaped into the trench and moved toward the emplacement. Encountering a squad of enemy riflemen, he fearlessly attacked them with handgrenades and bayonet, killed 8 and forced 3 to surrender. Continuing along the trench, he single-handedly forced the surrender of 32 more riflemen, captured the machine gunners, and opened the way for the leading elements of the battalion to advance and secure its objective. The extraordinary gallantry and aggressiveness displayed by T/Sgt. Peregory are exemplary of the highest tradition of the armed forces.

*PEREZ, MANUEL, JR.

Rank and organization: Private First Class, U.S. Army, Company A 511th Parachute Infantry, 11th Airborne Division. Place and date: Fort William McKinley, Luzon, Philippine Islands, 13 February 1945. Entered service at. Chicago, Ill. Born: 3 March 1923 Oklahoma City, Okla. G.O. No.: 124, 27 December 1945. Citation: He was lead scout for Company A, which had destroyed 11 of 12 pillboxes in a strongly fortified sector defending the approach to enemy-held Fort William McKinley on Luzon, Philippine Islands. In the reduction of these pillboxes, he killed 5 Japanese in the open and blasted others in pillboxes with grenades. Realizing the urgent need for taking the last emplacement, which contained 2 twin-mount .50-caliber dual-purpose machineguns, he took a circuitous route to within 20 yards of the position, killing 4 of the enemy in his advance. He threw a grenade into the pillbox, and, as the crew started withdrawing through a tunnel just to the rear of the emplacement, shot and killed 4 before exhausting his clip. He had reloaded and killed 4 more when an escaping Japanese threw his rifle with fixed bayonet at him. In warding off this thrust, his own rifle was knocked to the ground. Seizing the Jap rifle, he continued firing, killing 2 more of the enemy. He rushed the remaining Japanese, killed 3 of them with the butt of the rifle and entered the pillbox, where he bayoneted the 1 surviving hostile soldier. Single-handedly, he killed 18 of the enemy in neutralizing the position that had held up the advance of his entire company. Through his courageous determination and heroic disregard of grave danger, Pfc. Perez made possible the successful advance of his unit toward a valuable objective and provided a lasting inspiration for his comrades.

*PETERS, GEORGE J.

Rank and organization: Private, U.S. Army, Company G, 507th Parachute Infantry, 17th Airborne Division. Place and date: Near Fluren, Germany,

24 March 1945. Entered service at: Cranston, R.I. Birth: Cranston, R.I. G.O. No.: 16, 8 February 1946. Citation: Pvt. Peters, a platoon radio operator with Company G, made a descent into Germany near Fluren, east of the Rhine. With 10 others, he landed in a field about 75 yards from a German machinegun supported by riflemen, and was immediately pinned down by heavy, direct fire. The position of the small unit seemed hopeless with men struggling to free themselves of their parachutes in a hail of bullets that cut them off from their nearby equipment bundles, when Pvt. Peters stood up without orders and began a 1-man charge against the hostile emplacement armed only with a rifle and grenades. His single-handed assault immediately drew the enemy fire away from his comrades. He had run halfway to his objective, pitting rifle fire against that of the machinegun, when he was struck and knocked to the ground by a burst. Heroically, he regained his feet and struggled onward. Once more he was torn by bullets, and this time he was unable to rise. With gallant devotion to his self-imposed mission, he crawled directly into the fire that had mortally wounded him until close enough to hurl grenades which knocked out the machinegun, killed 2 of its operators, and drove protecting riflemen from their positions into the safety of a woods. By his intrepidity and supreme sacrifice, Pvt. Peters saved the lives of many of his fellow soldiers and made it possible for them to reach their equipment, organize, and seize their first objective.

*PETERSON, GEORGE

Rank and organization: Staff Sergeant, U.S. Army, Company K, 18th Infantry, 1st Infantry Division. Place and date: Near Eisern, Germany, 30 March 1945. Entered service at: Brooklyn, N.Y. Birth: Brooklyn, N.Y. G.O. No.: 88, 17 October 1945. Citation: He was an acting platoon sergeant with Company K, near Eisern, Germany. When his company encountered an enemy battalion and came under heavy small-arms, machinegun, and mortar fire, the 2d Platoon was given the mission of flanking the enemy positions while the remaining units attacked frontally. S/Sgt. Peterson crept and crawled to a position in the lead and motioned for the 2d Platoon to follow. A mortar shell fell close by and severely wounded him in the legs, but, although bleeding and suffering intense pain, he refused to withdraw and continued forward. Two hostile machineguns went into action at close range. Braving this grazing fire, he crawled steadily toward the guns and worked his way alone to a shallow draw, where, despite the hail of bullets, he raised himself to his knees and threw a grenade into the nearest machinegun nest, silencing the weapon and killing or wounding all its crew. The second gun was immediately turned on him, but he calmly and deliberately threw a second grenade which rocked the position and killed all 4 Germans who occupied it. As he continued forward he was spotted by an enemy rifleman, who shot him in the arm. Undeterred, he crawled some 20 yards until a third machinegun opened fire on him. By almost superhuman effort, weak from loss of blood and suffering great pain, he again raised himself to his knees and fired a grenade from his rifle, killing 3 of the enemy guncrew and causing the remaining one to flee. With the first objective seized, he was being treated by the company aid man when he observed 1 of his outpost men seriously wounded by a mortar burst. He wrenched himself from the hands of the aid man and began to crawl forward to assist his comrade, whom he had almost reached when he was struck and fatally wounded by an enemy bullet. S/Sgt. Peterson, by his gallant, intrepid actions, unrelenting fighting spirit, and outstanding initiative, silenced 3 enemy machineguns against great odds and while suffering from severe wounds, enabling his company to advance with minimum casualties.

*PETERSON, OSCAR VERNER

Rank and organization: Chief Watertender, U.S. Navy. Born: 27 August 1899, Prentice, Wis. Accredited to: Wisconsin. Citation: For extraordinary courage and conspicuous heroism above and beyond the call of duty while in charge of a repair party during an attack on the U .S .S.

Neosho by enemy Japanese aerial forces on 7 May 1942. Lacking assistance because of injuries to the other members of his repair party and severely wounded himself, Peterson, with no concern for his own life, closed the bulkhead stop valves and in so doing received additional burns which resulted in his death. His spirit of self-sacrifice and loyalty, characteristic of a fine seaman, was in keeping with the highest traditions of the U.S. Naval Service. He gallantly gave his life in the service of his country.

*PETRARCA, FRANK J.

Rank and organization: Private First Class, U.S. Army, Medical Detachment, 145th Infantry, 37th Infantry Division. Place and date: At Horseshoe Hill, New Georgia, Solomon Islands, 27 July 1943. Entered service at: Cleveland, Ohio. Birth: Cleveland, Ohio. G.O. No.: 86, 23 December 1943. Citation: For conspicuous gallantry and intrepidity in action above and beyond the call of duty. Pfc. Petrarca advanced with the leading troop element to within 100 yards of the enemy fortifications where mortar and small-arms fire caused a number of casualties. Singling out the most seriously wounded, he worked his way to the aid of Pfc. Scott, Iying within 75 yards of the enemy, whose wounds were so serious that he could not even be moved out of the direct line of fire Pfc Petrarca fearlessly administered first aid to Pfc. Scott and 2 other soldiers and shielded the former until his death. On 29 July 1943, Pfc. Petrarca. during an intense mortar barrage, went to the aid of his sergeant who had been partly buried in a foxhole under the debris of a shell explosion, dug him out, restored him to consciousness and caused his evacuation. On 31 July 1943 and against the warning of a fellow soldier, he went to the aid of a mortar fragment casualty where his path over the crest of a hill exposed him to enemy observation from only 20 yards distance. A target for intense knee mortar and automatic fire, he resolutely worked his way to within 2 yards of his objective where he was mortally wounded by hostile mortar fire. Even on the threshold of death he continued to display valor and contempt for the foe, raising himself to his knees, this intrepid soldier shouted defiance at the enemy, made a last attempt to reach his wounded comrade and fell in glorious death.

PHARRIS, JACKSON CHARLES

Rank and organization: Lieutenant, U.S. Navy, U.S.S. California. Place and date: Pearl Harbor, Territory of Hawaii, 7 December 1941. Entered service at: California. Born: 26 June 1912, Columbus, Ga. Citation: For conspicuous gallantry and intrepidity at the risk of his life above and beyond the call of duty while attached to the U.S.S. California during the surprise enemy Japanese aerial attack on Pearl Harbor, Territory of Hawaii, 7 December 1941. In charge of the ordnance repair party on the third deck when the first Japanese torpedo struck almost directly under his station, Lt. (then Gunner) Pharris was stunned and severely injured by the concussion which hurled him to the overhead and back to the deck. Quickly recovering, he acted on his own initiative to set up a hand-supply ammunition train for the antiaircraft guns. With water and oil rushing in where the port bulkhead had been torn up from the deck, with many of the remaining crewmembers overcome by oil fumes, and the ship without power and listing heavily to port as a result of a second torpedo hit, Lt. Pharris ordered the shipfitters to counterflood. Twice rendered unconscious by the nauseous fumes and handicapped by his painful injuries, he persisted in his desperate efforts to speed up the supply of ammunition and at the same time repeatedly risked his life to enter flooding compartments and drag to safety unconscious shipmates who were gradually being submerged in oil. By his inspiring leadership, his valiant efforts and his extreme loyalty to his ship and her crew, he saved many of his shipmates from death and was largely responsible for keeping the California in action during the attack. His heroic conduct throughout this first eventful engagement of

World War 11 reflects the highest credit upon Lt. Pharris and enhances the finest traditions of the U.S. Naval Service.

*PHELPS, WESLEY

Rank and organization: Private, U.S. Marine Corps Reserve. Born: 12 June 1923, Neafus, Ky. Accredited to: Kentucky. Citation: For conspicuous gallantry and intrepidity at the risk of his life above and beyond the call of duty while serving with the 3d Battalion, 7th Marines, 1st Marine Division, in action against enemy Japanese forces on Peleliu Island, Palau Group, during a savage hostile counterattack on the night of 4 October 1944. Stationed with another marine in an advanced position when a Japanese handgrenade landed in his foxhole Pfc. Phelps instantly shouted a warning to his comrade and rolled over on the deadly bomb, absorbing with his own body the full, shattering Impact of the exploding charge. Courageous and indomitable, Pfc. Phelps fearlessly gave his life that another might be spared serious injury, and his great valor and heroic devotion to duty in the face of certain death reflect the highest credit upon himself and the U.S. Naval Service. He gallantly gave his life for his country.

*PHILLIPS, GEORGE

Rank and organization: Private, U.S. Marine Corps Reserve. Born 14 July 1926, Rich Hill, Mo. Entered service at: Labadie, Mo. Citation. For conspicuous gallantry and intrepidity at the risk of his life above and beyond the call of duty while serving with the 2d Battalion, 28th Marines, 5th Marine Division, in action against enemy Japanese forces during the seizure of Iwo Jima in the Volcano Islands, on 14 March 1945. Standing the foxhole watch while other members of his squad rested after a night of bitter handgrenade fighting against infiltrating Japanese troops, Pvt. Phillips was the only member of his unit alerted when an enemy handgrenade was tossed into their midst. Instantly shouting a warning, he unhesitatingly threw himself on the deadly missile, absorbing the shattering violence of the exploding charge in his own body and protecting his comrades from serious injury. Stouthearted and indomitable, Pvt. Phillips willingly yielded his own life that his fellow marines might carry on the relentless battle against a fanatic enemy. His superb valor and unfaltering spirit of self-sacrifice in the face of certain death reflect the highest credit upon himself and upon the U.S. Naval Service. He gallantly gave his life for his country.

PIERCE, FRANCIS JUNIOR

Rank and organization: Pharmacist's Mate First Class, U.S. Navy serving with 2d Battalion, 24th Marines, 4th Marine Division. Place and date: Iowa Jima, 15 and 16 March 1945. Entered service at Iowa Born: 7 December 1924, Earlville, Iowa. Citation: For conspicuous gallantry and intrepidity at the risk of his life above and beyond the call of duty while attached to the 2d Battalion, 24th Marines, 4th Marine Division, during the Iwo Jima campaign, 15 and 16 March 1945. Almost continuously under fire while carrying out the most dangerous volunteer assignments, Pierce gained valuable knowledge of the terrain and disposition of troops. Caught in heavy enemy rifle and machinegun fire which wounded a corpsman and 2 of the 8 stretcher bearers who were carrying 2 wounded marines to a forward aid station on 15 March, Pierce quickly took charge of the party, carried the newly wounded men to a sheltered position, and rendered first aid. After directing the evacuation of 3 of the casualties, he stood in the open to draw the enemy's fire and, with his weapon blasting, enabled the litter bearers to reach cover. Turning his attention to the other 2 casualties he was attempting to stop the profuse bleeding of 1 man when a Japanese fired from a cave less than 20 yards away and wounded his patient again. Risking his own life to save his patient, Pierce deliberately exposed himself to draw the attacker from the cave and destroyed him with the last of his ammunition Then lifting the wounded man to his back, he advanced unarmed through deadly rifle fire across 200 feet of open terrain. Despite exhaustion and in the face of warnings against such a suicidal mission, he again traversed the same fire-swept path to rescue the remaining marine. On the following morning, he led a combat patrol to the sniper nest and, while aiding a stricken marine, was seriously wounded. Refusing aid for himself, he directed treatment for the casualty, at the same time maintaining protective fire for his comrades. Completely fearless, completely devoted to the care of his patients, Pierce inspired the entire battalion. His valor in the face of extreme peril sustains and enhances the finest traditions of the U.S. Naval Service.

*PINDER, JOHN J., JR.

Rank and organization: Technician Fifth Grade, U.S. Army, 16th Infantry, 1st Infantry Division. Place and date: Near Colleville-sur-Mer, France, 6 June 1944. Entered .service at: Burgettstown, Pa. Birth: McKees Rocks, Pa. G.O. No.: 1, 4 January 1945. Citation: For conspicuous gallantry and intrepidity above and beyond the call of duty on 6 June 1944, near Colleville-sur-Mer, France. On D-day, Technician 5th Grade Pinder landed on the coast 100 yards off shore under devastating enemy machinegun and artillery fire which caused severe casualties among the boatload. Carrying a vitally important radio, he struggled towards shore in waist-deep water. Only a few yards from his craft he was hit by enemy fire and was gravely wounded. Technician 5th Grade Pinder never stopped. He made shore and delivered the radio. Refusing to take cover afforded, or to accept medical attention for his wounds, Technician 5th Grade Pinder, though terribly weakened by loss of blood and in fierce pain, on 3 occasions went into the fire-swept surf to salvage communication equipment. He recovered many vital parts and equipment, including another workable radio. On the 3rd trip he was again hit, suffering machinegun bullet wounds in the legs. Still this valiant soldier would not stop for rest or medical attention. Remaining exposed to heavy enemy fire, growing steadily weaker, he aided in establishing the vital radio communication on the beach. While so engaged this dauntless soldier was hit for the third time and killed. The indomitable courage and personal bravery of Technician 5th Grade Pinder was a magnificent inspiration to the men with whom he served.

POPE, EVERETT PARKER

Rank and organization: Captain, U.S. Marine Corps, Company C, 1st Battalion, 1st Marines, 1st Marine Division. Place and date: Peleliu Island, Palau group, 19-20 September 1944. Entered service at: Massachusetts. Born: 16 July 1919, Milton, Mass. Citation: For conspicuous gallantry and intrepidity at the risk of his life above and beyond the call of duty while serving as commanding officer of Company C, 1st Battalion, 1st Marines, 1st Marine Division, during action against enemy Japanese forces on Peleliu Island, Palau group, on 19-20 September 1944. Subjected to pointblank cannon fire which caused heavy casualties and badly disorganized his company while assaulting a steep coral hill, Capt. Pope rallied his men and gallantly led them to the summit in the face of machinegun, mortar, and sniper fire. Forced by widespread hostile attack to deploy the remnants of his company thinly in order to hold the ground won, and with his machineguns out of order and insufficient water and ammunition, he remained on the exposed hill with 12 men and 1 wounded officer determined to hold through the night. Attacked continuously with grenades, machineguns, and rifles from 3 sides, he and his valiant men fiercely beat back or destroyed the enemy, resorting to hand-to-hand combat as the supply of ammunition dwindled, and still maintaining his lines with his 8 remaining riflemen when daylight brought more deadly fire and he was ordered to withdraw. His valiant leadership against devastating odds while protecting the units below from heavy Japanese attack reflects the highest credit upon Capt. Pope and the U.S. Naval Service.

*POWER, JOHN VINCENT

Rank and organization. First Lieutenant, U.S. Marine Corps. Born: 20 November 1918, Worcester, Mass. Appointed from: Massachusetts. Citation: For conspicuous gallantry and intrepidity at the risk of his life above and beyond the call of duty as platoon leader, attached to the 4th Marine Division, during the landing and battle of Namur Island, Kwajalein Atoll, Marshall Islands, 1 February 1944. Severely wounded in the stomach while setting a demolition charge on a Japanese pillbox, 1st Lt. Power was steadfast in his determination to remain in action. Protecting his wound with his left hand and firing with his right, he courageously advanced as another hostile position was taken under attack, fiercely charging the opening made by the explosion and emptying his carbine into the pillbox. While attempting to reload and continue the attack, 1st Lt. Power was shot again in the stomach and head and collapsed in the doorway. His exceptional valor, fortitude and indomitable fighting spirit in the face of withering enemy fire were in keeping with the highest traditions of the U.S. Naval Service. He gallantly gave his life for his country.

*POWERS, JOHN JAMES

Rank and organization: Lieutenant, U.S. Navy. Born: 13 July 1912, New York City, N.Y. Accredited to: New York. Other Navy award: Air Medal with 1 gold star. Citation: For distinguished and conspicuous gallantry and intrepidity at the risk of his life above and beyond the call of duty, while pilot of an airplane of Bombing Squadron 5, Lt. Powers participated, with his squadron, in 5 engagements with Japanese forces in the Coral Sea area and adjacent waters during the period 4 to 8 May 1942. Three attacks were made on enemy objectives at or near Tulagi on 4 May. In these attacks he scored a direct hit which instantly demolished a large enemy gunboat or destroyer and is credited with 2 close misses, 1 of which severely damaged a large aircraft tender, the other damaging a

20,000-ton transport. He fearlessly strafed a gunboat, firing all his ammunition into it amid intense antiaircraft fire. This gunboat was then observed to be leaving a heavy oil slick in its wake and later was seen beached on a nearby island. On 7 May, an attack was launched against an enemy airplane carrier and other units of the enemy's invasion force. He fearlessly led his attack section of 3 Douglas Dauntless dive bombers, to attack the carrier. On this occasion he dived in the face of heavy antiaircraft fire, to an altitude well below the safety altitude, at the risk of his life and almost certain damage to his own plane, in order that he might positively obtain a hit in a vital part of the ship, which would insure her complete destruction. This bomb hit was noted by many pilots and observers to cause a tremendous explosion engulfing the ship in a mass of flame, smoke, and debris. The ship sank soon after. That evening, in his capacity as Squadron Gunnery Officer, Lt. Powers gave a lecture to the squadron on point-of-aim and diving technique. During this discourse he advocated low release point in order to insure greater accuracy; yet he stressed the danger not only from enemy fire and the resultant low pull-out, but from own bomb blast and bomb fragments. Thus his low-dive bombing attacks were deliberate and premeditated, since he well knew and realized the dangers of such tactics, but went far beyond the call of duty in order to further the cause which he knew to be right. The next morning, 8 May, as the pilots of the attack group left the ready room to man planes, his indomitable spirit and leadership were well expressed in his own words, "Remember the folks back home are counting on us. 1 am going to get a hit if 1 have to lay it on their flight deck." He led his section of dive bombers down to the target from an altitude of 18,000 feet, through a wall of bursting antiaircraft shells and into the face of enemy fighter planes. Again, completely disregarding the safety altitude and without fear or concern for his safety, Lt. Powers courageously pressed home his attack, almost to the very deck of an enemy carrier and did not release his bomb until he was sure of a direct hit. He was last seen attempting recovery from his dive at the extremely low altitude of 200 feet, and amid a terrific barrage of shell and bomb fragments, smoke, flame and debris from the stricken vessel.

POWERS, LEO J.

Rank and organization: Private First Class, U.S. Army, 133d Infantry, 34th Infantry Division. Place and date: Northwest of Cassino, Italy, 3 February 1944. Entered service at: Alder Gulch, Mont. Birth: Anselmo, Nebr. G.O. No.: 5, 15 January 1945. Citation: For conspicuous gallantry and intrepidity at risk of life above and beyond the call of duty. On 3 February 1944, this soldier's company was assigned the mission of capturing Hill 175, the key enemy strong point northwest of Cassino, Italy. The enemy, estimated to be at least 50 in strength, supported by machineguns emplaced in 3 pillboxes and mortar fire from behind the hill, was able to pin the attackers down and inflict 8 casualties. The company was unable to advance, but Pfc. Powers, a rifleman in 1 of the assault platoons, on his own initiative and in the face of the terrific fire, crawled forward to assault 1 of the enemy pillboxes which he had spotted. Armed with 2 handgrenades and well aware that if the enemy should see him it would mean almost certain death, Pfc. Powers crawled up the hill to within 15 yards of the enemy pillbox. Then standing upright in full view of the enemy gunners in order to throw his grenade into the small opening in the roof, he tossed a grenade into the pillbox. At this close, the grenade entered the pillbox, killed 2 of the occupants and 3 or 4 more fled the position, probably wounded. This enemy gun silenced, the center of the line was able to move forward again, but almost immediately came under machinegun fire from a second enemy pillbox on the left flank. Pfc. Powers, however, had located this pillbox, and crawled toward it with absolutely no cover if the enemy should see him. Raising himself in full view of the enemy gunners about 15 feet from the pillbox, Pfc. Powers threw his grenade into the pillbox, silencing this gun, killing another German and probably wounding 3 or 4 more who fled. Pfc. Powers, still acting on his own initiative, commenced crawling toward the third enemy pillbox in the face of heavy machine-pistol and machinegun fire. Skillfully availing himself of the meager cover and concealment, Pfc. Powers crawled up to within 10 yards of this pillbox fully exposed himself to the enemy gunners, stood upright and tossed the 2 grenades into the small opening in the roof of the pillbox. His grenades killed 2 of the enemy and 4 more, all wounded, came out and surrendered to Pfc. Powers, who was now unarmed. Pfc. Powers had worked his way over the entire company front, and against tremendous odds had single-handedly broken the backbone of this heavily defended and strategic enemy position, and enabled his regiment to advance into the city of Cassino. Pfc. Powers' fighting determination and intrepidity in battle exemplify the highest traditions of the U.S. Armed Forces.

PRESTON, ARTHUR MURRAY

Rank and organization: Lieutenant, U.S. Navy Reserve, Torpedo Boat Squadron 33. Place and date. Wasile Bay, Halmahera Island, 16 September 1944. Entered service at: Maryland. Born: 1 November 1913, Washington, D.C. Citation: For conspicuous gallantry and intrepidity at the risk of his life above and beyond the call of duty as commander, Motor Torpedo Boat Squadron 33, while effecting the rescue of a Navy pilot shot down in Wasile Bay, Halmahera Island, less than 200 yards from a strongly defended Japanese dock and supply area, 16 September 1944. Volunteering for a perilous mission unsuccessfully attempted by the pilot's squadron mates and a PBY plane, Lt. Comdr. (then Lieutenant) Preston led PT-489 and PT-363 through 60 miles of restricted, heavily mined waters. Twice turned back while running the gauntlet of fire from powerful coastal defense guns guarding the 11-mile strait at the entrance to the bay, he was again turned back by furious fire in the immediate area of the downed airman. Aided by an aircraft smokescreen, he finally succeeded in reaching his objective and, under vicious fire delivered at 150-yard range, took the pilot aboard and cleared the area, sinking a small hostile cargo vessel with 40-mm. fire during retirement. Increasingly vulnerable when covering aircraft were forced to leave because of insufficient fuel, Lt. Comdr. Preston raced PT boats 489 and 363 at high speed for 20 minutes through shell-splashed water and across minefields to safety. Under continuous fire for 2l/2 hours, Lt. Comdr. Preston successfully achieved a mission considered suicidal in its tremendous hazards, and brought his boats through without personnel casualties and with but superficial damage from shrapnel. His exceptional daring and great personal valor enhance the finest traditions of the U.S. Naval Service.

*PRUSSMAN, ERNEST W.

Rank and organization: Private First Class, U.S. Army, 13th Infantry, 8th Infantry Division. Place and date: Near Les Coates, Brittany, France, 8 September 1944. Entered service at: Brighton, Mass. Birth: Baltimore, Md. G.O. No.: 31, 17 April 1945. Citation: For conspicuous gallantry and intrepidity at risk of life above and beyond the call of duty on 8 September 1944, near Les Coates, Brittany, France. When the advance of the flank companies of 2 battalions was halted by intense enemy mortar, machinegun, and sniper fire from a fortified position on his left, Pfc. Prussman maneuvered his squad to assault the enemy fortifications. Hurdling a hedgerow, he came upon 2 enemy riflemen whom he disarmed. After leading his squad across an open field to the next hedgerow, he advanced to a machinegun position, destroyed the gun, captured its crew and 2 riflemen. Again advancing ahead of his squad in the assault, he was mortally wounded by an enemy rifleman, but as he fell to the ground he threw a handgrenade, killing his opponent. His superb leadership and heroic action at the cost of his life so demoralized the enemy that resistance at this point collapsed, permitting the 2 battalions to continue their advance.

*PUCKET, DONALD D. (Air Mission)

Rank and organization: First Lieutenant, U.S. Army Air Corps, 98th, Bombardment Group. Place and date: Ploesti Raid, Rumania, 9 July 1944. Entered service at: Boulder, Colo. Birth: Longmont, Colo. G.O. No.: 48, 23 June 1945. Citation: He took part in a highly effective attack against vital oil installation in Ploesti, Rumania, on 9 July 1944. Just after "bombs away," the plane received heavy and direct hits from anti-aircraft fire. One crewmember was instantly killed and 6 others severely wounded. The airplane was badly damaged, 2 were knocked out, the control cables cut, the oxygen system on fire, and the bomb bay flooded with gas and hydraulic fluid. Regaining control of his crippled plane, 1st Lt. Pucket turned its direction over to the copilot. He calmed the crew, administered first aid, and surveyed the damage. Finding the bomb bay doors jammed, he used the hand crank to open them to allow the gas to escape. He jettisoned all guns and equipment but the plane continued to lose altitude rapidly. Realizing that it would be impossible to reach friendly territory he ordered the crew to abandon ship. Three of the crew, uncontrollable from fright or shock, would not leave. 1st Lt. Pucket urged the others to jump. Ignoring their entreaties to follow, he refused to abandon the 3 hysterical men and was last seen fighting to regain control of the plane. A few moments later the flaming bomber crashed on a mountainside. 1st Lt. Pucket, unhesitatingly and with supreme sacrifice, gave his life in his courageous attempt to save the lives of 3 others.

RAMAGE, LAWSON PATERSON

Rank and organization: Commander, U.S. Navy, U.S.S. Parche. Place and date: Pacific, 31 July 1944. Entered service at: Vermont. Born: 19 January 1920, Monroe Bridge, Mass. Citation: For conspicuous gallantry and intrepidity at the risk of his life above and beyond the call of duty as commanding officer of the U.S.S. Parche in a predawn attack on a Japanese convoy, 31 July 1944. Boldly penetrating the screen of a heavily escorted convoy, Comdr. Ramage launched a perilous surface attack by delivering a crippling stern shot into a freighter and quickly following up with a series of bow and stern torpedoes to sink the leading tanker and damage the second one. Exposed by the light of bursting flares and bravely defiant of terrific shellfire passing close overhead, he struck again, sinking a transport by two forward reloads. In the mounting fury of fire from the damaged and sinking tanker, he calmly ordered his men below, remaining on the bridge to fight it out with an enemy now disorganized and confused. Swift to act as a fast transport closed in to ram, Comdr. Ramage daringly swung the stern of the speeding Parche as she crossed the bow of the onrushing ship, clearing by less than 50 feet but placing his submarine in a deadly crossfire from escorts on all sides and with the transport dead ahead. Undaunted, he sent 3 smashing "down the throat" bow shots to stop the target, then scored a killing hit as a climax to 46 minutes of violent action with the Parche and her valiant fighting company retiring victorious and unscathed.

*RAY, BERNARD J.

Rank and organization: First Lieutenant, U.S. Army, Company F, 8th Infantry, 4th Infantry Division. Place and date: Hurtgen Forest near Schevenhutte, Germany, 17 November 1944. Entered service at: Baldwin, N.Y. Birth: Brooklyn, N.Y. G.O. No.: 115, 8 December 1945. Citation: He was platoon leader with Company F, 8th Infantry, on 17 November 1944, during the drive through the Hurtgen Forest near Schevenhutte, Germany. The American forces attacked in wet, bitterly cold weather over rough, wooded terrain, meeting brutal resistance from positions spaced throughout the forest behind minefields and wire obstacles. Small arms, machinegun, mortar, and artillery fire caused heavy casualties in the ranks when Company F was halted by a concertina-type wire barrier. Under heavy fire, 1st Lt. Ray reorganized his men and prepared to blow a path through the entanglement, a task which appeared impossible of accomplishment and from which others tried to dissuade him. With implacable determination to clear the way, he placed explosive caps in his pockets, obtained several bangalore torpedoes, and then wrapped a length of highly explosive primer cord about his body. He dashed forward under direct fire, reached the barbed wire and prepared his demolition charge as mortar shells, which were being aimed at him alone, came steadily nearer his completely exposed position. He had placed a torpedo under the wire and was connecting it to a charge he carried when he was severely wounded by a bursting mortar shell. Apparently realizing that he would fail in his self-imposed mission unless he completed it in a few moments he made a supremely gallant decision. With the primer cord still wound about his body and the explosive caps in his pocket, he completed a hasty wiring system and unhesitatingly thrust down on the handle of the charger, destroying himself with the wire barricade in the resulting blast. By the deliberate sacrifice of his life, 1st Lt. Ray enabled his company to continue its attack, resumption of which was of positive significance in gaining the approaches to the Cologne Plain.

*REESE, JAMES W.

Rank and organization. Private, U.S. Army, 26th Infantry, 1st Infantry Division. Place and date. At Mt. Vassillio, Sicily, 5 August 1943. Entered service at: Chester, Pa. Birth: Chester, Pa. G.O. No.: 85, 17 December 1943. Citation: For conspicuous gallantry and intrepidity at the risk of life. above and beyond the call of duty in action involving actual conflict with the enemy. When the enemy launched a counterattack which threatened the position of his company, Pvt. Reese, as the acting squad leader of a 60-mm. mortar squad, displaying superior leadership on his own initiative, maneuvered his squad forward to a favorable position, from which, by skillfully directing the fire of his weapon, he caused many casualties in the enemy ranks, and aided materially in repulsing the counterattack. When the enemy fire became so severe as to make his position untenable, he ordered the other members of his squad to withdraw to a safer position, but declined to seek safety for himself. So as to bring more effective fire upon the enemy, Pvt. Reese, without assistance, moved his mortar to a new position and attacked an enemy machinegun nest. He had only 3 rounds of ammunition but secured a direct hit with his last round, completely destroying the nest and killing the occupants. Ammunition being exhausted, he abandoned the mortar. seized a rifle and continued to advance, moving into an exposed position overlooking the enemy. Despite a heavy concentration of machinegun, mortar, and artillery fire, the heaviest experienced by his unit throughout the entire Sicilian campaign, he remained at this position and continued to inflict casualties upon the enemy until he was killed. His bravery, coupled with his gallant and unswerving determination to close with the enemy, regardless of consequences and obstacles which he faced, are a priceless inspiration to our armed forces.

*REESE, JOHN N., JR.

Rank and organization: Private First Class, U.S. Army, Company B, 148th Infantry, 37th Infantry Division. Place and date: Paco Railroad Station, Manila, Philippine Islands. 9 February 1945. Entered service at: Pryor, Okla. Birth. Muskogee, Okla. G.O. No.: 89, 19 October 1945. Citation. He was engaged in the attack on the Paco Railroad Station, which was strongly defended by 300 determined enemy soldiers with machineguns and rifles, supported by several pillboxes, 3 20mm. guns, 1 37-mm. gun and heavy mortars. While making a frontal assault across an open field, his platoon was halted 100 yards from the station by intense enemy fire. On his own initiative he left the platoon. accompanied by a comrade, and continued forward to a house 60 yards from the objective. Although under constant enemy observation. the 2 men remained in this position for an hour, firing at targets of opportunity, killing more than 35 Japanese and wounding many more. Moving closer to the station and discovering a group of Japanese replacements attempting to reach pillboxes, they opened heavy fire, killed more than 40 and stopped all subsequent attempts to man the emplacements. Enemy fire became more intense as they advanced to within 20 yards of the station. From that point Pfc. Reese provided effective covering fire and courageously drew enemy fire to himself while his companion killed 7 Japanese and destroyed a 20-mm. gun and heavy machinegun with handgrenades. With their ammunition running low, the 2 men started to return to the American lines, alternately providing covering fire for each other as they withdrew. During this movement, Pfc. Reese was killed by enemy fire as he reloaded his rifle. The intrepid team, in 2 1/2 hours of fierce fighting, killed more than 82 Japanese, completely disorganized their defense and paved the way for subsequent complete defeat of the enemy at this strong point. By his gallant determination in the face of tremendous odds, aggressive fighting spirit, and extreme heroism at the cost of his life, Pfc. Reese materially aided the advance of our troops in Manila and providing a lasting inspiration to all those with whom he served.

*REEVES, THOMAS JAMES

Rank and organization: Radio Electrician (Warrant Officer) U.S. Navy. Born: 9 December 1895, Thomaston, Conn. Accredited to: Connecticut. Citation: For distinguished conduct in the line of his profession, extraordinary courage and disregard of his own safety during the attack on the Fleet in Pearl Harbor, by Japanese forces on 7 December 1941. After the mechanized ammunition hoists were put out of action in the U.S.S. California, Reeves, on his own initiative, in a burning passageway, assisted in the maintenance of an ammunition supply by hand to the antiaircraft guns until he was overcome by smoke and fire, which resulted in his death.

*RICKETTS, MILTON ERNEST

Rank and organization: Lieutenant, U.S. Navy. Born: 5 August 1913, Baltimore, Md. Appointed from: Maryland. Citation: For extraordinary and distinguished gallantry above and beyond the call of duty as Officer-in-Charge of the Engineering Repair Party of the U.S.S. Yorktown in action against enemy Japanese forces in the Battle of the Coral Sea on 8 May 1942. During the severe bombarding of the Yorktown by enemy Japanese forces, an aerial bomb passed through and exploded directly beneath the compartment in which Lt. Ricketts' battle station was located, killing, wounding or stunning all of his men and mortally wounding him. Despite his ebbing strength, Lt. Ricketts promptly opened the valve of a near-by fireplug, partially led out the fire hose and directed a heavy stream of water into the fire before dropping dead beside the hose. His courageous action, which undoubtedly prevented the rapid spread of fire to serious proportions, and his unflinching devotion to duty were in keeping with the highest traditions of the U.S. Naval Service. He gallantly gave his life for his country.

*RIORDAN, PAUL F.

Rank and organization: Second Lieutenant, U.S. Army, 34th Infantry Division Place and date: Near Cassino, Italy, 3-8 February 1944. Entered service at. Kansas City, Mo. Birth: Charles City, Iowa. G.O. No.. 74, 11 September 1944. Citation: For conspicuous gallantry and intrepidity above and beyond the call of duty. In the attack on the approaches to the city of Cassino on 3 February 1944, 2d Lt. Riordan led 1 of the assault platoons. Attacking Hill 175, his command was pinned down by enemy machinegun fire from the hill and from a pillbox about 45 yards to the right of the hill. In the face of intense fire, 2d Lt. Riordan moved out in full view of the enemy gunners to reach a position from where he could throw a handgrenade into the pillbox. Then, getting to his knees, he hurled the grenade approximately 45 yards, scoring a direct hit. The grenade killed 1 and wounded the other 2 Germans in the nest and silenced the gun. Another soldier then cleaned out the enemy pillboxes on the hill itself, and the company took its objective. Continuing the assault into Cassino itself on 8 February 1944, 2d Lt. Riordan and his platoon were given the mission of taking the city jail house, one of the enemy's several strongpoints. Again 2d Lt. Riordan took the lead and managed to get through the ring of enemy fire covering the approaches and reached the building. His platoon, however, could not get through the intense fire and was cut off. 2d Lt. Riordan, aware that his men were unable to follow, determined to carry on single-handed, but the numerically superior enemy force was too much for him to overcome, and he was killed by enemy small-arms fire after disposing of at least 2 of the defenders. 2d Lt. Riordan's bravery and extraordinary heroism in the face of almost certain death were an inspiration to his men and exemplify the highest traditions of the U.S. Armed Forces.

*ROAN, CHARLES HOWARD

Rank and organization: Private First Class, U.S. Marine Corps Reserve. Born: 16 August 1923, Claude, Tex. Accredited to. Texas. Citation: For conspicuous gallantry and intrepidity at the risk of his life above and beyond the call of duty while serving with the 2d Battalion, 7th Marines, 1st Marine Division, in action against enemy Japanese forces on Peleliu, Palau Islands, 18 September 1944. Shortly after his leader ordered a withdrawal upon discovering that the squad was partly cut off from their company as a result of the rapid advance along an exposed ridge during an aggressive attack on the strongly entrenched enemy, Pfc. Roan and his companions were suddenly engaged in a furious exchange of handgrenades by Japanese forces emplaced in a cave on higher ground and to the rear of the squad. Seeking protection with 4 other marines in a depression in the rocky, broken terrain, Pfc. Roan was wounded by an enemy grenade which fell close to their position and, immediately realizing the eminent peril to his comrades when another grenade landed in the midst of the group, unhesitatingly flung himself upon it, covering it with his body and absorbing the full impact of the explosion. By his prompt action and selfless conduct in the face of almost certain death, he saved the lives of 4 men. His great personal valor reflects the highest credit upon himself and the U.S. Naval Service. He gallantly gave his life for his comrades.

*ROBINSON, JAMES E., JR.

Rank and organization: First Lieutenant, U.S. Army, Battery A, 861st Field Artillery Battalion, 63d Infantry Division. Place and date: Near Untergriesheim, Germany, 6 April 1945. Entered service at: Waco, Tex. Birth: Toledo, Ohio. G.O. No.: 117, 11 December 1945. Citation: He was a field artillery forward observer attached to Company A, 253d Infantry, near Untergriesheim, Germany, on 6 April 1945. Eight hours of desperate fighting over open terrain swept by German machinegun, mortar, and small-arms fire had decimated Company A, robbing it of its commanding officer and most of its key enlisted personnel when 1st Lt. Robinson rallied the 23 remaining uninjured riflemen and a few walking wounded, and, while carrying his heavy radio for communication with American batteries, led them through intense fire in a charge against the objective. Ten German infantrymen in foxholes threatened to stop the assault, but the gallant leader killed them all at point-blank range with rifle and pistol fire and then pressed on with his men to sweep the area of all resistance. Soon afterward he was ordered to seize the defended town of Kressbach. He went to each of the 19 exhausted survivors with cheering words, instilling in them courage and fortitude, before leading the little band forward once more. In the advance he was seriously wounded in the throat by a shell fragment, but, despite great pain and loss of blood, he refused medical attention and continued the attack, directing supporting artillery fire even though he was mortally wounded. Only after the town had been taken and he could no longer speak did he leave the command he had inspired in victory and walk nearly 2 miles to an aid station where he died from his wound. By his intrepid leadership 1st Lt. Robinson was directly responsible for Company A's accomplishing its mission against tremendous odds.

RODRIGUEZ, CLETO

Rank and organization: Technical Sergeant (then Private), U.S. Army, Company B, 148th Infantry, 37th Infantry Division. Place and date: Paco Railroad Station, Manila, Philippine Islands, 9 February 1945. Entered service at: San Antonio, Tex. Birth: San Marcos, Tex. G.O. No.: 97, 1 November 1945. Citation: He was an automatic rifleman when his unit attacked the strongly defended Paco Railroad Station during the battle for Manila, Philippine Islands. While making a frontal assault across an open field, his platoon was halted 100 yards from the station by intense enemy fire. On his own initiative, he left the platoon, accompanied by a comrade, and continued forward to a house 60 yards from the objective. Although under constant enemy observation, the 2 men remained in this position for an hour, firing at targets of opportunity, killing more than 35 hostile soldiers and wounding many more. Moving closer to the station and discovering a group of Japanese replacements attempting to reach pillboxes, they opened heavy fire, killed more than 40 and stopped all subsequent attempts to man the emplacements. Enemy fire became more intense as they advanced to within 20 yards of the station. Then, covered by his companion, Pvt. Rodriguez boldly moved up to the building and threw 5 grenades through a doorway killing 7 Japanese, destroying a 20-mm. gun and wrecking a heavy machinegun. With their ammunition running low, the 2 men started to return to the American lines, alternately providing covering fire for each other's withdrawal. During this movement, Pvt. Rodriguez' companion was killed. In 2 1/2 hours of fierce fighting the intrepid team killed more than 82 Japanese, completely disorganized their defense, and paved the way for the subsequent overwhelming defeat of the enemy at this strongpoint. Two days later, Pvt. Rodriguez again enabled his comrades to advance when he single-handedly killed 6 Japanese and destroyed a well-placed 20-mm. gun by his outstanding skill with his weapons, gallant determination to destroy the enemy, and heroic courage in the face of tremendous odds, Pvt. Rodriguez, on 2 occasions, materially aided the advance of our troops in Manila.

*ROEDER, ROBERT E.

Rank and organization: Captain, U.S. Army, Company G, 350th Infantry, 88th Infantry Division. Place and date: Mt. Battaglia, Italy, 27-28 September 1944. Entered service at: Summit Station, Pa. Birth: Summit Station, Pa. G.O. No.: 31, 17 April 1945. Citation: for conspicuous gallantry and intrepidity at risk of life above and beyond the call of duty. Capt. Roeder commanded his company in defense of the strategic Mount Battaglia. Shortly after the company had occupied the hill, the Germans launched the first of a series of determined counterattacks to regain this dominating height. Completely exposed to ceaseless enemy artillery and small-arms fire, Capt. Roeder constantly circulated among his men, encouraging them and directing their defense against the persistent enemy. During the sixth counterattack, the enemy, by using flamethrowers and taking advantage of the fog, succeeded in overrunning the position Capt. Roeder led his men in a fierce battle at close quarters, to repulse the attack with heavy losses to the Germans. The following morning, while the company was engaged in repulsing an enemy counterattack in force, Capt. Roeder was seriously wounded and rendered unconscious by shell fragments. He was carried to the company command post, where he regained consciousness. Refusing medical treatment, he insisted on rejoining his men although in a weakened condition, Capt. Roeder dragged himself to the door of the command post and, picking up a rifle, braced himself in a sitting position. He began firing his weapon, shouted words of encouragement, and issued orders to his men. He personally killed 2 Germans before he himself was killed instantly by an exploding shell. Through Capt. Roeder's able and intrepid leadership his men held Mount Battaglia against the aggressive and fanatical enemy attempts to retake this important and strategic height. His valorous performance is exemplary of the fighting spirit of the U.S. Army.

*ROOKS, ALBERT HAROLD

Rank and organization: Captain, U.S. Navy. Born: 29 December 1891, Colton, Wash. Appointed from: Washington. Citation: for extraordinary heroism, outstanding courage, gallantry in action and distinguished service in the line of his profession, as commanding officer of the U.S.S. Houston during the period 4 to 27 February 1942, while in action with superior Japanese enemy aerial and surface forces. While proceeding to attack an enemy amphibious expedition, as a unit in a mixed force, Houston was heavily attacked by bombers; after evading 4 attacks, she was heavily hit in a fifth attack, lost 60 killed and had 1 turret wholly disabled. Capt. Rooks made his ship again seaworthy and sailed within 3 days to escort an important reinforcing convoy from Darwin to Koepang, Timor, Netherlands East Indies. While so engaged, another powerful air attack developed which by Houston's marked efficiency was fought off without much damage to the convoy. The commanding general of all forces in the area thereupon canceled the movement and Capt. Rooks escorted the convoy back to Darwin. Later, while in a considerable American-British-Dutch force engaged with an overwhelming force of Japanese surface ships, Houston with H.M.S. Exeter carried the brunt of the battle, and her fire alone heavily damaged 1 and possibly 2 heavy cruisers. Although heavily damaged in the actions, Capt. Rooks succeeded in disengaging his ship when the flag officer commanding broke off the action and got her safely away from the vicinity, whereas one-half of the cruisers were lost.

*ROOSEVELT, THEODORE, JR.

Rank and organization: brigadier general, U.S. Army. Place and date: Normandy invasion, 6 June 1944. Entered service at: Oyster Bay, N.Y. Birth: Oyster Bay, N.Y. G.O. No.: 77, 28 September 1944. Citation: for gallantry and intrepidity at the risk of his life above and beyond the call of duty on 6 June 1944, in France. After 2 verbal requests to accompany the leading assault elements in the Normandy invasion had been denied, Brig. Gen. Roosevelt's written request for this mission was approved and he landed with the first wave of the forces assaulting the enemy-held beaches. He repeatedly led groups from the beach, over the seawall and established them inland. His valor, courage, and presence in the very front of the attack and his complete unconcern at being under heavy fire inspired the troops to heights of enthusiasm and self-sacrifice. Although the enemy had the beach under constant direct fire, Brig. Gen. Roosevelt moved from one locality to another, rallying men around him, directed and personally led them against the enemy. Under his seasoned, precise, calm, and unfaltering leadership, assault troops reduced beach strong points and rapidly moved inland with minimum casualties. He thus contributed substantially to the successful establishment of the beachhead in France .

ROSS, DONALD KIRBY

Rank and organization: Machinist, U.S. Navy, U.S.S. Nevada. Place and date: Pearl Harbor, Territory of Hawaii, 7 December 1941. Entered service at: Denver, Colo. Born: 8 December 1910, Beverly, Kans. Citation: For distinguished conduct in the line of his profession, extraordinary courage and disregard of his own life during the attack on the Fleet in Pearl Harbor, Territory of Hawaii, by Japanese forces on 7 December 1941. When his station in the forward dynamo room of the U.S.S. Nevada became almost untenable due to smoke, steam, and heat, Machinist Ross forced his men to leave that station and performed all the duties himself until blinded and unconscious. Upon being rescued and resuscitated, he returned and secured the forward dynamo room and proceeded to the after dynamo room where he was later again rendered unconscious by exhaustion. Again recovering consciousness he returned to his station where he remained until directed to abandon it.

ROSS, WILBURN K.

Rank and organization: Private, U.S. Army, Company G, 350th Infantry, 3d Infantry Division. Place and date: Near St. Jacques, France, 30 October 1944. Entered service at: Strunk, Ky. Birth: Strunk, Ky. G.O. No.: 30, 14 April 1945. Citation: For conspicuous gallantry and intrepidity at risk of life above and beyond the call of duty near St. Jacques, France. At 11:30 a.m. on 30 October 1944, after his company had lost 55 out of 88 men in an attack on an entrenched. full-strength German company of elite mountain troops, Pvt. Ross placed his light machinegun 10 yards in advance of the foremost supporting riflemen in order to absorb the initial impact of an enemy counterattack. With machinegun and small-arms fire striking the earth near him, he fired with deadly effect on the assaulting force and repelled it. Despite the hail of automatic fire and the explosion of rifle grenades within a stone's throw of his position, he continued to man his machinegun alone, holding off 6 more German attacks. When the eighth assault was launched, most of his supporting riflemen were out of ammunition. They took positions in echelon behind Pvt. Ross and crawled up, during the attack, to extract a few rounds of ammunition from his machinegun ammunition belt. Pvt. Ross fought on virtually without assistance and, despite the fact that enemy grenadiers crawled to within 4 yards of his position in an effort to kill him with handgrenades, he again directed accurate and deadly fire on the hostile force and hurled it back. After expending his last rounds, Pvt. Ross was advised to withdraw to the company command post, together with 8 surviving riflemen, but, as more ammunition was expected, he declined to do so. The Germans launched their last all-out attack, converging their fire on Pvt. Ross in a desperate attempt to destroy the machinegun which stood between them and a decisive breakthrough. As his supporting riflemen fixed bayonets for a last-ditch stand, fresh ammunition arrived and was brought to Pvt. Ross just as the advance assault elements were about to swarm over his position. He opened murderous fire on the oncoming enemy; killed 40 and wounded 10 of the attacking force; broke the assault single-handedly, and forced the Germans to withdraw. Having killed or wounded at least 58 Germans in more than 5 hours of continuous combat and saved the remnants of his company from destruction, Pvt. Ross remained at his post that night and the following day for a total of 36 hours. His actions throughout this engagement were an inspiration to his comrades and maintained the high traditions of the military service.

ROUH, CARLTON ROBERT

Rank and organization: First Lieutenant, U.S. Marine Corps Reserve, 1st Battalion, 5th Marines, 1st Marine Division. Place and date: Peleliu Island, Palau group, 15 September 1944. Entered service at: New Jersey. Born: 11 May 1919, Lindenwold, N.J. Citation: For conspicuous gallantry and intrepidity at the risk of his life above and beyond the call of duty while attached to the 1st Battalion, 5th Marines, 1st Marine Division, during action against enemy Japanese forces on Peleliu Island, Palau group, 15 September 1944. Before permitting his men to use an enemy dugout as a position for an 81-mm. mortar observation post, 1st Lt. Rouh made a personal reconnaissance of the pillbox and, upon entering, was severely wounded by Japanese rifle fire from within. Emerging from the dugout, he was immediately assisted by 2 marines to a less exposed area but, while receiving first aid, was further endangered by an enemy grenade which was thrown into their midst. Quick to act in spite of his weakened condition, he lurched to a crouching position and thrust both men aside, placing his own body between them and the grenade and taking the full blast of the explosion himself. His exceptional spirit of loyalty and self-sacrifice in the face of almost certain death reflects the highest credit upon 1st Lt. Rouh and the U.S. Naval Service.

RUDOLPH, DONALD E.

Rank and organization: Second Lieutenant, U.S. Army, Company E, 20th Infantry, 6th Infantry Division. Place and date: Munoz, Luzon, Philippine Islands, 5 February 1945. Entered service at: Minneapolis, Minn. Birth: South Haven, Minn. G.O. No.: 77, 10 September 1945. Citation: 2d Lt. Rudolph (then T/Sgt.) was acting as platoon leader at Munoz, Luzon, Philippine Islands. While administering first aid on the battlefield, he observed enemy fire issuing from a nearby culvert. Crawling to the culvert with rifle and grenades, he killed 3 of the enemy concealed there. He then worked his way across open terrain toward a line of enemy pillboxes which had immobilized his company. Nearing the first pillbox, he hurled a grenade through its embrasure and charged the position. With his bare hands he tore away the wood and tin covering, then dropped a grenade through the opening, killing the enemy gunners and destroying their machinegun. Ordering several riflemen to cover his further advance, 2d Lt. Rudolph seized a pick mattock and made his way to the second pillbox. Piercing its top with the mattock, he dropped a grenade through the hole, fired several rounds from his rifle into it and smothered any surviving enemy by sealing the hole and the embrasure with earth. In quick succession he attacked and neutralized 6 more pillboxes. Later, when his platoon was attacked by an enemy tank, he advanced under covering fire, climbed to the top of the tank and dropped a white phosphorus grenade through the turret, destroying the crew. Through his outstanding heroism, superb courage, and leadership, and complete disregard for his own safety, 2d Lt. Rudolph cleared a path for an advance which culminated in one of the most decisive victories of the Philippine campaign.

*RUHL, DONALD JACK

Rank and organization: Private First Class, U.S. Marine Corps Reserve. Born 2 July 1923, Columbus, Mont. Accredited to: Montana. Citation: For conspicuous gallantry and intrepidity at the risk of his life above and beyond the call of duty while serving as a rifleman in an assault platoon of Company E, 28th Marines, 5th Marine Division, in action against enemy Japanese forces on Iwo Jima, Volcano Islands, from 19 to 21 February 1945. Quick to press the advantage after 8 Japanese had been driven from a blockhouse on D-day, Pfc. Ruhl single-handedly attacked the group, killing 1 of the enemy with his bayonet and another by rifle fire in his determined attempt to annihilate the escaping troops. Cool and undaunted as the fury of hostile resistance steadily increased throughout the night, he voluntarily left the shelter of his tank trap early in the morning of D-day plus 1 and moved out under a tremendous volume of mortar and machinegun fire to rescue a wounded marine lying in an exposed position approximately 40 yards forward of the line. Half pulling and half carrying the wounded man, he removed him to a defiladed position, called for an assistant and a stretcher and, again running the gauntlet of hostile fire, carried the casualty to an aid station some 300 yards distant on the beach. Returning to his platoon, he continued his valiant efforts, volunteering to investigate and apparently abandoned Japanese gun emplacement 75 yards forward of the right flank during consolidation of the front lines, and subsequently occupying the position through the night to prevent the enemy from repossessing the valuable weapon. Pushing forward in the assault against the vast network of fortifications surrounding Mt. Suribachi the following morning, he crawled with his platoon guide to the top of a Japanese bunker to bring fire to bear on enemy troops located on the far side of the bunker. Suddenly a hostile grenade landed between the 2 marines. Instantly Pfc. Ruhl called a warning to his fellow marine and dived on the deadly missile, at-sorbing the full impact of the shattering explosion in his own body and protecting all within range from the danger of flying fragments although he might easily have dropped from his position on the edge of the bunker to the ground below. An indomitable fighter, Pfc. Ruhl rendered heroic service toward the defeat of a ruthless enemy, and his valor, initiative and unfaltering spirit of self-sacrifice in the face of almost certain death sustain and enhance the highest traditions of the U.S. Naval Service. He gallantly gave his life for his country.

RUIZ, ALEJANDRO R. RENTERIA

Rank and organization: Private First Class, U.S. Army, 165th Infantry, 27th Infantry Division. Place and date: Okinawa, Ryukyu Islands, 28 April 1945. Entered service at: Carlsbad, N. Mex. Birth: Loving, N. Mex. G.O. No.: 60, 26 June 1946. Citation: When his unit was stopped by a skillfully camouflaged enemy pillbox, he displayed conspicuous gallantry and intrepidity above and beyond the call of duty. His squad, suddenly brought under a hail of machinegun fire and a vicious grenade attack, was pinned down. Jumping to his feet, Pfc. Ruiz seized an automatic rifle and lunged through the flying grenades and rifle and automatic fire for the top of the emplacement. When an enemy soldier charged him, his rifle jammed. Undaunted, Pfc. Ruiz whirled on his assailant and clubbed him down. Then he ran back through bullets and grenades, seized more ammunition and another automatic rifle, and again made for the pillbox. Enemy fire now was concentrated on him, but he charged on, miraculously reaching the position, and in plain view he climbed to the top. Leaping from 1 opening to another, he sent burst after burst into the pillbox, killing 12 of the enemy and completely destroying the position. Pfc. Ruiz's heroic conduct, in the face of overwhelming odds, saved the lives of many comrades and eliminated an obstacle that long would have checked his unit's advance.

*SADOWSKI, JOSEPH J.

Rank and organization: Sergeant, U.S. Army, 37th Tank Battalion, 4th Armored Division. Place and date: Valhey, France, 14 September 1944. Entered service at: Perth Amboy, N.J. Birth: Perth Amboy, N.J. C o. No.: 32, 23 April 1945. Citation: For conspicuous gallantry and intrepidity at the risk of his life above and beyond the call of duty at Valhey, France. On the afternoon of 14 September 1944, Sgt. Sadowski as a tank commander was advancing with the leading elements of Combat Command A, 4th Armored Division, through an intensely severe barrage of enemy fire from the streets and buildings of the town of Valhey. As Sgt. Sadowski's tank advanced through the hail of fire, it was struck by a shell from an 88-mm. gun fired at a range of 20 yards. The tank was disabled and burst into flames. The suddenness of the enemy attack caused confusion and hesitation among the crews of the remaining tanks of our forces. Sgt. Sadowski immediately ordered his crew to dismount and take cover in the adjoining buildings. After his crew had dismounted, Sgt. Sadowski discovered that 1 member of the crew, the bow gunner, had been unable to leave the tank. Although the tank was being subjected to a withering hail of enemy small-arms, bazooka, grenade, and mortar fire from the streets and from the windows of adjacent buildings, Sgt. Sadowski unhesitatingly returned to his tank and endeavored to pry up the bow gunner's hatch. While engaged in this attempt to rescue his comrade from the burning tank, he was cut down by a stream of machinegun fire which resulted in his death. The gallant and noble sacrifice of his life in the aid of his comrade, undertaken in the face of almost certain death, so inspired the remainder of the tank crews that they pressed forward with great ferocity and completely destroyed the enemy forces in this town without further loss to themselves. The heroism and selfless devotion to duty displayed by Sgt. Sadowski, which resulted in his death, inspired the remainder of his force to press forward to victory, and reflect the highest tradition of the armed forces.

*SARNOSKI, JOSEPH R. (Air Mission)

Rank and organization: Second Lieutenant, U.S. Army Air Corps, 43rd Bomber Group, Place and date: Over Buka Area, Solomon Islands, 16 June 1943. Entered service at: Simpson, Pa. Born. 30 January 1915, Simpson, Pa. G.O. No.: 85, 17 December 1943. Citation: For conspicuous gallantry and intrepidity in action above and beyond the call of duty. On 16 June 1943, 2d Lt. Sarnoski volunteered as bombardier of a crew on an important photographic mapping mission covering the heavily defended Buka area, Solomon Islands. When the mission was nearly completed, about 20 enemy fighters intercepted. At the nose guns, 2d Lt. Sarnoski fought off the first attackers, making it possible for the pilot to finish the plotted course. When a coordinated frontal attack by the enemy extensively damaged his bomber, and seriously injured 5 of the crew, 2d Lt. Sarnoski, though wounded, continued firing and shot down 2 enemy planes. A 20-millimeter shell which burst in the nose of the bomber knocked him into the catwalk under the cockpit. With indomitable fighting spirit, he crawled back to his post and kept on firing until he collapsed on his guns. 2d Lt. Sarnoski by resolute defense of his aircraft at the price of his life, made possible the completion of a vitally important mission.

*SAYERS, FOSTER J.

Rank and organization: Private First Class, U.S. Army, Company L, 357th Infantry, 90th Infantry Division. Place and date: Near Thionville, France, 12 November 1944. Entered service at: Howard, Pa. Birth: Marsh Creek, Pa. G.O. No.: 89, 19 October 1945. Citation: He displayed conspicuous gallantry above and beyond the call of duty in combat on 12 November 1944, near Thionville, France. During an attack on strong hostile forces entrenched on a hill he fearlessly ran up the steep approach toward his objective and set up his machinegun 20 yards from the enemy. Realizing it would be necessary to attract full attention of the dug-in Germans while his company crossed an open area and flanked the enemy, he picked up his gun, charged through withering machinegun and rifle fire to the very edge of the emplacement, and there killed 12 German soldiers with devastating close-range fire. He took up a position behind a log and engaged the hostile infantry from the flank in an heroic attempt to distract their attention while his comrades attained their objective at the crest of the hill. He was killed by the very heavy concentration of return fire; but his fearless assault enabled his company to sweep the hill with minimum of casualties, killing or capturing every enemy soldier on it. Pfc. Sayers' indomitable fighting spirit, aggressiveness, and supreme devotion to duty live on as an example of the highest traditions of the military service.

SCHAEFER, JOSEPH E.

Rank and organization: Staff Sergeant, U.S. Army, Company I, 18th Infantry, 1st Infantry Division. Place and date: Near Stolberg, Germany, 24 September 1944. Entered service at: Long Island, N.Y. Birth: New York, N.Y. G.O. No.: 71, 22 August 1945. Citation: He was in charge of a squad of the 2d Platoon in the vicinity of Stolberg, Germany, early in the morning of 24 September 1944, when 2 enemy companies supported by machineguns launched an attack to seize control of an important crossroads which was defended by his platoon. One American squad was forced back, another captured, leaving only S/Sgt. Schaefer's men to defend the position. To shift his squad into a house which would afford better protection, he crawled about under heavy small-arms and machinegun fire, instructed each individual, and moved to the building. A heavy concentration of enemy artillery fire scored hits on his strong point. S/Sgt. Schaefer assigned his men to positions and selected for himself the most dangerous one at the door. With his Ml rifle, he broke the first wave of infantry thrown toward the house. The Germans attacked again with grenades and flame throwers but were thrown back a second time, S/Sgt. Schaefer killing and wounding several. Regrouped for a final assault, the Germans approached from 2 directions. One force drove at the house from the front, while a second group advanced stealthily along a hedgerow. Recognizing the threat, S/Sgt. Schaefer fired rapidly at the enemy before him, killing or wounding all 6; then, with no cover whatever, dashed to the hedgerow and poured deadly accurate shots into the second group, killing 5, wounding 2 others, and forcing the enemy to withdraw. He scoured the area near his battered stronghold and captured 10 prisoners. By this time the rest of his company had begun a counterattack; he moved forward to assist another platoon to regain its position. Remaining in the lead, crawling and running in the face of heavy fire, he overtook the enemy, and liberated the American squad captured earlier in the battle. In all, single-handed and armed only with his rifle, he killed between 15 and 20 Germans, wounded at least as many more, and took 10 prisoners. S/Sgt. Schaefer's indomitable courage and his determination to hold his position at all costs were responsible for stopping an enemy breakthrough.

SCHAUER, HENRY

Rank and organization: Private First Class, U.S. Army, 3d Infantry Division. Place and date: Near Cisterna di Littoria, Italy, 23-24 May 1944. Entered service at: Scobey, Mont. Born: 9 October 1918, Clinton, Okla. G.O. No.: 83, 27 October 1944. Citation: For conspicuous gallantry and intrepidity at risk of life above and beyond the call of duty. On 23 May 1944, at 12 noon, Pfc. (now T/Sgt.) Schauer left the cover of a ditch to engage 4 German snipers who opened fire on the patrol from its rear. Standing erect he walked deliberately 30 yards toward the enemy, stopped amid the fire from 4 rifles centered on him, and with 4 bursts from his BAR, each at a different range, killed all of the snipers. Catching sight of a fifth sniper waiting for the patrol behind a house chimney, Pfc. Schauer brought him down with another burst. Shortly after, when a heavy enemy artillery concentration and 2 machineguns temporarily halted the patrol, Pfc. Schauer again left cover to engage the enemy weapons single-handed. While shells exploded within 15 yards, showering dirt over him, and strings of grazing German tracer bullets whipped past him at chest level, Pfc. Schauer knelt, killed the 2 gunners of the machinegun only 60 yards from him with a single burst from his BAR, and crumpled 2 other enemy soldiers who ran to man the gun. Inserting a fresh magazine in his BAR, Pfc. Schauer shifted his body to fire at the other weapon 500 yards distant and emptied his weapon into the enemy crew, killing all 4 Germans. Next morning, when shells from a German Mark VI tank and a machinegun only 100 yards distant again forced the patrol to seek cover, Pfc. Schauer crawled toward the enemy machinegun. stood upright only 80 yards from the weapon as its bullets cut the surrounding ground, and 4 tank shells fired directly at him burst within 20 yards. Raising his BAR to his shoulder, Pfc. Schauer killed the 4 members of the German machinegun crew with 1 burst of fire.

SCHONLAND, HERBERT EMERY

Rank and organization: Commander, U.S. Navy, U.S.S. San Francisco Place and date: Savo Island, 12-13 November 1943. Entered service at. Maine. Born: 7 September 1900, Portland, Maine. Citation: For extreme heroism and courage above and beyond the call of duty as damage control officer of the U.S.S. San Francisco in action against greatly superior enemy forces in the battle off Savo Island, 12-13 November 1942. In the same violent night engagement in which all of his superior officers were killed or wounded, Lt. Comdr. Schonland was fighting valiantly to free the San Francisco of large quantities of water flooding the second deck compartments through numerous shell holes caused by enemy fire. Upon being informed that he was commanding officer, he ascertained that the conning of the ship was being efficiently handled, then directed the officer who had taken over that task to continue while he himself resumed the vitally important work of maintaining the stability of the ship. In water waist deep, he carried on his efforts in darkness illuminated only by hand lanterns until water in flooded compartments had been drained or pumped off and watertight integrity had again been restored to the San Francisco. His great personal valor and gallant devotion to duty at great peril to his own life were instrumental in bringing his ship back to port under her own power, saved to fight again in the service of her country.

*SCHWAB, ALBERT EARNEST

Rank and organization: Private First Class, U.S. Marine Corps Reserve. Born: 17 July 1920, Washington, D.C. Entered service at: Tulsa, Okla. Citation: For conspicuous gallantry and intrepidity at the risk of his life above and beyond the call of duty as a flamethrower operator in action against enemy Japanese forces on Okinawa Shima in the Rykuyu Islands, 7 May 1945. Quick to take action when his company was pinned down in a valley and suffered resultant heavy casualties under blanketing machinegun fire emanating from a high ridge to the front, Pfc. Schwab, unable to flank the enemy emplacement because of steep cliffs on either side, advanced up the face of the ridge in bold defiance of the intense barrage and, skillfully directing the fire of his flamethrower, quickly demolished the hostile gun position, thereby enabling his company to occupy the ridge. Suddenly a second enemy machinegun opened fire, killing and wounding several marines with its initial bursts. Estimating with split-second decision the tactical difficulties confronting his comrades, Pfc. Schwab elected to continue his l-man assault despite a diminished supply of fuel for his flamethrower. Cool and indomitable, he moved forward in the face of a direct concentration of hostile fire, relentlessly closed the enemy position and attacked. Although severely wounded by a final vicious blast from the enemy weapon, Pfc. Schwab had succeeded in destroying 2 highly strategic Japanese gun positions during a critical stage of the operation and, by his dauntless, single-handed efforts, had materially furthered the advance of his company. His aggressive initiative, outstanding valor and professional skill throughout the bitter conflict sustain and enhance the highest traditions of the U.S. Naval Service.

*SCOTT, NORMAN

Rank and organization: Rear Admiral, U.S. Navy. Born: 10 August 1889, Indianapolis, Ind. Appointed from: Indiana. Citation: For extraordinary heroism and conspicuous intrepidity above and beyond the call of duty during action against enemy Japanese forces off Savo Island on the night of 11-12 October and again on the night of 12-13 November 1942. In the earlier action, intercepting a Japanese Task Force intent upon storming our island positions and landing reinforcements at Guadalcanal, Rear Adm. Scott, with courageous skill and superb coordination of the units under his command, destroyed 8 hostile vessels and put the others to flight. Again challenged, a month later, by the return of a stubborn and persistent foe, he led his force into a desperate battle against tremendous odds, directing close-range operations against the invading enemy until he himself was killed in the furious bombardment by their superior firepower. On each of these occasions his dauntless initiative, inspiring leadership and judicious foresight in a crisis of grave responsibility contributed decisively to the rout of a powerful invasion fleet and to the consequent frustration of a formidable Japanese offensive. He gallantly gave his life in the service of his country.

*SCOTT, ROBERT R.

Rank and organization: Machinist's Mate First Class, U.S. Navy. Born: 13 July 1915, Massillon, Ohio. Accredited to Ohio. Citation: For conspicuous devotion to duty, extraordinary courage and complete disregard of his own life, above and beyond the call of duty, during the attack on the Fleet in Pearl Harbor by Japanese forces on 7 December 1941. The compartment, in the U.S.S. California, in which the air compressor, to which Scott was assigned as his battle station, was flooded as the result of a torpedo hit. The remainder of the personnel evacuated that compartment but Scott refused to leave, saying words to the effect "This is my station and I will stay and give them air as long as the guns are going."

SCOTT, ROBERT S.

Rank and organization: Captain (then Lieutenant), U.S. Army, 172d Infantry, 43d Infantry Division. Place and date. Near Munda Air Strip, New Georgia, Solomon Islands, 29 July 1943. Entered service at. Santa Fe, N. Mex. Birth: Washington, D.C. G.O. No.: 81, 14 October 1944. Citation: For conspicuous gallantry and intrepidity at the risk of his life above and beyond the call of duty near Munda Airstrip, New Georgia, Solomon Islands, on 29 July 1943. After 27 days of bitter fighting, the enemy held a hilltop salient which commanded the approach to Munda Airstrip. Our troops were exhausted from prolonged battle and heavy casualties, but Lt. Scott advanced with the leading platoon of his company to attack the enemy position, urging his men forward in the face of enemy rifle and enemy machinegun fire. He had pushed forward alone to a point midway across the barren hilltop within 75 yards of the enemy when the enemy launched a desperate counterattack, which f successful would have gained undisputed possession of the hill. Enemy riflemen charged out on the plateau, firing and throwing grenades as they moved to engage our troops. The company withdrew, but Lt. Scott, with only a blasted tree stump for cover, stood his ground against the wild enemy assault. By firing his carbine and throwing the grenades in his possession he momentarily stopped the enemy advance using the brief respite to obtain more grenades. Disregarding small-arms fire and exploding grenades aimed at him, suffering a bullet wound in the left hand and a painful shrapnel wound in the head after his carbine had been shot from his hand, he threw grenade after grenade with devastating accuracy until the beaten enemy withdrew. Our troops, inspired to renewed effort by Lt. Scott's intrepid stand and incomparable courage, swept across the plateau to capture the hill, and from this strategic position 4 days later captured Munda Airstrip.

SHEA, CHARLES W.

Rank and organization: Second Lieutenant, U.S. Army, Company F, 350th Infantry. 88th Infantry Division. Place and date: Near Mount Damiano, Italy, 12 May 1944. Entered service at: New York, N.Y. Birth: New York, NY. G.O. No.: 4, 12 January 1945. Citation: For conspicuous gallantry and intrepidity at risk of life above and beyond the call of duty, on 12 May 1944, near Mount Damiano, Italy. As 2d Lt. Shea and his company were advancing toward a hill occupied by the enemy, 3 enemy machineguns suddenly opened fire, inflicting heavy casualties upon the company and halting its advance. 2d Lt. Shea immediately moved forward to eliminate these machinegun nests in order to enable his company to continue its attack. The deadly hail of machinegun fire at first pinned him down, but, boldly continuing his advance, 2d Lt. Shea crept up to the first nest. Throwing several hand grenades, he forced the 4 enemy soldiers manning this position to surrender, and disarming them, he sent them to the rear. He then crawled to the second machinegun position, and after a short fire fight forced 2 more German soldiers to surrender. At this time, the third machinegun fired at him, and while deadly small arms fire pitted the earth around him, 2d Lt. Shea crawled toward the nest. Suddenly he stood up and rushed the emplacement and with well-directed fire from his rifle, he killed all 3 of the enemy machine gunners. 2d Lt. Shea's display of personal valor was an inspiration to the officers and men of his company.

*SHERIDAN, CARL V.

Rank and organization: Private First Class, U.S. Army, Company K, 47th Infantry, 9th Infantry Division. Place and date: Frenzenberg Castle, Weisweiler, Germany, 26 November 1944. Entered service at: Baltimore,

Md. Birth: Baltimore, Md. G.O. No.: 43, 30 May 1445. Citation: Attached to the 2d Battalion of the 47th Infantry on 26 November 1944, for the attack on Frenzenberg Castle, in the vicinity of Weisweiler, Germany, Company K, after an advance of 1,000 yards through a shattering barrage of enemy artillery and mortar fire, had captured 2 buildings in the courtyard of the castle but was left with an effective fighting strength of only 35 men. During the advance, Pfc. Sheridan, acting as a bazooka gunner, had braved the enemy fire to stop and procure the additional rockets carried by his ammunition bearer who was wounded. Upon rejoining his company in the captured buildings, he found it in a furious fight with approximately 70 enemy paratroopers occupying the castle gate house. This was a solidly built stone structure surrounded by a deep water-filled moat 20 feet wide. The only approach to the heavily defended position was across the courtyard and over a drawbridge leading to a barricaded oaken door. Pfc. Sheridan, realizing that his bazooka was the only available weapon with sufficient power to penetrate the heavy oak planking, with complete disregard for his own safety left the protection of the buildings and in the face of heavy and intense small-arms and grenade fire, crossed the courtyard to the drawbridge entrance where he could bring direct fire to bear against the door. Although handicapped by the lack of an assistant, and a constant target for the enemy fire that burst around him, he skillfully and effectively handled his awkward weapon to place two well-aimed rockets into the structure. Observing that the door was only weakened, and realizing that a gap must be made for a successful assault, he loaded his last rocket, took careful aim, and blasted a hole through the heavy planks. Turning to his company he shouted, "Come on, let's get them!" With his .45 pistol blazing, he charged into the gaping entrance and was killed by the withering fire that met him. The final assault on Frezenberg Castle was made through the gap which Pfc. Sheridan gave his life to create.

*SHOCKLEY, WILLIAM R.

Rank and organization: Private First Class, U.S. Army, Company L, 128th Infantry, 32d Infantry Division. Place and date: Villa Verde Trail, Luzon, Philippine Islands, 31 March 1945. Entered service at: Selma, Calif. Birth: Bokoshe, Okla. G.O. No.: 89, 19 October 1945. Citation: He was in position with his unit on a hill when the enemy, after a concentration of artillery fire, launched a counterattack.. He maintained his position under intense enemy fire and urged his comrades to withdraw, saying that he would "remain to the end" to provide cover. Although he had to clear two stoppages which impeded the reloading of his weapon, he halted one enemy charge. Hostile troops then began moving in on his left flank, and he quickly shifted his gun to fire on them. Knowing that the only route of escape was being cut off by the enemy, he ordered the remainder of his squad to withdraw to safety and deliberately remained at his post. He continued to fire until he was killed during the ensuing enemy charge. Later, 4 Japanese were found dead in front of his position. Pfc. Shockley, facing certain death, sacrificed himself to save his fellow soldiers, but the heroism and gallantry displayed by him enabled his squad to reorganize and continue its attack.

SHOMO, WILLIAM A. (Air Mission)

Rank and organization: Major, U.S. Army Air Corps, 82d Tactical Reconnaissance Squadron. Place and date: Over Luzon, Philippine Islands, 11 January 1945. Entered service at: Westmoreland County, Pa. Birth: Jeannette, Pa. G.O. No.: 25, 7 April 1945. Citation: For conspicuous gallantry and intrepidity at the risk of his life above and beyond the call of duty. Maj. Shomo was lead pilot of a flight of 2 fighter planes charged with an armed photographic and strafing mission against the Aparri and Laoag airdromes. While en route to the objective, he observed an enemy twin engine bomber, protected by 12 fighters, flying about 2,500 feet above him and in the opposite direction Although the odds were 13 to 2, Maj. Shomo immediately ordered an attack. Accompanied by his wingman he closed on the enemy formation in a climbing turn and scored hits on the leading plane of the third element, which exploded in midair. Maj. Shomo then attacked the second element from the left side of the formation and shot another fighter down in flames. When the enemy formed for Counterattack, Maj. Shomo moved to the other side of the formation and hit a third fighter which exploded and fell. Diving below the bomber he put a burst into its underside and it crashed and burned. Pulling up from this pass he encountered a fifth plane firing head on and destroyed it. He next dived upon the first element and shot down the lead plane; then diving to 300 feet in pursuit of another fighter he caught it with his initial burst and it crashed in flames. During this action his wingman had shot down 3 planes, while the 3 remaining enemy fighters had fled into a cloudbank and escaped. Maj. Shomo's extraordinary gallantry and intrepidity in attacking such a far superior force and destroying 7 enemy aircraft in one action is unparalleled in the southwest Pacific area.

*SHOUP, CURTIS F

Rank and organization: Staff Sergeant, U.S. Army, Company I, 346th Infantry, 87th Infantry Division. Place and date: Near Tillet, Belgium, 7 January 1945. Entered service at: Buffalo, N.Y. Birth: Napenoch, N.Y. G.O. No.: 60, 25 July 1945. Citation: On 7 January 1945, near Tillet, Belgium, his company attacked German troops on rising ground. Intense hostile machinegun fire pinned down and threatened to annihilate the American unit in an exposed position where frozen ground made it impossible to dig in for protection. Heavy mortar and artillery fire from enemy batteries was added to the storm of destruction falling on the Americans. Realizing that the machinegun must be silenced at all costs, S/Sgt. Shoup, armed with an automatic rifle, crawled to within 75 yards of the enemy emplacement. He found that his fire was ineffective from this position, and completely disregarding his own safety, stood up and grimly strode ahead into the murderous stream of bullets, firing his low-held weapon as he went. He was hit several times and finally was knocked to the ground. But he struggled to his feet and staggered forward until close enough to hurl a grenade, wiping out the enemy machinegun nest with his dying action. By his heroism, fearless determination, and supreme sacrifice, S/Sgt. Shoup eliminated a hostile weapon which threatened to destroy his company and turned a desperate situation into victory.

SHOUP, DAVID MONROE

Rank and organization: Colonel, U.S. Marine Corps, commanding officer of all Marine Corps troops on Betio Island, Tarawa Atoll, and Gilbert Islands, from 20 to 22 November 1943. Entered service at: Indiana. Born: 30 December 1904, Tippecanoe, Ind. Citation: For conspicuous gallantry and intrepidity at the risk of his life above and beyond the call of duty as commanding officer of all Marine Corps troops in action against enemy Japanese forces on Betio Island, Tarawa Atoll, Gilbert Islands, from 20 to 22 November 1943. Although severely shocked by an exploding enemy shell soon after landing at the pier and suffering from a serious, painful leg wound which had become infected, Col. Shoup fearlessly exposed himself to the terrific and relentless artillery, machinegun, and rifle fire from hostile shore emplacements. Rallying his hesitant troops by his own inspiring heroism, he gallantly led them across the fringing reefs to charge the heavily fortified island and reinforce our hard-pressed, thinly held lines. Upon arrival on shore, he assumed command of all landed troops and, working without rest under constant, withering enemy fire during the next 2 days, conducted smashing attacks against unbelievably strong and fanatically defended Japanese positions despite innumerable obstacles and heavy casualties. By his brilliant leadership daring tactics, and selfless devotion to duty, Col. Shoup was largely responsible for the final decisive defeat of the enemy, and his indomitable fighting spirit reflects great credit upon the U.S. Naval Service.

SIGLER, FRANKLIN EARL

Rank and organization: Private, U.S. Marine Corps Reserve, 2d Battalion, 26th Marines, 5th Marine Division. Place and date: Iwo Jima, Volcano Islands, 14 March 1945. Entered service at: New Jersey. Born: 6 November 1924, Glen Ridge, N.J. Citation: For conspicuous gallantry and intrepidity at the risk of his life above and beyond the call of duty while serving with the 2d Battalion, 26th Marines, 5th Marine Division, in action against enemy Japanese forces during the seizure of Iwo Jima in the Volcano Islands on 14 March 1945. Voluntarily taking command of his rifle squad when the leader became a casualty, Pvt. Sigler fearlessly led a bold charge against an enemy gun installation which had held up the advance of his company for several days and, reaching the position in advance of the others, assailed the emplacement with handgrenades and personally annihilated the entire crew. As additional Japanese troops opened fire from concealed tunnels and caves above, he quickly scaled the rocks leading to the attacking guns, surprised the enemy with a furious 1-man assault and, although severely wounded in the encounter, deliberately crawled back to his squad position where he steadfastly refused evacuation, persistently directing heavy machinegun and rocket barrages on the Japanese cave entrances. Undaunted by the merciless rain of hostile fire during the intensified action, he gallantly disregarded his own painful wounds to aid casualties, carrying 3 wounded squad members to safety behind the lines and returning to continue the battle with renewed determination until ordered to retire for medical treatment. Stouthearted and indomitable in the face of extreme peril, Pvt. Sigler, by his alert initiative, unfaltering leadership, and daring tactics in a critical situation, effected the release of his besieged company from enemy fire and contributed essentially to its further advance against a savagely fighting enemy. His superb valor, resolute fortitude, and heroic spirit of self-sacrifice throughout reflect the highest credit upon Pvt. Sigler and the U.S. Naval Service.

SILK, EDWARD A.

Rank and organization: First Lieutenant, U.S. Army, Company E, 398th Infantry, 100th Infantry Division. Place and date: Near St. Pravel, France, 23 November 1944. Entered service at: Johnstown, Pa. Born: 8 June 1916, Johnstown, Pa. G.O. No.: 97, 1 November 1945. citation. 1st Lt. Edward A. Silk commanded the weapons platoon of Company E, 398th Infantry, on 23 November 1944, when the end battalion was assigned the mission of seizing high ground overlooking Moyenmoutier France, prior to an attack on the city itself. His company jumped off in the lead at dawn and by noon had reached the edge of a woods in the vicinity of St. Pravel where scouts saw an enemy sentry standing guard before a farmhouse in a valley below. One squad, engaged in reconnoitering the area, was immediately pinned down by intense machinegun and automatic-weapons fire from within the house. Skillfully deploying his light machinegun section, 1st Lt. Silk answered enemy fire, but when 15 minutes had elapsed with no slackening of resistance, he decided to eliminate the strong point by a 1-man attack. Running 100 yards across an open field to the shelter of a low stone wall directly in front of the farmhouse, he fired into the door and windows with his carbine; then, in full view of the enemy, vaulted the wall and dashed 50 yards through a hail of bullets to the left side of the house, where he hurled a grenade through a window, silencing a machinegun and killing 2 gunners. In attempting to move to the right side of the house he drew fire from a second machinegun emplaced in the woodshed. With magnificent courage he rushed this position in the face of direct fire and succeeded in neutralizing the weapon and killing the 2 gunners by throwing grenades into the structure. His supply of grenades was by now exhausted, but undaunted, he dashed back to the side of the farmhouse and began to throw rocks through a window, demanding the surrender of the remaining enemy. Twelve Germans, overcome by his relentless assault and confused by his unorthodox methods, gave up to the lone American. By his gallant willingness to assume the full burden of the attack and the intrepidity with which he carried out his extremely hazardous mission, 1st Lt. Silk enabled his battalion to continue its advance and seize its objective.

SJOGREN, JOHN C.

Rank and organization: Staff Sergeant, U.S. Army, Company I, 160th Infantry, 40th Infantry Division. Place and date: Near San Jose Hacienda, Negros, Philippine Islands, 23 May 1945. Entered service at: Rockford, Mich. Birth: Rockford, Mich. G.O. No.: 97, 1 November 1945. Citation: He led an attack against a high precipitous ridge defended by a company of enemy riflemen, who were entrenched in spider holes and supported by well-sealed pillboxes housing automatic weapons with interlocking bands of fire. The terrain was such that only 1 squad could advance at one time; and from a knoll atop a ridge a pillbox covered the only approach with automatic fire. Against this enemy stronghold, S/Sgt. Sjogren led the first squad to open the assault. Deploying his men, he moved forward and was hurling grenades when he saw that his next in command, at the opposite flank, was gravely wounded. Without hesitation he crossed 20 yards of exposed terrain in the face of enemy fire and exploding dynamite charges, moved the man to cover and administered first aid. He then worked his way forward and, advancing directly into the enemy fire, killed 8 Japanese in spider holes guarding the approach to the pillbox. Crawling to within a few feet of the pillbox while his men concentrated their bullets on the fire port, he began dropping grenades through the narrow firing slit. The enemy immediately threw 2 or 3 of these unexploded grenades out, and fragments from one wounded him in the hand and back. However, by hurling grenades through the embrasure faster then the enemy could return them, he succeeded in destroying the occupants. Despite his wounds, he directed his squad to follow him in a systematic attack on the remaining positions, which he eliminated in like manner, taking tremendous risks, overcoming bitter resistance, and never hesitating in his relentless advance. To silence one of the pillboxes, he wrenched a light machinegun out through the embrasure as it was firing before blowing up the occupants with handgrenades. During this action, S/Sgt. Sjogren, by his heroic bravery, aggressiveness, and skill as a soldier, single-handedly killed 43 enemy soldiers and destroyed 9 pillboxes, thereby paving the way for his company's successful advance.

SKAGGS, LUTHER, JR.

Rank and organization: Private First Class, U.S. Marine Corps Reserve, 3d Battalion, 3d Marines, 3d Marine Division. Place and date: Asan-Adelup beachhead, Guam, Marianas Islands, 21-22 July 1944. Entered service at: Kentucky. Born: 3 March 1923, Henderson, Ky. Citation: For conspicuous gallantry and intrepidity at the risk of his life above and beyond the call of duty while serving as squad leader with a mortar section of a rifle company in the 3d Battalion, 3d Marines, 3d Marine Division, during action against enemy Japanese forces on the Asan-Adelup beachhead, Guam, Marianas Islands, 21-22 July 1944. When the section leader became a casualty under a heavy mortar barrage shortly after landing, Pfc. Skaggs promptly assumed command and led the section through intense fire for a distance of 200 yards to a position from which to deliver effective coverage of the assault on a strategic cliff. Valiantly defending this vital position against strong enemy counterattacks during the night, Pfc. Skaggs was critically wounded when a Japanese grenade lodged in his foxhole and exploded, shattering the lower part of one leg. Quick to act, he applied an improvised tourniquet and, while propped up in his foxhole, gallantly returned the enemy's fire with his rifle and handgrenades for a period of 8 hours, later crawling unassisted to the rear to continue the fight until the Japanese had been annihilated. Uncomplaining and calm throughout this critical period,

Pfc. Skaggs served as a heroic example of courage and fortitude to other wounded men and, by his courageous leadership and inspiring devotion to duty, upheld the high traditions of the U.S. Naval Service.

SLATON, JAMES D.

Rank and organization: Corporal, U.S. Army, 157th Infantry, 45th Infantry Division. Place and date: Near Oliveto, Italy, 23 September 1943. Entered service at: Gulfport, Miss. Born: 2 April 1912, Laurel, Miss G.O. No.: 44, 30 May 1944. Citation: For conspicuous gallantry and intrepidity at the risk of life above and beyond the call of duty in action with the enemy in the vicinity of Oliveto, Italy, on 23 September 1943. Cpl. Slaton was lead scout of an infantry squad which had been committed to a flank to knock out enemy resistance which had succeeded in pinning 2 attacking platoons to the ground. Working ahead of his squad, Cpl. Slaton crept upon an enemy machinegun nest and, assaulting it with his bayonet, succeeded in killing the gunner. When his bayonet stuck, he detached it from the rifle and killed another gunner with rifle fire. At that time he was fired upon by a machinegun to his immediate left. Cpl. Slaton then moved over open ground under constant fire to within throwing distance, and on his second try scored a direct hit on the second enemy machinegun nest, killing 2 enemy gunners. At that time a third machinegun fired on him 100 yards to his front, and Cpl. Slaton killed both of these enemy gunners with rifle fire. As a result of Cpl. Slaton's heroic action in immobilizing 3 enemy machinegun nests with bayonet, grenade, and rifle fire, the 2 rifle platoons which were receiving heavy casualties from enemy fire were enabled to withdraw to covered positions and again take the initiative. Cpl. Slaton withdrew under mortar fire on order of his platoon leader at dusk that evening. The heroic actions of Cpl. Slaton were far above and beyond the call of duty and are worthy of emulation.

*SMITH, FURMAN L.

Rank and organization: Private, U.S. Army, 135th Infantry, 34th Infantry Division. Place and date: Near Lanuvio, Italy, 31 May 1944. Entered service at: Central, S.C. Birth: Six Miles, S.C. G.O. No.: 6, 24 January 1945. Citation: For conspicuous gallantry and intrepidity at the risk of his life above and beyond the call of duty. In its attack on a strong point, an infantry company was held up by intense enemy fire. The group to which Pvt. Smith belonged was far in the lead when attacked by a force of 80 Germans. The squad leader and 1 other man were seriously wounded and other members of the group withdrew to the company position, but Pvt. Smith refused to leave his wounded comrades. He placed them in the shelter of shell craters and then alone faced a strong enemy counterattack, temporarily checking it by his accurate rifle fire at close range, killing and wounding many of the foe. Against overwhelming odds, he stood his ground until shot down and killed, rifle in hand.

SMITH, JOHN LUCIAN

Rank and organization: Major, U.S. Marine Corps, Marine Fighter Squadron 223, Place and date: In the Solomon Islands area, August-September 1942. Entered service at: Oklahoma. Born: 26 December 1914, Lexington, Okla. Other Navy award: Legion of Merit. Citation: For conspicuous gallantry and heroic achievement in aerial combat above and beyond the call of duty as commanding officer of Marine Fighting Squadron 223 during operations against enemy Japanese forces in the Solomon Islands area, August-September 1942. Repeatedly risking his life in aggressive and daring attacks, Maj. Smith led his squadron against a determined force, greatly superior in numbers, personally shooting down 16 Japanese planes between 21 August and 15 September 1942. In spite of the limited combat experience of many of the pilots of this squadron, they achieved the notable record of a total of 83 enemy aircraft destroyed in this period, mainly attributable to the thorough training under Maj. Smith and to his intrepid and inspiring leadership. His bold tactics and indomitable fighting spirit, and the valiant and zealous fortitude of the men of his command not only rendered the enemy's attacks ineffective and costly to Japan, but contributed to the security of our advance base. His loyal and courageous devotion to duty sustains and enhances the finest traditions of the U.S. Naval Service.

SMITH, MAYNARD H. (Air Mission)

Rank and organization. Sergeant, U.S. Army Air Corps, 423d Bombardment Squadron, 306th Bomber Group. Place and date: Over Europe, 1 May 1943. Entered service at: Cairo, Mich. Born: 1911, Cairo Mich. G.O. No.: 38, 12 July 1943. Citation: For conspicuous gallantry and intrepidity in action above and beyond the call of duty. The aircraft of which Sgt. Smith was a gunner was subjected to intense enemy antiaircraft fire and determined fighter airplane attacks while returning from a mission over enemy-occupied continental Europe on 1 May 1943. The airplane was hit several times by antiaircraft fire and cannon shells of the fighter airplanes, 2 of the crew were seriously wounded, the aircraft's oxygen system shot out, and several vital control cables severed when intense fires were ignited simultaneously in the radio compartment and waist sections. The situation became so acute that 3 of the crew bailed out into the comparative safety of the sea. Sgt. Smith, then on his first combat mission, elected to fight the fire by himself, administered first aid to the wounded tail gunner, manned the waist guns, and fought the intense flames alternately. The escaping oxygen fanned the fire to such intense heat that the ammunition in the radio compartment began to explode, the radio, gun mount, and camera were melted, and the compartment completely gutted. Sgt. Smith threw the exploding ammunition overboard, fought the fire until all the firefighting aids were exhausted, manned the workable guns until the enemy fighters were driven away, further administered first aid to his wounded comrade, and then by wrapping himself in protecting cloth, completely extinguished the fire by hand. This soldier's gallantry in action, undaunted bravery, and loyalty to his aircraft and fellow crewmembers, without regard for his own personal safety, is an inspiration to the U.S. Armed Forces.

SODERMAN, WILLIAM A.

Rank and organization: Private First Class, U.S. Army, Company K, 9th Infantry, 2d Infantry Division. Place and date: Near Rocherath, Belgium, 17 December 1944. Entered service at: West Haven, Conn. Birth: West Haven, Conn. G.O. No.: 97, 1 November 1945. Citation: Armed with a bazooka, he defended a key road junction near Rocherath, Belgium, on 17 December 1944, during the German Ardennes counteroffensive. After a heavy artillery barrage had wounded and forced the withdrawal of his assistant, he heard enemy tanks approaching the position where he calmly waited in the gathering darkness of early evening until the 5 Mark V tanks which made up the hostile force were within pointblank range. He then stood up, completely disregarding the firepower that could be brought to bear upon him, and launched a rocket into the lead tank, setting it afire and forcing its crew to abandon it as the other tanks pressed on before Pfc. Soderman could reload. The daring bazookaman remained at his post all night under severe artillery, mortar, and machinegun fire, awaiting the next onslaught, which was made shortly after dawn by 5 more tanks Running along a ditch to meet them, he reached an advantageous point and there leaped to the road in full view of the tank gunners, deliberately aimed his weapon and disabled the lead tank. The other vehicles, thwarted by a deep ditch in their attempt to go around the crippled machine, withdrew. While returning to his post Pfc. Soderman, braving heavy fire to attack an enemy infantry platoon from close range, killed at least 3 Germans and wounded several others with a round from his bazooka. By this time, enemy pressure had made Company K's position untenable. Orders were issued for withdrawal to an assembly area, where Pfc. Soderman was located when he once more heard enemy tanks approaching. Knowing that elements of the company had not completed their disengaging maneuver and were consequently extremely vulnerable to an armored attack, he hurried from his comparatively safe position to meet the tanks. Once more he disabled the lead tank with a single rocket, his last; but before he could reach cover, machinegun bullets from the tank ripped into his right shoulder. Unarmed and seriously wounded he dragged himself along a ditch to the American lines and was evacuated. Through his unfaltering courage against overwhelming odds, Pfc. Soderman contributed in great measure to the defense of Rocherath, exhibiting to a superlative degree the intrepidity and heroism with which American soldiers met and smashed the savage power of the last great German offensive

SORENSON, RICHARD KEITH

Rank and organization: Private, U.S. Marine Corps Reserve, 4th Marine Division. Place and date: Namur Island, Kwajalein Atoll Marshall Islands, 1-2 February 1944. Entered service at: Minnesota. Born: 28 August 1924, Anoka, Minn. Citation: For conspicuous gallantry and intrepidity at the risk of his life above and beyond the call of duty while serving with an assault battalion attached to the 4th Marine Division during the battle of Namur Island, Kwajalein Atoll, Marshall Islands, on 1-2 February 1944. Putting up a brave defense against a particularly violent counterattack by the enemy during invasion operations, Pvt. Sorenson and 5 other marines occupying a shellhole were endangered by a Japanese grenade thrown into their midst. Unhesitatingly, and with complete disregard for his own safety, Pvt. Sorenson hurled himself upon the deadly weapon, heroically taking the full impact of the explosion. As a result of his gallant action, he was severely wounded, but the lives of his comrades were saved. His great personal valor and exceptional spirit of self-sacrifice in the face of almost certain death were in keeping with the highest traditions of the U.S. Naval Service.

*SPECKER, JOE C.

Rank and organization: Sergeant, U.S. Army, 48th Engineer Combat Battalion. Place and date: At Mount Porchia, Italy, 7 January 1944. Entered service at: Odessa, Mo. Birth: Odessa, Mo. G.O. No.. 56, 12 July 1944. Citation: For conspicuous gallantry and intrepidity at risk of life, above and beyond the call of duty, in action involving actual conflict. On the night of 7 January 1944, Sgt. Specker, with his company, was advancing up the slope of Mount Porchia, Italy. He was sent forward on reconnaissance and on his return he reported to his company commander the fact that there was an enemy machinegun nest and several well-placed snipers directly in the path and awaiting the company. Sgt. Specker requested and was granted permission to place 1 of his machineguns in a position near the enemy machinegun. Voluntarily and alone he made his way up the mountain with a machinegun and a box of ammunition. He was observed by the enemy as he walked along and was severely wounded by the deadly fire directed at him. Though so seriously wounded that he was unable to walk, he continued to drag himself over the jagged edges of rock and rough terrain until he reached the position at which he desired to set up his machinegun. He set up the gun so well and fired so accurately that the enemy machine-gun nest was silenced and the remainder of the snipers forced to retire, enabling his platoon to obtain their objective. Sgt. Specker was found dead at his gun. His personal bravery, self-sacrifice, and determination were an inspiration to his officers and fellow soldiers.

SPURRIER, JUNIOR J.

Rank and organization: Staff Sergeant, U.S. Army, Company G, 134th Infantry, 35th Infantry Division. Place and dare: Achain, France, 13 November 1944. Entered service at: Riggs, Ky. Birth: Russell County, Ky.

G.O. No.: 18, 15 March 1945. Citation: For conspicuous gallantry and intrepidity at risk of his life above and beyond the call of duty in action against the enemy at Achain, France, on 13 November 1944. At 2 p.m., Company G attacked the village of Achain from the east. S/Sgt. Spurrier armed with a BAR passed around the village and advanced alone. Attacking from the west, he immediately killed 3 Germans. From this time until dark, S/Sgt. Spurrier, using at different times his BAR and Ml rifle, American and German rocket launchers, a German automatic pistol, and handgrenades, continued his solitary attack against the enemy regardless of all types of small-arms and automatic-weapons fire. As a result of his heroic actions he killed an officer and 24 enlisted men and captured 2 officers and 2 enlisted men. His valor has shed fresh honor on the U.S. Armed Forces.

*SQUIRES, JOHN C.

Rank and organization: Sergeant (then Private First Class), U.S. Army, Company A, 30th Infantry, 3d Infantry Division. Place and date: Near Padiglione, Italy, 23-24 April 1944. Entered service at: Louisville, Ky. Birth: Louisville, Ky. G.O. No.: 78, 2 October 1944. Citation: For conspicuous gallantry and intrepidity at risk of life above and beyond the call of duty. At the start of his company's attack on strongly held enemy positions in and around Spaccasassi Creek, near Padiglione, Italy, on the night of 23-24 April 1944, Pfc. Squires, platoon messenger, participating in his first offensive action, braved intense artillery, mortar, and antitank gun fire in order to investigate the effects of an antitank mine explosion on the leading platoon. Despite shells which burst close to him, Pfc. Squires made his way 50 yards forward to the advance element, noted the situation, reconnoitered a new route of advance and informed his platoon leader of the casualties sustained and the alternate route. Acting without orders, he rounded up stragglers, organized a group of lost men into a squad and led them forward. When the platoon reached Spaccasassi Creek and established an outpost, Pfc. Squires, knowing that almost all of the noncommissioned officers were casualties, placed 8 men in position of his own volition, disregarding enemy machinegun, machine-pistol, and grenade fire which covered the creek draw. When his platoon had been reduced to 14 men, he brought up reinforcements twice. On each trip he went through barbed wire and across an enemy minefield, under intense artillery and mortar fire. Three times in the early morning the outpost was counterattacked. Each time Pfc. Squires ignored withering enemy automatic fire and grenades which struck all around him, and fired hundreds of rounds of rifle, Browning automatic rifle, and captured German Spandau machinegun ammunition at the enemy, inflicting numerous casualties and materially aiding in repulsing the attacks. Following these fights, he moved 50 yards to the south end of the outpost and engaged 21 German soldiers in individual machinegun duels at point-blank range, forcing all 21 enemy to surrender and capturing 13 more Spandau guns. Learning the function of this weapon by questioning a German officer prisoner, he placed the captured guns in position and instructed other members of his platoon in their operation. The next night when the Germans attacked the outpost again he killed 3 and wounded more Germans with captured potato-masher grenades and fire from his Spandau gun. Pfc. Squires was killed in a subsequent action.

*STEIN, TONY

Rank and organization: Corporal, U.S. Marine Corps Reserve. Born: 30 September 1921, Dayton, Ohio. Accredited to: Ohio. citation: For conspicuous gallantry and intrepidity at the risk of his life above and beyond the call of duty while serving with Company A, 1st Battalion, 28th Marines, 5th Marine Division, in action against enemy Japanese forces on Iwo Jima, in the Volcano Islands, 19 February 1945. The first man of his unit to be on station after hitting the beach in the initial assault, Cpl. Stein, armed with a personally improvised aircraft-type weapon, provided rapid covering fire as the remainder of his platoon attempted to move into position. When his comrades were stalled by a concentrated machinegun and mortar barrage, he gallantly stood upright and exposed himself to the enemy's view, thereby drawing the hostile fire to his own person and enabling him to observe the location of the furiously blazing hostile guns. Determined to neutralize the strategically placed weapons, he boldly charged the enemy pillboxes 1 by 1 and succeeded in killing 20 of the enemy during the furious single-handed assault. Cool and courageous under the merciless hail of exploding shells and bullets which fell on all sides, he continued to deliver the fire of his skillfully improvised weapon at a tremendous rate of speed which rapidly exhausted his ammunition. Undaunted, he removed his helmet and shoes to expedite his movements and ran back to the beach for additional ammunition, making a total of 8 trips under intense fire and carrying or assisting a wounded man back each time. Despite the unrelenting savagery and confusion of battle, he rendered prompt assistance to his platoon whenever the unit was in position, directing the fire of a half-track against a stubborn pillbox until he had effected the ultimate destruction of the Japanese fortification. Later in the day, although his weapon was twice shot from his hands, he personally covered the withdrawal of his platoon to the company position. Stouthearted and indomitable, Cpl. Stein, by his aggressive initiative sound judgment, and unwavering devotion to duty in the face of terrific odds, contributed materially to the fulfillment of his mission, and his outstanding valor throughout the bitter hours of conflict sustains and enhances the highest traditions of the U.S. Naval Service.

STREET, GEORGE LEVICK, III

Rank and organization: Commander, U.S. Navy, U.S.S. Tiranle. Place and date: Harbor of Quelpart Island, off the coast of Korea, 14 April 1945. Entered service at: Virginia. Born: 27 July 1913, Richmond, Va. Other Navy awards: Navy Cross, Silver Star with 1 Gold Star. Citation. For conspicuous gallantry and intrepidity at the risk of his life above and beyond the call of duty as commanding officer of the U.S.S. Tirante during the first war patrol of that vessel against enemy Japanese surface forces in the harbor of Quelpart Island, off the coast of Korea, on 14 April 1945. With the crew at surface battle stations, Comdr. (then Lt. Comdr.) Street approached the hostile anchorage from the south within 1,200 yards of the coast to complete a reconnoitering circuit of the island. Leaving the 10-fathom curve far behind he penetrated the mined and shoal-obstructed waters of the restricted harbor despite numerous patrolling vessels and in defiance of 5 shore-based radar stations and menacing aircraft. Prepared to fight it out on the surface if attacked, Comdr. Street went into action, sending 2 torpedoes with deadly accuracy into a large Japanese ammunition ship and exploding the target in a mountainous and blinding glare of white flames. With the Tirante instantly spotted by the enemy as she stood out plainly in the flare of light, he ordered the torpedo data computer set up while retiring and fired his last 2 torpedoes to disintegrate in quick succession the leading frigate and a similar flanking vessel. Clearing the gutted harbor at emergency full speed ahead, he slipped undetected along the shoreline, diving deep as a pursuing patrol dropped a pattern of depth charges at the point of submergence. His illustrious record of combat achievement during the first war patrol of the Tirante characterizes Comdr. Street as a daring and skilled leader and reflects the highest credit upon himself, his valiant command, and the U.S. Naval Service.

*STRYKER, STUART S.

Rank and organization. Private First Class, U.S. Army, Company E, 513th Parachute Infantry, 17th Airborne Division. Place and date: Near Wesel, Germany, 24 March 1945. Entered service at: Portland, Oreg. Birth. Portland, Oreg. G.O. No.: 117, 11 December 1945. Citation. He was a platoon runner, when the unit assembled near Wesel, Germany after a descent east of the Rhine. Attacking along a railroad, Company E reached a point about 250 yards from a large building used as an enemy headquarters and manned by a powerful force of Germans with rifles, machineguns, and 4 field pieces. One platoon made a frontal assault but was pinned down by intense fire from the house after advancing only 50 yards. So badly stricken that it could not return the raking fire, the platoon was at the mercy of German machine gunners when Pfc. Stryker voluntarily left a place of comparative safety, and, armed with a carbine, ran to the head of the unit. In full view of the enemy and under constant fire, he exhorted the men to get to their feet and follow him. Inspired by his fearlessness, they rushed after him in a desperate charge through an increased hail of bullets. Twenty-five yards from the objective the heroic soldier was killed by the enemy fusillades. His gallant and wholly voluntary action in the face of overwhelming firepower, however, so encouraged his comrades and diverted the enemy's attention that other elements of the company were able to surround the house, capturing more than 200 hostile soldiers and much equipment, besides freeing 3 members of an American bomber crew held prisoner there. The intrepidity and unhesitating self-sacrifice of Pfc. Stryker were in keeping with the highest traditions of the military service.

SWETT, JAMES ELMS

Rank and organization: First Lieutenant, U.S. Marine Corps Reserve, Marine Fighter Squadron 221, with Marine Aircraft Group 12, 1st Marine Aircraft Wing. Place and date: Solomon Islands area, 7 April 1943. Entered service at: California. Born: 15 June 1920, Seattle, Wash. Other Navy award: Distinguished Flying Cross with 1 Gold Star. Citation: For extraordinary heroism and personal valor above and beyond the call of duty, as division leader of Marine Fighting Squadron 221 with Marine Aircraft Group 12, 1st Marine Aircraft Wing, in action against enemy Japanese aerial forces in the Solomons Islands area, 7 April 1943. In a daring flight to intercept a wave of 150 Japanese planes, 1st Lt. Swett unhesitatingly hurled his 4-plane division into action against a formation of 15 enemy bombers and personally exploded 3 hostile planes in midair with accurate and deadly fire during his dive. Although separated from his division while clearing the heavy concentration of antiaircraft fire, he boldly attacked 6 enemy bombers, engaged the first 4 in turn and, unaided, shot down all in flames. Exhausting his ammunition as he closed the fifth Japanese bomber, he relentlessly drove his attack against terrific opposition which partially disabled his engine, shattered the windscreen and slashed his face. In spite of this, he brought his battered plane down with skillful precision in the water off Tulagi without further injury. The superb airmanship and tenacious fighting spirit which enabled 1st Lt. Swett to destroy 7 enemy bombers in a single flight were in keeping with the highest traditions of the U.S. Naval Service.

*TERRY, SEYMOUR W.

Rank and organization: Captain, U.S. Army, Company B, 382d Infantry, 96th Infantry Division. Place and date: Zebra Hill, Okinawa, Ryukyu Islands, 11 May 1945. Entered service at: Little Rock, Ark. Birth: Little Rock, Ark. G.O. No.: 23, 6 March 1946. Citation: 1st Lt. Terry was leading an attack against heavily defended Zebra Hill when devastating fire from 5 pillboxes halted the advance. He braved the hail of bullets to secure satchel charges and white phosphorus grenades, and then ran 30 yards directly at the enemy with an ignited charge to the first stronghold, demolished it, and moved on to the other pillboxes, bombarding them with his grenades and calmly cutting down their defenders with rifle fire as they attempted to escape. When he had finished this job by sealing the 4 pillboxes with explosives, he had killed 20 Japanese and destroyed 3 machineguns. The advance was again held up by an intense grenade barrage which inflicted several casualties. Locating the source of enemy fire in trenches on the reverse slope of the hill, 1st Lt. Terry, burdened by 6 satchel charges launched a 1-man assault. He wrecked the enemy's defenses by throwing explosives into their positions and himself accounted for 10 of the 20 hostile troops killed when his men overran the area. Pressing forward again toward a nearby ridge, his 2 assault platoons were stopped by slashing machinegun and mortar fire. He fearlessly ran across 100 yards of fire-swept terrain to join the support platoon and urge it on in a flanking maneuver. This thrust, too, was halted by stubborn resistance. 1st Lt. Terry began another 1-man drive, hurling grenades upon the strongly entrenched defenders until they fled in confusion, leaving 5 dead behind them. Inspired by this bold action, the support platoon charged the retreating enemy and annihilated them. Soon afterward, while organizing his company to repulse a possible counterattack, the gallant company commander was mortally wounded by the burst of an enemy mortar shell. By his indomitable fighting spirit, brilliant leadership, and unwavering courage in the face of tremendous odds, 1st Lt. Terry made possible the accomplishment of his unit's mission and set an example of heroism in keeping with the highest traditions of the military service.

*THOMAS, HERBERT JOSEPH

Rank and organization: Sergeant, U.S. Marine Corps Reserve. Born: 8 February 1918, Columbus, Ohio. Accredited to: West Virginia. Citation: For extraordinary heroism and conspicuous gallantry above and beyond the call of duty while serving with the 3d Marines, 3d Marine Division, in action against enemy Japanese forces during the battle at the Koromokina River, Bougainville Islands, Solomon Islands, on 7 November 1943. Although several of his men were struck by enemy bullets as he led his squad through dense jungle undergrowth in the face of severe hostile machinegun fire, Sgt. Thomas and his group fearlessly pressed forward into the center of the Japanese position and destroyed the crews of 2 machineguns by accurate rifle fire and grenades. Discovering a third gun more difficult to approach, he carefully placed his men closely around him in strategic positions from which they were to charge after he had thrown a grenade into the emplacement. When the grenade struck vines and fell back into the midst of the group, Sgt. Thomas deliberately flung himself upon it to smother the explosion, valiantly sacrificing his life for his comrades. Inspired by his selfless action, his men unhesitatingly charged the enemy machinegun and, with fierce determination, killed the crew and several other nearby-defenders. The splendid initiative and extremely heroic conduct of Sgt. Thomas in carrying out his prompt decision with full knowledge of his fate reflect great credit upon himself and the U.S. Naval Service. He gallantly gave his life for his country.

*THOMAS, WILLIAM H.

Rank and organization: Private First Class, U.S. Army, 149th Infantry, 38th Infantry Division. Place and date: Zambales Mountains Luzon, Philippine Islands, 22 April 1945. Entered service at: Ypsilanti, Mich. Birth. Wynne, Ark. G.O. No.: 81, 24 September 1945. Citation: He was a member of the leading squad of Company B, which was attacking along a narrow, wooded ridge. The enemy strongly entrenched in camouflaged emplacements on the hill beyond directed heavy fire and hurled explosive charges on the attacking riflemen. Pfc. Thomas, an automatic rifleman, was struck by 1 of these charges, which blew off both his legs below the knees. He refused medical aid and evacuation, and continued to fire at the enemy until his weapon was put out of action by an enemy bullet. Still refusing aid, he threw his last 2 grenades. He destroyed 3 of the enemy after suffering the wounds from which he died later that day. The effective fire of Pfc. Thomas prevented the repulse of his platoon and assured the capture of the hostile position. His magnificent courage and heroic devotion to duty provided a lasting inspiration for his comrades.

*THOMASON, CLYDE

Rank and organization: sergeant, U.S. Marine Corps Reserve. Born: 23 May 1914, Atlanta, Ga. Accredited to: Georgia. Citation: For conspicuous heroism and intrepidity above and beyond the call of duty during the Marine Raider Expedition against the Japanese-held island of

Makin on 17-18 August 1942. Leading the advance element of the assault echelon, Sgt. Thomason disposed his men with keen judgment and discrimination and, by his exemplary leadership and great personal valor, exhorted them to like fearless efforts. On 1 occasion, he dauntlessly walked up to a house which concealed an enemy Japanese sniper, forced in the door and shot the man before he could resist. Later in the action, while leading an assault on an enemy position, he gallantly gave his life in the service of his country. His courage and loyal devotion to duty in the face of grave peril were in keeping with the finest traditions of the U.S. Naval Service.

THOMPSON, MAX

Rank and organization: Sergeant, U.S. Army, Company K, 18th Infantry, 1st Infantry Division. Place and date: Near Haaren, Germany, 18 October 1944. Entered service at: Prescott, Ariz. Birth: Bethel, N.C. G.O. No.: 47, 18 June 1945. Citation: On 18 October 1944, Company K, 18th Infantry, occupying a position on a hill near Haaren, Germany, was attacked by an enemy infantry battalion supported by tanks. The assault was preceded by an artillery concentration, lasting an hour, which inflicted heavy casualties on the company. While engaged in moving wounded men to cover, Sgt. Thompson observed that the enemy had overrun the positions of the 3d Platoon. He immediately attempted to stem the enemy's advance single-handedly. He manned an abandoned machinegun and fired on the enemy until a direct hit from a hostile tank destroyed the gun. Shaken and dazed, Sgt. Thompson picked up an automatic rifle and although alone against the enemy force which was pouring into the gap in our lines, he ??fired burst after burst, halting the leading elements of the attack and dispersing those following. Throwing aside his automatic rifle, which had jammed, he took up a rocket gun, fired on a light tank, setting it on fire. By evening the enemy had been driven from the greater part of the captured position but still held 3 pillboxes. Sgt. Thompson's squad was assigned the task of dislodging the enemy from these emplacements. Darkness having fallen and finding that fire of his squad was ineffective from a distance, Sgt. Thompson crawled forward alone to within 20 yards of 1 of the pillboxes and fired grenades into it. The Germans holding the emplacement concentrated their fire upon him. Though wounded, he held his position fearlessly, continued his grenade fire, and finally forced the enemy to abandon the blockhouse. Sgt. Thompson's courageous leadership inspired his men and materially contributed to the clearing of the enemy from his last remaining hold on this important hill position.

*THORNE, HORACE M.

Rank and organization: Corporal, U.S. Army, Troop D, 89th Cavalry Reconnaissance Squadron, 9th Armored Division. Place and date: Near Grufflingen, Belgium, 21 December 1944. Entered service at: Keyport, N.J. Birth. Keansburg, N.J. G.O. No.: 80, 19 September 1945. Citation. He was the leader of a combat patrol on 21 December 1944 near Grufflingen, Belgium, with the mission of driving German forces from dug-in positions in a heavily wooded area. As he advanced his light machinegun, a German Mark III tank emerged from the enemy position and was quickly immobilized by fire from American light tanks supporting the patrol. Two of the enemy tankmen attempted to abandon their vehicle but were killed by Cpl. Thorne's shots before they could jump to the ground. To complete the destruction of the tank and its crew, Cpl. Thorne left his covered position and crept forward alone through intense machinegun fire until close enough to toss 2 grenades into the tank's open turret, killing 2 more Germans. He returned across the same fire-beaten zone as heavy mortar fire began falling in the area, seized his machinegun and, without help, dragged it to the knocked-out tank and set it up on the vehicle's rear deck. He fired short rapid bursts into the enemy positions from his advantageous but exposed location, killing or wounding 8. Two enemy machinegun crews abandoned their positions and retreated in confusion. His gun Jammed; but rather than leave his self-chosen post he attempted to clear the stoppage; enemy small-arms fire, concentrated on the tank, killed him instantly. Cpl. Thorne, displaying heroic initiative and intrepid fighting qualities, inflicted costly casualties on the enemy and insured the success of his patrol's mission by the sacrifice of his life.

*THORSON, JOHN F.

Rank and organization: Private First Class, U.S. Army, Company G, 17th Infantry, 7th Infantry Division. Place and date: Dagami, Leyte, Philippine Islands, 28 October 1944. Entered service at: Armstrong, Iowa Birth: Armstrong, Iowa. G.O. No.: 58, 19 July 1945. Citation: He was an automatic rifleman on 28 October 1944, in the attack on Dagami Leyte, Philippine Islands. A heavily fortified enemy position consisting of pillboxes and supporting trenches held up the advance of his company. His platoon was ordered to out-flank and neutralize the strongpoint. Voluntarily moving well out in front of his group, Pvt. Thorson came upon an enemy fire trench defended by several hostile riflemen and, disregarding the intense fire directed at him, attacked single-handed He was seriously wounded and fell about 6 yards from the trench. Just as the remaining 20 members of the platoon reached him, 1 of the enemy threw a grenade into their midst. Shouting a warning and making a final effort, Pvt. Thorson rolled onto the grenade and smothered the explosion with his body. He was instantly killed, but his magnificent courage and supreme self-sacrifice prevented the injury and possible death of his comrades, and remain with them as a lasting inspiration.

*TIMMERMAN, GRANT FREDERICK

Rank and organization: Sergeant, U.S. Marine Corps. Born: 14 February 1919, Americus, Kans. Accredited to: Kansas. Other Navy award: Bronze Star Medal. Citation: For conspicuous gallantry and intrepidity at the risk of his life above and beyond the call of duty as tank commander serving with the 2d Battalion, 6th Marines, 2d Marine Division, during action against enemy Japanese forces on Saipan, Marianas Islands, on 8 July 1944. Advancing with his tank a few yards ahead of the infantry in support of a vigorous attack on hostile positions, Sgt. Timmerman maintained steady fire from his antiaircraft sky mount machinegun until progress was impeded by a series of enemy trenches and pillboxes. Observing a target of opportunity, he immediately ordered the tank stopped and, mindful of the danger from the muzzle blast as he prepared to open fire with the 75mm., fearlessly stood up in the exposed turret and ordered the infantry to hit the deck. Quick to act as a grenade, hurled by the Japanese, was about to drop into the open turret hatch, Sgt. Timmerman unhesitatingly blocked the opening with his body holding the grenade against his chest and taking the brunt of the explosion. His exception valor and loyalty in saving his men at the cost of his own life reflect the highest credit upon Sgt. Timmerman and the U.S. Naval Service. He gallantly gave his life in the service of his country.

*TOMICH, PETER

Rank and organization: Chief Watertender, U.S. Navy. Born: 3 June 1893, Prolog, Austria. Accredited to: New Jersey. Citation: For distinguished conduct in the line of his profession, and extraordinary courage and disregard of his own safety, during the attack on the Fleet in Pearl Harbor by the Japanese forces on 7 December 1941. Although realizing that the ship was capsizing, as a result of enemy bombing and torpedoing, Tomich remained at his post in the engineering plant of the U.S.S. Utah, until he saw that all boilers were secured and all fireroom personnel had left their stations, and by so doing lost his own life.

TOMINAC, JOHN J.

Rank and organization: First Lieutenant, U.S. Army, Company I, 15th Infantry, 3d Infantry Division. Place and date: Saulx de Vesoul, France, 12 September 1944. Entered service at: Conemaugh, Pa. Birth: Conemaugh,

Pa. G.O. No.: 20, 29 March 1945. Citation: For conspicuous gallantry and intrepidity at risk of life above and beyond the call of duty on 12 September 1944, in an attack on Saulx de Vesoul, France 1st Lt. Tominac charged alone over 50 yards of exposed terrain onto an enemy roadblock to dispatch a 3-man crew of German machine gunners with a single burst from his Thompson machinegun after smashing the enemy outpost, he led 1 of his squads in the annihilation of a second hostile group defended by mortar, machinegun automatic pistol, rifle and grenade fire, killing about 30 of the enemy. Reaching the suburbs of the town, he advanced 50 yards ahead of his men to reconnoiter a third enemy position which commanded the road with a 77-mm. SP gun supported by infantry elements. The SP gun opened fire on his supporting tank, setting it afire with a direct hit. A fragment from the same shell painfully wounded 1st Lt. Tominac in the shoulder, knocking him to the ground. As the crew abandoned the M-4 tank, which was rolling down hill toward the enemy, 1st Lt. Tominac picked himself up and jumped onto the hull of the burning vehicle. Despite withering enemy machinegun, mortar, pistol, and sniper fire, which was ricocheting off the hull and turret of the M-4, 1st Lt. Tominac climbed to the turret and gripped the 50-caliber antiaircraft machinegun. Plainly silhouetted against the sky, painfully wounded, and with the tank burning beneath his feet, he directed bursts of machinegun fire on the roadblock, the SP gun, and the supporting German infantrymen, and forced the enemy to withdraw from his prepared position. Jumping off the tank before it exploded, 1st Lt. Tominac refused evacuation despite his painful wound. Calling upon a sergeant to extract the shell fragments from his shoulder with a pocketknife, he continued to direct the assault, led his squad in a hand grenade attack against a fortified position occupied by 32 of the enemy armed with machineguns, machine pistols, and rifles, and compelled them to surrender. His outstanding heroism and exemplary leadership resulted in the destruction of 4 successive enemy defensive positions, surrender of a vital sector of the city Saulx de Vesoul, and the death or capture of at least 60 of the enemy.

*TOWLE, JOHN R.

Rank and organization: Private, U.S. Army, Company C, 504th Parachute Infantry, 82d Airborne Division. Place and date: Near Oosterhout, Holland, 21 September 1944. Entered service at: Cleveland, Ohio. Birth: Cleveland, Ohio. G.O. No.: 18, 15 March 1945. Citation. For conspicuous gallantry and intrepidity at the risk of life above and beyond the call of duty on 21 September 1944, near Oosterhout, Holland. The rifle company in which Pvt. Towle served as rocket launcher gunner was occupying a defensive position in the west sector of the recently established Nijmegen bridgehead when a strong enemy force of approximately 100 infantry supported by 2 tanks and a half-track formed for a counterattack. With full knowledge of the disastrous consequences resulting not only to his company but to the entire bridgehead by an enemy breakthrough, Pvt. Towle immediately and without orders left his foxhole and moved 200 yards in the face of Intense small-arms fire to a position on an exposed dike roadbed. From this precarious position Pvt. Towle fired his rocket launcher at and hit both tanks to his immediate front. Armored skirting on both tanks prevented penetration by the projectiles, but both vehicles withdrew slightly damaged. Still under intense fire and fully exposed to the enemy, Pvt. Towle then engaged a nearby house which 9 Germans had entered and were using as a strongpoint and with 1 round killed all 9. Hurriedly replenishing his supply of ammunition, Pvt. Towle, motivated only by his high conception of duty which called for the destruction of the enemy at any cost, then rushed approximately 125 yards through grazing enemy fire to an exposed position from which he could engage the enemy half-track with his rocket launcher. While in a kneeling position preparatory to firing on the enemy vehicle, Pvt. Towle was mortally wounded by a mortar shell. By his heroic tenacity, at the price of his life, Pvt. Towle saved the lives of many of his comrades and was directly instrumental in breaking up the enemy counterattack.

TREADWELL, JACK L.

Rank and organization: Captain, U.S. Army, Company F, 180th Infantry, 45th Infantry Division. Place and date: Near Nieder-Wurzbach, Germany, 18 March 1945. Entered service at: Snyder. Okla. Birth: Ashland, Ala. G.O. No.: 79, 14 September 1945. Citation: Capt. Treadwell (then 1st Lt.), commanding officer of Company F, near Nieder-Wurzbach, Germany, in the Siegfried line, single-handedly captured 6 pillboxes and 18 prisoners. Murderous enemy automatic and rifle fire with intermittent artillery bombardments had pinned down his company for hours at the base of a hill defended by concrete fortifications and interlocking trenches. Eight men sent to attack a single point had all become casualties on the hare slope when Capt. Treadwell, armed with a submachinegun and handgrenades, went forward alone to clear the way for his stalled company. Over the terrain devoid of cover and swept by bullets, he fearlessly advanced, firing at the aperture of the nearest pillbox and, when within range, hurling grenades at it. He reached the pillbox, thrust the muzzle of his gun through the port, and drove 4 Germans out with their hands in the air. A fifth was found dead inside. Waving these prisoners back to the American line, he continued under terrible, concentrated fire to the next pillbox and took it in the same manner. In this fort he captured the commander of the hill defenses, whom he sent to the rear with the other prisoners. Never slackening his attack, he then ran across the crest of the hill to a third pillbox, traversing this distance in full view of hostile machine gunners and snipers. He was again successful in taking the enemy position. The Germans quickly fell prey to his further rushes on 3 more pillboxes in the confusion and havoc caused by his whirlwind assaults and capture of their commander. Inspired by the electrifying performance of their leader, the men of Company F stormed after him and overwhelmed resistance on the entire hill, driving a wedge into the Siegfried line and making it possible for their battalion to take its objective. By his courageous willingness to face nearly impossible odds and by his overwhelming one-man offensive, Capt. Treadwell reduced a heavily fortified, seemingly impregnable enemy sector.

*TRUEMPER, WALTER E. (Air Mission)

Rank and organization Second Lieutenant, U.S. Army Air Corps. 510th Bomber Squadron, 351st Bomber Group. Place and date: Over Europe, 20 February 1944. Entered service at: Aurora, Ill. Born: 31 October 1918, Aurora, Ill. G.O. No.: 52, 22 June 1944. Citation: For conspicuous gallantry and intrepidity at risk of life above and beyond the call of duty in action against the enemy in connection with a bombing mission over enemy-occupied Europe on 20 February 1944. The aircraft on which 2d Lt. Truemper was serving as navigator was attacked by a squadron of enemy fighters with the result that the copilot was killed outright, the pilot wounded and rendered unconscious, the radio operator wounded and the plane severely damaged Nevertheless, 2d Lt. Truemper and other members of the crew managed to right the plane and fly it back to their home station, where they contacted the control tower and reported the situation. 2d Lt. Truemper and the engineer volunteered to attempt to land the plane. Other members of the crew were ordered to jump, leaving 2d Lt. Truemper and the engineer aboard. After observing the distressed aircraft from another plane, 2d Lt. Truemper's commanding officer decided the damaged plane could not be landed by the inexperienced crew and ordered them to abandon it and parachute to safety. Demonstrating unsurpassed courage and heroism, 2d Lt. Truemper and the engineer replied that the pilot was still alive but could not be moved and that they would not desert him. They were then told to attempt a landing. After 2 unsuccessful efforts their plane crashed into an open field in a third attempt to land. 2d Lt. Truemper, the engineer, and the wounded pilot were killed.

*TURNER, DAY G.

Rank and organization: Sergeant, U.S. Army, Company B, 319th Infantry, 80th Infantry Division. Place and date: At Dahl, Luxembourg, 8 January 1945. Entered service at. Nescopek, Pa. Birth: Berwick, Pa. G.O. No.: 49, 28 June 1945. Citation: He commanded a 9-man squad with the mission of holding a critical flank position. When overwhelming numbers of the enemy attacked under cover of withering artillery, mortar, and rocket fire, he withdrew his squad into a nearby house, determined to defend it to the last man. The enemy attacked again and again and were repulsed with heavy losses. Supported by direct tank fire, they finally gained entrance, but the intrepid sergeant refused to surrender although 5 of his men were wounded and 1 was killed. He boldly flung a can of flaming oil at the first wave of attackers, dispersing them, and fought doggedly from room to room, closing with the enemy in fierce hand-to-hand encounters. He hurled handgrenade for handgrenade, bayoneted 2 fanatical Germans who rushed a doorway he was defending and fought on with the enemy's weapons when his own ammunition was expended. The savage fight raged for 4 hours, and finally, when only 3 men of the defending squad were left unwounded, the enemy surrendered. Twenty-five prisoners were taken, 11 enemy dead and a great number of wounded were counted. Sgt. Turner's valiant stand will live on as a constant inspiration to his comrades His heroic, inspiring leadership, his determination and courageous devotion to duty exemplify the highest tradition of the military service .

TURNER, GEORGE B.

Rank and organization: Private First Class, U.S. Army, Battery C, 499th Armored Field Artillery Battalion, 14th Armored Division. Place and date. Philippsbourg, France, 3 January 1945. Entered service at: Los Angeles, Calif. Born: 27 June 1899, Longview, Tex. G.O. No.: 79, 14 September 1945. Citation: At Phillippsbourg, France, he was cut off from his artillery unit by an enemy armored infantry attack. Coming upon a friendly infantry company withdrawing under the vicious onslaught, he noticed 2 German tanks and approximately 75 supporting foot soldiers advancing down the main street of the village. Seizing a rocket launcher, he advanced under intense small-arms and cannon fire to meet the tanks and, standing in the middle of the road, fired at them, destroying 1 and disabling the second. From a nearby half-track he then dismounted a machinegun, placed it in the open street and fired into the enemy infantrymen, killing or wounding a great number and breaking up the attack. In the American counterattack which followed, 2 supporting tanks were disabled by an enemy antitank gun. Firing a light machinegun from the hip, Pfc. Turner held off the enemy so that the crews of the disabled vehicles could extricate themselves. He ran through a hail of fire to one of the tanks which had burst into flames and attempted to rescue a man who had been unable to escape; but an explosion of the tank's ammunition frustrated his effort and wounded him painfully. Refusing to be evacuated, he remained with the infantry until the following day, driving off an enemy patrol with serious casualties, assisting in capturing a hostile strong point, and voluntarily and fearlessly driving a truck through heavy enemy fire to deliver wounded men to the rear aid station. The great courage displayed by Pfc. Turner and his magnificently heroic initiative contributed materially to the defense of the French town and inspired the troops about him.

URBAN, MATT

Rank and organization: Lieutenant Colonel (then Captain), 2d Battalion, 60th Infantry Regiment, 9th Infantry Division, World War II. Place and date: Renouf, France, 14 June to 3 September 1944. Entered service at: Fort Bragg, North Carolina, 2 July 1941. Date and place of birth: 25 August 1919, Buffalo, New York. Lieutenant Colonel (then Captain) Matt Urban, 1 12-22-2414, United States Army, who distinguished himself by a series of bold, heroic actions, exemplified by singularly outstanding combat leadership, personal bravery, and tenacious devotion to duty, during the period 14 June to 3 September 1944 while assigned to the 2d Battalion, 60th Infantry Regiment, 9th Infantry Division. On 14 June, Captain Urban's company, attacking at Renouf, France, encountered heavy enemy small arms and tank fire. The enemy tanks were unmercifully raking his unit's positions and inflicting heavy casualties. Captain Urban, realizing that his company was in imminent danger of being decimated, armed himself with a bazooka. He worked his way with an ammo carrier through hedgerows, under a continuing barrage of fire, to a point near the tanks. He brazenly exposed himself to the enemy fire and, firing the bazooka, destroyed both tanks. Responding to Captain Urban's action, his company moved forward and routed the enemy. Later that same day, still in the attack near Orglandes, Captain Urban was wounded in the leg by direct fire from a 37mm tank-gun. He refused evacuation and continued to lead his company until they moved into defensive positions for the night. At 0500 hours the next day, still in the attack near Orglandes, Captain Urban, though badly wounded, directed his company in another attack. One hour later he was again wounded. Suffering from two wounds, one serious, he was evacuated to England. In mid-July, while recovering from his wounds, he learned of his unit's severe losses in the hedgerows of Normandy. Realizing his unit's need for battle-tested leaders, he voluntarily left the hospital and hitchhiked his way back to his unit hear St. Lo, France. Arriving at the 2d Battalion Command Post at 1130 hours, 25 July, he found that his unit had jumped-off at 1100 hours in the first attack of Operation Cobra." Still limping from his leg wound, Captain Urban made his way forward to retake command of his company. He found his company held up by strong enemy opposition. Two supporting tanks had been destroyed and another, intact but with no tank commander or gunner, was not moving. He located a lieutenant in charge of the support tanks and directed a plan of attack to eliminate the enemy strong-point. The lieutenant and a sergeant were immediately killed by the heavy enemy fire when they tried to mount the tank. Captain Urban, though physically hampered by his leg wound and knowing quick action had to be taken, dashed through the scathing fire and mounted the tank. With enemy bullets ricocheting from the tank, Captain Urban ordered the tank forward and, completely exposed to the enemy fire, manned the machine gun and placed devastating fire on the enemy. His action, in the face of enemy fire, galvanized the battalion into action and they attacked and destroyed the enemy position. On 2 August, Captain Urban was wounded in the chest by shell fragments and, disregarding the recommendation of the Battalion Surgeon, again refused evacuation. On 6 August, Captain Urban became the commander of the 2d Battalion. On 15 August, he was again wounded but remained with his unit. On 3 September, the 2d Battalion was given the mission of establishing a crossing-point on the Meuse River near Heer, Belgium. The enemy planned to stop the advance of the allied Army by concentrating heavy forces at the Meuse. The 2d Battalion, attacking toward the crossing-point, encountered fierce enemy artillery, small arms and mortar fire which stopped the attack. Captain Urban quickly moved from his command post to the lead position of the battalion. Reorganizing the attacking elements, he personally led a charge toward the enemy's strong-point. As the charge moved across the open terrain, Captain Urban was seriously wounded in the neck. Although unable to talk above a whisper from the paralyzing neck wound, and in danger of losing his life, he refused to be evacuated until the enemy was routed and his battalion had secured the crossing-point on the Meuse River. Captain Urban's personal leadership, limitless bravery, and repeated extraordinary exposure to enemy fire served as an inspiration to his entire battalion. His valorous and intrepid actions reflect the utmost credit on him and uphold the noble traditions of the United States.

*VALDEZ, JOSE F.

Rank and organization: Private First Class, U.S. Army, Company B, 7th Infantry, 3d Infantry Division. Place and date: Near Rosenkrantz, France, 25 January 1945. Entered service at: Pleasant Grove, Utah. Birth: Governador, N. Mex. G. O. No.: 16, 8 February 1946. Citation: He was on outpost duty with 5 others when the enemy counterattacked with overwhelming strength. From his position near some woods 500 yards beyond the American lines he observed a hostile tank about 75 yards away, and raked it with automatic rifle fire until it withdrew. Soon afterward he saw 3 Germans stealthily approaching through the woods. Scorning cover as the enemy soldiers opened up with heavy automatic weapons fire from a range of 30 yards, he engaged in a fire fight with the attackers until he had killed all 3. The enemy quickly launched an attack with 2 full companies of infantrymen, blasting the patrol with murderous concentrations of automatic and rifle fire and beginning an encircling movement which forced the patrol leader to order a withdrawal. Despite the terrible odds, Pfc. Valdez immediately volunteered to cover the maneuver, and as the patrol 1 by 1 plunged through a hail of bullets toward the American lines, he fired burst after burst into the swarming enemy. Three of his companions were wounded in their dash for safety and he was struck by a bullet that entered his stomach and, passing through his body, emerged from his back. Overcoming agonizing pain, he regained control of himself and resumed his firing position, delivering a protective screen of bullets until all others of the patrol were safe. By field telephone he called for artillery and mortar fire on the Germans and corrected the range until he had shells falling within 50 yards of his position. For 15 minutes he refused to be dislodged by more than 200 of the enemy; then, seeing that the barrage had broken the counter attack, he dragged himself back to his own lines. He died later as a result of his wounds. Through his valiant, intrepid stand and at the cost of his own life, Pfc. Valdez made it possible for his comrades to escape, and was directly responsible for repulsing an attack by vastly superior enemy forces.

*VANCE, LEON R., Jr (Air Mission)

Rank and organization: Lieutenant Colonel, U.S. Army Corps, 489th Bomber Group. Place and date: Over Wimereaux. France, 5 June 1944. Entered service at. Garden City, N.Y. Born: 11 August 1916, Enid, Okla . G.O. No. . 1, 4 January 1 945. Citation: For conspicuous gallantry and intrepidity above and beyond the call of duty on 5 June 1944, when he led a Heavy Bombardment Group, in an attack against defended enemy coastal positions in the vicinity of Wimereaux, France. Approaching the target, his aircraft was hit repeatedly by antiaircraft fire which seriously crippled the ship, killed the pilot, and wounded several members of the crew, including Lt. Col. Vance, whose right foot was practically severed. In spite of his injury, and with 3 engines lost to the flak, he led his formation over the target, bombing it successfully. After applying a tourniquet to his leg with the aid of the radar operator, Lt. Col. Vance, realizing that the ship was approaching a stall altitude with the 1 remaining engine failing, struggled to a semi-upright position beside the copilot and took over control of the ship. Cutting the power and feathering the last engine he put the aircraft in glide sufficiently steep to maintain his airspeed. Gradually losing altitude, he at last reached the English coast, whereupon he ordered all members of the crew to bail out as he knew they would all safely make land. But he received a message over the interphone system which led him to believe 1 of the crewmembers was unable to jump due to injuries; so he made the decision to ditch the ship in the channel, thereby giving this man a chance for life. To add further to the danger of ditching the ship in his crippled condition, there was a 500-pound bomb hung up in the bomb bay. Unable to climb into the seat vacated by the copilot, since his foot, hanging on to his leg by a few tendons, had become lodged behind the copilot's seat, he nevertheless made a successful ditching while lying on the floor using only aileron and elevators for control and the side window of the cockpit for visual reference. On coming to rest in the water the aircraft commenced to sink rapidly with Lt. Col. Vance pinned in the cockpit by the upper turret which had crashed in during the landing. As it was settling beneath the waves an explosion occurred which threw Lt. Col. Vance clear of the wreckage. After clinging to a piece of floating wreckage until he could muster enough strength to inflate his life vest he began searching for the crewmember whom he believed to be aboard. Failing to find anyone he began swimming and was found approximately 50 minutes later by an Air-Sea Rescue craft. By his extraordinary flying skill and gallant leadership, despite his grave injury, Lt. Col. Vance led his formation to a successful bombing of the assigned target and returned the crew to a point where they could bail out with safety. His gallant and valorous decision to ditch the aircraft in order to give the crewmember he believed to be aboard a chance for life exemplifies the highest traditions of the U.S. Armed Forces.

VANDEGRIFT, ALEXANDER ARCHER

Rank and organization: Major General, U.S. Marine Corps, commanding officer of the 1st Marine Division. Place and date: Solomon Islands, 7 August to 9 December 1942. Entered service at: Virginia. Born: 13 March 1887, Charlottesville, Va. Citation: For outstanding and heroic accomplishment above and beyond the call of duty as commanding officer of the 1st Marine Division in operations against enemy Japanese forces in the Solomon Islands during the period 7 August to 9 December 1942. With the adverse factors of weather, terrain, and disease making his task a difficult and hazardous undertaking, and with his command eventually including sea, land, and air forces of Army, Navy, and Marine Corps, Maj. Gen. Vandegrift achieved marked success in commanding the initial landings of the U.S. forces in the Solomon Islands and in their subsequent occupation. His tenacity, courage, and resourcefulness prevailed against a strong, determined, and experienced enemy, and the gallant fighting spirit of the men under his inspiring leadership enabled them to withstand aerial, land, and sea bombardment, to surmount all obstacles, and leave a disorganized and ravaged enemy. This dangerous but vital mission, accomplished at the constant risk of his life, resulted in securing a valuable base for further operations of our forces against the enemy, and its successful completion reflects great credit upon Maj. Gen. Vandegrift, his command, and the U.S. Naval Service.

*VAN NOY, JUNIOR

Rank and organization: Private, U.S. Army, Headquarters Company, Shore Battalion, Engineer Boat and Shore Regiment. Place and date: Near Finschafen, New Guinea, 17 October 1943. Entered service at: Preston, Idaho. Birth: Grace, Idaho. G.O. No.: 17, 26 February 1944. Citation: For conspicuous gallantry and intrepidity above and beyond the call of duty in action with the enemy near Finschafen, New Guinea, on 17 October 1943. When wounded late in September, Pvt. Van Noy declined evacuation and continued on duty. On 17 October 1943 he was gunner in charge of a machinegun post only 5 yards from the water's edge when the alarm was given that 3 enemy barges loaded with troops were approaching the beach in the early morning darkness. One landing barge was sunk by Allied fire, but the other 2 beached 10 yards from Pvt. Van Noy's emplacement. Despite his exposed position, he poured a withering hail of fire into the debarking enemy troops. His loader was wounded by a grenade and evacuated. Pvt. Van Noy, also grievously wounded, remained at his post, ignoring calls of nearby soldiers urging him to withdraw, and continued to fire with deadly accuracy. He expended every round and was found, covered with wounds dead beside his gun. In this action Pvt. Van Noy killed at least half of the 39 enemy taking part in the landing. His heroic tenacity at the price of his life not only saved the lives of many of his comrades, but enabled them to annihilate the attacking detachment.

*VAN VALKENBURGH, FRANKLIN

Rank and organization: Captain, U.S. Navy. Born: 5 April 1888, Minneapolis, Minn. Appointed from: Wisconsin. Citation: For conspicuous devotion to duty, extraordinary courage and complete disregard of his own life, during the attack on the Fleet in Pearl Harbor T.H., by Japanese forces on 7 December 1941. As commanding officer of the U.S.S. Arizona, Capt. Van Valkenburgh gallantly fought his ship until the U.S.S. Arizona blew up from magazine explosions and a direct bomb hit on the bridge which resulted in the loss of his life.

*VAN VOORHIS, BRUCE AVERY

Rank and organization: Lieutenant Commander, U.S. Navy. Born: 29 January 1908, Aberdeen, Wash. Appointed from: Nevada. Citation: For conspicuous gallantry and intrepidity at the risk of his life above and beyond the call of duty as Squadron Commander of Bombing Squadron 102 and as Plane Commander of a PB4Y-I Patrol Bomber operating against the enemy on Japanese-held Greenwich Island during the battle of the Solomon Islands, 6 July 1943. Fully aware of the limited chance of surviving an urgent mission, voluntarily undertaken to prevent a surprise Japanese attack against our forces, Lt. Comdr. Van Voorhis took off in total darkness on a perilous 700-mile flight without escort or support. Successful in reaching his objective despite treacherous and varying winds, low visibility and difficult terrain, he fought a lone but relentless battle under fierce antiaircraft fire and overwhelming aerial opposition. Forced lower and lower by pursuing planes, he coolly persisted in his mission of destruction. Abandoning all chance of a safe return he executed 6 bold ground-level attacks to demolish the enemy's vital radio station, installations, antiaircraft guns and crews with bombs and machinegun fire, and to destroy 1 fighter plane in the air and 3 on the water. Caught in his own bomb blast, Lt. Comdr. Van Voorhis crashed into the lagoon off the beach, sacrificing himself in a single-handed fight against almost insuperable odds, to make a distinctive contribution to our continued offensive in driving the Japanese from the Solomons and, by his superb daring, courage and resoluteness of purpose, enhanced the finest traditions of the U.S. Naval Service. He gallantly gave his life for his country.

*VIALE, ROBERT M.

Rank and organization: Second Lieutenant, U.S. Army, Company K, 148th Infantry, 37th Infantry Division. Place and date: Manila, Luzon, Philippine Islands, 5 February 1945. Entered service at: Ukiah, Calif. Birth: Bayside, Calif. G.O. No.: 92, 25 October 1945. Citation: He displayed conspicuous gallantry and intrepidity above and beyond the call of duty. Forced by the enemy's detonation of prepared demolitions to shift the course of his advance through the city, he led the 1st platoon toward a small bridge, where heavy fire from 3 enemy pillboxes halted the unit. With 2 men he crossed the bridge behind screening grenade smoke to attack the pillboxes. The first he knocked out himself while covered by his men's protecting fire; the other 2 were silenced by 1 of his companions and a bazooka team which he had called up. He suffered a painful wound in the right arm during the action. After his entire platoon had joined him, he pushed ahead through mortar fire and encircling flames. Blocked from the only escape route by an enemy machinegun placed at a street corner, he entered a nearby building with his men to explore possible means of reducing the emplacement. In 1 room he found civilians huddled together, in another, a small window placed high in the wall and reached by a ladder. Because of the relative positions of the window, ladder, and enemy emplacement, he decided that he, being left-handed, could better hurl a grenade than 1 of his men who had made an unsuccessful attempt. Grasping an armed grenade, he started up the ladder. His wounded right arm weakened, and, as he tried to steady himself, the grenade fell to the floor. In the 5 seconds before the grenade would explode, he dropped down, recovered the grenade and looked for a place to dispose of it safely. Finding no way to get rid of the grenade without exposing his own men or the civilians to injury or death, he turned to the wall, held it close to his body and bent over it as it exploded. 2d Lt. Viale died in a few minutes, but his heroic act saved the lives of others.

*VILLEGAS, YSMAEL R.

Rank and organization: Staff Sergeant, U.S. Army, Company F, 127th Infantry, 32d Infantry Division. Place and date: Villa Verde Trail, Luzon, Philippine Islands, 20 March 1945. Entered service at: Casa Blanca, Calif. Birth: Casa Blanca, Calif. G.O. No.: 89, 19 October 1945. Citation: He was a squad leader when his unit, in a forward position, clashed with an enemy strongly entrenched in connected caves and foxholes on commanding ground. He moved boldly from man to man, in the face of bursting grenades and demolition charges, through heavy machinegun and rifle fire, to bolster the spirit of his comrades. Inspired by his gallantry, his men pressed forward to the crest of the hill. Numerous enemy riflemen, refusing to flee, continued firing from their foxholes. S/Sgt. Villegas, with complete disregard for his own safety and the bullets which kicked up the dirt at his feet, charged an enemy position, and, firing at point-blank range killed the Japanese in a foxhole. He rushed a second foxhole while bullets missed him by inches, and killed 1 more of the enemy. In rapid succession he charged a third, a fourth, a fifth foxhole, each time destroying the enemy within. The fire against him increased in intensity, but he pressed onward to attack a sixth position. As he neared his goal, he was hit and killed by enemy fire. Through his heroism and indomitable fighting spirit, S/Sgt. Villegas, at the cost of his life, inspired his men to a determined attack in which they swept the enemy from the field.

VLUG, DIRK J.

Rank and organization: Private First Class, U.S. Army, 126th Infantry, 32d Infantry Division. Place and date. Near Limon, Leyte, Philippine Islands, 15 December 1944. Entered service at: Grand Rapids, Mich. Birth: Maple Lake, Minn. G.O. No.: 60, 26 June 1946. Citation: He displayed conspicuous gallantry and intrepidity above and beyond the call of duty when an American roadblock on the Ormoc Road was attacked by a group of enemy tanks. He left his covered position, and with a rocket launcher and 6 rounds of ammunition, advanced alone under intense machinegun and 37-mm. fire. Loading single-handedly, he destroyed the first tank, killing its occupants with a single round. As the crew of the second tank started to dismount and attack him, he killed 1 of the foe with his pistol, forcing the survivors to return to their vehicle, which he then destroyed with a second round. Three more hostile tanks moved up the road, so he flanked the first and eliminated it, and then, despite a hail of enemy fire, pressed forward again to destroy another. With his last round of ammunition he struck the remaining vehicle, causing it to crash down a steep embankment. Through his sustained heroism in the face of superior forces, Pfc. Vlug alone destroyed 5 enemy tanks and greatly facilitated successful accomplishment of his battalion's mission.

VOSLER, FORREST T. (Air Mission)

Rank and organization: Technical Sergeant, U.S. Army Air Corps. 358th Bomber Squadron, 303d Bomber Group. Place and date. Over Bremen, Germany, 20 December 1943. Entered service at: Rochester, N.Y. Born: 29 July 1923, Lyndonville, N.Y. G.O. No.: 73, 6 September 1944. Citation: For conspicuous gallantry in action against the enemy above and beyond the call of duty while serving as a radio operator-air gunner on a heavy bombardment aircraft in a mission over Bremen, Germany, on 20 December 1943. After bombing the target, the aircraft in which

T/Sgt. Vosler was serving was severely damaged by antiaircraft fire, forced out of formation, and immediately subjected to repeated vicious attacks by enemy fighters. Early in the engagement a 20-mm. cannon shell exploded in the radio compartment, painfully wounding T/Sgt. Vosler in the legs and thighs. At about the same time a direct hit on the tail of the ship seriously wounded the tail gunner and rendered the tail guns inoperative. Realizing the great need for firepower in protecting the vulnerable tail of the ship, T/Sgt. Vosler, with grim determination, kept up a steady stream of deadly fire. Shortly thereafter another 20-mm. enemy shell exploded, wounding T/Sgt. Vosler in the chest and about the face. Pieces of metal lodged in both eyes, impairing his vision to such an extent that he could only distinguish blurred shapes. Displaying remarkable tenacity and courage, he kept firing his guns and declined to take first-aid treatment. The radio equipment had been rendered inoperative during the battle, and when the pilot announced that he would have to ditch, although unable to see and working entirely by touch, T/Sgt. Vosler finally got the set operating and sent out distress signals despite several lapses into unconsciousness. When the ship ditched, T/Sgt. Vosler managed to get out on the wing by himself and hold the wounded tail gunner from slipping off until the other crewmembers could help them into the dinghy. T/Sgt. Vosler's actions on this occasion were an inspiration to all serving with him. The extraordinary courage, coolness, and skill he displayed in the face of great odds, when handicapped by injuries that would have incapacitated the average crewmember, were outstanding.

WAHLEN, GEORGE EDWARD

Rank and organization: Pharmacist's Mate Second Class, U.S. Navy, serving with 2d Battalion, 26th Marines, 5th Marine Division. Place and date: Iwo Jima, Volcano Islands group, 3 March 1945. Entered service at: Utah. Born: 8 August 1924, Ogden, Utah. Citation: For conspicuous gallantry and intrepidity at the risk of his life above and beyond the call of duty while serving with the 2d Battalion, 26th Marines, 5th Marine Division, during action against enemy Japanese forces on Iwo Jima in the Volcano group on 3 March 1945. Painfully wounded in the bitter action on 26 February, Wahlen remained on the battlefield, advancing well forward of the frontlines to aid a wounded marine and carrying him back to safety despite a terrific concentration of fire. Tireless in his ministrations, he consistently disregarded all danger to attend his fighting comrades as they fell under the devastating rain of shrapnel and bullets, and rendered prompt assistance to various elements of his combat group as required. When an adjacent platoon suffered heavy casualties, he defied the continuous pounding of heavy mortars and deadly fire of enemy rifles to care for the wounded, working rapidly in an area swept by constant fire and treating 14 casualties before returning to his own platoon. Wounded again on 2 March, he gallantly refused evacuation, moving out with his company the following day in a furious assault across 600 yards of open terrain and repeatedly rendering medical aid while exposed to the blasting fury of powerful Japanese guns. Stouthearted and indomitable, he persevered in his determined efforts as his unit waged fierce battle and, unable to walk after sustaining a third agonizing wound, resolutely crawled 50 yards to administer first aid to still another fallen fighter. By his dauntless fortitude and valor, Wahlen served as a constant inspiration and contributed vitally to the high morale of his company during critical phases of this strategically important engagement. His heroic spirit of self-sacrifice in the face of overwhelming enemy fire upheld the highest traditions of the U.S. Naval Service.

WAINWRIGHT, JONATHAN M.

Rank and organization: General, Commanding U.S. Army Forces in the Philippines. Place and date: Philippine Islands, 12 March to 7 May 1942. Entered service at: Skaneateles, N.Y. Birth: Walla Walla, Wash. G.O. No.: 80, 19 September 1945. Citation: Distinguished himself by intrepid and determined leadership against greatly superior enemy forces. At the repeated risk of life above and beyond the call of duty in his position, he frequented the firing line of his troops where his presence provided the example and incentive that helped make the gallant efforts of these men possible. The final stand on beleaguered Corregidor, for which he was in an important measure personally responsible, commanded the admiration of the Nation's allies. It reflected the high morale of American arms in the face of overwhelming odds. His courage and resolution were a vitally needed inspiration to the then sorely pressed freedom-loving peoples of the world.

*WALKER, KENNETH N. (Air Mission)

Rank and organization: Brigadier General, U.S. Army Air Corps, Commander of V Bomber Command. Place and date: Rabaul, New Britain, 5 January 1943. Entered service at. Colorado. Birth: Cerrillos, N. Mex. G.O. No.: 13, 11 March 1943. Citation: For conspicuous leadership above and beyond the call of duty involving personal valor and intrepidity at an extreme hazard to life. As commander of the 5th Bomber Command during the period from 5 September 1942, to 5 January 1943, Brig. Gen. Walker repeatedly accompanied his units on bombing missions deep into enemy-held territory. From the lessons personally gained under combat conditions, he developed a highly efficient technique for bombing when opposed by enemy fighter airplanes and by antiaircraft fire. On 5 January 1943, in the face of extremely heavy antiaircraft fire and determined opposition by enemy fighters, he led an effective daylight bombing attack against shipping in the harbor at Rabaul, New Britain, which resulted in direct hits on 9 enemy vessels. During this action his airplane was disabled and forced down by the attack of an overwhelming number of enemy fighters.

*WALLACE, HERMAN C.

Rank and organization: Private First Class, U.S. Army, Company B, 301st Engineer Combat Battalion, 76th Infantry Division. Place and date: Near Prumzurley, Germany, 27 February 1945. Entered service at: Lubbock, Tex. Birth: Marlow, Okla. G.O. No.: 92, 25 October 1945. Citation: He displayed conspicuous gallantry and intrepidity. While helping clear enemy mines from a road, he stepped on a well-concealed S-type antipersonnel mine. Hearing the characteristic noise indicating that the mine had been activated and, if he stepped aside, would be thrown upward to explode above ground and spray the area with fragments, surely killing 2 comrades directly behind him and endangering other members of his squad, he deliberately placed his other foot on the mine even though his best chance for survival was to fall prone. Pvt. Wallace was killed when the charge detonated, but his supreme heroism at the cost of his life confined the blast to the ground and his own body and saved his fellow soldiers from death or injury.

WALSH, KENNETH AMBROSE

Rank and organization: First Lieutenant, pilot in Marine Fighting Squadron 124, U.S. Marine Corps. Place and date: Solomon Islands area, 15 and 30 August 1943. Entered service at: New York. Born: 24 November 1916, Brooklyn, N.Y. Other Navy awards: Distinguished Flying Cross with 5 Gold Stars. Citation: For extraordinary heroism and intrepidity above and beyond the call of duty as a pilot in Marine Fighting Squadron 124 in aerial combat against enemy Japanese forces in the Solomon Islands area. Determined to thwart the enemy's attempt to bomb Allied ground forces and shipping at Vella Lavella on 15 August 1943, 1st Lt. Walsh repeatedly dived his plane into an enemy formation outnumbering his own division 6 to 1 and, although his plane was hit numerous times, shot down 2 Japanese dive bombers and 1 fighter. After developing engine trouble on 30 August during a vital escort mission, 1st Lt. Walsh landed his mechanically disabled plane at Munda, quickly replaced it with another, and proceeded to rejoin his flight over Kahili. Separated from his escort group when he encountered approximately 50 Japanese Zeros, he unhesitatingly attacked, striking with relentless fury in his lone battle against a powerful force. He destroyed 4 hostile fighters before cannon shellfire forced him to make a dead-stick landing off Vella Lavella where he was later picked up. His valiant leadership and his daring skill as a flier served as a source of confidence and inspiration to his fellow pilots and reflect the highest credit upon the U.S. Naval Service.

*WALSH, WILLIAM GARY

Rank and organization: Gunnery Sergeant, U.S. Marine Corps Reserve. Born: 7 April 1922, Roxbury, Mass. Accredited to: Massachusetts. Citation: For extraordinary gallantry and intrepidity at the risk of his life above and beyond the call of duty as leader of an assault platoon, attached to Company G, 3d Battalion, 27th Marines, 5th Marine Division, in action against enemy Japanese forces at Iwo Jima, Volcano Islands on 27 February 1945. With the advance of his company toward Hill 362 disrupted by vicious machinegun fire from a forward position which guarded the approaches to this key enemy stronghold, G/Sgt. Walsh fearlessly charged at the head of his platoon against the Japanese entrenched on the ridge above him, utterly oblivious to the unrelenting fury of hostile automatic weapons fire and handgrenades employed with fanatic desperation to smash his daring assault. Thrown back by the enemy's savage resistance, he once again led his men in a seemingly impossible attack up the steep, rocky slope, boldly defiant of the annihilating streams of bullets which saturated the area. Despite his own casualty losses and the overwhelming advantage held by the Japanese in superior numbers and dominant position, he gained the ridge's top only to be subjected to an intense barrage of handgrenades thrown by the remaining Japanese staging a suicidal last stand on the reverse slope.

When 1 of the grenades fell in the midst of his surviving men, huddled together in a small trench, G/Sgt. Walsh, in a final valiant act of complete self-sacrifice, instantly threw himself upon the deadly bomb, absorbing with his own body the full and terrific force of the explosion. Through his extraordinary initiative and inspiring valor in the face of almost certain death, he saved his comrades from injury and possible loss of life and enabled his company to seize and hold this vital enemy position. He gallantly gave his life for his country.

*WARD, JAMES RICHARD

Rank and organization: Seaman First Class, U.S. Navy. Born: 10 September 1921, Springfield, Ohio. Entered service at: Springfield, Ohio. Citation: For conspicuous devotion to duty, extraordinary courage and complete disregard of his life, above and beyond the call of duty, during the attack on the Fleet in Pearl Harbor by Japanese forces on 7 December 1941. When it was seen that the U.S.S. Oklahoma was going to capsize and the order was given to abandon ship, Ward remained in a turret holding a flashlight so the remainder of the turret crew could see to escape, thereby sacrificing his own life.

WARE, KEITH L.

Rank and organization: Lieutenant Colonel, U.S. Army, 1st Battalion, 1 5th Infantry, 3d Infantry Division. Place and date: Near Sigolsheim, France, 26 December 1944. Entered service at: Glendale, Calif. Born: 23 November 1915, Denver, Colo. G.O. No.: 47, 18 June 1945. Citation: Commanding the 1st Battalion attacking a strongly held enemy position on a hill near Sigolsheim, France, on 26 December 1944, found that 1 of his assault companies had been stopped and forced to dig in by a concentration of enemy artillery, mortar, and machinegun fire. The company had suffered casualties in attempting to take the hill. Realizing that his men must be inspired to new courage, Lt. Col. Ware went forward 150 yards beyond the most forward elements of his command, and for 2 hours reconnoitered the enemy positions, deliberately drawing fire upon himself which caused the enemy to disclose his dispositions. Returning to his company, he armed himself with an automatic rifle and boldly advanced upon the enemy, followed by 2 officers, 9 enlisted men, and a tank. Approaching an enemy machinegun, Lt. Col. Ware shot 2 German riflemen and fired tracers into the emplacement, indicating its position to his tank, which promptly knocked the gun out of action. Lt. Col. Ware turned his attention to a second machinegun, killing 2 of its supporting riflemen and forcing the others to surrender. The tank destroyed the gun. Having expended the ammunition for the automatic rifle, Lt. Col. Ware took up an Ml rifle, killed a German rifleman, and fired upon a third machinegun 50 yards away. His tank silenced the gun. Upon his approach to a fourth machinegun, its supporting riflemen surrendered and his tank disposed of the gun. During this action Lt. Col. Ware's small assault group was fully engaged in attacking enemy positions that were not receiving his direct and personal attention. Five of his party of 11 were casualties and Lt. Col. Ware was wounded but refused medical attention until this important hill position was cleared of the enemy and securely occupied by his command.

*WARNER, HENRY F.

Rank and organization: Corporal, U.S. Army, Antitank Company, 2d Battalion, 26th Infantry, 1st Infantry Division. Place and date: Near Dom Butgenbach, Belgium, 20-21 December 1944. Entered service at: Troy, N.C. Born: 23 August 1923, Troy, N.C. G.O. No.: 48, 23 June 1945. Citation: Serving as 57-mm. antitank gunner with the 2d Battalion, he was a major factor in stopping enemy tanks during heavy attacks against the battalion position near Dom Butgenbach, Belgium, on 20-21 December 1944. In the first attack, launched in the early morning of the 20th, enemy tanks succeeded in penetrating parts of the line. Cpl. Warner, disregarding the concentrated cannon and machinegun fire from 2 tanks bearing down on him, and ignoring the imminent danger of being overrun by the infantry moving under tank cover, destroyed the first tank and scored a direct and deadly hit upon the second. A third tank approached to within 5 yards of his position while he was attempting to clear a jammed breach lock. Jumping from his gun pit, he engaged in a pistol duel with the tank commander standing in the turret, killing him and forcing the tank to withdraw. Following a day and night during which our forces were subjected to constant shelling, mortar barrages, and numerous unsuccessful infantry attacks, the enemy struck in great force on the early morning of the 21st. Seeing a Mark IV tank looming out of the mist and heading toward his position, Cpl. Warner scored a direct hit. Disregarding his injuries, he endeavored to finish the loading and again fire at the tank whose motor was now aflame, when a second machinegun burst killed him. Cpl. Warner's gallantry and intrepidity at the risk of life above and beyond the call of duty contributed materially to the successful defense against the enemy attacks.

WATSON, WILSON DOUGLAS

Rank and organization: Private, U.S. Marine Corps Reserve, 2d Battalion, 9th Marines, 3d Marine Division. Place and date: Iwo Jima, Volcano Islands, 26 and 27 February 1945. Entered service at: Arkansas. Born: 18 February 1921, Tuscumbia, Ala. Citation: For conspicuous gallantry and intrepidity at the risk of his life above and beyond the call of duty as automatic rifleman serving with the 2d Battalion, 9th Marines, 3d Marine Division, during action against enemy Japanese forces on Iwo Jima, Volcano Islands, 26 and 27 February 1945. With his squad abruptly halted by intense fire from enemy fortifications in the high rocky ridges and crags commanding the line of advance, Pvt. Watson boldly rushed 1 pillbox and fired into the embrasure with his weapon, keeping the enemy pinned down single-handedly until he was in a position to hurl in a grenade, and then running to the rear of the emplacement to destroy the retreating Japanese and enable his platoon to take its objective. Again pinned down at the foot of a small hill, he dauntlessly scaled the jagged incline under fierce mortar and machinegun barrages and, with his assistant BAR man, charged the crest of the hill, firing from his hip. Fighting furiously against Japanese troops attacking with grenades and knee mortars from the reverse slope, he stood fearlessly erect in his exposed position to cover the hostile entrenchments and held the hill under savage fire for 15 minutes, killing 60 Japanese before his ammunition was exhausted and his platoon was able to join him. His courageous initiative and valiant fighting spirit against devastating odds were directly responsible for the continued advance of his platoon, and his inspiring leadership throughout this bitterly fought action reflects the highest credit upon Pvt. Watson and the U.S. Naval Service.

*WAUGH, ROBERT T.

Rank and organization: First Lieutenant, U.S. Army, 339th Infantry, 85th Infantry Division. Place and date: Near Tremensucli, Italy, 11-14 May 1944. Entered service at: Augusta, Maine. Birth: Ashton, R.I. G.O. No.: 79, 4 October 1944. Citation: For conspicuous gallantry and intrepidity at risk of life above and beyond the call of duty in action with the enemy. In the course of an attack upon an enemy-held hill on 11 May, 1st Lt. Waugh personally reconnoitered a heavily mined area before entering it with his platoon. Directing his men to deliver fire on 6 bunkers guarding this hill, 1st Lt. Waugh advanced alone against them, reached the first bunker, threw phosphorus grenades into it and as the defenders emerged, killed them with a burst from his tommygun. He repeated this process on the 5 remaining bunkers, killing or capturing the occupants. On the morning of 14 May, 1st Lt. Waugh ordered his platoon to lay a base of fire on 2 enemy pillboxes located on a knoll which commanded the only trail up the hill. He then ran to the first pillbox, threw several grenades into it, drove the defenders into the open, and killed them. The second pillbox was next taken by this intrepid officer by similar methods. The fearless actions of 1st Lt. Waugh broke the Gustav Line at that point, neutralizing 6 bunkers and 2 pillboxes and he was personally responsible for the death of 30 of the enemy and the capture of 25 others. He was later killed in action in Itri, Italy, while leading his platoon in an attack.

WAYBUR, DAVID C.

Rank and organization: First Lieutenant, U.S. Army, 3d Reconnaissance Troop, 3d Infantry Division. Place and date: Near Agrigento, Sicily, 17 July 1943. Entered service at: Piedmont, Calif. Birth: Oakland, Calif. G.O. No.: 69, 21 October 1943. Citation: For conspicuous gallantry and intrepidity at the risk of life above and beyond the call of duty in action involving actual conflict with the enemy. Commander of a reconnaissance platoon, 1st Lt. Waybur volunteered to lead a 3-vehicle patrol into enemy-held territory to locate an isolated Ranger unit. Proceeding under cover of darkness, over roads known to be heavily mined, and strongly defended by road blocks and machinegun positions, the patrol's progress was halted at a bridge which had been destroyed by enemy troops and was suddenly cut off from its supporting vehicles by 4 enemy tanks. Although hopelessly outnumbered and out-gunned, and himself and his men completely exposed, he quickly dispersed his vehicles and ordered his gunners to open fire with their .30 and .50 caliber machineguns. Then, with ammunition exhausted, 3 of his men hit and himself seriously wounded, he seized his .45 caliber Thompson submachinegun and standing in the bright moonlight directly in the line of fire, alone engaged the leading tank at 30 yards and succeeded in killing the crewmembers, causing the tank to run onto the bridge and crash into the stream bed. After dispatching 1 of the men for aid he rallied the rest to cover and withstood the continued fire of the tanks till the arrival of aid the following morning.

*WEICHT, ELLIS R.

Rank and organization: Sergeant, U.S. Army, Company F, 142d Infantry, 36th Infantry Division. Place and date St. Hippolyte, France, 3 December 1944. Entered service at: Bedford, Pa. Birth: Clearville, Pa. G.O. No.: 58, 19 July 1945. Citation: For commanding an assault squad in Company F's attack against the strategically important Alsatian town of St. Hippolyte on 3 December 1944. He aggressively led his men down a winding street, clearing the houses of opposition as he advanced. Upon rounding a bend, the group was suddenly brought under the fire of 2 machineguns emplaced in the door and window of a house 100 yards distant. While his squad members took cover, Sgt. Weicht moved rapidly forward to a high rock wall and, fearlessly exposing himself to the enemy action, fired 2 clips of ammunition from his rifle. His fire proving ineffective, he entered a house opposite the enemy gun position, and, firing from a window, killed the 2 hostile gunners. Continuing the attack, the advance was again halted when two 20-mm. guns opened fire on the company. An artillery observer ordered friendly troops to evacuate the area and then directed artillery fire upon the gun positions. Sgt. Weicht remained in the shelled area and continued to fire on the hostile weapons. When the barrage lifted and the enemy soldiers attempted to remove their gun, he killed 2 crewmembers and forced the others to flee. Sgt. Weicht continued to lead his squad forward until he spotted a road block approximate 125 yards away. Moving to the second floor of a nearby house and firing from a window, he killed 3 and wounded several of the enemy. Instantly becoming a target for heavy and direct fire, he disregarded personal safety to continue his fire, with unusual effectiveness, until he was killed by a direct hit from an antitank gun.

*WETZEL, WALTER C.

Rank and organization: Private First Class, U.S. Army, 13th Infantry, 8th Infantry Division. Place and date: Birken, Germany, 3 April 1945. Entered service at: Roseville, Mich. Birth: Huntington, W. Va. G.O. No.: 21, 26 February 1946. Citation: Pfc. Wetzel, an acting squad leader with the Antitank Company of the 13th Infantry, was guarding his platoon's command post in a house at Birken, Germany, during the early morning hours of 3 April 1945, when he detected strong enemy forces moving in to attack. He ran into the house, alerted the occupants and immediately began defending the post against heavy automatic weapons fire coming from the hostile troops. Under cover of darkness the Germans forced their way close to the building where they hurled grenades, 2 of which landed in the room where Pfc. Wetzel and the others had taken up firing positions. Shouting a warning to his fellow soldiers, Pfc. Wetzel threw himself on the grenades and, as they exploded, absorbed their entire blast, suffering wounds from which he died. The supreme gallantry of Pfc. Wetzel saved his comrades from death or serious injury and made it possible for them to continue the defense of the command post and break the power of a dangerous local counterthrust by the enemy. His unhesitating sacrifice of his life was in keeping with the U.S. Army's highest traditions of bravery and heroism.

WHITELEY, ELI

Rank and organization: First Lieutenant, U.S. Army, Company L, 15th Infantry, 3d Infantry Division. Place and date: Sigolsheim, France, 27 December 1944. Entered service at: Georgetown, Tex. Birth: Florence, Tex. G.O. No.: 79, 14 September 1945. Citation: While leading his platoon on 27 December 1944, in savage house-to-house fighting through the fortress town of Sigolsheim, France, he attacked a building through a street swept by withering mortar and automatic weapons fire. He was hit and severely wounded in the arm and shoulder; but he charged into the house alone and killed its 2 defenders. Hurling smoke and fragmentation grenades before him, he reached the next house and stormed inside, killing 2 and capturing 11 of the enemy. He continued leading his platoon in the extremely dangerous task of clearing hostile troops from strong points along the street until he reached a building held by fanatical Nazi troops. Although suffering from wounds which had rendered his left arm useless, he advanced on this strongly defended house, and after blasting out a wall with bazooka fire, charged through a hail of bullets. Wedging his submachinegun under his uninjured arm, he rushed into the house through the hole torn by his rockets, killed 5 of the enemy and forced the remaining 12 to surrender. As he emerged to continue his fearless attack, he was again hit and critically wounded. In agony and with 1 eye pierced by a shell fragment, he shouted for his men to follow him to the next house. He was determined to stay in the fighting, and remained at the head of his platoon until forcibly evacuated. By his disregard for personal safety, his aggressiveness while suffering from severe wounds, his determined leadership and superb courage, 1st Lt. Whiteley killed 9 Germans, captured 23 more and spearheaded an attack which cracked the core of enemy resistance in a vital area.

WHITTINGTON, HULON B.

Rank and organization: Sergeant, U.S. Army, 41st Armored Infantry 2d Armored Division. Place and date: Near Grimesnil, France, 29 July 1944. Entered service at: Bastrop, La. Born: 9 July 1921, Bogalusa, La. G.O. No.: 32, 23 April 1945. Citation: For conspicuous gallantry and intrepidity at the risk of life above and beyond the call of duty. On the night of 29 July 1944, near Grimesnil, France, during an enemy armored attack, Sgt. Whittington, a squad leader, assumed command of his platoon when the platoon leader and platoon sergeant became missing in action. He reorganized the defense and, under fire, courageously crawled between gun positions to check the actions of his men. When the advancing enemy attempted to penetrate a roadblock, Sgt.

Whittington, completely disregarding intense enemy action, mounted a tank and by shouting through the turret, directed it into position to fire pointblank at the leading Mark V German tank. The destruction of this vehicle blocked all movement of the remaining enemy column consisting of over 100 vehicles of a Panzer unit. The blocked vehicles were then destroyed by handgrenades, bazooka, tank, and artillery fire and large numbers of enemy personnel were wiped out by a bold and resolute bayonet charge inspired by Sgt. Whittington. When the medical aid man had become a casualty, Sgt. Whittington personally administered first aid to his wounded men. The dynamic leadership, the inspiring example, and the dauntless courage of Sgt. Whittington, above and beyond the call of duty, are in keeping with the highest traditions of the military service.

WIEDORFER, PAUL J.

Rank and organization: Staff Sergeant (then Private), U.S. Army, Company G, 318th Infantry, 80th Infantry Division. Place and date: Near, Chaumont, Belgium, 25 December 1944. Entered service at: Baltimore, Md. Birth: Baltimore, Md. G.O. No.: 45, 12 June 1945. Citation: He alone made it possible for his company to advance until its objective was seized. Company G had cleared a wooded area of snipers, and 1 platoon was advancing across an open clearing toward another wood when it was met by heavy machinegun fire from 2 German positions dug in at the edge of the second wood. These positions were flanked by enemy riflemen. The platoon took cover behind a small ridge approximately 40 yards from the enemy position. There was no other available protection and the entire platoon was pinned down by the German fire. It was about noon and the day was clear, but the terrain extremely difficult due to a 3-inch snowfall the night before over ice-covered ground. Pvt. Wiedorfer, realizing that the platoon advance could not continue until the 2 enemy machinegun nests were destroyed, voluntarily charged alone across the slippery open ground with no protecting cover of any kind. Running in a crouched position, under a hail of enemy fire, he slipped and fell in the snow, but quickly rose and continued forward with the enemy concentrating automatic and small-arms fire on him as he advanced. Miraculously escaping injury, Pvt. Wiedorfer reached a point some 10 yards from the first machinegun emplacement and hurled a handgrenade into it. With his rifle he killed the remaining Germans, and, without hesitation, wheeled to the right and attacked the second emplacement. One of the enemy was wounded by his fire and the other 6 immediately surrendered. This heroic action by 1 man enabled the platoon to advance from behind its protecting ridge and continue successfully to reach its objective. A few minutes later, when both the platoon leader and the platoon sergeant were wounded, Pvt. Wiedorfer assumed command of the platoon, leading it forward with inspired energy until the mission was accomplished.

*WIGLE, THOMAS W.

Rank and organization: Second Lieutenant, U.S. Army, Company K, 135th Infantry, 34th Infantry Division. Place and date: Monte Frassino, Italy, 14 September 1944. Entered service at: Detroit, Mich. Birth: Indianapolis, Ind. G.O. No.: 8, 7 February 1945. Citation: For conspicuous gallantry and intrepidity at the risk of life above and beyond the call of duty in the vicinity of Monte Frassino, Italy. The 3d Platoon, in attempting to seize a strongly fortified hill position protected by 3 parallel high terraced stone walls, was twice thrown back by the withering crossfire. 2d Lt. Wigle, acting company executive, observing that the platoon was without an officer, volunteered to command it on the next attack. Leading his men up the bare, rocky slopes through intense and concentrated fire, he succeeded in reaching the first of the stone walls. Having himself boosted to the top and perching there in full view of the enemy, he drew and returned their fire while his men helped each other up and over. Following the same method, he successfully negotiated the second. Upon reaching the top of the third wall, he faced 3 houses which were the key point of the enemy defense. Ordering his men to cover him, he made a dash through a hail of machine-pistol fire to reach the nearest house. Firing his carbine as he entered, he drove the enemy before him out of the back door and into the second house. Following closely on the heels of the foe, he drove them from this house into the third where they took refuge in the cellar. When his men rejoined him, they found him mortally wounded on the cellar stairs which he had started to descend to force the surrender of the enemy. His heroic action resulted in the capture of 36 German soldiers and the seizure of the strongpoint.

WILBUR, WILLIAM H.

Rank and organization: Colonel, U.S. Army, Western Task Force, North Africa. Place and date: Fedala, North Africa, 8 November 1942. Entered service at: Palmer, Mass. Birth: Palmer, Mass. G.O. No.: 2, 13 January 1943. Citation: For conspicuous gallantry and intrepidity in action above and beyond the call of duty. Col. Wilbur prepared the plan for making contact with French commanders in Casablanca and obtaining an armistice to prevent unnecessary bloodshed. On 8 November 1942, he landed at Fedala with the leading assault waves where opposition had developed into a firm and continuous defensive line across his route of advance. Commandeering a vehicle, he was driven toward the hostile defenses under incessant fire, finally locating a French officer who accorded him passage through the forward positions. He then proceeded in total darkness through 16 miles of enemy-occupied country intermittently subjected to heavy bursts of fire, and accomplished his mission by delivering his letters to appropriate French officials in Casablanca. Returning toward his command, Col. Wilbur detected a hostile battery firing effectively on our troops. He took charge of a platoon of American tanks and personally led them in an attack and capture of the battery. From the moment of landing until the cessation of hostile resistance, Col. Wilbur's conduct was voluntary and exemplary in its coolness and daring.

*WILKIN, EDWARD G.

Rank and organization: Corporal, U.S. Army, Company C, 157th Infantry, 45th Infantry Division. Place and date: Siegfried Line in Germany, 18 March 1945. Entered service at: Longmeadow, Mass. Birth: Burlington, Vt. G.O. No.: 119, 17 December 1945. Citation: He spearheaded his unit's assault of the Siegfried Line in Germany. Heavy fire from enemy riflemen and camouflaged pillboxes had pinned down his comrades when he moved forward on his own initiative to reconnoiter a route of advance. He cleared the way into an area studded with pillboxes, where he repeatedly stood up and walked into vicious enemy fire, storming 1 fortification after another with automatic rifle fire and grenades, killing enemy troops, taking prisoners as the enemy defense became confused, and encouraging his comrades by his heroic example. When halted by heavy barbed wire entanglements, he secured bangalore torpedoes and blasted a path toward still more pillboxes, all the time braving bursting grenades and mortar shells and direct rifle and automatic-weapons fire. He engaged in fierce fire fights, standing in the open while his adversaries fought from the protection of concrete emplacements, and on 1 occasion pursued enemy soldiers across an open field and through interlocking trenches, disregarding the crossfire from 2 pillboxes until he had penetrated the formidable line 200 yards in advance of any American element. That night, although terribly fatigued, he refused to rest and insisted on distributing rations and supplies to his comrades. Hearing that a nearby company was suffering heavy casualties, he secured permission to guide litter bearers and assist them in evacuating the wounded. All that night he remained in the battle area on his mercy missions, and for the following 2 days he continued to remove casualties, venturing into enemy-held territory, scorning cover and braving devastating mortar and artillery bombardments. In 3 days he neutralized and captured 6 pillboxes single-handedly, killed at least 9 Germans, wounded 13, took 13 prisoners, aided in the capture of 14 others, and saved many American lives by his fearless performance as a litter bearer. Through his superb fighting skill, dauntless courage, and gallant, inspiring actions, Cpl. Wilkin contributed in large measure to his company's success in cracking the Siegfried Line. One month later he was killed in action while fighting deep in Germany.

*WILKINS, RAYMOND H. (Air Mission)

Rank and organization: Major, U.S. Army Air Corps. Place and date: Near Rabaul, New Britain, 2 November 1943. Entered service at: Portsmouth, Va. Born: 28 September 1917, Portsmouth, Va. G.O. No.: 23, 24 March 1944. Citation: For conspicuous gallantry and intrepidity above and beyond the call of duty in action with the enemy near Rabaul, New Britain, on 2 November 1943. Leading his squadron in an attack on shipping in Simpson Harbor, during which intense antiaircraft fire was expected, Maj. Wilkins briefed his squadron so that his airplane would be in the position of greatest risk. His squadron was the last of 3 in the group to enter the target area. Smoke from bombs dropped by preceding aircraft necessitated a last-second revision of tactics on his part, which still enabled his squadron to strike vital shipping targets, but forced it to approach through concentrated fire, and increased the danger of Maj. Wilkins' left flank position. His airplane was hit almost immediately, the right wing damaged, and control rendered extremely difficult. Although he could have withdrawn, he held fast and led his squadron into the attack. He strafed a group of small harbor vessels, and then, at low level, attacked an enemy destroyer. His 1,000 pound bomb struck squarely amidships, causing the vessel to explode. Although antiaircraft fire from this vessel had seriously damaged his left vertical stabilizer, he refused to deviate from the course. From below-masthead height he attacked a transport of some 9,000 tons, scoring a hit which engulfed the ship in flames. Bombs expended, he began to withdraw his squadron. A heavy cruiser barred the path. Unhesitatingly, to neutralize the cruiser s guns and attract its fire, he went in for a strafing run. His damaged stabilizer was completely shot off. To avoid swerving into his wing planes he had to turn so as to expose the belly and full wing surfaces of his plane to the enemy fire; it caught and crumpled his left wing. Now past control, the bomber crashed into the sea. In the fierce engagement Maj. Wilkins destroyed 2 enemy vessels, and his heroic self-sacrifice made possible the safe withdrawal of the remaining planes of his squadron.

*WILL, WALTER J.

Rank and organization: First Lieutenant, U.S. Army, Company K 18th Infantry, 1st Infantry Division. Place and date: Near Eisern, Germany, 30 March 1945. Entered service at: West Winfield, N.Y. Birth: Pittsburgh, Pa. G.O. No.: 88, 17 October 1945. Citation: He displayed conspicuous gallantry during an attack on powerful enemy positions. He courageously exposed himself to withering hostile fire to rescue 2 wounded men and then, although painfully wounded himself, made a third trip to carry another soldier to safety from an open area. Ignoring the profuse bleeding of his wound, he gallantly led men of his platoon forward until they were pinned down by murderous flanking fire from 2 enemy machineguns. He fearlessly crawled alone to within 30 feet of the first enemy position, killed the crew of 4 and silenced the gun with accurate grenade fire. He continued to crawl through intense enemy fire to within 20 feet of the second position where he leaped to his feet, made a lone, ferocious charge and captured the gun and its 9-man crew. Observing another platoon pinned down by 2 more German machineguns, he led a squad on a flanking approach and, rising to his knees in the face of direct fire, coolly and deliberately lobbed 3 grenades at the Germans, silencing 1 gun and killing its crew. With tenacious aggressiveness, he ran toward the other gun and knocked it out with grenade fire. He then returned to his platoon and led it in a fierce, inspired charge, forcing the enemy to fall back in confusion. 1st Lt. Will was mortally wounded in this last action, but his heroic leadership, indomitable courage, and unflinching devotion to duty live on as a perpetual inspiration to all those who witnessed his deeds.

WILLIAMS, HERSHEL WOODROW

Rank and organization: Corporal, U.S. Marine Corps Reserve, 21st Marines, 3d Marine Division. Place and date: Iwo Jima, Volcano Islands, 23 February 1945. Entered service at: West Virginia. Born: 2 October 1923, Quiet Dell, W. Va. Citation: For conspicuous gallantry and intrepidity at the risk of his life above and beyond the call of duty as demolition sergeant serving with the 21st Marines, 3d Marine Division, in action against enemy Japanese forces on Iwo Jima, Volcano Islands, 23 February 1945. Quick to volunteer his services when our tanks were maneuvering vainly to open a lane for the infantry through the network of reinforced concrete pillboxes, buried mines, and black volcanic sands, Cpl. Williams daringly went forward alone to attempt the reduction of devastating machinegun fire from the unyielding positions. Covered only by 4 riflemen, he fought desperately for 4 hours under terrific enemy small-arms fire and repeatedly returned to his own lines to prepare demolition charges and obtain serviced flamethrowers, struggling back, frequently to the rear of hostile emplacements, to wipe out 1 position after another. On 1 occasion, he daringly mounted a pillbox to insert the nozzle of his flamethrower through the air vent, killing the occupants and silencing the gun; on another he grimly charged enemy riflemen who attempted to stop him with bayonets and destroyed them with a burst of flame from his weapon. His unyielding determination and extraordinary heroism in the face of ruthless enemy resistance were directly instrumental in neutralizing one of the most fanatically defended Japanese strong points encountered by his regiment and aided vitally in enabling his company to reach its objective.

Cpl. Williams' aggressive fighting spirit and valiant devotion to duty throughout this fiercely contested action sustain and enhance the highest traditions of the U.S. Naval Service.

*WILLIAMS, JACK

Rank and organization: Pharmacist's Mate Third Class, U.S. Naval Reserve. Born: 18 October 1924, Harrison, Ark. Accredited to: Arkansas. Citation: For conspicuous gallantry and intrepidity at the risk of his life above and beyond the call of duty while serving with the 3d Battalion 28th Marines, 5th Marine Division, during the occupation of Iwo Jima Volcano Islands, 3 March 1945. Gallantly going forward on the frontlines under intense enemy small-arms fire to assist a marine wounded in a fierce grenade battle, Williams dragged the man to a shallow depression and was kneeling, using his own body as a screen from the sustained fire as he administered first aid, when struck in the abdomen and groin 3 times by hostile rifle fire. Momentarily stunned, he quickly recovered and completed his ministration before applying battle dressings to his own multiple wounds. Unmindful of his own urgent need for medical attention, he remained in the perilous fire-swept area to care for another marine casualty. Heroically completing his task despite pain and profuse bleeding, he then endeavored to make his way to the rear in search of adequate aid for himself when struck down by a Japanese sniper bullet which caused his collapse. Succumbing later as a result of his self-sacrificing service to others, Williams, by his courageous determination, unwavering fortitude and valiant performance of duty, served as an inspiring example of heroism, in keeping with the highest traditions of the U.S. Naval Service. He gallantly gave his life for his country.

*WILLIS, JOHN HARLAN

Rank and organization: Pharmacist's Mate First Class, U.S. Navy. Born: 10 June 1921, Columbia, Tenn. Accredited to: Tennessee. Citation: For conspicuous gallantry and intrepidity at the risk of his life above and beyond the call of duty as Platoon Corpsman serving with the 3d Battalion, 27th Marines, 5th Marine Division, during operations against enemy Japanese forces on Iwo Jima, Volcano Islands, 28 February 1945. Constantly imperiled by artillery and mortar fire from strong and mutually supporting pillboxes and caves studding Hill 362 in the enemy's cross-island defenses, Willis resolutely administered first aid to the many marines wounded during the furious close-in fighting until he himself was struck by shrapnel and was ordered back to the battle-aid station. Without waiting for official medical release, he quickly returned to his company and, during a savage hand-to-hand enemy counterattack, daringly advanced to the extreme frontlines under mortar and sniper fire to aid a marine lying wounded in a shellhole. Completely unmindful of his own danger as the Japanese intensified their attack, Willis calmly continued to administer blood plasma to his patient, promptly returning the first hostile grenade which landed in the shell-hole while he was working and hurling back 7 more in quick succession before the ninth 1 exploded in his hand and instantly killed him. By his great personal valor in saving others at the sacrifice of his own life, he inspired his companions, although terrifically outnumbered, to launch a fiercely determined attack and repulse the enemy force. His exceptional fortitude and courage in the performance of duty reflect the highest credit upon Willis and the U.S. Naval Service. He gallantly gave his life for his country.

*WILSON, ALFRED L.

Rank and organization: Technician Fifth Grade, U.S. Army, Medical Detachment, 328th Infantry, 26th Infantry Division. Place and date: Near Bezange la Petite, France, 8 November 1944. Entered service at: Fairchance, Pa. Birth: Fairchance, Pa. G.O. No.: 47, 18 June 1945. Citation: He volunteered to assist as an aid man a company other than his own, which was suffering casualties from constant artillery fire. He administered to the wounded and returned to his own company when a shellburst injured a number of its men. While treating his comrades he was seriously wounded, but refused to be evacuated by litter bearers sent to relieve him. In spite of great pain and loss of blood, he continued to administer first aid until he was too weak to stand. Crawling from 1 patient to another, he continued his work until excessive loss of blood prevented him from moving. He then verbally directed unskilled enlisted men in continuing the first aid for the wounded. Still refusing assistance himself, he remained to instruct others in dressing the wounds of his comrades until he was unable to speak above a whisper and finally lapsed into unconsciousness. The effects of his injury later caused his death. By steadfastly remaining at the scene without regard for his own safety, Cpl. Wilson through distinguished devotion to duty and personal sacrifice helped to save the lives of at least 10 wounded men.

WILSON, LOUIS HUGH, JR.

Rank and organization: Captain, U.S. Marine Corps, Commanding Rifle Company, 2d Battalion, 9th Marines, 3d Marine Division. Place and date: Fonte Hill, Guam, 25-26 July 1944. Entered service at: Mississippi. Born: 11 February 1920, Brandon, Miss. Citation: For conspicuous gallantry and intrepidity at the risk of his life above and beyond the call of duty as commanding officer of a rifle company attached to the 2d Battalion, 9th Marines, 3d Marine Division, in action against enemy Japanese forces at Fonte Hill, Guam, 25-26 July 1944. Ordered to take that portion of the hill within his zone of action, Capt. Wilson initiated his attack in mid-afternoon, pushed up the rugged, open terrain against terrific machinegun and rifle fire for 300 yards and successfully captured the objective. Promptly assuming command of other disorganized units and motorized equipment in addition to his own company and 1 reinforcing platoon, he organized his night defenses in the face of continuous hostile fire and, although wounded 3 times during this 5-hour period, completed his disposition of men and guns before retiring to the company command post for medical attention. Shortly thereafter, when the enemy launched the first of a series of savage counterattacks lasting all night, he voluntarily rejoined his besieged units and repeatedly exposed himself to the merciless hail of shrapnel and bullets, dashing 50 yards into the open on 1 occasion to rescue a wounded marine lying helpless beyond the frontlines. Fighting fiercely in hand-to-hand encounters, he led his men in furiously waged battle for approximately 10 hours, tenaciously holding his line and repelling the fanatically renewed counterthrusts until he succeeded in crushing the last efforts of the hard-pressed Japanese early the following morning. Then organizing a 17-man patrol, he immediately advanced upon a strategic slope essential to the security of his position and, boldly defying intense mortar, machinegun, and rifle fire which struck down 13 of his men, drove relentlessly forward with the remnants of his patrol to seize the vital ground. By his indomitable leadership, daring combat tactics, and valor in the face of overwhelming odds, Capt. Wilson succeeded in capturing and holding the strategic high ground in his regimental sector, thereby contributing essentially to the success of his regimental mission and to the annihilation of 350 Japanese troops. His inspiring conduct throughout the critical periods of this decisive action sustains and enhances the highest traditions of the U.S. Naval Service.

*WILSON, ROBERT LEE

Rank and organization: Private First Class, U.S. Marine Corps. Born: 24 May 1921, Centralia, Ill. Accredited to: Illinois. Citation For conspicuous gallantry and intrepidity at the risk of his life above and beyond the call of duty while serving with the 2d Battalion, 6th Marines, 2d Marine Division, during action against enemy Japanese forces at Tinian Island, Marianas Group, on 4 August 1944. As 1 of a group of marines advancing through heavy underbrush to neutralize isolated points of resistance,

Pfc. Wilson daringly preceded his companions toward a pile of rocks where Japanese troops were supposed to be hiding. Fully aware of the danger involved, he was moving forward while the remainder of the squad, armed with automatic rifles, closed together in the rear when an enemy grenade landed in the midst of the group. Quick to act, Pfc. Wilson cried a warning to the men and unhesitatingly threw himself on the grenade, heroically sacrificing his own life that the others might live and fulfill their mission. His exceptional valor, his courageous loyalty and unwavering devotion to duty in the face of grave peril reflect the highest credit upon Pfc. Wilson and the U.S. Naval Service. He gallantly gave his life for his country.

WISE, HOMER L.

Rank and organization: Staff Sergeant. U.S. Army, Company L, 142d Infantry, 36th Infantry Division. Place and date: Magliano, Italy, 14 June 1944. Entered service al: Baton Rouge, La. Birth: Baton Rouge La. G.O. No.: 90, 8 December 1944. Citation: While his platoon was pinned down by enemy small-arms fire from both flanks, he left his position of comparative safety and assisted in carrying 1 of his men, who had been seriously wounded and who lay in an exposed position, to a point where he could receive medical attention. The advance of the platoon was resumed but was again stopped by enemy frontal fire. A German officer and 2 enlisted men, armed with automatic weapons, threatened the right flank. Fearlessly exposing himself, he moved to a position from which he killed all 3 with his submachinegun. Returning to his squad, he obtained an Ml rifle and several antitank grenades, then took up a position from which he delivered accurate fire on the enemy holding up the advance. As the battalion moved forward it was again stopped by enemy frontal and flanking fire. He procured an automatic rifle and, advancing ahead of his men, neutralized an enemy machinegun with his fire. When the flanking fire became more intense he ran to a nearby tank and exposing himself on the turret, restored a jammed machinegun to operating efficiency and used it so effectively that the enemy fire from an adjacent ridge was materially reduced thus permitting the battalion to occupy its objective.

*WITEK, FRANK PETER

Rank and organization: Private First Class, U.S. Marine Corps Reserve. Born: December 1921, Derby, Conn. Accredited to: Illinois. Citation: For conspicuous gallantry and intrepidity at the risk of his life above and beyond the call of duty while serving with the 1st Battalion, 9th Marines, 3d Marine Division, during the Battle of Finegayen at Guam, Marianas, on 3 August 1944. When his rifle platoon was halted by heavy surprise fire from well-camouflaged enemy positions, Pfc. Witek daringly remained standing to fire a full magazine from his automatic at point-blank range into a depression housing Japanese troops, killing 8 of the enemy and enabling the greater part of his platoon to take cover. During his platoon's withdrawal for consolidation of lines, he remained to safeguard a severely wounded comrade, courageously returning the enemy's fire until the arrival of stretcher bearers, and then covering the evacuation by sustained fire as he moved backward toward his own lines. With his platoon again pinned down by a hostile machinegun, Pfc. Witek, on his own initiative, moved forward boldly to the reinforcing tanks and infantry, alternately throwing handgrenades and firing as he advanced to within 5 to 10 yards of the enemy position, and destroying the hostile machinegun emplacement and an additional 8 Japanese before he himself was struck down by an enemy rifleman. His valiant and inspiring action effectively reduced the enemy's firepower, thereby enabling his platoon to attain its objective, and reflects the highest credit upon Pfc. Witek and the U.S. Naval Service. He gallantly gave his life for his country.

*WOODFORD, HOWARD E.

Rank and organization: Staff Sergeant, U.S. Army, Company I, 130th Infantry, 33d Infantry Division. Place and date: Near Tabio, Luzon, Philippine Islands, 6 June 1945. Entered service at: Barberton, Ohio. Birth: Barberton, Ohio. G.O. No.: 14, 4 February 1946. Citation: He volunteered to investigate the delay in a scheduled attack by an attached guerrilla battalion. Reaching the line of departure, he found that the lead company, in combat for the first time, was immobilized by intense enemy mortar, machinegun, and rifle fire which had caused casualties to key personnel. Knowing that further failure to advance would endanger the flanks of adjacent units, as well as delay capture of the objective, he immediately took command of the company, evacuated the wounded, reorganized the unit under fire, and prepared to attack. He repeatedly exposed himself to draw revealing fire from the Japanese strongpoints, and then moved forward with a 5-man covering force to determine exact enemy positions. Although intense enemy machinegun fire killed 2 and wounded his other 3 men, S/Sgt. Woodford resolutely continued his patrol before returning to the company. Then, against bitter resistance, he guided the guerrillas up a barren hill and captured the objective, personally accounting for 2 hostile machinegunners and courageously reconnoitering strong defensive positions before directing neutralizing fire. After organizing a perimeter defense for the night, he was given permission by radio to return to his battalion, but, feeling that he was needed to maintain proper control, he chose to remain with the guerrillas. Before dawn the next morning the enemy launched a fierce suicide attack with mortars, grenades, and small-arms fire, and infiltrated through the perimeter. Though wounded by a grenade, S/Sgt. Woodford remained at his post calling for mortar support until bullets knocked out his radio. Then, seizing a rifle he began working his way around the perimeter, encouraging the men until he reached a weak spot where 2 guerrillas had been killed. Filling this gap himself, he fought off the enemy. At daybreak he was found dead in his foxhole, but 37 enemy dead were lying in and around his position. By his daring, skillful, and inspiring leadership, as well as by his gallant determination to search out and kill the enemy, S/Sgt. Woodford led an inexperienced unit in capturing and securing a vital objective, and was responsible for the successful continuance of a vitally important general advance.

YOUNG, CASSIN

Rank and organization: Commander, U.S. Navy. Born: 6 March 1894, Washington, D.C. Appointed from: Wisconsin. Other Navy award: Navy Cross. Citation: For distinguished conduct in action, outstanding heroism and utter disregard of his own safety, above and beyond the call of duty, as commanding officer of the U.S.S. Vestal, during the attack on the Fleet in Pearl Harbor, Territory of Hawaii, by enemy Japanese forces on 7 December 1941. Comdr. Young proceeded to the bridge and later took personal command of the 3-inch antiaircraft gun. When blown overboard by the blast of the forward magazine explosion of the U.S.S. Arizona, to which the U.S.S. Vestal was moored, he swam back to his ship. The entire forward part of the U.S.S. Arizona was a blazing inferno with oil afire on the water between the 2 ships; as a result of several bomb hits, the U.S.S. Vestal was afire in several places, was settling and taking on a list. Despite severe enemy bombing and strafing at the time, and his shocking experience of having been blown overboard, Comdr. Young, with extreme coolness and calmness, moved his ship to an anchorage distant from the U.S.S. Arizona, and subsequently beached the U.S.S. Vestal upon determining that such action was required to save his ship.

*YOUNG, RODGER W.

Rank and organization: Private, U.S. Army, 148th Infantry, 37th Infantry Division. Place and date: On New Georgia, Solomon Islands, 31 July 1943. Entered service at: Clyde, Ohio. Birth: Tiffin, Ohio. G.O. No.: 3, 6

January 1944. Citation: On 31 July 1943, the infantry company of which Pvt. Young was a member, was ordered to make a limited withdrawal from the battle line in order to adjust the battalion's position for the night. At this time, Pvt. Young's platoon was engaged with the enemy in a dense jungle where observation was very limited. The platoon suddenly was pinned down by intense fire from a Japanese machinegun concealed on higher ground only 75 yards away. The initial burst wounded Pvt. Young. As the platoon started to obey the order to withdraw, Pvt. Young called out that he could see the enemy emplacement, whereupon he started creeping toward it. Another burst from the machinegun wounded him the second time. Despite the wounds, he continued his heroic advance, attracting enemy fire and answering with rifle fire. When he was close enough to his objective, he began throwing handgrenades, and while doing so was hit again and killed. Pvt. Young's bold action in closing with this Japanese pillbox and thus diverting its fire, permitted his platoon to disengage itself, without loss, and was responsible for several enemy casualties.

ZEAMER, JAY JR. (Air Mission)

Rank and organization: Major, U.S. Army Air Corps. Place and date: Over Buka area, Solomon Islands, 16 June 1943. Entered service at: Machias, Maine. Birth: Carlisle, Pa. G.O. No.: 1, 4 January 1944. Citation: On 16 June 1943, Maj. Zeamer (then Capt.) volunteered as pilot of a bomber on an important photographic mapping mission covering the formidably defended area in the vicinity of Buka, Solomon Islands. While photographing the Buka airdrome. his crew observed about 20 enemy fighters on the field, many of them taking off. Despite the certainty of a dangerous attack by this strong force, Maj. Zeamer proceeded with his mapping run, even after the enemy attack began. In the ensuing engagement, Maj. Zeamer sustained gunshot wounds in both arms and legs, 1 leg being broken. Despite his injuries, he maneuvered the damaged plane so skillfully that his gunners were able to fight off the enemy during a running fight which lasted 40 minutes. The crew destroyed at least 5 hostile planes, of which Maj. Zeamer himself shot down 1. Although weak from loss of blood, he refused medical aid until the enemy had broken combat. He then turned over the controls, but continued to exercise command despite lapses into unconsciousness, and directed the flight to a base 580 miles away. In this voluntary action, Maj. Zeamer, with superb skill, resolution, and courage, accomplished a mission of great value.

*ZUSSMAN, RAYMOND

Rank and organization: Second Lieutenant, U.S. Army, 756th Tank Battalion. Place and date: Noroy le Bourg, France, 12 September 1944. Entered service at: Detroit, Mich. Birth: Hamtramck, Mich. G.O. No.: 42, 24 May 1945. Citation: On 12 September 1944, 2d Lt. Zussman was in command of 2 tanks operating with an infantry company in the attack on enemy forces occupying the town of Noroy le Bourg, France. At 7 p.m., his command tank bogged down. Throughout the ensuing action, armed only with a carbine, he reconnoitered alone on foot far in advance of his remaining tank and the infantry. Returning only from time to time to designate targets, he directed the action of the tank and turned over to the infantry the numerous German soldiers he had caused to surrender. He located a road block and directed his tanks to destroy it. Fully exposed to fire from enemy positions only 50 yards distant, he stood by his tank directing its fire. Three Germans were killed and 8 surrendered. Again he walked before his tank, leading it against an enemy-held group of houses, machinegun and small arms fire kicking up dust at his feet. The tank fire broke the resistance and 20 enemy surrendered. Going forward again alone he passed an enemy-occupied house from which Germans fired on him and threw grenades in his path. After a brief fire fight, he signaled his tank to come up and fire on the house. Eleven German soldiers were killed and 15 surrendered. Going on alone, he disappeared around a street corner. The fire of his carbine could be heard and in a few minutes he reappeared driving 30 prisoners before him. Under 2d Lt. Zussman's heroic and inspiring leadership, 18 enemy soldiers were killed and 92 captured.